Comprehensive in scope yet readable in tone! This is a solid introduction to Catholic history that will benefit anyone who reads it.

— Trent Horn, author of *Why We're Catholic: Our Reasons for Faith, Hope, and Love*

Steve Weidenkopf has emerged as an elite historian of the Catholic Church, and *Timeless* is his masterwork. From infancy to maturity, this comprehensive volume illustrates the significance of each milestone in the life of the Body of Christ with remarkable narrative that is vivid and inspiring, boldly netting the troubling controversies that crippled it and the glorious triumphs that enable it to be the sole preserver of Western culture and the salvation of all mankind. The search is over — this chronicle is the most accessible and readable history of the Church available.

— Shaun A. McAfee, author of *Reform Yourself!* and other best-selling titles, and Instructor of Media at Sacred Heart Institute

Steve Weidenkopf has once again demonstrated his ability to write a clear, powerful, well-documented history book. Above all, he has again shown that Christ and his Church are at the center of history, and that whenever the Church undergoes a crucifixion, it is always followed by a resurrection, a much-needed lesson.

— Anne W. Carroll, author of *Christ the King: Lord of History* and *Christ and the Americas*, and founder of Seton School

I have been waiting for this book, and I didn't think it could be done. But here it is: a one-volume history of the Catholic Church that I can recommend without reservation! No sneering triumphalism. No groveling apologies. Just the glorious story of the greatest institution in history, written how history should be written — lively, compelling, inspiring, and true.

— Christopher Check, president of Catholic Answers

In a single volume and from a thoroughly Catholic perspective, professor Steve Weidenkopf provides an engaging and thoughtful history of the Catholic Church and its interactions with the world around it. The work is wonderfully organized in such a way that readers can select a per_____ _____ __ _____ ____ __ ___ Early ___ ___ Ages or the French Revolution, and read det__ _____ events as they related to the Catholic Churc_ _____ _____ _____ walks the reader through often complex maj__ ___ _____ ___ __g not

D1153502

only the events and people associated with each of them, but also making clear why such disputes mattered for the life of the Church and its members. Weidenkopf does not shy away from addressing the most controversial events in the long history of Catholicism but, in the style of great Catholic writers like Hilaire Belloc or Warren H. Carroll, is careful to explain them in a context that illuminates such events in a way that hostile modern popular narratives fail to do. Modern Catholics wishing to get a better understanding of both the history and historical nature of their faith would do well to read this book.

— Andrew Holt, professor of history at Florida State College at Jacksonville

If you want to learn Church history, but do not wish to wade through dense scholarly volumes to do it, *Timeless: A History of the Catholic Church* is the book for you. Steve Weidenkopf masterfully unveils Catholicism's two-thousand-year drama in a single, gripping, easy-to-read volume without neglecting the key events that every Catholic ought to know. I highly recommend this book.

— Gary Michuta, Catholic author, apologist, and speaker

Ignorance of history is ignorance of the Church. Steve Weidenkopf takes us through the great pilgrimage of the Church through time, showing her organic development and helping us to overcome serious misconceptions. The Church's story is one of hope, as we recognize how God's providence makes good come out of evil, particularly through the witness of the saints. Learning about the Church will inspire us to follow Christ more faithfully in the midst of the difficulties of our time.

— R. Jared Staudt, PhD, Archdiocese of Denver and
Augustine Institute, author of *The Beer Option*

The attempt to write a history of the Catholic Church in a single volume is no small task. It requires not only a depth of knowledge but prudence in one's selection of data and its analysis. Fortunately, Steve Weidenkopf has succeeded in doing just that. Written with a Catholic vision of history and a lucid, popular narrative, his work brings to life two thousand years of history that both inspires and informs. The Church in her heroic struggle in this fallen world with her successes and failures is clearly set forth. This book's Christocentric vision of history is a rare gem, to be read and treasured by the faithful and all who seek the deeper meaning of Western Christian civilization.

— Timothy T. O'Donnell, President, Christendom College

TIMELESS

A HISTORY
OF THE
CATHOLIC
CHURCH

STEVE WEIDENKOPF

Our
Sunday
Visitor

www.osv.com
Our Sunday Visitor Publishing Division
Our Sunday Visitor, Inc.
Huntington, Indiana 46750

Except where noted, the Scripture citations used in this work are taken from the *Revised Standard Version of the Bible — Second Catholic Edition* (Ignatius Edition), copyright © 1965, 1966, 2006 National Council of the Churches of Christ in the United States of America. Used by permission. All rights reserved.

Every reasonable effort has been made to determine copyright holders of excerpted materials and to secure permissions as needed. If any copyrighted materials have been inadvertently used in this work without proper credit being given in one form or another, please notify Our Sunday Visitor in writing so that future printings of this work may be corrected accordingly.

Copyright © 2018 by Steve Weidenkopf

23 22 21 20 19 18   1 2 3 4 5 6 7 8 9

All rights reserved. With the exception of short excerpts for critical reviews, no part of this work may be reproduced or transmitted in any form or by any means whatsoever without permission from the publisher. For more information, visit: www.osv.com/permissions.

Our Sunday Visitor Publishing Division
Our Sunday Visitor, Inc.
200 Noll Plaza
Huntington, IN 46750
1-800-348-2440

ISBN: 978-1-68192-148-8 (Inventory No. T1868)
eISBN: 978-1-68192-150-1
LCCN: 2018957747

Cover design: Amanda Falk
Cover art: Shutterstock
Interior design: Amanda Falk

PRINTED IN THE UNITED STATES OF AMERICA

"Historical analysis is never an end in itself; it is not made solely with a view to knowing the past; rather, it focuses decisively on conversion and on an authentic witness of Christian life on the part of the faithful."

Pope Benedict XVI, 2007

To my sons: Maximilian, Luke, Jeb, and Martin

May the story of the Church and the actions of
your brothers in the Lord, who came before you,
inspire you to manfully defend the Faith and live it
throughout your lives.

Contents

Author Preface

> *"The historian, like the novelist, tells a story; a story of some portion of the past; he describes (rather than defines). The novelist has it easier: he can invent people who did not exist and events that did not happen. The historian cannot describe people and events that did not exist; he must limit himself to men and women who really lived; he must depend on evidences of their acts and words — though, like the novelist, he too must surmise something about their minds."[1]*
>
> JOHN LUKACS, 2011

From the beginning of the Church, Christians have told her story, because history is integral to the Faith. God does not ignore his creation, but rather entered human history in a unique manner in the Incarnation, intimately involving himself in that history. The writing of Church history should acknowledge this

---

1. John Lukacs, *The Future of History* (New Haven, CT: Yale University Press, 2011), 109.

supernatural reality and follow certain principles, such as accepting the miraculous in human affairs, seeing the impact of the actions of the saints, and recognizing the primacy of the Vicar of Christ (the pope) in the life of the Church and Western Civilization.[2]

Saint Luke provided the first example of Christian historical writing when he recorded the events of the early Church in the Acts of the Apostles. Early Church historians concentrated on recording the lives and deaths of the martyrs, so that their heroic sacrifices could be remembered through the centuries. Romans, such as Tacitus and Suetonius, wrote histories of their empire and the emperors who ruled it. Similarly, Christians began to write histories of the Church. The "Father of Church History" is Eusebius of Caesarea (263–339). His *Ecclesiastical History* is a gold mine of information about the Church in the time of Roman persecution, and the Empire's eventual conversion.

In later centuries, many other great historians have contributed their time and efforts to telling the story of the Catholic Church. The pantheon of Church historians includes such men as Saint Augustine of Hippo (354–430), Saint Gregory of Tours (538–594), Saint Bede, called the Venerable (672–735), Cardinal Baronius (1538–1607), Ludwig von Pastor (1854–1928), Hilaire Belloc (1870–1953), Christopher Dawson (1889–1970), Henri Daniel-Rops (1901–1965), and Warren H. Carroll (1932–2011).[3] These authors followed the Catholic principles of history, and wrote books whose influence continues to the modern world.

It is a daunting and humbling task to write a one-volume history of the Church, and I recognize the immense duty (and honor) entrusted to me in this endeavor. This book is not meant to be an exhaustive study of the history of the Catholic Church through the last two thousand years; rather, it is designed to provide a de-

---

2. These principles are from Warren H. Carroll and Anne Carroll, *The Crisis of Christendom: A History of Christendom*, vol. 6 (Front Royal, VA: Christendom Press, 2013), 813–822.
3. This list is not meant to be exhaustive. The reader may want to add or subtract to it, but the list represents the men I believe to be true "greats" in the history profession.

tailed narrative of the main events that have shaped the Church and the world. The focus of this book is on the Church in the Western world, specifically Europe. This approach is not meant to deny the universality of the Church nor the contributions of the East to Church history, but rather is the result of a need to focus the book on a main area of activity — and a recognition that history in the Western world over the last 500 years has been told through a mostly Protestant perspective. Many Catholics are unaware that what they believe to be the history of the Church is a false narrative created as a result of the Protestant Reformation and the Enlightenment.[4] My hope is that this work inspires you to grow in your Catholic identity, to understand that Church history is your family history, and to take pride in the actions of your brothers and sisters in the Faith who came before you. Armed with this knowledge, I pray that we may defend the Church when attacked by false narratives and historical myths and grow deeper in our love for the Lord Jesus Christ and the Church he founded.

---

4. This is particularly true in regard to certain historical events such as the Crusades, the Inquisition, the Protestant Reformation, etc.

Introduction

> *"The Christian is someone who has a good memory, who loves history and seeks to know it."*[1]
>
> POPE BENEDICT XVI, 2010

O ften, we view the study of history as something mundane and tiresome. This is partially due to the way history is taught in the modern world. Teachers have limited time for instruction and are restricted by standards that require meeting objectives set by authorities outside the educational environment. As a result, the teaching of history is reduced to requiring students to memorize information — that is, names, dates, and events — with no meaningful link to their personal lives. The result is that students study to pass their tests and then quickly forget the material. History is just another boring subject. Historians also make history boring by writing for each other in thick, academic, and mundane

---

1. Benedict XVI, *Address at a Meeting with Young People*, Cathedral of Sulmona, July 4, 2010.

tomes. Nonprofessional historians write many of the popular history books, because they are writers who desire to tell a historical story. These books sell because history is presented as it should be: a dramatic story of heroes and villains, told in a way that resonates with the reader and explains the makeup of the modern world by providing the context of the past. In a world focused on the sciences and business, history may be seen as a quaint subject. But in reality it is *the* subject, along with theology and philosophy, that can provide a sense of our human identity. Identifying with the Catholic Church is an important part of our faith lives, but that can be difficult if we do not know the history of the Church. You may have participated in Bible studies or learned Church doctrines or apologetics, but you are not alone if you have never studied Church history. This may be the result of the daunting task associated with learning two thousand years' worth of events and people! Where does one begin? Perhaps we should first explore what we mean by "the Church."

WHAT IS THE CHURCH?

In a document from the Second Vatican Council (1962–1965), titled *Lumen Gentium* (Dogmatic Constitution on the Church), the conciliar fathers wrote about the mystery of the Church, her hierarchical structure, the universal call to holiness of all members of the People of God, and the role of the Blessed Mother in the plan of salvation. Early in the document, the conciliar bishops provide a succinct definition of the Church: "Christ, the one Mediator, established and continually sustains here on earth His holy Church, the community of faith, hope and charity, as an entity with visible delineation through which He communicates truth and grace to all."[2] With this in mind, what is the Church? She was established by Christ — not created by a group of people who decided to get together and believe the

2. *Lumen Gentium*, 8.

same things. Rather, God himself founded the Church and sustains her in existence. The Church lives out the theological virtues of faith, hope, and love communally and through the actions of her individual members. She is an organization with a visible and hierarchical structure (pope, bishops, priests, deacons, laity). The Church's structure is not the work of a committee or majority vote; it was divinely instituted, and is not subject to change by human whim. The definition from *Lumen Gentium* also answers the question of why Christ founded the Church: The Church is the instrument through which he communicates truth and grace (through the sacraments) to the world. The Church has a salvific mission, which is a continuation of Christ's own mission of salvation. *Lumen Gentium* also describes the Church as a "complex reality" composed of both visible and invisible elements, which we describe as the Communion of Saints. The Church exists in three states: you and I are a part of the Church Militant (those on earth), while those who have died are members of the Church Suffering (souls in purgatory), and the Church Triumphant (the saints in heaven). The study of Church history is mostly concerned with the visible element of the past actions of the Church Militant, but it cannot ignore the invisible reality of the Church. The *Catechism of the Catholic Church* reminds us that "the Church is in history, but at the same time she transcends it. It is only 'with the eyes of faith' that one can see her in her visible reality and at the same time in her spiritual reality as bearer of divine life."[3]

The Church is a living Church — she is neither confined to one historical era, nor does she remain static through the centuries. The story of the Church comprises the actions of the men and women who lived the Faith. Although the dogmas and doctrines of the Church are immutable, the presentation of those teachings and their lived expression by the faithful change and develop through the centuries of human existence, so that she presents the timeless treasures of the Faith to each new human

---

3. *Catechism of the Catholic Church*, Second Edition (New York: Doubleday, 1995), 470.

generation. Therefore, we should not be alarmed at the changes that occur in the Church (although not in her essential elements) as she marches through human history.[4]

Finally, the Church is comprised of fallen, yet redeemed, human persons. As a result, the study of Church history is the study of their actions, both good and bad, and the effects of those actions on the life of the Church. The story of the Church is the story of saints and sinners and, more often than not, sinners who became saints! Studying the lives of those who came before us should encourage us in our struggles, and help us realize the need to continually fight against temptation and live our vocation to holiness in imitation of Christ. Through two thousand years of the Christian faith, there have been those, even in the highest office of the Church, who did not authentically live their vocation to holiness. There were popes who lived immorally, and an authentic study of Church history cannot gloss over their actions or make excuses. Rather, it should analyze them in order to learn from their mistakes and to defend the Church.

Ultimately, the study of the history of the Church — our own family history — should help us grow in our devotion and love of the Holy Spirit, who guides, guards, and animates the Church. For without the Third Person of the Holy Trinity, the Church would be simply a human institution, and would have disintegrated long ago. Indeed, as the Catholic historian Hilaire Belloc (1870–1953) wrote, "When one remembers how the Catholic Church has been governed, and by whom, one realizes that it must be divinely inspired to have survived at all."[5]

WHAT IS HISTORY?

Did you know that there is a Catholic understanding of history?

---

4. See Cardinal Walter Brandmüller, *Light and Shadows: Church History amid Faith, Fact and Legend*, trans. Michael J. Miller (San Francisco: Ignatius Press, 2009 [2007]), 17.
5. Quoted in Desmond Seward, *The Monks of War: The Military Religious Orders* (New York: Penguins Books, 1995 [1972]), 222.

In the ancient world, Greeks and Romans viewed history as a series of repetitive cycles with no beginning, central event, or end — they believed that human events repeated themselves in a never-ending cycle. History in the pagan world had no central meaning. The modern understanding of history is myopically narrow on the modern era and views the past with disdain, clinging to the supposed superiority of the present. A Catholic understanding of history, on the other hand, recognizes the central role of God. Presented originally by Saint Augustine of Hippo in his epic work *The City of God*, history is linear — it has a beginning and an end. God oversees and is involved in human history, proving his love for humanity and his intimate involvement in human affairs by sending the Second Person of the Trinity to take on human flesh. Christ's Incarnation is the central event in human history — all history radiates outward (both forward and backward) from this crucial event. The climax of the Incarnation provides meaning to human history and a path out of the circular view of history espoused by the pagans. Christ came in "the fullness of time," when the world was composed of the three great civilizations of the Jews, Greeks, and Romans. This is illustrated by the placard placed on Jesus' cross by Pontius Pilate, identifying him as the "King of the Jews," written in the three languages of those civilizations. The establishment of the Church ushered in a new civilization, forming a new culture out of the ancient world.[6] The history of the Church is the study of this new civilization and its impact.

History, in the Catholic sense, is more than just the recording of human events. We refer to it as salvation history — the unfolding of God's plan for his people, their sanctification, and their eventual union with him in heaven. Salvation history began with God's act of creation *ex nihilo* (out of nothing). God created the world, plants, and animal life, and then man and woman in his

---

6. See Robert Louis Wilken, *The First Thousand Years: A Global History of Christianity* (New Haven, CT: Yale University Press, 2012), 2.

image and likeness. Unfortunately, the disobedient act of our first parents broke the relationship between humanity and God, but God did not leave us to our own devices. He sent his only begotten Son to restore that relationship and our chance for a share in the heavenly kingdom. In time, the created world will come to an end with the Second Coming of Christ, who will usher in a new heaven and a new earth. We must keep in mind this divine dimension of human history, especially when studying Church history. This is not merely one subject among many; it is a way to grow deeper in relationship with the Holy Trinity by recognizing and discerning the spiritual meaning of human affairs.

OUR FAMILY HISTORY

Given the importance of learning Church history, and the method by which it should be learned, we can ask another question: "How should we view Church history?" This book seeks to tell the story of the Catholic Church through the actions of the men and women who came before us in faith. Christ revealed God to be a loving Father, and we are adopted sons and daughters in Christ and heirs to the kingdom of heaven. We all live in the family of God, the Church. When we study the actions and events of our brothers and sisters in the Faith, we are studying our spiritual genealogy. Many people spend hours and resources tracing their earthly lineage, but, more importantly, because we hope to live with them in eternity, we should study the history of our spiritual family. Viewing Church history in this manner helps us understand that history is the subject by which we grow in our Catholic identity.

Part of our Catholic identity involves using the proper terms when learning Church history. As an example, the term "Christianity" is an unhistorical, post-Reformation term that "connotes an opinion or a theory; a point of view; an idea."[7] The Catholic faith

---

7. Hilaire Belloc, *Europe and the Faith* (Rockford, IL: TAN Books and Publishers, 1992 [1920]), 38–39.

is none of those things, as Catholics are not attached to an idea or a philosophy but to a *Person* (Christ) and to a *thing* (the Church). Additionally, "Christianity" implies a multiplicity of ways of living the Faith — that is, "Catholic Christianity," "Protestant Christianity" — but there is only one Church that contains the fullness of Christ's revelation, authority, and grace. Therefore, the term "Christianity" is not used in this book; rather, "the Faith" is utilized in accordance with the historical understanding of the Church.

THE IMPORTANCE OF LEARNING CHURCH HISTORY

Now that we understand the definitions of the Church and history, we must ask and answer another question: Why study Church history?

Learning Church history is vital for the modern-day Catholic for the four following reasons:

1. To make sense of our world
2. To know Christ better
3. To defend the Faith and the Church
4. To know who we are

The knowledge of our Catholic story gives meaning to the present age, which allows us to view modern-day problems with a deeper and more accurate perspective. Additionally, knowing the past can help shape our future decisions so that we can benefit the Church and the world. This worldview is not common thinking in our current culture, but is essential for the modern-day Catholic. Today's society condenses complex issues and policy decisions into thirty-second sound bites. But focusing on the present is ultimately detrimental, since it makes humanity "lose their sense of the past, of history; but by doing so it also deprives them of the ability to understand themselves, to perceive problems and to build the future."[8]

---

8. Benedict XVI, *Address at a Meeting with Young People*, Cathedral of Sulmona, July 4, 2010.

Since "Christ is the foundation and center of human history, [and] he is its meaning and ultimate goal," studying Church history leads to greater knowledge of Jesus, which is the consummate goal of any Christian study.[9] It can be difficult to see Christ in every event and human activity in the Church's history, especially when those actions are not in conformity with Jesus' example and teachings, but he is always present in his Mystical Body. Learning Church history allows us to grow deeper in love with the Lord and his Church.

Most Catholics in the United States learned non-Catholic history in school (unless they went to a Catholic school that taught them authentic Catholic history) because history as a whole is taught in the American educational system from an English Protestant perspective. As an example, I remember learning in secondary school about the cruelty and barbarism of the reign of "Bloody Mary" Tudor and the cultured, civilized court of her half-sister Elizabeth I. The standard Protestant (false) historical narrative paints "Good Queen Bess" as one of England's greatest monarchs: a strong, intelligent woman with excellent judgment who led England into an era of prosperity and who was beloved by her people because she exhibited their strong Protestant convictions. This narrative is a "monstrous scaffolding of poisonous nonsense [that] has … been foisted on posterity."[10] In reality, the "Virgin Queen" was a figurehead, used and controlled by powerful men behind the scenes. Under her reign, the first state-sponsored persecution of the Catholic Church in Europe since the Roman Empire was undertaken. Elizabeth and her thugs killed, tortured, and imprisoned thousands of English subjects simply because they were Catholic (although Elizabeth's Catholic half-sister Mary was inappropriately given the nickname "bloody"). Unfortunately, that historical truth is rarely presented in today's history class. It is vital for us as

---

9. John Paul II, *Novo Millennio Ineunte*, 5.
10. Hilaire Belloc, *Characters of the Reformation: Historical Portraits of 23 Men and Women and Their Place in the Great Religious Revolution of the 16ᵗʰ Century* (Rockford, IL: TAN Books and Publishers, Inc., 1992 [1936]), 102.

Catholics to be able to defend the Church when she is maligned or misrepresented, and when myths are presented as historical fact. Catholics have an obligation to embrace the truths, both good and bad, about our past, and retake the historical narrative from the dominant Protestant (and increasingly secular) view.

The Church is called to continue Christ's salvific mission, and each Catholic is given a role to play in that important drama. Before we can play our part, though, we need to know who we are — we must have a sense of Catholic identity, which we can find in Church history. The modern Western world exhibits cultural and historical amnesia on a national level. Nations that separate themselves from their Christian origins are apt to embrace immoral and totalitarian political systems, which erode individual rights and place the individual at the service of the state. In order to regain its identity, the Western world must relearn its Catholic history and hold in high esteem the supernatural and transcendent character of history — the recognition that God acts throughout human history. We must embrace what Hilaire Belloc termed "the Catholic Conscience of History," wherein the Catholic understands the history of Western civilization from within precisely because it is the story of the Catholic Church and her influence on that civilization. Belloc believed that a rightly formed Catholic should have "an intimate knowledge [of history] through identity."[11] Learning Church history from an authentic Catholic perspective should produce a deeper personal identity with the Church and lead to a "new, forceful consciousness of being Catholic."[12]

THE BEST METHOD OF LEARNING CHURCH HISTORY

In any form of catechesis, the method of teaching should be established in the example of the Master Catechist, Christ. The

---

11. Belloc, *Europe and the Faith*, 1.
12. Brandmüller, *Light and Shadows*, 84.

Gospels provide numerous examples of Jesus' teaching methods, which usually varied depending on his audience. To his apostles Jesus was very direct, so that they would have complete understanding of what he was trying to convey (though they still did not seem to grasp it at times). To the larger crowds of people who gathered to see and hear him, he spoke in a simpler manner — he told stories. People remember stories because we are relational beings, who build relationships with others through shared experiences that are recounted as stories. For example, a photo of siblings at a hockey game, viewed years later, will produce stories from that shared experience ("Remember when Dad took us to that game?"). History is best taught and learned as story. Indeed, for most of human existence, history was conveyed through oral tradition (stories) and, when written down, continued to be told in a narrative format.

Until the late eighteenth century, history was seen as a form of literature and taught under that genre. In the nineteenth century, German nationalist and Lutheran author Leopold von Ranke (1795–1886) changed history to a form of science, where textual criticism and primary source material dominated the field.[13] Ranke taught at the University of Berlin, which had been opened in 1810, a few years after the Prussian Army was defeated by Napoleon. The purpose of the Berlin institution was to train and educate citizens and civil servants to staff the Prussian state bureaucracy. This university instituted a change in the role of higher education. Previously, universities "served the common good by passing on a shared intellectual heritage,"[14] a cultural identity. The new university was less concerned with handing on the cultural identity of a civilization, instead focusing on the "development of new knowledge through original scientific research."[15] This

---

13. Ranke was known for his *History of the Popes* (pub. 1834–1839), which were answered by a Catholic series written by Ludwig von Pastor (1854–1928) in the late nineteenth century.
14. Christopher Shannon and Christopher O. Blum, *The Past as Pilgrimage: Narrative, Tradition & the Renewal of Catholic History* (Front Royal, VA: Christendom Press, 2014), 40.
15. Ibid.

scientific focus moved the study and teaching of history from literature — a narrative retelling of a national, racial, and religious identity — to an "objective science" focused on written sources. Indeed, this shift in understanding the historical profession was a deliberate rejection of the "traditional approach to history."[16]

This shift continues into the modern world, where narrative history is seen as biased, and history written or taught by a believing Christian is doubly suspect. The modern-day belief that historians of no faith are more "objective" than historians of faith is a fallacy, for "the rejection of some or all religious truth is every bit as much an intellectual position as is the acceptance of religious truth. Both the believer and the non-believer have a point of view. … Objectivity does not derive from having no point of view."[17] It has been forgotten that all presentations of history rest on the worldview of the historian. The task of the historian is to review available sources and find a way to craft a comprehensible narrative from the mass of raw materials. The crafting of the subject into a readable and presentable book is heavily influenced by the worldview of the author, who, if honest, will openly communicate that worldview to the reader or student. I am a faithful Catholic, and as such I approach the subject of Church history from that perspective. That does not mean that I will ignore or gloss over the negative events or actions in the history of Church, but it does mean that I will interpret those events in light of my faith and the unique role of the Church in human history.

---

16. Ibid.
17. Warren H. Carroll, *The Founding of Christendom: A History of Christendom*, vol. 1 (Front Royal, VA: Christendom College Press, 1985), 11–12.

ONE

The Beginning — Pentecost and the Spread of the Gospel

"You shall be my witnesses in Jerusalem and in all Judea and Samaria and to the end of the earth."[1]

JESUS CHRIST

The fisherman had experienced a range of emotions over the last few months. Years ago, he had met the man who changed his life, who gave it meaning — the man who gave his authority to the fisherman and commanded him to lead a new community that would change the course of human history. Little did the fisherman know that hundreds of men would follow in his shoes and his name would be remembered and recalled for thousands of years. None of that occupied the fisherman's

---

1. Acts 1:8

mind at the moment. Instead, he was focused on the crowd in front of him: several thousand people from around the known world, enraptured by his tale of the Christ, by a miracle of the Holy Spirit hearing him in their native language. Peter had experienced every emotion during his friendship with Jesus. He had learned from the Master, lived and eaten with him, and loved him. Weakened by fear and consumed by self-preservation, he had denied knowing the man who had given him everything. But the Christ had forgiven him, and that act of mercy motivated Peter. He recalled vividly the day he heard the Master's body was not in the tomb and how he ran as fast as he could to see for himself the emptiness. Then, Jesus appeared to him and the other apostles and spent time with them, and then he left again. But he promised to send the Spirit, and when the Spirit came ten days later, Peter and the others were changed men. No longer afraid of the Jews, they were emboldened for the epic adventure Jesus called them to undertake. It began in Jerusalem in front of a large crowd, where the once simple fisherman proclaimed Jesus Christ crucified, died, and resurrected.

Every story has a beginning. Our family history begins some two thousand years ago in the imperial Roman province of Judea, an unimportant backwater in the imperial system. It was a place of frequent violence and home to a group of people who, unique in the Empire, were allowed to worship their one God. If asked, no one alive at the time would have thought that a motley collection of "nobodies" could lead a cultural and religious revolution that would change the Empire and sweep the world. In the first century A.D., a document known as the Acts of Caesar Augustus was published in order to honor the emperor and encourage others to imitate his virtues.[2] In the same century, a physician named Luke wrote another document with a similar title. It recorded the actions of a band of brothers — witnesses to the life and teachings of Jesus Christ, filled with the Holy Spirit — who spread his Good News throughout the world and provided a blueprint of life in the new kingdom.

---

2. Tim Gray and Jeff Cavins, *Walking with God: A Journey through the Bible* (West Chester, PA: Ascension Press, 2010), 262.

A REPLACEMENT FOR THE BETRAYER

P eter and the other apostles knew that in the new kingdom
they were not merely witnesses to the deeds of Jesus — they
were also endowed with authority as representatives of Christ.
The college of apostles had been incomplete since the death
of Judas the betrayer. Someone was needed to restore the college to its fullness and take Judas's place. The Eleven, recognizing their office as not merely organizational but also priestly,[3]
cast lots in accordance with the Davidic custom, where priestly
duties were assigned by lot. The lot fell on Matthias, who had
been one of the earliest disciples of Jesus. The college was now
complete, and the apostles waited the promised sending of the
Spirit.

PENTECOST — BIRTHDAY OF THE CHURCH

Under the Old Covenant, the feast of Pentecost celebrated the
giving of the Law by God to the Jewish people through Moses
(the Torah) fifty days after the first Passover. Ten days after Jesus
ascended into heaven (fifty after his resurrection) a group of 120
disciples, including the apostles and the Blessed Mother, gathered in Jerusalem. We know the story from the second chapter
of the Acts of the Apostles: they heard a mighty wind and were
shocked when tongues of fire descended on them. They began
speaking in other languages. This event alludes to the Tower
of Babel in the Old Testament, when human communication
was garbled because of mankind's sinfulness. But now, in the
New Covenant, God restored the community of humanity in a
shared language of the Gospel in the Church.[4] Tradition holds
that the event took place in the Upper Room where Jesus and
the apostles celebrated the Last Supper; however, an alterna-

---

3. Ibid., 264.
4. Ibid., 266.

tive theory proposes that the location was actually the Temple.[5] Filled with the Spirit, the apostles began preaching, which the assembled diverse crowd heard in their own native languages. This miracle captured the attention of the crowd, and Peter began the Church's evangelization efforts by proclaiming Jesus Christ crucified, died, and resurrected. After hearing Peter's testimony, the people asked him what they should do. He invited them to repent and be baptized. The Acts of the Apostles records that three thousand souls were added to the membership of the Church on the day of Pentecost.[6]

THE FIRST MARTYRS

As the Christian family grew in numbers, so did the pastoral needs of the community. The apostles knew their own chief mission was preaching, so they ordained seven men "full of the Spirit and of wisdom" to serve the needs of the community as deacons.[7] Stephen, one of the seven, was later arrested by the Jewish authorities for allegedly teaching against Moses — that is, the Law — and the Temple. Brought before the high priest and the Sanhedrin, Stephen presented a catechesis of Christ, illustrating that "the mystery of the Cross stands at the center of the history of salvation as recounted in the Old Testament ... that Jesus, Crucified and Risen, is truly the goal of all this history."[8] Enraged by Stephen's testimony, the assembly rushed him outside the city and stoned him, while a man named Saul watched over their garments. Saint Stephen, the first martyr of the Church, forgave his attackers before he died.

---

5. This makes sense when reading the narrative in the Acts of the Apostles, which describes a large number of people hearing the apostles speaking in their native languages — such a number would not have fit inside the Upper Room. Cisterns were also near the Temple, which could have been used for the baptisms that occurred after Peter's preaching. See Gray and Cavins, 265.

6. Acts 2:41.

7. Acts 6:3.

8. Benedict XVI, Wednesday General Audience on Stephen the Protomartyr, January 10, 2007, in *Jesus, the Apostles, and the Early Church* (San Francisco: Ignatius Press, 2007), 136.

The first apostle to give the ultimate witness of love for Christ and the Church was Saint James the Greater, the son of Zebedee and brother of Saint John the Beloved. The Roman Emperor Claudius (r. A.D. 41–54) made Herod Agrippa (r. A.D. 41–44), king of the Jews; shortly thereafter, Herod began a persecution of the Church in Jerusalem in order to quash a movement that reverenced a different King. He ordered the beheading of James and the imprisonment of Peter, who was miraculously freed.[9] Tradition holds that before his martyrdom in Jerusalem, James embarked on a missionary journey to the far reaches of the western Mediterranean and brought the Gospel to the shores of the Roman province of Hispania. Tradition further attests that after his death in Judea, the relics of James were miraculously translated to Spain, where they were discovered in the ninth century. Eventually, a grand cathedral arose at the spot, known as Santiago de Compostela, which has remained a popular pilgrimage destination since the Middle Ages.[10]

THE SPREAD OF THE GOSPEL

Jesus Christ never intended his saving message to remain only in the Roman province of Judea. Motivated by the command of Christ and emboldened by the indwelling of the Holy Spirit, the apostles left Jerusalem to spread the Gospel into the world.[11] Amazingly, these men traveled not only throughout the expansive Roman Empire, which had organized the known world and provided well-kept roads for travelers, but also beyond its borders. Tradition holds that John the Beloved traveled throughout Asia Minor, Andrew preached in Greece and modern-day Ukraine, Bartholomew went south to Arabia and perhaps India as well,

---

9. Acts 12.
10. James became the patron saint of Spain, known as "the Moor-slayer," as his intercession was invoked throughout the *Reconquista*, the centuries-long war of liberation by Catholic forces against the Muslim occupiers.
11. The Church used to celebrate the feast of the Dispersion of the Apostles liturgically on July 15.

Jude made his way to Mesopotamia and perhaps Armenia and Iran, Matthew may have traveled to Ethiopia, Philip journeyed to Asia Minor, Simon trekked to Iran, and Thomas spread the Good News in southern Iran and India.[12] Although it is interesting to note how far the apostles traveled, and to imagine the hardships they endured for love of Christ, it is vital for us to focus on what they did: preach. Their preaching was not to spread an idea or philosophy, since the Christian faith is neither of those things; rather, they gave witness to the person of Jesus. The Christian faith is ultimately the belief in the person of Jesus Christ and the modification of one's life to reflect his teachings. The apostles, Christ's closest friends on earth, concentrated on telling as many people as possible about the God-man whom they knew and loved.

THE GREATEST MISSIONARY

When we read the Scriptures, we notice repeated examples of God taking the seemingly insignificant and endowing it with great significance, or taking the weak to humble the strong, or asking the unlikely to undergo a great mission. One of the best examples of that divine strategy is the calling of Saint Paul as the Church's greatest missionary.

Saul, a Pharisee, was a zealous defender of the Jewish faith. Born in the city of Tarsus in the southeast corner of Asia Minor, Saul was well-educated, spoke Greek and Hebrew, and held Roman citizenship. Saul, filled with zeal to crush the blaspheming (in his eyes) followers of Jesus, was given the mission by the high priest to persecute Christians in Damascus, a city in Syria with a sizable Jewish population. So, Saul embarked on a journey to Damascus where, along the way, as we read in Acts, he encountered the Lord in a dramatic and shocking way. Profoundly changed by

---

12. See Warren H. Carroll, *The Founding of Christendom: A History of Christendom*, vol. 1 (Front Royal, VA: Christendom College Press, 1985), 406.

this encounter, Saul transformed from persecutor to missionary, and over the rest of his life he suffered for the Faith with repeated imprisonments, floggings, beatings, shipwrecks, and stoning.[13] Ultimately, he made three missionary journeys to strategic centers of Roman rule, preaching first to the Jewish communities and, after rejection by the Jews, focusing on the Gentiles.[14]

Saul's first missionary journey took place on the island of Cyprus, where he also changed his name to Paul. In the ancient world, Jews frequently had Greek names along with their given Jewish names. Saul's name was similar to the Greek *saulos*, a derogatory word for the way prostitutes walk.[15] Recognizing that his Jewish name might pose difficulties in preaching to the Gentiles, Saul changed his name to Paul, perhaps in honor of the Roman governor of Cyprus, Sergius Paulus, who converted as a result of Paul's preaching.[16] Paul's second missionary journey encompassed several locations, including Galatia, Philippi, Thessalonica, and the city of Corinth, which had been initially established by Julius Caesar as a Roman colony where freed slaves and army veterans settled. Paul's last missionary journey was a three-year stay at Ephesus.

Paul's missionary activity produced three vital effects in the early Church. First, his tireless journeying spread the Faith throughout the Roman Empire in centers of political and economic importance, which allowed for the rapid growth of the Church as the Faith spread easily along the Roman roads and waterways of commerce and government business. Second, Paul did not simply preach the Gospel and leave the new converts to their own devices. Rather, he chose and mentored men, known as "elders" (in Greek, *presbuteroi*, from which the word "presbyters," or "priests," derives) to lead their communities, providing continuity and an established hierarchical foundation. Third, Paul kept in contact with his nascent Christian communities by

---

13. See 2 Cor 11:23–29.
14. Paul's focus on the strategic centers of Roman rule is found in Gray and Cavins, 282.
15. Gray and Cavins, 275.
16. Ibid.

writing letters, which comprise thirteen of the twenty-seven in-spired books in the New Testament. Paul's missionary journeys successfully solidified the Faith in the Roman world. His suc-cess was grounded in the saving message of Jesus itself and was aided by Paul's versatility and adaptability; "he had the power to translate the Palestinian Gospel into language intelligible to the Greek world."[17] We cannot overstate the importance of Paul to the history of the Church. The Apostle to the Gentiles was "the greatest of converts, the greatest of disciples, greatest of missionaries [and] the follower in whom more than any other is mirrored the Master."[18]

A GENTILE CONVERTS

The presence of Jewish communities throughout the Roman Empire helped the early Church grow by providing groups in major centers where the first Christian missionaries could bring the Gospel. The earliest members and converts to the Faith were Jews, and the early Christians were very conscious of their connection to Judaism. But Paul's experience had proved that the Faith met resistance in the Jewish synagogues of the Roman Empire, so his missionary focus shifted to the Gentiles, who eagerly responded to the message and became members of the Church. One early Gentile conversion is recorded in the Acts of the Apostles and involves a vision received by Peter.

The Jewish people were a separated people in the ancient world. Their kosher laws forbade the eating of foods common in the Gentile world, which had produced a division between Jew and Gentile. When Peter was near the city of Joppa, he fell into a trance while waiting for something to eat. He saw the sky open and a blanket coming down from heaven filled with animals. A voice commanded him to get up and eat, but Peter refused,

17. Henry Chadwick, *The Early Church*, revised edition (New York: Penguin Books, 1993), 20.
18. Philip Hughes, *A History of the Church: Volume 1: The Church and the World in which the Church was Founded*, second edition (London: Sheed and Ward, 1998), 20.

for the food was unclean. The scene repeated itself three times before the vision ended. Eventually, Peter realized that the larger meaning of the vision was that the divide between Jews and Gentiles was over because of Christ. The purpose of the dietary laws, to remind the Jewish people of their salvation from slavery in Egypt by the Lord, was abrogated by the New Covenant of Christ. After the vision, men sent by a Roman centurion came to the house where Peter was staying and asked him to come to Caesarea. The centurion had received a visit by an angel, directing him to send for Peter.[19]

A Roman centurion was akin to a noncommissioned officer in our modern militaries. To be a centurion, a soldier was required to have at least sixteen years of military service. These officers were the backbone of the Roman military structure. A Roman legion, comprised nominally of five thousand soldiers, was organized into ten cohorts with six "centuries" per cohort. Within a century, a centurion commanded eighty men (originally, it was one hundred, hence the term "centurion").[20] Cornelius, the centurion who sent for Peter, was a member of the Italian cohort, and therefore a foreigner, but was known as a "God-fearing" man by the Jews. When Peter entered his home, Cornelius fell on his knees before him. He told Peter about his angelic visitor. Peter then realized the importance of his own vision of unclean food — there was to be no partiality between Jew and Gentile in the New Covenant. Peter preached about Christ to Cornelius's household, during which the Holy Spirit descended upon the inhabitants and all were baptized. The conversion of Cornelius the centurion was a monumental event in the life of the Church. It signified that the Gospel was meant not just for Jews but for the whole world. The conversion brought division within the Church, which faced an important test in her early life.

---

19. Acts 10:1–8.
20. For the Roman legion military structure, see Adrian Goldsworthy, *The Complete Roman Army* (London: Thames & Hudson, 2003), 46–47.

THE COUNCIL OF JERUSALEM

Throughout Church history, the Church faced many important questions, the answers to which impacted her life for centuries. In the early days, the first question was what to do with the Gentiles. Paul's missionary activity and Peter's visit to Cornelius's household, among other evangelization efforts, brought Gentile converts to the Faith. However, some believed these new Christians should adopt the Jewish dietary restrictions and the law of circumcision. This group, known as the Circumcision Party, was angry that Peter ate with Gentiles, and criticized him upon his return to Jerusalem. In an attempt to placate the Circumcision Party, when Peter later went to Antioch, he refused to eat with the Gentile converts there. Paul, in a spirit of fraternal correction, rebuked Peter for this action.[21] The issue became a debate as groups formed around James the Less, bishop of Jerusalem, who believed that all Christians should follow the Jewish customs, and Paul, who argued that Christ had fulfilled the Law and instituted the New Covenant, thereby abrogating the need to follow the dietary restrictions and circumcision of the Old Covenant.

In an effort to resolve the conflict, the apostles gathered in Jerusalem, where, after some debate, Peter spoke in favor of not requiring the Gentiles to be circumcised and abide by the dietary restrictions. James agreed, but proposed that Gentile converts follow the traditional law of "strangers among the Jews" as given by Moses — that is, do not eat meat offered to false gods or the flesh of strangled animals, and refrain from engaging in temple prostitution.[22] James's amendment was accepted, and the apostles promulgated their decision by sending Paul, Barnabas, and a few other men with letters to Antioch to inform the Christian

---

21. See Galatians 2. This episode is sometimes overblown by Protestants, who use it to illustrate 1) that Peter's primacy was not respected in the early Church or his leadership was suspect, because he gave in to the Circumcision Party; and 2) that Paul was the real leader of the early Church. Paul's rebuke of Peter is nothing more than fraternal correction, which even popes are liable to experience.
22. See Robert Louis Wilken, *The First Thousand Years: A Global History of Christianity* (New Haven, CT: Yale University Press, 2012), 21.

community in the city. The Council of Jerusalem set the procedure for how disagreements and questions of importance would be settled by the Church's leadership: collegiality with Petrine leadership.

In these first decades, the family of God had undergone an amazing transformation. What began as a small sect within a recognized group in the Roman Empire evolved into a separate community. Commanded by the Lord to take the Gospel to the four corners of the world, the Church's mission of evangelization resulted in converts from every walk of life and nationality embracing Christ and joining the new family of God. An important question concerning the addition of the Gentiles was settled through an exercise of apostolic leadership. The family was small but growing and would soon come into contact with the world's only superpower.

TWO

The Empire and the Church

> *"Two ways there are, one of life and one of death, but there is a great difference between the two ways."*[1]
>
> THE *DIDACHE*

The philosophy teacher was perplexed. He had mastered ancient Greek thought, but this new teaching threatened to turn the philosophical world upside down. How was he to interpret this new way of life? It gave purpose and meaning to his life in a way the Greeks had never done. His contact with the God-man Jesus, in the sacraments and teachings of the Catholic Church, led him to understand that the only authentic source of philosophical truth was Christ. He believed it was his duty to share that truth with others. As a young man, he had left his native Pal-

---

1. The *Didache*. Translated from the Greek text by Roswell D. Hitchcock, 1884, accessed September 18, 2018, http://reluctant-messenger.com/didache.htm.

estine to study philosophy in Ephesus. After his conversion at the age of thirty-eight, he settled in Rome, where he opened a school of Christian philosophy and allowed students to attend free of charge — because the truth of Christ was so important, it had to be made accessible to all. The philosopher poured his life into studying the Scripture, where he saw how the life of Jesus fulfilled the ancient Old Testament prophecies. He studied history and was the first to understand that there is a twofold dimension to history: sacred and secular, with Christ at the center.[2] He utilized his intellectual talents to combat early heresies, and when the Roman Empire turned its violent attention to the nascent Church, he wrote to defend and explain the Faith to the emperor and pagan society. When persecution came under the reign of Marcus Aurelius (r. 161–180), the philosopher's ardent love for Christ drove him to give his life in martyrdom. He is forever known as Saint Justin Martyr (100–165).

WHAT WAS THE ROMAN EMPIRE?

In his study of the impact of the Catholic faith on Europe, the historian Hilaire Belloc asked two important questions: "What was the Roman Empire?" and "What was the Church in the Roman Empire?" Answering these questions helps us understand the history of the early Church.

In the centuries before Christ, the city of Rome was a republic governed by elected magistrates, advised by the Senate. This form of government was designed to prevent one person or group from gaining supreme power. The Roman Republic began to change during the life of the outstanding general Julius Caesar, whose conquests (especially of Gaul) increased the power, prestige, and wealth of Rome. After Caesar's murder in 41 B.C., three men, Marc Antony (one of Caesar's generals), Octavian (Caesar's nephew and adopted son), and Marcus Aemilius Lepidus (a close ally of Caesar), stepped into the political void caused by Caesar's death and established a dictatorship known as the Second Triumvirate.

---

2. See Henry Chadwick, *The Early Church*, revised edition (New York: Penguin Books, 1993), 78.

Eventually, infighting and civil war ensued among the three, which ended when Octavian exiled Lepidus and defeated Marc Antony at the Battle of Actium in 31 B.C. Octavian was acknowledged as *imperator* (emperor) by the army and given the title "Augustus" by the Senate years later. Although Octavian kept the outward governmental framework of the Republic, he was a military dictator; thus the Roman Empire was born. The Empire reached its height of power, influence, and expanse in the mid-second century, when it encompassed all of Europe west of the Rhine and south of the Danube Rivers, including most of Britain, as well as North Africa, Greece, Asia Minor, Syria, and Palestine. The Empire was organized into forty provinces with a total population of sixty million people, most of whom lived an agrarian lifestyle (only 15 percent of the Empire lived in cities).[3] Above all, the Empire united a vast, diverse civilization in a "common mode of life," consisting of shared language, culture, and commerce, which all citizens embraced and preserved.[4] The Roman army was the foundation of the Empire. It was deployed in garrisons in cities that were connected by a well-maintained and extensive road network, allowing the free flow of resources and ideas.[5] It was into this political organization that the Church grew, and that growth raised the ire of the Empire, with violent results.

THE BURNING OF ROME

The night of July 18, A.D. 64, began 250 years of government-sanctioned persecution against the Catholic Church. On that night, a great fire flared up in the city of Rome. The fire raged for days,

---

3. For total population of the Empire, see Adrian Goldsworthy, *How Rome Fell: Death of a Superpower* (New Haven, CT: Yale University Press, 2009), 41. For percentage of the population who lived in cities, see Peter S. Wells, *Barbarians to Angels: The Dark Ages Reconsidered* (New York: W.W. Norton & Company, 2008), 72.
4. See Hilaire Belloc, *Europe and the Faith* (Rockford, IL: TAN Books and Publishers, Inc., 1992 [1920]), 22.
5. See Brennan Pursell, *History in His Hands: A Christian Narrative of the West* (New York: Crossroad, 2011), 81.

ultimately destroying several districts of the city and causing serious property damage as well as loss of life. When it subsided, the angry populace demanded answers about the fire's origin. Rumors circulated that the emperor was to blame for the fire, as it was known he wanted to remake the city according to his own design and even rename it after himself ("Neropolis").[6] In an effort to deflect criticism, the emperor fabricated a scapegoat. He blamed the fire on a small sect in the city that refused to honor the pagan gods: the Christians.

Nero became emperor of Rome in A.D. 54 at the young age of seventeen. The history of the Roman emperors illustrates that many men who came to the throne before the age of thirty-five went insane.[7] Nero certainly fits that description — the man was a psychopath. He was known to practice all forms of vice and was a cruel, "neurotic hedonist" who poisoned his brother, ordered the murder of his mother, and kicked his pregnant wife, Poppaea, to death because she scolded him for coming home late from the races one night.[8] Nero was a man "of about average height, his body was pockmarked and smelly, while he had light yellow hair, good but not handsome features, blue, rather weak eyes, too thick a neck, a big belly, and spindly legs" and was "ridiculously fussy about his person and his clothes, having his hair done in rows of curls."[9]

Nero blamed the Christians for the great fire and initiated the first of many persecutions against the early Church. He outlawed the Christian faith, ordering the arrest and imprisonment of Christians in Rome.[10] Those arrested who refused to abandon the Faith were horribly tortured and killed. Tacitus, a Roman sen-

---

6. See Tim Gray and Jeff Cavins, *Walking with God: A Journey through the Bible* (West Chester, PA: Ascension Press, 2010), 287.

7. Examples include Domitian (age 30), Commodus (age 19), and Elagabalus (age 17). It is interesting to note that the United States Constitution (Article II, Section 1.5) stipulates that only those who have reached the age of thirty-five can assume the office of President. I am convinced the Founding Fathers were well aware of Roman history when they stipulated that particular age requirement.

8. Desmond Seward, *Jerusalem's Traitor: Josephus, Masada and the Fall of Judea* (Cambridge, MA: Da Capo Press, 2009), 34 & 36.

9. Suetonius, *Lives of the Caesars*, VI, Nero, li., quoted in Seward, *Jerusalem's Traitor*, 37.

10. Nero's law against the Faith would remain Roman law until the early fourth century. Nero's persecution was limited to Rome; it was not Empire-wide.

ator and historian, described the horrors suffered by Christians under Nero: "[they] were covered with wild beasts' skins and torn to death by dogs; or they were fastened on crosses, and, when daylight failed, were burned to serve as lamps by night."[11] Although Nero tried to use the Christians as a scapegoat for the fire, his punishments served to bring about "a sentiment of pity [among the Roman people], due to the impression that they [Christians] were being sacrificed not for the welfare of the state but to the ferocity of a single man."[12]

Tradition holds that during Nero's persecution the twin pillars of the early Church, Saints Peter and Paul, were martyred in Rome. Peter demanded to be crucified upside down, and Paul, as a Roman citizen, was executed by beheading. Before their martyrdom, Peter and Paul had worked to strengthen the Christian community in the imperial capital and mentored elders to lead the flock after their deaths. As a result, the bishop of Rome, Linus (67–76), became the successor to Saint Peter and the universal pastor of the Christian community.

THE JEWISH REVOLT

A few years after Nero's persecution of Christians in Rome, a devastating event occurred in the Holy Land that would forever shape the history and worship of the Jewish people, and also influence the early Church.

Gessius Florus, the Roman Procurator of Judea, was a wicked man. He disliked the Jewish people and wanted to goad them into rebellion against Rome. Florus provoked the people by commandeering money from the Temple treasury in the name of the emperor. The people, incensed, rioted in the streets of Jerusalem. Florus demanded that the Jews hand over the leaders of the demonstrations. When the people refused, he ordered Ro-

---

11. Tacitus, *Annals*, XV, 44, quoted in Jean Comby, *How to Read Church History: From the Beginnings to the Fifteenth Century*, vol. 1 (New York: Crossroads, 2001), 38.
12. Ibid.

man troops to restore order. The army killed thousands of Jews in Jerusalem, even crucifying Roman citizens, which was against imperial law. This was the tipping point for the Jews, and more men joined the rebellion. The rebels quickly overwhelmed the small Roman garrison in Jerusalem. Word reached the Roman legate in Syria that the situation in Judea was out of control, so he ordered the Twelfth Legion, augmented by mercenaries and auxiliary troops, to quell the Jewish rebellion. On the march to Judea, Jewish rebels at the pass of Beth-Horon ambushed and slaughtered the legion.[13] News of the massacre of the Roman legion spread throughout Judea, encouraging more people to join the rebellion, which now became a full-scale war.

Rome never allowed those who defeated a legion to remain unpunished. When word of the Twelfth's defeat reached the capitol, Nero ordered General Titus Flavius Vespasian to Judea. Vespasian was "a no-nonsense sort of man, tough, shrewd, and efficient, with a caustic wit, a soldier's soldier who always led from the front and had been wounded several times."[14] Vespasian was a confident and experienced combat commander, a veteran of thirty battles fought in Germania and Britain against some of Rome's fiercest foes. He took command of several legions and ordered his son, Titus, to lead the Fifteenth Legion from Egypt to Judea. Nearly sixty thousand Roman troops were dispatched to Judea to put down the Jewish revolt. Vespasian embarked on a systematic campaign, initially refusing to attack the main rebel stronghold of Jerusalem and focusing instead on controlling the surrounding areas and strategic towns on the approach to the great city.

The main source of information for the Great Jewish Revolt is from the writings of Josephus (A.D. 37–100), a Levite and a Jewish nobleman (a descendant of the famous Maccabee kings on his mother's side), whose many books include *The Wars of the*

---

13. This was the same location where Joshua in the Old Testament commanded the sun to stand still so the Israelites could defeat the Amorites (see Jos 10:10).
14. Seward, *Jerusalem's Traitor*, 78.

Jews.[15] Josephus had lived in Rome in the years before the Jewish rebellion, so he was intimately aware of the power of the Empire. He returned to his homeland and tried in vain to convince his countrymen that war against Rome was futile. But Josephus believed it was his duty to defend his nation, so he joined the rebellion and took command of the city of Jotapata (also known as Yodfat), which the Romans besieged for forty-seven days. Eventually, Roman soldiers broke into the city and killed most of the city's population. Josephus survived and was taken prisoner. He soon gained favor with Vespasian for his knowledge, respect for Rome, and clever mind. The Romans used Josephus to convince other Jewish towns to surrender, so most Jews saw him as a traitor. At the end of the war, Josephus settled in Rome, became an imperial citizen, and took as his own the imperial family name, Flavius, in honor of their patronage.

THE HOLY CITY DESTROYED

After three years of fighting, Vespasian's systematic campaign in Judea came to its culmination with the siege of Jerusalem. The situation in the city at the arrival of the Roman legions was desperate. Zealots inside the city had unleashed ferocious class warfare, breaking into rival factions so that the Jews in the city were fighting not only the Romans, but also each other. As Vespasian's army prepared for siege, word reached the general that Nero had committed suicide, triggering a year of civil war among rival claimants to the throne. Vespasian left the Judean campaign and placed his son Titus in command of the siege. Eventually, Vespasian emerged victorious from the civil war and became emperor in the summer of A.D. 69. Titus embarked on the biggest siege to date in Roman history. He placed the Tenth Legion, "Caesar's Own," on the lower slopes of the Mount of Olives. The soldiers used wood from the

---

15. His other famous works are *The Antiquities of the Jews* (a history of the Jewish people from the creation accounts in Genesis to his own time) and *The Life of Flavius Josephus* (an autobiography).

Garden of Gethsemane to build siege engines.

Conditions in the city went from desperate to horrific. A large number of people had come to the city for the Passover feast when the Romans began the siege. As months passed, starvation reigned. People ate leather and hay, and even sifted through cow dung looking for scraps of food — for "what had once revolted them now became their normal diet."[16] There was even a ghastly account of a mother, delirious from hunger, who ate her infant child.[17] The death toll climbed until the Jewish soldiers were forced to walk over corpses to sally forth from the city. After six months of siege, the Romans prepared their final assault. Titus personally led the way and ordered that the Temple was not to be destroyed. Unfortunately, those orders were not obeyed, and the Roman troops rampaged through the city. The destruction of the Temple, which had been only recently completed in A.D. 64, was a watershed moment in the life of the children of Israel, although it was not the first time the Temple had been destroyed. In fact, the Babylonians destroyed the first Temple on August 10, 587 B.C. The second Temple was destroyed 657 years later on the same day. The loss of the Temple fundamentally changed the practice of Judaism from a worship that required animal sacrifice to an observance of the Law as the defining characteristic of Jewish faith. Titus triumphantly marched back to Rome in A.D. 71 and carried with him the great menorah from the Temple.[18]

Although Jerusalem had fallen to the Roman legions, a group of Jews led by Eleazar ben Ya'ir took refuge in the isolated rock plateau fortress of Masada for three years. The Romans, under the command of Lucius Flavius Silva, built an impressive 400-foot ramp in order to enter the fortress. Knowing the final Roman assault was near, Eleazar ordered his troops to commit suicide with

---

16. Seward, *Jerusalem's Traitor*, 200.
17. Josephus, *The Wars of the Jews*, Book 6, Chapter 3.4, trans. William Whiston, A.M. (Peabody, MA: Hendrickson Publishers, 2006), 737.
18. Genseric the Vandal took the menorah to Carthage in A.D. 455 when he sacked Rome. It was recovered by the Byzantine general Belisarius in 533 and sent back to Jerusalem by Emperor Justinian. Unfortunately, the menorah vanished after the Islamic invasion in the seventh century.

their families to avoid capture. When the Romans broke into Masada in the morning, a ghastly sight greeted them.

After years of continued clashes, another Jewish revolt commenced in A.D. 132 under the leadership of Simon bar Kokhba. Once more, the Romans violently put down the rebellion, this time leveling the entire city of Jerusalem. It was replaced by a new city, founded by Emperor Hadrian, and renamed Aelia Capitolina.

Over one million Jews died in the Great Jewish Revolt, and tens of thousands were sold into slavery. Christian inhabitants of Jerusalem, remembering Jesus' prophetic words, fled to the countryside before the siege and were not deeply impacted by the war. The destruction of the Temple and the subsequent change in Judaism helped solidify the distinction between Jews and Christians. Originally viewed as a Jewish phenomenon, the Christian faith became a permanent separate entity as a result of the Jewish war with Rome.

THE *DIDACHE*

The early Church produced an interesting document known as the *Didache*, or *The Teaching of the Twelve Apostles*.[19] The *Didache* outlines the choice each person faces — the way of life and the way of death. The way of life involves living out the Ten Commandments, whereas the way of death involves living by the sins of pride, lust, lying, stealing, murder, adultery, sodomy, and abortion. From the earliest days of the Faith, as the *Didache* illuminates, Christian living was focused on morality, on living in accordance with the example of Christ and the teachings of the Church. The *Didache* also provides information on the worship and sacramental life of the early Church. The document exhorts Christians to pray every day — especially the Lord's Prayer, which should be recited three times a day. The Sacrament of Baptism and its ap-

---

19. There is no known author of the *Didache*. It was discovered in a monastery in Constantinople in 1883. An excellent website with multiple translations of the *Didache* is http://www.earlychristianwritings.com/.

plication is mentioned in the *Didache*. The candidate was required to fast before reception of the sacrament and was baptized in the Trinitarian formula with water. Prayers for the celebration of the Eucharist on the Lord's Day are found in the *Didache*, along with the admonition that only those who are baptized can receive the Lord's body and blood. Finally, the document also testifies to the practice of the early Church that only worthy, morally upright men should be appointed as bishops and deacons in the Church.

THE FAITH SPREADS

The Faith spread rapidly within the Roman Empire for several reasons. The Empire itself provided a universal organized structure for the rapid spread of ideas. Although many groups of people lived within the confines of the Empire, each with their own culture and language, all shared the common tongue, Greek, which was the language for business, education, and everyday life (at this time, Latin was the official state language and used primarily for political purposes). Moreover, the initial decades of the Church were times of peace in the Empire, which afforded people the time to ask important life questions and seek answers. The Roman Empire was overall a religious society. Romans understood that there was a connection between religious faith and morality, and between conduct in life and one's fate in the afterlife. Religion had a political dimension as well; participation in the state cults was viewed as a civic duty. All forms of religious cults existed in the Empire, from nature-worship to emperor-worship. The mystery religions that originated in Egypt and Persia were also popular and contained rites of initiation, sacred food, sacrifices, and a hierarchical structure, elements found also in the Faith, which assisted in conversions. Within the Roman religious environment, several groups were predisposed to accept the Gospel, such as the "proto-Christians," known to Jews as "God-fearers." These proto-Christians were Gentiles (Roman pagans) who, as a result of contact with Judaism, came to adore the one true God. They read the Old Testament and tried to live in accordance with the Ten

Commandments.[20] Additionally, Hellenized Jews had been part of the Jewish Diaspora and were considered half-pagan by Palestine Jews. Hellenized Jews took Greek names, spoke Latin and Greek, and dressed like the pagans. The several large communities of Hellenized Jews throughout the Empire provided rich evangelization opportunities for the missionaries of the early Church.

Pagans were attracted to the Faith by the witness of the early Christians, especially the martyrs. Romans were also astounded by how the Christians treated the poor with a dignity unknown to the pagan world.[21] Christian charity toward pagans was a deeply effective form of evangelization. Pagans understood Christians caring for Christians, but when believers also cared for pagans during plagues and other times of need, the pagans were intrigued. Indeed, "the practical application of charity was probably the most potent single cause of Christian success."[22] Ultimately, what allowed the Faith to spread rapidly in its first few decades was the fact that the Gospel was inclusive — it was meant for everyone. Roman society was very class-oriented, and religious cults were organized similarly. In contrast, the Catholic Church accepted everyone regardless of race, class status, education, or profession. That openness was unique and intriguing to people in the first-century Roman Empire.

MORE PERSECUTION

Vespasian, the Roman general who had quashed the Great Jewish Revolt, reigned as emperor for a decade (A.D. 69–79). Upon his death, his son Titus, commanding general of the Roman forces that had taken Jerusalem, succeeded to the imperial purple. Titus became the first Roman emperor to succeed his biological father,

---

20. See Rod Bennett, *The Apostasy that Wasn't: The Extraordinary Story of the Unbreakable Early Church* (El Cajon, CA: Catholic Answers Press, 2015), 52.
21. See Robert Louis Wilken, *The First Thousand Years: A Global History of Christianity* (New Haven, CT: Yale University Press, 2012), 156–158.
22. Chadwick, *The Early Church*, 56.

in what became known as the Flavian dynasty. Titus's brief reign lasted only two years, but during those two years the Flavian amphitheater (also known as the Colosseum) in Rome was completed and Mount Vesuvius erupted. After Titus died of fever, his younger brother Domitian became emperor. Domitian struggled with his mental health while emperor and was an "unpredictable and treacherous, [and] a truly horrible man who delighted in cruelty."[23] He was the first Roman emperor to deify himself with the title "Lord and God" during his reign.[24] Domitian was paranoid; he spent his last days in a specially constructed hall of polished surfaces that acted as mirrors so he could see anyone trying to sneak up on him. He also delighted in the sadistic task of catching flies and spearing them with a special needle. Domitian initiated a limited persecution of the Church by striking down members of the imperial family who had become Christians. It was during his fifteen-year reign that the beloved Saint John the Evangelist was exiled to the island of Patmos. Eventually, imperial officials grew angry at the whims of the mentally ill Domitian. He was assassinated in 96, and was succeeded by his adviser Nerva.

THE EPISTLE OF SAINT CLEMENT OF ROME

Before the turn of the century, a man in Rome named Clement, who had known Peter and Paul, was selected to become the fourth bishop of the city.[25] Clement was aware that his position

---

23. Seward, *Jerusalem's Traitor*, 264.
24. Previous emperors were deified after their deaths, never while alive.
25. Historians debate the dating of Clement's *Epistle*. The original letter was lost sometime during the Middle Ages and the most recent copy is from the seventeenth century. The traditional view holds to a date of A.D. 96 because Eusebius of Caesarea indicated that Clement wrote the letter toward the end of Emperor Domitian's reign. An alternative date of A.D. 70 was proposed by Msgr. Thomas J. Herron, who was the English language secretary in the Congregation for the Doctrine of the Faith under Cardinal Joseph Ratzinger, in his book *Clement and the Early Church of Rome: On the Dating of Clement's First Epistle to the Corinthians*. Msgr. Herron argues that since the letter favorably mentions Jewish temple practices, which seems odd if the Temple was destroyed, the letter must have been written before the destruction of the Jerusalem Temple in A.D. 70. Additionally, Msgr. Herron points out that the *Epistle* relies heavily on quotations from the Old Testament but not the Gospels, which is a curious omission if written in the year 96. Msgr. Herron deduces that Clement does not quote from the Gospels because his letter was written before them.

was unique in the Church. It required diligent oversight of the other Christian communities scattered throughout the Empire, which is why he was greatly troubled by reports from the Christian community in Corinth (initially established by Saint Paul). Word had reached Rome that the Corinthians were openly rebelling against their priests. This uprising threatened not only to tear apart the Church in Corinth, but also to affect the Church's evangelization mission, so Clement resolved to act quickly. He sent a firm and fatherly reprimand to the Corinthians that became known as the *Epistle of Saint Clement of Rome*. Clement focused his letter on the theme of order. Order, according to Clement, is the expression of the will of God and is good, whereas disorder is the expression of the will of the devil and is bad. The Corinthians were giving in to the temptations of the Evil One by their rebellion, which was weakening the unity of the Church and causing scandal among the pagans. Clement wrote, "Disgraceful, beloved, indeed, exceedingly disgraceful and unworthy of your training in Christ, is the report that the well-established and ancient Church of the Corinthians is ... in revolt against the presbyters. And this report has reached not only us but also people that differ from us in religion."[26]

Clement's letter illustrates three fundamental Catholic doctrines. First, it affirms the apostolic teaching that the clergy derive their authority from God and not from the people. In other words, "the Church's structure was sacramental not political."[27] Second, Clement reminds the Corinthians that the Church's organization is apostolic. The apostles handed on their authority through ordination to other men in the communities they established. This is known as apostolic succession. Finally, Clement's letter is the "first exercise of the Roman primacy after Saint Peter's death" and proves the early Church believed in papal pri-

26. Saint Clement of Rome, *The Epistle to the Corinthians*, 47, trans. James A. Kleist, S.J. (New York: Paulist Press, 1946), 38.
27. Benedict XVI, Wednesday General Audience on Saint Clement, Bishop of Rome, March 7, 2007, in *Church Fathers: From Clement of Rome to Augustine* (San Francisco: Ignatius Press, 2008), 10.

macy and universal jurisdiction.[28] Clement may have been writing on an internal matter of a particular church, but his letter clearly indicates he knew he had the authority to command the Corinthians to stop their rebellion. He wrote, "If some shall disobey the words which have been spoken by him [Christ] through us [Clement], let them know they will involve themselves in no small transgression and danger."[29] Saint John the Beloved was still alive at the time of the Corinthian uprising, but it was Clement, the bishop of Rome, rather than the living apostle, who wrote the admonition. The Corinthians acknowledged Clement's epistle as authoritative; they ended their rebellion and restored the ousted priests upon receipt of the letter, which was still being read in the city a century later.[30]

WHAT WAS THE CHURCH
IN THE ROMAN EMPIRE?

With the closing of the first century, we can clearly answer Catholic historian Hilaire Belloc's question, "What was the Church in the Roman Empire?" Belloc first assessed what the Church was *not*. The Church was not an opinion, a fashion, a philosophy, or a theory; instead, she was a "clearly delineated body corporate based on numerous exact doctrines, extremely jealous of its unity and of its precise definitions, and filled, as was no other body of men at that time, with passionate conviction."[31] The Church was a distinct and unique organism within the Roman Empire. She was organized in a hierarchical structure centered on bishops, the chief of whom was the bishop of Rome. Most cults in the Empire were local and attached to specific places; however, the Church's structure, doctrine, and worship were not dependent

---

28. Ibid., 8.
29. Saint Clement of Rome, *The Epistle to the Corinthians*, 59.
30. The epistle was revered throughout the early Church to the point where some considered it canonical, although it was not ultimately included in the canon of Scripture.
31. Belloc, *Europe and the Faith*, 35.

on geography but were the same throughout the Empire. At the end of the first century, there were fewer than 10,000 Christians, comprising only 0.0017 percent of the total imperial population of 60 million. By the end of the second century, the Church had grown to 200,000 members, though still less than 1 percent of the Roman population. At the time of the first Empire-wide persecution, initiated in 250 by the Emperor Decius (r. 249–251), there were more than one million Christians (2 percent of the imperial population). By the beginning of the fourth century, the Church was home to six million people, or 10 percent of the population of the Roman Empire.[32] The Church came into conflict with Roman society because her teachings and lifestyle were in opposition to societal norms. Roman society "believed man to be sufficient to himself and all belief to be mere opinions." Conversely, the Church "proposed statement instead of hypothesis, affirmed concrete historical facts instead of suggesting myths, and treated its ritual of 'mysteries' as realities instead of [merely] symbols."[33]

PAGAN ATTACKS ON THE CHURCH

The growing Catholic population became a concern for certain pagan authors who were dumbfounded that people would join what they saw as such a nonsensical religion. They attacked the Church in order to dissuade Romans from joining this new religion. The three main critics of the Church and her teaching, who wrote various books, pamphlets, and tracts against her, were Celsus (second century), Porphyry (234–305), and Julian the Apostate (r. 361–363).[34]

Celsus, a second-century philosopher, wrote the first major pagan attack against the Catholic Church. Most of what we know about Celsus and his anti-Catholic work *True Doctrine* (c. A.D.

---

32. Data on the numbers of Christians is found in Robert Louis Wilken, *The First Thousand Years: A Global History of Christianity* (New Have, CT: Yale University Press, 2012), 65–66.
33. Belloc, *Europe and the Faith*, 38. This is also a sentiment embraced by the modern world.
34. Julian's attack on the Church and her teaching is discussed in Chapter Three.

170) comes from the writings of the Catholic apologist Origen (185–254), who wrote a work known as *Contra Celsum* that refuted Celsus's criticisms of the Church. Celsus utilized popular critiques as well as intellectual arguments in his attack on the Church. He viewed Jesus as a low-grade magician who duped people into believing he could actually perform miracles.[35] Celsus considered Christians a revolutionary fad, a threat to the ancient culture and traditions of Rome. Romans believed that religion and the nation were linked — one could not exist without the other — therefore, an extraterritorial group like the Catholic Church was an odd, seditious, and potentially threatening institution. Celsus also believed the newness of the Faith made it untrustworthy. The only acceptable and authentic religions, in the eyes of Celsus, were those whose teachings had been passed down from multiple generations. "Greco-Roman society revered the past. The older something was, the better it was thought to be … [because] those who lived very long ago, were thought to have been closer to the gods."[36]

Celsus extended his theological criticisms of the Church to foundational doctrinal teachings, such as the Incarnation, the Resurrection, and Jesus' divinity. Celsus questioned the timing of the Incarnation, asking: "Is it only now after such a long age that God has remembered to judge the human race? Did he not care before?" He found the Incarnation unreasonable: "The assertion that some God or son of God has come down to earth as judge of mankind is most shameful, and no lengthy argument is required to refute it. What is the purpose of such a descent on the part of God? Was it in order to learn what

35. Roman society was tolerant of various practices, but magic was not one of them. The practice of magic was a criminal offense, and calling someone a magician was a grave insult. See Robert Louis Wilken, *The Christians as the Romans Saw Them*, Second Edition (New Haven, CT: Yale University Press, 1984), 99. Additionally, the Roman legal system inflicted capital punishment on those convicted of practicing magic. The penalties included exposure to wild beasts, slitting the throat, or being burned alive. See the *Sentential* of Julius Paullus, 5, 23, 17, quoted in Gary Michuta, *Hostile Witnesses: How the Historic Enemies of the Church Prove Christianity* (El Cajon, CA: Catholic Answers Press, 2016), 64.

36. Wilken, *The Christians as the Romans Saw Them*, 122.

was going on among men? Does he now know everything?"[37] Celsus considered the resurrection of Jesus an unnatural and therefore suspect event. Celsus did not dispute the claim that a man could be God or that men should worship him, but he doubted Jesus' divinity because the Savior ate normal human food and spoke in a normal human voice. According to Celsus, "A divine figure would have had an enormously loud speaking voice!"[38] He opined that it would have been better for the Christians to worship Jonah or Daniel from the Old Testament, men who had accomplished astounding feats, rather than Jesus. Finally, Celsus attacked the Faith because he saw it as nothing more than an apostate group from Judaism. Celsus viewed Christian repudiation of circumcision and Jewish dietary laws as proof that the movement was illegitimate and that no self-respecting Roman should join it.[39]

Porphyry (234–305) was born in Tyre (modern-day Lebanon) on the coast of the Mediterranean Sea, and was a Neoplatonic philosopher. He wrote a scathing critique of the Catholic Church titled *Against the Christians*, which was refuted by a long list of Christian apologists and intellectuals, including Eusebius of Caesarea, Saint Jerome, and Saint Augustine. Porphyry's anti-Catholic work is known only from these Christian writers because Emperors Constantine and Theodosius II ordered copies of his work to be burned in the fourth and fifth centuries.[40] Porphyry attacked the Scriptures with literary and historical criticism, arguing that they did not provide a reliable historical account of Jesus. Porphyry believed such central Christian doctrines as the Incarnation and the Resurrection were fabrications. He was stupefied that Christians would believe Jesus was an incarnate god:

---

37. *Contra Celsum*, Chapter 4 in Comby, 32.
38. See Henry Chadwick, *The Church in Ancient Society: From Galilee to Gregory the Great* (Oxford: Oxford University Press, 2001), 113.
39. Wilken, *The Christians as the Romans Saw Them*, 116.
40. For the imperial book burning see Wilken, *The Christians as the Romans Saw Them*, 126, and Michuta, *Hostile Witnesses*, 125.

Even supposing that some Greeks were stupid enough to think that gods dwell in statues, this would be a purer conception than to accept that the divine had descended into the womb of the Virgin Mary, that he had become an embryo, that after his birth he had been wrapped in swaddling clothes, stained with blood, bile and worse. ... Why, when he was taken before the high priest and governor, did not the Christ say anything worthy of a divine man ... ? He allowed himself to be struck, spat upon on the face, crowned with thorns. ... Even if he had to suffer by order of God, he should have accepted the punishment but should not have endured his passion without some bold speech, some vigorous and wise word addressed to Pilate his judge, instead of allowing himself to be insulted like one of the rabble off the streets.[41]

The Church endured general criticisms from a host of pagan authors in addition to Celsus and Porphyry, which included the charges that Christians were atheists, ignorant and poor people, bad citizens, cannibals, and sexual deviants. These pagan critics believed Christians were atheists because they did not participate in the traditional and imperial polytheistic religious cults. This angered the Romans, since they thought the Christian lack of faith in the gods could bring divine wrath and vengeance on the Empire. Pagan critics attempted to dissuade members of the upper class from joining the Church by arguing — falsely — that only members of the socially inferior class (women, children, slaves, the poor) were attracted to the Christian faith. Imperial Roman society and its religious cults were highly class-stratified. The Church, teaching that all believers were equal regardless of social standing, threatened the established social order. Additionally, pagan authors charged Christians with a lack of patriotism

41. Comby, 33.

because they refused to worship the emperor, which was considered blasphemy and treason, and were allegedly not interested in political affairs or the welfare of the Empire. In reality, Christians were very much concerned with state affairs and, despite the persecutions, prayed for the prosperity of the Empire and the well-being of the emperor.

Early Christians believed in the Real Presence of Jesus in the Eucharist — that they were eating and drinking the body and blood of Christ. Pagans, misunderstanding, applied the charge of cannibalism to the Eucharist. Roman society tolerated many vices, but cannibalism was something not even immoral Rome abided. One of the earliest Christian apologists, Marcus Minucius Felix (c. 200), was a lawyer who wrote a dialogue between a Christian and a pagan, addressing the primary attacks of Roman pagans on the Church. The pagan labeled Christians as sexual deviants, baby-killers, and cannibals:

> The story about the initiation of new recruits is as detestable as it is well known. An infant, covered with flour, in order to deceive the unwary, is placed before the one who is to be initiated into the mysteries. Deceived by this floury mass, which makes him believe that his blows are harmless, the neophyte kills the infant. They avidly lick up the blood of the infant and argue over how to share its limbs. By this victim they are pledged together, and it is because of their complicity in this crime that they keep mutual silence! Everyone knows about their banquets, and these are talked of everywhere. On festivals they assemble for a feast with all their children, their sisters, their mothers, people of both sexes and every age. After eating their fill, when the excitement of the feast is at its height and their drunken ardor has inflamed incestuous passions, they provoke a dog which has been tied to a lampstand to leap, throwing it a piece of meat be-

yond the length of the cord which holds it. The light which could have betrayed them having thus been extinguished, they then embrace one another, quite at random. If this does not happen in fact, it does so in their minds, since that is their desire.[42]

Despite these libelous attacks, by the third century, the Christian apologist Tertullian could boast "we are but of yesterday and we have filled all you have — cities, islands, forts, towns, assembly halls, even military camps, tribes, town councils, the palace, senate and forum. We have left you nothing but the temples."[43]

THE TIME OF MAJOR PERSECUTIONS

From the first to the fourth centuries, there were twelve major imperial Roman persecutions of the Catholic Church. Many of these were confined to Rome and the surrounding areas or particular provinces, but some were Empire-wide. At times, Christians were ignored by the state, although Nero's law against the Church remained on the books. At other times, Christians were violently persecuted because they were an identifiable minority; or because they were suspected of nefarious activity (they necessarily maintained a certain secrecy due to their illegal status); or because Romans considered them antisocial, since they tended to live close together while rejecting elements of Roman society, such as the public baths, and spectacles like the gladiatorial games. Saint Justin commented, "The world suffers nothing from Christians but hates them because they reject its pleasures."[44] Frequently, imperial politics and affairs of state determined whether Christians were persecuted or left in peace. Christians were

---

42. *Octavius* 9,6, quoted in Comby, 30.
43. Tertullian, *Apologia*, 37.
44. Justin Martyr, *Epistle to Diogentes*, 6, quoted in Diane Moczar, *Ten Dates Every Catholic Should Know: The Divine Surprises and Chastisements that Shaped the Church and Changed the World* (Manchester: NH, 2005), 4.

easy scapegoats, blamed for various regional and national events. Tertullian mocked the Roman tendency to scapegoat Christians when he wrote: "If the Tiber rises too high or the Nile too low, the cry is 'the Christians to the lion.' All of them to a single lion?"[45]

THE PERSECUTION OF TRAJAN

Early in the second century, Emperor Trajan sent a man known as Pliny (called "the Younger" to distinguish him from his well-known uncle, Pliny the Elder, who had died in the blast of Mount Vesuvius in 79) to be the imperial legate in the province of Bithynia (modern-day Turkey). Pliny the Younger was instructed to conduct a financial audit, examine local governments, stop political disorder, and investigate the military situation. Soon after his arrival in the region, a group of butchers filed a complaint against Christians. The butchers were angry because the new sect was gaining converts, which impacted their business; pagan converts to the Faith refused to buy their sacrificial meat for use in the pagan temples. Pliny knew that Christians were an illegal sect, but wondered whether he needed to initiate a new persecution. He wrote a letter to Trajan, requesting instruction. The emperor responded with a benign neglect policy, telling Pliny to not actively pursue Christians if they were quiet and not public in the manifestation of their faith. But if the Christians caused trouble, Pliny was to arrest them.[46] Trajan's sensible policy, designed to limit the unnecessary involvement of the state in private affairs, was discarded several years later when a large earthquake rocked the city of Antioch in Bithynia. Aftershocks from the earthquake continued for days, causing the city to suffer terrible destruction and many deaths. Trajan had been visiting the city and was injured when the natural disaster struck. The people were angry. They

---

45. Chadwick, *The Early Church*, 29.
46. Trajan's policy is the first "don't ask/don't tell" policy in history.

believed the pagan gods had allowed the earthquake because the city housed a significant number of Christians.[47] Trajan acquiesced to the blood lust of the people and ordered a persecution of Christians in the city. He arrested the long-standing and well-known bishop of the city, Ignatius. The elderly bishop, who had direct apostolic ties as a disciple of Saint John the Evangelist, had overseen the Antiochene Christian community for three decades. Trajan wanted to make an example of Ignatius, so he commanded the bishop be taken to Rome under armed guard and executed in the Flavian amphitheater. That decision proved providential for the history of the Church, since during his long journey to the capital Ignatius wrote letters to six Christian communities (the Ephesians, Magnesians, Trallians, Romans, Philadelphians, and Smyrnaeans), and to one fellow bishop, Saint Polycarp.

These letters not only provide detail into the life of the early Church, but also illustrate Ignatius's deep love of Christ and the Church. His letters verify early Christian belief in the central doctrines of the Faith, such as the Trinity, the Incarnation, the Divinity of Christ, the Real Presence of Christ in the Eucharist, and the hierarchical structure of the Church (unified by the primacy of the bishop of Rome).[48] Ignatius uses special language in his letter to the Romans, referring to the Roman Church as "worthy of God, worthy of honor, worthy of being called blessed, worthy of praise, worthy of success, worthy of veneration."[49] Ignatius was concerned that influential members of the Church in Rome might try to intervene on his behalf and prevent his martyrdom. He had embraced his cross and desired to fulfill the Lord's plan for the end of this earthy life, writing, "God's wheat I am, and by the teeth of wild beasts I am

---

47. Antioch had been the home of Saint Peter for a time and was the place where the followers of Jesus first received the name "Christians." See Acts 11:26.

48. Ignatius's letters so thoroughly prove that the early Church was the Catholic Church that the sixteenth-century Protestant revolutionary John Calvin tried to discredit them by writing "[there is] nothing more nauseating, than the absurdities which have been published under the name of Ignatius [of Antioch]." John Calvin, *Institutes of the Christian Religion*, i. 13.29, accessed April 27, 2017, http://www.ccel.org/ccel/calvin/institutes/.

49. Margherita Guarducci, *The Primacy of the Church of Rome: Documents, Reflections, Proofs*, trans. Michael J. Miller (San Francisco: Ignatius Press, 2003), 27–28.

to be ground that I may prove Christ's pure bread."[50] Ignatius also exhorted his fellow Christians to remain obedient to their bishops and priests. He gave the Church her name — the Catholic Church — when he wrote to the Smyrnaeans, "Where the bishop appears, there let the people be, just as where Jesus Christ is, there is the Catholic Church."[51] Ignatius's letter to the Philadelphians contains one of the earliest references to the belief in the Real Presence of Jesus in the Eucharist. The Sacred Liturgy was the center of Christian life in the early Church, and Ignatius exhorted his brothers and sisters to "take care, then, to partake of one Eucharist, for, one is the Flesh of Our Lord Jesus Christ, and one the cup to unite us with His Blood."[52] This man of deep faith and love for the Church arrived in Rome and was martyred by lions in the Colosseum in the year 116.[53]

EARLY HERESIES

The early Church dealt not only with external Roman persecution, but also with internal persecution in the form of false teachings, known as heresies. One of the earliest falsehoods that sought to reshape the Church's fundamental teachings was Gnosticism (from the Greek *gnosis*, which means "knowledge"). Gnostics held to a negative view of the material world and believed it was the creation of an evil god, whereas spiritual things were positive and

---

50. Ignatius of Antioch, *Epistle to the Romans*, 4, trans. James A. Kleist, S.J. (New York: Paulist Press, 1946), 82.

51. Ignatius of Antioch, *Epistle to the Smyrnaeans*, 8. Catholic is derived from the Greek term for "universal." Many mistakenly believe the Church's name is the Roman Catholic Church. That term is a Protestant one developed in the nineteenth century by Anglican (Church of England) theologians studying ecclesiology who posited the Church was one tree with several branches (their teaching is known as the "branch theory"), which they identified as Anglo-Catholic (Church of England and Episcopalians in the United States), Orthodox, and Roman Catholic, or those united with the pope. The term "Roman Catholic" from this theory became the standard English language term for the Church in the twentieth century, but it is not a Catholic term and is never used officially by the Church.

52. Ignatius of Antioch, *Epistle to the Philadelphians*, 4.

53. Saint Ignatius'a death is usually cited as A.D. 107, but Warren Carroll supports, convincingly, a later date of 116. See Warren H. Carroll, *The Founding of Christendom: A History of Christendom*, vol. 1 (Front Royal, VA: Christendom College Press, 1985), 480.

the work of a benevolent god. The dualist construct of the Gnostics presented the history of the world as a battle between the God of Goodness and Light and the God of Evil and Darkness. They believed that human souls were good (because they were spiritual) but imprisoned in evil, material human bodies.

Gnosticism was an ancient belief that predated the Faith and proved resilient because it assimilated teachings of various religions in order to accumulate adherents. It attempted to present Jesus as a spiritual being who only appeared human (thus denying the Incarnation) and who came to earth to provide the way to free the spirit from the evils of the material world. Those who joined the group were promised this secret knowledge of Jesus. Gnostics did not practice baptism and did not hold to the centrality of the Eucharist, since a good spiritual god would never imprison his presence in an evil material object. Their rejection of the material world led to the renunciation of marriage and the sexual act between man and woman — that union, in their eyes, might result in a good soul's imprisonment in an evil body in the form of an infant. Additionally, their view of material things led to the bizarre belief that the highest form of worship was suicide, which freed the good soul from the bad body.[54]

The early Christian bishop Irenaeus (140–202), born in Smyrna, was a disciple of Saint Polycarp, who in turn had been a disciple of Saint John the Evangelist. Irenaeus was the bishop of Lyons in the imperial province of Gaul (modern-day France). He was an exceptional scholar, educated at Rome in philosophy and literature. He oriented his writing on the tasks of defending "true doctrine from the attacks of heretics" and explaining "the truth

---

54. The eradication of heresy is a difficult task, as the history of the Church illustrates. Heresies that are refuted and condemned in one century arise and return with a vengeance in later centuries, making heresy akin to the carnival/arcade game Whack-a-Mole. The Church addresses the false teaching definitely and "whacks" it down, but it reappears later in a mutated form. Gnosticism is a prime example, as it is refuted in the second century but returns in the form of Manichaeism in the fourth century, and then as Albigensianism (or Catharism) in the thirteenth century, and even makes an appearance in the twentieth century with the Heaven's Gate cult.

of the faith clearly."[55] In *Against Heresies*, his elaborate five-part survey of Gnosticism, he accurately identified the core teaching of the heresy: the origin of evil.[56] Gnosticism sought to explain why evil exists in the world by attributing evil to material things. Irenaeus refuted this tenet by illustrating that the origin of evil is the wrong use of free will. Evil exists because men and women, given free will by a loving Creator, choose to perform evil actions — there is nothing inherently evil about material things.

Irenaeus also included a list of the Roman pontiffs, beginning with Saint Peter and ending with the reigning pope at the time of his writing, Eleutherius (r. 175–189). Interestingly, only four of the thirteen popes listed were born in the city of Rome, which illustrates the universality of the Church at this early stage. Irenaeus also presented the features of a true Church, in order to help Christians and new converts discern which communities were orthodox and which were heretical. He stressed that an authentic Christian community was one that preached a consistent message throughout the world and was founded upon apostolic succession — certainty of truth in doctrinal matters rests with churches that can trace apostolic origins. Irenaeus stressed that Christian teaching must be public — not secret like the Gnostics preached — guided by the Holy Spirit, and completely united:

> The Church, though dispersed throughout the world … having received [this faith from the apostles] … as if occupying but one house, carefully preserves it. She also believes these points [of doctrine] just as if she had but one soul and one and the same heart, and she proclaims them and teaches them and hands them down with perfect harmony as if she possessed only one mouth.[57]

---

55. Benedict XVI, Wednesday General Audience on Saint Irenaeus of Lyons, March 28, 2007, in *Church Fathers: From Clement of Rome to Augustine* (San Francisco: Ignatius Press, 2008), 22.
56. The original title was *An Exposition and Refutation of What is Falsely Called Knowledge*.
57. Irenaeus, *Against Heresies*, I, 10, 1–2.

Most importantly, Irenaeus highlighted the primacy of the Church in Rome, which is "the greatest and most important and best known of all, founded and organized by the two most glorious apostles, Peter and Paul. For with this Church [Rome], because of her more powerful preeminence all churches must agree."[58] Irenaeus's *Against Heresies* clearly illustrates that the early Christians believed the test of orthodoxy was unity with the Church in Rome and her bishop, the pope.

MARCION THE HERETIC

Marcion, a wealthy shipowner from Constantinople and the son of the bishop of Sinope (in modern-day Turkey), came to Rome in the year 135. He had semi-Gnostic tendencies, believing the material world was evil. These tendencies led him into heresy when he denied the humanity of Jesus, believing Christ's human body was an optical illusion. Marcion is best known for his false interpretation of Scripture. He preached a dichotomy of the Old and New Testaments, arguing that the God portrayed in the Old Testament was a stern, wrathful judge, whereas the God of the New Testament was a loving father. The difference could only be explained by recognizing they were two different gods, a belief that still finds adherence in the modern world. He tried to convince the Roman Church that his interpretation was correct, but when his heresy was rejected in the summer of 144, he established his own church. Marcion's church imitated the hierarchical structure of the Catholic Church with Marcion, of course, as the head. Marcionites practiced a rigorous moral life and reserved baptism for celibates, eunuchs, and dedicated widows.

SAINT POLYCARP (D. 155)

Polycarp, bishop of Smyrna (modern-day Turkey), was a disci-

58. Irenaeus, *Against Heresies*, III, 3.2; translation in Guarducci, *The Primacy of the Church of Rome*, 19.

ple of Saint John the Evangelist, the recipient of one of Saint Ignatius of Antioch's letters, and one of the most respected members of the Church. He had spent some time in Constantinople, where he met Marcion. Toward the middle of the second century, Polycarp was an elderly man near ninety when, shortly before his death, he made a journey to Rome to discuss an important matter with the pope.

While in Rome, Polycarp saw Marcion walking down the street, but made no move to acknowledge him. Marcion, offended, maneuvered to cross paths with the saintly bishop. When he was near Polycarp, Marcion called out, "Don't you recognize me?" Polycarp responded, "I do indeed: I recognize the firstborn of Satan!"[59] Polycarp, who preached strenuously against heresy, had no time for the egotistical founder of a heresy itself.

Soon after Polycarp returned home from his consultation with the pope, a persecution of Christians began in Smyrna. At a festival held in honor of Emperor Antoninus Pius (r. 138–161), anti-Christian outbursts erupted from a mob. Christians were arrested and martyred by being thrown to wild beasts in the arena; however, the mob's bloodlust was not slaked. They demanded the life of the aged and venerable Polycarp. The bishop was sentenced to die by burning at the stake, but when all the preparations had been made and the fire lit, it miraculously failed to touch him. He was cut down from the stake and killed by the executioner's dagger.[60]

MONTANISM

The late second century was witness to another heresy that greatly affected the Church. Montanus was a recent convert to the Faith who, along with two women, Maximilla and Prisca, who had left their husbands to follow him, began to utter prophecies

---

59. Carroll, *The Founding of Christendom*, 460.
60. Ibid., 461.

and claim direct revelations from the Holy Spirit. Montanus argued that private revelations held equal authority to Scripture and the teaching of the Church. Montanus's followers practiced a strict asceticism with severe penitential disciplines, including extreme fasting. Montanus believed sins committed after baptism could not be forgiven. This rigorist position produced a conflict in the Church between those favoring mercy toward Christians who gave in during the persecutions (known as *lapsi*), and rigorists who believed the *lapsi* could not reenter communion. Montanus also called his followers to renounce material goods, marriage, and the marital act, and to seek out martyrdom. Ultimately, Montanus's insistence on equal authority of private revelation and Scripture helped to "reinforce the conviction that revelation had come to an end with the apostolic age, and so to foster the creation of a closed canon of the New Testament."[61]

Although a variety of heresies challenged the unity of the Church and posed significant problems, they also provided opportunities for the Church to affirm her teaching in definitive terms. The result was a benefit to the faithful, who clearly knew what to believe in order to remain in communion with the apostolic faith.

THE ANTIPOPE WHO BECAME A SAINT

Not much is known about the life of Hippolytus, an early Christian theologian and scholar, but his writings provide details about the liturgical customs of the Roman Church and the heresies afflicting the Church in the late second and early third centuries. In his *Apostolic Tradition*, Hippolytus describes the rite of baptism used by the early Church in Rome. His book also provides details concerning the structure of the liturgy, which involved a prayer of thanksgiving, the invocation of the Holy Spirit on the offering, the recitation of Jesus' words of consecration for the Eucharist, as

---

61. Chadwick, *The Early Church*, 53.

THE EMPIRE AND THE CHURCH | 65

well as a memorial acclamation. Hippolytus exhorted the faithful
to show reverence to the Eucharist and to receive it worthily, not
dropping the host or spilling the Precious Blood.

Many of the heresies in the early Church dealt with Jesus'
relationship to the Father. The Church wrestled with discerning
the correct terminology to apply to the truth the apostles had
passed down: that Jesus is true God and true man. In many cases,
it was difficult to determine whether a teaching or theological
opinion was truly heretical. The heresy of Modalism blurred the
distinctions between Father and Son in the Trinity, to the point
where it posited they were actually one person who appeared in
different modes.[62]

Hippolytus wanted Pope Zephyrinus (r. 198–217) to strongly rebuke and condemn the Modalists, and grew upset when the
pontiff failed to do so. After Zephyrinus died, the clergy and
people of Rome elected the former slave Callistus I (r. 217–222)
to succeed him. Hippolytus soon disagreed with the new pope
(and his successors) on the issue of absolution and readmittance
of Christians who had committed serious sins. Hippolytus was a
"rigorist" and believed that those who had greatly sinned should
not be absolved or readmitted to communion, despite their genuine contrition and repentance. Callistus, remembering the actions
of Christ, embraced a policy of mercy. Hippolytus was so angry at
Callistus's election and decisions that he gathered a group of followers, who elected him pope, and claimed Callistus was unworthy of the office due to his embattled past.[63] Hippolytus opened
the door to the concept of the "antipope," a concept that would
rear its ugly head throughout Church history. Ultimately, Hippolytus's schism would last for nineteen years and through three
pontificates.[64]

---

62. The heresy was also known as Monarichianism, Patripassianism, or Sabellianism (for Sabellius,
the main proponent of the heresy in Rome in the early third century). A Modalist, for example,
believed that God the Father appeared in the mode of God the Son on earth.
63. It was believed that as a slave Callistus had embezzled his master's money.
64. The pontificates of Saint Callistus I (r. 217–222), Saint Urban I (r. 222–230), and Saint Pontian (r.
230– 235).

Maximinus Thrax, a career soldier, was proclaimed emperor by the legions in Germania in 235. Shortly afterward, he turned his attention to the Church, and began a persecution targeting the clergy. Callistus's successor, Pontian (r. 230–235), and the antipope Hippolytus, were arrested and sent to the mines on the island of Sardinia. Amid the suffering and hardship of the mines, Hippolytus renounced his schism and papal claim. He was then reconciled to the Church by Pontian. Both men ultimately succumbed to the harsh conditions, and when their remains were transported back to Rome for burial, they were both honored as martyrs and saints of the Church. Saint Hippolytus is the first antipope, and the only antipope ever canonized.

THE APOLOGISTS

The criticism of Roman pagan authors against the Church and her teaching produced one positive effect: it gave rise to the apologists. Apologists were educated Christians who wrote an *apologia*, a defense of the Faith from the attacks of pagan authors. These early Christian apologists tried to make the teachings of the Church understandable and accessible to the Greco-Roman mind. They worked to refute the false claims of authors like Celsus and Porphyry and convince the emperors to pursue policies of tolerance. They did not write for catechetical purposes nor to present a systematic exposition of all Christian teachings. Rather, they emphasized the existence of one God, the nature of God, the immortality of the soul, and the Christian ideal of holy living.

One of the first apologists was Justin (100–165), a learned philosopher born in Palestine. Justin converted to the Faith at the age of thirty-eight and moved to Rome. There, he opened a school to teach Christian philosophy, free of charge. Justin did not repudiate the Greek philosophy he had previously taught, but now "claimed with power and clarity that he had found in

the Christian faith 'the only sure and profitable philosophy.'"[65]
Justin studied Scripture and believed that Christ was the fulfillment of the Old Testament prophecies. He posited that the
Old Testament and Greek philosophy could be used together
like "two paths that lead to Christ, to the Logos."[66] Justin was
the first intellectual to see history as twofold — sacred and secular, with Christ at the center of all human history.[67] He also
produced works defending the apostolic faith against heresies,
though he is best known for his apologetic work written to Emperor Antonius Pius. In his *First Apology*, Justin responds to the
false charges leveled against Christians by pagan authors and
explains the Christian understanding of the Eucharist:

> And this food is called among us the Eucharist,
> of which no one is allowed to partake but the man
> who believes that the things which we teach are true,
> and who has been washed with the washing that is for
> the remission of sins, and unto regeneration, and who
> is so living as Christ has enjoined. For not as com-
> mon bread and common drink do we receive these;
> but in like manner as Jesus Christ, our Savior, having
> been made flesh by the Word of God, had both flesh
> and blood for our salvation, so likewise have we been
> taught that the food which is blessed by the prayer
> of His word, and from which our blood and flesh by
> transmutation are nourished, is the flesh and blood of
> that Jesus who was made flesh.[68]

Justin's deep faith and love of Christ were tested during the reign

---

65. Justin, *Dialogue* 8, 1, quoted in Benedict XVI, Wednesday General Audience on Saint Justin,
Philosopher and Martyr, March 21, 2007, in *Church Fathers: From Clement of Rome to Augustine* (San
Francisco: Ignatius Press, 2008), 19.
66. Ibid.
67. Chadwick, *Early Church*, 78.
68. Justin Martyr, *First Apology*, Chapter 66, accessed September 18, 2018, http://www.newadvent.
org/fathers/0126.htm.

of Emperor Marcus Aurelius (r. 161–180), when he was arrested and martyred during a persecution of the Church. He is known as Saint Justin Martyr.

Another early apologist was Tertullian of Carthage (163–230), the son of a Roman army centurion. Tertullian, like Justin, converted to the Faith in his thirties. A few years later, Tertullian was ordained a priest. His writings discussed the proper behavior of Christians in a pagan world, defending the Faith from pagan attacks and heresies, and covered various theological topics. Tertullian was the first Christian writer to use the terms "Trinity" and "person" to explain the relationship in the Godhead, writing that God is "one substance consisting of three persons."[69] Tertullian reveled in the apparent paradoxes inherent in the Church's teachings, such as the fact that God is one yet three, that Christ is man yet God, and that the eternal God could suffer and die. In the mind of Tertullian, these "absurdities" were what made the Faith believable.[70] Unlike other apologists, Tertullian had no use for pagan philosophy and did not believe the Faith needed to be reconciled to it, writing, "What indeed has Athens to do with Jerusalem?"[71] A focus on philosophy, he believed, led to heresies.

In his apologetic works, Tertullian focused on educating the Roman populace about Christians, illustrating that they were no different from any other Romans, apart from their religious beliefs. Christians were not a secret organization bent on the destruction of the Empire but rather "a body knit together by the sense of one belief, united in discipline, bound together by a common hope. We pray, too, for the emperors. ... We live with you, eat the same food, wear the same clothing, have the same way of life as you. We live in the same world as you. We sail with you, we serve as soldiers with you, and till the ground and engage

69. Tertullian, *Against Praxeas*, 2. He was also the first Church Father to write in Latin rather than Greek.
70. See Mike Aquilina, *The Fathers of the Church: An Introduction to the First Christian Teachers*, Expanded Edition (Huntington, IN: Our Sunday Visitor, 2006), 92.
71. Ibid.

in trade."[72] Tertullian informed his pagan readers that persecutions would not eradicate the Christians: "your cruelty serves no purpose. On the contrary, for our community, it is an invitation. We multiply every time one of us is mowed down. The blood of the martyrs is the seed of Christians."[73] Unfortunately, Tertullian agreed with the Montanist assessment that the Church was too lax in her enforcement of penitential discipline, and joined the heretical group in the year 211. While a Montanist, he even repudiated teachings he had held during his orthodox days, including whether or not Christians could serve in the military. Ultimately, even the Montanists were too lax for Tertullian, so he left them and founded his own group. Although he was an astute defender of the Faith in his early Christian life, Tertullian provides an example to all Christians, especially theologians, about the need for humility and adherence to the Church's teachings.

The apologist Origen (185–254) had personally experienced the persecutions. His father, a catechist, had been arrested and martyred under the Emperor Septimius Severus (r. 193–211) when Origen was a young man. Much of what we know about Origen is because the "Father of Church History," Eusebius of Caesarea, discussed the apologist and his works at length in the book *Ecclesiastical History*. Origen was born in the great city of Alexandria in Egypt and, like his father, was a catechist. Origen became head of a famous catechetical school in Alexandria, and was a prolific writer. Saint Jerome later remarked, "Who could ever read all that Origen wrote?"[74] Origen wrote apologies defending the Faith against pagan attacks, along with theological treatises. He was a systematic theologian, constructing a vast synthesis of the Faith in order to display the harmony of Christian teaching. Ultimately, theology, for Origen, was the handmaid of Scripture and was utilized in order to explain and understand the sacred word. Origen was the first Christian scholar to write commentaries on the books of the Old Testament. He believed it

---

72. Tertullian, *Apology* 37, 39, 42.
73. Ibid., 50:13.
74. Chadwick, *The Early Church*, 109.

was vital for Christians to have accurate translations of the Jewish texts, so he created a work known as the *Hexapla* that contained six parallel columns: four Greek versions of the Old Testament along-side two Hebrew translations. Scholars could use the work to see in one glance how a certain passage was translated among the various texts. Origen believed that the unity of the Old and New Testaments was found in Christ, and that the prime purpose of Scripture was to convey spiritual truth. The scholar, he thought, must approach inter-pretation of Scripture prayerfully in order to understand accurately the truths God wishes to convey in the sacred pages.

Although Origen was a gifted scholar, he, like Tertullian, chose a path that led him into conflict with the Church. Origen's troubles in-volved disobedience to Demetrius, the bishop of Alexandria, whom he "thought a worldly, power-hungry prelate consumed with pride in his own self-importance, enjoying the honor of presiding over a wealthy community in a great city."[75] Origen decided to escape the situation and travel, making his way to Rome and then to the east, where (although a layman) he was allowed to preach. In Palestine, he was ordained to the priesthood without Demetrius's permission, which greatly angered the bishop. Upon return to Egypt, Origen quickly realized that the situation with his bishop was untenable. He left and returned to Caesarea in Palestine, where he was welcomed. While living in the Holy Land, Origen composed his famous apol-ogetic work *Contra Celsum* ("Against Celsus," countering the pagan Roman author discussed earlier). In the mid-third century, Origen was caught up in the general persecution of Decius and was arrest-ed, imprisoned, and horribly tortured. Origen was an influential and important early Christian scholar and apologist. He suffered for the Faith heroically and died in 254 from the effects of his imprisonment and torture.[76]

---

75. Ibid.
76. There is much debate about Origen's alleged self-mutilation. Eusebius of Caesarea records a story that Origen, taking the Lord's explication of chastity in Matthew 19:12 literally, castrated himself in order to ensure chastity while catechizing women. Other accounts indicate Origen did not castrate himself, but that he took drugs to maintain celibacy.

THE FIRST EMPIRE-WIDE PERSECUTION

The mid-third century witnessed the short reign of Decius as Roman emperor. Decius (r. 249–251) was a strong and inflexible man with little administrative experience. He desired unity in the Empire and disliked the presence of the Christians, who refused to worship the state gods. So, he issued an edict in January 250 that required every citizen in the Empire to make a public sacrifice before the idols of the pagan gods. All those who sacrificed received a certificate, known as the *libellus*, documenting their adherence to Decius's edict. Failure to comply resulted in arrest, torture, and execution. This edict produced the first extensive Empire-wide persecution of the Church. Previously, persecution of Christians had been confined to particular cities or provinces but was not applied uniformly throughout the Empire. Decius, in an attempt to solidify support for his reign and to reassure the public of the security of the Empire, believed the edict would root out unpatriotic elements in Roman society.

The edict produced mass confusion, chaos, and fear in the Church. Pope Saint Fabian (r. 236–250) refused to sacrifice and was martyred. However, other Christians, including bishops, offered the sacrifice in order to save their lives. Wealthy Christians offered bribes to others to sacrifice in their names, or had their slaves sacrifice, thinking that by not personally sacrificing, they could avoid moral culpability. Most Christians resisted the edict. Those who had given in caused scandal and a challenge to the Church when the persecution ended and they requested readmittance. The persecution stopped at the death of Decius, who, while campaigning in the Balkans against the barbarian Goths, disappeared in a swamp — his body was never recovered. Later Christian authors highlighted the fact that Decius was the first Roman emperor to be killed by a foreign enemy and indicated this fate was the result of his persecution of the Church.

VALERIAN PERSECUTES THE CHURCH

A few years after the death of the tyrant Decius, a man from a noble senatorial family ascended the throne as emperor. Valerian (r. 253–260) was friendly to Christians at first, but when political and military problems plagued the Empire he, like previous emperors, utilized the Church as a scapegoat. Various barbarian tribes, including the Franks, were on the move along the northern border and had made incursions across the Rhine River. The Persians had launched an invasion in the east, conquering and destroying territory (including the city of Antioch). Valerian distracted the populace from the politico-military situation by issuing an edict ordering the execution of all Christian bishops, priests, and deacons in 257. The saintly bishop of Rome, Sixtus II (r. 257–258), was executed by a group of soldiers while meeting with his flock in a Roman cemetery along the Appian Way. A Roman deacon, Lawrence, was ordered to gather the wealth of the Church and bring it to the Roman authorities several days later. At the appointed time, Lawrence arrived with a group of poor people, indicating the Church's riches lay not in material goods but in the corporal works of mercy undertaken for the benefit of others. The authorities were not amused at Lawrence's behavior. They ordered his execution: burning alive on a gridiron. Tradition attests that Lawrence, in the midst of the excruciating experience, joked with his executioners, asking them to turn him over since he was done on that side.

A few years later, Valerian and the legions were defeated by the Persians at the Battle of Edessa. Valerian was captured by the Persian king Shapur I (r. 240–270) and subjected to humiliating treatment throughout five years of captivity, including being used as a footstool by Shapur when mounting his horse. When Valerian died in captivity, Shapur ordered the flaying and stuffing of his corpse for a war trophy. Once more, a Roman emperor who had sought the destruction of the Church suffered an ignoble end.

DIOCLETIAN'S DIVISION AND
GREAT PERSECUTION

The Roman Empire experienced a profound political crisis of instability in the third century. Over twenty emperors were murdered, and a new emperor, on average, put on the purple every three years. For over two hundred years (31 B.C.–A.D. 180), there had been only sixteen emperors, but in the ninety years encompassing most of the third century, there were twenty-eight! The man who became emperor in the year 284 was acutely aware of this volatile situation and the need for greater political security in the Empire. Diocles was thirty-eight when he was proclaimed emperor, upon which he changed his name to Diocletian. As the son of slaves (his father rose to be a freedman), he was familiar with the necessity of hard work and sacrifice. Diocletian joined the army, becoming known as an exceptional administrator who loved the imperial traditions of Rome and who earnestly desired to return the Empire to its former strength and glory. Diocletian lived in ways unlike those of previous emperors; he was not known to drink alcohol and was devoted to his family, refusing to take mistresses (a rare occurrence among the Roman nobility). He was fiscally frugal and ran the imperial court like his army headquarters, establishing a multilayered bureaucracy with strict ceremonies and rituals. Vvery few people were granted audiences, and those who did were required to prostrate themselves before him.[77]

Diocletian made a decision in the late third century that had a lasting impact on the Empire, the Church, and the world. Realizing that the Roman Empire was too large and cumbersome to be governed by one man, he divided the Empire in two. The western half encompassed what became Europe and parts of North Africa. The eastern half of the Empire contained Greece, Asia

---

77. See Adrian Goldsworthy, *How Rome Fell: Death of a Superpower* (New Haven, CT: Yale University Press, 2009), 158.

Minor, the Holy Land, and Egypt. He also established smaller regional jurisdictions in each half of the Empire, named "dioceses"
after himself.[78] There were twelve dioceses in all, each ruled by a
vicar. Diocletian's reorganization increased the imperial bureaucracy to over thirty thousand officials — as one contemporary
wrote, "more numerous than flies on sheep in springtime."[79]As
part of the reorganization of the Empire, Diocletian also created
the tetrarchy, a political structure designed to provide a smooth
transition of power upon the death of the emperor and prevent
the recurrent civil wars. The tetrarchy was a system based on four
rulers, two emperors (*augusti*), one for each half of the Empire,
and two caesars, who acted as deputies to the *augusti*. When an
emperor died, his caesar would automatically become emperor
and would then appoint a new caesar.

Diocletian chose to rule the eastern half of the Empire and
appointed Galerius as his caesar. In the west, Diocletian's friend
Maximian was named *augustus*, with Constantius as his caesar. In
order to further strengthen the tetrarchy and prevent civil war,
Diocletian bolstered the political bond between the men through
marriage. Constantius married Maximian's daughter Fausta, and
Galerius married Diocletian's daughter Valeria. Additionally, each
caesar was adopted by his *augusti*. Diocletian chose to make his
imperial home in the city of Nicomedia and only visited the capital city of Rome once, during the celebration of his twentieth
anniversary as emperor. Galerius, his caesar, resided in Sirmium
(modern-day Serbia). In the west, Maximian made his residence
in Milan, whereas Constantius lived in Trier (modern-day Germany). Rome, the ancient capital, was discarded as an imperial
residence but retained influence due to its large population and
the presence of the Senate.

Diocletian was tolerant of Christians for the first nineteen
years of his reign, and there is speculation that members of his

---

78. The Church adopted the imperial structure and retained the name for administrative regions
when the Empire collapsed in the West in the late fifth century.
79. Goldsworthy, *How Rome Fell*, 164.

immediate family may have been Christian. Everything changed, however, when Galerius, known by one later Christian writer as "the Beast," persuaded Diocletian to initiate what became known as the Great Persecution because of a military readiness problem in the eastern legions. Some Christians in the east refused military service, which was causing a manpower shortfall in the army. Christians who had joined the army refused to sacrifice to the pagan gods before battle (per army custom and tradition), which affected unit morale and cohesiveness. Galerius believed the issue in the army was a crisis, so he asked Diocletian to deal with the Church once and for all.

Diocletian issued the first edict of persecution on February 23, 303, ordering the closing of all known Christian churches and buildings. He demanded that all copies of the Scriptures be handed over to Roman authorities for destruction. Further edicts ordered first the imprisonment of the clergy, and then torture and execution of bishops, priests, and deacons. A final edict was passed that mimicked Decius's general order in the previous century, requiring all Romans to sacrifice to the pagan gods. Persecution of the Church was widespread in the eastern half of the Empire, especially in North Africa (Egypt), where more than two hundred bishops were martyred. It was more sporadic in the west since the western emperor, Constantius, did not vigorously enforce the edicts.[80]

We have historical knowledge of the Great Persecution from three main sources: the writings of Eusebius of Caesarea and Lactantius (c. 250–c. 330), and the *Acts of the Martyrs*. Eusebius was an eyewitness to the persecutions in Palestine and Egypt. He wrote of the violence in his works *Ecclesiastical History* and *The Martyrs of Palestine*. Lactantius was a North African teacher of rhetoric who became the tutor to Constantine's son Crispus. He wrote about the Great Persecution in his *De mortibus persecutorum*, positing the belief that emperors who persecuted the Church ended their lives

---

80. Wilken, *The First Thousand Years*, 76.

in a violent and horrible fashion as punishment from God. The *Acts of the Martyrs* was a compilation of stories about the martyrs. Verbal transcripts of exchanges between arrested Christians and Roman officials, eyewitness accounts, and even imaginary narratives were utilized in crafting these works. These sources allowed later Christians to understand the ferocity unleashed by the Roman Empire on the Church in the early fourth century.

Christians who suffered through the Great Persecution were divided into groups, depending on how they responded during the crisis. Some refused to give in to the edicts requiring submission to the pagan gods and, as a result, were killed for the Faith. Known as *martyrs* ("witnesses"), these brave Christians suffered horrible deaths by fire, wild beasts, beheading, and other manners of painful death. Not every Christian arrested during the persecutions died, but many, known as the *confessors*, were imprisoned and suffered the tortures of racking, beating, scourging, or having their fingernails ripped out. Christian women were frequently sent to brothels. Men were oftentimes sent to the mines, where the tendon of their left foot was cauterized to prevent escape. Those who toiled in the mines also had their right eye ripped out, and the wound burned with a hot iron. Sometimes they suffered the horror of castration. Despite their harsh treatment, Christians in the mines (who were ministered to by clandestine aid from their brethren) continued to preach the Gospel and brought fellow prisoners to Christ. Unfortunately, under extreme stress, some Christians gave in to the dictates of the persecution edicts and apostatized. They were known as *traditores* ("traitors") from the Latin *tradere*, "to hand over." There were different classes of *traditore* — those who handed over copies of the sacred Scripture, those who handed over the sacred vessels used in the celebration of Mass, and those who revealed the names of Christians who had such items in their possession. The extensive destruction of copies of the Scriptures during the Great Persecution was remembered for centuries. Finally, some Christians, known as the *lapsi*, gave in during the persecutions and, after they ended, desired readmittance. The subsequent discussion of how to handle their request for return to communion dominated the early life of the Church, in essence centering on whether the Church was a "society of saints or a school for sinners."[81]

The question of how to handle the *lapsi* was an issue after the first general persecution under Emperor Decius in the mid-third century. Pope Saint Cornelius (r. 251–253) believed it was his pastoral duty to restore to communion those who fell during the persecution. He thought their participation in the Eucharist, after a suitable period of penance, would strengthen them in the event of future attacks. Saint Cyprian (200–258), bishop of Carthage, also believed the Church should follow the road of mercy for the *lapsi*. During the Decian persecution, Cyprian had fled his see and was criticized for abandoning his flock. After the persecution ended, Cyprian focused on restoring unity in his diocese by urging mercy and patience, especially for the *lapsi*. He gathered fellow bishops in North Africa in a local council to discuss the *lapsi*. They decided that those who had received the *libellus* but did not personally sacrifice could be readmitted to communion after a period of penance. Those who had sacrificed were required to undertake a prolonged period of penance and could be reconciled on their deathbeds.[82] When the persecution under Valerian began, Cyprian refused to leave Carthage and became the first African bishop martyred during the persecution. Both Cornelius and Cyprian imitated the Lord's mercy in their dealings with the *lapsi*, and their example set the policy for the Church in later persecutions. Their emphasis on unity and mercy — as opposed to the rigorists, who wanted permanent expulsion of the *lapsi* — helped the Church settle this critical question. As a result, the Church honors their sanctity by a shared feast day (September 16) on the liturgical calendar.

The Great Persecution of Diocletian witnessed the martyr-

---

81. Chadwick, *The Church in Ancient Society*, 692.
82. Wilken, *The First Thousand Years*, 70–71.

doms of saints such as Agnes, a young virgin; Sebastian, a centurion; and Lucy, a young woman betrayed to the authorities by her betrothed. The killing was especially terrible in North Africa, where Eusebius recorded the extermination of entire towns populated by Christians. Indeed, he records that "so many were killed on a single day that the axe, blunted and worn out by the slaughter, was broken in pieces, while the exhausted executioners had to be periodically relieved."[83] The torments and methods of execution were horrific, as Eusebius describes in his *Ecclesiastical History*:

> Immense numbers of men, women, and children, despising this transient life, faced death in all its forms for the sake of our Savior's teaching. Some were scraped, racked, mercilessly flogged, subjected to countless other torments too terrible to describe in endless variety, and finally given to the flames; some were submerged in the sea; others cheerfully stretched out their necks to the headman's axe; some died under torture; others were starved to death; others again were crucified, some as criminals usually are, some with still greater cruelty nailed the other way up, head down, and kept alive till they starved to death on the very cross.[84]

The Great Persecution ended because Diocletian wanted to retire to his cabbage farm in Dalmatia. He abdicated in 305, becoming the first emperor to voluntarily give up power. His caesar, Galerius, succeeded him in accordance with the dictates of the tetrarchy. Galerius reigned for a few years, until he died from the effects of venereal disease. Before he died, Galerius issued an edict of toleration of Christians, in the hopes that their prayers might assuage

---

83. Eusebius, *The History of the Church from Christ to Constantine*, trans. G. A. Williamson (New York: Penguin, 1965), Book VIII, 9, p. 265.
84. Ibid., VIII, 8.

God to spare him during his illness (since prayers for his recovery to the pagan gods had had no effect on his health).[85] This act of desperation provided for the freedom of worship and conscience for Christians in the Roman Empire, but did not yet provide the Church with legal rights to exist as a corporate body.

Surveying the death and destruction wrought on the family of God by the Roman persecutions leads to the question, "Why?" Why did God allow this massacre to take place? Why, in the very infancy of the Church, when she was seemingly at her most vulnerable, did the Lord allow such ferocious violence against his Mystical Body? Tertullian provides the answer: "The blood of the martyrs is the seed of Christians."[86] The experience of the persecution laid the foundation for the eventual conversion of the Empire. The Church would grow from a hunted sect to an official state religion in just over three hundred years. The conversion of the Roman Empire, one of the most monumental events in the history of the world, was made possible by the witness of those early Christians who stood firm in the midst of persecution, motivated by their love of Christ and his Church.

---

85. Michael Grant, *Constantine the Great: The Man and His Times* (New York: Charles Scribner's Sons, 1993), 137.
86. Tertullian, *Apology* 37, 39, 42.

THREE

Conversions

"*Jesus Christ, you who Clotilda maintains to be the Son of the living God ... I beg the glory of your help. If you will give me victory over my enemies ... then I will believe in you and I will be baptized in your name. I have called upon my own gods, but, as I see only too clearly, they have no intention of helping me. I therefore cannot believe that they possess any power, for they do not come to the assistance of those who trust in them. I now call upon you. I want to believe in you, but I must first be saved from my enemies.*"[1]

CLOVIS, KING OF THE FRANKS

The dream confirmed his deepest desires. As a little boy, he had wandered off from his parents and gone missing for several days. But to the

---

1. Gregory of Tours, *History of the Franks*, Book II, 30, trans. Lewis Thorpe (New York: Penguin Books, 1974), 143.

surprise of his pagan parents, he was found inside a Christian church. The curious boy, son of a Roman soldier stationed in Gaul, had been enamored with the stories he heard of Christian monks and their unique lifestyle. Now, after giving half his military-issued cloak to a freezing beggar who had been ignored by other passersby, the young soldier received confirmation in a dream that his future would be guided by service to the poor as a Christian. However, the young man would soon learn that what he wanted to do was not exactly what the Lord required of him. He found solace as a hermit, but his holiness attracted attention. When the venerable bishop of Poitiers died, the people demanded the former-soldier-turned-monk become their bishop. Beloved by his people, the reluctant bishop spread the Gospel throughout the countryside and also became one of the most beloved saints in the history of the Church. The shrine of his relics at Tours was one of the most visited during the Middle Ages. Saint Martin is a shining example of the amazing saints who illuminate this era in Church history, which produced two conversions that shaped the history of Western civilization.

VICTORY AT THE BRIDGE

Diocletian's dream of an Empire free from political turmoil and civil war was dead. His abdication in 305 pushed the Empire into another period of instability, as men, empowered by their legions, fought for political supremacy. Constantius, the western Augustus, was garrisoned with his soldiers in Britain and fell ill. He desired to see his son, Constantine, once more before he died, but the young man was in Nicomedia in the east and under close watch by Galerius, who was paranoid that the son of Constantius would usurp him. When news reached Constantine that his father was ill, he made plans to leave the imperial palace. When the time was right, Constantine fled Nicomedia and began the long and arduous journey to Britain. He reached the garrison in time to see his father before his death, but was surprised that when Constantius died, contrary to the established policy of the tetrarchy, the British legions named him Augustus. When news of Constantine's proclamation as emperor reached Rome, another son of an emperor was angry. Maxientius, the son-in-law of Galerius and the son of the former emperor Maximian (who had abdicated in the same year as Diocletian), believed he should rule the Western Empire. Maxientius conspired with the Praetorian Guard and was proclaimed Emperor. The Western Empire now contained two men, with large numbers of troops, claiming to be emperor. The explosive situation needed swift resolution.

Constantine held a council of war in Britain, where he asked the advice of his generals. Should they march on Rome and engage Maxientius's forces in combat to determine who would rule the Western Empire, or should they bide their time and gather additional forces? The generals advised the more cautious military strategy, but, recognizing that fortune favors the brave, Constantine decided to leave Britain, march through Gaul into Italy, and attack Rome — a risky campaign, but one that, if victorious, would give Constantine the imperial purple.

Constantine's army left their garrison in Roman Britain and sailed across the channel to Gaul. On their march through Gaul, they witnessed a miracle that changed the future of the Empire forever. Constantine and his soldiers saw a cross mysteriously appear in the sky with puzzling phrase *in hoc signo vinces*, "In this sign, you will conquer."[2] Constantine was not a Christian, though he was aware of the group and, no doubt, had Christians in his army. Constantine's father had not vigorously enforced Diocletian's persecution edits in the west, so Constantine was, at the least, not ill disposed to the Church. It is believed that Constantine had a strong devotion to only one pagan god, Sol, making

---

2. There are two main sources for the vision. Eusebius records the vision in his *Life of Constantine*, written twenty years after the battle but told to him by Constantine himself, who provided the account to Eusebius under oath. The other source is provided by Lactantius in his *De mortibus persecutorum*. Some authors believe that the sign was a natural event known as a "halo-phenomenon" in which the "sun is surrounded by a circle of light that has two lesser suns on a horizontal axis to the right and left. When all three are visible the points of light extending out from the center form an image that resembles a cross in a circle." See Robert Louis Wilken, *The First Thousand Years: A Global History of Christianity* (New Haven, CT: Yale University Press, 2012), 82.

him already semi-monotheistic in his religious views. He came to believe the sign was indication of the Christian God's favor in the coming battle with Maxentius, and in order to show his belief, he ordered his soldiers to paint the symbol of the Chi-Rho — the monogram formed from the first two letters of the Greek word for Christ — on their shields.

This Christian symbol became extremely popular after Constantine's usage. Reproductions of it are found everywhere in the Roman world from the fourth century onward (indeed, it is still used in Catholic churches today and on liturgical vestments). The adoption of a Christian symbol by a Roman army marked a dramatic turning point in the history of the Church. The Roman army had been the instrument of state persecution of the Church, and less than a decade previously, had killed thousands of Christians. Now, troops from this same organization marched to battle with the sign of Christ on their shields. The victor of the coming fight could lay sole claim to the western throne.

THE BATTLE OF MILVIAN BRIDGE

It was October 28, 312, six years to the day of his accession to imperial power, and Maxentius felt lucky. News of Constantine's forces approaching the city had reached him. He believed victory was certain because the pagan priests had told him the enemy of the Romans would die this day. Naturally, Maxentius believed this prophecy referred to the upstart Constantine and his legions from Britain. (He should have realized he was not popular among the people of Rome, and perhaps the prophecy was applicable to him.) Confident of victory, Maxentius defied sound military tactics. Instead of remaining within the fortified city walls and enduring a siege, he marched his army out of the city in order to engage Constantine in open combat. Because the stone bridge in that area, known as the Milvian Bridge (from whence the battle received its name), had been partially destroyed to prevent its use by the invading army, Maxentius's forces crossed the Tiber on a wooden pontoon bridge. Constantine and his soldiers were also confident of victory, despite being outnumbered, because of their miraculous vision. Maxentius arrayed his forces too close to the river, which hampered their battlefield maneuvers. As it became apparent that the combat favored Constantine's army, Maxentius ordered a retreat. But the wooden pontoon bridge collapsed under the assembled weight of the heavy cavalry and infantry, and Maxentius was thrown into the Tiber, where he drowned. His body was later recovered, decapitated, and taken into the city by Constantine as a sign of his victory. The Roman populace hailed Constantine as a deliverer and recognized him as the sole ruler of the Western Empire. In a move that signaled the dawn of a new era, Constantine did not go to the Capitol to offer the traditional sacrifice to the pagan gods in thanksgiving for his victory.

CONSTANTINE AND THE CHURCH

Constantine attributed his victory over Maxentius to the intercession of the Christian God and, as a result, he favored the Church. Miraculously, the Faith went from a persecuted sect, hounded by the Roman emperors, to the favored organization of a Roman emperor! Constantine even embraced the Faith, receiving instruction under the spiritual guidance of bishop Hosius of Cordova (c. 257–358). Constantine became a catechumen, but he did not receive baptism until on his deathbed in 337.[3] Although he was truly grateful for his victory over Maxentius, Constantine's ambition had not been sated by becoming the western emperor, and he viewed the Church as an institution he could use to bring unity and reform to the Empire. Constantine's vision of the Church and his involvement in her internal affairs became known as *caesaro-papism* — a situation where the emperor reigned supreme in both the temporal and spiritual realms. *Caesaro-papism* became the norm in the eastern half of the Empire, but not in the

---

3. He was baptized by the Arian heretic Eusebius of Nicomedia.

western half, and as such the development of the Church differed in the two parts of the Empire.

Constantine legislated Christian morality: crucifixion as a form of punishment was outlawed, gladiatorial games were suspended, temple prostitution was ended, and chastity laws were enacted. He also outlawed the ancient pagan *pater familias* custom. In this practice, the father of the household (which included immediate family members as well as all servants) was able to reject any child born in his household by refusing to hold the infant after birth. The rejected infant was then exposed outside the city walls and left to die. Although Constantine favored the Church, paganism continued to exist, and Constantine served in the traditional imperial role as Pontifex Maximus, or "bridge-builder," between the various cults. However, his focus was on the Church. His favoritism extended to granting the Lateran palace, property of his wife, Fausta, to the bishop of Rome and building a church on that location for the pope, which became (and still is) the pope's cathedral diocesan church, known as Saint John Lateran. The emperor made Sunday a legal holiday on which government offices and businesses were closed. Additionally, the Church was exempt from taxation and received funding from the state. Constantine also reshaped the imperial bureaucracy by appointing Christians to positions of importance as counsels and prefects.[4] Constantine pursued these policies, seeing himself as "God's special servant and attendant and friend and representative."[5]Although Constantine favored the Church and took instruction in the Christian faith after his victory at Milvian Bridge, there was a dark side to the man that was intent on personal ambition, power, and control. Constantine was a "coldly intelligent organizer, a man of action who possessed the advantage of being absolutely tireless. [He was] dedicated to his own personal

---

4. Over 50 percent of his appointments to these positions were given to Christians. See Rodney Stark, *Bearing False Witness: Debunking Centuries of Anti-Catholic History* (West Conshohocken, PA: Templeton, 2016), 57.

5. Michael Grant, *Constantine the Great: The Man and His Times* (New York: Charles Scribner's Sons, 1993), 151.

success and despotically determined at all costs to achieve it."[6]

THE DONATIST CONTROVERSY

After each major persecution by the Roman Empire against the Church, two groups formed: the rigorists and the laxists. Rigorists believed that the *lapsi* should not be readmitted to communion after the persecution ended. Instead, they should be excommunicated, and if the *lapsi* were clergy, they should forfeit their ecclesiastical offices. This inflexible position embraced the heretical view that lapsed clergy could not validly celebrate the sacraments. The rigorist position was widely held in North Africa, a site of intense persecution (especially under Diocletian), and caused a challenging problem for the Church in the early fourth century. In some ways, rigorist thinking was understandable, since those who had suffered during the imperial persecutions looked with great suspicion on those who lapsed. The loss of a loved one as a martyr to the imperial authorities could easily foster feelings of anger or resentment toward the *lapsi*. Laxists believed that *lapsi* should undergo a period of penance before readmittance to the Church, but did not embrace the rigorist beliefs.

Donatus, a man "with a genius for organization and propaganda," was one of the leaders of the rigorist movement in North Africa.[7] The rigorist/laxist issue came to the forefront in the year 312 when Caecilian, the bishop of Carthage, was ordained. The rigorists objected to Caecilian's ordination, holding that it was null and void because one of his episcopal consecrators, Felix, was supposedly a member of the *lapsi*. Allegedly, Felix had handed over the Scriptures during the Great Persecution, but the charge was false. Nonetheless, the taint of being a *lapsi* hovered over Felix; the rigorists refused to recognize Caecilian's ordination, and elected Donatus bishop. The scandal of two bishops in Carthage

---

6. Ibid., 105–107.
7. Philip Hughes, *A History of the Church, Volume II: The Church and the World the Church Created* (London: Sheed and Ward, 1993 [1979]), 3.

produced a schism in the Church in Africa. In an effort to solve the situation, those who favored Donatus (known as Donatists) appealed to the emperor to solve the conundrum.

In an example of *caesaro-papsim*, Constantine accepted the case because he feared the loss of God's favor and the ascendancy of a rival if he did not act. Constantine wanted to use the Church to foster unity under his leadership of the Empire and would not tolerate disunity in the Church.[8] Eventually, Constantine ruled in favor of Caecilian, much to the chagrin of the Donatists, who appealed the decision. The emperor turned the appeal over to Pope Miltiades (r. 311–314), who convened a council in Rome to discuss the matter. Donatus traveled to Rome and presented his case, but the assembled clerics were not convinced, and, once more, Caecilian's ordination was held to be valid. The Donatists refused to accept Rome's decision and continued to cause problems in Carthage. Their continued resistance caused such agitation for Constantine that the emperor reopened the case. He called for a group of bishops to meet at Arles to once more hear the Donatists' arguments. The local council of Arles met, with forty-six bishops in attendance, and once more upheld the validity of Caecilian's consecration. They also condemned and excommunicated the Donatists in the hopes of ending the controversy. Unfortunately, the Donatists persisted in their rigorist views and heretical teachings, which impacted Church unity for the next century.

THE EDICT OF MILAN

Constantine knew that, despite his favoritism toward the Catholic Church, she still did not have a legal right to exist in the Empire due to Nero's law instituted nearly three hundred years earlier. Constantine remedied that situation when he met with the eastern Emperor Licinius in Rome at the marriage of Licinius

---

8. Ibid., 4.

to Constantine's sister, Constantia. The two emperors issued a joint declaration on religion, granting "to Christians and others, full authority to observe that religion which each preferred."[9] Although the edict allowed for religious toleration of all faiths, the co-emperors clearly specified Christians in the document: "We have given to those Christians free and unrestricted opportunity of religious worship."[10] Moreover, Christian property taken during the Great Persecution under Diocletian was restored in the edict. This imperial action legalized the Faith and allowed the Church to exist as a legally recognized corporation within the Empire. Paganism was allowed to continue, but the Church was placed on equal legal footing with the pagan cults. Most importantly, Christians were free to publicly worship without fear of government persecution. Just a decade earlier, such an act on the part of a Roman emperor, let alone both emperors, would have been unthinkable and improbable — but through the miracle of the cross in the sky and Constantine's victory over Maxentius, the unthinkable and improbable became reality.

SOLE EMPEROR

With the Edict of Milan, Christians in the Roman Empire assumed the horrible days of persecution were over. Unfortunately, for the Christians in the eastern provinces, this was not the case. Licinius had co-issued the edict with Constantine, but he was no friend of the Church. Instead, his childhood friendship with Galerius, the initiator of the Great Persecution, was the defining relationship in his life. Several years after the edict of toleration at Milan, Licinius initiated a persecution of Christians in his territory and engaged in conflict with Constantine over who would rule

---

9. Lactantius, *De Mort. Pers.*, ch. 48. opera, ed. 0. F. Fritzsche, II, p 288 sq. (Bibl Patr. Ecc. Lat. XI). Translated in University of Pennsylvania. Dept. of History: *Translations and Reprints from the Original Sources of European History*, (Philadelphia, University of Pennsylvania Press [1897?–1907?]), Vol 4:, 1, pp. 28–30.
10. Ibid.

the Empire. After a few battles and an uneasy truce, the forces of Licinius and Constantine finally clashed decisively at the Battle of Adrianople on July 3, 324. Licinius lost and, with the remnant of his army, retreated to the town of Byzantium. A few months later, in the final battle of the civil war, Constantine overwhelmingly defeated Licinius, who begged for his life. Constantine allowed his brother-in-law to live, no doubt influenced by the pleadings of his sister, but the reprieve was short-lived. Within a year, Constantine ordered Licinius's execution. The death of Licinius and the supremacy of Constantine's army produced an event not seen in the Empire for the last generation: a sole emperor.

Constantine's desire to rule a united empire had come to pass, and he endeavored to build a worthy monument to the accomplishment of that goal. He spared no expense to build a magnificent new city on the site of the town of Byzantium. Several years of construction produced a city so vast and massive that Saint Jerome would later remark, "in clothing Constantinople the rest of the world was left naked."[11] The city, now the capital seat of the Empire, was consecrated in the year 330 as "New Rome." Later, the city would take on the name of its founder and be known as Constantinople.[12]

HERESY

The Church had confronted heresy in her first centuries, but the impact had been limited. Now that the emperor favored the Church and converts came from all strata of society, the danger of heresy and its impact were compounded. False teaching

---

11. Abbot Giuseppe Ricciotti, *The Age of the Martyrs: Christianity from Diocletian (284) to Constantine (337)*, trans. Rev. Anthony Bull, C.R.L. (Rockford, IL: TAN Books and Publishers, Inc., 1999 [1959]), 220.

12. Constantine and his saintly mother, Helena, also engaged in other building projects that directly benefited the Church. Constantine built the first churches dedicated to Saints Peter and Paul in Rome. Helena traveled to the Holy Land, where she was able to locate many relics, including the True Cross. A large basilica was built that incorporated the site of Jesus' crucifixion as well as his tomb. The structure was consecrated in the year 336 and became a favored place of pilgrimage for Christians from the west for centuries.

destroyed communion and threatened the security of the social order, necessitating a response from secular government. Unfortunately, a heresy that began in the early fourth century proved a "pernicious attack" that would consume the Church for the next five hundred years. The Church assembled in ecumenical councils to combat the spread of heresy and to define her teachings,[13] mostly in response to the question of who Jesus is — or, more precisely, what words should be used to describe who Jesus is, and what relationship he has to the Father and the Holy Spirit. Theologians, priests, and monks sought to answer the question, but their teachings were not always in conformity with the apostolic faith.

ARIUS THE HERETIC

As a priest in Alexandria, Egypt, Arius had seen firsthand the impact of the recent wave of converts resulting from imperial favoritism of the Church. He knew that many educated Romans steeped in Greco-Roman philosophy and logic struggled with the Church's teachings — namely, the Trinity, and the concept of Jesus as both God and man — because these posed paradoxes for the Roman mind. He tried to explain these teachings in a book entitled *Thalia*. Arius's teachings became very popular and were even set to music as a memory aid. (The tune used was from an old drinking song, which helped even the uneducated sailors and stevedores of the bustling port remember them.)[14] As a master propagandist graced with a dynamic personality, Arius spread his teachings throughout the diocese. They were soon embraced in other areas of the Empire as well. Arius tried to solve the question

---

13. A distinction that will be useful for the reader: a synod can be a meeting of local or regional bishops or even representative bishops from throughout the world (but not all bishops). Small "c" councils are meetings of local bishops (synod and council can be synonymous). Big "C" Councils are ecumenical (all the bishops in world are invited). Synods and councils are only authoritative for the area or region.

14. See Rod Bennett, *The Apostasy that Wasn't: The Extraordinary Story of the Unbreakable Early Church* (El Cajon, CA: Catholic Answers Press, 2015), 130.

of who Jesus is in relationship to the Father by declaring that God was not always Father, and there was a time when the Son was not in existence but, rather, had been brought into existence by the Father. This teaching appeared logical, but makes Christ into a creature (albeit the first and most perfect creature of the Father, but a creature nonetheless). Arius argued that "the Son who is tempted, suffers and dies, however exalted he may be, is not to be equal to the immutable Father."[15] Arius demoted the Holy Spirit by teaching that the Spirit was also created and was the second most perfect creature. Arius simplified the Trinity by exalting the Father and teaching that the Son and Holy Spirit were creatures of the Father, not coeternal with him. This made the doctrine of the Trinity more palatable to the educated Roman converts, but by making the Son and Holy Spirit creatures, Arius developed a "clever attempt to save paganism, to allow men to go on worshipping a creature rather than the Creator."[16] Bishop Alexander quickly identified the heretical nature of Arius's teachings, condemning them in 318, and also ordered Arius to cease their propagation. However, the popularity of the teachings brought Arius recognition and fame — and, vain man that he was, he refused to acquiesce to his bishop. News of the theological squabble reached Constantine, who could not tolerate internal ecclesial dissension. The emperor wrote a letter to Arius and Alexander, urging them to reconcile. The emperor remonstrated the pair for even raising such questions in the first place, which he thought were provoked by idleness, made for the "sake of a philosophical exercise," and were brought "imprudently to the ears of the people."[17] Constantine demanded an end to the bickering so that he could have "back peaceful nights and days without care [so] that I may keep some pleasure in the pure light and joy of a tranquil life."[18] Unfortunately for Constantine and the Church, Arius's teachings did

---

15. Henry Chadwick, *The Early Church*, revised edition (New York: Penguin Books, 1993), 124.
16. Bennett, 138.
17. Grant, *Constantine the Great*, 171–172.
18. Ibid.

not vanish; they spread rapidly, and the emperor would deal with this issue for the rest of his life.

Arius's teachings were popular and widespread partly because the Empire was at peace. Tranquil times allow people to engage in activities normally considered superfluous during times of stress and difficulty. Many newly converted Romans were educated in the art of rhetoric and debate, and they joyfully engaged in the discussion over Arius's opinion that Jesus was the first most perfect creature of God. Some even used Scripture to support their arguments. Saint Jerome (347–420) later bemoaned the use of personal interpretation of the Word of God contrary to the teaching authority of the Church: "Builders, carpenters, workers in metal and wood, websters, and fullers, makers of anything, cannot become an expert without a teacher; physicians are trained by physicians. The art of the Scripture is the only art which is claimed by all."[19]

Arianism is an example of a top-down heretical movement, meaning that the higher elements of Roman society — that is, the nobility, army, parts of the episcopacy — embraced the newfangled idea while the general populace remained orthodox.[20] The Roman nobility believed Arianism was more sophisticated than the orthodox beliefs of the masses. Arius provided the well-educated, class-conscious, newly converted nobles another way to separate themselves from the common and poor people, who remained solidly Catholic. Arianism's rapid spread was also due to the Roman army. The army, like the nobility, prided itself on being different from the masses of Roman society, and was central to the life of the Empire, even though the legionaries numbered just a fraction of the population. The army embraced Arianism. Since the troops were stationed across the Empire, Arius's teachings gained footing in numerous parts of the world. Acceptance of Arianism became so widespread that even bishops began to

---

19. Jerome, *Ad Paulium*, epistle 5, quoted in Ricciotti, *The Age of Martyrs*, 247.
20. See Bennett, 214.

agree with it. If Arianism had "prevailed, the whole nature of the [Christian] religion would have been transformed. It would not only have been transformed, it would have failed, and with its failure would have followed the breakdown of that civilization which the Catholic Church was to build up."[21] The attack on the Faith by the North African priest demanded an answer.

THE COUNCIL OF NICAEA

Constantine, desiring peace, invited all the bishops in the Empire to the city of Nicaea to discuss Arius's heresy. Nicaea was an easily accessible town, connected by imperial roads to all the provinces, and only twenty-five miles from the imperial palace at Nicomedia. In order to facilitate maximum episcopal participation, Constantine paid all the bishops' travel expenses. Due to Nicaea's location, most of the assembled bishops came from the east, but over ten western bishops, including Constantine's close friend, Hosius of Cordova, and the papal legates Vitus and Vincent of Capua, attended. Pope Sylvester I (r. 314–335) approved the calling of this council by the emperor. Tradition holds that 318 total bishops were present.[22] Hosius, along with the papal legates, presided over the proceedings, and Constantine attended the first and last sessions of the council. One attendee noted, "The council looked like an assembled army of martyrs."[23] Many of the assembled bishops had suffered during the Great Persecution. Hosius had been a confessor; other bishops had been imprisoned, sent to the mines, or had gone into hiding. Many bishops had suffered horrible tortures, including the loss of limbs and the gouging out of eyes. Only twenty years previously, an emperor had tried with all his might to eradicate the Catholic Church. Now, an emperor

---

21. Hilaire Belloc, *The Great Heresies* (Rockford, IL: TAN Books and Publishers, Inc., 1991 [1938]), 11.
22. Other sources indicate the number was a little more than 200. See Wilken, *The First Thousand Years*, 91.
23. Theodoret, *Ecclesiastical History*, I:10, quoted in Bennett, 128.

had called the bishops together to settle a doctrinal controversy and achieve peace and unity in the Church and Empire.

Arius was invited to the council to present his teachings to the assembled bishops, some of whom were active supporters. Numerous other attendees were sympathizers, known as "semi-Arians," who wanted compromise and peace above all else. After Arius's presentation, the council fathers debated his teachings. Some, including Eusebius of Nicomedia, defended his position. Ultimately, the bishops decided to develop a written statement of belief, but agreement on terminology proved elusive. The most interesting aspect of the council is perhaps the fact that the fiercest debate centered not on whether Arius's teachings were orthodox (they clearly were not) but on what word should be used to describe the relationship of Jesus with the Father. The western bishops preferred the word *homoousios* (in Greek; or consubstantial, from the Latin), which meant the *Logos* (the Word of God, the Son) had the same nature as the Father but was not the same person. The term was not found in Scripture, but it was favored in order to force the Arians to deny Arius's central heretical proposition — that the *Logos* was a created being of the Father.

Unfortunately, the word did not have the same meaning in the east as in the west; it had been condemned in the east as heretical in the third century. The worldly Paul of Samosata (200–275) had been the bishop of Antioch and a proponent of the heresy known as Modalistic Monarchianism. This belief emphasizes the oneness of God to the point where the Father, Son, and Holy Spirit are modes of the one God, not separate, yet united persons in the Trinity.[24] Paul used the term *homoousios* (consubstantial) to deny the distinct divine personality of the Son, indicating that Father, Son, and Holy Spirit are the same person. A local council of bishops in Antioch in 268 had condemned Paul of Samosata and the word *homoousios*. Understandably, many of the eastern bishops present at Nicaea bristled at the use of *homoousios*, even with the

---

24. Other names for the heresy are Sabellianism and Patripassianism.

western understanding of the word. The Semi-Arians preferred the term *homoiousios*, which meant "of *like* substance," but this term was rejected by the orthodox, since it did not clearly and definitively indicate that the Father, Son, and Holy Spirit are co-eternal and of the *same* substance. Eventually, *homoousios* was used in the final written statement of faith developed at the council.

The statement of belief, known as the Nicene Creed, was written and voted on by the bishops, who overwhelmingly approved it (316 of the 318 bishops voted in favor).[25] Hosius of Cordova was the first whose signature was affixed to the document, followed by Vitus and Vincent, the papal legates. Two bishops, Theonas and Secundus, refused to sign and were sent into exile — a momentous event, as it marked the first time in Church history that a secular punishment (exile) was applied to an ecclesiastical crime (heresy).[26]

The council fathers also discussed other matters while assembled at Nicaea, including the dating of Easter and a series of discipline canons. The question of when Easter should be celebrated dominated the early Church and was a source of friction between the western and eastern halves of the Church.[27] The eastern dating method, which followed the practice of the Apostle John, celebrated the feast on the fourteenth day of the Jewish month of Nisan, regardless of the day of the week. Those who followed this dating method were known as Quatrodecimans (from the Latin for "fourteen," *quattuordecim*). The western method moved Easter to the first Sunday after the first full moon of the vernal equinox, in order to clearly link the celebration with the day of the week of the first Easter. The bishops ruled at Nicaea that the western

---

25. The Nicene Creed is still recited at Mass today. Dan Brown in his *The Da Vinci Code* has a fictional dialogue between two characters who discuss the deliberations at the Council of Nicaea. Brown writes that the vote taken by the bishops was a "relatively close vote" — not only is his book pure fiction, but apparently his math is off as well! See Dan Brown, *The Da Vinci Code* (New York: Doubleday, 2003), 233.
26. This precedent would become significant in future centuries during the medieval period and the establishment of papal inquisitors.
27. Saint Polycarp traveled to Rome to discuss the matter with Pope Saint Pius I in the second century.

method would be used universally throughout the Church so that all Christians would celebrate the feast on the same day.

The discipline canons of Nicaea were enforced throughout the universal Church — the first time in Church history this had occurred. The twenty total canons at Nicaea dealt with clerical behavior and liturgical practice. Some examples of the Nicene canons include:

- Members of the clergy must not keep in their house a woman who is not their mother, sister, aunt, or a woman above all suspicion.
- Clerics who practice usury (loaning money at exorbitant interest) are to be deposed.
- Deacons are not to sit with the priests and are not to distribute the Eucharist to them.
- The ancient custom must be observed of praying while standing and not kneeling on Sundays and in the fifty days after Easter.[28]

The last day of the council coincided with the twentieth anniversary of Constantine's accession of imperial power (as proclaimed by the legions in Britain). In celebration of this milestone and of the completion of their conciliar efforts, the emperor held a banquet for the bishops. Constantine believed the council had achieved peace and unity in the Church and Empire.

THE BEGINNINGS OF MONASTICISM

During the Roman persecutions, many Christians witnessed to their faith by shedding their blood, the ultimate price for refusing to repudiate their beliefs. Now that the Faith was legalized and the Church was recognized as a corporate institution in the Empire, "red martyrdom" was temporarily at an end. Christians

28. Ricciotti, 269–270.

still desired to give their lives totally to Christ in a radical and unique manner, however, so a lifestyle of self-sacrifice and renunciation developed in the form of monasticism — a word derived from the Greek *monachos*, meaning "solitary."[29] Christian monks practiced what became known as "white martyrdom" — a complete self-sacrifice and renunciation of the things of the world, dying to self in order to grow closer to Christ and the Church. The founder of monasticism is usually identified as Saint Anthony the Abbot (250–356), an Egyptian Christian from a wealthy family in Alexandria who, at the age of nineteen, gave his wealth to the poor and began to live an ascetical life. He lived a strict penitential life in the midst of the bustling city and was engaged in spiritual combat against demons for nearly fifteen years. At the age of thirty-five, he left the city and spent the next seven decades in the wild, only returning to Alexandria twice: the first time to encourage his fellow Christians to remain strong in the midst of Diocletian's Great Persecution, and later to support his bishop, Athanasius, in the fight against the Arians.[30] In the desert, Anthony lived a solitary, silent, and penitential life, sustaining his health on a daily meal of bread, seasoned with salt, and water. He did not eat meat or drink wine. His day was spent in prayer.[31] Although his life appeared lonely, Anthony sought solitude in order to grow closer to God. Unfortunately for Anthony, this way of life attracted attention, and soon a large following of men appeared in the desert seeking to emulate him.[32] Anthony wanted to remain solitary with the Lord, but he realized he had an obligation to assist these men in some way. He organized communal times of prayer,

---

29. Wilken, *The First Thousand Years*, 99.

30. Saint Athanasius spent some time with Anthony in the desert before he became bishop. He also wrote a popular biography of the great saint in which he recorded that the hermit told the Alexandrians to "have no fellowship with the most impious Arians. For there is no communion between light and darkness." Athanasius, *Life of Saint Anthony*, 69, quoted in Warren H. Carroll, *The Building of Christendom: A History of Christendom*, vol. 2 (Front Royal, VA: Christendom College Press, 1987), 21.

31. Wilken, *The First Thousand Years*, 101.

32. This is just one example of many in the lives of the saints of the axiom that holiness attracts. There is a deep desire in all human beings for communion with God, as we are all created in his image and likeness. Saints like Anthony illustrate through their lives that communion with God is possible, albeit in an imperfect manner this side of the veil, and that example attracts others.

song, and spiritual conferences, while maintaining the eremetical environment.

Another hermit who developed an early form of cenobitic monasticism (monks living in community) was Saint Pachomius (290–348). Pachomius's first monastic community, established in the year 318, soon grew to over a hundred monks. He realized that a monastery of that size was burdensome, so he created a more manageable structure. Pachomius divided his community into a complex of buildings with individual houses, wherein no more than forty monks had individual cells. Each monk wore the same simple habit. Eventually, Pachomius founded nine other similar monasteries. He composed the first monastic rule, which provided for a life of daily spiritual exercises for the monks, with regular times for prayer, work, and communal meals. Upon his death in the mid-fourth century, Pachomius's monasteries housed thousands of monks.

While Anthony and Pachomius are credited with establishing the first forms of monasticism, other groups of Christians, especially in Egypt, Palestine, and Syria, practiced very different ways of holy living. There arose some monastic extremists, including such groups as the Dendrites (from the Greek *dendron*, meaning "tree"), who escaped the world by living in trees and practiced extreme forms of asceticism. Another group, the Adamites, believed that through holy living they could regain Adam's original innocence in the Garden before the Fall, so they walked around naked. Perhaps the most famous are the Stylites, or "pillar hermits," who lived on platforms on top of pillars. These men practiced extreme fasting, living on the contributions of passersby who would put food and other necessities in a bucket, which had been lowered down by a rope. The most well-known Stylite was Saint Simeon (d. 459). Annoyed with numerous people disturbing his hermetical life to seek guidance on holy living, he ascended a twenty-eight-foot platform, where he lived for thirty-six years!

Although many monastic groups sought to live out the Christian life in a unique manner, one man would be known as the "Father of Eastern Monasticism," Saint Basil the Great (329–378). Basil came from a holy family; his grandfather had been martyred, and his grandmother, parents, and siblings are also saints. One of his brothers was also a Church Father and extraordinary theologian, Saint Gregory of Nyssa (335–394). Despite the sanctity of his family, Basil embraced the world in his early life. Undoubtedly, the prayers of his parents brought about his eventual complete conversion. Basil dedicated his life to God by becoming a monk, which he believed would help him fulfill the Christian vocation to embrace "likeness to God as far as possible."[33] Basil wanted to live the monastic life with all excellence, since "mediocrity brings the Christian faith into discredit."[34] So, he founded a new community of monks whose lives were governed by one rule, so that they all could pursue holiness in a common life.

Basil's rule contributed two important developments to monasticism: the novitiate and organized community life. Basil recognized that new members who wished to join the monastic community should undergo a period of testing and initiation to determine if the monastic life suited them, and if they truly belonged in the community. If a novice was not able to live peacefully in accordance with the rule, then he was not allowed to permanently join the group. Basil wanted the monks to be in communion, rather than remaining a group of disparate hermits who occasionally gathered for certain times or events. He restricted the number of monks living in community to no more than forty and created a life centered on a spirit of moderation, which was balanced between an active and contemplative lifestyle. Basil organized times of common prayer for his monks. He stressed the need for spiritual direction and proper holy living, including the practice of celibacy. He emphasized living a simple life of moderate food consumption and wearing no ostentatious clothing. Basil even forbade his monks from loud laughing, as it

---

33. Basil, *Homily on the Creation of Man* 1.17.
34. Basil, *Epistle* 190.1.

would disturb the prayerful atmosphere of the community, although smiling was permitted.[35]

Basil also created a lasting societal organization to care for the sick and dying — the hospital. Because the first monks were separated from major urban areas, they had to care for their own sick and developed a rudimentary healthcare system. In some monasteries, a separate building, the infirmary, was constructed to care for the sick members of the community. Basil was aware of early monastic health care but wanted to improve upon it by providing a safe place for all the ill, injured, and dying to receive proper medical treatment by trained professionals, offered at no charge.[36] Basil was able to support his hospital by utilizing his family's wealthy connections with the imperial government. The land for the hospital was donated to Basil by the state; he convinced the provincial governor to grant tax-exempt status to the new institution by highlighting the public impact of the hospital, which would care for the sick and poor and provide jobs in the local economy. The new health complex was known as the *Basileias*, in honor of Basil, and became the model for the Byzantine healthcare system for centuries.[37] Basil was known as "the Great" during his lifetime because his contemporaries appreciated his singular brilliance and holy efforts.

ARIANISM CONTINUES

Although the Council of Nicaea had definitively condemned Arius and his false teachings, many eastern bishops voiced their displeasure with the council's work, especially with the use of the word *homoousios*. These bishops had signed the Creed, despite their misgivings and Semi-Arian leanings, but, after the council, worked to undermine the orthodox teaching by gaining favor with Constan-

35. Henry Chadwick, *The Church in Ancient Society: From Galilee to Gregory the Great* (Oxford: Oxford University Press, 2001), 335.
36. Wilken, *The First Thousand Years*, 160.
37. Ibid., 160–162.

tine and persecuting the orthodox bishops. Eusebius of Nicomedia, one of the leading Semi-Arians, formulated a plan to restore Arius to communion, spread his teachings, and rid the Church of the supporters of Nicaea. He influenced the emperor to allow Arius an audience, wherein the condemned cleric made an ambiguous profession of faith that did not contain the word *homoousios* and was not a clear acceptance of the orthodox faith confirmed at Nicaea. Constantine was no theologian and did not understand the subtleties, so he ordered Arius's bishop to reinstate him to active priestly ministry. This exercise of *caesaro-papism* proved disastrous for the Church — "whenever Constantine meddled in Church affairs, he only made matters worse."[38] The bishop of Arius's home diocese (Alexandria, Egypt) was a strong supporter of Nicaea and had been present at the council as a deacon assistant to the original combatant of Arius, Bishop Alexander. This new bishop, Athanasius, refused to obey the imperial order.

ATHANASIUS — DEFENDER OF ORTHODOXY

More than likely, the young bishop of Alexandria never dreamed that, one day, he would be alone against his brother bishops in the fight to preserve Nicene orthodoxy in the east. Happily, Athanasius (297–373) possessed the mind and fortitude to tangle with the impious Arians. He was a talented theologian, known for his treatise on the Incarnation, in which he wrote that God "was made man so that we might be made God."[39] The redheaded, blue-eyed bishop loved the people of his diocese immensely and, as a result of the Arian conflict, would suffer much for them.

Eusebius of Nicomedia planned to attack the Nicene bishops by pressuring Constantine to depose them for secular reasons. The Arians accused Athanasius of committing murder and sorcery, concocting a bizarre plot around the bishop Arsenius. The

---

38. Ricciotti, 273.
39. Athanasius, *De Incarnatione*, 54, 3.

Arians whisked Arsenius into hiding. They accused Athanasius of killing Arsenius and mutilating the body by cutting off his right hand, which they said he would use in acts of sorcery. The Arians went so far as to produce a blackened mummified hand as proof.[40] Athanasius became aware of the Arian plot when his friend, Governor Archelaus, found Arsenius hiding in Tyre. Archelaus arrested Arsenius secretly so that the Arians could be denounced in a public setting. The local council of Tyre in 335 provided such a venue. The emperor was present to celebrate his thirtieth anniversary of imperial accession and the tenth anniversary of the Council of Nicaea. Among the conciliar business was the trial of Athanasius, who was present to answer the charges of the Arians. The mummified hand was presented as proof of Athanasius's nefarious conduct. However, unbeknownst to the Arians, Athanasius and his supporters had brought Arsenius to the council disguised in a cloak. After the charges against Athanasius were presented, he was allowed time to make a defense. The embattled bishop of Alexandria asked his brother bishops if they knew Arsenius and would recognize him. When the assembly murmured agreement, Athanasius brought the cloaked figure before them, uncovered his head, and said: "Is this the right Arsenius? Is this the man I murdered? Is this the man [who I] mutilated after his murder by cutting off his right hand?" Athanasius then pulled off the cloak completely from Arsenius, pointed to the man's two intact hands, and said to the Arians, "Let no one seek for a third hand, for man has received two hands from the Creator and no more."[41]

The Arians were incensed that their plan against Athanasius had backfired. They rushed toward the Alexandrian prelate, screaming, spitting, and calling him possessed by the devil. They threatened Athanasius with bodily harm, but imperial officials escorted him out of the room. The Arian bishops then condemned and deposed him. As a result, Athanasius was forced into his first

---

40. Bennett, 171.
41. Theodoret, *Ecclesiastical History*, I:28, quoted in Carroll, *The Building of Christendom*, 18.

of five total exiles by numerous emperors, beginning with Constantine, for his adherence to the orthodox faith. He spent his exiles, which spanned nearly half of his time as bishop of Alexandria, in Gaul, Rome, and the Egyptian desert.[42] Most of the laity in the east remained faithful, as did the monks, but Athanasius was almost alone among the eastern episcopacy in maintaining the Nicene faith. Athanasius's efforts earned him the moniker "Defender of Orthodoxy," and in all of Church history, "few more gifted men have ever lived."[43]

THE END OF THE HERETIC AND THE EMPEROR

A year after Athanasius's exile to Gaul, Arius was in Constantinople and felt the urge to go to the bathroom. He left his attendant servant outside the public facility, but the servant soon heard shouting and screaming. He ran into the restroom and saw Arius dead on the ground, surrounded by his entrails.[44] The orthodox supporters of Nicaea took the death of Arius in the capital city as a sign. Even Constantine "is reported to have looked upon the event as a significant proof of the Nicene doctrine."[45] Unfortunately, Arius's death did not end belief in his teachings, and even the emperor's newfound orthodoxy would not prove decisive. The following year, the emperor became gravely ill. Now in his sixties after a lifetime of ruling the Roman Empire, Constantine decided the time was right to receive baptism. He went to confession and traveled to Nicomedia, where he was baptized by the Arian sympathizer Eusebius of Nicomedia, becoming the first Roman emperor to receive the Sacraments of Initiation in the Catholic Church. He refused to discard his white baptismal gown, never again wearing the imperial purple.[46] This man who had witnessed the miracle of the cross on his way to the Milvian

---

42. Athanasius was bishop for forty-five years and spent twenty of them in exile.
43. Carroll, *The Building of Christendom*, 15.
44. Ricciotti, 280.
45. G.P. Baker, *Constantine the Great and the Christian Revolution* (New York: Cooper Square Press, 2001), 292.
46. Ibid., 309.

Bridge, who had favored and legalized the Catholic Church in the Roman Empire, passed to his eternal reward on Pentecost Sunday 337. At the time of the Battle of Milvian Bridge in 312, Christians numbered only nine million, fifteen percent of the total imperial population. At the time of Constantine's death, Christians comprised thirty percent of the population.[47] The Senate declared Constantine divine, the last time that honor was bestowed on an emperor. The purging of a dead emperor's extended relatives by his immediate family was common after his death in order to cull the field of potential candidates for the throne. Constantine's two brothers and his sister's husband, along with three of his five nephews, were killed. The youngest of the surviving nephews, a young boy of six, would never forget the death of his family members. When Julian became emperor nearly twenty-five years later, he would use his power to take revenge on those he blamed for the killings — Christians.

The Empire was divided among the three sons of Constantine, who had been raised in the orthodox faith of Nicaea. Constantine II ruled Gaul, Britain, and Spain; Constantius II was given the eastern provinces; and Constans governed in Italy and Africa. However, this three-part arrangement did not last long. The brothers engaged in warfare against one another, and Constantine II was killed in 340 while fighting against Constans, who was then killed by assassins a decade later. In the year 350, Constantius II found himself sole emperor like his father, and reigned for twenty-four years. He married an Arian sympathizer who turned him toward that false teaching. Constantius II then began a systematic campaign against the adherents of the Nicene faith.

PERSECUTION OF THE ORTHODOX

Constantius II, like his father, desired unity in the empire, and he pursued that end by persecuting bishops who supported Ni-

---

47. Rodney Stark, *Bearing False Witness: Debunking Centuries of Anti-Catholic History* (West Conshohocken, PA: Templeton Press, 2016), 53.

caea so that Arianism could unite the Church. Because most of the eastern bishops had already embraced the heresy, save the valiant and still living Saint Athanasius, Constantius II began his campaign in the west in 355 when he called a local council to meet at Milan. The council was called primarily to force the western bishops to condemn Athanasius and the word *homoousios* (consubstantial). The emperor ordered the assembled three hundred western bishops to sign the condemnation.[48] Although some bishops gave into the demands of the emperor, others held fast and refused. Dionysius, the bishop of Milan, refused to sign, and he was deposed by the emperor and replaced by an Arian bishop. Hilarius, a deacon who was vocal in his opposition to Arianism, was stripped, tied to a pillar, and flogged. Despite being a hundred years old, the venerable Hosius, who had presided at the Nicene proceedings, was arrested and tortured until he signed the condemnation of Athanasius. Vincent of Capua, one of the papal legates at Nicaea, was tricked into signing the condemnation by assurance that Arianism would also be condemned.[49] The council of Milan was a success for Constantius II; nearly half of the assembled bishops signed the condemnation of Athanasius. The bishops who refused were exiled. In order to ensure the complete eradication of the orthodox faith among the episcopacy in the west, Constantius II turned his attention to the Roman pontiff, Liberius (r. 352–366).

The pope was in a precarious position. He initially defended Athanasius, but severe imperial pressure was brought upon him to sign the condemnation. He was bribed with cash, but he threw it into the street.[50] Because he refused to sign, Liberius was seized in the middle of the night by imperial officials and sent to Thrace, while one of his deacons, Felix, was installed as an antipope. In exile, Liberius was threatened with death. After two years of overwhelming imperial pressure, he signed a condemnation of

---

48. Bennett, 216.
49. Ibid.
50. Ibid., 218.

Athanasius that rejected both the words *homoousios* and *homoiousios*.[51] After his signature, Liberius was allowed to return to Rome, where the people, who were likely unaware the pontiff had given in to the emperor, greeted him warmly. Constantius II's persecution of the Church brought a scathing written rebuke from Athanasius, who compared the emperor to other nefarious enemies of the Church, such as Pharaoh in the Book of Exodus, Herod, and Pilate. Athanasius considered Constantius II a tool of Satan and a precursor of the Antichrist. Constantius II did not appreciate the criticism. He sent imperial troops to once more depose and exile the orthodox defender of Nicaea. An unqualified man, known as George the Pork Dealer, was made bishop of Alexandria, but the people rejected him and longed for the return of their saintly bishop. It would be another six years before Athanasius returned to his episcopal see in 362. Unfortunately, this hero of the Church was exiled twice more but returned home before he passed to his eternal reward in 373.

The Arian crisis continued to plague the Church after the death of the great defender of orthodoxy. Saint Basil the Great's brother, Gregory of Nyssa, remarked, "Whenever you went to the money changer, to the butcher's shop, or to the thermal baths, people asked you whether the Father is greater than the Son, or whether the Son proceeded from nothing!"[52] A century later, Saint Jerome, commenting on the Arian crisis, wrote, "the whole world groaned when, to its astonishment, it discovered that it was Arian … the little ship of the apostles was in peril."[53] The speed and widespread acceptance of Arianism was impressive. The Church

---

51. Known as the Second Formula of Sirmium. There is some debate of whether Liberius actually signed the condemnation. Some sources indicate the story was propaganda created by the Arians citing the fact that when Liberius returned to Rome from exile he was treated as a conqueror. Athanasius and others believed Liberius signed the condemnation. Athanasius wrote, "Liberius, having been exiled, gave in after two years, and, in fear of the death with which he was threatened, signed." (*Hist. Ar.*, xli). He is the first pope not considered a saint, which is an indication that he likely did sign, although under extreme duress.

52. Régine Pernoud, *Martin of Tours: Soldier, Bishop, Saint*, trans. Michael J. Miller (San Francisco: Ignatius Press, 2006), 42.

53. Jerome, *Dialogue Against the Luciferians*, 19.

was actively engaged in the Arian crisis for nearly fifty years, and its effects lasted for three centuries before finally being checked by heroic bishops, monks, and laity.

THE APOSTATE EMPEROR

Julian was an angry child. His father, Julius, the half-brother of Constantine, had been murdered upon the emperor's death, along with one of his sons (Julian's half-brother), by Christian members of the imperial household; another half-brother was executed later in 354. Julian blamed the deaths of his family members on these Christians and later said, "There are no wild beasts so hostile to mankind as are most Christians in their hatred for each other."[54] Sadly, the violent actions of Christians in Julian's early life produced bitter fruit and persecution for the Church. Julian was baptized, but his family adhered to the Arian heresy, which clouded his understanding of the Catholic faith. After the death of his father, Julian was educated in Greek literature by a pagan tutor, who acted as a father figure for the impressionable young boy. Julian grew fond of pagan authors; at the age of twenty, he "embrace[d] paganism with enthusiasm."[55]

Julian's political career began in 355 when Constantius II appointed him caesar of the west. He also married Constantius's sister, Helena, the same year. Julian proved to be an effective administrator, streamlining bureaucracy and reducing taxes. He illustrated his military prowess by retaking Cologne in 356 from the barbarians and defeating a 35,000-man Alemanni army with only 13,000 troops at the Battle of Strasbourg in 357. The Persians were causing trouble in the eastern provinces, so Constantius launched a military campaign. The emperor, concerned about Julian's successes, feared that the caesar might become too powerful. Constantius ordered Julian's western legions to

54. Bennett, 207.
55. Robert Louis Wilken, *The Christians as the Romans Saw Them*, Second Edition (New Haven, CT: Yale University Press, 1984), 164.

move east to fight the Persians. The intention of the emperor was obvious, as there were troops closer to the eastern provinces who were better rested than Julian's legions in Germania. Julian's men did not appreciate the emperor's punitive orders, and rebelled by proclaiming Julian emperor. They made plans to march on Constantinople in order to install Julian as emperor, but before they reached the capital city, news arrived that Constantius II had died on November 3, 361. Julian was thirty years old and now reigned as Roman emperor. Julian's reign lasted a brief eighteen months, but in that short period of time he left his mark on imperial and ecclesiastical history.

Julian's singular focus after becoming emperor was the persecution of the Catholic Church, which he both hated and feared. He tried to nullify his baptism by engaging in the initiation rite for the cult of Cybele, an Anatolian goddess, which required bathing in bull's blood.[56] Julian even wrote a book attacking the Faith entitled *Against the Galilaeans*, in which he opined that the Christian faith was nothing more than a "fabrication [and] a fiction of men, composed by wickedness."[57] He desired to return to the ancient ways of Rome and embraced paganism with a fury. He stopped shaving and grew a beard in the tradition of the ancient Greeks, although it prompted the creation of the nickname "goat" from his subjects.[58] He wore pagan philosopher clothing, instead of traditional Roman attire, ordered the rebuilding of dismantled pagan temples, and brought back public sacrifices to the pagan deities. The emperor passed several anti-Christian edicts, including one that required referring to Christians as "Galilaeans" — his favorite pejorative for the believers in Christ. His persecution of the Church involved a three-pronged strategy: the reorganization of paganism, the

---

56. Wilken, *The First Thousand Years*, 119.
57. Julian, *Against the Galilaeans*, 39A, quoted in Adrian Murdoch, *The Last Pagan: Julian the Apostate and the Death of the Ancient World* (Rochester, VT: Inner Traditions, 2008), 132.
58. Adrian Goldsworthy, *How Rome Fell: Death of a Superpower* (New Haven, CT: Yale University Press, 2009), 225.

marginalization of Catholics, and an alliance with the Jews.

Julian's plan to restore paganism revolved around making it like the Catholic Church. He composed standard prayer books for use in pagan temples throughout the Empire and engaged in charitable works, such as founding homes for single mothers, establishing pagan prison ministries, and even created a pagan military chaplaincy.[59] But "the thing he planned to revive had never existed" — there had never been a hierarchically structured corporate body in paganism like the Church.[60] The emperor believed that if he made paganism like the Catholic Church, people would return to the pagan cults; but he failed to understand that the Faith was more than just an external organization promoting charitable works.

The second element of Julian's strategy was to marginalize Catholics in Roman society. He stopped promotions of Catholic soldiers and refused to appoint any Catholic as provincial governor or magistrate. Catholics were also banned from practicing law. In June 362, the emperor issued an edict forbidding Catholics from teaching rhetoric, grammar, and philosophy in schools. The short-term goal was to force ambitious Christians to allow pagans to educate their children.[61] Julian hoped that, in the long-term, the edict would prevent educated people from remaining or becoming Catholic, which would stagnate the Church and eventually cause her demise. This edict was problematic for Catholic parents; education was critical for advancement in Roman society. Thankfully, the edict did not have the intended effect, as its enforcement did not last long.

Finally, Julian believed he could neutralize the Church by entering into an alliance with the Jews. He wrote letters to Jewish leaders in Jerusalem, exhorting them to begin training a new class of priests, since he intended to rebuild the Temple and reinstate an-

---

59. Bennett, 252.
60. Hughes, *A History of the Church*, vol. I, 179.
61. Goldsworthy, *How Rome Fell*, 236.

imal sacrifices.[62] Julian thought that a rebuilt Temple would nullify Christ's prophecy concerning the destruction of the Holy City and lessen the credibility of the Catholic faith. He financed construction efforts to rebuild the Temple, but the work did not progress due to sudden, unnatural events. The Roman soldier and historian Ammianus Marcellinus (c. 330–390) recorded that soon after construction began an earthquake damaged the site. When the work continued, mysterious balls of fire burst from the foundation and burned the workmen.[63] The damage to the foundation and the fiery death of several workers permanently halted construction.

Julian's persecution of the Church, which included the torture and exile of bishops and execution of Christians in Syria, produced the opposite effect he had hoped to achieve. Persecution strengthened the Church and the resolve of Christians, counteracting the emperor's longed-for return of a vibrant paganism. Julian's decision to restore exiled Nicene bishops to their sees, which he hoped would sow division in the Church, was welcomed by the faithful and undercut the authority of Arian bishops. In the end, the Church was not greatly affected by the apostate's anti-Christian policies and edicts. This illustrates how deeply the Faith was inculcated into Roman society less than a century after Constantine's victory at Milvian Bridge. Julian's persecution of the Church also failed because he reigned for only eighteen months. He launched a military campaign against the Persians in the summer of 363, and at the Battle of Samarra foolishly charged into an enemy retreat without his armor. He was struck with a double-bladed spear that pierced his ribs and struck his liver. The wound proved fatal. The emperor, forever known as Julian the Apostate, died uttering, "You have won, O Galilean" as his final words.[64]

---

62. See Bennett, 240, for the rebuilding of the Temple, and Wilken, *The First Thousand Years*, 120, for reinstatement of animal sacrifices.
63. Ammianus Marcellinus, *Res Gestae*, book 23, chapter 1. Sozomen (c. 400–450), a Christian writer, confirms Marcellinus's account. See Gary Michuta, *Hostile Witnesses: How the Historic Enemies of the Church Prove Christianity* (El Cajon, CA: Catholic Answers Press, 2016), 149.
64. The phrase may be legend. See Bennett, 256.

THE END OF PAGANISM

In less than twenty years after the death of Julian the Apostate, the paganism he had endeavored to revitalize was stamped out. Theodosius (r. 379–392) was an orthodox Catholic from Spain who became co-emperor with Gratian (r. 367–383) in 379. Theodosius was a soldier and spent time with his father, a Roman general, on campaign in Britain, Gaul, and the Balkans. He eventually became sole emperor, the last man to rule a united empire. Despite his political and military success, Theodosius considered it "more important to be a member of the Church than to be lord of the world."[65] He illustrated this belief at the very beginning of his reign when he became the first emperor to refuse the pagan title Pontifex Maximus.[66] Theodosius desired religious unity in the Empire, and issued the Edict of Thessalonica in 380, which declared the Catholic faith to be the sole religion of the Empire:

> It is Our will that all the people who are ruled by the administration of Our Clemency shall practice that religion which the divine Peter the Apostle transmitted to the Romans. We command that those persons who follow this rule shall embrace the name of Catholic Christians. The rest, however, whom We adjudge demented and insane, shall sustain the infamy of heretical dogmas, their meeting places shall not receive the name of churches, and they shall be smitten first by divine vengeance and secondly by the retribution of Our own initiative.[67]

Theodosius's edict also outlawed paganism, declaring pagan sac-

---

65. Augustine, *The City of God*, 5.26.
66. Wilken, *The First Thousand Years*, 95.
67. Theodosian Code XVI, 1, 2, quoted in Jean Comby, *How to Read Church History: From the Beginnings to the Fifteenth Century*, vol. I (New York: Crossroads, 2001), 73.

rifice a capital offense.[68] In only sixty-eight years, the Catholic faith had gone from persecuted minority to state-established religion!

A year later, the great emperor hoped to end the Arian controversy within the Church by calling a second ecumenical council at Constantinople. The Arians also erroneously believed that the Holy Spirit was not coeternal and of the same substance as the Father. In order to reassert the orthodox faith as defined at Nicaea, 148 eastern bishops met and added to the Nicene Creed words about the Holy Spirit, indicating that he "proceeds from the Father, [and] who with the Father and the Son is adored and glorified."[69]

CHURCH FATHERS

During this time in Church history, the Holy Spirit raised up saintly men who guided, loved, protected, and disciplined the faithful. These men, many of whom we have met already, were "heirs to the apostles, the leaders and teachers of the early Church," and are known as Church Fathers.[70] The age of the Fathers extends from the first through eighth centuries of Church history. Nearly ninety men are considered to be Church Fathers, grouped into categories such as hermits and monks, popes, apologists, preachers, philosophers, lawyers, scholars, theologians, and saints. They wrote in a variety of languages, including Greek, Latin, Syrian, and Armenian. Their writings consist of Scripture commentaries, theological works, and attacks against heresies. Pope Saint Gelasius I (r. 492–496) was the first to compile a listing of the Fathers,

---

68. Chadwick, *The Church in Ancient Society*, 514.
69. The Council was later affirmed by the pope, but the Constantinople canon, which declared the bishop of Constantinople to have second rank in the Church after the pope and referred to Constantinople as "New Rome," was rejected by Pope Saint Damasus in 382. The phrase "and the Son," known as the *filioque*, in terms of the procession of the Holy Spirit, was added in the West later and has been the source of much antagonism between the Eastern and Western halves of the Church.
70. Mike Aquilina, *The Fathers of the Church: An Introduction to the First Christian Teachers*, Expanded Edition (Huntington, IN: Our Sunday Visitor, 2006), 15.

and Saint Vincent of Lérins (d. 450) defined Church Fathers as "those alone who, though in diverse times and places, yet persevering in the communion and faith of the one Catholic Church have been approved teachers."[71] In order for an early Christian writer to be considered a Church Father, he must meet four basic criteria: orthodoxy, holiness of life, Church approval, and antiquity.[72] The work of the Church Fathers continues to be read and studied today.[73]

THE SOLDIER, BISHOP, AND SAINT

The soldier was filled with joy at the birth of his son and named him "Martin," or "little Mars," to honor the favorite pagan deity of the Roman military. Little did the soldier know that his son would be forever remembered as a man of peace and love, not war and violence. Martin's life was radically altered when he turned fifteen and was forced to enlist in the Roman army. Because the army suffered from a manpower shortage, Constantine had issued an edict in 331 requiring the sons of soldiers to enlist. Martin dutifully joined the service and became a member of the Imperial Guard, an elite cavalry unit charged with protecting the emperor on campaign. Although Martin did his duty, he did not want to join the army. It was the first instance in which "Martin would never be able to act as he intended; he could never decide his own destiny."[74]

Four years later, Martin was stationed at Amiens. During that winter, while out of the garrison riding, Martin passed by a poor man, half-naked, shivering in the cold, asking passersby for alms. People ignored the man and his pitiable condition, but Martin

---

71. *Nicene and Post-Nicene Fathers*, Series 2, 11:132, quoted in Aquilina, 18.
72. In most instances Saint John Damascene (d. 749) is considered the last Church Father, but some hold that distinction should be given to Saint Bernard of Clairvaux (d. 1153).
73. Nearly 40 percent of the Doctors of the Church are Church Fathers. The current *Catechism of the Catholic Church* contains three hundred quotes from the writings of the Fathers, of which ninety are from Saint Augustine alone.
74. Pernoud, *Martin of Tours*, 23.

took his military winter cloak and cut it in two, giving one half to the poor man. He was ridiculed for such a foolish act, but later that night, in a dream, Martin saw Christ clothed in the cloak he had given to the poor man. The experience roused Martin to embrace the Faith, and he was baptized.

Martin struggled with his military service after his baptism, because he found it incompatible with Christian living. A visit from the western caesar before a battle gave him the opportunity he needed to end his military career. Germanic tribes were making incursions across the frontier, raiding Roman territory in Gaul. Julian the Apostate mustered his forces at Worms for a decisive battle and ordered the Imperial Guard into combat. Before the battle, Julian appeared before the men to pay them a combat bonus, but he was confronted with an unanticipated situation. Martin's later biographer Sulpicius Severus recorded the story:

> There he [Julian] began to distribute a bonus to the soldiers. They were called up one by one in the usual way until Martin's turn came. But he thought it would be a suitable time for applying for his discharge, for he did not think that it would be honest for him to take the bonus if he was not going to fight. So he said to the Caesar: "I have been your soldier up to now. Let me now be God's. Let someone who is going to fight have your bonus. I am Christ's soldier." These words put the tyrant into a rage and he said that it was from fear of the battle that was to be fought the next day that he wanted to quit the service, not from religious motives. But Martin was undaunted; in fact, he stood all the firmer when they tried to frighten him. "If it is put down to cowardice," he said, "and not to faith, I will stand unarmed in front of the battle line tomorrow and I will go unscathed through the enemy's columns in the name of the Lord Jesus,

protected by the sign of the Cross instead of by shield and helmet."[75]

Confronted with Martin's strong faith, Julian relented, allowing him to muster out of the army after serving twenty-five years. Martin left the military and embraced the monastic lifestyle, settling in the town of Poitiers. Martin's reputation for holiness increased, and he soon came to the attention of the saintly and beloved bishop Hilary of Poitiers (310–368). Upon Hilary's death in 368, the people wanted someone special to take his place, and they quickly agreed it should be Martin. Martin had no interest in the episcopacy and wanted to remain a monk, but "once again he would be obliged to do something he had not wanted to do: he would be a bishop in spite of himself."[76] Despite his hesitance, Martin was an effective and popular bishop, contrary to the other bishops in Gaul who tended to be worldly and stayed in the cities. Martin believed the function of a bishop was to minister to the people, not to spend time in meetings with other bishops. He refused to go to local synods and other gatherings of the episcopacy. He initiated a plan of evangelization to bring the Gospel to the *pagani* in the countryside: "One could sum up Martin's apostolate by noting that he did not take the Roman road, but, rather, the Gaulish byway."[77] The saintly man almost singlehandedly brought the Faith out of the city and into the countryside, where he worked many miracles, including the raising of three people from the dead.[78] Martin's efforts ensured the Church would not remain an urban phenomenon, but rather be the foundation of a post-imperial society.

The beloved bishop passed to his eternal reward on November 8, 397. He was buried on November 11, and his shrine be-

---

75. Ibid., 31–32.
76. Ibid., 54.
77. Ibid., 85.
78. Ibid., 102.

came one of the most important pilgrimage places in Christendom.[79] The Church recognized Martin's sanctity immediately, a unique honor usually reserved for martyrs or popes.[80] Martin was "an everyday saint" who humbly submitted to God's plan for his life, despite his desires, so that "forced to do something he did not want to do, he accomplished much more than he could have dared to hope."[81]

THE UNLIKELY BISHOP, PROTECTOR OF THE CHURCH

In the same year of Martin's death, another man who had not wanted to be a bishop died in the city of Milan. Born in Trier, Ambrose came from a prominent Roman Christian family who counted martyrs among its ancestors. His father, Aurelius Ambrosius, was the praetorian prefect of Gaul during the reign of Constantius II. When Aurelius died, the family moved to Rome. Ambrose's sister became a religious, receiving her veil from the hands of Pope Liberius.[82] Like his father, Ambrose embraced a secular career in politics. He studied grammar, rhetoric, and law, and he even learned Greek. His brilliance and talents earned him a position on the staff of the praetorian prefect of Italy. At the age of twenty-nine, Ambrose was appointed governor of the provinces of Liguria and Emelia with the regional seat at Milan. Ambrose gained a reputation as an efficient, fair, and conscientious governor.

Following the death of Auxentius, the Arian bishop of Milan, in 373, the clergy and people gathered in the cathedral to elect his successor. The orthodox contingent saw Auxentius's death as an opportunity to get rid of the Arians and elect a bishop who supported Nicaea. The Arians wanted to retain control of Milan

---

79. Unfortunately, his tomb and the accompanying basilica were thoroughly destroyed by French Protestants in the sixteenth century.
80. In fact, Martin was the first nonpapal, non-martyred saint in the Church.
81. Pernoud, *Saint Martin of Tours*, 150,179.
82. Wilken, *The First Thousand Years*, 127.

and were opposed to any candidate in favor of the orthodox creed. Both sides were unwilling to compromise, and the deliberations turned violent. Hoping to quell the riot, Ambrose, who had been present observing the proceedings, rose to address the assembly, urging peace and unity. His speech had the desired effect, along with an unintended consequence. Tradition holds that a small child cried out, "Ambrose for bishop!" and the people agreed.[83] Ambrose was stupefied at his unexpected election by popular acclamation, especially given his status as a catechumen. Ambrose left the cathedral without accepting the election; however, the clergy and people were determined to see him bishop. They sent a petition to Emperor Valentinian, requesting his assistance in the matter. The emperor sent a letter to Ambrose that told him to accept, so he did. He was baptized on Sunday, ordained a priest a few days later, and then consecrated bishop the following Sunday.[84]

Ambrose quickly embraced the clerical life thrust upon him. He sold his worldly possessions and gave the money to the poor. He diligently studied the Scriptures and theological works. He developed a prayer life rooted in the Scriptures, known as *lectio divina*, (or divine reading), which remains a popular devotion. His primary objective was to root out Arianism and unite the Milanese under the banner of Nicaean orthodoxy. Ambrose, like Irenaeus, defined membership in the Church as communion with Rome, writing, "Where Peter is, there is the Church."[85] Ambrose also wanted to combine the public duties of a bishop with the life of a monk. He lived simply, focused on his personal prayer life, and devoted hours to performing corporal works of mercy. He taught his people primarily through preaching, which influenced a young teacher named Augustine. His relationship with this young teacher would be one of the most important friendships in Church history.

Ambrose understood the secular political world due to his previous profession. As bishop, he engaged in not only ensuring

---

83. Ibid., 128.
84. Ibid.
85. Ambrose, *Sermon on the Psalms*, 40.30.

the independence of the Church from secular control, but also in reminding the emperor that he was not above critique from the episcopacy. He established the principle that even the most powerful political ruler is subject to the bishops of the Church in matters of faith. Ambrose rejected the eastern notion of *caesaro-papism* when he wrote: "In cases where matters of faith are in question, it is the custom for bishops to judge emperors when the emperors are Christian, and not for emperors to judge bishops. The Emperor is within the Church and not above the Church."[86] He instituted this policy in two high-profile cases of conflict with the emperor.

The Roman Senate house contained a statue of the pagan goddess Victoria, where senators used to offer incense at her altar upon entering the building. Constantius II removed the statue at the urging of Christian senators in 357, but it was later restored. Emperor Gratian ordered its removal once more; however, during the reign of Valentinian, a group of pagan senators wanted to hold a procession to the statue. News reached Ambrose that the emperor was considering granting the request. The bishop wrote a letter, exhorting him to forbid the procession — and if the emperor refused, then he could "come to church if you wish, but you will not find a bishop there, or if so, it will be one who resists you."[87]

In 390, the local military commander, Butheric, arrested a popular charioteer in Thessalonica on charges of sexual impropriety, resulting in a riot that led to Butheric's death and the mutilation of his corpse, which was dragged through the streets. Emperor Theodosius, incensed at the treatment of his official, ordered the army to massacre every Thessalonian who attended the next series of games. Several thousand people, including women and children, were put to the sword. Ambrose was horrified when he heard the news and sent a scathing personal letter to Theodosius, calling him to repentance for this sinful act:[88]

---

86. Ambrose, *Epistle* 75.
87. Wilken, *The First Thousand Years*, 132–133.
88. The document was not included in Ambrose's official correspondence but was sent directly to Theodosius. See Wilken, *The First Thousand Years*, 135.

A deed has been perpetrated at Thessalonica, which has no parallel in history. Put away this sin from your kingdom. You may do that by humbling your soul before God. You are a man, and temptation has come to you; now get the better of it. Tears and penitence alone can take away sin. I dare not offer the Sacrifice [of the Mass] if you attend. For can it possibly be right, after the slaughter of so many, to do that which may not be done after the blood of only one innocent person has been shed?[89]

Theodosius was moved by Ambrose's letter. He made a public profession of penance by coming to Milan on Christmas Day 390, where he prostrated himself before the bishop, wearing simple clothing. Ambrose joyfully absolved the emperor and readmitted him to communion. The image of the most powerful man in the world humbly submitting himself in penance before the Church must have moved the entire Church, as news spread of the action — such an act would have been unthinkable even twenty years before! Ambrose's strong defense of the Church, as well as his leadership in restricting *caesaro-papism* in the west, is his most enduring legacy. The saintly bishop of Milan died in 397. His friend, Saint Augustine, whom he helped bring into the Church, wrote of Ambrose that "he was one of those [men], who speak the truth, and speak it well, judiciously, pointedly, and with beauty and power of expression."[90]

THE GOLDEN-MOUTHED

John (347–390) loved his home city of Antioch, but God's plan for his life would lead him far from home and involve much suffering. He studied the law with a mind to pursue public service, but felt

---

89. F. Homes Dudden, *The Life and Times of St. Ambrose*, II (Oxford, 1935), 385–386, quoted in Carroll, *The Building of Christendom*, 65.
90. Augustine, *Christian Doctrine*, IV.21.

the call to the life of a hermit and monk. His brilliance and holy living attracted the attention of his bishop, who ordained him a deacon in 381 and then a priest five years later. He would have been content to remain in his beloved Antioch, ministering to the people. But when Nectarius, the archbishop of Constantinople, died in 397, John was chosen to succeed him. Initially, John refused the appointment, prompting the emperor to send an armed guard to escort him to the capital city. In Constantinople, John found a lax clergy, so his first task as archbishop was to reform the presbyterate. John desired to live a simple eremetical life as archbishop, but that caused friction with the wealthy Christians of Constantinople, who expected their archbishop to host lavish parties for their entertainment. The archbishop exhorted the rich to forgo their extravagant lifestyle (he mocked their use of silver chamber pots) in order to help the poor. John's preaching lost the support of many powerful and influential Christians in the city. John also preached against the vanity of women and their extravagant dress. Many believed this was directed at the empress Eudoxia, who was known for her ostentatious lifestyle. Eudoxia and her ecclesial supporters held a synod (known as the Synod of the Oak) wherein they persuaded Emperor Arcadius (r. 395–408) to depose and banish the archbishop. When news of John's exile reached the people, they disagreed so vehemently that the empress fearfully ordered John's return. The beloved archbishop cautiously returned to the city and continued his preaching. A few months later, a silver statue of Eudoxia was erected near the cathedral and the attendant celebrations caused a commotion. John complained about the situation to the prefect of the city, who in turn informed the empress the archbishop was unhappy with the celebrations. Eudoxia used the opportunity to get rid of John, convincing Arcadius to exile the archbishop once more. This time, John was sent to exile in the farthest regions of the Empire, attended by a vicious guard, who mistreated him during the long journey. Eventually, the experience was too much for the aged archbishop. John died in the year 407, giving glory to God with his dying breath.

John's preaching earned him the moniker "Golden-Mouthed," or "Chrysostom." His sermons were popular with the common people because he concentrated on practical, everyday matters, and provided guidance on how to live the Christian faith daily. His sermon topics included conducting transactions in the marketplace in accordance with the Church's moral teachings, utilizing monetary blessings for the good of others, avoiding vanity, and living a holy Christian marriage. John urged husbands to love their wives and encouraged young men to choose a spouse wisely: "Love based on physical beauty belong[s] to unchaste souls. Seek instead for beauty of soul. Do you not see how many, after living with beautiful wives, have ended their lives pitiably, and how many, who have lived with those of no great beauty, have run on to extreme old age with great enjoyment."[91] Saint John Chrysostom's preaching ensured that his fame and sanctity would be recognized in the Church for centuries.

THE IRASCIBLE TRANSLATOR

Eusebius Sophronius Hieronymus (342–420) was born in Dalmatia to a Christian family. He was a well-educated young man who lived a worldly lifestyle, which, no doubt, caused consternation for his parents. Eventually, the young man known to history as Jerome was baptized in Rome in 360. A brilliant student, Jerome turned his attention to studying theology, which he undertook with vigor. After a few years in Rome, he traveled east and settled in Antioch for five years, living an ascetical life as a hermit in the desert. During this time, he was ordained to the priesthood. He left the ancient Christian city and spent time in Constantinople. During his sojourn in the east, he met some of the leading theologians of the day, including Gregory Na-

---

91. John Chrysostom, *Homily on Letter of Saint Paul to the Ephesians* in Nicene and Post-Nicene Fathers, Series 1, 13:143–152, quoted in Aquilina, 183,184.

zianzen and Gregory of Nyssa. Jerome's theological mind and intellectual skills drew the attention of Pope Saint Damasus I (r. 366–384), who appointed him papal secretary. Jerome's studies continued, and he learned Greek and Hebrew. Damasus asked Jerome to utilize his language skills in undertaking the translation of the Scripture into the language of the people, which was Latin.[92] Jerome began work on the audacious project in 382. Two years later, he published a translated version of the Gospels. A few years later, Jerome began the translation of the Old Testament books. Jerome's work became known as the Vulgate edition of the Bible, which has been the standard text of Scripture from the sixth century to the modern day.

When Pope Damasus died, the situation in Rome became untenable for Jerome, who had many enemies in the Eternal City. Jerome's anger-management problem, and unapologetic manner of speaking and writing, were well known. When the Roman lawyer Helvidius argued that the Blessed Mother gave birth to additional children after Jesus, Jerome wrote an eviscerating response: "To defend his position, [Helvidius] piles up text upon text, waves his sword like a blindfolded gladiator, rattles his noisy tongue, and ends by wounding no one but himself."[93] Jerome also criticized high profile members of the Church. When Ambrose the civilian was acclaimed bishop of Milan, Jerome penned his disgust: "[A] catechumen today becomes a bishop tomorrow; yesterday at the amphitheater, today in the church; in the evening at the circus, in the morning at the altar; a little time ago patron of actors, now dedicator of virgins."[94] Without his papal patron, Jerome left Rome and settled in Bethlehem, living in a monastery near a convent established by two female friends, Paula and her daughter Eustochium. Jerome spent the remainder of his days practicing asceticism. Despite his irascible

---

92. The pope also decreed that Latin was the standard language of the liturgy instead of Greek. See Chadwick, *The Church in Ancient Society*, 319.
93. Quoted in Aquilina, 199.
94. Jerome, *Epistle* 69.9.

nature, Jerome performed an admirable task in translating the Scriptures into Latin and providing the Church with a standard edition of the Word of God. Jerome's writings illustrate his filial obedience to the bishop of Rome and provide additional evidence of the early Christians' belief in Petrine primacy. He wrote, "I know that on this rock [Saint Peter's See] the Church is built" and "I am with whoever is united to the teaching of Saint Peter."[95]

THE SACK OF ROME

Germanic tribes east of the Rhine desired admittance into the Roman Empire due to the economic advantages and security found within the imperial borders; over the centuries, Roman policy allowed for their entry in exchange for military service. In the late fourth century, an ethnically German warrior (Roman by birth) commanded a Roman auxiliary force at the Battle of the Frigid River. At the end of the first day of battle, the commander, Alaric (d. 410), had lost nearly half his men in the fighting, and was upset that his forces had been used in a manner that limited the casualties of the regular Roman forces. Like other auxiliary commanders before him, Alaric desired a regular Roman military commission, along with the title *Magister Militum* (Master of Soldiers) in recognition of his service to Rome. When the emperor denied his request, Alaric left the army and went east to raid. Alaric returned to the western half of the Empire in the early fifth century and marched on Rome with an army of thirty thousand warriors.[96] When Alaric captured Rome's port city Ostia, a delegation from Rome appeared in his camp, asking for terms. Alaric told the delegates that he required all movable wealth in the city and the return of all Germanic slaves held in Rome. One of the ambassadors, aghast at the terms, asked Alaric what he intended to leave the Romans with. Alaric respond-

---

95. Jerome, *Epistle* 15, 2 and *Epistle* 16.
96. He actually marched on the city three times; the third march resulted in the sacking of the great city and much consternation throughout the Empire.

ed, "Your lives."[97] The delegation returned to the city with Alaric's terms, but the Senate countered with an offer of 5,000 pounds of gold, 30,000 pounds of silver, 4,000 silk tunics, 3,000 scarlet hides, and 3,000 pounds of black pepper.[98] The counteroffer did not change Alaric's mind. He unleashed his troops to rampage, pillage, and murder within the city for three days. Interestingly, Alaric gave strict orders for his troops not to destroy churches or hurt the clergy in the city, which they obeyed.[99] Rome had not been sacked in eight hundred years — its destruction caused Saint Jerome to weep when news of the calamity reached him in Bethlehem. Distraught, the Church Father wrote, "In one city the whole world has perished" and questioned, "If Rome can perish, what can be safe?"[100] The news of Rome's sacking was so upsetting that some wondered whether the end of the world was at hand. Others remarked that the city never suffered such indignity when the pagan gods were honored, and blamed the disaster on the Christians. This opinion gained traction in the Empire, but one man stood up to answer that claim.

THE GREATEST PAGAN CONVERT

The son born to Patricius and Monica on November 13, 354, in the town of Thagaste in Roman Numidia (modern-day Algeria) would become known as one of the most distinguished theologians, spiritual writers, and saints in Church history. Monica, a Christian, prayed fervently for her husband, two sons, and daughter to embrace the Faith. Her son Augustine was "intellectually precocious, with the temperament of the artist, and all the frank sensuality of the pagan."[101] As a young man, Augustine lived an

97. Arthur Ferrell, *The Fall of the Roman Empire: The Military Explanation* (London: Thames and Hudson, 1986), 103.
98. Ibid.
99. Goldsworthy, *How Rome Fell*, 301.
100. First quote is from Jerome's *Prologue to Commentary on Ezekiel*, quoted in Chadwick, *The Church in Ancient Society*, 513. Second quote from Wilken, *The First Thousand Years*, 189.
101. Hughes, *History of the Church*, vol. II, 8.

immoral life, which caused his mother much pain. His father died when he was sixteen, but not before Monica's prayers had been answered and Patricius had received baptism. At seventeen, Augustine entered into a relationship with a young woman of lower social status. It was not uncommon for young men to take a concubine until they had the means to make a living and acquire a socially acceptable wife.[102] Augustine loved the girl deeply, and they spent the next fourteen years together. The relationship produced a child, a son they named Adeodatus, which means "God's gift" (a common name in North Africa at the time). A few years after his son's birth, Augustine joined a Gnostic sect known as the Manichaeans, much to the chagrin of his mother, who prayed for his conversion during the decade he spent as a member of the group.

Augustine had a keen mind that he utilized to make a living as a teacher. He taught grammar in his hometown of Thagaste for a time and then rhetoric in Carthage, Rome, and Milan. Milan was the imperial residence during this time, and it was in this city that Augustine heard the preaching of Saint Ambrose, who became his friend. Augustine treasured his relationship with the saintly bishop of Milan, who helped him along the path of faith. Eventually, on the Easter Vigil in 387, the prayers of Monica were answered. Augustine, along with Adeodatus, was baptized by Ambrose. A few months after Augustine's conversion, Monica remarked to her son: "There was indeed one thing for which I wished to wait in this life, and that was that I might see you a Catholic before I died. My God has exceeded this abundantly, so that I see you despising all earthly happiness, for you have been made his servant. What am I doing here?"[103] Her life's wish realized, Monica died at the age of fifty-six.

After his conversion, Augustine returned to North Africa to the town of Hippo, where he wished to live a simple monastic

---

102. Chadwick, *The Church in Ancient Society*, 472.
103. Augustine, *Confessions* IX, 10.26.

life in communion with God. However, like many other saints in Church history, God had planned a different path for Augustine. He was ordained a priest in 391 and, four years later, made bishop of Hippo. Even as the chief ecclesial leader in Hippo, Augustine continued to live a simple monastic life while he undertook the administrative and financial duties of the episcopacy. In one moment of exasperation, Augustine commented on the difficulties of being a bishop: "No one who has not been a bishop would believe what we are expected to do."[104] As bishop, Augustine arbitrated disputes among his flock and interfaced with the civil authorities. He devoted his time and energy to reforming the clergy of his diocese and exhorting his people to live the Faith authentically. He bemoaned the Christians who only attended the Sacrifice of the Mass on Christmas and Easter.[105] He reminded his flock that attending Mass to please a patron, secure a wife, or attain physical healing were not proper motivations, and called them to attend Mass to praise God and to reform themselves, saying, "A convert will find many good Christians in the Church if he sets out to become one himself."[106]

Augustine was a prolific writer whose works greatly influenced the development of doctrine and Christian spirituality. He was the Church's unmatched thinker and theologian for eight hundred years, the "bridge between the old world (Roman) and the new world (Catholic)."[107] Augustine's two most famous works are *Confessions* and *The City of God.* His *Confessions* was written a decade after his conversion to the Faith, when he had been a priest for eight years. It is "a sort of autobiography in the form of a dialogue with God."[108] In this prose-poem, Augustine writes of the fundamental truth that "the soul that has lost God has lost

---

104. Chadwick, *The Church in Ancient Society,* 477.
105. See Henry Chadwick, *Augustine of Hippo: A Life* (New York: Oxford University Press, 2009), 69.
106. Augustine, *De catechizandis rudibus,* 7.11.
107. Philip Hughes, *A Popular History of the Catholic Church* (Garden City, NY: Image Books, 1947), 59.
108. Benedict XVI, Wednesday General Audience on Saint Augustine, February 20, 2008, in *Church Fathers: From Clement of Rome to Augustine* (San Francisco: Ignatius Press, 2008), 186.

its roots and therefore has lost itself."[109] True happiness is found
not in oneself but in relationship with God. Only God fulfills the
soul's longing: "You have made us for yourself, and our heart finds
no rest until it rests in you."[110] Even the soul that has wandered
far from God can be made whole again by entering into a relationship with the loving God, as Augustine explained in a letter
about his book: "See what I was in myself and by myself. I had
destroyed myself, but he who made me remade me."[111] Augustine's *Confessions* became the most popular and standard manual
for Christian spirituality for the next thousand years.[112]

Alaric's sack of Rome in 410 was met with cries of indignation
directed at Christians and God. Many in the Empire argued that
the city had been protected from harm when the pagan deities
were worshiped. Now that they had been ignored in favor of the
Christian God, the deities had withdrawn their protection, and
the city was destroyed. Augustine recognized that argument as
fallacious, and he wrote a rebuttal to ensure a proper interpretation of the calamity. His work, written over a decade, encompassed twenty-two books and is known as *The City of God: Against
the Pagans*. The *City* is divided into two parts. The first is a defense
of the Faith against the pagan claim that conversion was the reason for the Empire's destruction. The second part is an explication of the two cities — the "City of Man," founded on self-love,
pride, ambition, greed, and other vices, and the "City of God,"
founded on love of God, selflessness, humility, sacrifice, and obedience. These "cities" are distinct yet comingled in time, and each
individual struggles as a citizen of both. Augustine's work laid the
foundation for a proper interpretation of human history. God is
involved in history, and the Faith is the key to understanding the
events that occur in the world. All events must be understood in

109. Chadwick, *Augustine*, 91.
110. Augustine, *Confessions*, I.
111. Christopher Rengers, O.F.M. Cap., *The 33 Doctors of the Church* (Rockford, IL: TAN Books and
Publishers, 2000), 117.
112. Ibid.

light of the Gospel and God's plan for humanity. History is the "drama of sin and redemption," and a city's destruction is not due to the withdrawal of the gods' protection but to the freely willed choices of men loved by God.[113]

Augustine's days were filled not only with writing but also with protecting his flock from the heretical teachings of three groups: the Manichaeans, the Donatists, and the Pelagians. Mani (216–276), a Persian raised in a Christian/Jewish sect, left the group in his early twenties to found his own movement. Mani's Gnostic teachings embraced a dualist understanding of the world, with a belief that material things are evil and spiritual things are good. The core believers of Mani's religion were the elect, who possessed the secret knowledge he shared with them. The elect were bound to live in accordance with Manichaean principles, including celibacy, vegetarianism, abstinence from alcohol, no land ownership, and refraining from picking or eating apples because of the fruit's alleged role in original sin.[114] The vast majority of Mani's followers did not want to live the strict life of the elect, so they were known as "hearers." The hearers obeyed Mani's teaching of using contraception to prevent pregnancy and, if that failed, abortion, because the marital act, according to Manichaeism, could result in the imprisonment of a good spiritual soul in a bad material body. Additionally, the hearers followed a vegetarian diet and acted as the servants of the elect. This strict and radical life, along with the emphasis on possessing secret knowledge, fostered growth in membership — but the Manichaeans ran into trouble with the Roman authorities. The sect was seen as a dangerous foreign element by Emperor Diocletian, who issued an edict of suppression at the end of the third century. Augustine was well aware of Manichaean teaching and the danger it presented to the faithful because he had been a member of the group for a decade in his youth. He worked diligently to combat Manichaeism and

---

113. Chadwick, *The Early Church*, 226–227.
114. Chadwick, *The Church in Ancient Society*, 171. Catholics could easily spot a Manichaean attending Mass as they refused to receive the Precious Blood at Communion.

protect his people from the nefarious cult.

The Donatists were an extremist group that had developed in North Africa in the early fourth century, after the Great Persecution. They developed as a result of the ongoing question concerning the *lapsi*. Donatists argued that the handing over of the sacred objects and the Scriptures during the Great Persecution was an unforgiveable mortal sin. Additionally, the Donatists believed that if a member of the *lapsi* was a cleric, he could not continue in ministry, because the sacraments celebrated by a lapsed priest were invalid due to his personal failings and unworthiness. Despite imperial and papal condemnation of their teachings, the group persisted and proved a difficult opponent for Augustine in Hippo. The Donatists thrived on being a small, constantly persecuted group. Adherents engaged in self-inflicted martyrdom by making themselves known to the authorities in order to be killed, and even practiced immolation and drowning. They despised Catholics and engaged in open warfare against them. Catholic travelers moving through Donatist territory were frequently ambushed and blinded by Donatists throwing a mixture of lime and vinegar into their eyes.[115] When Donatists captured Catholic churches, they first used a disinfectant, the same used in public restrooms, to cleanse the space before utilizing it.[116] They also smashed altars and threw away consecrated oils and the Eucharist because they believed the items to be profaned from the unworthiness of the Catholic minister.[117] The situation was akin to a civil war. Hippo was split between Donatists and Catholics, "and each body treasured the memory of every single insult."[118] Augustine worked tirelessly to end the infighting and to bring the Donatists into communion with the Church. Augustine wrote books undermining the Donatists' extremist views, which resulted in many conversions from the group.

---

115. Chadwick, *Augustine*, 103.
116. Ibid.
117. Chadwick, *The Church in Ancient Society*, 385.
118. Chadwick, *The Early Church*, 219.

Augustine also wrote against the teachings of the British monk Pelagius, a tall and corpulent man who Jerome described as being "weighed down with Scottish porridge."[119] Pelagius visited Rome sometime in the early fifth century and was disillusioned by the decadent lifestyle of Roman Christians. Pelagius wrote the book *On Nature* in 415. In it, he said that original sin was not communicated to the entire human race, but was only the personal sin of Adam. He advocated that Christ's mission was not salvific, but only provided a good example for moral living. Pelagius also denied the operative power of grace. He believed man has the capacity, through his own will, to live a life of perfection and attain heaven — God's grace is unnecessary. Pope Zosimus (r. 417–418) condemned Pelagianism in 418, which resulted in a famous phrase attributed to Augustine (although he probably never wrote the exact words): "Rome has spoken, the case is closed."[120] Augustine's writings against Pelagianism were so effective that he is known as the "Doctor of Grace."

Augustine devoted the last thirty-five years of his life to his flock in Hippo. He died as the Arian Vandals were besieging his beloved city. In the eyes of his friend and biographer, Posidius, Augustine was a "heroic pastor," who left the Church in Hippo in far better shape than it had been when he became its bishop.[121] Few members of the family of God have shone more brightly than the great Saint Augustine.

MARY IS THE MOTHER OF GOD — THE COUNCIL OF EPHESUS

On Christmas Day in the year 428, the newly consecrated patriarch of Constantinople gave a homily. Nestorius, a monk originally from Antioch, had been chosen patriarch by Emperor Theodosius II (r. 408–450) for his reputation for holiness and excellent

119. Ibid., 448. It is possible that Pelagius was Irish rather than British.
120. Rengers, 124.
121. See Posidius, *Vita* 31, 8.

preaching. Nestorius was particular about language, exhibiting
a "semantic fussiness" and "arrogant intellectualism [that] drove
him from mere idiosyncrasy into explicit heresy."[122] In his first
Christmas as patriarch, Nestorius attacked the use of the word
Theotokos to describe Mary as "the Mother of God": "They ask
whether Mary may be called God-bearer. But has God, then, a
Mother? Mary did not bear God — the creature did not bear the
Creator, but the man, who is the instrument of the Godhead. He
who was formed in the womb of Mary was not God himself, but
God assumed him."[123]

Nestorius's attack on the Blessed Mother was, in reality, an
attack on Christ. He was fond of saying that "God is not a baby
two or three months old."[124] This view was influenced by Nestorius's Arian educational background in Antioch. Nestorius could
not reconcile the fact that Jesus, as true God and true man, was
born of Mary. He believed that Mary provided merely the human "fleshy garment" of Christ, since "the Eternal God cannot
be born, suffer, and die."[125] Mary, according to Nestorius, was
Christotokos, or "Christ-bearer" — not *Theotokos*, or "God-bearer."[126] When news of Nestorius's preaching reached Saint Cyril
of Alexandria (r. 412–444), the patriarch of Alexandria, he became alarmed and wrote to Nestorius: "These things I write out
of love in Christ, exhorting you as a brother and calling upon
you before Christ and the elect angels, to hold and teach these
things with us, in order to preserve the peace of the churches
and that the priests of God may remain in an unbroken bond of
concord and love."[127]

Known as the "guardian of exactitude," Cyril sought to vigor-

122. Aquilina, 187.
123. Charles J. Hefele, *A History of the Councils of the Church*, III (Edinburgh, 1896), 12–13, quoted in
Carroll, *The Building of Christendom*, 92.
124. Chadwick, *The Early Church*, 198.
125. B. J. Kidd, *A History of the Church to A.D. 461*, III (Oxford, 1922), 204, quoted in Carroll, *The
Building of Christendom*, 93.
126. Nestorius's position was radical, as Mary had been referred to as *Theotokos* since the third century. See Wilken, *The First Thousand Years*, 193.
127. Aquilina, 191.

ously combat Nestorius's false preaching and ensure the Church did not suffer another far-reaching and destructive heresy like Arianism. When Nestorius failed to correct his error, Cyril sent letters to the emperor and Pope Saint Celestine I (r. 422–432). Cyril wanted the pope's opinion on Nestorius's teaching before he publicly condemned it:

> We do not openly and publicly break off communion with [Nestorius] before bringing these things to the notice of Your Holiness. Deign therefore to prescribe what you feel in the matter, so that it may be clearly known to us whether we must hold communion with him, or whether we should freely declare to him that no one can remain in communion with one who cherishes and preaches suchlike erroneous doctrine.[128]

Celestine responded that Nestorius's teachings were not in conformity with the apostolic Catholic faith. As a result, Cyril condemned Nestorius's heretical teachings about Mary, which he correctly discerned were really an attack on Christ himself, writing to his monks, "I am astonished that the question should ever have been raised as to whether the Holy Virgin should be called Mother of God, for it really amounts to asking, is her Son God, or is he not?"[129] Cyril's letters and writings were instrumental in defeating Nestorianism. They received definitive acclamation at the third ecumenical council, convened by Emperor Theodosius II at Ephesus in 431. Cyril acted as papal legate, and in short order the assembled council fathers condemned Nestorius, deposed him, and then excommunicated him. He retired to his former monastery in Antioch. The Council of Ephesus affirmed Mary as *Theotokos*, Mother of God, in accordance with the apostolic faith.

---

128. Hughes, *The History of the Church*, vol. I, 241.
129. Cyril of Alexandria, *Epistle* 1, 4, quoted in Carroll, *The Building of Christendom*, 93.

THE FIRST GREAT POPE

A decade after the Council at Ephesus, Leo I (r. 440–461) began his twenty-one-year pontificate, exerting papal supremacy throughout the Church, enforcing ecclesiastical discipline, fighting heresies, and protecting Rome. Leo had been a deacon of the Roman Church during the pontificate of Pope Celestine I and was known to be an excellent preacher. He was in Gaul, representing papal interests, when news came of Celestine's death and his election to the papacy.

An abbot of an influential monastery in Constantinople began teaching that Jesus had only one nature, a divine one (Monophysitism). The monk, Eutyches (378–454), taught that Jesus' human nature was absorbed by his divine nature "like a drop of water mingled in a cup of wine."[130] Eutyches's teaching flowed from the Arian controversy concerning the nature of Christ, as theologians continued struggling to find the language to express the faith of Nicaea. In an effort to dispel any notion of Jesus being two persons, Eutyches preached Monophysitism, which essentially repudiated Christ's humanity — if Christ is true God and true man, then it logically follows he must have both a divine and human nature. News of Eutyches's teaching reached Rome, which prompted Pope Leo to write a theological treatise, known as the *Tome*, on the subject. Leo sent his book to Saint Flavian, the patriarch of Constantinople, who, in turn, excommunicated and deposed Eutyches. However, the influential monk appealed this action to the emperor and requested an ecumenical council to settle the matter. Emperor Theodosius II called a council to meet in Ephesus in 449. Leo sent representatives with a copy of his *Tome*, which he expected to be read and accepted as definitive teaching. Eutyches and his supporters objected to the reading of the papal document and highjacked the proceedings of the coun-

---

130. Eamon Duffy, *Saints and Sinners: A History of the Popes* (New Haven, CT: Yale University Press, 2006), 49.

cil which then ruled in favor of the heretical monk and ordered the deposition and exile of Saint Flavian! When news of the irregular proceedings at Ephesus reached Pope Leo, he condemned the council, referring to it as "*non judicium, sed latrocinium*" ("not a judicial gathering, but a council of thieves [or robbers]").[131]

Eventually, another meeting was called at Chalcedon in 451. This gathering was the most well-attended ecumenical council to date, with more than five hundred bishops present. At this council, Leo's *Tome* was read to the assembled council fathers, who, moved by the Holy Spirit, shouted with one voice after the reading: "Behold the Faith of the Fathers; the Faith of the Apostles! So do we too, all of us believe, all who are orthodox believe the same! Anathema to whoever believes otherwise! Thus through Leo has Peter spoken!"[132] Leo had developed a way to express the apostolic faith concerning the nature of Jesus. In the hypostatic union, confirmed in the proceedings at Chalcedon, Leo taught that Jesus is one divine person, the Second Person of the Blessed Trinity, with two natures — divine and human. Jesus is "truly God and truly man" and must be "acknowledged in two natures, without confusion, without change, without division, without separation."[133] Leo's contribution to theology is one of the most significant teachings of the successors of Peter.

The council also passed discipline canons, but one in particular raised the ire of Pope Leo. The (mostly eastern) bishops in attendance at Chalcedon passed a canon that equated the see of Constantinople with that of Rome. This was done for political reasons, as the city was the capital of the Empire, but it implied that the patriarch of Constantinople was equal in authority to the pope. Leo rightly understood that if this canon were accepted, the hierarchical structure of the Church established by Christ would be altered. Jesus had chosen Peter to be the visi-

---

131. This gathering is known as the "Robber Council" of 449. Wilken, *The First Thousand Years*, 169.
132. *Acts of the Council*, Session 2, quoted in Hughes, *History of the Church*, vol. I, 256.
133. J. Neuner, S.J., and J. Dupuis, S.J., *The Christian Faith in the Doctrinal Documents of the Catholic Church*, sixth edition (New York: Alba House, 1996), 203.

ble head of the Church on earth, and his authority, power, and mission were handed down to his successors, whose identities are not based on political considerations — that is, which city is the capital of the Roman Empire — but rather on where Peter was bishop. Papal rejection of this canon continued the tension between east and west, Constantinople and Rome, which would linger for centuries.

During the pontificate of Leo, the Huns, a nomadic people, left the Mongolian steppe and began a six-thousand-mile march to Rome. The Romans were dreadfully afraid of the Huns, who were described by the Roman historian Ammianus Marcellinus as "abnormally savage [and] totally ignorant of the distinction between right and wrong [and] are under no restraint from religion or superstition."[134] The Huns were skilled horsemen, who allegedly slept in the saddle and ate half-raw meat they warmed under the saddle of their horse; excellent archers, shooting with impressive rapidity and accuracy while riding at high speed; and skilled engineers, using siege towers, battering rams, and scaling ladders in their attacks against fortified cities.

These fearsome warriors were led by Attila, a highly intelligent man. He was described by the Roman diplomat Priscus of Panium as "a lover of war, [who] was personally restrained in action, most impressive in counsel, gracious to supplicants, and generous to those who he had once given his trust,"[135] but merciless to those whose loyalty was not absolute. Physically, Attila was "short of stature with a broad chest, massive head, and small eyes."[136] As a young man, Attila had lived in Rome as a hostage, where he learned Latin and Roman culture. He returned to his people and eventually became their sole ruler in 445 when he killed his brother in order to assume control

134. Quoted in Diane Moczar, *Ten Dates Every Catholic Should Know: The Divine Surprises and Chastisements that Shaped the Church and Changed the World* (Manchester: Sophia Institute Press, 2005), 24.
135. Quoted in Peter S. Wells, *Barbarians to Angels: The Dark Ages Reconsidered* (New York: W.W. Norton & Company, 2008), 25–26.
136. Ibid.

of the tribe. In 451, Attila invaded Gaul in search of booty and plunder, and marched toward Paris. News of the Huns' arrival sent the Parisians into a panicked mass exodus. However, the holy woman Saint Geneviève (422–502) rallied the people, urging them to pray and perform penance so that God might protect the city.[137] Abruptly, the Huns changed direction and instead marched down the Rhineland, sacking Reims, Mainz, Strasbourg, Cologne, Worms, and Trier instead. A year later, Attila invaded Italy and led his army to the outskirts of Rome. Pope Leo received reports about the march of the Huns. When Attila was still some distance away, Leo left the city with a small entourage and walked to the Huns' camp. History does not record what the great pope said to the great warrior, but after the papal visit, Attila's army broke camp and marched away. Leo had saved Rome.

Unfortunately, the respite proved fleeting, as another group of warriors arrived three years later. Genseric was the Arian ruler of the destructive Vandals. The Vandals approached Rome, and once again the saintly pope marched out. Leo's mission was only partly successful this time, as Genseric decided to loot the city but not destroy it. The Vandals ravaged the city for fourteen days, carrying off enormous amounts of wealth and goods, including the famous menorah from the Temple of Jerusalem that Titus had brought to Rome after the conquest of Judea in the first century. Over the next several years, Leo worked tirelessly to restore and rebuild Rome, prioritizing the repair and construction of new churches. His pontificate was the most important of the century and one of the most momentous in all Church history. The saintly pope, the protector of Rome, eminent theologian, Doctor of the Church, and luminous Christian, passed to his eternal reward on November 10, 461.

---

137. Geneviève lived as a religious from an early age and was known for acts of piety and charity. When her parents died, she moved to Paris to live with her grandmother. The bishop of Paris asked Geneviève to look after the consecrated virgins in the city. She received visions of saints and angels and was known for her holiness.

THE COLLAPSE OF THE
WESTERN ROMAN EMPIRE

Thirty-five years after the death of Pope Saint Leo the Great, the political environment in the western world changed dramatically. When General Orestes made his son, sixteen-year-old Romulus, emperor in 475, the young man took control of a Roman Empire vastly different from that established by Octavian Augustus in 27 B.C. Rome in the fifth century was a fatigued state, riven by political intrigue and controlled by an army whose core membership consisted of ethnically German warriors. Their commanders demanded increased recognition and authority from the Roman government for their services. In 476, Odoacer, a Roman auxiliary commander, demanded to rule a large portion of Italy and was rebuffed by General Orestes. Angered, Odoacer rebelled against Rome, killed Orestes, and overthrew the boy-emperor Romulus (commonly known as "Augustulus" or "little Augustus"). Odoacer declared himself King of Italy. Over time, central governing authority in Rome collapsed, and political power devolved to the local Germanic chieftains, the former commanders of Roman auxiliary troops.[138] There were many causes for the collapse of the Empire in the west in the late fifth century, but the historical evidence does not support the popular myths that hordes of greedy, savage German barbarians invaded Roman territory and eventually conquered it in a bloody spasm of violence, or that the Empire became enfeebled by embracing the Faith.

In the early Empire, the army had been composed of Roman citizens who saw military service as a duty of citizenship. By the third century, the army was professionalized, drawing recruits not from ordinary citizenry but from slaves and poor freemen. Recruiting became so difficult that imperial bureaucrats developed the idea of offering the Germanic tribes entrance into the con-

---

138. The following section is adapted from my *The Real Story of Catholic History: Answering Twenty Centuries of Anti-Catholic Myths* (El Cajon, CA: Catholic Answers Press, 2017), 49–53.

fines of the Empire in exchange for military service. Meanwhile, political and military policies sent the Empire into a cycle of civil wars as the legions pulled back from the frontier. By the fifth century, the Roman army in its vital components was staffed by ethnic Germans, who had been raised in the Empire and self-identified as Roman but were not beholden to the wealthy Roman nobility or the imperial bureaucracy.[139]

The change in the army reflected the overall change in Roman society. After five hundred years of rule, the Roman Empire started to buckle in exhaustion.[140] Romans simply lost confidence in their society. It was this exhaustion and lack of confidence, not the Church or invading hordes of barbarians, that broke the Roman system:

> Civilization requires confidence in the society in which one lives, belief in its philosophy, belief in its laws, and confidence in one's own mental powers. Vigor, energy, vitality: all the great civilizations — or civilizing epochs — have a weight of energy behind them. So if one asks why the civilization of Greece and Rome collapsed, the real answer is that it was exhausted.[141]

The ethnically German, yet Roman, local chieftains were forced to forge a new identity and social structure as a result of the Empire's collapse. The Church, with her bishops and dioceses (organized according to the imperial governmental structure), was the only transnational organization in existence — and her unity in belief, practice, and way of life provided a glimmer of hope and light in

---

139. This account of the stages in the transformation of the Roman army is from Arthur Ferrill, *The Fall of Rome: The Military Explanation* (London: Thames and Hudson, 1986).
140. Joseph Cardinal Ratzinger recognized that fatigue was the cause of Rome's collapse when he wrote, "in its final days, Rome still functioned as a great historical framework, but in practice, it was already subsisting on models that were destined to fail. Its vital energy had been depleted." See Joseph Ratzinger and Marcello Pera, *Without Roots: The West, Relativism, Christianity, Islam* (New York: Basic Books, 2007), 66-67.
141. Kenneth Clark, *Civilisation: A Personal View* (New York: Harper & Row, 1969), 4.

the chaos caused by the collapse of the Western Roman Empire.[142]

TWO SWORDS

Twenty years after Odoacer's rebellion, Pope Saint Gelasius (r. 492–496) formulated a new political principle in the West known as the "Two Powers." Gelasius wrote to the Eastern Emperor Anastasius I (r. 491–518), explaining: "There are two powers, august Emperor, by which this world is chiefly ruled, namely the sacred authority of the priests and the royal power. Of these, that of the priests is the more weighty, since they have to render an account for even the kings of men in the divine judgment."[143] Pope Saint Gelasius's letter to the emperor was another development of the relationship between the ecclesial and civil authorities. Ambrose had advocated that the emperor, if Christian, was not above rebuke from the Church in certain matters, but Gelasius went further and argued that ecclesial power is higher and more important than civil power because the Church answers to God for the actions of men. This created a (mostly healthy) tension in the West between the Church and the civil political power, in contrast to the East, where the Church was subservient to the emperors' policy of *caesaro-papism*.

THE GERMANIC TRIBES

The area once controlled by the Western Roman Empire was now governed by various Germanic tribes. The Goths were composed of the Visigoths, who settled in parts of Hispania, and southern and western Gaul; and the Ostrogoths, who lived in Italy. The Vandals were originally from southern Scandinavia but crossed

---

142. The Eastern Empire continued in existence until the fifteenth century when the Ottoman Turks conquered it. The Eastern Empire is commonly referred to in the West as the "Byzantine Empire." However, the German Protestant scholar Hieronymus Wolf created that term in 1557. The "Byzantines" always saw themselves as Roman.
143. J. H. Robinson, *Readings in European History*, (Boston: Ginn, 1905), 72–73.

the Rhine early in the fifth century. They migrated to Hispania soon thereafter and invaded North Africa. Under the leadership of Genseric, they sacked the city of Rome in 455. The Burgundians were also originally from Scandinavia, but had migrated to Poland and the Rhône valley in Gaul in the early fifth century. Their king, Chilperic II, received the title "general" from one of the last western emperors, Julius Nepos. Chilperic was Arian, but married Caretena, a Catholic. Their daughter, Clotilda, would play a vital role in Church history as the wife of Clovis, king of the Franks. The Franks, whose name derives from an old German word that meant "savage,"[144] were comprised of a confederation of tribes that were mostly hostile to Rome. One tribe, known as the Salian Franks, invaded Roman Gaul in the fifth century and eventually ruled northern Gaul. They became Roman auxiliary troops, fighting for Rome against Attila and the Huns. Southern Gaul was controlled by the Gallo-Romans, a Catholic people with strong ties to Rome and Roman culture. Perhaps the most famous Gallo-Roman was Saint Gregory of Tours (538–594), who wrote the *History of the Franks*, an invaluable resource for the history of these peoples. The Franks were a pagan people completely indifferent to the Faith, yet they "would become, not only the champions of Catholicism, but the future saviors of classical civilization."[145]

Most of these Germanic tribes (except the Franks and some Burgundians) were converted to Arianism by the missionary Ulfilas (311–383), the "Apostle to the Goths." Ulfilas was an educated and intelligent man who had spent time in Constantinople. He was eventually ordained bishop by Eusebius of Nicomedia (the famed friend of the heretic Arius), and he spent forty years evangelizing the Goths. He invented Gothic script and translated the Scripture into Gothic to aid in his evangelization efforts. The Arian Goths influenced other Germanic tribes to embrace not only Arianism,

---

144. J. M. Wallace-Hadrill, *The Barbarian West 400–1000* (Cambridge: Basil Blackwell, 1985), 65.
145. Moczar, *Ten Dates*, 35.

but also hostility toward Roman culture and the Catholic Church.

The Franks resisted the Arianism of the Goths, holding fast to their pagan beliefs and customs. By the late fifth century, the Merovingian family became dominant among the Salian Franks, and in the year 482 the grandson of Merovech became king. Clovis (466–511) was only fifteen years old when he ascended the throne. The son of King Childeric I (436–482) and Basina, Queen of Thuringia, he became the most powerful political and military ruler in Western Europe. Clovis embodied his name (which means "noble warrior") but was known to be ruthless, even to his own warriors.

When Clovis became king of the Salian Franks, he received a letter from Remigius (Remy), a Gallo-Roman bishop in the city of Reims. Remigius focused much of his episcopacy on the conversion of the Franks to the Catholic faith, recognizing that if they became Arian like the other Germanic tribes the Church would suffer and perhaps be extinguished in large parts of the world. Remigius desired Clovis's conversion for this reason, but he also wanted to be on friendly terms with the warlike chief who intended to conquer all of Gaul. So, Remigius's letter was diplomatic and calculating, containing flattery and advice on ruling well to ensure a long, successful reign:

> Great news has reached us. You have just been placed at the head of the Frankish armies. None are surprised to see you become what your fathers were. Take for counselors those whose choice does honor to your discernment. Be prudent, chaste, moderate; honor bishops and do not disdain their advice. As long as you live on good terms with them, the affairs of state will prosper. Raise up the souls of your peoples, relieve the widows, feed the orphans. Later on they will serve you, and thus you will conquer the hearts of the very ones who fear you. Let justice be done both in your heart and by your lips. To your pleasures and games invite, if you like, young men of your own age,

but only discuss business matters with the elders. It is thus that you will reign gloriously.[146]

Remigius continued to pray for Clovis's conversion and strove to keep the Church on good terms with his administration.

Within a few years of Remigius's letter, Clovis's armies had conquered most of Gaul. The Franks defeated the Gallo-Romans at the Battle of Soissons in 486, which gave them control of most of northern Gaul. Clovis marched on the important town of Paris, but, like Attila the Hun before him, his plans were thwarted by the saintly Geneviève. This beautiful woman of God had vowed that pagans would never set foot in her beloved city, and despite the Frankish siege, she maintained that resolve. When the city's food situation became critical, Geneviève courageously commanded twelve ships up the Seine River, loaded supplies onboard, and sailed back to Paris. Eventually, the Frankish siege lost momentum, and Clovis was forced to retreat. Once again, Geneviève had saved Paris. She devoted the few remaining years of her life to praying for Clovis's conversion. Despite the setback at Paris, by the early sixth century Clovis's dream of a Frankish kingdom, where all tribes were united under his leadership and that of his progeny, was realized.

CLOTILDA AND THE CONVERSION OF CLOVIS

Saint Clotilda (474–545) is one of the most important saints in Church history but is, sadly, not well-known outside of France.[147] Born a Burgundian princess, Clotilda was pledged in marriage to Clovis of the Franks, who was a few years her senior, to strengthen the alliance between the two peoples. They married in the late fifth century. Clotilda was Catholic, despite the fact that most Burgundians were Arian. Raised by her Catholic mother, Clo-

---

146. Remigius, *Letter to Clovis*, 481, quoted in Moczar, *Ten Dates*, 37.
147. It is a travesty that very few parishes in the United States bear the name of this exemplary woman.

144 | CHAPTER THREE

tilda held strongly to the Faith and prayed constantly for Clovis's conversion. She also tried to reason with Clovis: "The gods
whom you worship are no good. They haven't even been able to
help themselves, let alone others. They are carved out of stone
or wood or some old piece of metal. The very names, which you
have given them were the names of men, not gods. You ought
instead to worship him who created at a word and out of nothing
heaven, the earth, the sea."[148]

Clovis was not swayed by Clotilda's reasoning. He gave a
rather weak response, arguing that God "can do nothing, and,
what is more, there is no proof that he is God at all."[149] Clovis's
intransigence only motivated Clotilda all the more. She continued to argue with, reason with, and, most importantly, pray for
her husband. One prayer was answered when Clovis agreed to
allow the baptism of their firstborn son, but the boy died shortly
after receiving the sacrament. Clovis viewed his son's death as
proof that Clotilda's God was false, arguing that "if he had been
dedicated in the name of my gods, he would have lived without
question."[150] The saintly Clotilda answered this charge with abiding faith:

> I give thanks to Almighty God, the Creator of all
> things, who has not found me completely unworthy,
> for he has deigned to welcome to his Kingdom the
> child conceived in my womb. I am not at all cast down
> in my mind because of what has happened, for I know
> that my child, who was called away from this world
> in his white baptismal robes, will be nurtured in the
> sight of God.[151]

Despite the tension in her marriage and the death of her son,

---

148. Gregory of Tours, *History of the Franks*, Book II, 29, pp. 141–142.
149. Ibid.
150. Ibid., 142.
151. Ibid.

Clotilda did not waver from her love of God and the Church.

Toward the end of the fifth century, Clovis led his army in a campaign against the Alemanni, another Germanic tribe that obstructed the consolidation of his power in Gaul. In the pivotal battle of the campaign, the Alemanni gained the upper hand and Clovis recognized his troops' desperate situation. Near the edge of despair, Clovis reached out to the heavens, invoking Clotilda's God.[152] Almost immediately the battle swung in his favor as the Franks defeated the Alemanni. When he returned home, Clovis told Clotilda what had occurred, and she quickly dispatched a message to bishop Remigius to come and instruct Clovis in the Faith so he could receive baptism. During his baptismal preparation, Clovis had one overarching concern: How would his warriors react? Clovis was anxious that his troops might overthrow him for rejecting their ancestral gods, or they might allow his conversion but not accept the Faith themselves, which would cause division in the tribe. So, Clovis called his warriors together. He informed his warriors of his intention to convert, and asked their opinion. The king was overjoyed to learn that the soldiers not only agreed with his plan but accepted conversion as well. On Christmas Day 496, the prayers of Clotilda, Remigius, and Geneviève were answered. Clovis, King of the Franks, was baptized in Reims, along with three thousand Frankish warriors. Legend holds the cathedral was so packed with people that the cleric holding the sacred chrism could not get through the crowd, but Remigius looked to heaven and saw a dove descending with a vial of oil. Remigius took the oil from the dove and used it to anoint Clovis. This holy oil was used for the next 1,300 years to anoint the kings of France. After his baptism, Clovis worked to establish a strong relationship with the Church in several ways, such as instituting reforms and recognizing the independence of the Church in his territory.[153]

---

152. See the quote at the beginning of this chapter.
153. As a result of Clovis's baptism and the subsequent strong relationship between the papacy and the Frankish kings, France became known as the "Eldest Daughter of the Church."

The kingdom of the Franks, according to custom, was divided among the sons of Clovis upon the great king's death. But the brothers quarreled, and Queen Clotilda witnessed bloody infighting among her sons over Gaul.[154] The saintly wife of Clovis outlived him by thirty-four years — decades she spent financing the construction of churches and monasteries and living a penitential life of prayer, first in Paris and then at the Shrine of Saint Martin of Tours. By her prayers, exemplary Christian living, and wifely vocation, she changed the course of Church history.

The impact of Clovis's conversion on the Church was immense.[155] He was the only Catholic king in the west, and his conversion legitimatized the Faith in the eyes of his people, who had previously viewed it as the religion of the weak and conquered Gallo-Romans. The Franks would dominate the Continent for centuries, which contributed to the eventual conversion of the Arian Germanic tribes.

---

154. Theuderic controlled Metz; Chlodomer ruled Orleans; Childebert received Paris; and Clotaire, Soissons.
155. The event is so important that Pope Saint John Paul II traveled to France in 1996 to celebrate the 1,500th anniversary of Clovis's baptism.

FOUR

Bright Lights in a Dark Time

"The Greeks thought of everything, the Romans did everything, and Christian monks saved their best achievements from oblivion."[1]

BRENNAN PURSELL

The six-year-old boy was awestruck. Priests and bishops were not unusual sights, but this was the Vicar of Christ himself. The bishop of Rome rarely left the city — let alone Italy — but here he was in France, the first pope to visit the land of Clovis and his descendants. The pope came to discuss important matters with the young boy's father, who had been anointed king of the Franks a few years before by the holy missionary bishop Boniface. Soon after the anointing, the pope had granted the

---

1. Brennan Pursell, *History in His Hands: A Christian Narrative of the West* (New York: Crossroad, 2011), 108.

| 147 |

former imperial title *patricius Romanorum* ("Patrician of the Romans") to the king and to his sons, Charles and Carloman. The boy's father had developed a special relationship with the bishop of Rome, protecting him from the violent Lombards and donating land in northern and central Italy to the patrimony of the pope. Now, the pope came to anoint the sons of the great king Pepin as kings of the Franks, though the title would not be assumed until Pepin's death fourteen years later. Eventually, Charles, who had met the pope when he was six, would be the only one of his brothers to live past the age of twenty, and would assume sole kingship of the mighty Franks. In time, Charles would have another encounter with a different successor of Saint Peter, who would crown him emperor. Charles' name and legend would extend through the centuries, making him known as the "Father of Europe" — Charlemagne.

"DARK AGES"?

The era from the collapse of the Western Roman Empire to the beginning of the eleventh century is frequently and erroneously referred to as the "Dark Ages." The term originated with the Italian poet Petrarch (1304–1374) and was subsequently utilized by the Englishman Thomas Sprat (1635–1713), who wrote that the period was "quiet as the dark of night."[2] The myth of the Dark Ages is founded on the presumption that we gain knowledge of a time period mostly through written sources. Because there is a dearth of known manuscripts dating from this period, the assumption is that these centuries were a "period of decline and darkness" — but archaeological and other sources show that the so-called Dark Age was in fact marked by "immense cultural, economic, and political development."[3] Significant challenges faced the peo-

2. Thomas Sprat, *History of the Royal Society* (London, 1667), 14, quoted in Joseph and Frances Gies, *Cathedral, Forge, and Waterwheel: Technology and Invention in the Middle Ages* (New York: Harper Collins, 2010), loc. 1, Kindle.
3. Peter S. Wells, *Barbarians to Angels: The Dark Ages Reconsidered* (New York: W.W. Norton & Company, 2008), xiv and 5.

ple who lived in the centuries after the collapse of the Empire in the West. They lived in a difficult and at times "dark" period, witnessing and suffering from the frequent invasions and raids of the Vikings and Magyars and the rise of Islam. However, they also encountered the bright lights of Catholic missionaries who spread the Gospel and converted the remaining pagan and Arian Germanic tribes. This was also a time of technological advances, such as the harnessing of water and wind to create power and the introduction of the open-field system of agriculture.[4] Although the population of major cities in Western Europe declined due to radical changes in commerce, cities still served as administrative, trading, and manufacturing centers. One significant achievement by the end of this time period was the eradication of slavery in Europe. The Roman Empire had been built on slave labor and completely depended on it for the continuance of society. The post-Roman world, dominated by the Church, witnessed the end of slavery in the European mainland. Western European society did change after the end of the Empire, becoming less urban and more rural with less general literacy. But to describe this change as ushering in a "dark age" is incompatible with the historical record and the role and achievements of the Church during this time period.

PATRICK AND THE IRISH

A young man, born in the late fourth century in Britain, whose father was a Roman city official and a deacon of the Church, evangelized an island that would later become the "nursery of saints."[5] When sixteen years old, Patrick was captured by Irish raiders and taken to the island to tend sheep as a slave. His years of slavery

---

4. The *Domesday Book* compiled in 1086 recorded 5,624 water-powered mills in England. See Gies, *Cathedral, Forge, and Waterwheel*, 134.
5. Warren H. Carroll, *The Building of Christendom: A History of Christendom*, vol. 2 (Front Royal, VA: Christendom College Press, 1987), 181.

were "also the years of his conversion and he looked back upon this stage in his spiritual development as the most important and critical in his life."[6] After six years in captivity, Patrick escaped and made his way back to Britain. Home at last, Patrick discerned a call to the priesthood and was eventually consecrated bishop. Eighteen years after his escape, he returned to the Emerald Isle, this time not as a slave, but as a missionary. Patrick had "strength of will, energy of action, resolution without overconfidence, and the capacity for resisting pressure from others" that served him well in his evangelization.[7]

Contrary to popular belief, Patrick was not the first Christian missionary in Ireland. Pope Saint Celestine I (r. 422–432) had sent the missionary Palladius to the Irish in 431, several decades before Patrick. However, Patrick "secured its [the Faith's] permanence, shaped its course, and made it a power in the land."[8] Patrick achieved three main objectives in Ireland: he organized the Church there, converted the remaining pagan tribes, and, most importantly, connected the Church in Ireland with the Church in Rome, making Ireland fully, unmistakably, and devotedly Catholic.

Patrick knew that for the Faith to succeed and attain permanence on the island, a native clergy was required. However, developing an Irish clergy required time and funding. The best source of funding was land, so Patrick sought the conversion of tribal kings and clan chiefs, which required a herculean evangelization effort, as there were 150 kings in Ireland at the time.[9] Besides his missionary activity, Patrick was also known for his *Confession*, which illustrated his love and overwhelming sense of gratitude to God for his life. He intended the *Confession* to be a personal

6. J.B. Bury, *Ireland's Saint: The Essential Biography of St. Patrick*, ed. Jon M. Sweeney (Brewster, MA: Paraclete Press, 2010), 53.
7. Ibid.,187.
8. Ibid., 22.
9. J.B. Bury points out Patrick sought the conversion of kings and chiefs in order to acquire land (See Bury, *Ireland's Saint*, 90), and Wilken notes the number of kings in Ireland at the time (see Robert Louis Wilken, *The First Thousand Years: A Global History of Christianity* [New Have, CT: Yale University Press, 2012], 271).

statement aimed at the communities in Britain who criticized his work among the Irish. The date of Patrick's death is uncertain, but his legacy is clearly recognizable.[10] Within a half-century of his death, the entire island had converted to the Catholic faith and their ties to Rome were solidified: "Their conversion was far from being virtually instantaneous, as later legends would suggest; but it was unusually rapid, unusually thorough, and above all peaceful. No tradition with any color of historical reliability speaks of martyrdom in connection with the conversion of Ireland."[11]

The Irish founded monasteries and convents throughout the island and lived strict, organized lifestyles that embraced ascetical practices. They focused on reading, writing, and copying manuscripts, and their work helped to ensure the survival of ancient Greco-Roman literature and culture. Saint Patrick's work also created a generation of missionaries who regularly sailed to Scotland, Wales, and the Continent in order to spread the Faith. Saint Columba (521–597) founded the monastery at Iona and evangelized in Scotland; Saint Columbanus (543–615), along with twelve companions, traveled to the Continent and introduced private and frequent auricular confession; and Saint Brendan (484–577) sailed to Iceland and possibly even North America.

THE FATHER OF WESTERN MONASTICISM

Although monasticism still flourished in the East as a result of the efforts of Saint Basil the Great, its influence on the Church in the West was not as comprehensive until the arrival of the great Saint Benedict of Nursia (480–543). Benedict came from a noble Roman family, but renounced his worldly life and lived in solitude as a hermit for three years. During his solitude, he overcame major temptations to selfishness, sensuality, and anger. Holiness attracts

10. Some sources indicate Patrick died in 461; others indicate 493. One can safely indicate the great saint died before the end of the fifth century.
11. Carroll, *The Building of Christendom*, 123.

— when news of the saintly hermit reached the ears of the faithful, they flocked to Benedict. Eventually, Benedict realized the need for a community of dedicated men who could focus on deepening their relationships with God. He founded the monastery at Monte Cassino in 530 as a "school of divine service" where monks in obedience practiced the faith in love in order to achieve holy humility.[12] Benedict's twin sister, Scholastica, followed his lead, dedicating her life to holy living and founding communities of women dedicated to the same ideal as Benedict's monks. Benedict's most lasting contribution to the monastic movement was the writing of his *Rule*. The *Rule* highlighted the importance of the role of abbot to the monastic community; the abbot was elected for life and was expected to act as a father figure to his brother monks.[13] Saint Benedict exhorted the abbot to rule as a servant leader in imitation of Christ, who came not to be served but to serve. Benedict also established an organized life for the monastery in his *Rule*. The monks oriented their lives on the motto *ora et labora* ("prayer and work") and structured their day into a routine of prayer, work, study, and ascetical practices such as fasting, with the ultimate goal of imitating the life of Christ by chastity, prayer, work, temperance, and obedience. Controversially, Benedict required his monks to engage in manual labor, a radical idea at the time as only slaves performed hard labor — a free or educated man would never work with his hands. Benedict understood the value of hard work not only for the good of the community but also for the individual.

A major work in Benedictine monasteries was the painstaking endeavor of manuscript copying. Scriptoriums were instituted to provide the monks with a source of manual labor and to preserve

---

12. The monastery itself has a fascinating history. It has been rebuilt time and again after it was sacked by the Lombards in 539, destroyed by Muslim invaders in 884, demolished in an earthquake in 1349, pillaged by Napoleon's troops in 1799, and reduced to rubble by an Allied bombardment in 1944. For the purpose of life at Monte Cassino, see Benedict XVI, Wednesday General Audience on Saint Benedict of Norcia, April 9, 2008, in *Church Fathers and Teachers: From Saint Leo the Great to Peter Lombard* (San Francisco: Ignatius Press, 2010), 22–23.

13. See *The Rule of Saint Benedict*, Chapters 2 and 64, trans. Anthony C. Meisel and M.L. del Mastro (New York: Image Books, 1975), 48–51.

the Scriptures and other literary works, including the works of Greco-Roman authors, the cultural heritage of European society. Copying the Scriptures, on average, took a monk ten months to complete.[14] The work was mentally and physically exhausting, as one monk recorded: "He who does not know how to write imagines it to be no labor; but though three fingers only hold the pen, the whole body grows weary."[15]

Benedict could not have predicted the impact of his monastic movement on the Church and Western civilization. By the fourteenth century, his order had produced twenty-four popes, 200 cardinals, 7,000 archbishops, 15,000 bishops, 37,000 monasteries, and 1,500 canonized saints![16] Pope Paul VI proclaimed Saint Benedict the patron saint of Europe in 1964. His contribution to the Church and Europe cannot be overstated:

> The saint's work and particularly his *Rule* were to prove the heralds of an authentic spiritual leaven which, in the course of the centuries, far beyond the boundaries of his country and time, changed the face of Europe following the fall of the political unity created by the Roman Empire, inspiring a new spiritual and cultural unity, that of the Christian faith shared by the peoples of the Continent. This is how the reality we call "'Europe'" came into being.[17]

GREGORY THE GREAT

Gregory came from a rich Roman patrician family and saintly

14. Henry G. Graham, *Where We Got the Bible: Our Debt to the Catholic Church* (Rockford, IL: TAN Books and Publishers, 2004 [1992]), 78.
15. Charles Montalembert, *The Monks of the West: From Saint Benedict to Saint Bernard*, vol. 5 (London: Nimmo, 1896), 151–152, quoted in Thomas E. Woods Jr., *How the Catholic Church Built Western Civilization* (Washington, DC: Regnery Publishing, 2005), 39.
16. Woods, 28.
17. Benedict XVI, Wednesday General Audience on Saint Benedict of Norcia, April 9, 2008, in *Church Fathers and Teachers*, 20.

parents, Saints Gordian and Sylvia. Gregory was drawn to a life of service and, in 572, became the prefect of Rome, responsible for the city and its inhabitants. Although he was an excellent civil servant, Gregory soon felt called to a deeper level of service — not to the state, but to God. In 575, he resigned his secular office and became a monk, years which, he later remarked, were the happiest of his life. However, Gregory was not allowed to remain an anonymous monk. Pope Pelagius II (r. 579–590) sent Gregory to Constantinople to be his personal representative to the emperor. Gregory's years as prefect and the skills he had acquired in politics served him well in this new diplomatic role. Gregory was fiercely loyal to Rome and did not trust the Greeks, writing that they were "too clever to be honest."[18] Throughout his six years in Constantinople, Gregory refused to learn Greek, instead relying on translators. His time in the imperial capital was not joyful, and he concluded: "How can anyone be seduced by Constantinople and how can anyone forget Rome. I do not know."[19]

In 590, Pope Pelagius II died from an outbreak of the plague. Gregory returned to his beloved Rome to discover that the clergy had elected him bishop. Gregory had no interest in the papacy and, after his diplomatic adventures in Constantinople, wanted nothing more than to return to the simple monastic life. He wrote a letter to the emperor, asking him to repudiate the election, but the emperor refused. Gregory fled the city and hid in a cave for three days, believing another man would be chosen during his absence. Eventually realizing that the monastery was not God's plan for his life, he agreed to assume the papacy.

Gregory (r. 590–604) was the first monk to be elected pope. His pontificate was one of the most important in Church history, as he strove to defend the Church and the papacy against secular rulers. In his fourteen-year reign, he restored prestige and respect to the papacy and the city of Rome. In the civil arena,

---

18. Henry Chadwick, *The Early Church*, revised edition (New York: Penguin Books, 1993), 254.
19. P. Llewellyn, *Rome in the Dark Ages* (London, 1993), 90, quoted in Eamon Duffy, *Saints and Sinners: A History of the Popes*, 3rd ed. (New Haven, CT: Yale University Press, 2006), 62.

he organized a system of relief for the poor, whom he held in special esteem, even inviting twelve poor people to eat a meal with him each day.[20] He established hospitals to care for the sick and injured. His efforts succeeded in rebuilding Rome into an important and proud city after years of neglect. Although he initially did not want to be pope, Gregory took his office seriously and recognized that the pope is a servant leader in imitation of Christ, beginning the tradition of the pope's use of the title *Servus Servorum Dei* ("Servant of the Servants of God"). As pope, Gregory reinforced the primacy of the Roman See throughout the Church. He rebuked the patriarch of Constantinople, John the Faster, for using the title "ecumenical patriarch" — which, at best, asserted the equality of the patriarch with the pope and, at worst, implied the bishop of Constantinople was superior to the bishop of Rome. Gregory's rebuke of the patriarch resulted in Emperor Phocas acknowledging the pope as "the head of all the Churches."[21]

Gregory also sought Church reform. He removed unworthy clergy and reformed the liturgy and music, introducing what became known as Gregorian chant. Gregory also spent time contemplating the role of a bishop, and wrote a work known as *Pastoral Care*. Gregory believed a bishop should prepare himself for ruling his flock by first ruling himself in humility. A bishop must be a man of meditation, steeped in Scripture, and devoted to preaching, teaching, and correcting the faults of his flock. A bishop should be concerned for the welfare of all the people in his diocese, even those who do not embrace the Christian faith. Gregory put his own counsel into practice by protecting the large Jewish population in Rome and speaking out against the forced baptism of Jews in France.[22]

Gregory understood the importance of evangelization in

---

20. Duffy, *Saints and Sinners*, 64.
21. Henri Pirenne, *Mohammed and Charlemagne* (Mineola, NY: Dover Publications, 2001 [1954]), 213.
22. Ibid., 84.

the life of the Church. He sent missionaries to the Visigoths in Spain as well as to the Franks, Saxons, and Lombards. Perhaps his most important missionary contribution occurred among the Anglo-Saxons of Britain. Before he became pope, Gregory was walking through the slave markets of Rome with a friend when he noticed a group of fair-haired youths from the north. Their appearance was unlike that of any people he had ever seen. Gregory asked his friend who these people were, and his companion told him they were "Angles" — a pagan, ethnic German tribe that had left the Continent in the fifth and sixth centuries (along with the Saxons and Jutes) and settled in Celtic Britain. Gregory responded to his friend with a play on words, describing the "Angles" as "angels" and stating, "How sad it was that beings with such bright faces should be slaves of the prince of darkness when they should be co-heirs with the angels in heaven."[23] He vowed that if he were ever in a position to help these people embrace the light of Christ, he would do so. Five years into his pontificate, he commissioned his steward in Gaul to purchase Angle slave boys so that they could be educated in monasteries and eventually sent back to England as missionaries. Gregory also commissioned Saint Augustine of Canterbury (d. 604) and forty monks to travel to England in 597 on an evangelization mission. Augustine and his companions successfully traveled to the island and made contact with King Ethelbert of Kent, who accepted Christ and was baptized on Christmas Day. The Faith had reached England prior to Augustine, but his successful mission to King Ethelbert led to the widespread acceptance of the Gospel. By the late seventh century, the complete conversion of the tribes in England was accomplished.

Augustine's mission in England produced unique situations he was unsure how to handle, so he sent letters to Gregory, asking advice. The pope's response formed the basis of Catholic

---

23. F. Homes Dudden, *Gregory the Great: His Place in History and Thought* (New York, 1905, 1967), I, 196–197, quoted in Carroll, *The Building of Christendom*, 197.

missionary principles and policies for centuries. Augustine asked the pope whether he should destroy pagan temples or consecrate them as churches. Gregory replied with a wise strategy:

> Destroy as few pagan temples as possible; only destroy their idols, sprinkle them with holy water, build altars and put relics in the buildings, so that, if the temples have been well built, you are simply changing their purpose, which was the cult of demons, in order to make a place where from henceforth the true God will be worshiped. Thus the people, seeing that their places of worship have not been destroyed, will forget their errors and, having attained knowledge of the true God, will come to worship him in the very places where their ancestors assembled.[24]

Augustine also inquired about pagan customs and festivals. Once more, Gregory replied with prudence, telling the missionary to "Christianize" the celebrations by holding them on the feast days of saints and the Blessed Mother. Gregory's contribution to missionary activity, his defense of the primacy of the papacy, and other reforms gave the Church a firm foundation during the turbulent years between the collapse of central governing power from Rome and the rise of the Frankish kingdom, and provided God's people with much needed hope. For his tireless efforts on behalf of the Church and the family of God, he is forever known as "Gregory the Great."

THE APOSTLE TO THE GERMANS

Although the contributions of Saint Patrick and the Irish missionaries were important, "probably the greatest missionary since

---

24. Gregory, *Letters* XI, 56, quoted in Jean Comby, *How to Read Church History: From the Beginnings to the Fifteenth Century*, vol. I (New York: Crossroads, 2001), 123.

St. Paul" was an Anglo-Saxon known as the "Apostle to the Germans" for his extensive travels and successful evangelization efforts in what is modern-day Germany.[25] In the late seventh century, a young man named Winfrid entered a Benedictine monastery, despite the objections of his parents. Winfrid grew in holiness and piety and was ordained a priest, but he yearned to leave the monastery and bring the Light of Christ to the pagan Germans, just as Augustine of Canterbury and his monks had brought the Faith to England a century earlier. Winfrid heard reports that Pope Gregory II (r. 715–731) had sent missionaries to Bavaria in 716, so he traveled to Rome. Pope Gregory was delighted at the arrival of the eager Winfrid. After a period of intense theological study, Winfrid was commissioned by the pope to preach the Gospel in the regions of Thuringia, Bavaria, Franconia, and Hesse. In recognition of his special missionary commission, the pope also changed Winfrid's name to Boniface.[26]

The newly named monk traveled to Hesse (central Germany) in 721, and "with his tireless activity, his gift for organization, and his adaptable, friendly, yet firm character" achieved astounding success, including the conversion of the twin chieftains Dettic and Deorulf.[27] Boniface also established Benedictine monasteries, including the great monastery of Fulda in 744.[28] News of his achievements traveled to Rome, and he was recalled by Pope Gregory to provide a status report. Impressed and pleased with Boniface's efforts, Gregory consecrated him archbishop of all Germany east of the Rhine (without a specific episcopal seat) and placed his territory under papal jurisdiction. Invested with this

---

25. John Vidmar, OP, *The Catholic Church Through the Ages* (New York/Mahwah, NJ: Paulist Press, 2005), 83.

26. The following section is adapted from my article, "St. Boniface and the Christmas Tree," Catholic Answers online magazine, June 5, 2014, https://www.catholic.com/magazine/online-edition/st-boniface-and-the-christmas-tree.

27. Pope Benedict XVI Wednesday Audience on Saint Boniface, the Apostle of the Germans, on March 11, 2009, in *Church Fathers and Teachers*, 80.

28. Boniface placed Fulda under the direct jurisdiction of the papacy, a novel concept at the time. This was the same arrangement for the more well-known monastery at Cluny later in the early tenth century.

new authority and pontifical mandate, Boniface returned to Germany in 723 and spent the rest of his life evangelizing the areas of modern Germany and the Netherlands. He also became a friend of the Frankish court, helping reform and reorganize the Church in that area by holding several reforming synods.

As a result of his missionary travels, Boniface knew that in winter the inhabitants of the village of Geismar gathered around a huge old oak tree knon as the "Thunder Oak," dedicated to the god Thor. This annual event of worship offered a human sacrifice, usually a small child, to the pagan god. Boniface desired to convert the village by destroying the Thunder Oak, so he gathered a few companions and journeyed to Geismar. His fellow missionaries, fearful that the Germans might kill them, balked at moving forward when they reached the outskirts of the village on Christmas Eve. Boniface steadied the nerves of his friends as they approached the pagan gathering, saying, "Here is the Thunder Oak; and here the cross of Christ shall break the hammer of the false god Thor."[29] Boniface and his friends arrived at the time of the sacrifice, which was interrupted by their presence. In a show of amazing trust in God and zeal to enkindle the fire of Christ in the German pagans, Boniface grabbed an axe and chopped down the Thunder Oak of mighty Thor. The Germans were astounded that a lightning bolt from Thor did not strike the Christian dead. The holy bishop then preached the Gospel to the people, using a little fir tree behind the now felled oak tree. Tradition holds that he pointed to the fir tree and said: "This little tree, a young child of the forest, shall be your holy tree tonight. It is the wood of peace. It is the sign of an endless life, for its leaves are evergreen. See how it points upward to heaven. Let this be called the tree of the Christ-child; gather about it, not in the wild wood, but in your own homes; there it will shelter no deeds of blood, but loving gifts and rites of kindness."[30] Awed by the destruction of

29. Fr. William P. Saunders, "The Christmas Tree," *Straight Answers* article in the *Arlington Catholic Herald*, http://www.holyspiritinteractive.org/library/976#.W9m0D2JKiks.
30. Ibid.

the oak tree, and heeding Boniface's preaching, the inhabitants of Geismer were baptized.[31]

Boniface continued his missionary efforts into his old age. In 754, he left for a trip to Frisia with fifty monks. Their work was successful; many pagans agreed to receive baptism. When the appointed time came to celebrate the sacrament, a large armed crowd of pagans approached the missionaries. Knowing his time to die was at hand, Boniface discouraged his followers from fighting and said: "Cease my sons, from fighting, give up warfare for the witness of Scripture recommends that we do not give an eye for an eye but rather good for evil. Here is the long-awaited day; the time of our end has now come; courage in the Lord!"[32] The ferocious pagan attack left Boniface and his fellow companions dead, martyrs for the Faith. His later biographer, Othlo, recalled Boniface's deep love for the people whom he endeavored for so long to bring to Christ: "The holy bishop Boniface can call himself father of all the inhabitants of Germany, for it was he who first brought them forth in Christ with the words of his holy preaching; he strengthened them with his example; and lastly, he gave his life for them; no greater love than this can be shown."[33]

THE RISE OF ISLAM

In the seventh century, a militaristic and imperialistic movement

31. The Catholic tradition of using an evergreen tree to celebrate the birth of Jesus spread throughout Germany over the centuries after the miraculous event at Geismar. German immigrants in the eighteenth century brought the custom to the New World. Although there are many stories, legends, and myths surrounding the founding of the Christmas tree, including the *Washington Post* claiming the custom originated with the sixteenth-century Protestant revolutionary Martin Luther, there is only one story revolving around a historical person (Boniface) and a historical event (the felling of Thor's Thunder Oak). For the false attribution of the Christmas Tree to Martin Luther, see *The Washington Post: The Mini Page*, "O Tannenbaum!", December 6, 2009, SC5. For Boniface chopping the oak tree, see Fr. John Laux, *Church History: A Complete History of the Catholic Church to the Present Day* (Rockford, IL: TAN Books and Publishers, Inc., 1989), 221 and Carroll, *The Building of Christendom*, 276.
32. Willibald, *Vita S. Bonifatii, ed. cit.*, 46, quoted in, Pope Benedict XVI, Wednesday Audience on Saint Boniface, March 11, 2009.
33. Othlo, *Vita S. Bonifatii, ed. cit.*, lib. I, 158, quoted in, Pope Benedict XVI, Wednesday Audience on Saint Boniface, March 11, 2009.

known as Islam developed in the Arabian Peninsula.[34] Islam's entrance onto the world stage is steeped in mystery. The standard historical narrative presents the story of a solitary Arab receiving alleged divine inspiration and revelations, which spontaneously produced a radically new civilization in the seventh century. Recent scholarship challenges this narrative and posits that Islam grew out of existing surrounding civilizations, taking elements from them and reshaping them into a new community: "The puzzle of Islam's origins might be viewed... as a black hole sucking in a great spiraling swirl of influences before casting them back out in a radically different form."[35] Over the last generation, much of what has traditionally been understood about the origins of Islam and its founder Muhammad has come into question, so much so that one historian has remarked, "Nowadays, it is hard to think of any other field of history so riven by disagreement as is that of early Islam."[36] Modern studies on the origins of Islam have led historians to even question the existence of Muhammad.[37] Although this question might have seemed fanciful and unthinkable a generation ago, it is based in the fact that the first recorded public reference to Muhammad occurred sixty years after his death, and the first biographies about him were not written until 150 years later.[38]

The traditional Muslim narrative of Muhammad describes a man born in the city of Mecca (in the Arabian Peninsula) in the late sixth century. He was a member of an important and wealthy tribe who participated in lucrative trade with pilgrims who came to Mecca to worship the pantheon of Arabian gods at the Kaaba shrine. At this time, the Arabian Peninsula contained various no-

34. The following section is adapted from my book *The Glory of the Crusades* (El Cajon, CA: Catholic Answers Press, 2014), 31–34.

35. Tom Holland, *In the Shadow of the Sword: The Birth of Islam and the Rise of the Global Arab Empire* (New York: Doubleday, 2012), loc. 952, Kindle.

36. Ibid., loc. 792, Kindle.

37. A professor at the University of Münster has recently opined that Muhammad is a figure of myth. See Holland, loc. 764, Kindle.

38. Ibid., loc. 721, Kindle.

madic tribes who were "the most superstitious and ignorant in the world."[39] They were also vicious and ruthless warriors who found employment in the Roman Empire as auxiliary troops, augmenting the Roman legions when the need arose.[40] In 610, Muhammad allegedly experienced "history's most epochal mid-life crisis"[41] in a cave near Mecca. Later Muslim tradition (the story is not recounted in the Qur'an) records that Muhammad was awoken from a deep sleep by the voice of a heavenly messenger, later identified as the Archangel Gabriel, who informed him of his calling as the messenger of God. Muhammad's initial reactions to this voice were terror and belief that he was possessed by an evil spirit. Distraught, he contemplated suicide: "I will go to the top of the mountain and throw myself down that I may kill myself and gain rest."[42] The messenger consoled Muhammad and ordered him to recite the words of God. Muhammad continued to receive private revelations for the following three years. Finally in 613, Muhammad was ordered to make his revelations public.

Muhammad revealed the contents of his private revelations in Mecca, which were initially met with indifference. However, the frequency and urgency of his radical and revolutionary teachings eventually drew heightened responses. He claimed there was only one God, and it was the one who did not have an idol in the Kaaba. Muhammad also demanded total submission (*islam*) to the will of God. His call to abandon tribal relationships was "the most stomach-churning prospect imaginable for any Arab."[43] Those who submitted to the will of God joined a unique community (*umma*), where all were considered equal. The formation of this community created a sharp distinction between Muslims

---

39. The opinion of a sixth-century Christian as quoted in Holland, *In the Shadow of the Sword*, loc. 3792, Kindle.

40. It was reported that they drank their victims' blood during battle. See Holland, *In the Shadow of the Sword*, loc. 3792, Kindle.

41. Holland, *In the Shadow of the Sword*, loc. 3800, Kindle.

42. Ibn Ishaq, *The Life of Muhammad: A Translation of Ibn Ishaq's Sirat Rasul Allah*, A. Guillaume, trans. (Oxford University Press, 1955), 106, quoted in Robert Spencer, *The Truth about Muhammad: Founder of the World's Most Intolerant Religion* (Washington, DC: Regnery Publishing, Inc., 2006), 42.

43. Holland, *In the Shadow of the Sword*, loc. 5623, Kindle.

and nonbelievers. Those in the community lived in the House of Islam; those outside it lived in the House of War. This relationship presupposed a permanent state of conflict between the two houses. The unity of the *umma*, in theory, prevented infighting and led to outward expansion from the beginnings of Islam.

Islamic tradition records that in 620 Muhammad experienced the "Night Journey," in which he allegedly was miraculously transported from Mecca to Jerusalem, where he ascended into heaven from the Temple Mount, Muhammad supposedly met the first man, Adam; the prophets Joseph, Moses, and Abraham; as well as Jesus. This alleged journey solidified Jerusalem as a holy place in Islam and led to a rivalry with Christians and Jews over the Holy City. A few years later, Muhammad fled Mecca, in what is known as the *Hijra*, in fear of his life. Along with some of his original followers, Muhammad settled in Medina, which later became known as the "City of the Prophet." Medina had been settled by Jews and was part of an important merchant route to Syria. It became the place of Muhammad's militant revelations and his base of combat operations. According to a later biographer, Muhammad personally led nine combat raids from Medina while wielding his favorite sword, known as "the Cleaver of Vertebrae."[44] Another biographer quotes Muhammad as saying, "… the gates of Paradise lie in the shadow of the sword."[45] In 624, Muhammad ordered an attack on a merchant convoy during the pagan holy month, in which it was forbidden to shed blood. Muhammad justified the raid by declaring he had received a revelation from God of his approval of the attack. This attack and justification set the pattern in Islam, wherein good became identified with anything benefiting the *umma*, and evil anything that harmed or did not advance Islam.

Muhammad shared his revelations with the Jewish popula-

---

44. For numbers of raids, see Ibn Ishaq in Tom Holland, *The Forge of Christendom: The End of Days and the Epic Rise of the West* (New York: Doubleday, 2008), 424. For the name of Muhammad's sword, see Holland, *The Forge of Christendom*, 82.
45. Salih Muslim in Holland, *In the Shadow of the Sword*, loc. 64, Kindle.

tion in Medina, in the hopes that they would join his community. When he was rebuffed, he adopted a number of Jewish practices in the hopes that that would persuade them to join his cause. He ordered his followers to practice fasting, to follow Jewish dietary laws (no pork), and to pray toward Jerusalem. Even the adoption of these practices did not sway the Jews to his side; instead, they became harsh critics of Muhammad's teachings. A Meccan army arrived at the gates of Medina in 627, but were successfully rebuffed. After the siege, Muhammad made his move against the Jews. He charged them with collaborating with the Meccans, despite the fact that many Jews had bravely defended Medina, and ordered the execution of hundreds of Jewish men; the women and children were sold into slavery. Muhammad's anger toward the Jews continued throughout his life and culminated in his deathbed order of their expulsion from Arabia.

Muhammad's personal life shaped Muslim behavior and formed the foundation for Islamic cultural practice. He preached polygamy and had fourteen wives, including a nine-year-old girl whom he married when she was six but with whom he waited until she was nine (he was in his fifties) to consummate the marriage.[46] He also married his daughter-in-law after receiving a "revelation" from God to do so. Muhammad ruthlessly ordered the assassinations of his political and personal opponents and at the end of his life, instructed his followers to "fight all men until they say there is no God but Allah."[47] This statement was later written into the Qur'an as "fight those who believe not in God."[48] During his life, Muhammad embodied these words in his campaigns against his fellow Arabs as well as against Jews. Muhammad's militaristic teachings and actions set the example for his followers who

---

46. According to al-Bukhari's *ahadith*, vol. 7, Book 62, Number 64. Child marriage is still practiced in many Muslim nations. As an example, article 1041 of the Civil Code of the Islamic Republic of Iran allows for marriage at nine for girls and fourteen for boys.

47. Muhammad ibn Umar al-Waqidi, *Kitab al-Maghazi*, vol. 3 (London: Oxford University Press, 1966), 1113, quoted in Efraim Karsh, *Islamic Imperialism: A History* (New Haven, CT: Yale University Press, 2006), 19.

48. Qur'an 9.29.

sought to emulate the *jihad* undertaken by the prophet. *Jihad* and imperial expansion of the *umma* promised not only material but also spiritual riches for the Muslim — heaven awaited him if he died on *jihad*, and hell awaited those who fought against him.[49]

Christians who encountered Islam in its first centuries did not acknowledge the movement as a new religion, instead seeing it as a heresy, "a perversion of Christian doctrine."[50] A seventh-century Greek text records one view that "there is no truth in the so-called prophet. There is only the shedding of blood."[51] Saint John Damascene described Muhammad as the "forerunner of the Antichrist" and "false" since "prophets do not come armed with a sword."[52] In the twelfth century, Peter the Venerable (1092–1156) described Islam as "the error of errors, the sewer into which the waste of all previous heresies flowed."[53] Saint Thomas Aquinas (1225–1274), in his *Summa Contra Gentiles* described Muhammad as a false prophet:

> As for proofs of the truth of his doctrine, he brought forward only such as could be grasped by the natural ability of anyone with a very modest wisdom. Indeed, the truths that he taught he mingled with many fables and with doctrines of the greatest falsity. He did not bring forth any signs produced in a supernatural way, which alone fittingly gives witness to divine inspiration. What is more, no wise man, men trained in things divine and human, believed in him from the beginning. Those who believed in him were brutal

---

49. See Qur'an quote in Karsh, 19.

50. Hilaire Belloc, *The Great Heresies* (Rockford, IL: TAN Books and Publishers, Inc., 1991 [1938]), 42.

51. Patricia Crone and Michael Cook, *Hagarism: The Making of the Islamic World* (Cambridge, UK: Cambrigde University Press, 1977), 3–4, quoted in Holland, *The Forge of Christendom*, 82.

52. John Damascene, *On the Heretics*, quoted in Holland, *The Forge of Christendom*, 82 and Wilken, *The First Thousand Years*, 308.

53. M. Uebel, "Unthinking the Monster: twelfth-century responses to Saracen alterity," in J. J. Cohen, ed., *Monster Theory* (Minneapolis, MN: University of Minnesota Press, 1996), 264–291, quoted in Norman Housley, *Fighting for the Cross: Crusading to the Holy Land* (New Haven, CT: Yale University Press, 2008), 212.

men and desert wanderers, utterly ignorant of all divine teaching, through whose numbers Mohammed
forced others to become his followers by the violence
of his arms. He perverts almost all the testimonies of
the Old and New Testaments by making them into
fabrications of his own. It is thus clear that those who
place any faith in his words believe foolishly.[54]

Even a Byzantine emperor, Manuel II Paleologus (r. 1391–1425),
realized that Islam was not a new religion, but a repackaging of
Jewish and Christian beliefs spread by bloody conquest.[55] Islam
achieved a sudden and overwhelming success because it conquered territory, expanded violently, offered a sense of relief and
equality to all classes of people, consisted of simple doctrine, and
absorbed (rather than completely eradicated) the cultures it conquered.[56]

Muhammad's teachings on the *umma* and *jihad* oriented Islam
toward imperialistic expansion. The conflict between the House
of Islam and the House of War began during Muhammad's lifetime when Islamic forces raided into Palestine and Syria. Within
a decade of Muhammad's death in 632, Muslim armies conquered
the Christian areas of Syria (635), Jerusalem (638), and Egypt
(642). In 674, Muslim forces even laid siege to the capital city of
the Byzantine Empire, Constantinople, but were repulsed. Islam
also expanded westward through North Africa, sweeping away all
resistance so that the last Christian stronghold fell by 700. Former pagan nomads from the Arabian Peninsula now ruled the
ancient Roman provinces, which had once been converted to the
Catholic faith by the blood of the martyrs. Early in the eighth
century, Islamic forces crossed into Hispania and began the con-

---

54. Thomas Aquinas, *Summa Contra Gentiles*, Book 1, Chapter 6.
55. Manuel II wrote, "Show me just what Mohammed brought that was new, and there you will
find things only evil and inhuman, such as his command to spread by the sword and the faith he
preached," quoted by Pope Benedict XVI in his *Regensburg Address*, September 12, 2006.
56. These reasons for Islam's success are taken from Hilaire Belloc, *The Great Heresies*, 50–51.

quest of Visigothic Spain, which was completed by 711. Muslim forces practiced "shock and awe" tactics in the conquest of Spain. They destroyed churches or turned them into mosques, burned books, established *sharia* law, enslaved people, and persecuted Christians with mass crucifixions and beheadings.

Muslims now controlled Spain, except for a small enclave in the mountainous north that became known as Asturias. It was from this area that the longest war in human history, known as the *Reconquista* ("re-conquest"), would begin.[57] Islamic forces soon crossed the Pyrenees and conducted a series of raids into southern France. In 718, a Muslim army attacked the city of Narbonne, massacred all the adult male inhabitants, and sold the women and children into slavery. Three years later, Prince Eudes of Aquitaine defeated a large Muslim invasion force at Toulouse. A decade later, another Muslim invasion force, under the command of Abdul al-Rahman, defeated Prince Eudes's army and attacked Bordeaux, killing many inhabitants and burning churches in the city. Prince Eudes rode northward to discuss the situation with Charles, the mayor of the Frankish palace.

THE BATTLE OF POITIERS

Abdul al-Rahman's strategic objective was to raid deep into France to soften its defenses for a later full-scale invasion. His immediate tactical objective was to plunder the shrine of Saint Martin of Tours, because of its reported wealth and the psychological impact its destruction would produce on the inhabitants of France. His army, comprised of mobile armored cavalry, archers, and infantry, relied on rapid, violent raids to terrify the populace and make the enemy submissive. This sizable force of nearly thirty thousand men seemingly had victory within its grasp.[58]

---

57. It was a 780-year war. Christians were able to liberate the important city of Toledo in 1085 and won the decisive battle of Las Navas de Tolosa in the summer of 1212. By the fifteenth century, only a small Islamic enclave remained at Granada, which was liberated in 1492.
58. Victor Davis Hanson, *Carnage and Culture* (New York: Anchor Books, 2001), 141.

Prince Eudes made his way to the Merovingian court of the Frankish kingdom, where he briefed Charles on the military situation developing near the towns of Tours and Poitiers. As "mayor of the palace," Charles held the roles of commander-in-chief of the military and prime minister of government; he was the most powerful person in the kingdom. The Franks mustered a number of troops equal to that of al-Rahman's invasion force, professional (not conscripted) soldiers, seasoned from the constant combat over the previous eighteen years in the effort to unite all the tribes of Gaul. Frankish warriors were required to arm themselves and to provide three months of military service to the kingdom each year. Unlike the Muslims, who relied on the strength of their cavalry, the Frankish military was based on heavily armored infantry.

The two forces met near the town of Poitiers (120 miles southwest of Paris). Al-Rahman attacked the Franks with his cavalry, but the Frankish infantry maintained good order and discipline, arraying themselves into protective squares. One commentator wrote that the Franks were "an immovable sea. [They] stood one close to another and stiffened like a wall. As a mass of ice, they stood firm together."[59] Charles's men withstood repeated cavalry charges by the Muslim army. When the Muslims were exhausted from the repeated assaults, Charles ordered an advance. The Franks assaulted the main Muslim camp and killed Abdul al-Rahman, along with ten thousand Muslim troops. The remaining Muslim forces rallied and beat the Franks back. In the evening, each army rested and waited for dawn. When the Franks awoke the next morning, they discovered the Muslim army had retreated in the middle of the night. The victory was complete. Muslim casualties were so high that they referred to the battle as "the Road of the Martyrs."[60]

Charles's fame spread as a result of the battle, and he was given the name "Martel," which means "hammer," since "as a hammer

---

59. *The Chronicle of the Continuator of Isidore*, quoted in Hanson, *Carnage and Culture*, 138.
60. David Nicolle, *Poitiers AD 732: Charles Martel Turns the Islamic Tide* (New York: Osprey Publishing, 2008), 80.

breaks and crushes iron, steel, and other metals, so did he break up and crush his enemies."[61] The Battle of Poitiers was one of the most important battles in Western European history. If al-Rahman's forces had won that day, their strategic objective — providing a path for a larger invasion force to wreak havoc and possibly destroy the Frankish kingdom — might have been achieved. The fall of the Frankish kingdom would have been devastating and all of European and Church history completely changed. Charles Martel and his Franks succeeded in preserving Western civilization against the forces of Islam at Poitiers.[62]

In the ninth century, Islamic forces raided throughout the Mediterranean, invading Sicily in 831 and conquering most of the island by 878. A Muslim force first invaded the mainland of Italy in 841 and returned in 846 for an attack on Rome. A small force landed at Ostia and marched from that port city to Rome, where they plundered the city and profaned the churches of old Saint Peter's and Saint Paul's. The desecration of the churches and the destruction of the city prompted Pope Leo IV (r. 847–855) to organize the city's defenses. He ordered the construction of defensive walls forty feet high and twelve feet thick, ringed by forty-four defensive towers.[63] Islamic military activity in Italy continued throughout the ninth century, culminating in the destruction of Saint Benedict's monastery at Monte Cassino in 884. Finally, in the early tenth century, a coalition Christian army — raised and led into battle by Pope John X (r. 914–928) — defeated a large Muslim invasion force at the Battle of Garigliano.

Life for Christians and Jews in Muslim-occupied territory was marked by subjection and humiliation. Non-Muslims had few rights and were harassed, insulted, and belittled by their Mus-

---

61. *Chronicle of Saint-Denis*, quoted in Nicolle, *Poitiers AD 732*, 20.
62. Most historians until modern times recognized the significance of Charles's victory, but some modern historians (Philip Hitti and Franco Cardini, et al.) think the battle was minor, with no real long-term significance. I think this criticism stems from a bias embraced by many in academia against Christians and the Church, entrenched in a false narrative that Islam is superior and enlightened.
63. Duffy, *Saints and Sinners*, 99. These defenses were known as the "Leonine Walls" and one can still visit their remnants in Rome today.

lim neighbors. Water, food, garments, and utensils touched by a non-Muslim were considered polluted and could not be used by Muslims.[64] Christians and Jews, since they were people of the Book — that is, the Bible — were afforded "special protected" status in Islamic society and were known as *dhimmis*, but the price for protection was an annual tax called the *jizya*. The tax was required of all Christian and Jewish men, women, and children — including widows, orphans, and the dead. Humiliating treatment accompanied the payment of the tax, as described by a thirteenth-century Muslim jurist: "The infidel who wishes to pay his poll tax must be treated with disdain by the collector: the collector remains seated and the infidel remains standing in front of him, his head bowed and his back bent. The collector holds him by the beard and strikes him on both cheeks."[65]

Christians and Jews were forbidden to have weapons and could not testify in court. Although churches were sometimes left standing (when not converted into mosques), no new church construction was allowed, nor could bells be rung to call the faithful to Mass. In seventh-century Egypt, every publicly visible cross was destroyed, and every church was required to bear this inscription denying the Incarnation on its doors: "Mohammed is the great apostle of God, and Jesus also is the apostle of God. But truly God is not begotten and does not beget."[66] At times, Christians and Jews were required to wear clothing specifying their identities, which reinforced their separation from society. Certain professions and jobs were also barred to Christians and Jews, whose societal status was barely above the level of slaves. As a result, there was heavy societal pressure to convert to Islam. Some did, but most Christians maintained their faith for centu-

---

64. Darío Fernández-Morera, *The Myth of the Andalusian Paradise: Muslims, Christians, and Jews under Islamic Rule in Medieval Spain* (Wilmington, DE: ISI Books, 2016), 212.
65. Bat Ye'or, *Islam and Dhimmitude: Where Civilizations Collide* (Madison, NJ, 2002), 70, quoted in Andrew G. Bostom, MD, ed., *The Legacy of Jihad: Islamic Holy War and the Fate of Non-Muslims* (Amherst, NY: Prometheus Books, 2005), 29.
66. L.W. Barnard, *The Greco-Roman and Oriental Background of the Iconoclastic Controversy* (London, 1974), 18, quoted in Carroll, *The Building of Christendom*, 264.

ries before a majority of the population embraced Islam.[67]

THE MUSLIM WORLD AFTER MUHAMMAD

Muhammad's effort to build a community united in political and military purpose through religion was tested mightily after his death, as competing families engaged in a game of thrones. The immediate successors of Muhammad, known as the "right-ly-guided" caliphs, did not rule long, and the death of the last led to a fracturing of Islam into two sects. The first successor of Muhammad was his longtime friend and father of his favorite wife, Abu Bakr (r. 632–634). Umar (r. 634–644), the brother-in-law of Muhammad, succeeded Abu Bakr. The next caliph, Uthman (r. 644–656), established the Umayyad dynasty in Arabia (651–750) (later ruling in Spain), which was comprised of the Meccan tribes that initially opposed Muhammad. The last "rightly-guided" caliph was Ali (r. 656–661), the cousin and son-in-law of Muhammad, who had been the first male convert to Islam (as a nine-year-old). Opponents assassinated him in 661, and his death brought about the Shi'a party in Islam, a group that considered themselves the only true Muslims and waged war against the other Muslims, known as the Sunnis.[68] The pursuit of power produced conquered territories that, although originally provinces of a united Muslim empire, soon became independent, competing territories. The Muslim world was broken into regional centers of power: the Abbasid (Sunni) caliphate in Baghdad (750–1258), the Fatimid (Shi'ite) caliphate in Egypt (909–1171), and the Umayyad caliphate of Cordoba in Spain. Islam broke onto the world stage from a remote backwater, but its conquests thrust the movement into the forefront of European and Christian thought.

---

67. Richard Bulliet's data in his *Conversion to Islam in the Medieval Period: An Essay in Quantitative History* (Cambridge, MA: Harvard University Press, 1979) showed it took an average of 243 years for 50 percent of the Christian population to convert to Islam in Syria, Iraq, Iran, Egypt, and Spain. Bulliet's data is quoted in Rodney Stark, *God's Battalion: The Case for the Crusades* (New York: HarperOne, 2009), 32.

68. The Shi'ites also believe that only a direct descendant of Muhammad can become the caliph.

THE SECOND COUNCIL OF CONSTANTINOPLE

In the middle of the sixth century, the theological issue surrounding the question "Who is Jesus?" continued to dominate the Church's development of doctrine, and even occupied the attention of the Roman Emperor in Constantinople. Although the theological matter involved the nature of Jesus, a political and ecclesial question was concerned as well: Who determines theological orthodoxy — the emperor or the pope?

Justinian, the nephew and adopted son of Emperor Justin (r. 518–527), was "a man of such restless energy that he famously never slept. His tirelessness was rivaled only by the soaring scale of his ambition."[69] Upon Justin's death, Justinian became the Roman emperor (r. 527–565) and embarked on an ambitious agenda. On the military front, in 533, Justinian sent General Belisarius to North Africa to fight the Vandals and reclaim imperial territory. Belisarius's successful campaign in Africa led to a twenty-year combat operation in Italy to wrest imperial territory from the local ethnic Germanic chieftains, who had ruled imperial lands since the collapse of the Western Empire in the late fifth century. Regarding theology, Justinian desired to end the religious squabbling between the Monophysites and the orthodox, a conflict that dominated imperial society despite the earlier condemnation of Monophysitism at the Council of Chalcedon in 451. Justinian's position on the theological controversy was clouded by his relationship with his wife, Theodora. Despite her notorious past as a former actress and dancer known for her sexual adventures, Theodora was a Monophysite and maintained a group of Monophysite monks at the imperial palace. In the question of the "two powers" of Church and state, Justinian viewed the state as the more powerful. To him, it was the emperor's responsibility to choose and oversee bishops and to establish and maintain orthodoxy in faith. The emperor, not the pope, was Christ's vicar on

---

69. Holland, *In the Shadow of the Sword*, loc. 2326, Kindle.

earth, ruling over one empire, one law, and one Church.

Monophysites believed that the Church had embraced Nestorianism when she had declared Christ to have two natures, human and divine.[70] Monophysites believed that Jesus is one person (divine) with only one nature (divine), rejecting his fully human nature. Justinian believed the Monophysites were not actually heretics, just misunderstood, and he desired to reconcile their beliefs with the magisterially defined teachings of previous Church councils. So, he issued an edict that he believed was a compromise to the problem. His edict confirmed the teachings of Chalcedon, which the orthodox supported, and condemned the writings of three theologians, known as the "Three Chapters," whom the Monophysites believed were heretics. The writings comprising the Three Chapters included the teachings of Theodore of Mopsuestia, a friend and teacher of Nestorius; some writings of Theodoret of Cyrus; and a letter of Ibas of Edessa. Although Chalcedon had condemned Nestorius, the council had not condemned the writings of his teacher Theodore of Mopsuestia, which the Monophysites believed was a significant omission. They were also upset that Theodoret of Cyrus, a friend and defender of Nestorius, had not been condemned but rather restored to his episcopal see. Finally, the letter of Ibas of Edessa in support of Nestorius had not been addressed by the council, which the Monophysites argued indicated tacit support. Justinian believed he had found a way to reunite the orthodox and Monophysites by condemning the Three Chapters. But although that position made the Monophysites happy, it upset the orthodox, who saw the emperor's edict as inappropriately modifying the work of an ecumenical council. Some bishops in the east, including the patriarch of Constantinople, initially refused to sign the condemnation of the Three Chapters, but were eventually coerced.

When the emperor sent the edict to Rome for papal approval,

---

70. Nestorius taught that Mary gave birth to the human Christ, not the divine Jesus, which amounts to teaching that Jesus is two persons (human and divine).

there began an epic struggle between pope and emperor concerning the question of who should determine theological orthodoxy. Pope Vigilius (r. 537–555) had previously been the papal legate to Constantinople and a friend of Theodora. He had ingratiated himself with Theodora by posing as a Monophysite sympathizer — he knew her support would be crucial to his papal ambitions. When Pope Agipatus I (r. 535–536) died on a visit to the capital city, Vigilius believed his accession to the See of Rome was guaranteed. Vigilius accompanied the body of the pope back to Rome, but he was infuriated when Silverius (r. 536–537) was elected pope instead. Vigilius then concocted a plan to get rid of Silverius. He persuaded General Belisarius, who was campaigning in Italy against the Goths, to arrest Silverius on the trumped-up charges of plotting with the Goths against the Empire. Silverius was arrested and sent into exile in Anatolia. Under pressure from General Belisarius, the Roman clergy elected Vigilius pope (although, in effect, he was an antipope while Silverius lived since Silverius did not abdicate the office).[71] Despite the machinations leading to his election, Vigilius had no desire to accept the emperor's edict condemning the Three Chapters, because he believed it to be a repudiation of the work of Chalcedon.[72] When Justinian ordered Vigilius to appear in Constantinople to discuss the matter, he demurred. The emperor then ordered his arrest, which occurred while he was celebrating Mass in Rome, and his forcible removal to the capital city. Vigilius would spend the next decade in imperial captivity. When in Constantinople, Vigilius agreed to issue a condemnation of the Three Chapters, along with an explicit statement that the judgment had no impact on the teachings of Chalcedon. Many Western bishops did not agree with the pope's decision and rose up against it. In 550, Vigilius proposed the calling of an ecumenical council to resolve the issue, but the emperor did not agree. Eventually, Vigilius tried to escape

71. Carroll, *The Building of Christendom*, 170.
72. The lack of the knowledge of Greek by Western bishops and theologians hampered Western understanding of this matter.

BRIGHT LIGHTS IN A DARK TIME | 175

Constantinople and return to Rome. He was only able to get as far as Chalcedon, where he stayed in the same church used by the council in 451. Finally, the emperor agreed to the meeting of an ecumenical council at Constantinople in 553. The council condemned the writings of the Three Chapters, and also reiterated the teachings of the Councils of Ephesus and Chalcedon. After the council, Vigilius was allowed to leave Constantinople and return to Rome, but he died on the journey, never reaching the city.

While a complicated theological affair, the Three Chapters controversy also illustrated the tension between the emperor and the pope concerning authority. The East continued to view the Church as an organ of the state and implemented the policy of *caesaro-papism*. The emperor believed he had the right and power to control the Church, even to the point of determining correct doctrine. However, the West viewed the Church as separate from, and even above, the secular authority, with the pope as leader of the universal Church.

THE THIRD COUNCIL OF CONSTANTINOPLE

Nearly a century after the Three Chapters controversy, the Church was once again thrust into theological debate when Patriarch Sergius of Constantinople proposed a new teaching known as Monothelitism. Sergius was concerned with the issues raised by the Monophysites, so he tackled the issue from another angle. He proposed that Christ had only one will (Monothelitism), a divine will. However, the problem with Monothelitism was the same problem present in Monophysitism: it denied the true humanity of Jesus. If the Lord only has one divine will, then the Church cannot teach that Jesus was true God and true man. Many Eastern bishops and theologians embraced Sergius's teaching, but others rejected it. Saint Maximus the Confessor (580–662) even suffered physical violence (his tongue and right hand were cut off) and exile for refusing to embrace Monothelitism. Sergius sent a letter to Pope Honorius (r. 625–638), requesting his approval of Monothelitism. Honorius provided an ambiguous reply, causing speculation as to whether the pope even understood Sergius's theological argument, which produced a source of disagreement and conflict in the Church for the next fifty years. Emperor Heraclius (r. 610–641) agreed with Sergius and, in an exercise of *caesaro-papism*, proclaimed Monothelitism as official doctrine.

The controversy was still raging when Martin was elected pope in 649. An accomplished scholar and former papal envoy to Constantinople, Martin grasped the error of Monothelitism. In October 649, Martin gathered 105 bishops at the Lateran Palace to discuss the heresy. It was condemned, and Martin took the bold step of excommunicating the sitting patriarch of Constantinople, Paul II, for purveying the erroneous teaching. Emperor Constans II (r. 641–668), displeased with Martin's pronouncement, began a campaign to get rid of the meddlesome pope. The Byzantine governor Olympius devised a nefarious plan to murder Martin. Olympius's sword-bearer was to go to Mass, get in line to receive the Eucharist from Martin, and then strike him dead. However, the plan failed when, at the moment of reception, the sword-bearer miraculously could not see the pope.[73] A few years later, another governor dispatched a large body of troops to Rome, where they arrested Martin, placed him on a ship, and sent him to the island of Naxos in the Aegean, where he remained for a year.

After a year had passed without any communication from the pope, the clergy of Rome assumed Martin had died, so they elected Eugenius I as his successor. News of this election reached Martin after another year. The Church was in a unique situation: two men acting as pope, neither one an antipope. Martin was still pope, since, once elected, a man remains pope until death or resignation. In reality, Eugenius was not pope but merely the ecclesial administrator of Rome (he later became the

---

73. Carroll, *The Building of Christendom*, 243

pope when Martin died). In September 654, Martin was finally escorted to Constantinople, where he spent three months in jail. Eventually, he was placed on trial before an imperial official. Martin was accused of plotting rebellion, entering into treasonable communication with Muslims, and refusing to acknowledge Mary as *Theotokos* (God-bearer), but the real reason for his arrest was his opposition to Monothelitism. Martin was found guilty and sentenced to death. The pope was taken to the public square, stripped naked, beaten, weighed down with heavy chains, and dragged to prison. Patriarch Paul, near death, pleaded with Constans II to spare the pope's life. The emperor agreed to commute the death sentence, but ordered Martin into exile at Cherson in the Crimea. Before his departure, the pope was given one last chance to embrace the Monothelite heresy. He refused. In the spring of 655, Martin was placed on a ship for the Crimea. He spent several months in exile before finally succumbing to the horrible treatment by the Byzantines. The saintly Martin, defender of orthodoxy, was the last martyred pope in Church history.

The theological conflict was finally resolved a quarter-century later at the Third Council of Constantinople in 681. Emperor Constantine IV (r. 652–685) called the council, which was approved by Pope Saint Agatho (r. 678–681). The conciliar fathers condemned Monothelitism and also condemned Pope Honorius as a heretic, writing, "It is our unanimous decree that there shall be expelled from the Church and anathematized Honorius, formerly Pope of Old Rome, because we find in his letter to Sergius, that in all respects he followed his view and confirmed his impious doctrines."[74] The papal legates signed the decrees of the council and sent them to Rome for final approval by the pope. While the council was in session, Pope Saint Agatho died and was succeeded by Pope Saint Leo II (r. 681–683),

---

74. Charles J. Hefele, *A History of the Councils of the Church*, vol. V (Edinburgh, UK: T. & T. Clark, 1896), 150–152, quoted in Carroll, *The Building of Christendom*, 253.

who was fluent in Greek. Leo confirmed the decree that condemned the heresy of Monothelitism, but he changed the wording in the decree about Pope Honorius. Instead of condemning Honorius outright and declaring him a heretic, Leo indicated that Honorius had not accepted the heretical teaching; he had only refrained from condemning it when given the opportunity: "Honorius who did not extinguish the fire of heretical teaching, as behooved one who exercised the authority of the apostles, but by his negligence blew the flames still higher."[75] According to Leo, Honorius had been negligent in safeguarding the Faith but was not a heretic.[76]

By the end of the seventh century, the Church had officially answered the question "Who is Jesus?" — or, more accurately, developed and approved theological language to describe the relationship between the Persons of the Trinity as well as the Person of Jesus himself. Jesus is a Divine Person with a divine and human nature and will. Additional theological controversies and heresies would capture the Church's attention in the centuries ahead, but the work of the first six ecumenical councils had placed the Church's teachings on sure footing.

THE POLITICAL SITUATION OF THE FRANKISH KINGDOM

In the mid-seventh century, the kings of the Franks were weak and ineffective. Einhard, the later biographer of Charlemagne, wrote of these Merovingian kings, "nothing was left to the king except to be happy with the royal title and to sit on his throne with his flowing hair and to behave as if he had authority."[77] In the early sixth century, the kingdom of the Franks had been di-

---

75. Philip Hughes, *A History of the Church, Volume 1: The World in Which the Church was Founded* (London: Sheed and Ward, 1979 [1948]), 302.
76. This is an important distinction, as many with an animus against the Church cite the case of Honorius as proof against papal infallibility.
77. Quoted in Wilken, *The First Thousand Years*, 333–334.

vided into three parts (the division was made permanent in 614), comprising Burgundy, Neustria, and Austrasia, each region being assigned its own mayor of the palace.[78] The mayor of the palace originated in the *maior domus*, or the head of the household, role, and grew in power over the kings in the latter sixth century when a series of underage children came to the throne.

The end of the monarchy began in 639 with the death of King Dagobert. His successors were known as the "Do-Nothing" kings whose reigns led to the end of the Merovingian dynasty. Charles Martel, the victor over the Muslims at the Battle of Poitiers in 732, became mayor of the palace in 714 and ruled the kingdom with an iron fist. When King Theoderic IV died in 737, Charles refused to invest another king. His military exploits expanded Frankish territory but cost the kingdom revenue, so Charles turned to the Church and her property to finance his expeditions. Charles died in 741, leaving two legitimate sons: Carloman (c. 713–754) and Pepin (718–768) (known as "the Short" because he kept his hair short, unlike the Frankish custom of long hair and beards). The brothers knew the great Saint Boniface well and worked with him to organize and reform the Church in the kingdom. Both brothers realized the kingdom needed a king, so they raised a Merovingian, Childeric III, to the throne, but he was not to reign long.

Carloman was known for his ruthlessness, as evidenced by his actions against the Alemanni in 746. Frustrated by their frequent rebellions, Carloman invited the Alemanni nobility to a meeting at Cannstatt (modern-day Stuttgart), where he arrested and tried them for treason. Upon their conviction, he massacred thousands of the Alemanni nobility. A year later, moved by contrition under the spiritual direction of Saint Boniface, Carloman renounced his earthly titles, performed penance, and traveled to Rome. At a meeting with Pope Zachary (r. 741–752), he received the tonsure

---

78. Geoffrey Barraclough, *The Crucible of Europe: The Ninth and Tenth Centuries in European History* (Berkeley, CA: University of California Press, 1976), 11.

and habit of a Benedictine monk and spent his remaining years at the monastery of Monte Cassino.

Pepin was now sole ruler of the Frankish kingdom, but he did not hold the title "king" because he was not of royal blood. Pepin thought it ridiculous that the official who actually wielded power in the kingdom was not considered king simply because of his birth, so he sent a letter to the pope with a question: who should be king — the man who wields power, or the one simply born into a royal family but who wields no real power? Pope Zachary responded to his inquiry by writing, "It is better that he who had the power should bear the royal name than he who remained without power."[79] Using the papal response as justification, Pepin deposed the last Merovingian king, Childerich III, in 751, solemnly cut Childerich's hair (the Franks traditionally believed the king possessed magical power, which depended on his long hair and beard), and sent him to a monastery.[80] On Christmas Day 751, Saint Boniface anointed Pepin King of the Franks. A year later, Pope Stephen III (r. 752–757) traveled to the Frankish kingdom (the first pope to do so) to ask Pepin to undertake a military campaign in northern Italy against the Lombards, who were harassing and threatening the papacy. Pepin's sons, Charles and Carloman, were present at the meeting with the pope and received, along with their father, the title *patricius Romanorum* ("Patrician of the Romans") from Pope Stephen. The title denoted Pepin and his sons as the personal protectors of the pope. Prior to this, the pope and the city of Rome had been protected by the Roman emperor in Constantinople. However, the constant harassment from Muslim forces in the east prevented the emperor from assisting the pope on a consistent basis, so the successor of Saint Peter looked to the Franks. The Islamic invasions and conquest of Christian territory along the Mediterranean spawned a shift of

---

79. Wilken, *The First Thousand Years*, 334.
80. Matthias Becher, *Charlemagne* (New Haven, CT: Yale University Press, 2003), 37.

political power to the north. This marked a significant change from the Empire, which was a Mediterranean entity.[81] Pepin's military campaign in Italy was successful, resulting in a peace treaty with the Lombards. The areas controlled by the Franks were given to the pope in what became known as the Donation of Pepin. This donation created the "Papal States" — territory directly controlled by the pope, who now assumed the role of secular lord while remaining universal shepherd of the Church. The Papal States would exist until the late nineteenth century and involve the pope in temporal affairs (not always in a positive way) over the next several centuries.

CHARLES THE GREAT

Although Pope Stephen II had anointed the sons of Pepin (Charles and Carloman) king in 754, they did not assume the title until Pepin's death in 768. Carloman, the second son, died at a young age, making Charles the sole king of the Franks. Charles reigned as king for over forty years. He made the Frankish kingdom into an empire and is known in history as Charles the Great, or Charlemagne.

In his *Vita Karoli magni* ("Life of Charles the Great"), a favorable biography of the great ruler, Charles's friend Einhard described Charlemagne physically as "exceptionally tall" — he was over seven feet in height, with a "firm gait, a thoroughly manly manner of holding himself, and, a high voice which did not really correspond to the rest of his body."[82] Charlemagne was known to be talkative, interested in astronomy and theology (especially the works of Saint Augustine).[83] He was married multiple times, kept multiple concubines, and fathered twelve children, four boys and eight girls. He loved his daughters deeply and refused marriage for them, preferring they remain with

---

81. See Barraclough, *The Crucible of Europe*, Chapter 1.
82. Becher, 2.
83. Ibid., 5.

him at court. Charlemagne's reign and legacy were shaped by his Saxon campaigns, his relationship with the pope, and the Carolingian Renaissance.

A year after becoming sole king, Charlemagne embarked on a military campaign to subdue, pacify, and convert the barbarian Saxons. The costly and protracted experience took thirty years to complete. The Saxons lived just beyond the Frankish borders in the territory between the Rhine and Elbe Rivers, north of Cologne and east of the modern-day Netherlands. They were a disparate people with no central king, which was one of the reasons why it took Charlemagne so long to incorporate them into the Frankish empire. The Saxons were fierce pagans who practiced human sacrifice and ritual cannibalism. In 772, the Saxons crossed the Frankish border, looting, killing, and burning, prompting Charlemagne's military campaign that destroyed a major Saxon pagan shrine at Irminsul. The Saxons revolted against the Franks in 778, destroying the Karlsburg fortification that had been erected during Charlemagne's first Saxon campaign. A few years later, a Saxon ruler named Widukind rebelled against the Franks, which caused another military expedition by Charlemagne, which culminated this time in the beheading of 4,500 Saxon nobles at Verdun — all in a single day.

The violent conflict and Saxon intransigence led Charlemagne to believe that the only way to fully pacify the barbarous Saxons was to convert them by force, since previous missionary endeavors had proved fruitless. His decision to use force was not the standard policy when subduing non-Christian tribes encountered by the Franks, and was controversial; even his friend and adviser, Alcuin of York, wrote that "faith arises from the will, not from compulsion. You can persuade a man to believe, but you cannot force him. You can haul him to the waters of baptism but not to faith itself."[84] Finally, in 785, Widukind accepted baptism, and the long, violent campaigns came to an end for a period of

---

84. Alcuin of York, *Letter*, 113.

time.[85] Charlemagne enacted conversion laws, known as capitularies, to ensure that the Saxons remained in the Faith. These
capitularies included the strict admonition that "anyone who, in
contempt of the Christian faith, refuses to respect the holy fast of
Lent and eats meat shall be put to death."[86] The Saxon campaigns
occupied a significant amount of Charlemagne's energy and time,
but eventually the Saxons accepted the Faith and ended their violence.

   Charlemagne's relationship with the bishop of Rome was
marked by his role as personal protector of the pope. At the end
of the eighth century, news reached his court that Pope Saint
Leo III (r. 795–816) had been attacked by a Roman mob. Leo
had been a long-serving member of the Roman Church but was
not from one of the leading Roman noble families, who resented
his election and accused him of perjury and adultery.[87] Leo had
been leading a procession through the city streets when he was
attacked. Thugs tried to cut off his tongue and gouge out his eyes.
His supporters dragged him to a nearby church, where they were
astonished to learn the pope suffered no permanent injury. Leo
fled the city and made his way to the Frankish kingdom. Outraged, Charlemagne sent Leo back to Rome under armed escort,
secure in the knowledge the king would come to the Eternal City
to help settle the issue.

   Charlemagne arrived at Rome in November 800 and was met
by Pope Leo III twelve miles from the city — double the distance the ancient Roman emperors were traditionally met by a
city delegation upon their return home.[88] Pope and king shared a
meal and discussed business before the pope returned to Rome.
Upon his arrival in the city, Charlemagne attended an assembly
of clergy and noblemen, where Leo III proclaimed under oath

---

85. Charlemagne would make one more military campaign to Saxony in 804 due to another Saxon
uprising.
86. Jean Comby, *How to Read Church History: From the Beginnings to the Fifteenth Century*, vol. I (New
York: Crossroads, 2001), 123.
87. Becher, 8.
88. Ibid., 13.

his innocence of the charges leveled against him. This settled the matter. While at the meeting, Charlemagne was encouraged by the pope and noblemen to assume the title of emperor due to his power, prestige, and his role as protector of the pope. He agreed to do so. A little while later, on Christmas Day 800, Charlemagne was crowned emperor by Pope Leo III. After a gap of 324 years, the Western world witnessed imperial rule. The people attending the ceremony cheered, "To Charles the most pious Augustus, crowned by God, the great and pacific emperor, life and victory!"[89] After crowning Charlemagne, Pope Leo prostrated himself before the emperor. This act of respect and recognition challenged the authority of the Eastern emperor, although Westerners argued that the title was vacant since a woman, Empress Irene, ruled the Eastern Empire at this time.[90]

Charlemagne's empire would become known in history as the Holy Roman Empire, wherein the Church and Empire would exist in a mostly friendly environment, respectful of each entity's authority in its particular sphere of influence. Charlemagne's empire relied on vassals in a form of early feudalism, as opposed to the old Roman Empire, which had relied on a centralized bureaucracy governed from a central location. Charlemagne did not have a central or permanent capital, instead constructing palaces in multiple locations, such as Frankfurt, Ingelheim, Diedenhofen, Worms, and Aachen. Charlemagne minted coins, set currency rates, and organized the military by introducing a general military obligation for men in the Empire. Charlemagne also worked closely with the Church in his realm to pursue ecclesial reform. He asked the pope for a copy of canon law, as well as a missal, that he intended to be used throughout the Empire. He required bishops to spend time in their dioceses ministering to their flock and banned the practice of pluralism.[91] Charlemagne's vast Empire

---

89. Ibid., 7.
90. See Becher, 14–15.
91. Becher, 115–117. Pluralism is an ecclesiastical abuse wherein one man is bishop of multiple dioceses.

encompassed one million square kilometers and contained 180 dioceses; 700 monasteries; 750 royal estates; 150 palaces; and 150 administrative districts in Italy, 20 in Spain, and 500 in Gaul.[92] He established diplomatic relations with the Abbasid caliphate in Baghdad and was granted administrative control of the Church of the Holy Sepulchre in Jerusalem by caliph Harun al-Rashid in 802.[93] Overseeing this enormous empire was Charles, "the most merciful, awe-inspiring, great, and pacific emperor crowned by God, who rules the Roman Empire and who [is] king of the Franks and Lombards by the grace of God."[94]

Charlemagne united this empire through a revival of art, architecture, and education in the Carolingian Renaissance. The emperor wanted both boys and girls to learn at his palace schools, and he desired a standardized curriculum throughout the empire. He invited scholars of all nationalities, including Theodulf of Orléans (Visigoth), Paulinus of Aquilea (Lombard), Dungal (Irish), and the Anglo-Saxon Alcuin of York (732–804), to teach in the schools. Alcuin, who was influenced by the writings of the notable Saint Bede (c. 673–735), had become the director of the monastic library at York in 767. Charlemagne recruited Alcuin to become the head of the palace school in Aachen in the early 780s. The scholar from York was given the task of creating a standardized curriculum, which he divided into two parts: the *trivium* and *quadrivium*. The *trivium* consisted of the study of grammar, logic, and rhetoric; the *quadrivium* included arithmetic, geometry, astronomy, and music. The learning plan created by Alcuin of York formed the foundation of the liberal arts curriculum that is still utilized in many colleges and universities in the modern world.

Charlemagne also demanded that the clerics in his realm know how to read and write. He even required bishops to test their priests to ensure their proficiency. Although the emperor

92. Ibid., 118.
93. Ibid., 97.
94. Ibid., 17.

valued the importance of education, and could read, he never mastered the art of writing despite diligent nightly practice.
Charlemagne patronized Benedictine monasteries and fostered
their growth throughout the Empire. This allowed for the prolif-
eration of libraries and *scriptoria*, where the Scriptures and ancient
Greco-Roman manuscripts were copied and preserved. Most of
modern-day knowledge of classical literature derives from copies
made in the *scriptoria* of Charlemagne.[95] The monks in the Holy
Roman Empire recognized the need for a new and easier-to-read
script that would also ensure fewer errors when copying texts,
so they developed what became known as Carolingian minis-
cule. The new script, which was clear and uniform, with rounded shapes, capital letters, and spaces between words, created a
disciplined and legible writing style, and was used for 400 years.
Charlemagne's impact on Western civilization also included the
adoption of the *Anno Domini* dating system, first developed by the
sixth-century monk Dionysius Exiguus. Dionysius replaced the
standard dating method (centered on the reign of Emperor Diocletian) by ordering the calendar around the Incarnation of Jesus.
The Synod of Whitby in 664 had made the dating system official
in England, but Charlemagne's acceptance brought the method
to the European continent.[96]

When Charles was fifty-eight years old, he divided his empire among his three sons, per Frankish custom. Charles the
Younger received control of the core lands of the kingdom (from
the Loire to the Rhine); Pepin received Italy and Bavaria; and
Louis was granted Aquitaine, Provence, and parts of Burgundy. A few years later Pepin and then Charles the Younger died,
so the Empire in total fell to Louis, who was nicknamed "the
Pious" for his devout adherence to and practice of the Faith.
On January 28, 814, Charlemagne died after contracting a fever
and suffering from an illness for a week. His body was washed,

95. Barraclough, 27.
96. Wilken, *The First Thousand Years*, 180.

prepared, and buried on his day of death in the church of Saint Mary in Aachen.[97] Louis the Pious reigned as emperor and king of the Franks, but, following custom, he divided the territory among his four sons in 817. This partitioning of the empire was made permanent in the Treaty of Verdun in 843. The sons of Louis the Pious met and signed the treaty, which recognized the coexistence of the independent states.[98] The united Holy Roman Empire of Charlemagne was relegated to the annals of history (the title remained but the territory was greatly reduced), despite a brief recurrence in the late tenth century under the leadership of Otto the Great.

Charlemagne's contribution to Western Civilization and Church history cannot be overstated. Along with Constantine, Charlemagne is considered the chief lay builder of Christendom, a "unity of spirit, [in] the hierarchical order and organic interrelationship of society" in which Church and state operated in close cooperation for the welfare of Christian people.[99] Christendom was the governmental and societal recognition of the reign of Christ the King among men, wherein the pope was the spiritual leader and the emperor the temporal leader, "each deriving their authority from God, consecrating it through the Church and then giving back its fruits to God."[100] Christendom was neither a utopia nor a perfect society, but it was a society centered in Christ and focused on the eternal — wherein Catholic kings were, at the very least, expected to protect and safeguard, rather than control, the Church. The healthy tension that existed between Church and state produced a vibrant society whose culture and civilization contributed to the betterment of humanity for centuries. Charlemagne's empire would last in various forms and locations for over a thousand years. He is rightly considered the "Father of Europe."[101]

---

97. Ibid., 132.
98. Barraclough, 69.
99. Carroll, *The Building of Christendom*, 328.
100. Ibid., 329.
101. The Holy Roman Empire was dissolved by Napoleon Bonaparte in 1806.

IMAGE BREAKING AND THE
SECOND COUNCIL OF NICAEA

Previously, when the Merovingian kings ruled the Frankish kingdom, and several years before the Battle of Poitiers, a violent heresy in the east rocked the Church.

A large volcanic eruption occurred in the Aegean Sea in the year 726. Emperor Leo III (r. 717–741) believed the cause was attributable to God's wrath over widespread idolatry in the Empire due to the presence of icons, though these holy images had adorned eastern churches and monasteries for centuries. Leo banned their creation after the natural disaster, influenced by the opinions of some theologians that icons led to idolatry. Leo III's unpopular order caused a revolt in Greece. Those who agreed with the emperor became known as *iconoclasts* ("image breakers"), whereas those who supported the creation and use of holy images were known as *iconodules* (or sometimes *iconophiles*). When news of Leo's destruction and ban on icons reached Rome, Pope Gregory II (r. 715–731) grasped the fallacy of the theological argument, and sent a letter to the emperor, condemning Leo's "image-breaking" (iconoclasm) policy:

> Christ knows that so often as we go into the Church of St. Peter, and see the picture of this saint, we are moved and tears flow from us. Christ has made the blind to see: you have made the seeing blind. You say: We worship stones and walls and boards. But it is not so, O Emperor; but they serve us for remembrance and encouragement, lifting our slow spirits upwards by those whose names the pictures bear. And we worship them not as God, as you maintain, God forbid! For we set not our hope on them; and if a picture of the Lord is there, we say: Lord Jesus Christ, help and save us. At a picture of His Holy Mother we say: Holy God-bearer, pray for us with

thy Son and so with a martyr. It would have been better for you to have been a heretic than a destroyer of images.[102]

The iconoclast controversy unleashed by Emperor Leo III continued for over fifty years and, ultimately, required an ecumenical council to resolve. Leo III died in 741 and was succeeded by Constantine V (r. 741–775). While Leo had been content to order the destruction of existing images and ban the creation of new ones, Constantine instituted active persecution of the *iconodules*. Monasteries and convents that refused to follow the imperial ban on images were seized; monks and nuns were arrested and executed. After Constantine died in 775, his successor, Leo IV (r. 775–780), was an *iconoclast*. However, Leo's wife, Irene, was orthodox and did not share her husband's negative view of icons. When Leo unexpectedly died in 780, his young son, Constantine VI, was made emperor, with Irene as regent, from 780–790. Irene attempted to end the iconoclast controversy by calling an ecumenical council in the year 787. Pope Adrian (r. 772–795) sent legates to the meeting held in Nicaea, site of the first ecumenical council more than 450 years previously.

The Second Council of Nicaea, attended by 350 bishops, worked to define the doctrine of worship and veneration.[103] The council distinguished between worship (*latria*), which is reserved for God alone; the special reverence (*hyperdulia*) due to Mary as the Mother of God; and the reverence (*dulia*) given to saints in veneration. The council fathers approved the use of icons, with the recognition that they are images used to aid Christians in devotion, to inspire love and devotion for God, Mary, and the saints:

As the figure of the sacred cross, so also the sacred

---

102. Charles J. Hefele, *A History of the Councils of the Church*, vol. V, 290–293, quoted in Carroll, *The Building of Christendom*, 277.
103. For the number of bishops see Wilken, *The First Thousand Years*, 305.

figures, whether of color or of stone or of any material, may be depicted on vessels, on clothes and walls, on tables, in houses and on roads, namely, the figures of Jesus Christ, of our immaculate Lady, of the venerable angels, and of all holy men. The oftener one looked on these representations, the more would the looker be stirred to the remembrance of the originals, and to the imitation of them, and to offer his greeting and his reverence to them, not the actual *latria* (worship) which belonged to the Godhead alone, for the honor which is shown to the figure passes over to the original, and whoever does reverence to an image does reverence to the person represented by it.[104]

The council fathers relied on the writings of Saint John Damascene (676–749), who wrote three *apologias* in 729, defending images against the policy of Leo III. John used arguments from reason, Scripture, and the tradition of the Church. He compared icons to the Incarnation and taught that "since the invisible God took on flesh, we may make images of Christ, who was visible, and picture him in all his activities."[105] John also argued that icons are necessary for catechesis, since "what a book is to those who can read, an image is to those who cannot read. The image speaks to the sight as words to the ear; it brings us understanding."[106] Saint John Damascene's defense of images earned him the title "Doctor of Christian Art." The use of his writings by the council fathers at Nicaea ensured that a beautiful and unique Christian art form survived the heresy that threatened to rob the faithful of images.

---

104. Hefele, *A History of the Councils of the Church*, vol. V, 374–375, quoted in Carroll, *The Building of Christendom*, 317.
105. Christopher Rengers, O.F.M. Cap., *The 33 Doctors of the Church* (Rockford, IL: TAN Books and Publishers, 2000), 234.
106. Ibid., 235.

THE PHOTIAN SCHISM AND THE
FOURTH COUNCIL OF CONSTANTINOPLE

In the year 858, Emperor Michael III (r. 842–867), nicknamed "the Drunkard," deposed Patriarch Ignatius of Constantinople because the emperor had been accused of incest and the bishop refused to give the emperor Communion as a result.[107] In his place, Michael appointed a layman, Photius, patriarch of Constantinople. Subsequently, Photius sent a letter to the pope, announcing his appointment, but Pope Saint Nicholas the Great (r. 858–867) was confused. He wanted to know what happened to his friend Ignatius, so he sent legates to the imperial capital to investigate. The legates were bribed by Photius to bring a favorable report back to the pope. However, Nicholas was not easily duped. The pope was known for his unwavering orthodoxy and steadfastness in the midst of controversy.[108]

Pope Nicholas, not content with the report from his bribed legates, responded to Photius's letter:

> We do not number Ignatius among the deposed, and as long as we are not in a position to ascertain, in all truth, his offense and his guilt, we refuse to pass sentence of condemnation; for we must beware lest an innocent man be condemned on false pretenses. As the Roman Church maintains him in his dignity, if no accusation against him is substantiated, so also she re-

---

107. Duffy, *Saints and Sinners*, 102.

108. A few years earlier, he had resisted the power of Lothair of Lorraine and demanded he hold to his valid marriage to Theutberga, the daughter of the Duke of Burgundy. Lothair, disappointed in his wife's failure to produce children, had divorced Theutberga on false charges of incest. Lothair married his concubine (who had already given him three children). Lothair convinced a synod of Frankish bishops to recognize the divorce, but Theutberga appealed to the pope, who ruled in her favor. The archbishops of Cologne and Trier arrived in Rome with the decree from the synod, supporting Lothair's divorce. Pope Nicholas responded by excommunicating the archbishops. The pope held firm, even when Emperor Louis II (r. 844–875), Lothair's brother, laid siege to Rome in order to change Nicholas's decision. Nicholas's defense of marriage and papal independence "made it unmistakably clear to all Christendom that kings as well as Christians were under the law of Christ and that his Vicar would enforce his law." See Carroll, *The Building of Christendom*, 351.

fuses to admit you to patriarchal honors, as you have come by them in reckless defiance of the traditions of the Fathers.[109]

Emperor Michael was not pleased with Nicholas's response and wrote to the pope, reminding him that the ecclesiastical affairs of the Church in Constantinople were not his concern, and threatening to attack Rome if Nicholas refused to ratify Photius' appointment. Nicholas was not persuaded by the emperor's threats. Photius, in 867, with the support of the emperor, issued a decree excommunicating Pope Nicholas and declared him deposed from his see for his meddling in the affairs of the Church in Constantinople (although the pope had died, unbeknownst to Photius). The Eastern Church was now in schism, since the patriarch was no longer in communion with the Roman Pontiff.[110] A month after Photius's schismatic actions, a palace coup initiated by Basil the Macedonian resulted in the death of Emperor Michael III and the restoration of Ignatius as patriarch. The new Emperor Basil wrote to Pope Adrian II (r. 867–872) suggesting an ecumenical council to definitively decide the Photius-Ignatius issue. The Fourth Council of Constantinople met in the year 869 and excommunicated Photius for his schismatic act (he later repented and was reconciled to the Church). The next council would not meet for more than 250 years. Pope Nicholas the Great was a man of integrity, a patient teacher, a defender of orthodoxy, an advocate of papal authority, and a saint. He and Pope Adrian III (r. 884–884) were the only saintly pontiffs in the 182 years from 867–1049, and Nicholas was the last pope to be given the title "the Great."[111]

---

109. Ibid., 356.

110. Photius also accused the pope of embracing heresy for accepting the *filioque*, which affirmed the Holy Spirit processed from the Father *and* the Son — a phrase that had been added to the Nicene Creed in the West in the sixth century in response to Arianism.

111. Although many Catholics acknowledge Pope Saint John Paul II (r. 1978–2005) as "the Great," most historians have not yet made that determination.

THE SLIDE TOWARDS CHAOS

Christian Europe in the ninth and tenth centuries was marked by violent physical struggle. These were times of attacks by Muslims, Magyars, and Vikings, which disrupted European society and contributed to the development of feudalism.

Muslim marauders terrorized the coastal areas of the Mediterranean Sea, disrupting European commerce, and, as mentioned earlier, were engaged in combat operations on the Italian mainland. The Magyars were a nomadic people who specialized in mobile military strikes. In the late ninth century they crossed the Carpathian Mountains and attacked German territory in a series of military raids. They achieved military successes in northern Italy, German areas, as well as Byzantine territory. However, they suffered a devastating defeat at the Battle of Lechfeld in 955, which halted their rampage through Europe. The bishop Piligrim of Passau eventually converted the tribe in the late tenth century. They settled along the Danube, forming the territory known as Hungary.

The Vikings began attacking England in the late eighth century and received their name from the Old English word for "robbers." They were pagans who practiced infanticide by throwing unwanted babies over the sides of their ships into the sea. Charlemagne had encountered the Vikings in 804 during his last campaign against the Saxons. Though he had sensed the danger of these people from the north, he was not equipped with a navy to effectively defend against their raiding. Numerous chronicles tell the tale of the Vikings who raided the English coast as well as France, raping, pillaging, destroying, and killing all in their path, especially targeting monasteries.[112] In the middle of the ninth century, a group of Vikings attacked the city of Nantes, broke into the cathedral during Mass, killed everyone inside, looted the city, and burned down the cathe-

---

112. Monasteries were particular targets because they were large structures, often conveniently located on coastlines, with plenty of moveable wealth.

dral. A few years later, the Vikings sailed down the Seine River with 120 ships and attacked Paris on Easter Sunday. They even built wooden siege towers to enter and sack the city.[113] These savage Northmen ravaged Christian Europe for 200 years, but were eventually converted by the efforts of Olaf Tryggvason (r. 995–1000), king of Norway, in the late tenth century, ending the incessant and disruptive raiding. Even after their eventual conversion, they found it difficult to fully accept the Faith — late medieval Viking gravestones have Christian symbols on one side and symbols of Wotan on the other (which is "called hedging your bets").[114]

European society changed as a result of the devastating raids of the ninth century. The protection desired by the population against the Muslims, Magyars, and Vikings came at the price of "subordination, subjection, and dependence," and led to the establishment of a class of people who could afford to purchase weapons and who had the time to learn to use them: the nobility.[115] Society gradually transitioned from being "taxed and administered by a regular government, to a society of fighting nobles and their descendants, organized upon a basis of independence and in a hierarchy of lord and overlord."[116] Feudal society revolved around the verbal pledge of allegiance and military service, known as the oath. The lord invested his vassal with a fief (a grant of land) in an "investiture ceremony" that involved the presentation of a staff, sword, spear, or other symbol of the transfer of land.[117] The vassal, in exchange for the fief, promised fealty and military service to the lord. The backbone of feudalism was the serf, who was not a slave but was recognized as a person with certain limited rights. The serf had the

113. John France, *Western Warfare in the Age of the Crusades, 1000–1300* (Ithaca, NY: Cornell University Press, 1999), 117.
114. Kenneth Clark, *Civilisation: A Personal View* (New York: Harper & Row, 1969), 14.
115. Barraclough, 86–87.
116. Belloc, *Europe and the Faith*, 136–137.
117. Uta-Renate Blumenthal, *The Investiture Controversy: Church and Monarchy from the Ninth to the Twelfth Century* (Philadelphia: University of Pennsylvania Press, 1995 [1988]), 28.

right to a family (slaves did not) and the right to hunt certain animals (boar and rabbits but not deer) for food.[118] Serfs were given tenure, which could be inherited. They also received their own small personal parcel of land in exchange for working most of their time on the lord's land. Serfs were stewards of the land only, and did not have the right to sell it. Their life of hard labor was difficult, but they received many benefits, including up to one hundred days of rest during the celebration of holy days and saints' feasts.[119] The lord promised his serfs a working mill (in order to make flour for bread) and a church and priest for their spiritual needs. The vassal owed military service to his lord, who, in turn, owed the same to the king. The feudal king was not an absolute monarch; rather, he was the overlord of other lords. He could not decree general laws, collect taxes on the whole kingdom, or levy an army.[120] Although feudal society provided protection and an organized manner of life, it depended on personal relationships and land, which made it unsteady — relationships could be influenced by emotions and changing circumstances.

Despite the social transition, all was not dark and horrible in the early Middle Ages, as is often portrayed. Agricultural advances improved the quality of life, allowing for increased production with less labor, which allowed people to focus on other tasks. Most significant was the moldboard plow that permitted the ability to work heavier and more productive soils. Europeans also created the horse collar, which enabled a faster and stronger animal than the ox to pull plows; and they developed the three-field system of agriculture, which left one field fallow on a rotating basis, allowing for better usage and restoration of the land.

---

118. Norman F. Cantor, *In the Wake of the Plague: The Black Death and the World It Made* (New York: Harper Perennial, 2002), 70.
119. Pursell, 145.
120. Régine Pernoud, *Those Terrible Middle Ages: Debunking the Myths*, trans. Anne Englund Nash (San Francisco: Ignatius Press, 2000 [1977]), 77.

THE YEAR OF HORROR

Social changes rippled across all levels and institutions, including the papacy, which witnessed a dark and tumultuous time in the ninth and tenth centuries. From the death of Pope Saint Nicholas the Great in 867 to the year 920, fifteen popes reigned, of whom four were murdered, with several more possibly suffering the same fate.[121] John VIII (r. 872–882) was bludgeoned to death by a member of his court; Stephen VII (r. 896–897) was strangled; Leo V (r. 903) was murdered by his successor; and John X (r. 914–928) was suffocated. The papacy became a pawn in the power politics of various noble Italian families, who saw the office as a position of power and temporal influence, rather than a spiritual office exercised for the welfare of the people of God. At the end of the ninth century, the papacy was witness to one of the most bizarre and macabre scenes in Church history.

Pope Formosus' (r. 891–896) five-year pontificate was dominated by the political situation of determining who would rule as Holy Roman Emperor. Formosus kept switching support among the four main claimants, which produced general discord and displeasure with the pope. Formosus died on Easter Sunday in the year 896 at the age of 80. His successor, Boniface VI, reigned for only two weeks before his death and was replaced by Stephen VII (r. 896–897). One of the rival claimants to the imperial title, Lambert II of Spoleto, entered Rome in 897 and demanded Stephen VII place Formosus, his deceased predecessor, on trial for alleged violations of canon law. Lambert wanted to make an example out of Formosus's waffling, while also illustrating the power of the secular sphere over the papacy. Unfortunately, Pope Stephen VII agreed to Lambert's demands. The corpse of Pope Formosus was exhumed, dressed in pontifical robes with his hair shirt underneath, and propped up in a seat for the trial. Since the dead pontiff could not speak in his defense, a deacon was appointed as his

---

121. Carroll, *The Building of Christendom*, 369.

lawyer. The trial was swift and Pope Stephen VII pronounced the corpse guilty. The pontifical robes were stripped off the body and three fingers of the right hand were cut off. The corpse was then dragged through the church of Saint Peter and thrown into a grave. Grave robbers later dug up the corpse and threw it into the Tiber River. A few months later, Pope Stephen VII was arrested, thrown into a dungeon, and strangled. The next two popes reigned for short periods (four months for Romanus and twenty days for Theodore II). Finally, John IX (r. 898–900) was elected, and he annulled and condemned the macabre event known as the "Synod of the Corpse."

The trouble in Rome during the ninth century continued into the tenth as the papacy lost its independence from secular control. Various noble families competed to control the papacy and have their members elected to the Chair of Saint Peter. One brazen example is provided by Alberc II, the duke of Spoleto, who, on his deathbed in 955, made his vassals swear an oath to ensure that his son, Octavian, became pope. The nobles granted Alberic's dying wish, installing Octavian as pope that same year. Octavian was only eighteen years old, and he took the name John. Previously, only one other pope — John II in 553 — had changed his name upon assuming the papacy, but this practice became the norm in the eleventh century. Octavian, now John XII (r. 955–963), was a very bad pope. He was "bold and brash as a pagan, addicted to hunting, hawking, and gambling; and [was] often immorally involved with women."[122] John's raucous lifestyle took its toll — the young pope died at the age of twenty-seven, allegedly while in bed with a married woman.[123] Before his death, John XII requested the aid of Otto, king of the Germans (known as Otto I, the Great) against the powerful nobleman Berengar of Ivrea, who was threatening the papacy. Otto marched his army to Rome, where John XII crowned him emperor in the year 962.

---

122. Carroll, *The Building of Christendom*, 416.
123. Duffy, *Saints and Sinners*, 105.

Otto's coronation as Holy Roman Emperor was significant because the title had been vacant for nearly a generation — in a game of politics with various Italian families, the popes had refused to anoint an emperor. Otto was a devout Catholic who was married to the granddaughter of King Alfred the Great of England. Otto's reign in Germany as emperor brought stability to central Europe; the dynasty he established united the imperial title with the rulers of German territory, and he once more gave the papacy a protector against scheming Italian noble families. The emperor favored the Church and used educated clergy as advisers. Otto contracted a fever in 973 and died at the age of sixty. Otto's reign was another bright light in a time of chaos. The relationship between the Holy Roman Emperor and the papacy, at times marked by both cooperation and conflict, would continue to dominate Church history in the following centuries.

CLUNY AND THE BEGINNING OF REFORM

In the early tenth century, Duke William of Aquitaine donated land for the construction of a monastery. William was grieved by a sin committed earlier in his life; in a fit of rage, he had killed a man. His desire to found a new monastery was partly influenced by the yearning for monks to pray for his soul after death. This action was not unique for the time period, but his choice of Berno, the abbot of a strict Benedictine community in Baume, as leader of the new monastery, was momentous. Many monasteries had become lax and worldly, but Berno was dedicated to reform and desired to return to the strict following of Saint Benedict's *Rule*. William allowed Berno to choose the land for the new monastery. The reform-minded monk picked an area in east-central France near the town of Cluny.

During the time of the Roman Empire, the Church had been centrally managed — monasteries and churches, along with their personnel and property, were subject to the local bishop. After the collapse of the central governing authority from Rome in the late fifth century, the Church was organized at a lower local level, with monasteries and churches subject to their landowner, which resulted in a loss of episcopal influence and oversight.[124] This resulted in more secular interference in monastic affairs, especially since monasteries were the economic engines in the early medieval period.[125] William desired a different path for Cluny. He wanted the monks to follow Berno's reform and to focus on spiritual, not temporal, matters. So, when he established the charter granting the land for the monastery at Cluny, William placed the temporal lordship of the land in the hands of the pope, freeing the monks from local temporal interference. In terms of spiritual matters, the monastery was still initially subject to the authority of the local ordinary. But, in 1024, the monastery received full freedom from diocesan jurisdiction by the pope.[126] This temporal and spiritual freedom from local control allowed the monastery at Cluny to flourish and properly pursue Berno's program of reform.

Cluny became a beacon for all those who desired to faithfully follow the Benedictine path to holiness. Eventually, Cluny grew in numbers and sent monks to establish other monasteries throughout Europe. These "daughter-houses" numbered 1,500 at the height of Cluny's power, and they were subject to the abbot of Cluny's authority. This placed significant power in the hands of the abbot of Cluny, who became one of the most important persons in all Christendom. The monastery constructed what was the largest church in Christendom until the sixteenth century Saint Peter's Basilica in Rome.[127] The monastery also housed one of the largest libraries in Christendom and was a center of learning and monastic reform. Cluny also influenced the Church liturgically. Abbot Odilo (c. 962–1049) mandated that a special Mass be cele-

---

124. Blumenthal, 5.
125. Benedict required his monks to work, which resulted in monasteries producing commercial items such as manuscripts, but also foodstuffs like wine, cheese, eggs, etc.
126. Ibid., 11.
127. Unfortunately, most of the magnificent church was destroyed during the anti-Catholic French Revolution in the eighteenth century.

brated in the monastery each year on November 2 to commemorate the monastery's dead. Eventually, this memorial became known as All Souls' Day and was placed on the Church's universal liturgical calendar. Cluny's influence gained new heights when three of its monks were elected to the papacy: Saint Gregory VII (r. 1073–1085), Blessed Urban II (r. 1088–1099), and Paschal II (r. 1099–1118).[128] These men made the Cluniac reform a universal Church reform that produced more faithful monasteries and an independent papacy.

The several centuries following the collapse of central governing authority from Rome had witnessed significant change in European society and difficult times. But there were many bright lights as the family of God developed a new society, preserved the civilization of the Greeks and Romans, and spread the Gospel to new places and peoples. The family had changed and suffered setbacks and heartbreak, but it was intact, ready to emerge into the glory of Christendom.

---

128. Cluny produced another pope in the fourteenth century, Blessed Urban V (r. 1363–1370).

FIVE

Cathedrals and Crusades

"It is a sign that man loves God, when he casts aside the world. It is a sure sign that he burns with love for God and with zeal when for God's sake he leaves his fatherland, possessions, houses, sons, and wife to go across the sea in the service of Jesus Christ."[1]

EUDES OF CHÂTEAUROUX

His mother had a strong devotion to the Blessed Virgin Mary and handed on that devotion to her son. The young man made a decision: he would leave the world and join a monastery. His decision was not motivated by a desire to flee his family; rather, this young man, one of seven children born to noble parents near Dijon, Burgundy, desired to more fully live out his love for God and the Blessed Mother. He wanted to join

---

1. Eudes of Châteauroux, "Sermo I," 130–132 in Crusade Propaganda and Ideology, ed. Christoph T. Maier (Cambridge, 2000), 184, quoted in Jonathan Riley-Smith, The Crusades, Christianity, and Islam (New York: Columbia University Press, 2008), 40–41.

a monastic order that was motivated by that same desire, so he chose the "white Benedictines," a reform-minded group that emphasized the strict interpretation and life of Saint Benedict's *Rule*. This group of monks was known as the Cistercians, from their original monastery's location near the village of Cîteaux in Burgundy. The young man's love and desire to join the monastery were contagious, and he appeared at Cîteaux with thirty companions, including four of his brothers and an uncle! When the twenty-year-old nobleman arrived at the monastery, he could not have known that he would become one of the most well-known men of his time and one of the most celebrated saints in Church history. Bernard did not seek fame, but rather service, through founding a famous monastery at Clairvaux; preaching the Second Crusade; and writing theological works, practical pastoral books, hymns, and prayers to Mary. He was one of the most remarkable men in a remarkable age of cathedrals and Crusades.

BUILDINGS FOR THE GLORY OF GOD

After the difficult times of struggle and chaos, Western civilization entered into a new phase during the eleventh and twelfth centuries, which was marked by intense activity in the military, spiritual, and intellectual areas. Additionally, technological advances were made that allowed for the building of immense structures dedicated to the glory of God: the cathedrals. Architectural and artisan techniques flourished during this period, resulting in magnificent churches throughout Christendom designed to lift man's gaze to the heavens. Intricate stained-glass windows, statuary, and paintings catechized the faithful about the Old Testament, Christ, and the saints, especially the Blessed Virgin Mary. An apt example of a town in this era is Chartres, an important religious and educational center in the twelfth and thirteenth centuries. The inhabitants of Chartres were a deeply religious people, who built a glorious Gothic cathedral over the course of nearly three decades, even harnessing themselves to carts to man-haul stone from the quarry during its construction.[2] The Chartres cathedral contained many relics venerated by the people and pilgrims from throughout Christendom, the most famous of which was the *sainte chemise*, or the robe, Mary wore when visited by the Archangel Gabriel during the Annunciation. Charles the Bald, grandson of Charlemagne, gave the relic to the town in 876. Its placement in the spectacular cathedral sparked the interest of pilgrims who traveled throughout Christendom to venerate the holy article and helped contribute to the spread of devotion to the Blessed Mother throughout the medieval period.[3] Each year during the octave of Pentecost the people of Chartres participated in a large diocesan pilgrimage, which united a mixed crowd of people from different social backgrounds. The cathedrals represent the great faith of medieval people and solidified this period of history as the Age of Faith.

SAINT PETER DAMIAN AND THE REFORM OF THE CLERGY

The promise of celibacy freely taken by the clergy dates back to the early Church and is based in Christian doctrine and tradition. As an ecclesial discipline, celibacy developed through the centuries. In the first three centuries of Church history, no law prohibited the ordination of married men, and many priests were married; however, marriage after ordination was never permitted.[4] Moreover, *all* priests — married, single, or widowed — practiced sexual abstinence after ordination. The first recorded Church legislation mandating clerical celibacy in the West was decreed at the Synod of Elvira in Spain around the year 300, and in the year 385, Pope Siricius (r. 384-399) mandated celibacy for all clergy in the West.

Despite the long-standing practice of the Church, celibacy

2. Kenneth Clark, *Civilisation: A Personal View* (New York: Harper & Row, Publishers, 1969), 56.
3. Ibid., 58.
4. This was true in both the Eastern and Western Churches. See Warren H. Carroll, *The Building of Christendom: A History of Christendom*, vol. 2 (Front Royal, VA: Christendom College Press, 1987), 97.

was often not lived faithfully in the early medieval era.[5] Pope Benedict VIII (r. 1012–1024) held a synod at Pavia, where he reinforced the rule of clerical celibacy and denounced the scandal of clerical marriage. By the time of Pope Saint Leo IX (r. 1049–1054), a lack of chastity among monks and the clergy, especially secular (diocesan) priests, was widespread. Many priests had not been properly trained or formed, and priests took mistresses and concubines who bore them children, causing terrible scandal. Moreover, priests engaged in sinful homosexual acts, and bishops and abbots seemed hesitant to act and restore virtue to the priesthood and monasteries. However, the Holy Spirit raised up a man whose divine mission was to end the scandal and put the Church's clergy on the path to authentic reform.

Peter was born in Ravenna and was orphaned while still a baby. An older brother and his concubine took him in, but they were cruel to Peter, starving and beating him. Peter was sent to work as a swineherd. Despite the hardships and abuse, Peter displayed virtue, charity, and a profound love for his deceased parents; he even gave a priest a precious coin he had found in the field so that a Mass could be offered for the repose of his parents' souls.[6] Peter found refuge from the drudgery and abuse when another older brother took him into his home. This brother loved and cared for Peter and sent him to school, where he proved to be a bright and diligent student. Peter was so grateful that he took his brother's name and became known as Peter Damian.[7] When Peter was twenty-eight, he joined the monastery and dedicated his life to the reform of the religious life and secular clergy. He was a lucid and persuasive writer and had a deep devotion to the

---

5. Medieval is another word for Middle Ages, as it derives from the Latin *medium+aevum* or middles age/era. Historians differ on the exact years of the Middle Ages (and some argue the term should not be used at all) but generally they encompass the time period of 500–1300. For a greater discussion about the term, its dating, and the impact on culture see Marcus Bull, *Thinking Medieval: An Introduction to the Study of the Middle Ages* (New York: Palgrave MacMillian, 2005).
6. Tom Holland, *The Forge of Christendom: The End of Days and the Epic Rise of the West* (New York: Doubleday, 2008), 337–338.
7. Matthew Cullinan Hoffman, trans., *The Book of Gomorrah and St. Peter Damian's Struggle Against Ecclesiastical Corruption* (New Braunfels, TX: Ite ad Thomam Books and Media, 2015), 10.

Cross of Christ, even describing himself as "Peter, servant of the servants of the Cross of Christ."[8]

Peter's love for the Cross led him to clamor for the reform of the clergy, calling for a more fervent living of the promise of celibacy. He wrote a letter to Pope Leo IX, exhorting him to root out the evil of sexual sins, including the taking of mistresses and homosexuality, from the clergy.[9] These sins were a plague in the Church, a "diabolical tyranny" that produced a "cancer of sodomitic impurity."[10] Peter condemned the perversion practiced by some members of the clergy in stark language, calling those who engage in homosexual acts "degenerate men [who] do not fear to perpetuate an act that even brute animals abhor. That which is done by the temerity of human depravity is condemned by the judgment of irrational cattle."[11] Peter not only condemned the sexual sins of the clergy, but also expressed deep compassion for those who had fallen — he desired their conversion and reconciliation to God and the Church. He advised brother priests who struggled with sexual sins and who were tempted by the devil to "immediately turn [your] eyes to the graves of the dead."[12] Pope Leo IX, who was dedicated to reform, favorably received Peter's letter and adopted many of his recommendations. Peter Damian's tireless efforts to reform the Church helped restore the quality of clergy.[13]

THE PAPAL REFORM MOVEMENT

Expelling sexual deviancy and immorality among the clergy was only one part of a large reform movement initiated in the Church

8. Benedict XVI, Wednesday General Audience on Saint Peter Damian, September 9, 2009, in *Church Fathers and Teachers: From Saint Leo the Great to Peter Lombard* (San Francisco: Ignatius Press, 2010), 136.
9. His letter is known as *The Book of Gomorrah*, although that was a title given to it in the fourteenth century.
10. Hoffman, 82.
11. Ibid., 129.
12. Ibid., 149.
13. Peter died in 1072 and was declared a Doctor of the Church in 1823 by Pope Leo XII.

by a series of popes in the mid-eleventh century. Eleven of the nineteen popes from 1073 to 1205 had spent time in the monastery and were free from the ecclesial abuses of simony, corruption, and lack of chastity prevalent in the secular clergy. These men were dedicated to establishing an independent papacy, free from secular control and interference and guided by the principle that "the Church shall be Catholic, chaste and free: Catholic in the faith and fellowship of the saints, chaste from all contagion of evil, and free from secular power."[14] The reform movement was initially centered on the papacy and a reorganization of the papal bureaucracy, which was centered on cardinals, who had become more prominent in the administration of the papal curia (court). Recognizing that the reform could not be permanent unless the papacy was free from secular interference and control, the reformers focused initially on changing the method of papal election.

For the first several centuries of Church history, the pope had been elected by the clergy and people of Rome, but in the tenth century powerful Roman aristocratic families appointed popes. Papal elections became farcical as families intrigued, bribed, and battled each other for control of the papacy, frequently resulting in a less than ideal candidate. The papacy became a pawn in the power politics of Roman families. The stature and effectiveness of the office of the universal shepherd was weakened. In the mid-eleventh century, the Holy Roman Emperor Henry III proposed a new method of election and convinced the reigning pontiff, Clement II, to accept it. Henry proposed that the emperor would nominate the pope. Although this method eliminated the power politics of the various Roman families, it was dangerously close to the *caesaro-papism* practiced in the east. The emperor had power over the Church, which in the hands of a virtuous and devout ruler could produce an acceptable papal candidate, but in

---

14. This quote is from Blessed Pope Urban II, one of the main reformers of this age, quoted in C. Morris, *The Papal Monarchy: The Western Church from 1050 to 1250* (Oxford, UK; Clarendon Press, 1991), 125, quoted in Eamon Duffy, *Saints and Sinners: A History of the Popes* (New Haven, CT: Yale University Press, 2006), 128.

other hands could produce the opposite effect. The emperor-appointed method was replaced in 1059 by a new electoral method developed by a monk named Hildebrand, adviser to Pope Nicholas II (r. 1058–1061) and the future Pope Saint Gregory VII. Hildebrand proposed that all secular and lay involvement in papal elections cease, and the responsibility be placed in the hands of the cardinals instead. Pope Nicholas agreed and issued a decree stipulating that the College of Cardinals would henceforth be charged with electing a new pope when the see became vacant.[15]

Now that papal elections were secure from secular interference, the papal reformers shifted their efforts toward the highly unstable papal finances. The bulk of funds used to support the pope and the curia came from the Papal States, which were always susceptible to invasion by powerful secular lords. The reformers wanted to develop more secure and independent revenue streams, so they instituted various fees for papal privileges and exemptions. Archbishops paid a fee to receive the pallium. Monasteries and churches that were under papal protection paid a census tax. Kingdoms and fiefs held by the pope paid feudal dues, and in some areas of Christendom a papal tax was levied on all churches and sent to Rome.[16] Although the establishment of these various taxes and fees was intended to secure an independent papacy, they would in fact lay the foundation for serious abuse in later centuries and eventually contribute to the sixteenth-century Protestant Revolt.

THE REFORM POPE

Bruno of Alsace had been noted for his piety before his papal election, which delighted those who desired reform in the Church. Taking the name Leo IX, the pope pursued three major issues during his pontificate: Church reform, the protection of the Papal States from the Normans, and the resolution of disputes with

---

15. This method, with slight modifications to the voting procedures, is still currently used for papal elections.
16. See Duffy, *Saints and Sinners*, 134.

the Byzantines.[17] With great zeal, the pope launched one of the most comprehensive reforms in Church history. Leo understood that authentic reform could not be simply mandated from afar but must be implemented locally, so he traveled throughout Italy, Germany, and France, holding synods.[18] Wherever he went, Pope Leo IX deposed immoral bishops and punished clerics engaged in simony, infidelity, and unchastity. His reform initiatives positively affected the Church, but were hampered by Leo's need to deal with the movement of the Normans against the Papal States.

The Normans were the conquerors of the eleventh century. Descendants of the Vikings who had ravaged Europe centuries earlier, the Normans continued their forefathers' military prowess and vicious raiding. Desiderius of Monte Cassino noted that the Normans "possess an insatiable enthusiasm for seizing what belongs to others."[19] William, Duke of Normandy, sailed a Norman invasion force across the English Channel in 1066, and, at great risk and daring, won the crown of England by defeating King Harold at the Battle of Hastings. The Normans invaded Sicily in the eleventh century and engaged in several independent military campaigns over the next several decades, eventually invading the Italian mainland as well. The presence of the Normans in Italy threatened the Papal States and the independence of the papacy. Pope Leo IX's hard work to reform the Church and keep the papacy free from secular control was endangered, so he raised an army to push them out of Italy. The papal army fought the Norman army, which was commanded by Robert Guiscard ("the Cunning One"), at the Battle of Civitate in 1053. Pope Leo was present with the army and refused a Norman offer of peace, primarily because the papal army greatly outnumbered the Normans. Despite their numerical inferiority, the Normans defeated the papal army, and Pope Leo IX

---

17. See Uta-Renate Blumenthal, *The Investiture Controversy: Church and Monarchy from the Ninth to the Twelfth Century* (Philadelphia: University of Pennsylvania Press, 1995 [1988]), 73.
18. Leo was so focused on reform that he spent only six months of his five-and-a-half-year pontificate in Rome!
19. Desiderius of Monte Cassino, *Dialogi de Miraculis Sancti Benedicti* in *Monumenta Germaniae Historica Scriptores* 30/2 (Leipzig, 1934), quoted in Holland, *The Forge of Christendom*, 272.

was taken captive. The pope was a prisoner of Robert Guiscard for nine months, eventually being released after recognizing the Norman conquests in Italy. He died shortly after returning to Rome. During Leo's captivity, significant problems developed between the western and eastern halves of the Church, which resulted in the first major separation of Christians. This division was avoidable but "occurred, more than for any other reason, because the pope was almost powerless to control or prevent it."[20]

THE GREAT SCHISM

Tension between the eastern and western halves of the Church had been building for centuries. The distinction between groups of Christians into East and West originated in Roman Emperor Diocletian's division of the Empire in the late third century. Constantine had moved the imperial capital to a new city at the former Byzantium (later renamed Constantinople) in the fourth century, which began a long process of Eastern assertion of superiority over the West. Besides the political situation, theological controversies impacted the relationship between East and West. Most of the heresies in the early Church developed in the East, and while Western bishops maintained the orthodox faith, the same could not be said of most of their Eastern counterparts. Church governance also developed differently in the two areas of the Empire. In the East, the emperor played a prominent role and viewed the Church as an organ of state. In many ways, the Eastern bishops acquiesced to imperial interference. When central governing authority from Rome collapsed in the West in the late fifth century, the pope became predominant in ecclesial and temporal affairs. As the centuries progressed, the East resolutely drew away from the West, and looked down upon the pope and Rome. Eastern bishops were angered by the addition of the *filioque* clause ("the Holy Spirit proceeds from the Father *and*

---

20. Carroll, *The Building of Christendom*, 478.

the Son") to the Nicene Creed, which had been an effort from Western bishops to combat Arianism.[21] The West was wary of the East due to numerous theological controversies, including iconoclasm and the Photian schism. The situation reached a boiling point during the patriarchy of Michael Cerularius (r. 1043–1058), the anti-western bishop of Constantinople, a "prickly, irascible, and intransigent" man who issued a decree in 1052 requiring all churches in Constantinople to follow Eastern liturgical practices, such as the use of leavened bread for the host at Mass.[22] Cerularius's decree, in effect, outlawed the celebration of the Latin Rite Mass in the imperial capital.

When news of Cerularius's decree reached Rome, Pope Leo IX directed his adviser, Cardinal Humbert, to write a reply to the patriarch. Leo did not know Greek (very few people in the west did at the time), but Humbert did. The cardinal was well-educated and a highly valued papal adviser, but the situation demanded a cool diplomatic personality, someone who listened more than talked and who practiced the virtues of discernment and prudence. Unfortunately, Humbert was hot-tempered, easily offended, and a zealous supporter of the papacy and Western Church. Leo IX realized the situation was too delicate and volatile to handle with written correspondence, so he sent a delegation to Constantinople in January 1054 with Humbert as lead ambassador. Humbert's temper was in full display in the imperial capital as he engaged in pen wars with Eastern churchmen. Nicetas Stethatos, a Byzantine monk, wrote Humbert, criticizing the Western use of unleavened bread:

---

21. The clause was originally added in Spain and then gradually accepted by the Church in the rest of the West. The Diocese of Rome was the last to accept the addition.

22. Holland, *The Forge of Christendom*, 279. The Byzantines took serious issue with the Western practice of using unleavened bread, which was based on the Jewish practice at Passover. Eastern theologians voiced the opinion that the use of unleavened bread was invalid matter. One bishop sent a letter to Pope Leo IX in 1053, accosting the pontiff for allowing the use of unleavened bread: "Straighten yourself out! Correct your errors! Abandon unleavened bread in order to put yourself in accord with true orthodoxy!" (E. Amann, "Michel Céulaire" in *Dictionnaire de Théologie catholique* X (2), 1683, quoted in Carroll, *The Building of Christendom*, 479.)

Those who still participate in the feast of the unleavened bread are under the shadow of the law and consume the feast of the Jews, not the spiritual and living food of God. How can you enter into communion with Christ, the living God, while eating the dead unleavened dough of the shadow of the law and not the yeast of the new covenant?[23]

Humbert responded by calling Stetatos a disciple of Muhammad.[24] While engaging in polemics with the easterners, Humbert received news in the summer of 1054 that, several months earlier, Pope Leo IX had died. This presented a crisis, as technically, the papal legates no longer had authority. Undaunted, Humbert remained in Constantinople for several more weeks. Recognizing the intransigence of Cerularius, Humbert was determined to be done with the affair. He drafted a letter of excommunication, although he had no authority to do so. The cardinal led the Western delegation to the Church of Hagia Sophia on July 16, 1054, and placed the document of excommunication on the altar. Humbert's letter made clear that Cerularius was responsible for the rift between the churches:

Being unable to bear these unprecedented injuries against the chief apostolic see, we sign against Michael and his supporters the anathema. May Michael the neophyte, who improperly bears the title patriarch and all those who follow him fall under the anathema, and all the heretics, and indeed with the devil and his angels, unless they return to their senses. Amen, Amen, Amen![25]

Michael responded to this grand insult and inappropriate gesture

23. Jean Comby, *How to Read Church History: From the Beginnings to the Fifteenth Century*, vol. I (New York: Crossroads, 2001), 132.
24. Holland, *The Forge of Christendom*, 279.
25. Comby, 133.

by burning the notice of excommunication and then issuing his own excommunication of Humbert. This action, coupled with a previous schismatic rejection of papal primacy years earlier, rendered the Church truly separated into halves.[26]

THE POPE — JUDGE OF KINGS

Nearly twenty years after the Great Schism, a new pope, who was a former monk of Cluny and adviser to Pope Nicholas II, was elected. Hildebrand, took the name Gregory and, like the first Pope Gregory, was motivated by ardent love for the Church. He knew the Church needed reform; he wanted to enforce clerical celibacy, and he sought complete independence from secular interference in Church affairs by eradicating lay appointment of clerics. Gregory VII (r. 1073–1085) spent his twelve-year pontificate struggling against secular rulers. As long as kings and princes could appoint bishops and abbots, the Church would not be free to be what she was meant to be: the City of God on earth. Gregory continued developing the "two powers" principle that had been established by Saint Ambrose in the fourth century and modified by Pope Saint Gelasius in the fifth century. Gregory VII elevated this principle by advocating that the pope is not merely responsible to God for the moral actions of secular rulers. He stipulated that the pope is the moral judge, not just the teacher, of kings, princes, and emperors. The pope has authority to absolve or condemn secular rulers and can impose either public or private sentences and penances, including excommunication, which would release a ruler's subjects from their oath of loyalty and provide moral legitimacy for open rebellion. Gregory VII enshrined this elevation of papal authority in Christendom in a series of decrees known as the *Dictatus Papae*, which stipulated that "the pope is the only man to whom all princes bend the knee; he is allowed to depose emperors; his sentence cannot be repealed by

---

26. Pope Paul VI and Patriarch Athenagoras annulled the mutual excommunications in 1965.

anyone and he alone can repeal all other sentences; and the pope must not be judged by anyone."[27]

Gregory's vision of papal authority was tested during the Investiture Controversy with Henry IV, King of the Germans (r. 1056–1105). Henry's father and grandfather had been crowned Holy Roman Emperors, but the title was not automatic; it required papal coronation. Henry believed this to be papal interference in secular affairs. His reign as king and eventual emperor was marked by near constant strife with the successors of Saint Peter (he was excommunicated a total of five times by three different popes). Pope Gregory and King Henry clashed over a particular practice established in the structure of feudal society. It was common practice in German areas for a nobleman to grant the insignia of ecclesiastical office (a ring and crozier) to bishops, saying, "Receive the church." The ring symbolized Christ's relationship to the Church, which the bishop was called to emulate; the crozier symbolized his pastoral responsibility for the faithful. The new bishop swore fealty to the secular ruler and was then ordained to the episcopacy. This ceremony was modeled on the similar secular investiture of vassals. Although the ecclesial ceremony was similar to the lay practice, the ceremony did not mean that ecclesiastical offices were considered fiefs of the secular ruler; rather, that the bishop was under the Lord's protection.[28] Despite the distinction, Pope Gregory feared the ceremony gave the appearance that the secular ruler was granting ecclesial offices and authority to the bishop, which amounted to asking whether the king or the pope truly appointed bishops. When the See of Milan fell vacant, Gregory and Henry disagreed over the selection of a suitable candidate, which, ultimately, led the pope to issue a ban against the lay investiture ceremony in 1075:

If anyone shall henceforth receive from the hand of

---

27. Comby, 137.
28. Blumenthal, 28,36.

any layman a bishopric or abbey, let him not be accounted a bishop or abbot. Further, if any emperor, duke, marquis, count, or any temporal lord, or indeed any secular power whatever, shall presume to give investiture of any bishopric or of any ecclesiastical dignity, let him understand that he is bound by the same sentence.[29]

Henry was greatly angered at Gregory's edict, viewing it as a threat to his authority and ability to govern. Recognizing the king's emotions might lead him to violence, Pope Gregory sent ambassadors to Henry to dissuade him from further action. He threatened the king with excommunication, should he not obey the ban against lay investiture. The impending conflict between the two men took a serious turn for the worse on Christmas Eve 1075, when, during Mass, Pope Gregory was violently attacked by armed men on horseback who broke into the church of Saint Mary Major. Gregory was gashed on the forehead, seized, and taken to a tower. Papal supporters rallied a group of armed men and rescued the pope in the morning. Although there was no direct evidence linking the attackers to King Henry, the general consensus was that Henry had a hand in the plot.

The king heard the words of the papal ambassadors with growing anger. He summoned an emergency imperial congress (known as a Diet) to meet in the city of Worms in 1076, where Henry denounced Gregory as a perjurer, adulterer, illegitimately elected, and a menace to the peace of Europe. The king then sent Gregory a letter that began, "to Hildebrand, at present not pope but false monk."[30] The letter was a long-winded diatribe against Gregory's actions as pope and how they impacted the king and the Church as a whole. Henry ended by advocating for Greg-

---

29. Horace K. Mann, *The Lives of the Popes in the Middle Ages*, VIII (London, 1902–1931), 78–79, quoted in Carroll, *The Building of Christendom*, 503.
30. *MG LL*, folio II, 47 ff; translated by Ernest F. Henderson, *Select Historical Documents of the Middle Ages* (London: George Bell and Sons, 1910), 372-372

ory's removal from the papacy: "Let another ascend the throne of Saint Peter, who shall not practice violence under the cloak of religion, but shall teach the sound doctrine of Saint Peter. I, Henry, king by the grace of God, do say unto thee, together with all our bishops: Descend, descend, to be damned throughout the ages."[31] Henry strongly encouraged the bishops of his realm to denounce Gregory publicly, but only one, William of Utrecht, did. Soon after the denouncement, William's cathedral was struck by lightning. A week later, the bishop suddenly suffered agonizing stomach cramps; a month later, he died.[32]

When the pope received Henry's letter, he excommunicated the king and absolved his subjects of their loyalty to him — the first (but not the last) time a pope had undertaken such a drastic action. Gregory's decree of excommunication allowed for rebellion in Germany, as vassals of the king no longer owed him fealty. Although there was some support for the overthrow of Henry, most of the nobles wanted peace. At the imperial Diet in the summer of 1076, they ordered the king to make peace with the pope or else be deposed. Several princes also asked Pope Gregory to come to the Diet the following year at Augsburg to preside over a trial of Henry. Gregory agreed to their request and began the journey, but decided to spend the winter in the northern Italian town of Canossa before crossing the Alps into German territory. When the king heard news of the pope's journey, he decided to meet with him at Canossa and reach a compromise. Henry and his party crossed the Alps in the dead of winter, at much personal risk; some members of his travel party lost limbs due to frostbite, as the winter of 1077 was severe. Henry, dressed in simple penitent's clothes, reached the castle at Canossa and begged forgiveness. Gregory forgave the king after making him wait outside the castle for three days. He may have delayed a response to Henry in order to teach him a lesson, or perhaps he was motivated out of indecision, knowing that granting

---

31. Ibid.
32. Holland, *The Forge of Christendom*, 369.

absolution would betray the German princes who supported the pope against the king. But refusing mercy to the king was a betrayal of his priestly ministry. The penitent king and the merciful pope met and were reconciled.

Unfortunately, once safe in his territory and after the threat of rebellion had subsided, the king continued his attacks against the pope and was once more excommunicated in the year 1080. This time, Henry responded by marching his army to Rome and laying siege to the city. After a protracted three-year siege, German forces breached the Roman defenses and captured the city. Gregory took refuge in Castel Sant'Angelo and waited for the Normans, with whom he had entered into an alliance, to come to the rescue. In Rome, Henry installed an antipope, who crowned him emperor, but Henry soon fled the city as the Norman army, under Robert Guiscard, marched near. The Normans arrived at Rome and proceeded to sack the city, which made Gregory an unpopular pontiff. The pope was forced to flee Rome for his own safety. He spent some time at the monastery of Monte Cassino before settling at Salerno, where he died the next year. Before his death, the saintly Gregory reminded the faithful in a letter that "my greatest concern has been that holy church, the bride of Christ, our lady and mother, should return to her true glory, and stand free, chaste, and catholic."[33]

THE CRUSADING MOVEMENT

The unique cultural and religious phenomenon of the crusading movement occupied a central place in European and Church

---

33. Gregory VII, *Epistolae Vagantes*, 54. The Investiture Controversy ended definitively with a compromise reached in the city of Worms in 1122 between Pope Callistus II (r. 1119–1124) and Henry V (r. 1111–1125) in which the king was allowed to invest candidates to the episcopacy, before their ordination, with a scepter but not the ring and crozier, and the pope allowed the presence of royal representatives at the elections of German bishops and abbots. The First Lateran Council confirmed the compromise reached at Worms, and the fifty-year struggle over this issue between king and pope came to an end.

history for nearly 600 years.[34] In essence, "a crusade was fought against those perceived to be the external or internal foes of Christendom for the recovery of Christian property or in defense of the Church or Christian people."[35] Those who participated in the Crusades were seen as pilgrims, and their journey was an armed pilgrimage. Crusaders indicated their commitment by first "taking the cross," which included a public ecclesiastical vow that bound the aspirant to undertake the armed pilgrimage. The vow was made to God (not to the pope, a bishop, or any secular lord) and was legally binding; to subsequently abandon it was to risk excommunication. They were marked by wearing a cloth cross on their garments, which would only be removed upon successful completion of their vow.

The origin of the Crusades as a movement was the papal reform program of the eleventh century, but the causes may be found in the teachings and history of Islam. Muhammad's worldview of a House of Islam versus a House of War presupposed a permanent state of war, wherein Muslims were obliged to engage in *jihad* so that the community (*umma*) could extend throughout the world. Muhammad's teachings led to the conquest of ancient Christian territory throughout the Mediterranean region. For centuries, Muslim overlords frequently harassed Christians. Although Christians were protected if they paid the annual tax (*jizya*), their status was barely above that of slaves. Christendom in its early centuries was not in a position to mount a strong defense against Islam, but the political, economic, and military situation toward the end of the eleventh century allowed a coordinated response from western knights.

Defensive campaigns to liberate ancient Christian territory from Muslim occupiers were motivated by several instances of Muslim destruction, harassment, and murder. In the early eleventh

---

34. The following sections are adapted from my book, *The Glory of the Crusades* (El Cajon, CA: Catholic Answers Press, 2014), 29–38; 42–48.
35. Jonathan Riley-Smith, *The Crusades: A History, Second Edition* (New Haven, CT: Yale University Press, 2005), xxxi.

century, Egypt was controlled by the demented caliph al-Hakim. Al-Hakim's reign was marked by bizarre regulations against his Muslim subjects and persecution against non-Muslims. He mandated Muslim women wear a veil in public, but then ordered them to not leave their homes.[36] He required all Christians and Jews to wear a black turban, and either a cross or a block of wood, in public.[37] Edicts passed in 1011 and 1012 prohibited the use of wine, even in the celebration of the Eucharist, and required the removal of all exterior crosses and destruction of all missals.[38] The persecution came to an end when al-Hakim was murdered in 1021.

In 1009, al-Hakim ordered the destruction of the Church of the Holy Sepulchre, known at the time in the Islamic world as the "church of the dung heap."[39] This destruction of one of the most important churches in Christendom and al-Hakim's persecution of indigenous Christians left a lasting imprint on the people of Europe. The danger grew exponentially for Holy Land Christians and the Byzantine Empire in the mid-eleventh century when a new group of people arrived on the world stage: the Seljuk Turks. The Seljuks were a nomadic people from the Asian steppe who had converted to Sunni Islam and consolidated their power in the Abbasid caliphate based in Baghdad. In the Holy Land, the Seljuks destroyed churches, killed priests, and harassed Western Christian pilgrims. One example of Seljuk brutality is illustrated in the story of Günther, bishop of Bamberg, who led a group of twelve thousand pilgrims to the Holy Land in 1065. The group managed to survive great trials in Hungary, mistreatment by the Byzantines, and the general discomfort and hardship involved in such a journey; but they were not to survive their

---

36. Holland, *The Forge of Christendom*, 235.

37. Ibid., 236.

38. Yahya ibn Said, ed. and trans. Ignati Kratchkovsky and Alexander Vasiliev, in *Patrologia Orientalis*, ed. René Graffin and François Nau (Paris, 1907-), 23:502—12, quoted in Andrew Jotischky, "The Christians of Jerusalem, the Holy Sepulchre and the Origins of the First Crusade," *Crusades*, vol. 7, The Society for the Study of the Crusades and the Latin East (Burlington, VT: Ashgate Publishing Company, 2008), 45.

39. Holland, *The Forge of Christendom*, 237. The church was rebuilt in 1048 and then renovated and expanded by the Crusaders after the liberation of Jerusalem.

encounter with the Seljuks, who massacred the entire group on Good Friday, only two days' march from Jerusalem.[40]

The Seljuks were not content with control of Armenia, Syria, and Palestine, soon setting their sights on Anatolia (modern-day Turkey), an important province of the Byzantine Empire. Unfortunately, the arrival of the Seljuks occurred at the worst possible time for the Byzantines, who were ruled in the latter eleventh century by a series of incompetent emperors who had allowed the army to decline. This decline in readiness was manifested at the Battle of Manzikert on August 19, 1071. Emperor Romanus IV Diogenes (r. 1068–1071) gathered a force of sixty thousand men, including western mercenaries, to fight the Turks. Despite intense fighting, the Seljuks were victorious. The Imperial Army was in shambles, the emperor had been captured, and the province that provided the bulk of military recruitment and economic prosperity was in enemy hands.

The Byzantine Empire began to recover under the vital leadership of Emperor Alexius I Comnenus (r. 1081–1118). Alexius knew that the dire threat the Seljuk Turks posed to the Empire required extreme measures and more manpower than he could raise or afford, so he sought help from the west. He sent ambassadors to the pope, the one person with the universal authority required to recruit and organize such an immense rescue effort.

RALLYING CHRISTENDOM

Blessed Pope Urban II (r. 1088–1099) had been born into a northern French noble family and, although he entered the service of the Church, he understood the martial class and how to motivate them.[41] He used this knowledge to considerable effect at the local council of French bishops at Clermont. On November 27, Urban

---

40. Jonathan Sumption, *Age of Pilgrimage: The Medieval Journey to God* (Mahwah, NJ: Hidden Spring Books, 2003), 257–258.
41. Jonathan Riley-Smith, *The Oxford Illustrated History of the Crusades* (New York: Oxford University Press, 1995), 1.

spoke to a large assembly in the open air and inaugurated the crusading movement. The pope's speech stressed three main themes: the liberation of the Holy City of Jerusalem, the violent activities of the Turks, and an exhortation to western warriors to take up arms.

The liberation of Jerusalem was paramount for Urban, and he knew this cause would resonate with the assembled French nobility and knights. There was much devotion to the Holy City in France. Pilgrimages were very popular, even among the nobles, many of whom had taken to naming their daughters "Jerusalem."[42] The Holy City was considered the center of the world. Its occupation by the Muslims was distasteful to the citizens of Christendom. Urban called the warriors to rouse from their slumber and selfish interests, to valiantly march to the east and restore ancient Christian lands (most importantly, Jerusalem) to Christ and the Church. Urban's preaching also emphasized the plight of Christians in the Holy Land who were subject to cruel tortures and punishments at the hands of the Turks. His graphic description of Turkish atrocities was designed to elicit a visceral response from his hearers so that they might take up their arms to liberate their Christian brothers and sisters.

Because participation would be voluntary, Urban needed to find ways to motivate the assembled warriors at Clermont to travel thousands of miles from home and risk certain death. Urban knew that few knights would undertake the arduous journey simply to help the schismatic Byzantine Christians. So, he appealed to the military adventures of the extraordinary warriors in French history in order to exhort his listeners to join the Crusade: "Let the deeds of your ancestors move you and incite your minds to manly achievements; Oh, most valiant soldiers and descendants of invincible ancestors, be not degenerate, but recall the valor of your progenitors."[43] Finally, Urban offered the spiritual incen-

---

42. Jonathan Riley-Smith, *The First Crusaders, 1095–1131* (Cambridge, UK: Cambridge University Press, 1997), 33.
43. Robert the Monk in Edward Peters, ed., *The First Crusade: The Chronicle of Fulcher of Chartres and Other Source Material*, Second Edition (Philadelphia: University of Pennsylvania Press, 1998), 27.

tive of a plenary indulgence for warriors who participated in the Crusade, a unique and powerful motivation. Through the power and authority of the Petrine Office, Urban decreed: "Whoever goes on the journey to free the church of God in Jerusalem out of devotion alone, and not for the gaining of glory or money, can substitute the journey for all penance for sin."[44]

Urban announced that what came to be known as the First Crusade would depart on the Feast of the Assumption of Mary, August 15, 1096, and appointed Bishop Adhemar de Monteil as leader of the expedition and the official papal representative.

RESPONDING TO THE SUMMONS

Urban knew his exhortation at Clermont would not produce enough warriors to ensure the success of the Crusade, so he planned an elaborate and lengthy road trip throughout France in order to recruit as many warriors as he could. His two-thousand-mile preaching tour required an entire year to complete, and made a huge impact on the people of France, most of whom had never seen the pope. Preachers were sent throughout Christendom, including England, Germany, Iceland, Sweden, and Italy. The response was immense. Some estimates indicate 100,000 people may have taken the cross, of whom 60,000 were warriors; of those, 6,000-7,000 were knights.[45] Although Urban desired and requested soldiers, the devotion to Jerusalem and desire for the indulgence was so widespread that large numbers of noncombatants also took the cross. Concerned for the well-being of women, Urban forbade married men from going on the Crusade without permission from their spouses.[46]

44. Canon 2 of the Council of Clermont.
45. John France, "Patronage and the Appeal of the First Crusade," in *The Crusades: The Essential Readings*, ed. Thomas F. Madden (Malden, MA: Blackwell Publishing, Ltd., 2006), 195–196.
46. J. A. Brundage, *Medieval Canon Law and the Crusader* (Madison: University of Wisconsin Press, 1969), 77, quoted in Norman Housley, *Contesting the Crusades* (Malden, MA: Blackwell Publishing, 2006), 15.

WHY DID THEY GO?

Although there is no simple explanation for the overwhelming response to Urban's call for the Crusade, one factor outweighs all others and provides the most meaningful answer: faith. Medieval people were steeped in the Catholic faith; it permeated every aspect of society and their daily lives. They saw Urban's call to the Crusade as a unique, once-in-a-lifetime opportunity to provide for their spiritual health and increase their chance of salvation. In this vicious and violent age, most laymen, especially the nobility, believed it was extremely difficult for those not in a monastery to go to heaven. The Church constantly warned warriors that warfare over land holdings against fellow Christians placed their souls in danger, providing sufficient motivation for many to take the cross.

Faith and love of God, neighbor, and self were the main reasons why medieval people participated in the Crusades. The knightly brothers Geoffrey and Guy indicated they were going to Jerusalem for "both the grace of the pilgrimage under the protection of God, to exterminate wickedness and unrestrained rage of the pagans by which innumerable Christians have already been oppressed, made captive and killed."[47] Odo of Burgundy explained that he undertook "the journey to Jerusalem as a penance for my sins ... since divine mercy inspired me that owing to the enormity of my sins I should go to the Sepulchre of Our Savior, in order that this offering of my devotion might be more acceptable in the sight of God."[48]

Popes, preachers, and saints throughout the crusading movement emphasized in their exhortations that service in God's army was born from love of God, love of neighbor, and concern for one's salvation. At Clermont, Urban urged knights to sacrifice themselves for Christ, as the Lord had done for them: "It ought to be

---

47. *Recueil des chartes de l'abbaye de Cluny*, ed. A Bruel, v (Paris 1894), 51-3, no. 3703; *Cartulaire de l'abbaye de Saint-Victor de Marseille*, ed. M. Guérard (Paris 1857), I, 167—168, no. 143, quoted in Christopher Tyerman, *God's War: A New History of the Crusades* (Cambridge, MA: Belknap Press, 2006), 27
48. Giles Constable, "Medieval Charters as a Source for the History of the Crusades," in *The Crusades: The Essential Readings*, ed. Madden, 148.

a beautiful ideal for you to die for Christ in that city where Christ died for you."[49] The chronicler Guibert of Nogent aptly summarized the purpose of the Crusade and why warriors took the cross when he wrote, "The Crusader set himself the task of winning back the earthly Jerusalem in order to enjoy the celestial Jerusalem."[50]

While the testimonies found in these written records is compelling, it is nonetheless wise to recognize that human motivations are usually complex and not always pure and virtuous. Some who went on the Crusade probably hoped they would benefit materially, although the historical record reflects the vast majority did not. Crusade expeditions were comprised of large bodies of warriors under the authority of their own lord. Although they may have been primarily motivated by holy reasons, they were not all saints. "They were men of the sword: pious and idealistic, but also crude, arrogant and at times savage."[51] Crusaders went to war not only for reasons that men have gone to war for centuries — glory, adventure, love of country — but also because they embraced the Crusade as a unique opportunity to participate in their salvation and give a witness of their love for God.

THE FIRST CRUSADE (1096–1102)

The warriors of the First Crusade knew they were involved in something exceptional and unique. They were members of "God's army" and "possessed a special sense of identity"; they were warriors of the Cross, fighting for God.[52]

Although the nations of Christendom were well represented in the armies of the First Crusade, the vast majority came

---

49. Baldric of Bourgueil, *Historia Jerosolimitana*, an account of the events of the First Crusade, quoted in Jonathan-Riley Smith, *The Crusades, Christianity and Islam*, 17.
50. Régine Pernoud, *The Crusaders*, trans. Enid Grant (San Francisco: Ignatius Press, 2003), 23.
51. Thomas F. Madden, *The New Concise History of the Crusades Updated Edition* (New York: Rowman & Littlefield Publishers, Inc., 2005), 13.
52. The following sections are adapted from my book, *The Glory of the Crusades*, 56–78. Raymond d'Aguilers, who was a participant, used the phrase "God's Army" in his chronicle of the First Crusade. For Crusaders possessing a special identity, see Tyerman, *God's War*, 105.

from France. The French were divided into two main groups, the northern and southern. Hugh of Vermandois (1053–1101), the younger brother of King Philip I the Fat, commanded the northern group. Count Raymond of Toulouse commanded the southern group. An old war wound that deprived him of one eyeball hampered the fifty-five-year-old Raymond, a veteran of conflicts against Muslims in Spain. Raymond's participation was marked by tension with his fellow Crusaders. He was one of the first warriors to take the cross at Clermont and was extremely wealthy. Unlike most Crusaders, Raymond traveled with his wife and planned to stay in the Holy Land. Joining his army was the papal legate Bishop Adhemar.

Godfrey de Bouillon (1058–1100) — whose father, Eustace, had fought with William the Conqueror, and whose mother, Ida of Lorraine, was a saint — led a group of Germans on the Crusade. His brothers, Eustace III and Baldwin, also took the Crusader vow and made the journey to Jerusalem. Crusade preaching was very effective in Godfrey's lands, which enabled him to assemble a vast army containing several thousand knights and soldiers, along with two future kings of Jerusalem.[53]

The infamous Norman warrior Bohemond commanded the last major army group. Bohemond was the son of Robert Guiscard, the leader of the Normans in southern Italy. "Bohemond," a nickname given to him by his father, referred to a legendary giant; the name was appropriate. His baptismal name was Mark.[54] Bohemond was perhaps the most fascinating Crusader; he personally knew Urban II, was fluent in Greek (a rarity among the western Crusaders), and was a brilliant military strategist and field commander.

The Crusaders were excited to reach the great city of Constantinople, which was larger and more majestic than any city in Christendom. The Byzantines were shocked and unprepared for

---

53. His brother Baldwin I and his cousin Baldwin Le Bourcq (II).
54. Tyerman, *God's War*, 114.

the arrival of such a large number of warriors from Western Europe. The Crusaders were unaware they had marched into a politically dangerous situation and were perplexed at the actions of Emperor Alexius (r. 1081–1118) upon their arrival. Alexius's primary aim was safeguarding his own position and power. He was not a great soldier and had no intention of placing his military reserves at the disposal of the Crusaders. A consummate politician, Alexius was wary of openly supporting the Crusaders because, if they failed, relations with the Seljuk Turks on his borders would become difficult. In addition, the presence of large foreign armies near his capital city made Alexius nervous about their intentions. In order to safeguard his throne, Alexius isolated the Crusade leaders and demanded their personal loyalty. Although some initially demurred, all the Crusade leaders eventually took the required oaths to ensure the transportation of their armies across the Bosporus.[55]

The Crusade leaders decided to liberate the ancient Christian city of Nicaea, the site of two ecumenical councils (in 325 and 787), as the first step on their long journey to Jerusalem. The siege of Nicaea lasted six weeks. While the Crusaders maintained the siege, Byzantine naval vessels on the Ascanian Lake prompted the Turkish garrison to open negotiations with imperial representatives for surrender terms. These negotiations were kept secret from the Crusaders, who continued to prepare for a general assault on the city walls. The emperor promised the Seljuk garrison safety of persons and property and ensured the Crusaders would not be allowed in the city. On June 19, 1097, the Crusaders awoke, stupefied to see imperial banners flying from the city walls.

Buoyed by the victory at Nicaea, the Crusaders began the second leg of their journey to Jerusalem at the end of June 1097, when they began the long march through Anatolia on their way

---

55. Raymond balked at the specific oath Alexius demanded, but he eventually swore a modified oath to respect the property and person of the emperor.

to Antioch. The Crusader march through Anatolia in the brutal summer heat was a nightmarish event for all involved. Food and water were scarce, as the Turks destroyed sources of food along the route. The lack of water caused many Crusader deaths. Some even died of excessive drinking when water sources were found. Crusaders suffered not only starvation and death, but also sickness.

During the march through Anatolia, forty-five miles southeast of Nicaea, Muslim forces set upon the Crusader vanguard commanded by Bohemond. Muslim troops were mostly fast-moving cavalry who relied on the bow to pepper the enemy with deadly volleys of arrows. These mounted archers loosed arrow volleys and then feigned withdrawal to entice their enemy to break ranks and advance in pursuit. Once the enemy took the bait, the archers moved to attack the enemy flanks and rear, with the goal of a complete encirclement and subsequent annihilation. Bohemond quickly assessed the situation and ordered the infantry, clerics, and noncombatants to make a defensive camp at a marsh, which also protected their rear and right flanks. Bohemond's warriors fought alone for several hours before the main body came to the rescue and beat back the Muslim assault. The Battle of Dorylaeum taught the Crusaders an invaluable lesson: if they maintained discipline, they could defeat the mounted Turkish warriors in open combat. News of the Crusader victory spread rapidly throughout Anatolia and caused panic in the Turkish world. Christian populations in towns with a Turkish garrison revolted against their Muslim overlords and welcomed the advancing Crusaders.

The main army arrived at the outskirts of the city of Antioch on October 20, 1097, after a grueling four-month march through the Anatolian plain. The Crusaders marched to the city walls, formed defensive positions around it, and settled in for a siege. Unfortunately, the Crusaders were ill prepared, and they soon found themselves engaged in a long-drawn-out stalemate of raiding, sallies, and counter-sallies. As the stalemate progressed through the winter, the Crusaders' sufferings intensified. By

Christmas, most of the available food near the city was consumed, and knights were forced to kill their horses. The lack of food resulted in many deaths in the Crusader camps. Those alive were forced to find and eat small amounts of food in the most disgusting of places.[56]

The rapidly deteriorating situation, the desire to end the months-long siege, and news of approaching Muslim reinforcements prompted Bohemond to craft a plan to liberate Antioch. He began negotiations with an Armenian tower guard captain near the Saint Paul gate to let the army into the city. The plan involved a commando-type raid where sixty knights climbed on a ladder to the tower just before dawn. The raid was successful. Once inside the city, the Crusaders moved rapidly while the remaining Turkish troops retreated to the citadel. The liberation of Antioch, brought about through the skilled negotiations of Bohemond, was a miracle. Achieving their objective, returning the ancient Christian city of Antioch to the Faith, was a momentous and happy occasion for the Crusaders. Unfortunately, their joy was soon forgotten.

The Muslim relief army arrived at Antioch on June 4, 1098, one day after the Crusaders had entered the city. The Crusaders who had been the besiegers now became the besieged, caught between the Muslim forces inside the citadel (who still held out and proved a nuisance), and the relief army. Once more, the situation looked hopeless, but, as the Lord had done throughout the expedition, God provided a way for the Crusade to continue. Peter Bartholomew, a layman, told the Crusade leaders that Saint Andrew had recently appeared and told him of the location of the holy lance of Saint Longinus, the Roman legionary who had pierced the side of Christ on the cross. Debate raged among

---

56. "At that time, the famished ate the shoots of beanseeds growing in the fields and many kinds of herbs unseasoned with salt; also thistles, which, being not well cooked because of the deficiency of firewood, pricked the tongues of those eating them; also horses, asses, and camels, and dogs and rats. The poorer ones ate even the skins of the beasts and seeds of grain found in manure." Fulcher of Chartres, *Chronicle*, Book I, XVI.2, quoted in Peters, *The First Crusade*, 73.

the Crusade leaders over the veracity of Peter's vision. Raymond of Toulouse believed Peter, and a search was conducted in the church of Saint Peter to find the lance. The Crusaders dug for hours throughout the morning and found nothing. As the day wore on, people began to lose hope. But just when the search was about to end, a worn lance head was found, which improved morale dramatically.

The time was at hand to deal with the relief army, so the Crusaders spiritually prepared for battle and then, following a battle plan devised by Bohemond, sallied forth from Antioch and engaged the Muslim army in combat. The numerically disadvantaged Crusaders slaughtered the Turks. After almost eight months of siege and constant combat, the Crusaders were victorious. Following the defeat of the relief army, the Crusaders rested and replenished their supplies while they planned for the eventual assault of Jerusalem.

The Crusaders began the march to Jerusalem, weakened from their losses on the campaign. The total number of warriors marching to Jerusalem was only 1,200 knights and 12,000 infantry, from an original force of 6,000–7,000 knights and 60,000 fighting men.[57] In early June, the lead elements of the Crusade army reached the inland road to Jerusalem. Their objective was within reach.

The Crusaders arrived at the walls of the Holy City on June 7, certainly aware that the liberation of Jerusalem was not an easy proposition. The city was surrounded by double walls and moats, and although the defenders were not as numerous as the attacking Crusaders, they were well supplied and prepared for a siege. The Fatimid governor made preparations for the impending siege and tried to make conditions intolerable to the Crusaders. He ordered all animal herds driven from the environs of the city in order to deny the Crusaders easy access to food, and he poisoned the wells near the city. As a result, the Crusaders were forced to haul water

---

57. Numbers marching to Jerusalem from Raymond d'Aguilers and quoted in France, *Victory*, 3.

from the Jordan River and other sources that were miles away from the city. Almost a week after their arrival on June 13, despite the lack of proper siege equipment, the Crusaders attacked the city but were repulsed. While the Crusaders pondered how they could possibly gain entry without proper siege equipment, the Lord once again provided. On June 17, six Genoese and English ships sailed into the port city of Jaffa. The ships carried not only provisions and wood for siege equipment, but also personnel who could construct proper siege engines and towers.

The death of Bishop Adhemar almost a year earlier at Antioch was still keenly felt throughout the Crusade armies, but the papal legate returned once more to exhort, lead, and encourage the Crusaders. The priest, Peter Desiderius, announced he had seen the spirit of Adhemar, who rebuked the Crusade leaders for their personal quarrels and told Peter that in order to capture the city the Crusaders needed to repent of their sins, fast, and walk barefoot around Jerusalem. The Crusaders heeded the advice of Adhemar in Peter's vision and on July 8 processed around the city, barefoot and unarmed, singing prayers and bearing relics, including the holy lance from Antioch. Five days later, they began their final assault on the city. Finally, after two days of combat, at 3:00 p.m., the hour of the Crucifixion — on Friday, July 15, the feast of the Dispersal of the Apostles — the Crusaders entered Jerusalem.[58]

After achieving their objective, the Crusaders were faced with the reality of protecting, consolidating, and organizing the territory they had liberated during the First Crusade. The commanders gathered two days after their momentous and miraculous victory to choose a leader for the city. The nobles looked to Godfrey, a warrior who had performed heroically throughout the Crusade. He was offered the crown and accepted, but re-

---

58. There was widespread killing once the Crusaders entered the city, as occurred in any medieval siege by every army (Christian and Muslim), but the modern world remembers the so-called Massacre of Jerusalem by the Crusaders. For an in-depth treatment on that topic, see my book, *The Glory of the Crusades*, 74–77.

fused to be called king. Rather, he took the title "Defender of the Holy Sepulchre."[59] Their vow fulfilled and Jerusalem secure, the vast majority of Crusaders who survived the grueling ordeal embarked on the journey home. Those who returned to see loved ones again were a blessed few, as 80 percent of those who participated in the First Crusade never returned.[60] Most Crusaders died from disease and starvation rather than from battle wounds. A few Crusaders stayed in the Latin East, but they were never numerous; the feudal territories they established, known in history as the Crusader States, always suffered from a lack of internal manpower to defend and expand their meager outposts.[61]

THE SECOND CRUSADE (1147–1149)

The Islamic world in the east was fractured in the late eleventh century by competing caliphs in Baghdad and Cairo.[62] Imad al-Din Zengi, the ruler of Mosul and Aleppo, sought to unify Muslims by calling for *jihad* against the Crusaders who had remained in the Latin East after the First Crusade. Zengi set his sights on the weakest of the Crusader States, Edessa. Once his army arrived at the city, Zengi's engineers began the task of undermining the walls by digging tunnels. On Christmas Eve, they succeeded in collapsing a portion of the walls. Zengi's army rampaged through the fallen city, pillaging, plundering, raping, and massacring six thousand Christian men, women, and children.[63]

Edessa had been the first Crusader State established, and after only forty years it was the first to fall back into Muslim hands.

---

59. Tradition holds that Godfrey refused the title of king because he "did not want to wear a crown of gold in the city where the Savior wore a crown of thorns."
60. Norman Housley, *Fighting for the Cross: Crusading to the Holy Land* (New Haven, CT: Yale University Press, 2008), 7.
61. The Crusader States were the County of Edessa (1098–1144), the Principality of Antioch (1098–1268), the Kingdom of Jerusalem (1099–1291), and the County of Tripoli (1100–1118).
62. The following sections are adapted from my book, *The Glory of the Crusades*, 87–105.
63. Amin Maalouf, *The Crusades through Arab Eyes*, trans Jon Rothschild (New York: Schocken Books, 1984), 135.

The fall of Edessa was a serious blow to the Christian strategic situation in the Latin East, since it guarded the approach to Antioch. The loss of Edessa demanded a Christian response. No new Crusade had been called in a generation, but the warriors of Christendom were asked once more to risk their lives to recover what had been lost.

Bernardo Paganelli was the first Cistercian monk elected pope, and took the name Eugenius III (r. 1145–1153). After receiving the news of the loss of Edessa, the pope issued the bull *Quantum praedecessores*, addressed to King Louis VII of France. Eugenius exhorted the warriors of France to take the cross and return Edessa to the patrimony of Christ. Since Jerusalem was still in Christian hands, the primary motivation for this expedition needed to be different from that of the First Crusade. Eugenius's exhortation challenged Christian warriors to recall the brave deeds of their ancestors and to embrace their sense of honor as Christian knights. Although an important document, *Quantum praedecessores* could not, on its own, motivate warriors to risk certain death thousands of miles from home — that would require the preaching of a saint.

Bernard of Clairvaux (1090–1153) was the greatest cleric of his age, well-known throughout Christendom as a preacher, theologian, reformer, devotee of Mary, and miracle worker.[64] Pope Eugenius asked Bernard to undertake a preaching tour in order to generate recruits for the new Crusade. Despite ill health, Bernard ventured across Christendom for nine months through the spring and winter of 1146 and into 1147, preaching numerous sermons and traveling several hundred miles. He also sent letters to those regions he could not personally visit, urging warriors to take up the cross to fight in a worthy cause. Bernard's preaching tour and written exhortations were a resounding success. Warriors took up the cross in large numbers, equaling and perhaps rivaling the total forces of the First Crusade. Many warriors who

---

64. Bernard also composed hymns and prayers and is the author of the *Memorare*.

responded to the call came from families who had sent young men east in the First Crusade.

No major monarch had marched in the First Crusade, but the two great kings of continental Europe at the time both joined the Second Crusade at the behest of Saint Bernard. The king of the Germans, Conrad III (r. 1138–1152), initially did not want to go on the Crusade, since there was a plethora of political issues to deal with in his own territory. Bernard had already preached the Crusade to King Louis VII of France (r. 1137–1180), who responded positively and was busy making preparations to depart. It was now time for Conrad III to follow suit. Bernard arrived at Conrad's Christmas Court in Speyer in December 1146 and met privately with the king. History does not record what was said between the powerful king and the humble preacher, but it does record the actions of both the next day. After celebrating Mass in the cathedral, Bernard turned toward Conrad, personally and publicly calling him to take the cross. Conrad responded, "I am ready to serve him!"[65] Bernard went to the altar, retrieved a prepared cloth cross, and pinned it on the king. The interaction made for excellent theater, which medieval people thoroughly enjoyed, but more than likely the king had already agreed to take the cross the day before, during his private meeting with Bernard. Now, preparations were undertaken to ready the massive German army for its march east.

Conrad's army left in the spring of 1147 and numbered 30,000–35,000 soldiers plus noncombatants.[66] The journey was a fairly uneventful trek through Eastern Europe, until they reached Byzantine territory. Once inside the Byzantine Empire, the Germans were harassed by imperial troops, yet they eventually reached Constantinople. Like Alexius I before him, Emperor Manuel was fearful, suspicious, and anxious about the Crusaders. He believed their true objective was to conquer Constantinople. In order to

---

65. *Vita Prima S. Bernardi*, quoted in Jonathan Phillips, *The Second Crusade: Extending the Frontiers of Christendom* (New Haven, CT: Yale University Press, 2007), 95.
66. Phillips, *The Second Crusade*, 169.

mitigate the risk of such an operation, Manuel entered into an alliance with the Turks and may have even supplied them with information on the numbers and route of the western armies.

Despite the distrust and treachery, the Byzantines transported the German army across the Bosporus, and the Crusaders made their way to Nicaea. Conrad's force left Nicaea, consuming too much food and marching too slowly, partly due to constant Turkish harassment. The slow march and rapid consumption of food and water sounded the death knell for the German army in the east. In late October, the army was badly mauled by the Turks near Dorylaeum, a site of victory for the First Crusaders fifty years before. Despite the heavy losses at Dorylaeum, Conrad's army continued the march for three more days, but it became apparent they should stop. The leading nobles demanded a council with Conrad to discuss the future of the army. Morale was low and casualties continued to mount. Things went from bad to worse when two Muslim arrows struck Conrad, one of which hit him in the head, causing a gruesome injury. The nobles begged to retreat, and Conrad agreed. The once-mighty German army, full of promise and hope of victory, was demolished as an effective fighting force. Conrad was still suffering from his arrow wound and went to Constantinople to convalesce, where he spent the rest of the winter and early spring. When he had recovered, he rejoined the Crusade and marched his forces to Acre and then to Jerusalem.

Although the French traveled a different route than the Germans, they did not have any greater success. The French army seemed to have all the ingredients for a successful Crusade. Twenty-six-year-old Louis VII was a pious and devoted Catholic, steeped in the crusading history of his ancestors. His pious and austere lifestyle contrasted with that of his wife, Eleanor of Aquitaine, the most famous woman of the medieval period. Unlike Conrad, who needed to be persuaded to join the Crusade, Louis VII was enthusiastic. Bernard traveled to Vézaly at Easter in 1146 to attend a massive assembly called by Louis

VII. Bernard eloquently prompted the nobility and clergy of France to respond to the summons. Indeed, the amazing fervor of the French manifested in an unexpected multitude of individuals taking the cross — so many, in fact, that the cloth crosses prepared beforehand ran out, and Saint Bernard improvised by tearing his own habit to make more![67] Even Eleanor of Aquitaine, along with several other women, joined the Crusade. Over the next fifteen months, Louis assembled the men and material needed to conduct combat operations in the east. Besides the military and political preparations, Louis focused on spiritual preparation. Demonstrating immense humility and penance, the king visited a leper house outside of Paris to minister to the poor souls by washing their feet.[68] In the summer of 1147, all was ready for the king of France and his mighty soldiers to march to war.

Like the Germans before them, the army experienced an uneventful march through Eastern Europe, but the situation changed drastically once they entered Byzantine territory. Despite Byzantine harassment, the French army arrived at Constantinople in early October 1147. They were transported to Anatolia and marched to Nicaea, where they watched in horror as the battered army of Conrad III returned from their disastrous march. Louis and his army moved inland and were constantly harassed by the Turks. They suffered a grievous setback at Mount Cadmus in southern Anatolia, where many nobles were wounded and killed and their supplies confiscated. The weakened army arrived in Antioch, home of Prince Raymond, the uncle of Eleanor of Aquitaine. Raymond tried to convince King Louis to attack Aleppo, which would have helped Raymond politically, but the king wanted to travel south to Jerusalem. Eleanor tried to persuade Louis to assist her uncle, but he refused. The issue, along with other things, caused a rift in their

---

67. Phillips, *The Second Crusade*, 63.
68. Ibid., 126–127.

marriage.[69]

By the summer of 1148, the Second Crusade was in a serious crisis. The major armies suffered horrific casualties during their marches through Anatolia; the remnants arrived in Jerusalem, disheartened and disheveled. Louis, Conrad, King Baldwin III of Jerusalem, and the local Christian nobility met to determine the course of the Crusade. The local Christian nobility made a compelling case to attack Damascus, so the armies set off to attack the city. The original goal of the Crusade, to liberate Edessa, had been tossed aside. The combined army arrived near Damascus on July 24, 1148. By the end of the first day of fighting, the Crusaders were in an excellent tactical position. They were in control of most of the orchards near the city and had pushed the outer defenses back to the city walls. On the second day of fighting, the defenders counterattacked and made small gains, but the Crusaders were still in a dominant position. By the third day, the Crusaders agreed to the suggestion of the local Christian nobles, to break camp and shift their point of attack to what they believed was a weaker section of the walls on the eastern side of the city. Unfortunately, the eastern walls were in fact heavily defended and Damascene troops reoccupied the orchards, preventing a return to their original attack position. Separated from their previously abundant food and water supply, and aware of advancing Muslim relief armies, Louis and Conrad made the heart-wrenching decision to end the siege and withdraw back to Jerusalem. The Crusade was over; it had accomplished nothing and was an abject disaster.

TROUBLE IN THE KINGDOM

Less than thirty years after the failure of the Second Crusade, the Christians of the Latin East found themselves surrounded by

---

69. Their marriage was not helped by the fact that Eleanor allegedly had an affair with Raymond, her uncle, who was eight years older. Louis and Eleanor received an annulment after the Crusade, and Eleanor married Henry Plantagenet, the future king of England, and bore him eight children, two of whom became kings of England: Richard I and John.

a unified Islam whose ruler pursued a campaign of *jihad* to push them out of the Holy Land forever. The man who would wreak havoc among the Christians in Outrémer was known as Yusuf Ibn Ayyub during his lifetime but became known in Western literature and history as "Saladin" from the Arabic title "Salah al-Din," meaning "The Restorer of Religion."[70] Saladin came to power in Egypt, where he overthrew the Shi'ite Fatimid caliphate and began the process of uniting the Muslim world in order to drive the Christians from the Latin East. In the year 1187, he took advantage of political issues in the Kingdom of Jerusalem and launched a major invasion aimed at recapturing the Holy City.

King Baldwin IV of Jerusalem (r. 1174–1185) was a leper, having been diagnosed by his tutor, William of Tyre, when Baldwin was still a child. In the early 1180s, the leprosy was consuming his body, and the political intrigue in the kingdom was consuming his mind and energy. It was his cross to bear that the heroic, morally strong, and faith-filled king was met with incompetence "whenever he tried to relinquish the increasingly intolerable burden" of responsibility.[71] Baldwin's fate was not to suffer in quiet agony the perils of his debilitating disease; instead, he spent his time dealing with the political intrigue of the factions within his court. The key actor in the kingdom's succession was Baldwin's sister, Sybilla, who had married William of Montferrat in 1176. The marriage ended with the untimely death of William in 1177, but the union produced a son, the later Baldwin V. Sybilla was too young, beautiful, and politically connected to remain a widow for the rest of her life. Three years after the death of her first husband, she met Guy de Lusignan, a handsome minor nobleman from Aquitaine who had left Europe in search of fame and fortune in the Latin East.[72] He found the vehicle through which he could accomplish his goals: a relationship with the young and widowed Sybilla.

---

70. Hannes Möhring, *Saladin: The Sultan and His Times, 1138–1193*, trans. David S. Bachrach, intro and preface Paul M. Cobb (Baltimore: Johns Hopkins University Press, 2005), xviii.
71. Tyerman, *God's War*, 356.
72. Madden, *New Concise History of the Crusades*, 72.

The sickly king was persuaded by his mother, Agnes, and sister Sybilla to appoint Guy regent in 1181, a bad decision since Guy was an ineffective ruler and an incompetent military commander. Baldwin IV could see the impending disaster. He knew Saladin was consolidating power and that it was only a matter of time before he launched a full-scale invasion of the kingdom, bent on its annihilation. Baldwin knew that dynastic disputes and court factions drained the kingdom of the unity it desperately needed in such a time. The leper king did what he could, but his earthly life came to an end on May 16, 1185, at the young age of twenty-four. King for eleven years, Baldwin tried to buttress the kingdom from the coming Islamic tide, but his actions came to naught when his successor, the boy Baldwin V, only eight years old, died in September 1186. In a political intrigue worthy of a Hollywood film Sybilla was crowned queen, but only after agreeing to divorce Guy, who was despised by the local nobility. She agreed on the condition that, after the coronation, she could choose a husband for herself. The nobility acquiesced. Once crowned, Sybilla chose Guy for her husband!

News of Saladin's invasion reached King Guy, who issued the summons for all able-bodied free men to muster for defense of the realm. The summons produced a grand army of 20,000 men, 1,200 of whom were knights (600 Templars and Hospitallers, and 600 local nobles).[73] It was the largest army ever assembled in the kingdom, and it depleted Christian garrisons throughout the Holy Land to only skeleton crews.

The Christian army was instructed to gather at Sephoria, where the kingdom's high command would meet to discuss the best course of action. A portion of Saladin's army besieged the city of Tiberias, which (except for the citadel) fell. Discussion raged over whether to move directly to Tiberias to break the siege. Some barons urged the king to march posthaste to Tibe-

---

73. Desmond Seward, *The Monks of War: The Military Religious Orders* (New York: Penguin Books, 1995), Seward, 53.

rias; others counseled caution. Eventually, the king chose the former option. He broke camp on July 3, 1187. The day was hot, and the march was across hilly terrain. The Christian force hoped to reach the water source at Hattin twelve miles away before the day ended. Saladin heard that Guy was on the move, so he broke off the siege of Tiberias and organized his army to meet the Christians. After an exhausting march, the Christians reached the "horns" of Hattin, a hill with two peaks, toward the end of July 3. On the morning of July 4, King Guy's army woke to the knowledge that they were surrounded by Saladin's troops. The Muslims taunted the tired and thirsty Christians by pouring out cups of water onto the ground.[74] Muslim forces added to the Christian discomfort by lighting fires (from gathered brushwood filled with dry thistles) in order to fill their camp with smoke.[75] Despite the intolerable conditions and psychological warfare, the Christians defended their position and tried to turn the conditions of battle to their favor, but they were so drained from the previous day's march and a lack of water that their defensive line broke. Saladin's forces swept through the army. Muslim soldiers found King Guy and his exhausted knights slumped on the ground, physically unable to continue the fight. The vast majority of the kingdom's forces were either killed or captured.[76] The defeat at Hattin also saw the capture of the relic of the True Cross, which was taken to Damascus and paraded through the city upside down in a gesture of ultimate insult.

Saladin now set his sights on capturing Jerusalem, and following the Christian losses at Hattin, the siege did not last long. Saladin's army arrived on September 20, 1187, and, nine days later, Muslim sappers opened a breach in the wall. Balian of Ibelin, commander of the defenses, asked for an audience with Saladin to discuss surrender terms. Saladin allowed the Christians to purchase their freedom; those who could not were sold

74. David Nicolle, *Hattin 1187: Saladin's Greatest Victory* (Oxford, UK: Osprey Publishing, 1993), 65.
75. Ibid., 64.
76. Ibid., 79.

into slavery. Saladin entered the city on October 2 and ordered the removal of every external Christian image and cross. Most of the churches in the city were turned into mosques, except the Church of the Holy Sepulchre. After the triumph of the First Crusade, the Holy City had remained in Christian hands for only eighty-eight years.

THE CRUSADE OF KINGS (1189–1192)

The defeat at Hattin, the loss of the True Cross, and the capture of the Holy City by Saladin shocked and horrified the inhabitants of Christendom.[77] Pope Urban III (r. 1185–1187) died in grief upon hearing the disastrous news. His successor, Gregory VIII (r. 1187), issued a summons for a new Crusade nine days later. The loss of Jerusalem awakened the warriors of Christendom in a way not seen for nearly a hundred years and impelled the unique participation of three of the major monarchs of Christendom: Frederick Barbarossa, Holy Roman Emperor; Philip I Augustus of France; and Richard I, the Lionhearted of England.

As a young man in his twenties, Frederick had taken the cross and participated in the Second Crusade in the army of his uncle, Conrad III. The failure of that campaign remained with him, and he vowed not to make the same mistakes. Frederick was the leading monarch of Christendom. Appointed King of the Germans in 1152 and anointed Holy Roman Emperor by Pope Alexander III in 1181, he controlled all of modern-day Germany and northern Italy. Frederick's Crusade essentially reenacted the First Crusade and re-fought the Second Crusade. The imperial army prepared to leave Germany in the spring of 1189. It was, by all accounts, a huge army, perhaps the largest ever assembled in Christendom during the crusading movement. One estimate puts the host at one hundred thousand men with twenty thousand cavalry — so large that it took three days for the army to pass a single point on

---

77. The following sections are adapted from my book, *The Glory of the Crusades*, 107–134.

the march.[78] The grand army reached enemy territory in April 1190 and won a battle at the city of Iconium. But success proved fleeting when, on June 10, 1190, the aged emperor died while fording the Saleh River. The loss of leadership was too much for the other German nobles to overcome. Most of the demoralized troops began the march home.

Richard (r. 1189–1199) was thirty-two years old when he assumed the throne of England upon the death of his father, Henry II. Richard's reign in England lasted a decade, but he only lived on the island for six months, as he preferred his extensive land holdings in France.[79] Richard's preparations for the Crusade were extensive. With the large amounts of money raised from the "Saladin tithe," a tithe on a tenth of income and property value for those who did not take the cross, and from selling his own lands, he raised a fleet of a hundred ships, with nine thousand sailors and soldiers, to transport his army to the Holy Land.[80] His army was ready, and the time to depart England and meet up with the French was at hand.

The twenty-five-year-old king of France was born of crusading stock — he was the son of Louis VII. Philip's reign was marked by political struggles with the kings of England, who were also his vassals as lords of Aquitaine. He was the polar opposite of Richard the Lionhearted. Philip was not an extraordinary warrior or military strategist like Richard, and he rarely took great risks. Instead, he was "a calculating, cautious and resourceful opportunist who tended to wait on favorable events rather than risk grand gestures."[81] The kings met and left France via ship, the first Crusade to travel by sea rather than over land, in the summer of 1190.

The campaign season of 1190 was a frustrating time for the

---

78. Estimate of strength from John France, *Victory in the East: A Military History of the First Crusade* (Cambridge, UK: Cambridge University Press, 1994), 136. For the army taking three days to pass a single point, see Tyerman, *God's War*, 418.

79. Although great English actors often portray him in Hollywood movies, Richard never learned to speak English, speaking only French.

80. Tyerman, *God's War*, 389–390.

81. Ibid., 378.

Christians besieging the city of Acre, who had arrived in the summer of 1189 under the banner of the released King Guy, who had been ransomed after his capture at the Battle of Hattin. Their action consisted of continually assaulting the walls to no effect and defending their fortified position from assaults by Saladin's relief army. The stalemate grated on the nerves of the soldiers, and one estimate indicates disease and starvation killed one hundred to two hundred warriors each day.[82] The intolerable situation needed to change, or else King Guy would be faced with another major military disaster. Thankfully, King Philip's Crusade army arrived on April 20, 1191. Philip's army built siege engines and a large siege tower to help with the assault on the walls. After a delay at Cyprus, which resulted in the capture of that strategic island, Richard reached the siege on June 8, 1191. The kings' arrival tilted the siege in favor of the Christians and finally brought it to a successful completion. Less than a month after the Muslims surrendered the city, the Christian camp was abuzz with the shocking news that King Philip was leaving the Crusade. Philip was ill and upset that Richard had received most of the glory and recognition for ending the siege at Acre. He also desired to gain control of Richard's land holdings in France.

Richard ordered his army to also leave Acre and march eighty miles to the port city of Jaffa. Control of Jaffa was necessary for logistical supply before any assault on Jerusalem could be attempted. Saladin's army shadowed the Crusaders, waiting for an opportunity to attack them decisively, which finally occurred at Arsuf. Although Saladin hoped for victory, he was outmaneuvered and defeated by Richard. After the Battle of Arsuf, Richard's army continued on to Jaffa to rest and resupply. At this point in the campaign, Richard continued to prosecute the military campaign simultaneously with diplomatic efforts, since he realized he did not have the manpower to liberate and hold Jerusalem. Recog-

---

82. Baha' al-Din Ibn Shaddad, *The Rare and Excellent History of Saladin*, tr. D.S. Richards (Aldershot, 2001), 143, quoted in Housley, *Fighting for the Cross*, 158.

nizing his military situation and conscious of reports from home about Philip's threats to his French land holdings, in early September 1192 Richard entered into a three-year truce with Saladin, known as the Treaty of Jaffa. The treaty allowed Muslim control of Jerusalem but permitted Christian access to the city. Most of the Crusaders used the truce to fulfill their vows by going to the Church of the Holy Sepulchre in Jerusalem before departing for home. Richard was not among them. He had sworn to restore Jerusalem to Christ and would not visit it until he had done so. His decision may have illustrated his belief that the Crusade was not complete, only suspended, until he could return and finish it.[83]

Unfortunately, the Lionhearted never returned to the Latin East to complete his Crusade. He died while besieging the castle of a rebellious vassal when he lowered his shield to applaud a lone crossbowman who had appeared on the ramparts without armor or shield. Unmoved by the show of appreciation, the crossbowman loosed his bolt and struck the king, who died from the infectious wound two weeks later. Richard left no children, and so the throne of England passed to his brother John, who was perhaps the worst monarch in English history.[84]

POPE INNOCENT III

Six years after the failure of the Third Crusade, a new pope focused his efforts on the crusading movement. Lothar of Segni was born into a noble Roman family who valued education. Lothar was sent to study theology at the University of Paris and later studied law at the University of Bologna. In 1198, he became the first pope with a university education and at the age of thirty-seven became the youngest pope in a century-and-a-half.[85] Lothar took the papal name Innocent III, and his pontificate (r. 1198–1216) was marked by his assertion of papal supremacy in the centuries-long struggle

---

83. See Möhring, 87.
84. John's legacy was so tainted that no future monarch ever used his name.
85. Duffy, *Saints and Sinners*, 145.

between pope and emperor. He was the first pope to systematically utilize and stress the title "Vicar of Christ." Like Gelasius and Gregory VII before him, Innocent advocated that spiritual power is above temporal power, and although secular authorities are autonomous within their own sphere, spiritual power is paramount not only in matters of faith and morals but also in temporal affairs. The pope can, and should, intervene in the temporal sphere and act as judge over secular rulers when circumstances dictate.

In concert with other reform initiatives, Innocent III devoted substantial energy to the crusading movement, exemplified not only by the many Crusades he called, but also by the innovations he brought to the movement.[86] Innocent envisioned armed pilgrimages managed and administered by the Church, a necessary innovation that, as events illustrated, was impractical to enforce. Money was always an issue during the Crusades, and Innocent tried to address that concern by taxing the Church and her clergy to finance them. Innocent increased access to the spiritual benefits accorded to Crusaders by granting indulgences, not only to those who fought in person, but also to those who paid for proxies to fight in their place, the proxies themselves, and even to those who provided material, donations, or alms to Crusaders.

THE DISASTER OF THE
FOURTH CRUSADE (1201–1205)

Innocent called a new Crusade on August 15, 1198, to once more liberate Jerusalem.[87] Unfortunately, it was the worst time to call a Crusade, as the political climate of Christendom was marked by conflict and confusion. Two men contested for the crown of the Holy Roman Emperor in Germany, and each claimed important allies. The boy king Frederick, with his mother, Constance, as regent, ruled the Kingdom of Sicily. The important Italian mar-

---

86. Among the Crusades called by Innocent are the major campaigns known as the Fourth and Fifth Crusades, as well as the infamous Albigensian Crusade against heretics in southern France.
87. This section adapted from my book *The Glory of the Crusades*, 135–161.

itime powers of Genoa and Pisa were locked in war, as were the kings of England and France. The possibility of accomplishing a Crusade seemed doubtful, but a local French baron, the brother of the former king of Jerusalem (Henry of Champagne), held a large and well-attended tournament, where he announced he was taking the cross.

Count Thibaut III of Champagne viewed participation in the Crusades as a family obligation. His decision to go on Crusade influenced other noblemen to take the cross. The French barons met to discuss operational plans for the Crusade and decided to travel by sea, like the Third Crusade, since a sea journey was substantially faster than a land march. The nobles agreed to pursue the sea route, but that decision required allied assistance since none had a fleet. The barons chose six men to travel to Italy and negotiate a contract for transport to Egypt. Genoa and Pisa were engaged in war, so the ambassadors decided to go to Venice, where they expected a warm reception by the ruler of the city, the aged, clever, and politically astute Enrico Dandolo (r. 1195–1205). The Crusade ambassadors arrived in Venice and requested transport for 4,500 horses, 4,500 knights, 9,000 squires, and 20,000 infantry, a combined force of 33,500 men. The Venetians agreed, negotiating a price of 85,000 marks of Cologne for their services. Both parties signed the Treaty of Venice. The large fleet of more than five hundred vessels, which required Venice to suspend their merchant activity for an entire year, would be ready in the summer of 1202.

The Crusade faced a severe crisis when Count Thibaut died unexpectedly on May 24, 1201. The expedition was in need of a new leader, and Boniface of Montferrat was suggested. He was an older man in his fifties and one of the best-known military commanders of the day. Boniface agreed to lead the Crusade, but his inability to speak French, along with his lack of personal commitment and a sense of detachment to the Crusade, became an issue.

As the Crusaders made their way to Venice in the summer of

1202, it soon became obvious that their numbers were substantially lower than the Crusade ambassadors had estimated. Ultimately, only 13,000 — a third of the expected 33,500 warriors assembled in Venice.[88] Because the expected number of Crusaders had not materialized, the Crusade leaders were unable to provide full payment in accordance with the treaty. Venice was faced with a financial disaster of epic proportions.

As summer turned to fall, the Venetian leader, Dandolo, concocted a plan to remedy the situation. He approached the Crusade nobles with a plan to capture the city of Zara, a town on the Dalmatian coast 165 miles southeast of Venice. The debt owed to the Venetians would be suspended until paid through the acquisition of booty. Dandolo was interested in Zara because it had been previously under Venetian control but had rebelled. Dandolo's plan seemed to solve the problems facing the Crusaders, but it produced a new and very serious problem. King Emeric of Hungary (r. 1196–1204), who had taken the cross in 1200, controlled Zara; therefore, the Church protected his lands. Attacking a Crusader's land resulted in excommunication. The Crusaders were faced with a serious moral quandary. They needed to fulfill their Crusader vow, but they needed Venetian ships in order to do so. They did not have the money to pay the Venetians, who now presented them with a plan to keep the Crusade from crumbling, but participation in that plan risked their souls. The choice was between an unfulfilled Crusade vow and desertion, or attacking a fellow Crusader. Debate raged among the Crusaders about the choices before them. Eventually, most accepted Dandolo's offer. Many believed keeping the Crusade intact was paramount, and if that involved attacking a Christian city to raise the money required for transport to Outrémer, then so be it. Innocent III did

---

88. Villehardouin, *Conquête de Constantinople*, sec. 56, I: 58. In Donald E. Queller and Thomas F. Madden, *The Fourth Crusade: The Conquest of Constantinople*, Second Edition (Philadelphia: University of Pennsylvania Press, 1997), 48. The reasons for the low turnout were numerous. Some chose not to fulfill their vows; others could not afford to fulfill their vows. There was no papal directive ordering warriors to assemble in Venice, so many troops found their own passage to the Holy Land.

not approve and wrote to the Crusade leaders, forbidding them from attacking Zara under the pain of excommunication.

As the Crusaders prepared their siege machines, sharpened their swords, and checked their armor in anticipation of the assault on Zara, the citizens of the city draped crosses over the city walls to remind the Crusaders they were attacking a Christian city.[89] The ingenious tactic did not stop the attack. Eventually, the Zarans sued for peace and surrendered on November 24 after a two-week siege. Travel in the Mediterranean Sea usually ceased for the winter from November to March, so the Crusaders had to winter in Zara.

At Zara, the Crusaders received envoys representing Alexius Angelus, fugitive from the Byzantine Empire and son of the deposed emperor. Alexius had fled the court of his uncle, Alexius III, in the fall of 1201. Alexius Angelus needed an army to free his father and return his family to power, and the Crusade army at Zara was in need of cash. The envoys asked the Crusaders to place the prince on the throne in Constantinople and presented Alexius's offer to help the Crusade leaders once they had installed him. He promised to unite the Byzantine Church with Rome; join the Crusade at the head of an army of 10,000 troops; permanently maintain a corps of 50 knights in the Holy Land; and pay 200,000 silver marks, enough to pay off the Venetian debt with a surplus to finance the campaign to the Holy Land. Alexius had previously visited Rome and asked Pope Innocent for assistance. The pope, unwilling to get involved in Byzantine politics, rebuffed the prince's request and told the Crusade leader Boniface of Montferrat to have nothing to do with the Byzantine refugee. Despite the papal warning, Boniface and the Crusade nobles agreed to help Alexius. When Innocent heard the news, he wrote a letter in the spring of 1203, in which he warned the nobles against traveling to Constantinople and "not to return to their previous sins (attacking another Christian city) like dogs returning to their own

---

89. Innocent III, *Register*, 5:160 (161), 316. In Queller and Madden, *The Fourth Crusade*, 77.

vomit."[90] The pope pointedly told the Crusaders to "give up these pointless diversions and feigned commitments: cross over to save the Holy Land."[91] Unfortunately, the Crusade leaders did not heed the pope's commands.

The Crusaders arrived at Constantinople on June 24, 1203. They were awestruck by the view. Constantinople was a majestic city, unlike anything the Crusaders knew in the west. It boasted a population of 500,000 in the city and another 300,000 in the surrounding "metro" area.[92] The Crusaders faced a formidable obstacle in the walls of the city and were outnumbered by the garrison three to one. In the city's nine-hundred-year history, a foreign army had never conquered Constantinople.

Based on Alexius's words and description of the situation in the city, the Crusaders initially believed that the installation of Alexius Angelus would be a peaceful coup. They soon found out his assessment was completely erroneous. The reigning emperor, Alexius III, was in no mind to give up power, and the people of Constantinople rejected the son of the former emperor who had arrived at the head of the large Western army. The rejection of Alexius Angelus at the walls dampened the Crusaders' spirits. A peaceful coup was no longer a viable tactic; the Crusaders now knew they would have to fight. Besieging Constantinople with an inferior force did not bode well. One participant in the Crusade summarized well their predicament: "Never have so many been besieged by so few."[93]

The attack began on July 17 when French Crusaders, using a battering ram and carrying scaling ladders, assaulted the walls of Constantinople. While the French were facing a determined defender, the Venetians attacked from the sea and succeeded in get-

90. Quoted in Queller and Madden, *The Fourth Crusade*, 102.
91. Innocent III Letter to Crusade Leaders in *Chronicles of the Crusades—Nine Crusades and Two Hundred Years of Bitter Conflict for the Holy Land Brought to Life Through the Words of Those Who Were Actually There*, ed. Elizabeth Hallam (New York: Weidenfeld and Nicolson, 1989), 211.
92. Queller and Madden, *The Fourth Crusade*, 108.
93. Villehardouin, *Conquête de Constantinople*, sec. 165, I:166. In Queller and Madden, *The Fourth Crusade*, 122.

ting into the city. They were met with stiff resistance and had to withdraw, but, as they did so, they set a fire in the city to separate their line of attack from the Greek defenders. The fire raged out of control, ultimately burning 120 acres and leaving 20,000 inhabitants homeless.[94] It was the first of three devastating fires the Crusaders would set in Constantinople. At the end of the day's battle, the Crusaders had suffered heavy casualties, the Venetian advance was halted, and the French were forced to abandon their assault and regroup. Nonetheless, the Crusaders were in a solid position, and the city was in danger. Alexius III took stock of his situation and decided fleeing was the better part of valor. This paved the way for the restoration of Isaac II, the deposed brother of Alexius III and father to Alexius Angelus.

A few weeks after his father's restoration to the throne, Alexius Angelus was crowned co-emperor, taking the name Alexius IV. Now that he was on the throne, it was time for Alexius IV to deliver on his promises to the Crusaders. A joint letter of obedience from Alexius and Patriarch John X Camaterus was sent to Pope Innocent III, reuniting the two churches. Although this official declaration of reunion was sent per his promise, Alexius IV and the patriarch made no effort to impose Roman doctrine and disciplines on the Byzantine people. Alexius paid half the amount of cash promised but still owed the Crusaders the enormous sum of one hundred thousand silver marks. The Crusaders used the payment to remunerate their debt to the Venetians. Although free from the burden of debt to Dandolo and the Venetian fleet, the Crusade leaders needed the remaining amount from Alexius IV in order to finance the Crusade to Jerusalem. Pressured by the Crusaders to pay his debt, Alexius sought ways to raise the necessary cash. He first turned to the nobility, taxing the wealthy families of Constantinople, but when even that proved unable to meet the

---

94. For the number of acres destroyed, see Tyerman, *God's War*, 546. For the number of homeless, see Thomas F. Madden, "The Fires of the Fourth Crusade in Constantinople, 1203—1204: A Damage Assessment," *Byzantinische Zeitschrift* 84/85 (1992): 73–74,88. In Queller and Madden, *The Fourth Crusade*, 125.

remaining amount, Alexius showed no shame in turning to the sacred. He ordered the tombs of past emperors opened in order to strip the corpses of their rich vestments and precious jewels. When that amount also proved wanting, Alexius commanded the confiscation of sacred icons and vessels whose rich ornamentation was taken for payment to the Crusaders.

At the beginning of 1204, Alexius IV was caught in a vicious cycle of trying to appease the anger of the mob over the presence of the Crusaders and desiring to not harm his former friends, to whom he owed his reign. Alexius's inability to decisively act either way led to the mob taking matters into their own hands. On January 25, 1204, a mob descended on Hagia Sophia and compelled the senate and clergy to meet and elect a new emperor. It took three days to find someone willing, but eventually, Nicholas Kannovos was acclaimed emperor. The news of a mob-elected emperor was a major shock to Alexius IV, who turned once again to his former Crusader friends for help. He offered them possession of the Blachernae imperial palace in exchange for their armed protection. He entrusted this proposal to Alexius Ducas, nicknamed Mourtzouphlus (because of his large bushy eyebrows that met in the middle of his forehead).[95] Unknown to Alexius IV, Mourtzouphlus hated the Crusaders and was the leader of one of the many anti-Latin groups in the city. Mourtzouphlus used his access to Alexius IV to stage a coup with the backing of the military, clergy, and civil service on the night and early morning of January 27/28, 1204. Alexius IV was imprisoned, and the popularly elected Nicholas Kannovos was arrested and killed. Mourtzouphlus was crowned emperor on February 5, taking the name Alexius V. Believing the Crusaders would leave if their ally Alexius IV was dead, Mourtzouphlus ordered the imprisoned former emperor strangled.

The Crusade leaders were furious to learn of Alexius IV's death. He still owed them money, and they were determined

95. Tyerman, *God's War*, 549.

to receive their promised payment from the Byzantines. The nobles knew they needed food, materials, and money for a successful expedition to the Holy Land, and they realized that the journey to Jerusalem lay through Constantinople. So, they once more laid siege to the city. On the second day of the siege, a small group of Crusaders found an undefended postern gate, and this brave band of warriors rushed into the city and opened one of the major city gates, allowing the Crusader army to enter Constantinople in a wild rampage. The next day, Alexius V fled the city, and the Crusaders initiated one of the most famous sacks in history.

The sack of Constantinople by the warriors of the Fourth Crusade took only three days, but set in motion centuries of acrimony and recriminations between East and West. The people of Constantinople were left relatively alone, for the Crusaders were more interested in the riches of the city than in its people. There was no wholesale massacre or slaughter, although people were killed and Byzantine women, including nuns, were publicly raped. The human toll of the sack was terrible, but more so was the economic toll, as the Crusaders sought to remove all the wealth and sacred relics they could carry and transport. Bronze statues throughout the city were melted down or shipped to the west. News of the conquest and sack made its way to Rome, where Innocent III was shocked, saddened, and angered by the actions of the Crusaders. The pope had conceived the Crusade six years earlier as an expedition to liberate Jerusalem. He did not envision — indeed, he actively worked against — the many diversions undertaken by the nobles. Innocent learned a valuable lesson about the crusading movement and, in future Crusades, worked to establish the Church's authority and oversight of the expeditions.

THE FIFTH CRUSADE (1218–1221)

Undeterred by the fiasco of the Fourth Crusade a decade earlier,

Innocent III preached a new Crusade that he hoped would liberate Jerusalem.[96] The pope marshaled all of Christendom in order to maximize the chance of success and to bring about a general spiritual awakening. Although the Fifth Crusade was designed by Innocent to be centrally administered by the Church and involved a huge recruiting effort throughout Christendom, there was no effort to appoint central secular leadership, which led to its ultimate failure.

Preaching the Fifth Crusade was a massive effort, encompassing every diocese in Christendom over eight years. Innocent ensured that those who preached were specially trained, forbidden to accept money, and instructed to travel moderately and behave piously. The massive preaching effort produced fruit in Austria, Germany, Hungary, and England. Unlike the Fourth Crusade, major secular rulers took the cross, including Frederick II, king of Germany and Sicily; Duke Leopold VI of Austria; King Andrew of Hungary; and King John of England. While the preaching campaign was in full swing and warriors throughout Christendom were taking the cross, the man who had influenced and supported the crusading movement more than any other, Pope Innocent III, died unexpectedly in the summer of 1216 at the age of fifty-five.

Despite the death of the pope, plans for the Crusade continued. Egypt was fixed as the immediate objective because it remained a source of military power and material aid for the Muslims in the Latin East, and was a major threat to the Crusader States. Conquering Egypt would not only liberate ancient Christian territory, but it would also provide a secure and important base of operations for the eventual liberation of Jerusalem and the Holy Land.

As mentioned, the Fifth Crusade suffered from a lack of strong secular leadership, and the ecclesial leadership actually hampered the efforts of the campaign. Two papal legates had been

---

96. The following section is adapted from my book *The Glory of the Crusades*, 169–178.

provided, Cardinal Robert from England and Cardinal Pelagius from Portugal, but soon after their arrival in Outrémer, "Cardinal Robert died, and Pelagius lived, which was a great pity, for he did much evil."[97] Pelagius was able to exercise control over the Fifth Crusade, not only due to the absence of major secular rulers but also because he controlled the money for the operation. His poor decision-making and generally negative demeanor contributed to the failure of the Crusade, and he was severely rebuked by Pope Honorius III (r. 1216–1227) after the expedition. The Crusaders arrived in Egypt in May 1218. They besieged the strategic city of Damietta by using their fleet to blockade the city, cutting off supplies in the hope that the city would surrender. The Muslim ruler of Egypt, al-Kamil, wanted the Crusaders to leave, so he offered a diplomatic solution. In return for the Crusader withdrawal from Egypt, al-Kamil offered to restore the previous territory of the Kingdom of Jerusalem, which was under his control. The offer was stunning since "al-Kamil offered to wipe away all of Saladin's conquests in Palestine for the Crusaders lifting of one siege in Egypt."[98] Cardinal Pelagius weighed the opinions and ruled against accepting al-Kamil's generous offer. He earnestly believed the Crusaders were in a position of strength and would emerge victorious.

As the siege wore on, the warriors were greeted by a strange sight in the late summer of 1219 when a group of twelve men in tattered clothing arrived. These twelve companions had come to the Crusade to witness to Christ among the Muslims, even to the point of martyrdom. Their leader was a man destined to be declared a saint by the Church: Francis of Assisi. Francis and his eleven friars traveled to Damietta to convert al-Kamil and end the Crusade. Francis discussed his desire to proclaim the Gospel to al-Kamil with Cardinal Pelagius, who urged him to abandon such plans, but Saint Francis and one of the friars, Brother Illumi-

---

97. Régine Pernoud, *The Crusaders*, trans. Enid Grant (San Francisco: Ignatius Press, 2003), 166.
98. Madden, *New Concise History of the Crusades*, 150.

nato, left the Crusader camp anyway. As they reached the Muslim sentries, they were taken into custody, beaten, and chained. Francis cried out to his captors: "I am a Christian. Take me to your master."[99] Brought before al-Kamil, Francis preached the Gospel through an interpreter for several days. The sultan listened attentively and responded personally and warmly to Francis, but he told the saint he could not convert to the Faith without deeply alienating his people. They would see the conversion as apostasy, which brings punishment by death in Islam. The dramatic interaction between the Catholic saint and the Muslim sultan did not produce the hoped-for fruit of conversion, nor did it end the Fifth Crusade, but it was an episode that illustrated the spiritual purpose of crusading.

Eighteen months after the first Crusaders arrived at Damietta, the city fell when a group of Crusaders noticed an unmanned defensive tower on the wall and stormed it. The city was taken without a fight, an unexpected development. The Crusaders soon discovered why the final assault was so easy. Once inside the city, the warriors were appalled to discover corpses everywhere. Eighteen months of blockade and siege had dwindled the food supplies within Damietta to dangerous levels, which had resulted in the starvation of fifty thousand people.[100] News of the fall of Damietta reached al-Kamil, who, once again, reached out to the Crusaders in an attempt to find a diplomatic solution. He offered the same terms as before, but this time sweetened the deal by promising to restore the True Cross, captured by Saladin at the Battle of Hattin in 1187. Cardinal Pelagius once again rejected al-Kamil's generous offer.

As summer approached, the troops were idle and restless, so Pelagius ordered the army to move out in a combat operation to capture al-Kamil's stronghold of Mansourah, which was halfway between Damietta and Cairo. The army approached Man-

---

99. Pernoud, *The Crusaders*, 267.
100. From a total population of sixty thousand. See Madden, *The New Concise History of the Crusades*, 151.

sourah and halted its advance in a precarious defensive position. The Crusaders were faced with the dilemma of attempting a difficult advance on Mansourah while separated from their line of supplies, digging in and waiting for reinforcements, or accepting tactical withdrawal. Because the army only had provisions for twenty days, Pelagius made the decision to retreat to Damietta. The retreat from Mansourah placed the Crusade in jeopardy, as the campaigning season came to a close and the army's strength was not enough to launch another operation against Cairo. So, Cardinal Pelagius pursued peace. Terms were reached on August 29, 1221: al-Kamil offered an eight-year truce, if the Crusaders surrendered Damietta and left Egypt; a prisoner exchange; and a promise to return the True Cross. Pelagius agreed to the terms, and the army left in September.

THE CRUSADER WITHOUT FAITH — FREDERICK II AND THE SIXTH CRUSADE (1228–1229)

One of the factors that significantly contributed to the failure of the Fifth Crusade was the absence of Holy Roman Emperor Frederick II's army.[101] Christendom and the warriors of the Fifth Crusade eagerly awaited the fulfillment of Frederick's vow, first taken in 1215. When these warriors returned home, the wait for Frederick II continued. The son of Henry VI (d. 1197) and Constance of Sicily (d. 1198) was something of a spectacle. Described as a "polymath, intellectual, linguist, scholar, falconry expert and politician of imagination, arrogance, ambition and energy," Frederick had been raised as a ward of the Church, with Innocent III as his guardian, since the age of four when his parents had died.[102] Frederick's political policies, individualistic demeanor, and spurious religious convictions were ahead of their time in the medieval period. Frederick's affinity with Islam was scandalous in an age

---

101. The following section is adapted from my book *The Glory of the Crusades*, 178–184.
102. Tyerman, *God's War*, 739.

permeated by the Catholic faith. His upbringing in Sicily had exposed him to Islamic culture, and he seemed to find himself more at ease in the company of Muslims than Christians. He spoke and wrote Arabic and traveled with a Muslim bodyguard.[103] After the death of his second wife, Isabella II, he instituted a harem stocked with Muslim women.

In 1221, Frederick met with his former tutor — who had been elected pope, taking the name Honorius III. Frederick once again renewed his Crusader vow and set a departure date of June 24, 1225. Frederick was a serial *crucesignati* ("crusader") whose first vow had been taken in 1215 during his coronation as King of the Germans at Aachen.[104] His second vow had come five years later during his coronation as Holy Roman Emperor in Rome. His meeting with Honorius III came after the Fifth Crusade's retreat from Egypt, and he later publicly promised to go to the Holy Land in 1225 and in 1227. As the departure date approached in the summer of 1225, Frederick was concerned about the lack of response for the campaign by the German nobility. He asked Honorius to grant him another extension. Honorius was willing to grant leniency to Frederick due to their long-standing relationship, but his successor was not as patient. In the spring of 1227, Honorius III died, and fifty-seven-year-old Cardinal Ugolino Conti was elected as his successor, taking the name Gregory IX (r. 1227–1241). Gregory IX was a proponent of the crusading movement and as a cardinal had preached the Fifth Crusade in Italy. Gregory's earnest support for the Crusades did not include patience for a preeminent Crusader like Frederick II to delay fulfillment of his vow (now twelve years old!), a fact he mentioned to the emperor in his first letter.

Frederick II made preparations to embark on his journey to Outrémer, which he envisioned to be limited in scope since his campaign was more about asserting his royal and imperial rights

103. Maalouf, *The Crusades through Arab Eyes*, 226.
104. Tyerman, *God's War*, 740.

than about the good of Christendom. As the troops assembled in Brindisi, the heat of the summer and squalid conditions in the camp produced a disease that ravaged the Crusader force. Many warriors died, including the husband of Saint Elizabeth of Hungary, Louis IV of Thuringia. The fate of the Crusade was seriously in doubt as a result of the debilitating disease. Soon after setting sail, Frederick became ill and canceled the campaign. This latest failure of Frederick II to fulfill his vow prompted Pope Gregory IX to issue the threatened excommunication. Frederick was undeterred by the ecclesiastical censure. He made preparations to travel east once healthy. In June 1228, the excommunicated emperor left Italy once more, despite the warnings of Gregory IX. Frederick arrived in the Holy Land in September. Technically, this journey was not a Crusade, since the excommunicated were not allowed to go on Crusade — but, true to form, Frederick II only cared about his own power and authority. He entered diplomatic negotiations with al-Kamil and eventually signed the Treaty of Jaffa, which provided for a ten-year truce and gave the emperor control of most of the city of Jerusalem in exchange for Frederick's military aid to al-Kamil. As during the Fifth Crusade, al-Kamil proved himself to be generous in diplomacy. Frederick's unofficial Crusade had reaped substantial dividends.

THE SAINTLY KING AND CRUSADER

Emperor Frederick's truce with al-Kamil expired in 1239.[105] Several years later, an Egyptian Muslim army conquered Jerusalem. When this news reached Europe, the king of France decided to take the cross. Louis had been ill when the vow was taken, which invalidated the oath according to some (including his mother, who did not want her son to go on Crusade). The king was undeterred and, once well, he took the cross again. Nothing could sway this saintly man from risking his fortune, kingdom, and life

---

105. The following section is adapted from my book *The Glory of the Crusades*, 185–199.

for the good of Christendom.

King Louis IX (r. 1226–1270) was blond, slender, handsome, gentle though firm, decisive in policy, and generous in charity. He was an extraordinarily devout and dutiful son, a loving husband and father. Along with the Holy Roman Emperor Frederick II, Louis was the most important political figure of the thirteenth century and the central figure in Christendom.[106] The two men could not have been more opposite in all aspects of their lives. Frederick was the "Crusader without faith," whereas Louis was the "Perfect Crusader."[107] One man seemed to eschew all religious faith, whereas the other embraced it and was declared a saint of the Church. Frederick kept a harem stocked with Muslim women, whereas, uncharacteristic of the age for royalty, Louis was a monogamous husband. The two men can be easily distinguished by their ultimate goals, "Frederick II thinking only of his imperial dream and Louis IX of his eschatological dream."[108] There was perhaps no greater king in the history of France. He governed his realm peacefully and justly for forty-four years, following three principles as monarch: devotion to God, self-discipline, and affection for and protection of his people.

Participation in the Crusades ran deep in Louis' family. His great-great-great-grandfather's brother had participated in the First Crusade; his great-grandfather, Louis VII, led the Second Crusade; his grandfather, Philip II, went on the Third Crusade; and his father, Louis VIII, fought in the Albigensian Crusade. Louis was motivated to participate in the Crusade not only because of family tradition, but more so because of his desire to liberate Jerusalem from Islam, an endeavor he saw as the greatest act of devotion to Christ. Louis began the massive material preparations required of the Crusade. He entered into agreements with

---

106. Jacques Le Goff, *Saint Louis*, trans. Gareth Evan Gollrad (Notre Dame, IN: University of Notre Dame, 2009), xxi.
107. The apt descriptive terms are from Régine Pernoud, *The Crusaders*, trans. Enid Grant (San Francisco: Ignatius Press, 2003).
108. Le Goff, 74.

the Italian cities of Genoa and Venice to provide transports for his army. Royal agents spent the following two years stockpiling food and supplies, especially in Cyprus.[109]

The Crusade army left France from the port of Aigues Mortes in 1248. They wintered in Cyprus and, in the spring of 1249, made the journey to Egypt. Louis decided to reenact the Fifth Crusade and liberate Egypt in order to use it as a base of operations for eventually liberating the Holy City. Although the king had well prepared for his expedition, he failed to learn the lessons of the Fifth Crusade and committed many of the same mistakes. This doomed his Crusade to the same fate as that of the earlier expedition. The French fleet arrived at Damietta in June 1249 and performed an amphibious landing, with Louis IX leading his troops from the front. The Muslim defenders withdrew from the city to the sultan's camp several miles away. The Crusaders entered the city and spent the summer in Damietta while waiting for reinforcements. As winter approached, Louis thought an attack on Cairo would give the Christians complete control of Egypt and finish the task left undone by the Fifth Crusade. He gave the command to march on Cairo in late November 1249.

The slow-moving Crusader army finally reached the outskirts of Mansourah in late December, where they planned an assault on the city, with Louis's brother, Robert of Artois, commanding the lead elements. Unfortunately, Robert disobeyed the king's orders and advanced on the town without waiting for the king and the main body of the army. His small force was annihilated in fierce urban combat. The loss of these troops sealed the fate of the entire Crusade. Louis did not have enough troops to successfully attack Mansourah, but he did not want to withdraw either, so he left the army in place for nearly two months. Eventually, their food supplies became critical and disease, particularly scurvy and dysentery, broke out in the camp. Even the king was afflicted, to the point where the back of his trousers was cut open

109. Tyerman, *God's War*, 781.

to deal with the nasty effects.[110] Louis, realizing that the tactical situation was untenable, ordered the retreat to Damietta. But the army was harassed by Muslim forces, and the only remaining option was surrender. Muslim warriors slaughtered the sick and wounded Crusaders, and sent Louis and the nobility to prison in Mansourah. Damietta was still in Christian control, so the sultan of Egypt, Turan Shah, chose to negotiate its return rather than undertake a costly siege. After a few weeks of captivity, Louis reached a deal with Turan Shah. The king agreed to return Damietta and to pay eight hundred thousand bezants for his freedom. Turan Shah agreed to release the king after payment of half the ransom, with the stipulation that Louis remain on board a ship off the coast of Damietta until the second half was paid.

Upon his release from prison, Louis discussed his plans with his nobles. The king was determined to stay in the Holy Land, but he allowed those who wanted to leave to do so. The king of Jerusalem at this time was Conrad II, the son of Frederick II, but, since he lived in Europe, the kingdom suffered from an absent monarch. Louis's leadership skills prompted him to take charge of the Christian areas in the kingdom. Although he had no legal authority to act as the king, he did have *gravitas*, which was recognized and welcomed by the Christians of Outrémer. The saintly king spent his time building up the kingdom's coastal city defenses. In the spring of 1253, Louis received news that his mother had died the previous fall. The news prompted Louis to make arrangements to leave Outrémer and return home after a six-year absence. The Holy Land continued to dominate his thoughts for his remaining years. He supported the Holy Land Christians with gifts of money and troops for the rest of his reign. Despite the king's preparations and best intentions, his first Crusade was a catastrophe, but his crusading career was not over, as he took the cross once more fifteen years later.

Baybars, a blue-eyed Russian Kipchak Turk, was the sultan

110. Ibid., 795.

of Egypt and Damascus. In the mid-thirteenth century, he began a campaign of *jihad* to eradicate Christians from the Holy Land. His preferred methods in dealing with Christian populations were massacre and enslavement, and he ordered the destruction of all captured Christian cities in order to prevent their liberation and resettlement. The Christians sent urgent appeals to Europe for another major Crusade while Baybars sacked Jaffa (1268) and captured the previously impregnable fortress of Krak des Chevaliers in the spring of 1271. Panic reached a height when the merciless Baybars sacked the city of Antioch following a four-day siege. His troops killed every Christian in the city, including all the women and children. It was the single worst massacre in crusading history.[111] The ancient Christian city would never be recovered. The Principality of Antioch, established after the First Crusade 170 years previously, was no more. The scourge of Baybars demanded a response.

News of Baybars's raids and destruction of Christian territory in Outrémer, along with the unfinished business of his first Crusade, prompted Louis to take the cross once more. He left Aigues Mortes on July 2, 1270, with a similar sized army as that of his first Crusade. After his departure, Louis announced that his initial objective was Tunis on the African coast opposite Sicily, where the army arrived in the summer of 1270. Louis spent two weeks at Tunis before advancing toward Carthage to wait for his brother Charles I's army from Sicily. Unfortunately, the wait proved fatal, as the "high summer, poor diet, and water contaminated by the immobile army soon stoked the outbreak of virulent disease, probably typhus or dysentery."[112] The Crusaders began

---

111. Baybars described the carnage to Bohemond VI, the absent ruler of Antioch: "You would have seen the crosses in your churches smashed, the pages of the false Testaments scattered, the Patriarch's tombs overturned. You would have seen your Muslim enemy trampling on the place where you celebrate the Mass, cutting the throats of monks, priests and deacons upon the altars. ... You would have seen fire running through your palaces, your dead burned in this world before going down to the fires of the next." Francesco Gabrieli, *Arab Historians of the Crusades* (Berkeley: University of California Press, 1984), 311, quoted in Madden, *The New Concise History of the Crusades*, 181–182.
112. Tyerman, *God's War*, 812.

to die — including Louis's son, Jean Tristan, and the papal legate. The saintly Crusader became sick and bedridden. Weakened from a month of illness, the king finally succumbed on August 25, 1270, at the age of fifty-six. He died at the hour of mercy while lying on a bed of ashes, mouthing the words, "Jerusalem, Jerusalem."[113] King Louis IX was the last monarch of Europe to go on Crusade to the Holy Land. Twenty-seven years after his death, Pope Boniface VIII canonized the king, who became the first saintly monarch in a century, and the last canonized monarch of the Middle Ages.

Saint Louis IX's death marked the end of the Crusades to the Holy Land. The crusading movement continued, but its emphasis changed to active defense of the homeland as the Ottoman Turks ravaged Eastern Europe and raided across the Mediterranean. The last Christian stronghold in Outrémer, the city of Acre, fell in 1291 after a ferocious five-week siege. The Crusader States disappeared, but the dream of liberating Jerusalem and returning it to Christ and his Church remained.

THE ALBIGENSIAN HERESY AND CRUSADE (1208–1229)

In the early thirteenth century, the king of France was not an absolute monarch; rather, he was a rich and influential ruler with limited power, especially in southern France, a region known as Languedoc. The people of Languedoc spoke a different laguage than other Frenchmen; it was more akin to Castilian. A merchant from southern France could be understood in Barcelona but would need an interpreter in Paris.[114] Languedoc was more

---

113. The hour of mercy is 3:00 p.m., the time when Jesus died on the cross. For Louis' death at that time, see *Vita* in *Recueil des historiens des Gaules et de la France*, 20:23. In Le Goff, *Saint Louis*, 226. For Louis' last words, see William of St. Pathus, *Vie de Saint Louis*, ed. Delaborde (Paris, 1899), 153–155, quoted in Steven Runciman, *A History of the Crusades Volume III: The Kingdom of Acre and the later Crusades* (London: The Folio Society, 1994), 244.

114. Joseph R. Strayer, *The Albigensian Crusades* (Ann Arbor: The University of Michigan Press, 1992 [1971]), 3.

urbanized than the rest of France, with towns that were run by city councils and acted like independent city states. The most important of these was Toulouse, which was overseen by a politically weak count. The Church in Languedoc was in a horrible state where corruption, worldliness, and greed were the norm. The clergy set a bad example for the people by openly flouting their promise of celibacy and being drunkards, gamblers, ignorant of Latin, and functionally illiterate. Bishops in the region were guilty of simony and absenteeism (spending inordinate amounts of time outside the diocese), and were described by Pope Innocent III as "blind men, dumb dogs who can no longer bark ... men who will do anything for money. They say the good is bad and the bad is good; they turn light into darkness and darkness into light, sweet to bitter and bitter to sweet."[115] The state of the clergy had much to do with the unique religious situation in southern France.

The region was rife with indifferentism, where Catholics and heretics interacted peacefully. Embracing heresy did not come with the normal legal, political, and social consequences as in other areas of Christendom — heretics were even members of the town council in Toulouse. Secular rulers in Languedoc were averse to fighting heresy, even though the Church looked to them to ensure the religious safety of society. Heresy was a major threat to society and the Church, and it was viewed throughout Christendom (except in Languedoc) as an active threat that had to be dealt with convincingly. Heresy often produced violence and threatened the welfare of society, not to mention the welfare of the eternal souls of those who embraced it. Failure to combat heresy and its spread was as bad as embracing heresy itself, but the secular rulers in Languedoc did not accept that generally held view. As a result, a pernicious heresy flared up, ingrained itself, and was eradicated only after a bloody civil war and the establishment of the medieval inquisitors.

A form of Gnosticism known as Catharism (from the Greek

---

115. Ibid., 19.

katharos, meaning "pure" or "clean," which described the devoted followers of the heresy, who were known as "the Pure") appeared in France in the early eleventh century. The heresy was also called Albigensianism, since it became entrenched around the town of Albi, forty-five miles east of Toulouse. In the early twelfth century, a local council of bishops in Toulouse had condemned the heretical teachings. The great Saint Bernard came to the region in 1145 and preached against Catharism. Twenty years later, however, it had become widespread and was openly preached. The Church continued to pursue a policy of patient (ultimately futile) preaching and teaching, but by the thirteenth century Pope Innocent III realized stronger measures were required.

The Cathari believed in a Gnostic-based dualist system of the world, where a good God of light created all spiritual things and Satan, the highest of all angels, created all material things, which were evil. The Cathari taught that Satan created the first man and woman from material elements alone and did not infuse their material body with souls. God took pity upon Adam and Eve and gave them good spiritual souls, but they rebelled against God by engaging in the sexual act, which imprisoned a good spiritual soul in a bad material body of a baby. The sexual act was viewed as the worst sin in Cathari morality; believers were obliged to forgo marriage as a result. If they were tempted sexually, recourse was made for homosexuality and bestiality, since procreation could not result.[116] In Cathari theology, God sent Jesus out of pity, to show man how to escape the power of Satan. Jesus was neither God nor man but a phantom who appeared on the earth. He preached spiritual release so that the soul could be freed from the confines of the evil prison of the body. The Catholic Church, which was the creation of Satan, had garbled Jesus' original message. Saint Dominic, while traveling through southern France in 1207, heard a Cathar say that "the Roman Church is the devil's church and her doctrines are those

---

116. See Warren H. Carroll, *The Glory of Christendom: A History of Christendom*, vol. 3 (Front Royal: Christendom Press, 1993), 165.

of demons, she is the Babylon whom Saint John called the mother of fornication and abomination, drunk with the blood of saints and martyrs."[117] The Cathari taught that they possessed the secret original knowledge of Jesus, which could be learned through membership in the Cathari church.

The priests of Catharism were known as "perfect" or "the pure" — men or women who renounced the world in a solemn public ceremony known as the *consolamentum*. The perfect could not own property or eat meat, eggs, or any other food derived from animal sexual intercourse. The *consolamentum* was a ritual akin to both baptism and ordination. It cleansed the perfect from sin and gave them authority to perform Cathari rituals. The perfect also promised to live free from the material world, including marriage and its benefits. The renunciation of marriage actually provided an easy means for those falsely accused of embracing Catharism to be acquitted of the heresy, as a man named John Texter proved when he said: "I am not a heretic, for I have a wife and I sleep with her. I have sons, I eat meat, and I lie and swear."[118] Ultimately, the perfect believed that the greatest act of worship was to commit suicide, which freed the good eternal soul from the bad material body.

Most Cathari were not members of the perfect. They were known as "believers," and participated in Cathari rituals, but were not required to follow the strict life of the Perfect. Catharism flourished in places without a strong central government (southern France and northwestern Italy) and where Catholic clergy were ill formed and provided bad examples of Christian living. The austere and apparent "holiness" of the perfect contrasted sharply with the greed and immorality of local Catholic clergy, whose ignorance of the Faith also allowed Cathari belief to grow unchecked.

Pope Innocent III sent missionaries to southern France to

117. Strayer, 22.
118. Ibid., 223.

preach the Faith and reformed the Church by deposing incompetent bishops. He also sent Blessed Pierre de Castelnau, a holy Cistercian monk, to the area as papal legate, with the mission to convert Cathari heretics. Pierre hoped the major secular ruler, Count Raymond VI of Toulouse, would support his mission, but Raymond was sympathetic to the Cathari because his wife was a perfect. In 1207, Pierre excommunicated Raymond for his failure to combat the heresy, placing his lands under interdict.[119] Early the next year, Pierre and Raymond met in the hopes of restoring communion, but the meeting was tense — especially when Raymond threatened Pierre, who was mysteriously murdered the next day by a servant of the count. No direct proof of Raymond's complicity in the murder was discovered, but popular opinion indicated Raymond was involved in some way. Innocent, furious at the death of his legate, denounced Raymond as a heretic and a murderer. Because the Cathari heresy threatened the souls of Catholics in southern France and all peaceful efforts had failed, Innocent proclaimed a Crusade to eradicate the false teaching.

The Albigensian Crusade lasted twenty years and was, in essence, a nasty, bloody civil war. The Crusade devolved into a series of sieges wherein Crusaders would make inroads but, as enlistments ended, the progress of the campaign would stall. Simon de Montfort, a man of "single-minded piety and unusually strict personal morality" who was "tenacious on campaign, resourceful in logistics, audacious in battle, inspiring to his followers, [and] ruthless to his enemies," was chosen in August 1209 to lead the Crusade.[120] Simon had been a participant in the Fourth Crusade but left after refusing to attack Zara.

The Crusaders won a decisive battle at Muret on September 12, 1213, when Simon's outnumbered army defeated the forces of King Peter II of Aragon.[121] Peter had marched to Languedoc

---

119. Interdict is an ecclesiastical punishment wherein the sacraments are forbidden to be celebrated in a specific territory.
120. Tyerman, *God's War*, 594.
121. The hero of the Battle of Las Navas de Tolosa against Muslim forces in Spain in 1212.

to help Raymond VI of Toulouse, his brother-in-law, but was killed in combat at Muret. As a result of the battle, Simon became the count of Toulouse and ruled the area with a heavy hand. Three years later, Raymond VII (the son of Raymond VI) began a rebellion against de Montfort and achieved early success, which included the liberation of Toulouse. While besieging his lost city, Simon was struck on the head by a stone from a mangonel and killed. Over the next four years, Raymond VII reconquered most of the territory that had been won by the Crusaders. The Crusade entered its final phase when King Louis VIII (r. 1223–1226) took the cross and marched his army southward. He captured the vital city of Avignon in September, but the Crusade stalled once more when the king unexpectedly died two months later, leaving his twelve-year-old son, Louis IX, as king. Eventually, the Crusade ended with the signing of the Peace of Paris treaty on April 12, 1229. Raymond VII made a public act of penance, received absolution, was reconciled to the Church, and was acknowledged as the legitimate count of Toulouse. The Albigensian Crusade strengthened the rule of the French king in the south of France, as his military involvement established royal control in a place heretofore independent of royal power. The Crusade did not, however, fully eradicate the Cathari heresy. This would require the actions of the medieval inquisitors.

THE MEDIEVAL INQUISITORS

It can be difficult for modern man to understand the establishment of the medieval inquisitors and the later institutional tribunals known as "the Inquisition," the most famous of which was the Spanish Inquisition.[122] This is due in part to the notion of religious freedom and expression, enshrined in most Western democratic forms of government — a relatively new understanding of

---

122. The following section is adapted from my book *The Real Story of Catholic History*, 111–122.

society.[123] Before the modern world, religious freedom was neither practiced nor tolerated, because unorthodox religious belief was not only a danger to souls, but to social order as well, since it often led to violent rebellion against civil authority. As such, heresy in the medieval and early-modern world was regarded as both an ecclesiastical and secular crime. The Church wanted to protect the souls of her flock from eternal damnation. The state wanted to safeguard the security of the realm and prevent violence. As such, it categorized heresy as treason, punishable by death.

The appointment of medieval inquisitors began in 1184 when Pope Lucius III (r. 1181–1185), in the bull *Ad abolendam*, sent a list of heresies to bishops throughout Christendom and ordered them to take an active role in determining the guilt of heretics, who were to be examined by trained theologians. Pope Gregory IX (r. 1227–1241) formally instituted the procedures for the inquisitors in 1231 in the bull *Ille humani generis*. The establishment of the medieval inquisitors was made possible when the Church adopted Roman legal procedures in her court system to deal with violators of ecclesiastical law, including heretics, in the twelfth century. The legal system, secular and ecclesial, changed from one based on accusatorial procedure to one based on inquisitorial procedure. Confession was elevated to the "queen of proofs," leading to the reappearance of the ancient practice of torture in judicial matters.[124] European criminal justice before the twelfth century had been an accusatorial procedure, by which the alleged victims of a crime went to court, made an accusation, and swore an oath to its truth. The accused was then called on to answer the charge. Swearing an oath that the charge was false was usually

---

123. The medieval inquisitors and the Inquisition, as a "historical phenomenon can be fathomed only when we look at it within the framework of its historical context and do not try to measure yesterday by today's standards. An essential step is to realize the unity of the medieval world, in which exclusion from the Church simultaneously meant exclusion from all human society. If someone attacked a dogma, he was attacking at the same time the foundations of the societal order and hence was considered a danger to the public." See Cardinal Walter Brandmüller, *Light and Shadows: Church History amid Faith, Fact and Legend*, trans. Michael J. Miller (San Francisco: Ignatius Press, 2009 [2007]), 100.

124. Edward Peters, *Torture*, expanded edition (Philadelphia: University of Pennsylvania Press, 1985), 41.

sufficient to get it dismissed. But, if doubts remained, a physical ordeal or judicial combat could occur, the outcome of which was considered God's judgment on the matter and sufficient to settle the claim.[125] This gave way to the inquisitorial procedure, by which a public official would collect evidence, receive testimony of at least two witnesses or a confession from the accused, and then pass judgment.

The pope-appointed inquisitors, usually Dominicans, were charged with preserving orthodoxy, protecting the unity of the Church and society, and rescuing the souls of alleged heretics from eternal damnation. An inquisitor had to be at least forty years old, well-schooled in theology and canon law, and morally upright.[126] These medieval inquisitors established the legal procedures that would influence later institutional tribunals. These procedures were just and charitable, recognized at the time as superior to the secular legal process. Initially, the inquisitors were itinerant, traveling to various locations where they preached to both clergy and laymen about the importance of truth and unity in faith and the danger of heresy, especially to one's immortal soul. Their jurisdiction extended only to Christians, not to practicing Jews or Muslims. As part of their preaching, the inquisitors established a "period of grace" of fifteen to forty days, a time of self-accusation and penance, during which the person could be reconciled to the Church. When the "period of grace" ended, witnesses could bring charges of heresy against persons to the attention of the inquisitors; if sufficient evidence existed, a trial would commence. Witnesses were called, whom the accused could cross-examine. The accused was also allowed to call supporting witnesses and, throughout the trial, was afforded multiple opportunities to repent. If, after repeated opportunities, he refused to confess, the inquisitors — in accordance with established legal process — could resort to using torture to elicit a confession.

---

125. Ibid., 42.
126. Brandmüller, 112.

Torture, in the medieval legal process, was used to elicit a confession and never as a punishment for heresy. Although torture was part of the ordinary criminal process in the secular world, its use in ecclesial courts for investigating heresy was not approved until 1252 — twenty years after the establishment of the medieval inquisitors — and it never became common.[127] Torture could not be applied by clergy and was governed by a series of strict protocols and protections for the accused. It was a "last resort" after every other means was used to discover the truth and elicit a confession. The decision to use torture could also be appealed by the accused. Several groups of people were also automatically exempted, including children, the elderly, pregnant women, knights, members of the nobility, and, in some cases, the clergy.[128] The judge accompanied the accused to the place of torture, and a notary was present to record the session. Moreover, a physician was present to ensure the accused was not killed or maimed.[129] The accused was shown the instruments of torture before application in the hopes it would engender a quick confession. If the accused confessed under torture, the confession had to be freely repeated the next day before it could be admissible in court. The methods of torture were various, and the judge, who was expected to take into consideration the severity of the crime and prescribe only standard methods based on local custom, made the selection in individual cases. Instruments included the *strappado*, in which the accused's hands were tied behind the back and attached to a rope that was slung over a beam in the ceiling, so that the accused could be lifted up and left hanging for a period of time. Occasionally, weights were attached to the feet to increase the strain on the arms and back.[130] Other forms of torture included keeping the accused awake for prolonged periods (but not more than forty hours) and stretching on the rack.

---

127. Edward Peters, *Inquisition* (Berkeley: University of California Press, 1988), 16.
128. Peters, *Torture*, 57.
129. Canon law specifically forbade the shedding of blood by ecclesial courts.
130. Peters, *Torture*, 68.

The purpose of the medieval inquisitors was to investigate heresy and, where it was found, to encourage voluntary confession, repentance, and reconciliation to the Church. Inquisitors failed in their mission if the accused persisted in heresy and refused to recant. Obstinate heretics who, after repeated opportunities to confess, refused to do so, were remanded to the state for punishment. Heresy was a capital offense in the secular world, so the death sentence was handed down and carried out by the state. The Church never executed any heretics. Though the popular notion is that millions of people were executed for heresy, the historical record proves that number to have been relatively few.[131] In the Diocese of Turin, Italy, for example, only twenty-two obstinate heretics were remanded to the state and executed during the entire fourteenth century.[132] The famous medieval inquisitor Bernard Gui (1261–1331), who wrote a "how-to" manual for inquisitors, passed 930 judgments in heresy cases throughout his career, while remanding only forty-two obstinate heretics to the state for punishment.[133] Secular courts were less just than ecclesial courts, and there are cases of criminals in secular prisons blaspheming or uttering heresies in order to be moved to the more humane and just ecclesial courts.[134] It was far more advantageous for a heretic to be interviewed by the inquisitors than by secular authorities.

The medieval inquisitors were originally established to combat the Albigensian heresy in southern France. Their work helped restore order and religious communion in the area so that, by the mid-fourteenth century, Cartharism was no longer an active threat to the people of Languedoc.

---

131. Critics of the Church use widely exaggerated numbers, ranging from 10,000 to 300,000, when estimating how many people were executed for heresy. See Rodney Stark, *Bearing False Witness: Debunking Centuries of Anti-Catholic History* (West Conshohocken, PA: Templeton Press, 2016), 118.
132. Brandmüller, *Light and Shadows*, 118.
133. Ibid.
134. See Henry Kamen, *The Spanish Inquisition: A Historical Revision* (New Haven, CT: Yale University Press, 1997), 184.

DEATH OF THE ARCHBISHOP —
THE TALE OF THOMAS BECKET

Thomas Becket was from a Norman family who had immigrated to England.[135] Becket was sent to school in Paris and eventually became a clerk for Theobald, the archbishop of Canterbury. Theobald noticed Becket's intellect and virtue and ordained him a deacon in 1154. When the young Henry Plantagenet became king in the same year, he chose Becket to be his chancellor. Despite their difference in age (Becket was twelve years senior), the two men became close friends and enjoyed their time together. Becket was handsome, tall, witty, and a good conversationalist. His personal piety was renowned; he eschewed foul language and acts of immorality. Despite his diaconal ordination, Becket led military expeditions for the king and participated in combat. When Theobald died in 1161, King Henry appointed Becket to the esteemed post of archbishop of Canterbury the following year. Becket had no desire for the post and made that known to the king, but Henry dismissed his concerns. Because Becket was only a deacon, he was first ordained a priest, and then, the following day, a bishop. A tremendous change occurred in Becket upon his assumption of the ancient see of Saint Augustine (the famous missionary sent to England by Pope Saint Gregory the Great in the late sixth century). He resigned his secular post as chancellor, much to the chagrin of Henry, and devoted his time to the poor, to ascetical spiritual practices like the wearing of a hair shirt, and to other penances.

One reason Henry appointed Becket to the important ecclesial post was, in part, because of the king's displeasure at ecclesial courts handling legal cases of crimes committed by clerics. Since the beginning of Henry's reign, a large number of murders had been committed by clerics in England. Henry believed the clerics

---

135. The 1964 movie *Becket*, with Richard Burton as Becket and Peter O'Toole as King Henry II, erroneously depicts him as a Saxon.

were receiving too-lenient sentences, since ecclesial courts were banned by canon law from utilizing the death penalty. The king wanted clerics accused of secular crimes to be tried in secular courts, and he demanded the compliance of the bishops of England. Although most bishops were willing to agree to the king's demand, Becket steadfastly refused to do so, telling the king: "The customs of Holy Church are fully set forth in the canons and decrees of the Fathers. It is not fitting for you, my lord king, to demand, nor for us to grant, anything that goes beyond these, nor ought we consent to any innovation."[136]

A short while later, the king demanded the bishops agree to sixteen propositions, known as the Constitutions of Clarendon. The Constitutions revealed the king was not merely interested in punishing wayward clerics, but also sought the complete control of the Church. Henry demanded, among other things, that the bishops agree that royal courts had jurisdiction over clerics accused of crimes, that the clergy could not leave England without the king's consent, and that there could be no appeal to the pope of decisions rendered in the royal courts without the king's permission. Becket refused to agree to the king's outrageous demands. As a result, the next several months involved the king persecuting Becket. False charges were levied against the archbishop, along with hefty fines for alleged wrongdoing as chancellor. Eventually, Becket was forced to flee England to escape the king's wrath. He sought shelter in France and brought his case before Pope Alexander III (r. 1159–1181). The pope supported Becket and implored Henry to cease his persecution against the Church. A delicate game of diplomacy and letters followed during the next four years among king, pope, and archbishop, ultimately ending with Becket's return to England in November 1170.

A month later, the king was campaigning with his army in Normandy when, perhaps influenced by a night of partying and

---

136. Richard Winston, *Thomas Becket* (New York, 1967), 150, quoted in Carroll, *The Glory of Christendom*, 93.

drinking, he indicated his displeasure with Becket to a group of his knights. The angry king said, "What disloyal cowards do I have in my court, that no one will free me of this lowborn priest!"[137] Four knights took the king's words as an imperative and left France, bound with royal vengeance for Becket. They returned to England and approached Becket on December 29 in his cathedral. As one knight raised his sword to cut down the archbishop, Becket cried out, "I commend myself and my church to God and the Blessed Mother."[138] The knight struck Becket in the head. The blow was so harsh that Becket was instantly decapitated, and the knight's sword snapped in two when it hit the stone floor of the cathedral. When the news reached Pope Alexander III, he was so horrified and angered by the killing that he banned anyone from mentioning Henry's name in his presence for a week.[139]

The murder of his once-close friend made Henry a "haunted man" for the remaining nineteen years of his life: "Every year he had to watch the growing stream of pilgrims to the shrine of the man for whose murder he knew himself to be ultimately responsible; every year he had to listen to the growing list of miracles wrought by Thomas Becket's intercession which led to his canonization just three years after his martyrdom."[140] Four years after the bloody affair, the king participated in an act of penance to atone for the murder of the archbishop. He processed barefoot and in penitential clothing to Canterbury cathedral, where he kissed the site of Becket's killing and was publicly whipped by several bishops, an abbot, and eighty monks. The knights who killed Becket went to confess their crime to the pope a year after the dreadful deed. Alexander III forgave them, instructing them to go on Crusade as penance. They joined the Knights Templars, one of the military religious orders committed to defending and

137. Winston, *Becket*, 318–320, 346–350, quoted in Carroll, *The Glory of Christendom*, 106.
138. Winston, *Becket*, 355–356, quoted in Carroll, *The Glory of Christendom*, 106.
139. Desmond Seward, *Eleanor of Aquitaine: The Mother Queen of the Middle Ages* (New York: Pegasus Books, 2014 [1978]), 120.
140. Carroll, *The Glory of Christendom*, 107.

fighting in the Holy Land, in defense of the inhabitants and pilgrims in the Latin East. Within three years, all had died.

THE BEGGAR MONKS — FRANCISCANS AND DOMINICANS

The medieval period witnessed one of the most profound religious revolutions in Church history — the beggar monks. The Holy Spirit brought two unique men to the story of the Church at the same time. Both became conscious of their special mission in the spring of 1206, and each would work for nearly two decades to change the Church and Western society forever. Their vocations and missions were different, but they shared the similarity of uniquely creating mendicant religious orders that were active in the world, rather than being separated from society behind the walls of the cloister. No religious order in the Church's history before this time had maintained its existence purely by begging others for sustenance and funding. Their success was not guaranteed, as many within the Church, especially the secular clergy, viewed the new orders with suspicion and jealousy. But the Franciscans, focused on holy living and preaching, and the Dominicans, focused on education and defense of the Faith, would shape the world and the Church through their tireless commitment to Christ.

The man who came to be known as Saint Francis of Assisi (1181–1226) came from a wealthy Italian family and spent his youth as a soldier. Captured at the Battle of Collestrada in 1202, Francis was held in captivity for a year in Perugia, during which time he contracted an illness that turned his thoughts to eternity. He recovered and made his way back to Assisi, still dreaming of fighting and earthly glory, but doing so with a changed heart. Gradually, the lure of the glory of war faded. Francis embraced simple living and personal piety. In 1205, on his way to Assisi, he stopped at a forgotten and run-down wayside chapel known as the Church of San Damiano. While there, he saw the large crucifix come alive and utter the words, "Francis, go, repair my house, which as you see, is falling completely to ruin."[141] Francis sold his possessions to provide money for the restoration of the chapel. His father was incensed by his actions and tried to prevent him from embracing the holy path he desired. Francis renounced his inheritance and in 1208 completely embraced "Lady Poverty" and the life of a beggar. Others, drawn to his holy living, joined him. He established the Order of Friars Minor, which focused on the works of preaching, begging, and serving the poor. Pope Innocent III approved the order in 1210, after the pontiff had a dream in which he witnessed the nine-hundred-year-old Lateran basilica leaning, swaying, ready to collapse before a little poor man set his shoulder to the church to support it. The next day, Innocent identified the man in his dream as Francis, who had come to Rome to ask the pope's approval for his new order — which was granted.[142] Francis' work also influenced a young woman from another wealthy aristocratic family. At the age of eighteen, Clare (1194–1253) left her home to embrace the holy lifestyle of Francis, who cut her hair and robed her in a penitential habit in the year 1211. A year later, Clare founded a religious order for women following the way of life of the Order of Friars Minor, with devotion to the Eucharist, and which became known as the Poor Clares.

Francis oriented his movement's actions on preaching in the vernacular, and "the love of Christ and the Church and his fellow man, by Christian joy, by the cheerful embracing of complete poverty, by a profound respect for the clergy, [and] above all by total fidelity to orthodox doctrine."[143] Francis wanted his friars to embrace holy poverty, telling them, "Know, my sons, that poverty is the special way to salvation; its fruit is manifold, but it is really well known only to a few."[144] Francis also had a great desire to

141. Frank M. Rega, *St. Francis of Assisi and the Conversion of the Muslims* (Rockford: TAN Books and Publishers, 2007), 10.
142. See Carroll, *The Glory of Christendom*, 163.
143. Carroll, *The Glory of Christendom*, 162.
144. Rega, 2.

bring the Gospel to Muslim territory, even to the point of martyrdom. He set out with some companions for Syria in 1212, but they were forced to return home when their ship ran into foul weather. The next year, he planned an expedition to Morocco by walking to Spain, but along the route he fell ill and canceled the journey. Finally, he traveled to the Crusader camp at Damietta during the Fifth Crusade, where he was able to preach the Gospel to al-Kamil.[145]

Francis' emphasis on preaching embraced forms of communication other than speaking, as evidenced by the creation of the first living Nativity scene in 1223. Francis established the crèche because he wanted to do "something that will recall to memory the of little Child who was born in Bethlehem and set before our bodily eyes in some way the inconveniences of his infant needs."[146] A year later, on the feast of the Exaltation of the Cross (September 14, 1224), Francis was gifted with the stigmata, or the wounds of Christ.[147] Francis suffered with the wounds of Christ for two years, until his death at the age of forty-five. Pope Gregory IX (r. 1227–1241) canonized Francis just two years later in 1228.

Dominic Guzman was born into a wealthy and noble family in Castile in the late twelfth century. He received a university education and was ordained a priest. The formative experience of his life was traveling with a bishop to southern France on a diplomatic mission, where he encountered the Cathari heretics. He soon recognized that the success of the heresy was due to ill-formed Catholic clergy, who did not live holy lives and were not well educated in the Faith. These priests were no match for the Cathari in apologetic debates. The Holy Spirit moved him to create a new religious order composed of men who could

145. Franciscans were martyred for the preaching activity among Muslims, even during the lifetime of Saint Francis. See Rega, 87.
146. Celano, First Life, Book One, Chapter 30, no. 86, 301. Omnibus, quoted in Rega, 102.
147. Francis was not the first holy individual to receive the wounds, but he is perhaps the most well-known of the stigmatics. An eleventh-century man named Dominic practiced severe penances and received the stigmata, as recorded by Saint Peter Damian in his Vita Dominici Loricatti.

effectively preach and defend the Faith. Pope Honorius III approved Dominic's new Order of Preachers in 1216, and gave it a universal mission to preach throughout Christendom. This was a unique and revolutionary action since, before the Franciscans and Dominicans, only secular clergy were regularly allowed to preach. Dominic wanted the men in his movement to focus on the study of theology and philosophy. Eventually, the order founded universities in order to educate others in these and other subjects. Dominic spent time in Languedoc during the Albigensian Crusade, and the great victory of Simon de Montfort at the Battle of Muret in 1213 was attributed to his intercession.

The Order of Preachers was the primary Catholic intellectual apostolate for centuries. Dominicans were chosen as the first papally appointed inquisitors. Dominic was named the Master of the Sacred Palace, or the pope's theologian, in 1217 and spent the majority of the rest of his life in Italy. Exhausted by years of severe penances, hard work, preaching throughout Christendom, and defending the Church from heretics, Dominic died in Bologna in 1221 and was canonized in 1234 by Pope Gregory IX.

Dominic's and Francis' religious orders revolutionized and helped reform the Church through a revitalized spirituality rooted in the embrace of Lady Poverty. A new standard for clerical living resulted from their work, and its impact remains to the present age.

TEACHING THE FAITH — THE RISE OF THE SCHOLASTICS

The teaching of theology and philosophy, the highest sciences of study, was concentrated in the monasteries during the ninth and tenth centuries. An educational revolution began in the late eleventh century with the creation of the universities.[148] The first university was founded at Bologna at the end of the eleventh century,

---

148. The word "university" is a condensed version of the Latin *universitas magisterium et scholarium*, or "a community of teachers and scholars." See Stark, *Bearing False Witness*, 140.

followed by the University of Paris in 1150, Oxford in 1167, and Cambridge in 1209. In total, eighty-one universities were founded before the mid-sixteenth century. The high value the medieval Church placed on universities is best illustrated in their description by Pope Innocent IV (r. 1243-1254) as "rivers of science which water and make fertile the soil of the universal Church."[149] In the thirteenth century, a new method of learning and investigation of knowledge was introduced in the universities. This new method, known as Scholasticism, was a synthesis of theology, Scripture, and Aristotelian philosophy, focused on developing precise definitions by using reason through questioning. At the age of twenty-seven, Saint Anselm of Canterbury (1037–1109), the "Father of Scholasticism," entered a Benedictine monastery and was ordained a priest. Eventually, his administrative skills and pious living were recognized and he was appointed archbishop of Canterbury in England in 1094. Anselm taught that faith and reason were harmonious and could be utilized together to answer questions about God, man, and the meaning of life. Anselm's philosophy was centered on the principle of *Fides quaerens intellectum* ("Faith seeking understanding"), wherein the believer seeks to grow deeper in faith by questioning, which leads to understanding. Faith, not doubt, is the starting point. He believed that the gift of faith is the first stage in studying theology, followed by experience, wherein the student lives out the teachings of Christ in his personal life; then, from faith and experience flow knowledge, which is the fruit of contemplative intuition. Anselm's famous works, *Cur Deus Homo* ("Why God Became Man") and the *Proslogion* (in which he developed a proof for the existence of God), became foundational documents in the study of theology and led to the Scholastic movement in the thirteenth century.[150]

Other notable theologians and thinkers contributed to the development and understanding of theology in the twelfth cen-

---

149. Ibid., 65.
150. Anselm proved the existence of God by declaring that "God is that than which nothing greater can be thought."

tury. Peter Lombard (d. 1160) was a distinguished professor at the University of Paris for nearly twenty years. His *Book of Sentences*, a collection of opinions from theologians and Church Fathers on matters of Divine Revelation, was the standard university theology textbook until the sixteenth century.

The great Scholastic thinkers of the thirteenth century included Saint Bonaventure (1217–1274) and Saint Thomas Aquinas (1225–1274). Bonaventure joined the Franciscans and studied at the University of Paris. He was concerned with the soul's mystical ascent to God and focused on synthesizing theology, philosophy, and mysticism. He left the academic world to become the seventh minister general of the Order of Friars Minor and is known as the "Doctor of Mystical Theology."

Thomas Aquinas was a humble and pious man who joined the Order of Preachers despite familial objection and became the greatest theologian in the Church since Saint Augustine.[151] Thomas's magnum opus was the *Summa Theologica*, which he wrote as a guide for students beginning advance work in theology. Comprised of three parts — on God, on the rational creature's ascent to God, and on Christ — the *Summa* tackled theological and philosophical questions, providing answers from the writings of the Church Fathers, Scripture, and Aristotelian philosophy. While known as a superb theologian, Thomas was not declared a saint of the Church due to his immense mind but because of his humility, devotion to the Eucharist, and deep prayer life.[152] Thomas suddenly stopped writing in 1273, when he received a mystical experience after celebrating Mass. A supernatural revelation left him with the understanding that everything he had written "was worthless."[153] Thomas' life and work is beautifully summarized in his favorite prayer: "Grant me, O Lord my God, a

---

151. His work is cited in the modern *Catechism of the Catholic Church* sixty-one times, which is the most of any individual author save Saint Augustine.
152. Thomas wrote the Eucharistic hymns *Tantum Ergo* and *Pange lingua*.
153. Benedict XVI, Wednesday General Audience on Saint Thomas Aquinas, June 2, 2010, in *Holy Men and Women of the Middle Ages and Beyond* (San Francisco: Ignatius Press, 2012), 7.

mind to know you, a heart to seek you, wisdom to find you, conduct pleasing to you, faithful perseverance in waiting for you, and a hope of finally embracing you."[154] The Angelic Doctor passed to his eternal reward in 1274 while on his way to attend the Second Council of Lyons.

The age of cathedrals and Crusades was the high-water mark for Christendom, when activity in the Church was focused on military, spiritual, and intellectual endeavors. People illustrated their deep faith in the construction of magnificent cathedrals throughout Christendom. Reform movements ensured the independence of the papacy, the restoration of the clerical life, and the eradication of heresy. The glory of Christendom in this age was soon tarnished, however, as the family of God weakened through the sinful actions of her most important and powerful members.

---

154. Ibid., June 16, 2010, 78.

SIX

The Family Weakens — Prelude to Division

"I have heard here that you have appointed the cardinals. I believe that it would honor God and profit us more if you would take heed always to appoint virtuous men. If the contrary is done, it will be a great insult to God, and disaster to Holy Church."[1]

CATHERINE OF SIENA TO POPE GREGORY XI

Born to a large family midway through the fourteenth century, on the feast of the Annunciation, the young woman suffered loss early in her life. Her twin sister died in infancy, and twelve of her twenty-three siblings did not live to see adulthood. Her family wanted her to marry when

---

1. Catherine of Siena, *Letter to Gregory XI, Saint Catherine of Siena as Seen in Her Letters*, ed. Vida D. Scudder (New York: E. P. Dutton & Co., 1906), 122.

she reached maturity, but she refused because she was drawn to the Dominican life as a tertiary. The young woman loved God, the poor, and, most especially, the sick. She cared for the sick throughout her hometown, even those with leprosy, and made an effort to bury the dead. She received locutions from Christ and visions of the Lord, Saint Mary Magdalene, Saint John the Beloved, Saints Peter and Paul, Saint Dominic, and the Blessed Virgin Mary. She became renowned throughout Christendom for wisdom and holiness. People, from the rich and powerful to the lowly, wrote letters to her. She dictated responses initially, until three years before her death when she learned to write (in a miraculous manner). Kings, dukes, princes, and popes received her letters; had these men heeded her advice, distress and suffering to Christendom would have been avoided. She left future Christian generations magnificent spiritual writings, including her dialogue with God on the spiritual life, which focused on authentic self-knowledge and guarding the soul by prudently and virtuously exercising the gift of free will. Catherine of Siena, one of the greatest female saints in the history of the Church, died at the early age of thirty-three. She accomplished much in her short time on earth. Perhaps her single most impactful earthly achievement was convincing the pope to return from France to his diocese in Rome, ending a seventy-year scandal. That action was one of the bright lights in a century full of darkness, a time that set the stage for even greater calamity in the future.

THE TROUBLED PAPACY

The fourteenth and fifteenth centuries witnessed terrible tribulation for the Church generally and the papacy particularly. Events that occurred in these centuries laid the foundation for the later Protestant Revolt and the great fractioning of Christendom in the sixteenth century. Many popes in this era were preoccupied with the temporal exercise of power and affairs of state, rather than the spiritual health of the Church. They frequently made imprudent decisions, and they used the spiritual weapons of interdict and excommunication as political weapons, which weakened men's adherence to their originally intended effects. Managing the papal curia and secular land holdings required massive revenue, which was raised through taxation, ecclesial fees, and loans with high interest rates from secular banking families. Papal taxation and the flow of money to Rome caused resentment in some areas of Christendom, becoming a source of discontent, especially from secular rulers, as the centuries progressed. Although the election of the pope by the cardinals removed overt secular interference in choosing a new pope, the College of Cardinals in this time was influenced by national interests. This resulted in long conclaves, as the factions could not agree on a candidate. The successor of Saint Peter is supposed to be a sign of unity in the Church. Unfortunately, in these centuries, more often than not, the pope was the source of conflict and division.

A POPE RESIGNS — THE STORY OF CELESTINE V

Some men aspire to become the pope. Some men reluctantly agree to their election as the successor of Saint Peter. Some men flee from the very thought of walking in the shoes of the Fisherman. Some men, like Saint Celestine V (r. 1294), are the least likely candidates for the office but are called by the Holy Spirit nonetheless. Peter Murrone, surnamed after Mount Murrone where he sought solitude, was a hermit, a simple, holy man living an ascetical life in the hills of Abruzzi. Peter had become a Benedictine monk at the age of seventeen, desiring a life of penance and solitude. In the summer of 1294, his life was abruptly interrupted, and he became the main actor in one of the most bizarre events in Church history.

Pope Nicholas IV (r. 1288–1292) had been dead for nearly two years. The cardinals meeting in conclave in Perugia could not agree on a successor. Unfortunately, national and political dynamics dominated the minds of the cardinals, and the Church was left without a universal shepherd. Disgusted by the prolonged papal vacancy and the scandal it presented to the Church, Peter wrote a letter to Cardinal Malabranca, bishop of Ostia, chastising the cardinals for their inability to elect a pope. He predicted an awful calamity for the Church if the cardinals persisted in their obstinacy.[2] Moved by the letter from the holy hermit, Cardinal Malabranca read its contents in the conclave, and then nominated Peter as a candidate for pope. The assembled cardinals agreed and elected Peter! A procession of dignitaries marched to his mountain retreat, where they presented Peter with the stunning news of his election as Supreme Pontiff. Of course, Peter demurred, as he had no interest in the papacy. But the cardinals persisted, and, in resignation to God's will, he accepted and took the name Celestine. As pope, Celestine lived in Naples, never setting foot in Rome. After only a five-month reign as the successor of Peter, Celestine was convinced he did not have the skill set to continue as pope. Overcome with the demands of the office, especially the political issues and affairs of state, and desiring to return to his former life of prayer and solitude, Celestine announced his resignation from the papacy to the cardinals on December 13, 1294. Peter Murrone would live for another two years after his resignation, eventually dying at the age of eighty-one.[3]

A TROUBLED PONTIFICATE

Ten days after Celestine V's resignation, the cardinals assembled in conclave once more and elected Cardinal Benedetto Gaetani pope, who then took the name Boniface VIII (r.1294–1303). Boniface made haste to Rome, having no idea he would be the last pontiff to live in the Eternal City for the next seventy years. Boniface loved the Church, and he desired her independence and recognition of papal supremacy above all else. Unfortunately, his actions lacked charity at times, and he unnecessarily made ene-

---

2. See Warren H. Carroll, *The Glory of Christendom: A History of Christendom*, vol. 3 (Front Royal, VA: Christendom Press, 1993), 326.
3. His reign was brief, but his action had lasting impact in the Church. Pope Benedict XVI fondly recalled the memory of Celestine V when he announced his own resignation from the papacy in 2013.

mies of those who were powerful, especially the king of France. His pontificate was one of the most turbulent in Church history, marked by political conflict with most of the major rulers of Christendom.[4]

Philip IV "the Fair" became king of France at the age of seventeen. This grandson of the saintly King Louis IX lacked his famous grandfather's love of the Church and unselfish love for his people. Philip was interested in ruling France absolutely, and he employed a man named Guillaume de Nogaret as an adviser. De Nogaret was described by a contemporary as a "body without a soul, who cares nothing about anyone's rights but only wants to increase the wealth of the King of France."[5] Trouble between Philip and Boniface began over the use of Church revenue. Philip taxed Church lands in France and used the proceeds to finance his various military campaigns. This action was clearly an attack on the independence of the Church, so Boniface issued a bull in 1296 entitled *Clericis laicos*, in which he stipulated that secular government could neither collect taxes from the Church without papal approval, nor could clergy pay a secular tax. Secular rulers who taxed the Church without permission and clergy who paid the tax were both liable to excommunication, with absolution reserved to the pope. Although the principle was correct, the application lacked charity. Boniface's bull did nothing more than raise the ire of Philip. Their relationship further deteriorated early in the fourteenth century when Philip arrested the papal legate on charges of inciting insurrection. Boniface demanded his release and threatened Philip with excommunition in the provocatively entitled bull *Ausculta fili*, or "Listen, son!" Boniface's new bull was burned upon delivery in France. A year later, with tensions still high, Boniface released

---

4. This included Dante, who placed Boniface, while he was still alive, in the eighth circle of hell, the pit of the simonists, in his *Inferno*. See *Inf.* 19.49–63.

5. Georges Digard, *Philippe le Bel et le Saint-Siège de 1285 à 1304* (Paris: Librairie du Recueil Sirey, 1936), quoted in Carroll, *The Glory of Christendom*, 334. There is some belief that de Nogaret may have been an adherent of Catharism, because his grandfather and parents were burned at the stake for embracing the heresy.

another imprudently worded bull *Unam sanctam*. Boniface VIII continued the formulation of the "two powers" theory, writing: "Spiritual power surpasses in dignity and in nobility any temporal power whatever. If the terrestrial power err, it will be judged by a superior spiritual power; but if the highest power of all err, it can be judged only by God, and not by man."[6] Boniface argued that although the secular ruler has power within the temporal arena, he only exercises it through the will of the spiritual power, the pope. Moreover, Boniface wrote, "We declare, state and define that it is absolutely necessary for the salvation of all human beings that they submit to the Roman Pontiff."[7]

It was clear to Philip that something had to be done with the overbearing and overreaching pope, so de Nogaret hatched a plan to seize Boniface and force him to resign. In September 1303, de Nogaret and one thousand troops launched an attack on the papal palace at Anagni. The attackers broke through the defenses by evening and rushed into the pope's room, where they were greeted by a defiant Boniface, who said: "Come forward, strike my head, I wish to suffer martyrdom, I wish to die for the Faith of Christ. ... Here is my neck; here is my head."[8] De Nogaret and his supporters contemplated what to do with the captured pontiff into the next day, but the townspeople of Anagni stormed the palace and liberated Boniface. De Nogaret escaped back to France, but the effects of the event lingered with the pope, who died in his sleep a little more than a month later. Philip, in ultimate disrespect, sent de Nogaret as his representative to the funeral. The strong relationship between French king and pope, which had been established long ago by Pepin the Short, was in a precarious position. It became more estranged by Philip's actions after Boniface's death.

---

6. Boniface VIII, *Unam sanctam*, in Mary M. Curley, *Conflict between Pope Boniface VIII and Philip IV the Fair* (Washington, 1927), 115–116, quoted in Carroll, *The Glory of Christendom*, 340.
7. Boniface VIII, *Unam sanctam*, in J. Neuner, S.J. and J. Dupuis, S.J., ed. *The Christian Faith in the Doctrinal Documents of the Catholic Church* (New York: Alba House, 1996), 281.
8. Digard, 182, quoted in Carroll, *The Glory of Christendom*, 343.

THE AVIGNON PAPACY

Boniface's pontificate was followed by the brief reign of Blessed Benedict XI (r. 1303–1304), who died mysteriously the day before he intended to excommunicate Guillaume de Norgaret. King Philip did not want another Boniface elected to the papacy, preferring a weaker candidate who would be more receptive of the persuasion of the French king and his policies. Philip was delighted when the cardinals elected the archbishop of Bordeaux, Bertrand de Got, who took the name Clement V (r. 1305–1314). Clement V was a weak leader and easily manipulated.

King Philip made it clear to Clement that he desired the pope to follow three courses of action, all of which favored the French monarch. Philip demanded Clement place Boniface VIII on trial for heresy, in a shocking reenactment of the ninth century Synod of Corpse. He also wanted the new pope to condemn the Knights Templars, in an effort to confiscate their wealth and land holdings in France. He asked Clement to move the papal residence from Rome to France. Clement agreed to all three requests. He opened proceedings against Boniface VIII, though he dragged his feet through the process, postponing several hearings due to stomachaches and nosebleeds. Clement was no fool, and recognized the show trial for what it was, especially when de Nogaret was given the role of chief prosecutor.

Philip did not wait for Clement to act against the Templars. On October 13, 1307, the king ordered the arrest of all the Templars in France. He had no authority to do so, as the Templars were an ecclesiastical organization and subject only to canon law. Philip ordered a royal investigation of the order. He tasked de Nogaret with determining whether the Templars denied Christ, spat on crucifixes, worshiped idols, and practiced sodomy. Eventually, Clement ordered an ecclesial investigation as well, which culminated in the suppression of the order at the ecumenical Council of Vienne in 1311. Philip's goal was partially realized —

the Templars were no more — but the pope did not pass judgment on their guilt or innocence, and gave their property to the Hospitallers. Philip cruelly kept the last Master of the Temple, Jacques de Molay (who was godfather to Philip's son), in prison for several years, before ordering his execution at the stake in 1314.

Philip's desire for Clement to move the papal residence to France was designed to allow the French king to access and pressure the pontiff. In 1308, Clement announced to his cardinals his intention to transfer his residence to the south of France, where he arrived in the spring of 1309. He established his court in the city of Avignon, which was legally a possession of the papacy and not an area controlled by the French monarch. The move was not intended to be a permanent relocation; no pope who reigned in Avignon gave up the idea of returning to Rome, although it took seventy years for the return to occur. The pope remained the bishop of Rome despite living in France. But the sight of the pope engaging in the ecclesiastical abuse of absenteeism caused consternation throughout Christendom and eventually weakened the papacy's prestige and respect. Rome itself was neglected during the long papal absence — cattle were stabled in the naves of Saint Peter's and Saint John Lateran! Many secular rulers believed the Avignon popes were puppets of the French king, which was not the case in most respects, but the image remained of the pope favoring one secular ruler over others. The College of Cardinals was greatly affected by the move to France. Nearly all the cardinals and Curia officials created during the seventy-year exile were French, which would be a major factor after the papacy returned to Rome.

THE BLACK DEATH

Europe suffered one of the world's most dramatic population upheavals in the fourteenth century with the arrival of what contemporaries called "the pestilence" and since the nineteenth century has been known as "the Black Death."[9] All the areas of Christendom were affected by the plague, but England was hit the hardest. Three waves of the pestilence wreaked havoc in the country from 1350–1450. England's population was six million in 1300; the plague so decimated the country that it did not recover its lost population for another five hundred years![10] Although the disease was the bubonic plague (which, in colder climates, turned into pneumonic plague), it is possible that, at least in England, the disease was actually combined with anthrax, which spread rapidly due to the large cattle population.[11] The incubation period for the plague was two to eight days, after which symptoms such as high fever, diarrhea and vomiting, headaches, convulsions, dizziness, restlessness, and delirium could be present in the patient. As the bacteria collected in the lymph nodes, especially in the groin, armpits, and neck, they produced buboes, which in rare cases were internal.[12] Death was near when the buboes burst and released pus, an immensely painful experience that occurred in fifty percent of cases within three to six days after onset of symptoms. The detrimental effect of the pestilence on Christendom's cities is reflected in the papal city of Avignon in March 1348. The mortality rate exceeded 50 percent; nearly 400 people died per day. During a five-week span, over 10,000 people were buried in a cemetery purchased by the pope for plague victims.[13]

In the heavily Jewish areas of southern France and Spain, people blamed the Jews for the devastating plague, which led to pogroms.[14] In Strasbourg, 900 Jews out of the nearly 2,000 in the city were burned by people angry at the pestilence. The *Chronicle of Strasbourg* recorded the contemporary belief that the Jews were

---

9. See Norman Cantor, *In the Wake of the Plague: The Black Death and the World It Made* (New York: Harper, 2001), 7.
10. Ibid., 8.
11. Ibid., 14–15.
12. Ibid., 12.
13. Carroll, *The Glory of Christendom*, 392.
14. Thirty percent of the 2.5 million Jews in Europe at the time lived in Spain and southern France. See Cantor, 150.

responsible for the Black Death:

> In the matter of this plague the Jews throughout the
> world were reviled and accused in all lands of having
> caused it through the poison which they are said to
> have put into the water and the wells — that is what
> they were accused of — and for this reason the Jews
> were burnt all the way from the Mediterranean into
> Germany, but not in Avignon, for the pope protected
> them there.[15]

Pope Clement VI (r. 1342–1352), appalled at the treatment of
the Jews, issued a bull on July 4, 1348, excommunicating anyone
who harassed the Jews on account of the plague. Some believed
that because the Jews suffered fewer deaths than Christians — the
result of their segregated living, personal cleanliness, good house-
keeping, and diet — they were responsible for the pestilence.[16]
Clement VI pointed out the absurdity of that belief; Jews were
suffering from the plague as well.

The Black Death killed over twenty-three million people
in Christendom, nearly a third of the total population, and
produced significant and lasting economic, legal, and spiritual effects.[17] The plague devastated the Church's clergy, as
they suffered a higher percentage of mortality than the laity.
The best priests disregarded the potential consequences of
the plague and ministered to the sick and dying. Their noble
and praiseworthy concern for the flock robbed the Church of
good priests, from which it took centuries to recover. Priests
in urban areas were affected the most — nearly 90 percent
died from the Black Death.[18] The priest shortage led to low-

---

15. Cantor, 149.
16. See Cantor, 163.
17. The number of dead is from Clement VI in 1351. See Carroll, *The Glory of Christendom*, 394.
18. Brennan Pursell, *History in His Hands: A Christian Narrative of the West* (New York: Crossroad, 2011), 151.

ering the minimum age for ordination, which then produced a Church staffed with undereducated and inexperienced clergy. The impact from the plague on the Church, along with other causes, laid the foundation for various ecclesiastical abuses in the fifteenth century.

THE WOMAN WHO BROUGHT THE POPE HOME

No one who witnessed the birth of Catherine Benincasa on the feast of the Annunciation in 1347 would have expected that the little girl from Siena would become one of the most famous female saints in Church history. Catherine was a typical child in a large Catholic family. When she reached maturity, her parents expected her to marry, but Catherine desired to enter the Third Order of the Dominicans and join the group in Siena known as the "Cloaked Sisters," who wore white woolen dresses with a white veil and black cape. These tertiaries lived in their own homes and performed acts of charity throughout the city. Eventually, Catherine's parents relented, and their daughter became a Cloaked Sister in 1366.

Catherine was focused on her spiritual life at an early age. At age seven, she asked the Blessed Mother to intercede for her so she could remain a virgin for life and be spiritually espoused to Jesus, which eventually occurred when she was twenty-one.[19] Catherine was given the gift of knowing the state of souls in her presence. Those in mortal sin would produce a foul, pungent odor, as occurred with the niece of a cardinal she met during her trip to Avignon. The smell was so horrific that Catherine had to flee from the woman's presence. The woman had committed adultery and was a priest's mistress.[20] Catherine practiced various forms of spiritual penances and mortifications, including refusing to drink wine, eating only bread and vegetables, and sleeping for only thir-

---

19. See Sigrid Undset, *Catherine of Siena*, trans. Kate Austin-Lund (San Francisco: Ignatius Press, 2009 [1954]), 16,49.
20. Undset, 77.

292 | CHAPTER SIX

ty minutes a night.[21] During a three-year stretch, she practiced complete silence, refusing to speak to anyone but her confessor and anyone he ordered her to speak with. Catherine was given the unique gift in 1370 of subsisting on the Blessed Sacrament as her only means of nourishment. Five years later, she received the stigmata, which she begged the Lord to keep invisible so that people would not be drawn to her (the wounds became visible on her body after death).

Catherine became well-known in Christendom due to her holiness and through her extensive letters, which made her the second greatest letter writer of the fourteenth century (behind Petrarch).[22] Catherine's letters found their way to kings, princes, popes, and everyday people. In addition to her extensive letters, Catherine also produced spiritual writings, the most famous of which was her *Dialogue of Divine Providence*, originally published in Italian in 1472. This book took the form of a dialogue between God and his creature. Catherine believed that the key to spiritual growth is true self-knowledge, in which the soul will "gain hatred of thy own fleshliness, and through hate will become a judge, and sit upon the seat of thy conscience, and pass judgment."[23] She also advocated that the soul can be joined to God intimately the more it hates sin. Catherine compared the soul to a city with many gates. Just as a city's gates allow people and goods to enter it, so does the soul, whose gates are memory, intellect, and will. All three gates can be attacked, and sometimes opened — except one, the Will, which cannot be violated unless the watchman of Free-Will, guarded by the dog Conscience, is derelict in his duty.[24]

Catherine lived during the Avignon papacy and realized the great scandal caused by the absent pope. She wrote letters to the pope in which she called him "our sweet Christ on earth" and

21. Ibid., 31.
22. Catherine dictated her correspondence for most of her life, until three years before her death when she was given the gift, in a miraculous manner, of writing.
23. Catherine of Siena, ed. Vida D. Scudder, *Letter to Gregory XI, Saint Catherine of Siena as Seen in Her Letters* (New York: E. P. Dutton, 1906), 27.
24. Ibid., 299–300.

"daddy" and was very direct in her assessment of the Church, her bishops, and her cardinals. She urged the pope to focus on spiritual matters, "for ever since Holy Church has aimed more at temporal than at spiritual things, matters have gone from bad to worse."[25] Catherine also pleaded for the pope to return to Rome, but she knew that letters alone would not prove decisive, so she travelled to France to confront the pope face to face.

Catherine was neither the first person to demand the pope's return to Rome during the Avignon papacy, nor was she the first holy woman to do so. Bridget of Sweden (1302–1373) had turned to a life of holiness after making a pilgrimage with her husband Ulf to Santiago de Compostela in 1343. She gave her possessions to the poor and entered a Cistercian convent, although she never became a consecrated religious. Bridget left Sweden and settled in Rome, where she began a concerted campaign to persuade the pope to leave France. Her letters were finally answered in 1367 when Pope Blessed Urban V (r. 1362–1370) left Avignon and triumphantly entered Rome. Unfortunately, he returned to France in 1370 due to the political instability in Italy, and died three months after resettling in Avignon. When Bridget died in 1373, it fell to Catherine to bring about the permanent return of the pontiffs.

Catherine left her beloved Siena and arrived in Avignon on June 18, 1376, where she stayed for three months in order to convince Pope Gregory XI (r. 1370–1378) to come home to Rome. Pierre Roger de Beaufort had been created a cardinal at the age of nineteen and then elected to the papacy nearly thirty years later. He was "modest, pious and prudent ... kindly and gracious on every occasion, but he also knew how to demonstrate the firmness, and even severity, which is sometimes demanded of great leaders."[26] When he met Catherine, he relied on her confessor to translate between the two of them, as he did not speak Ital-

---

25. Ibid., 129.
26. Henri Daniel-Rops, *The Protestant Reformation*, vol. 1, trans. Audrey Butler (New York: Image, 1963), 12.

ian and she did not speak French. Catherine urged Gregory to come home, telling him, "Who knows God's will so well as your Holiness, for have you not bound yourself by a vow?"[27] God had granted Catherine special knowledge of a private vow that Gregory had taken when he was a cardinal — that he would move the papal residency back to Rome if he were ever elected pope. The reminder of that vow to Gregory, in a manner that could only be ascribed to divine intervention, moved the pope to promise Catherine he would return.

A few months after returning to Siena, Catherine received word that Gregory was wavering in his commitment to move back to Rome. She wrote him strongly-worded letters, urging him to fulfill his promise to her and to God: "Do not delay, then, your coming. Do not believe the devil, who perceives his own loss, and so exerts himself to rob you of your possessions in order that you may lose your love and charity and your coming hindered. Respond to the Holy Spirit who calls you. I tell you, Come, come, come and do not wait for time, since time does not wait for you."[28] Catherine knew that the French cardinals were pressuring Gregory to remain in Avignon, and she begged the pope to pay no heed to those clamoring voices deceived and tempted by the devil: "I have prayed, and shall pray, sweet and good Jesus that He free you from all servile fear, and that holy fear alone remain. May ardor of charity be in you, in such wise as shall prevent you from hearing the voice of incarnate demons, and heeding the counsel of perverse counselors, settled in self-love, who, as I understand, want to alarm you, so as to prevent your return, saying, 'You will die.' Up, father, like a man! For I tell you that you have no need to fear."[29]

The holy virgin of Siena continued to write letters, calling on Gregory in direct and strong language to make good his promise. She grasped the difficulty of the decision, and eloquently wrote:

27. Undset, 210.
28. Scudder, 132.
29. Ibid., 165–166.

"I beg of you, on behalf of Christ crucified, that you be not a timorous child but manly. Open your mouth and swallow down the bitter for the sweet."[30] Catherine's persistence paid dividends when Gregory finally left Avignon for Italy, and returned the papal residence to Rome on January 17, 1377. Through the actions of this holy woman, the scandal of the pope living in France was at an end — but a worse problem loomed on the horizon.

THE GREAT WESTERN SCHISM

When Gregory XI returned the papal residence to Rome, ending the seventy-year Avignon papacy, there was much rejoicing in Christendom. Unfortunately, Gregory died a little over a year after his return. Before the pope died, he stipulated that the conclave should meet immediately upon his death and not wait for long-distance cardinals to arrive in Rome. He also instructed that the election should be decided by majority vote.[31] Only sixteen cardinals (eleven French, four Italian, and one Spaniard) were in Rome when Gregory died. They met in conclave and knew the Italian people wanted an Italian pope for fear that a Frenchman would move the residency back to Avignon. A large crowd gathered, making known to the assembled cardinals their desire for an Italian pope. The cardinals chose the Italian Bartholomew Prignano, the archbishop of Bari. Prignano took the name Urban VI (r. 1378–1389) and dedicated his papacy to reform. Urban knew that the Church had suffered greatly during the absence of the pope in France. He wanted to ensure the College of Cardinals would set the example of virtuous living for the entire Church. Unfortunately, his gruff demeanor lacked charity. He ruled with an iron first, elevating "the sledgehammer to the status of a tool of government."[32] He became abusive toward the cardinals, calling one a half-wit and another a liar, and mandated that no cardi-

---

30. Ibid., 185.
31. See Daniel-Rops, *The Protestant Reformation*, vol. 1, 45.
32. Daniel-Rops, *The Protestant Reformation*, vol. 1, 47.

nal should eat more than one course per meal. Catherine of Siena tried to warn the pontiff that his anger would produce negative effects for the Church, writing, "For the love of Jesus crucified, Holy Father, soften a little the sudden movements of your temper."[33] Urban VI did not heed the warning; indeed, several years into his pontificate, he famously arrested six cardinals on charges of plotting to kill him, and had them tortured and executed.[34]

The cardinals decided extreme measures had to be undertaken to deal with Urban's heavy-handedness. Five months after the conclave, fifteen cardinals (eleven French, three Italian, and one Spaniard) met secretly and declared that the election of Urban VI had been forced on them by the Roman mob and, therefore, was null and void. However, the cardinals had no authority to declare a papal election invalid and certainly no power to do what they did next — elect an antipope. One of the French cardinals, Robert of Geneva, was elected at this illegal conclave, and he took the name Clement VII. The Church had now entered the period that became known as the Great Western Schism. Clement VII was not the first antipope in Church history — indeed, there had been thirty-three antipopes before Clement VII, with the last one fifty years earlier, in 1328 — but the Great Western Schism lasted for a generation and was marked by hardened secular support for the various claimants. Christendom was rent asunder as secular rulers supported one papal claimant over another. Saints argued for the legitimacy of their candidate.[35] The major universities of Christendom tried to intervene to end the schism. The papacy, established by Christ to be a sign of unity and fraternity in the Church, was now the reason for disunity and division, and weakened people's love and respect for the Roman pontiff. Catherine of Siena wrote a scathing letter to the three malcontented Italian

33. Philip Hughes, *A Popular History of the Catholic Church* (New York: Image, 1947), 144.
34. Daniel-Rops, *The Protestant Reformation*, vol. 1, 49.
35. France, Scotland, Spain, and the Kingdom of Naples backed antipope Clement VII, and England, the Holy Roman Emperor, Hungary, and Poland supported Urban VI. Saints Catherine of Siena and Catherine of Sweden favored Urban, whereas Vincent Ferrer and Colette supported Clement.

cardinals who participated in the illegal conclave in 1378:

> You clearly know the truth, that Pope Urban VI is truly pope, chosen in orderly election, not influenced by fear. ... What made you do this? The poison of self-love, which has infected the world. That is what makes you pillars lighter than straw — flowers which shed no perfume, but stench that makes the whole world reek!
>
> Now you want to corrupt this truth, and make us see the opposite, saying that you chose Pope Urban from fear, which is not so. Return, return, and wait not for the rod of justice, since we cannot escape the hands of God.[36]

Unfortunately, the cardinals did not listen to Catherine's plea. When news reached Urban VI of the illegal conclave and the election of antipope Clement VII, he excommunicated the perpetrators and replaced the entire College of Cardinals. Antipope Clement VII declared war on Urban, raising an army that besieged Rome. The forces of the antipope were defeated, and Clement was forced to flee, first to Naples and then to Avignon. An opportunity arose to end the schism when antipope Clement VII died in 1394 during the reign of the valid pope Boniface IX (r. 1389–1404), who had replaced Urban VI. However, the cardinals in Avignon continued the schism by electing the one Spaniard who participated in the illegal conclave of 1376, Pedro de Luna, who took the name Benedict XIII. That same year, the faculty at the University of Paris drafted a memo with three options to solve the papal crisis. The first called for both claimants to abdicate, allowing for the election of a new pope recognized by all Christendom. The second option provided for a commission to

---

36. Scudder, 278.

be selected by both claimants, which would then decide between the two. The third option recommended the calling of an ecumenical council to solve the schism, which was eventually the option chosen, but not for another twenty years.

Another opportunity to end the schism arose in 1409, but the result was more confusion and another papal claimant. Pope Boniface IX died in 1404 and was succeeded by Innocent VII (r. 1404–1406), who was then succeeded by Gregory XII (r. 1406–1415). Antipope Benedict XIII resided in Avignon. Cardinals from Rome and Avignon agreed to meet in Pisa to try to end the schism. They declared both Gregory XII and Benedict XIII notorious schismatics and heretics, excommunicated them, and elected a new antipope: a Greek named Petros Philarges, the cardinal of Milan, who took the name Alexander V and resided in Pisa. Now three men claimed to be pope: Gregory XII in Rome, the valid pope; Benedict XIII in Avignon and Alexander V in Pisa, antipopes. Once again, a group of cardinals had grossly overstepped their authority and created a fiasco for the Church.

The schism caused theologians to question the constitution of the Church and how authority was exercised. Various scholars began to openly question previously accepted principles — that the Church is a monarchy, with the pope as the supreme visible governing authority; that the pope holds primacy throughout the Church; that councils are only authoritative if accepted by a pope who promulgates the decrees; and that no one can appeal a papal decision to a council or any other authority.[37] A heretical teaching known as conciliarism, or the belief that an ecumenical council wields supreme authority in the Church, became popular among scholars and theologians. This erroneous belief was in part fostered by the Avignon papacy and the Great Western Schism, which led to considerable doubt in the minds of people about the role and office of the papacy. Conciliarists were able to force recognition of some of their beliefs at the ecumenical coun-

---

37. These principles are outlined in Daniel-Rops, *The Protestant Reformation*, vol. 1, 54.

cil at Constance. Two decrees from that council, *Sacrosancta* and *Frequens*, discussed the role of a council in the Church and called for a regular meeting of councils every decade. Despite the decrees, the popes did not embrace these conciliarist ideas, so they were not implemented in the Church. Conciliarism as a whole was eventually condemned at the Fifth Lateran Council in the sixteenth century.

The Great Western Schism was finally resolved at the Council of Constance (1414–1418). Sigismund, the king of the Germans (and later Holy Roman Emperor), called the council in part to bring about a united Christendom that could help him defend his southern territory from the menacing Ottoman Turks. He chose the imperial city of Constance as the site of the gathering. The council was a huge affair; cardinals, bishops, theologians, priests and deacons, secular rulers, and others, totalling nearly one hundred thousand people, flocked to the city.[38] The number was so large that the council attendees agreed that voting would be performed by national bloc rather than by individuals. The council fathers solved the schism by first deposing the antipope John XXIII, who had replaced Alexander V in 1410. Antipope Benedict XIII in Avignon was also deposed (although he refused to acknowledge the conciliar decision). Pope Gregory XII, in Rome, sent legates to the council with a letter in two parts. The first part of the letter formally acknowledged the assembly, a necessary action to enable the council to be considered authentic and authoritative. In the second part of his letter, Gregory XII voluntarily abdicated the papal throne (the last pope to do so until Benedict XVI in 2013), paving the way for the election of a new pope to end the schism. The assembled delegates elected the twenty-five-year-old Otto Colonna, who took the name Martin V (r. 1417–1431). The Great Western Schism, after nearly forty years, was over. This century of papal crises had spawned heretical ideas, secular rulers independent of the Church, and a loss of

---

38. Daniel-Rops, *The Protestant Reformation*, vol. 1, 58.

respect and prestige for the papal office.

THE "PROTO-PROTESTANTS"

Before the rise of the Protestant movement in the sixteenth century, "proto-Protestants," specifically John Wyclif (or Wycliffe) and Jan Hus, began the formulation of the main tenents of what would later become Protestantism.[39] John Wyclif was born in Yorkshire, England, and studied at Oxford, where he was appreciated as an exceptional student and became a professor of philosophy and theology. Wyclif was a pure academic, an intellectual man who did not motivate or lead.[40] He provided the ideas and let others perform the actions.

At Oxford, Wyclif advocated several heretical teachings in lectures and books. Wyclif attacked the Eucharistic doctrine of transubstantiation in his book *On the Eucarhist*. He opined that the Real Presence of Jesus in the Eucharist was not a real flesh-and-blood presence but a symbolic one. Wyclif condemned the veneration of the saints, indulgences, and prayers for the dead, and adopted the Donatist heresy that the validity of a sacrament relies on the worthiness of the minister.

Wyclif's contributions to heresy mostly involved erroneous teachings concerning the Church. He defined the Church as an "invisible transcendent society" that is neither hierarchically structured nor united to the bishop of Rome, but is present in all the people of Christ.[41] Moreover, he attacked the papacy and referred to the pope as "the man of sin" and "Lucifer's member."[42] Wyclif believed that the state holds supremacy over the Church, and advocated for the confiscation of Church property. He also taught that the Bible is the only authoritative source of God's

---

39. The following section is adapted from my booklet *20 Answers: The Reformation* (El Cajon, CA: Catholic Answers Press, 2017), 20–24, 59–61.
40. See Daniel-Rops, *The Protestant Reformation*, vol. 1, 215.
41. Ibid., 217.
42. Ibid.

divine revelation (*sola scriptura*). Finally, he denied the existence of free will, opining that man is completely subject to the will of God. The archbishop of Canterbury censured Wyclif and his heretical teachings in 1377.

Wyclif gained popularity because he attacked ecclesiastical abuses, such as simony, and exploited latent nationalist anger at the papacy in the midst of its sojourn in Avignon. Groups of Wyclif followers, known as the "poor priests" and later as Lollards, traveled throughout England, preaching his heresy. Two of his followers undertook a new translation of Scripture into English, which the Church condemned — not because it was in the vernacular, but because the translation was rife with error.[43] In 1381, riots overran London, the archbishop of Canterbury was murdered, and violence spread in England. Although Wyclif did not personally endorse the violence, his teachings were viewed as a contribution. The violence was too much for those who had previously tolerated or backed Wyclif's teachings, and support for the professor waned. He was investigated by Oxford and eventually dismissed. The Council of London in 1382 condemned ten propositions derived from his teachings, although Wyclif was not mentioned by name.[44] Wyclif died of a stroke in 1384. The Council of Constance posthumously declared him a heretic. His body was exhumed by secular authorities and burned in 1424.

In 1382, King Richard II of England married Princess Anne of Bohemia and, as a result of the union, cultural and educational exchanges occurred between the two nations. Bohemian students came to Oxford to study, where they encountered the teachings of Wyclif. They brought these heretical teachings to Prague, where the priest, teacher, and popular preacher Jan Hus embraced and expounded upon them. Like Wyclif, Hus began preaching against

---

43. Although it is popular to believe that Wyclif's followers were the first to translate the Bible into English, Thomas More defuses that notion when he writes, "The whole Bible long before Wyclif's day was by virtuous and learned men translated into the English tongue, and by good and godly people with devotion and soberness well and reverently read." See Henry G. Graham, *Where We Got the Bible: Our Debt to the Catholic Church* (Rockford, IL: TAN Books and Publishers, 2004 [1992]), 104.
44. Daniel-Rops, *The Protestant Reformation*, vol. 1, 218.

corruption in the Church and ecclesial abuses.

Significant problems plagued the Church in Bohemia at the time. Clerical immorality was rampant, and there was widespread resentment against the Church, which owned nearly fifty percent of all land in the kingdom.[45] These issues, along with the presence of a heavy anti-German nationalist sentiment (the kingdom was part of the German-based Holy Roman Empire), produced a rich environment for revolutionaries and heretics.

Jan Hus studied philosophy and theology at the University of Prague, where he was appointed a professor in 1398. He rose through the university administration and became rector in 1402. He was a popular and commanding preacher. Adopting most of Wyclif's teachings, Hus challenged Catholic doctrine on papal authority, advocated *sola scriptura*, and denied sacred Tradition. He also condemned the veneration of the saints and the granting of indulgences. Like Wyclif, he viewed the hierarchy of the Church as ministers of Satan and denied the universal jurisdiction and primacy of the pope. Hus believed that the Church was built on the personal faith of Saint Peter and that Jesus had not instituted the Petrine office. The University of Prague condemned Wyclif's teachings in 1403, but Hus continued to propagate them. The archbishop of Prague excommunicated him in 1410. Violence erupted in the city and crowds burned copies of papal bulls. Hus was forced to flee the city in 1412 and stayed in the castle of a friend, where he wrote his heretical work *Treatise on the Church*.

Hus appealed to the newly convened council at Constance in 1414 concerning his teachings. He arrived there under an imperial order of safe conduct. Despite the guarantee of safety, he was arrested after questioning by an ecclesiastical tribunal and held in a Dominican monastery, where he spent the next six months. The council fathers charged Hus with heresy, and a trial commenced. The Bohemian heretic gave a spirited and frustrating defense of himself by evading and deflecting the questions from the pros-

---

45. Ibid., 220.

ecution. For example, accused of calling the pope "Antichrist," "Hus responded that he had not said it — all he had said was that a pope who sold benefices, who was arrogant, greedy, and otherwise contrary to Christ in way of life, was Antichrist."[46] The council condemned numerous teachings drawn from Hus' writings and demanded he repudiate them, including a teaching known as *utraquism*, which demanded Comunion under both species (Host and Precious Blood) for the laity. Despite repeated opportunities to recant his heresy and reconcile with the Church, Hus persisted in his error. Declared an obstinate heretic, Hus was remanded to the secular authorities and burned at the stake on July 6, 1415. Hus's death sparked a fifteen-year civil war in Bohemia, which became a microcosm of the spasm of violence that would engulf all of Christendom a century and a half later.[47]

THE MAID OF ORLÉANS — SAINT JOAN OF ARC

The fourteenth century witnessed the beginnings of a bloody conflict between England and France. The Hundred Years' War began during the reign of King Edward III (r. 1327–1377), a grandson of Philip IV of France. Edward laid claim to the French throne and began a series of military campaigns over the English monarch's right to rule France. The English appeared to have gained the upper hand in the conflict early in the fifteenth century, when King Henry V (r. 1413–1422) won a huge victory on the field of Agincourt in 1415. Henry's victory allowed for his marriage to Catherine, daughter of the French king Charles VI (r. 1380–1422). Henry was recognized as the heir to the French

---

46. Howard Kaminsky, *A History of the Hussite Revolution* (Berkeley, CA: 1967), 39-40, quoted in Warren H. Carroll, *The Glory of Christendom: A History of Christendom*, vol. 3 (Front Royal, VA: Christendom Press, 1993), 488.

47. In the twentieth century, as part of his desire to purify the memory of the Church in anticipation of the third millennium of the Christian faith, Pope Saint John Paul II (r. 1978–2005) expressed regret for the death of Jan Hus. See Pope John Paul II, *Address to an International Symposium on John Hus*, December 17, 1999, https://w2.vatican.va/content/john-paul-ii/en/speeches/1999/december/documents/hf_jp-ii_spe_17121999_jan-hus.html.

throne, but unexpectedly died at the age of thirty-five in 1422 and never became king of France. Despite their monarch's death, the English army continued campaigning in France, taking several cities in 1423 and 1424. By the following year, the French were in dire straits. France was seemingly on the verge of becoming a part of the patrimony of England.

In the summer of 1425, a thirteen-year-old French maiden, the daughter of Isabelle Romee and Jacques d'Arc, began to receive messages concerning her divine mission to save France. Joan received messages from Saint Michael the Archangel over the next three years, which, seemingly, prophesied the impossible. The archangel told Joan to "choose your standard and raise it boldly! You shall lead the Dauphin to Reims, that he may there receive the crown and unction that are his by right! You shall deliver France from the English!"[48] Michael also told Joan to inspire French soldiers to fight more bravely, that she would lead these soldiers into battle, and that God had chosen her for this special mission.

Four years later, Joan arrived at Chinon castle to meet with Dauphin Charles. The seventeen-year-old girl was examined by theologians from Poitiers who told her, "God cannot wish us to believe in you unless he sends us a sign."[49] Joan responded brusquely: "In God's name, I have not come to Poitiers to make signs. But lead me to Orléans (French city besieged by the English), and I will show you the signs I was sent to make."[50] Joan also made several predictions to the assembled theologians, including that the English would be defeated and the siege of Orléans lifted; the Dauphin would be anointed king at Reims; the city of Paris would return to the king's rule; and the Duke of Orléans, captured at Agincourt and held in England, would return to France. After their examination, the theologians declared

---

48. Daniel-Rops, *The Protestant Reformation*, vol. 1, 109.
49. Régine Pernoud, *The Retrial of Joan of Arc: Evidence for her Vindication*, trans. J.M. Cohen (San Francisco: Ignatius Press, 2007 [1955]), 113.
50. Ibid.

that "one can find no evil in her, but only goodness, humility, virginity, devoutness, honesty, and simplicity."[51] Joan was allowed to meet with Charles and told him "most noble Lord Dauphin, I have come and am sent by God to bring help to you and your kingdom."[52] She convinced the Dauphin of her authenticity by telling him a secret known only to him and God, of which the Lord had granted her knowledge.

A month after meeting the Dauphin, Joan was in charge of four thousand French soldiers on their way to lift the siege of Orléans, which had been under English attack for seven months. The English had designed the siege to starve the citizens of the city, and conditions were at the breaking point. Joan's forces fought the English outside of the city and won when the English withdrew from the siege. The victory at Orléans placed the English on the defensive and was a major turning point in the Hundred Years' War. Several months later, Dauphin Charles was crowned king of France as Charles VII (r. 1422–1461) in Reims cathedral, the traditional place of French coronations, with Joan at his side.

Joan's fortunes changed the following year while she commanded the defense of the city of Compiègne against a combined English and Burgundian siege. Joan led a sortie outside the gates. When her forces retreated, the city defenders were too quick in closing the gate, trapping Joan outside the walls of the city. Burgundian soldiers captured her and then sold her to the English for ten thousand gold crowns.[53] The English allowed the French collaborator Bishop Cauchon to begin heretical proceedings against Joan in January 1431. Cauchon had been forced from his diocese (Beauvais) by Joan's victories and had lent his support to the English, who he hoped would give him the Diocese of Rouen upon their total victory in France.

Cauchon transported Joan to Rouen, which had been un-

---

51. Ibid. 106.
52. Ibid., 116.
53. Or $225,000 in modern value. See Pernoud, *Retrial*, 192.

der English occupation since 1421, where she was held for three months and suffered through fifteen formal interrogation sessions. She was asked leading questions in an effort to trap and expose her, but Joan proved more than a match for Cauchon and his cronies. When asked if she was in God's grace, Joan wisely answered, "If I am in it, may God keep me in it, and if I am not, may it be God's will to put me in it."[54] Eventually, Joan was charged with four counts of "heresy," including defying the authority of the Church, being inspired by false and demonic voices, and wearing men's clothes.[55] After repeated sessions and interrogations, Joan finally broke and signed an act of abjuration, which she could not read. Found guilty of "errors of faith, of blasphemy, and of rebellion against the Church," she was sentenced to life imprisonment.[56] However, five days later, Joan recanted her confession. Cauchon declared her a relapsed heretic. On May 30, 1431, Joan was burned at the stake in Rouen. Her heart was found intact in the remains of the bier, and her ashes were scattered in the Seine River.

Nearly twenty years later, King Charles VII entered Rouen and immediately began a royal inquiry into Joan's death. The royal inquirers interviewed witnesses, reviewed the trial transcripts, and produced a report with findings that showed several irregularities in the trial of Joan. The partiality of her judges was questioned, and multiple defects in inquisitorial procedure were noticed, including Joan's imprisonment in a secular jail rather than an ecclesiastical one, where she should have been housed due to the charges of heresy. Joan had not been provided a defense counsel, and her appeal to Rome after sentencing had not been honored. Her immediate execution after her recantation was also highly irregular, as she should have been remanded to the state.

---

54. Pernoud, *Retrial*, 17.
55. This last charge was correct. Joan wore men's clothes on military campaign as a practical matter, but also as a guard to her chastity. She continued the practice in captivity as five Englishmen, one of whom attempted to rape her, guarded her.
56. Pernoud, *Retrial*, 30.

The presence of Bishop Cauchon at her execution was in violation of canon law, which forbade clerics from attending such activities. Finally, the royal inquiry deemed it highly irregular for an "unrepentant heretic" to have received the last sacraments. A papal commission established by Pope Callistus III (r. 1455–1458) continued the work of the royal inquiry in 1455. Twenty-five years after Joan's death, Bishop Jean Jouvenel of Rouen proclaimed the official verdict of the papal commission: "We, sitting on our judgment seat and with our thoughts only on God ... say, pronounce, decree, and declare the said trial and sentence (of condemnation) to be contaminated with fraud, calumny, wickedness, contradictions, and manifest errors of fact and law, and together with the abjuration, the execution, and all their consequences to have been and to be null, without value or effect, and to be quashed."[57]

In a symbolic gesture, the articles of Joan's accusation were torn in two. Joan the Maid's reputation was restored and her divine mission acknowledged. Her actions had saved France from English domination and very likely provided for the maintenance of the Catholic faith in France — for what would have been the fate of the eldest daughter of the Church had she failed and England succeeded? England separated itself from the Church through the actions of Henry VIII and his successors in the sixteenth century. France would also have fallen into the Protestant heresy, if not for the actions of Saint Joan of Arc.[58]

THE COUNCIL OF FLORENCE (1431–1445)

In the year of Joan's illegal execution, an ecumenical council gathered in Basel by order of Pope Martin V. The council's location was eventually transferred twice, first to Ferrara and then to Florence, from whence it takes its name. The council's main accomplishment was the unification of the two halves of

---

57. Ibid., 287–288.
58. Joan was beatified in 1909 by Pope Saint Pius X and canonized by Pope Benedict XV in 1920.
For Joan's actions saving France from the Protestant revolt, see Carroll, *The Glory of Christendom*, 522.

the Church, East and West. The long-sought-after reunion was briefly achieved previously at the Second Council of Lyons in 1274, when Emperor Michael VIII Palaeologus agreed to reunite in order to secure a papal alliance against Charles of Anjou. That thirteenth-century reunion lasted only eight years; Michael VIII's successor, Andronicus II, repudiated the unpopular reconciliation in 1282. In the fifteenth century, the Ottoman Turks pressed the Byzantines, and Emperor John VIII (r. 1425–1448) believed Western military aid would be forthcoming with an agreement to reunite. The Byzantine envoys to the council agreed to papal primacy. Pope Eugenius IV (r. 1431–1447) proclaimed the reunion on July 6, 1439. Despite the official reunion, many in the East were not happy, and Emperor Constantine XI (r. 1449–1453) deferred the publication of the decree for a time. Unfortunately, the Byzantine Empire soon ceased to exist after the Ottomans captured the capital city of Constantinople, an action that solidified the break between the two halves of the Church.

THE END OF THE EMPIRE — CONSTANTINOPLE FALLS

In the late thirteenth century, a Turkish emir known as Osman established a strong government, bolstered by an efficient and ruthlessly effective military.[59] Osman pushed westward and engaged the Byzantine Empire in the first of a long series of engagements.[60] By the late fourteenth century, the Ottomans were making incursions deep into imperial territory in the Balkan states. Military victories were the foundation of the Ottoman Empire, and the goal of every ruler was expansion, conquest, and world domination. The rise and advance of the Ottoman Turks necessitated an evolution in the crusading movement. Previously, the movement had focused on defensive wars to liberate ancient

---

59. The following section is adapted from my book *The Glory of the Crusades*, 208–214.
60. The Ottomans took their name from their first ruler, Osman.

Christian territories from the forces of Islam. With the Turks, however, the crusading movement focused on defensive wars to protect the European homeland and to survive.

Mehmet II, known as the "Drinker of Blood," became sultan of the Ottoman Empire in 1451. He embarked on a policy of total domination over the Byzantine Empire. He knew that the key to destroying Byzantium was the conquest of Constantinople, so he had been studying the city and planning his conquest ever since the young age of thirteen.[61] Mehmet knew that his army was superior to the Byzantines' in numbers of men, quality of officers, and expertise in siege tactics; however, he had also studied and learned from past military failures at Constantinople. Those armies had failed because they could not find a way past the massive Theodosian defensive walls. Mehmet had something in quantity and quality that those previous armies had not — cannons. Mehmet designed a siege that focused on destroying the walls using gunpowder, but he also knew that available cannons were not strong enough. He needed a bigger gun. A year before the siege, he had met a Hungarian engineer named Urban who was looking for work. Urban had recently offered his services to the Byzantine emperor, who had no use (or funds) for his skills, so Urban went to the Ottomans.[62] Mehmet ordered Urban to begin work on a super gun that would bring Constantinople to its knees. It took Urban three months of hard work, but he produced the largest bronze-cast cannon in the world. It was twenty-seven feet long, with a barrel of eight inches, and was thirty inches across the muzzle.[63] The cannon fired a solid shot eight feet in circumference (weighing 1,500 pounds) a full mile.[64] The cannon was so large it required sixty oxen and two hundred men to move it and could only travel two and half miles a day.[65] Firing the gun

---

61. Roger Crowley, *1453: The Holy War for Constantinople and the Clash of Islam and the West* (New York, 2005), 42.
62. Doukas, *Fragmenta Historicorum Graecorum*, vol. 5 (Paris, 1870), 247–248. In Crowley, *1453*, 90.
63. Crowley, *1453*, 93–94.
64. Ibid., 94
65. Ibid.

310 | CHAPTER SIX

was such a complex and labor-intensive evolution that it could only be fired seven times a day.[66] Mehmet now had a gun that could demolish the walls of Constantinople.

The Ottoman force arrived outside Constantinople on Easter Sunday, April 1, 1453. In accordance with the rules of war at the time, the city was asked to surrender, and it refused. The bombardment began in earnest and was nonstop from April 12 through April 18. The sixty-nine guns in the Turkish artillery fired 120 shots a day.[67] Urban's super gun hammered the Theodosian walls and caused extensive damage, but it developed cracks and ruptured early in the siege, robbing Mehmet of his special weapon.

A month into the siege, the defenders' situation was desperate. Food was scarce, supplies were dwindling, and the constant Turkish artillery barrage and assaults had taken their toll. Many soldiers left the wall at times to find food for their families, further weakening the defenses. A council of war recommended that Emperor Constantine XI leave the city, gather new troops, regroup, and strike the Turks from the rear, but the emperor refused to leave. As the siege approached its second month, both sides were eager for an end. Mehmet sent a proposal of surrender to the city that stipulated an annual tribute payment of one hundred thousand bezants and abandonment of the city. Constantine rejected the offer.

On May 29, Mehmet ordered a general assault. The Byzantine clergy prayed, blessed the city, and carried icons along the walls. The Ottomans kept coming, and at one point, a stone from one of Mehmet's big guns opened a breach in the inner enclosure. Almost immediately, three hundred Muslim warriors poured in through the gap, but were met with fierce Byzantine resistance. The defenders had been fighting for nearly four hours and were exhausted, but the Turks were unyielding. Mehmet ordered five

---

66. Ibid., 116.
67. Total number of guns from Crowley, *1453*, page 112, and shots per day from page 118.

thousand Janissaries forward. The crack troops gave out a yell that was heard five miles away.[68] Once more, the beleaguered Byzantine defenders beat back the Ottoman attack. The tide appeared to turn in favor of the Byzantines. Constantine could sense it, and he urged his warriors: "Brave soldiers, the enemy's army is weakening, the crown of victory is ours. God is on our side — keep fighting!"[69] In war, however, victory can be elusive and defeat sudden. Some Ottoman troops found an unguarded postern gate near the Blachernae Palace. In a repeat of the action that had led to the Crusader victory in 1204, they opened the gate and poured into the city, where they scaled the wall, tore down a Christian banner, and replaced it with the Ottoman standard. Ottoman troops surged past the defenders, and within fifteen minutes, thirty thousand Muslim warriors were in the city.[70] Horrified at the sudden change in the situation, Constantine rushed to the wall and disappeared in the melee, dying among his soldiers defending his beloved city.

The Muslim troops ran through the undefended city, slaughtering the inhabitants. Women, including nuns, and boys were savagely raped.[71] A large group of citizens trying to escape the Ottoman horde ran to Hagia Sophia, the sixth-century church built by Justinian the Great and the largest church in Christendom; some were killed, but most were captured as slaves. When news reached Mehmet that his troops were in the city, he rode straight for Hagia Sophia, which he entered and declared a mosque.[72] In the end, 4,000 Christians were killed and 50,000 seized, of whom 30,000 became slaves.[73] The Roman Empire was extinguished.

News of the fall of Constantinople shocked the West. The

---

68. Crowley, *1453*, 211.
69. Leonard of Chios, *De Capta a Mehemethe II Constantinopoli*, 44, quoted in Crowley, *1453*, 177.
70. Crowley, *1453*, 215.
71. Ibid., 220.
72. It remained a place of Muslim worship until 1935 when it was turned into a museum. Recent reports indicate a movement in Istanbul to return the space to a mosque.
73. Number of killed see Tyerman, *God's War*, 864. Number seized and enslaved see Crowley, *1453*, 233,235.

next three popes called for Crusades to liberate the city, but Western rulers were too preoccupied with their own concerns. Their selfishness allowed the travesty of the end of the Empire and the ascendancy of Islam to go unchallenged.

Five years after the loss of Constantinople, Aeneas Sylvius Piccolomini was elected pope, taking the name Pius II (r. 1458–1464). He was completely dedicated to the crusading ideal, and endeavored to organize a Crusade to liberate Constantinople. Pius II called the temporal rulers of Western Europe to gather at a congress in Mantua in 1459, to discuss plans for the liberation of Constantinople. Unfortunately, the response was less than enthusiastic, and none of the major rulers came to Mantua. At the Congress, Pius II gave a speech in which he blamed the conquest of Constantinople on the lack of Western response to the city in her hour of need, and he reminded his listeners of the savagery of the Turk.[74] Pius also recalled the heroes of the First Crusade in an effort to shame and motivate the absent secular leaders to take up arms in the cause of Christ: "Oh, that Godfrey, Baldwin, Eustace, Hugh, Bohemond, Tancred, and those other brave men who reconquered Jerusalem were here! Truly they would not need so many words to persuade them."[75] While exhorting the warriors of Christendom to take back Constantinople, Pius also engaged in evangelization in the hope of converting the Ottomans. In 1461, he sent a personal letter to Mehmet the Conqueror, urging him to abandon the false religion of Muhammad and embrace the true light of Christ. His request was denied.

After several fruitless years of cajoling, exhorting, and pleading with the secular rulers of Christendom to take the cross, Pius decided to take the cross himself. Pius addressed his reason for becoming a Crusader (an unprecedented action for a pope) in a letter: "Our cry, Go forth! has resounded in vain. Perhaps if the

---

74. Pius II in Franz Babinger, *Mehmet the Conqueror and His Time* 170–171, quoted in Crowley, *1453*, 242.

75. Quoted in Diane Moczar, *Islam at the Gates: How Christendom Defeated the Ottoman Turks* (Manchester, NH: Sophia Institute Press, 2008), 90.

word is, Come with me! It will have more effect. That is why we have determined to proceed in person against the Turks, and by word and deed to stir up all Christian princes to follow our example. It may be that, seeing their teacher and father, the Bishop of Rome, the Vicar of Christ, a weak and sickly old man, going to war, they will be ashamed to stay at home."[76]

He believed his personal example of taking the cross would be the impetus for others to do likewise. Pius's plan began to come to fruition when the rulers of Hungary, Venice, and Burgundy entered into an alliance with the Papal States to fight the Turks. The pope traveled to the muster site at Ancona in August 1464 to await the arrival of other Crusaders. Unfortunately, the pope's expectation for large numbers of Crusaders did not materialize, and those troops who did show quickly broke into fighting between national groups. As was common with large groups of soldiers gathered together in close quarters during the summer, disease broke out, and Crusaders died. The great Pius II contracted the plague and also died, and so ended his Crusade.

SAFEGUARDING THE FAITH — THE SPANISH INQUISITION

Fifteenth-century Spain was a unique and distinctive part of Christendom. The south, known as al-Andalus, was home to a Muslim-majority population of mostly farmers and silk producers. Central and northern Spain were Christian areas of six million people living in two kingdoms, Castile and Aragon. The Muslim conquest of Spain in the eighth century led to an uneasy coexistence among Muslims, Jews, and Christians. Christians living in Muslim-occupied territory were treated poorly, and there was overwhelming societal pressure to convert. At times, warriors entered into alliances with other warriors based on strategic or

76. Ludwig von Pastor, *History of the Popes*, vol. III (St. Louis, 1895–1935), 326, quoted in Carroll, *The Glory of Christendom*, 583.

economic concerns regardless of religion. The famous Christian warrior Rodrigo Díaz de Vivar, or "El Cid" (1043–1099), was a Castilian nobleman but served a Muslim ruler for a time, and then governed the city of Valencia as an independent ruler.

The Christian struggle to reconquer Spain from the forces of Islam constituted the longest war in human history — it was waged for 780 years (from 711 to 1492). By the mid-thirteenth century, Christian forces had pushed the Muslims to a southern enclave at Granada after liberating the key cities of Cordoba (1236), Valencia (1238), and Seville (1248). The military reality changed Spanish society, as the Christians now found themselves stronger than their Muslim overlords for the first time in centuries. This situation produced a social-perception change. Christians were no longer the servile group beholden to Muslims. Jews had been present in Spain since at least the third century, and by the Middle Ages Spain contained the largest population of Jews in Europe, although they were less than 2 percent of the total population.[77] Spanish Jews lived in urban areas, within separate communities, and could especially be found in the sectors of finance and medicine. Muslims, known in Spain as Moors, arrived in the early eighth century as part of the large Islamic military offensive, which had succeeded in conquering ancient Christian territory in lands that bordered the Mediterranean Sea. The successful *Reconquista* pushed Muslims into the south of Spain, where the last major stronghold at Granada surrendered on January 2, 1492.

King Fernando and Queen Isabel, who created the united Kingdom of Spain from their respective kingdoms of Aragon and Castile in 1479, initially favored a moderate approach in dealing with the defeated Muslims, but violent revolts in 1499, 1500, and 1501 changed their policy to one of forced conversions.[78] Major evangelization efforts were undertaken to convert the Muslim

---

77. Henry Kamen, *The Spanish Inquisition: A Historical Revision* (New Haven, CT: Yale University Press, 1997), 8.
78. The names of the monarchs are commonly Anglicized and rendered Ferdinand and Isabella, but I have chosen to use the Spanish version.

population. Those who received baptism were known as *Moriscos*, and, although they were Christian converts, they continued to live differently from the "Old Christians." *Moriscos* refrained from eating pork, the most common meat in Spain at the time; did not drink wine; and refrained from using butter or lard in cooking, preferring olive oil instead. In 1504, a Muslim scholar issued a *fatwa* (ruling) that, in times of persecution, such as in Spain, Muslims could conform to all outward rules of the Catholic faith without defecting from their true Islamic beliefs. This teaching, along with the large presence of *Moriscos* and *Marranos* (Jewish converts to the Faith), produced a general feeling of unease among the Spanish Christian population.[79] How could one know if a Jew or Muslim converted for authentic reasons and not for societal expediency? This situation led to the belief that *conversos*, Jewish and Muslim converts to the Faith, were not authentically Catholic, but posed as a "fifth element" in Spanish society that could undermine the crown and pose a national security threat to the country. Fear became a dominant emotion in Spanish society — fear that tens of thousands of people in Spain lived false lives by pretending to be Christian while still practicing their old faiths in secret. This belief was perpetuated by the structure of Spanish society, which prevented career advancement for non-Christians.

Many *conversos* became well-known and well-connected in Spanish society. One such *converso* was Salomon Halevi, the former rabbi of Burgos, who took the name Pablo de Santa Maria upon his baptism. He was ordained a priest, then later became the bishop of Burgos and papal legate. Some *conversos* retained their Jewish cultural traits and were treated as heretics by Old Christians. Sadly, Spanish neurosis concerning the *conversos* led to the forced expulsion of the remaining Jewish population by the crown in 1492. Fernando and Isabel were not personally anti-Semitic, but the presence of Jews in Spain, in their eyes, constituted

---

79. The Castilian-Portuguese word *marrano* meant "little pig." See Daniel-Rops, *The Protestant Reformation*, vol. 1, 324.

a national security threat and had a negative effect on the *converso* situation, as Jews could seduce converts to not live their new faith authentically.[80] The monarchs hoped the expulsion order would produce mass conversions rather than emigration, and nearly fifty percent of the Jewish population (totaling forty thousand) did convert and remain in Spain. The exiles found refuge in Italy, Portugal, and North Africa.[81]

In order to deal with the situation, Fernando and Isabel petitioned Pope Sixtus IV (r. 1471–1484) to establish an institutional tribunal in Spain, under the control of the crown, to investigate heresy and the *converso* problem. The tribunal, which came to be known as the Spanish Inquisition, "was not to act as a court of justice but as a disciplinary body called into existence to meet a national emergency."[82] The pope agreed to the crown's request and issued a bull establishing the Inquisition in Spain on November 1, 1478.

The creation of the Inquisition in Spain was driven by political, more than religious, concerns. National security and consolidation of power in the monarchy were the primary reasons for Fernando and Isabel's request.[83] The Spanish Inquisition was not created to enforce absolute uniformity in faith, as "the ruthless drive against 'heresy,' far from aiming at unification, was no more than the culmination of a long period of social and political pressure directed against the *conversos*."[84] The Inquisition was not an omnipotent tribunal affecting every aspect of Spanish life. Its work was focused mostly in southern Spain and in urban areas. Indeed, an individual living in the rural areas of Spain could go his entire life without ever seeing an inquisitor, and 95 percent of the population never had any contact with the Inquisition.[85]

The Inquisition did not have jurisdiction over practicing

---

80. See Kamen, *The Spanish Inquisition*, 20.
81. The Spanish expulsion of the Jews was not the first in European history, as both England in 1290 and France in 1306 had forced Jews out of those areas.
82. Ibid., 193.
83. Ibid., 45.
84. Ibid., 61.
85. Ibid., 280 and 282.

Muslims and Jews, only over baptized individuals. It existed under royal, not papal, control, as evidenced by the king's statement to newly appointed inquisitors: "Although you and the others enjoy the title of inquisitor, it is I and the queen who have appointed you, and without our support you can do very little."[86] The Inquisition was overseen by the *suprema*, a body of six members appointed by the king, with an inquisitor general, who was nominated by the king and appointed by the pope. The tribunals consisted of two inquisitors, usually trained lawyers and/or theologians, assisted by an assessor, a constable, and a prosecutor. There were never more than fifty inquisitors in Spain. Initially, the tribunals were itinerant, but by 1495 they were established in sixteen locations, subsequently reduced to only seven cities in the early sixteenth century.[87] The Inquisition initially focused on *conversos* but also acted as a disciplinary body for Old Christians to ensure right conduct and moral living. Sexual crimes, such as fornication, bigamy, and sodomy, were investigated, although the *suprema*, in 1509, ordered no action to be taken against homosexuals unless heresy was involved,[88] whereas secular courts treated sodomy as a capital offense.[89]

The legal procedure used by the Spanish Inquisition was similar to that developed by the medieval inquisitors in the thirteenth century. The inquisitor general established the specific procedures, the first set of which was issued by Tomás de Torquemada in 1484. When inquisitors went to a new area, they presented their credentials to the secular authorities. At the next Sunday Mass, after the homily or the recitation of the Creed, an inquisitor held aloft a crucifix to the assembly and asked everyone to raise his right hand, make the Sign of the Cross, and repeat a

---

86. J. Angel Sema Muñoz, *El establecimiento de la Inquisición en Aragón* (1484–1486) (*Documentos para su estudio*, Zaragoza, 1987), 229, quoted in Kamen, *The Spanish Inquisition*, 137.

87. See Kamen, *The Spanish Inquisition*, 142.

88. Henry Kamen, *The Phoenix and the Flame: Catalonia and the Counter Reformation* (New Haven, CT: Yale University Press, 1997), 268, cited in Stark, *Bearing False Witness*, 132.

89. Michael Goodish, "Sodomy in Medieval Secular Law," *Journal of Homosexuality* 1: 295–302, 1976, cited in Stark, *Bearing False Witness*, 132.

solemn oath to support the work of the Inquisition. The inquisitor then preached about the evils of heresy and issued an "edict of grace," which was a period of thirty to forty days when repentant heretics could voluntarily confess their crime to the inquisitors, receive a light penance, and be reconciled to the Church. After the edict of grace, denunciations by others were allowed so that "fear of neighbors, rather than of the Inquisition, was the first and constant concern of those denounced."[90] The names of witnesses who denounced others for heresy were kept secret from the accused in order to safeguard them from revenge.

The inquisitors then assessed the evidence against an individual. Material evidence included being caught in the act of heresy or immorality. Verbal evidence was the most common and illustrated the importance of words in Spanish society at the time. Verbal evidence could come from the statement of family members or the hearsay of neighbors. If the evidence supported the presence of heresy, the prosecutor for the Inquisition drew up charges and issued an arrest warrant for the accused, who was housed in an ecclesiastical jail until the hearing was completed. Conditions in ecclesiastical jails were far better than secular jails; in certain cases those accused of secular crimes, who were housed in secular jails, made heretical statements simply to be moved to ecclesiastical jails for better living conditions.[91] During incarceration and the trial, the accused's property and goods were seized by the Inquisition and inventoried. If the accused was acquitted or penanced, his goods were returned; if he were found guilty, his property was kept by the Inquisition, sold, and the proceeds turned into the crown, which then disbursed funds back to the Inquisition for its expenses. Confiscation of goods was the standard punishment for heresy in canon law, and many believed the Inquisition targeted the rich and well-off in order to finance its activities.[92]

---

90. Kamen, *The Spanish Inquisition*, 175.
91. Ibid., 184.
92. Ibid., 149.

The legal process of the Inquisition was fair and just, much more so than that of secular courts. The accused was allowed an advocate who could assist in their defense. The accused could call favorable witnesses to testify on their behalf. They could also disable hostile witnesses by providing a list of enemies to the inquisitors, who would then ignore the testimony of those witnesses. This was a very effective defense measure, as evidenced by the example of Gaspar Torralba, who, in 1531, gave a list of 152 enemies to the inquisitors. Most of the thirty-five witnesses against him were on his list. As a result, he received a light penitential sentence.[93] The accused could also present extenuating circumstances, such as drunkenness, insanity, or the excesses of youth, to explain their heretical utterances.

As with the medieval inquisitors, torture was allowed to elicit a confession but was never used as a form of punishment. Although allowed, torture could only be applied once, for no more than fifteen minutes and as last resort. It was rarely used (in only 2 percent of all cases), and much less frequently than in secular courts.[94] All torture sessions were carefully recorded and were always applied by the secular authorities in the presence of the inquisitors, a representative of the local bishop, and a physician. The torture session could not result in loss of limb or life, as canon law forbade the death penalty or shedding of blood by ecclesiastical tribunals.[95] The accused who confessed during a torture session had to repeat the confession the following day for its admissibility in court, as forced confessions were invalid. The methods utilized for torture included stretching, where the accused was hung by the wrists from a pulley on the ceiling, with heavy weights attached to the feet. The person was then slowly raised and suddenly dropped, which produced a jerking motion that stretched the body and could dislocate arms and legs. Water

---

93. Ibid., 195.
94. Thomas Madden, "The Truth About the Spanish Inquisition," *Crisis* Magazine, October 1, 2003, *http://www.catholicity.com/commentary/madden/03481.html.*
95. Kamen, *The Spanish Inquisition,* 190.

torture was also utilized, wherein a person was tied on a rack with their mouth forced open. A linen cloth was then put down the throat and water was slowly poured onto the cloth, giving the sensation of drownng. Binding was also utilized — ropes, which were tightened by the torturer, causing pain and discomfort, were bound to a person and bit into the body. Despite the use of torture, the Inquisition was the only criminal court of the time to put a limitation on the methods of torture.[96]

After the trial, sentencing occurred either privately or publicly in a ceremony known as the *auto-de-fé* ("act of faith"). The first *auto-de-fé* occurred on February 6, 1481, and consisted of a procession of penitents, the celebration of Mass, and an act of reconciliation. Unrepentant heretics were not executed during the ceremony; they were remanded to the state and burned at the stake, usually outside the city. *Auto-de-fé* ceremonies were popular because they celebrated public repentance and reinforced the Faith in Spanish society, but they were not a normal part of life. They were expensive to conduct and became a rare, once-in-a-lifetime experience.

There were many possible verdicts for those accused of heresy. If the evidence did not support a conviction, the accused was acquitted. Those accused who confessed to heresy and were repentant received a penitential sentence that could include swearing an oath to avoid sin; paying a fine; going into exile; enduring physical punishment, such as flogging (usually one hundred lashes); and serving prison time, which was not literally observed and was rarely served in an actual jail (usually served in the accused's own house or a monastery). Naval galley service was also imposed for the crimes of bigamy and sodomy. A common punishment was the public wearing of the *sanbenito*, a special yellow garment with one or two diagonal crosses. Penitents wore the *sanbenito* for a specified period of time (a few months to a lifetime), and once the period was completed, the *sanbenito* was frequently raised to

---

96. "The Holy See and the Spanish Inquisition," in *The Dublin Review* (July–October 1867), 198, cited in Gary Michuta, *Hostile Witnesses: How the Historic Enemies of the Church Prove Christianity* (El Cajon, CA: Catholic Answers Press, 2016), 192.

the rafters of the penitent's parish church.

The Church remanded obstinate heretics (those who refused multiple opportunities to repent) to the state for punishment. Although popular "black legends" paint the Spanish Inquisition as one of the greatest institutions of mass murder in history, the historical record proves otherwise. In the 44,674 cases brought before the Spanish Inquisition from 1540 to 1700, only 826 obstinate heretics were remanded to the state for execution.[97] In roughly the same period of time in Protestant England, there was an average of 750 hangings per year for various crimes.[98] During the height of the Inquisition's power and activity, from 1478 to 1528, it remanded a total of 1,500 obstinate heretics to the state, which equates to thirty people per year.[99]

Although some criticized the Inquisition and its penances, especially the wearing of the *sanbenito*, "the people as a whole gave their support to its existence. The tribunal was, after all, not a despotic body imposed on them tyrannically, but a logical expression of the social prejudices prevalent in their midst. It was created to deal with a problem of heresy, and as long as the problem was deemed to exist people seemed to accept it."[100] The Spanish Inquisition produced positive results not seen elsewhere in Christendom. The work of the inquisitors ensured that Spain experienced religious peace when the rest of Christendom was convulsed with spasms of violence from the Protestant Revolution. Unlike other areas of Christendom, Spain did not produce a native heresy, and the Protestant movement never gained ground in the country. On the contrary, while the rest of Christendom was fighting the Protestant heresy, Spain was engaged in an authentic

97. Jaime Contreras and Gustave Henningsen, "Forty-Four Thousand Cases of the Spanish Inquisition (1540–1700): Analysis of a Historical Data Bank," in *The Inquisition in Early Modern Europe: Studies on Sources and Methods*, ed. Gustave Henningsen and John Tedeschi (DeKalb, IL: Northern Illinois University Press, 1986), 100–129, cited in Stark, *Bearing False Witness*, 122.
98. V. A. C. Gatrell, *The Hanging Tree: Execution and the English People, 1770–1868* (Oxford, UK: Oxford University Press, 1994), 7, cited in Stark, *Bearing False Witness*, 122.
99. William E. Monter, *Frontiers of Heresy: The Spanish Inquisition from the Basque Lands to Sicily* (Cambridge, UK: Cambridge University Press, 1990), cited in Stark, *Bearing False Witness*, 121.
100. Kamen, *The Spanish Inquisition*, 314.

322 | CHAPTER SIX

Church reform that predated the reform decrees mandated at the Council of Trent in the mid-sixteenth century.

Myths about the Spanish Inquisition, which still cloud modern-day perceptions, began in the sixteenth century as Protestant propaganda illustrated the Inquisition (and the Catholic Church as a whole) as a threat to personal freedom and liberty. In particular, an exiled Spanish monk-turned-Lutheran, writing under the name Reginaldus Montanus, wrote what would became the standard narrative on the topic, *A Discovery and Plaine Declaration of Sundry Subtill Practices of the Holy Spanish Inquisition* (1567). Montanus's book was translated into English, French, Dutch, German, and Hungarian. It painted the Inquisition as hunting and killing Protestants — there was no mention in the book that the Inquisition focused on *conversos* and not Protestants. John Motley's 1855 book *The Rise of the Dutch Republic* laid the foundation for many myths about the Spanish Inquisition by describing horrible scenes of torture and execution in thoroughly unhistorical fiction. The historical record clearly shows that the Spanish Inquisition was not "an omniscient, omnipotent tribunal whose fingers reached into every corner of the land." Indeed, "for the Inquisition to have been a powerful as suggested, the fifty or so inquisitors in Spain would have had an extensive bureaucracy, a reliable system of informers, regular income, and the cooperation of the secular and ecclesiastical authorities. At no time did it have any of those."[101]

THE RENAISSANCE

A few hundred years earlier in Italy, the artist Giotto (1266–1337) started a revolution.[102] He wanted the viewer of his paintings to feel the human drama of his characters, but the flat style of painting borrowed from the Byzantines — in vogue at the time

---

101. Ibid., 315.
102. The word *Renaissance* is French in origin and means "rebirth," and was first used by Jean Michelet (1798–1874) in his book *History of France* (1855). The following section is adapted from my book *The Real Story of Catholic History*, 137–140.

in Italy — was inadequate for that goal. So, Giotto developed a new technique for rendering depth that allowed for unprecedented realism. His frescoes in Padua's Arena Chapel are among the most evocative in art history. Giotto was "one of the greatest masters of painted drama that has ever lived," and his "style was one of those feats of inspired originality that have occurred only two or three times in the history of art."[103] His techniques would be used in magnificent ways throughout the Renaissance. One might even think that Giotto was one of the most notable artists of the Renaissance, but, in reality, he lived a century before it began. His work illustrates that the Renaissance was not a break from the medieval world and the Church but a fulfillment of them.[104] Many innovations and achievements in art, architecture, and scholarship during medieval times laid the foundations for the Renaissance. The Renaissance is most associated with amazing works of art, especially in painting and sculpture, which never would have been possible save for the Catholic Church, which not only commissioned these works and provided their subject matter, but also defended the creation of art and artists.[105]

SECULAR PRINCES OR POPES?

A succession of ten popes from 1447 to 1521 are known as the "Renaissance Popes" not only because of their patronage of artists and their beautification efforts in Rome, but also because they primarily acted like secular princes instead of universal shepherds. Not every pope in this period was an immoral man, although some were, but all participated in the ecclesiastical abuses of the day, which, along with the fourteenth-century papal crisis, contributed to a loss of respect and prestige for the Roman pontiff throughout Christendom. In the end, their focus on tempo-

---

103. Kenneth Clark, *Civilisation: A Personal View* (New York: Harper & Row, 1969), 80.
104. See Thomas E. Woods, Jr., *How the Catholic Church Built Western Civilization* (Washington, DC: Regnery Publishing, 2005), 124.
105. Ibid., 115–118.

ral issues resulted in serious temporal loss for the Church and produced a divided Western Church that persists in the modern world.

Tommaso Parentucelli was a Dominican who studied at the University of Bologna and became an aide to a cardinal. He attended the Council of Florence. His promising ecclesiastical career culminated in his election as pope in 1447. Taking the name Nicholas V (r. 1447–1455), he focused particularly on controlling Italy, which, at the time, was a patchwork of kingdoms, duchies, and republics. The Republic of Venice and the Duchies of Milan, Genoa, and Savoy dominated northern Italy. The Kingdom of Naples controlled the south, and the Papal States comprised central Italy. Nicholas V also found time to patronize artists. He had a deep love for books and knowledge, so he began collecting manuscripts and rare books. His collection became the Vatican Library, which contained fifteen thousand volumes at his death.[106]

Alfonso de Borja (Italianized to "Borgia") was the first Spaniard elected to the papacy, taking the name Callistus III (r. 1455–1458). Callistus engaged in an offensive show of nepotism that became the staple policy of subsequent Renaissance popes. He gave important curial positions to members of his family, mostly nephews, one of whom later became pope. His pontificate was followed by Pius II (r. 1458–1464), who personally took the cross in an effort to shame Christendom's secular rulers, and Paul II (r. 1464–1471).

Francesco della Rovere loved his family. His two brothers and four sisters produced fifteen children. When della Rovere became pope, taking the name Sixtus IV (r. 1471–1484), he created two of his nephews cardinals, and one later became pope. In 1478, Christendom was scandalized to learn that the pope knew about a plot to assassinate Giuliano de' Medici, the brother of Lorenzo the Magnificent of Florence. One of the pope's nephews organized the plot; another nephew, a cardinal, was

---

106. Daniel-Rops, *The Protestant Reformation*, vol. 1, 258.

implicated. Sixtus knew his family members planned to kill the Medicis in church during Easter Sunday Mass.[107] The murder of Giuliano de' Medici illustrated the evils of a papacy focusing solely on temporal affairs. Sixtus's successor, Innocent VII (r. 1484–1491), was from Genoa and fathered two illegitimate children before becoming pope. He created Giovanni de' Medici, who later became the last Renaissance pope, a cardinal at the age of thirteen.

Rodrigo Borgia was a personally charming and shrewd politician. He was also a cardinal and bishop of the Church who was guilty of the ecclesiastical abuse of pluralism.[108] Borgia enjoyed life and the pleasures associated with it. His relationships with women, even as a cardinal, produced nine illegitimate children. Borgia wanted to be pope, and when Innocent VIII died in 1492, his desire was realized. One cardinal, who would later become pope himself, turned to a compatriot when Borgia was elected and said, "Flee! We are in the clutches of a wolf!"[109] The excitement of fulfilling his long-sought goal overwhelmed Borgia as he screamed, "I am Pope! I am Pope!" after the voting in the conclave revealed his victory.[110] Borgia took the name Alexander VI (r.1492–1503) not to honor previous popes but in memory of Alexander the Great. While pope, Alexander took Giulia Farnese as his mistress (she was nineteen, and he was in his sixties). Cesare Borgia, one of Alexander's illegitimate sons, terrorized Italian towns and villages with an armed band of violent brigands.[111] Alexander's pontificate was focused on temporal affairs and was the epitome of the Renaissance papacy. Machiavelli, after hearing the news of Alexander's death, summarized his pontificate and

107. See Daniel-Rops, *The Protestant Reformation*, vol. 1, 298.
108. Borgia held five wealthy dioceses, which is four too many, but far less than the record of twenty-three dioceses held by one man!
109. Michael Mallett, The Borgias: *The Rise and Fall of a Renaissance Dynasty* (New York, 1969), 118–120, quoted in Carroll, *The Glory of Christendom*, 639.
110. E. R. Chamberlin, *The Fall of the House of Borgia* (New York, 1974), 49, quoted in Carroll, *The Glory of Christendom*, 639.
111. One man who accompanied Cesare, Niccolò Machiavelli, wrote a book about political leadership titled *The Prince*, which may have been modeled on Cesare.

life well when he wrote, "The soul of the glorious Alexander was now borne among the choir of the blessed. Dancing attendance on him were his three devoted, favorite handmaidens: Cruelty, Simony, and Lechery."[112]

THE FIERY PREACHER OF FLORENCE

The young man experienced visions of God calling him to proclaim the "ruinous state of the Church" and to work for her reform.[113] A few years later, he joined the Dominicans and became a famous preacher. His fiery, apocalyptic sermons illustrated his oratorical gifts. He exuded the confidence of a prophet sent by God to proclaim a message of repentance, which, if not heeded, would lead to calamities. Girolamo Savonarola (1452–1498) loved Florence and the Church, but that love led to his violent end. Disgusted with the excesses of the Renaissance popes, especially Alexander VI, as well as the political grip of the de' Medici family on Florence, Savonarola's preaching turned radical in the late fifteenth century. He preached against immorality, corruption, and all forms of vanity expressed in Renaissance society, which led to his followers conducting "bonfires of the vanities," wherein the instruments of vanity, such as mirrors, makeup, wigs, dice, lewd books, immodest clothing, and paintings, were thrown into raging fires. Indicative of his fiery preaching was a sermon against the corruption in the Church, given in 1497:

> Come infamous Church, listen to the words of your Lord: "I have given you splendid robes, but you have made them cover idols; I have given you precious vessels, but you have used them to exalt your false pride. Your simony has profaned my sacraments; lechery has made of you a pockmarked harlot. And you no longer

112. Daniel-Rops, *The Protestant Reformation*, vol. 1., 309.
113. Ibid., 311.

even blush for your sins! Whore that you are! You sit on Solomon's throne, and beckon to all who pass you by. Those who have money you bid a welcome to, and have your pleasure of them; but the man of goodwill is cast outside your doors!"[114]

Savonarola's preaching contributed to the overthrow of the Medicis in 1494. He was invited to sit on the city council, but, in reality, the government of Florence became a dictatorship under Savonarola. His zeal spread through the city. "Bonfires of the vanities" increased, and he encouraged a radical following of the Gospel that included allowing wives to leave their husbands in order to enter the convent and allowing children to denounce their less-than-pious parents.[115]

Alexander VI's patience with Savonarola's attacks ended in 1495 when he summoned the preacher to come to Rome, but Savonarola ignored him. The pope forbade the fiery friar from preaching, but Savonarola ignored this directive as well. The pope's attempt to muzzle Savonarola only increased his zeal. He believed Rome was under the influence of the Antichrist in the person of Alexander VI. He attacked the pope, saying, "Once, anointed priests called their sons 'nephews'; but now they speak no more of nephews, but always of their sons ... O Prostitute Church."[116] In 1497, Alexander VI excommunicated Savonarola for his disobedience, but the Florentine preacher once more refused to waver. He declared Alexander to be a false pope. Mounting a pulpit erected in front of the cathedral in Florence, he raised aloft the Blessed Sacrament and said, "Lord, if my words are not yours, destroy me as I stand here now!"[117] He embraced the heresy of conciliarism by calling for an ecumenical council to meet

114. Ibid., 310.
115. Ibid., 315.
116. J. C. Olin (ed.), *The Catholic Reformation: Savonarola to Ignatius Loyola* (Westminster, MD, 1969), 9, quoted in Eamon Duffy, *Saints and Sinners: A History of the Popes*, 3rd ed. (New Haven, CT: Yale University Press, 2006), 197.
117. Daniel-Rops, *The Protestant Reformation*, vol. 1, 317.

and depose Alexander VI. Savonarola's attacks on the pope and his support of French King Charles VIII's invasion of Italy were deemed too radical. Popular support for his policies and preaching diminished after the Franciscans challenged him to walk through fire to prove his claim of prophecy from God. He refused, but one of his supporters accepted the challenge on the condition of being able to carry the Eucharist with him as he walked the coals. The Franciscans objected to the blasphemous condition. A debate ensued over the terms of the trial and took several hours, during which time a rain shower extinguished the prepared fire. The trial was called off, but the challenge succeeded in turning people away from Savonarola. Finally, Alexander VI informed the Florentines that their city would be placed under interdict if they refused to hand over the rebellious monk. City officials ordered Savonarola's arrest on Palm Sunday 1498. He was tortured, tried, condemned by the secular authorities as a heretic and schismatic, and burned at the stake on May 23, 1498. Savonarola's refusal to obey the pope led to his downfall, but his preaching tapped into the general consensus that the Church needed reform. Unfortunately, the Renaissance popes were not disposed to focus on the necessary reform of the Church.

THE WARRIOR POPE

Alexander VI died in 1503, and the nephew of Pius II was elected to succeed him. Taking the name Pius III (r. 1503) in honor of his uncle, the new pope expressed a desire to pursue the path of peace and to focus on Church reform. But the pope died twenty-six days after his election, serving one of the shortest pontificates in history. Once more, the cardinals gathered. This time they chose the nephew of Pope Sixtus IV, Giuliano della Rovere, who took the name Julius II (r. 1503–1513). The new pope had been guilty of the ecclesiastical abuse of pluralism, holding the sees of Avignon, Bologna, Lausanne, Coutances, Vivirs, Mende, Ostia, and Velletri, along with the abbotship of two monasteries.

Julius II was the epitome of the Renaissance man, with his taste for art, architecture, and carnal pleasures, and had fathered three illegitimate children in his youth. The pope recognized the need for reform in the Church, but instead made it the primary goal of his pontificate to restore the Papal States (which had been lost during the French invasion under Charles VIII) and secure an independent papacy.

Julius wanted to "see the Roman Pontiff the one and only permanent master of Italy," and he embarked on a series of military campaigns.[118] He personally rode into battle with full armor against various Italian towns.[119] His military prowess secured victory for the papal army; its coalition supporters and the Papal States remained firmly under papal control for the next 360 years. In 1506, Julius asked the Swiss Diet for a permanent corps of 200 Swiss mercenaries to form his personal bodyguard. The Swiss Guards swore allegiance to the pope and were given the title "Defenders of the Liberty of the Church."[120] The Swiss Guards have continuously protected the pope since the sixteenth century, and no pope has ever been killed on their watch.

Julius also spent considerable time as a patron of artists and architects. He commissioned multiple paintings, sculptures, and buildings in Rome for the glorification of God. He patronized Raphael and asked him to paint the walls of the papal palace at the Vatican. Most famously, he paid Michelangelo to paint the ceiling of the Sistine Chapel. Julius began a campaign to rebuild the basilica of Saint Peter in 1506, but did not live to see its completion. The Warrior Pope died in 1513, having succeeded in securing the independence of the papacy and keeping Italy free of foreign influence.

---

118. Ibid., 331.
119. The 1965 film *The Agony and the Ecstasy*, with Charlton Heston as Michelangelo and Rex Harrison as Julius II, magnificently captures the pope leading his army in the opening scene.
120. The Swiss were regarded from the thirteenth to the eighteenth centuries as the bravest and most reliable fighting men in Europe, with nearly one million men deployed throughout Christendom. See Robert Royal, *The Pope's Army: 500 Years of the Papal Swiss Guard* (New York: Crossroads, 2006), 36. The Swiss also fought in the American War of Independence.

THE LAST RENAISSANCE POPE

Giovanni de' Medici came from one of the most powerful families in Italy. His father, Lorenzo the Magnificent, was a diplomat,
politician, patron of several great Renaissance artists (including
Michelangelo), and ruler of the Florentine Republic. From an
early age, Giovanni was molded for a life in the Church, as he was
created a cardinal by Pope Innocent VIII at the age of thirteen
(though he did not officially assume the functions of the office
until he turned sixteen). In 1513, the College of Cardinals sat in
conclave to elect the successor of Pope Julius II. They were divided between a candidate favored by an older faction and Giovanni,
who was favored by the younger faction. Eventually, Giovanni
was elected at the age of thirty-seven and took the name Leo X (r.
1513–1521). Leo and his family were thrilled with his election, as
illustrated by a letter to his brother: "God has given us the papacy; let us use it to our advantage!"[121]

Leo was not overly involved in political affairs and did not
focus on the arts like his predecessors; instead, he focused on
pursuing his own agenda: benefiting his family. He did continue the work of the Fifth Lateran Council (1512–1517), initially
convoked by Julius II. The council produced several reform decrees in response to ecclesiastical abuses rampant at the time, but
ultimately its work was too little and too late, as the Protestant
Revolt began in Germany seven months after its conclusion. The
Germans had not been well-represented at the council and the
conciliar decrees were not well-received there.[122] The powder keg
of latent resentment, built up over the previous centuries against
the papacy, exploded in a revolt in German lands that dominated
the last five years of Leo's pontificate.

The century of papal crisis produced noteworthy problems
for the Church in the sixteenth century. The seventy-year Avi-

---

121. Daniel-Rops, *The Protestant Reformation*, vol. 1, 340.
122. Robert Herndon Fife, *The Revolt of Martin Luther* (New York: Columbia University Press, 1957),
390–391.

gnon papacy and the forty-year Great Western Schism resulted in a loss of respect and prestige. Secular rulers no longer obeyed the pope nor looked to the successor of Saint Peter as a unifying force in Christendom. The actions of the Renaissance popes fashioned the belief that the Roman pontiff was more concerned about temporal affairs than spiritual ones, which produced indifference. When the revolt against the Church began in Germany, the popes were not in a strong position to contain it, and the Church suffered greatly as a result. The abuses of the past centuries, along with resentment against the excesses of the Church and a change in the political structuring of Christendom, all factored into the grave crisis of the sixteenth century, when the family of God faced its biggest challenge.

SEVEN

The Great Divorce — Revolt against the Church

"Men must be changed by religion, not religion by men."[1]

GILES OF VITERBO, 1512

The young boy grew up near the city of Naples, and knew from an early age that he wanted to serve God in the Church. At sixteen, he entered the Order of Preachers, drawn to the order's intellectual focus and rigorous study of theology and philosophy. He avidly read the works of the great Dominican Saint Thomas Aquinas, later becoming the first theologian to write a detailed commentary on Aquinas's greatest work, the *Summa Theologiae* — a project that took fifteen years to

---

1. Quoted in Henri Daniel-Rops, trans. John Warrington, *The Catholic Reformation*, vol. 1 (Garden City, NY: Image Books, 1964), 17.

complete. He became a well-respected member of the order and, at the age of twenty-eight, was elected master general, holding the position for a decade. In the tumultuous year 1517, Pope Leo X created him a cardinal and, the following year, sent him on a diplomatic mission that came to define his life and legacy. Sent to imperial German lands to discuss the dire threat of the Ottoman Turks to Christendom, Thomas de Vio, known as Cajetan (from the Latinized version of his hometown Gaetano), met with an unruly professor from the University of Wittenberg in Electoral Saxony (in the northeast region of modern-day Germany) whose recent writings had caused a stir in Rome for their heretical teachings. His discussions with Martin Luther did not sway the wayward theologian to recant his heresy but frustrated and saddened Cajetan. The cardinal probably assumed that Luther's teachings could be contained, but, unfortunately for the unity of Christendom and future generations of Christians, the little-known university professor became a worldwide sensation who radically changed the world and the family of God.

THE PROTESTANT REVOLUTION

The events that happened in Electoral Saxony in the sixteenth century must be studied in depth, because they fundamentally altered Church and world history.[2] The movement is commonly referred to as the Protestant "Reformation," but that is a misnomer. What occurred was far from an authentic reform, which did occur later in the sixteenth century under the auspices of the Church. Rather, the movement should be known more accurately as the Protestant "Revolution" — for those who formed the main characters of

---

2. At the death of Frederick I the Warlike of the House of Wettin in 1428 a dispute arose among his family over territory. Eventually, the family lands were divided into east and west territories between the sons of Frederick II, Albert and Ernst, as a result of the Treaty of Leipzig in 1485. Initially, the Ernestine lands held one of the seven electoral positions for the Holy Roman Emperor. Their territory was known as Electoral Saxony to distinguish it from Albertine territory known as Ducal Saxony. In the mid-sixteenth century, the electorate changed hands to the Albertine line. Luther lived in Electoral Saxony under the rule of Elector Frederick III the Wise, whereas Ducal Saxony was ruled by Duke George.

this tragic drama sought to destroy the Church and replace her with their own creation.[3] The foundation of the Protestant movement rests on the false narrative that the Catholic Church was a corrupted version of the early Christian faith, which only those learned theologians who rebelled against the Church in the sixteenth century could restore. In essence, the Protestant movement was a religious revolution. Although social, cultural, and political factors were involved, the main issue was theological. The movement completely rejected Church authority and the entire sacramental system, a unique strategy compared to previous heresies.[4] The nature of the conflict between the revolutionaries and the Church consisted of two phases. The first was an internal conflict within the Church, as most people regarded the issues as a theological quarrel that would be quickly resolved. The second witnessed a separation of Christendom into Catholic and Protestant. What began as a "spiritual family quarrel" soon became a "spiritual family war" that devolved into an "actual civil war in arms."[5] The Church sought above all else to restore unity, before attempting the destruction of the heresy, as with previous false teachings. But her efforts ultimately failed, as the sins of men took root and the family of God divorced.

FACTORS THAT LED TO THE PROTESTANT REVOLUTION

A crisis of authority, unity, and spiritual life undergirded the Prot-

---

3. This is not a radical notion, as prior Catholic historians and even some Protestant historians acknowledged the true nature of the Protestant movement. Cardinal Walter Brandmüller, president emeritus of the Pontifical Committee on Historical Sciences, wrote, "Applied to the Church, reform consequently means an increasingly full understanding of the faith that has been handed down, and purer, more vigorous life based on that faith. ... Every development that would involve a contradiction, an opposition to the faith tradition that was foundational from the very beginning, to the traditional sacramental constitution and the basic hierarchical structure of the Church, should therefore be described not as reform but as revolution." Cardinal Walter Brandmüller, *Light and Shadows: Church History amid Faith, Fact, and Legend*, trans. Michael J. Miller (San Francisco: Ignatius Press, 2009), 141.
4. See Hilaire Belloc, *The Great Heresies* (Rockford, IL: TAN Books and Publishers, Inc., 1991 [1938]), 97.
5. Ibid., 110.

estant movement and led to serious questioning of the Church's role in society and in the souls of men.[6] Both secular and spiritual factors contributed to the revolution. For the last several centuries, secular governments had been exercising more autonomy. They were less easily influenced and more resistant to the wishes of the pope. Military technology increased, which allowed monarchs to build and sustain standing armies, thus increasing their internal and external power. Economically, Church teaching and policies regarding commerce on Sundays and usury irritated the growing and powerful merchant families of Europe. Secular rulers became envious of and greedy for the temporal wealth of the Church. Heavy taxes, including annates — the annual revenue from a diocese, provided by a newly ordained or installed bishop to Rome — were also a source of much abuse. Bishops, in order to pay the fees, heavily indebted their dioceses through loans from banking families, or participated in pluralism.

The papal crisis of the fourteenth century, which had witnessed the Avignon Papacy and the Great Western Schism, coupled with the Renaissance popes of the fifteenth century, severely weakened the Church. Ecclesiastical abuses became rampant and were easily exploited by Protestant revolutionaries. During the Renaissance papacy, nepotism flourished, as did pluralism, leading to the further abuse of absenteeism. The absence of a bishop from his diocese resulted in scandal and a weakening of respect for Church authority and teaching.[7] As in previous centuries, the promise of celibacy was not always practiced authentically.

Vernacular writers, such as Dante and Chaucer, parodied the poor example of the clergy, further eroding popular support and respect for the Church. Another popular author was Herasmus Gerritszoon, known as Erasmus (1466–1536). A gifted scholar and the son of a priest, he entered an Augustinian monastery but

---

6. Daniel-Rops, *The Protestant Reformation*, vol. 1, 42.
7. The grave scandal caused by absenteeism is shown by the example of Charles Borromeo, who became the first resident archbishop of Milan in nearly a century, and by a French bishop who entered his diocese for the first time at his funeral!

soon discovered he hated monastic life. He became the world's first successful itinerant man of letters, earning a living from his published works. His first bestseller was *Adagia* in 1500, followed by a devotional treatise published in 1504 known as the *Enchiridion Militis Christiani* (*Dagger for a Christian Soldier*). His 1516 Latin translation of the New Testament from the Greek was a well-read and utilized work, which he followed with a book on marriage titled *Encomium matrimonii* in 1518. Perhaps Erasmus's most famous book was his witty *In Praise of Folly*, which he wrote in 1511 at the home of Thomas More in England. This work utilized satire in an attempt to "use laughter to expose the absurdity and corruption" in the Church and "to tickle" her "into reforming herself."[8] Unfortunately, Erasmus's work was not taken seriously by Church leaders and instead lowered society's respect for the Church and her authority.

One factor that contributed to the Protestant movement, especially the speed of its advance and its ultimate success, was technology. The printing press had been invented earlier, but in the fifteenth century Johannes Gutenberg perfected the instrument by creating metal movable type, allowing for easier and faster production.[9] Book publishing became a popular and lucrative business, especially in Germany, which boasted one thousand printing houses by the year 1500.[10] The Bible was a major publishing success, as it was printed 1.3 million times in England between 1520 and 1649![11] The Protestant movement focused on the Bible, because "a religion of the book needs books."[12] The writings of one of the main Protestant revolutionaries, Martin Luther, formed a large corpus of printed works in the sixteenth

---

8. Eamon Duffy, *Saints and Sinners: A History of the Popes*, 3rd ed. (New Haven, CT: Yale University Press, 2006), 198.

9. Previously, printing utilized hand-carved wooden blocks, which made the process cumbersome and laborious. Metal moveable type allowed for an easier and faster process.

10. Henri Daniel-Rops, *The Protestant Reformation*, vol. 2, trans. Audrey Butler (New York: Image Books, 1963 [1958]), 31.

11. Ibid., 588.

12. Diarmaid MacCulloch, *The Reformation: A History* (New York: Penguin Books, 2003), 72.

century. In the year 1523 alone, Luther's writings were published in 390 editions; by 1525, three million copies of pamphlets about Luther's teachings were in circulation in Europe.[13] Luther's prolific writing was a publisher's dream. On average, he wrote a treatise every two weeks from 1516 to 1546. By the end of his life, his works represented one-third of all printed works in German.[14] There is no doubt that the printing press helped further the Protestant cause and ensured its success.

Luther was perhaps "the greatest master in the use of the German language in the entire history of the German-speaking peoples," and his role in the Protestant rebellion cannot be overstated.[15] Although political, social, and economic reasons all factored into the causes of Protestantism, it was in essence a theological revolution started by a university professor. Luther acknowledged that the true cause of the Protestant movement was not the abuses and corruption in the Church, as previous centuries had seen the same things. His interpretation of Divine Revelation paved the way for the great divorce and the fracturing of Christian unity:

> Someone said to me: "What a sin and scandal all these clerical vices are, the fornication, the drunkenness, the unbridled passion for sport!" Yes, I must confess that these are dreadful scandals, indeed, and they should be denounced and corrected. But the vices to which you refer are plain for all to see; they are grossly material, everyone perceives them, and so everyone is stirred to anger by them. Alas, the real evil, the incomparably more baneful and cruel canker, is the deliberate silence regarding the word of Truth, or else its adulteration. Yet who feel the horror of this?"[16]

---

13. Ibid., 152.
14. Steven Ozment, *The Serpent and the Lamb: Cranach, Luther, and the Making of the Reformation* (New Haven, CT: Yale University Press, 2011), 5.
15. Warren H. Carroll, *The Cleaving of Christendom: A History of Christendom*, vol. 4 (Front Royal, VA: Christendom Press, 2000), 3.
16. Daniel-Rops, *The Protestant Reformation*, vol. 2, 35–36.

THE REASONS FOR THE SUCCESS OF
THE PROTESTANT REVOLUTION

No one living in the sixteenth century could have predicted the outcome of the religious revolution taking place in Christendom, but we can assess why a family squabble turned into a full-blown rebellion that created a separate culture and religious identity. [17]

The rebellion began in the lands of the Germans (although it is convenient to name that territory "Germany," no such thing existed in the sixteenth century).[18] "Germany" at the time was a collection of nearly four hundred small areas controlled by princes, dukes, and lesser nobility, along with a few free individual city-states nominally led by the Holy Roman Emperor. Without a strong national leader in these areas to serve as a counterweight to the papacy, the patchwork of dukedoms, principalities, and other governing arrangements was a political playground of competing interests, into which resentment against foreign interference, especially from the papacy, was cultivated and stoked by German nationalists and satirists, such as Ulrich von Hutten (1488–1523). Hutten used this resentment to great effect in his various books and speeches, painting the papacy as the enemy of the German people. Hutten's propaganda against the papacy was effective; it even influenced Martin Luther. Hutten wrote that "three things are sold in Rome: Christ, the priesthood, and women. Three things are hateful to Rome: a general council, the reformation of the Church, and the opening of German eyes. Three ills I pray for Rome: pestilence, famine, and war. This be my trinity."[19]

The Church and her bishops were large landowners in Christendom, and the wealth generated by this land became a source of resentment for the nobility. Not just the wealth itself irritated the

---

17. The following sections are adapted from my booklet *20 Answers: The Reformation* (El Cajon, CA: Catholic Answers Press, 2017), 55–59.

18. The united nation of Germany did not come into existence until the late nineteenth century.

19. Ulrich von Hutten, *The Roman Trinity*, quoted in Roland H. Bainton, *Here I Stand: A Life of Martin Luther* (New York: Mentor Books, 1950), 101.

nobles, but also the accompanying power and prestige. Secular rulers were focused on consolidating their power, and the Church as an independent force blocked their desire for absolute control. Once the Protestant Revolt was in full swing, a similar pattern developed throughout Christendom: areas that turned Protestant forcibly confiscated Church property. Newly enriched noble families remained Protestant, because they feared that a return to the Catholic faith meant the loss of their newfound wealth back to the Church.

Another reason for the success of the Protestant Revolution was the military activity of the Ottoman Turks, which threatened the southern borders of the Holy Roman Empire. Emperor Charles V had to focus his efforts and energy on meeting the Turkish threat rather than on dealing swiftly and effectively with Luther, his heresy, and the revolt of the northern princes. A large Ottoman army even made its way to the gates of Vienna in 1529 during the height of the Protestant crisis. The Turkish siege at the gateway to Europe was broken, but the constant harassment from the Ottomans was a distraction that helped the Protestant movement gain ground. Luther believed that the Turkish threat was a just punishment from God for the sins and corruption of the Church. This belief emboldened him to continue his revolt even in the midst of a serious military situation. As G. K. Chesterton aptly noted, the Protestant Revolt "was a Christian mutiny during a Muslim invasion."[20]

MARTIN LUTHER — A TROUBLED SOUL

Hans Luder was a member of the mercantile class and was involved in the mining business. The firstborn son of Hans Luder was the second of his eight children,[21] and it is likely that Hans never thought his son would become one of the most well-known

---

20. G. K. Chesterton, *The Resurrection of Rome*, *CW* 21:349–350, quoted in G. K. Chesterton, *Lepanto*, ed. Dale Ahlquist (San Francisco: Ignatius Press, 2004), 85.

21. Martin's family name was Luder. When he enrolled at the University of Erfurt in 1501 he added an "h" to his name (Ludher) in keeping with the common practice in academia of "Latinizing" names. He began to spell his name "Luther" in 1518, which continued until the end of his life. See Heiko A. Oberman, *Luther: Man between God and the Devil* (New Haven, CT: Yale University Press, 1989), 86.

and studied figures in world history.[22] Born on November 10, 1480, the boy was named Martin, because his baptism occurred the following day on the feast of Saint Martin of Tours. By his own account, Martin Luther (1480–1546) had a difficult childhood, with verbally and physically abusive parents. In later years, Martin wrote: "My mother caned me for stealing a nut, until blood came. My father once whipped me so that I ran away and felt ugly toward him."[23] Martin's parents recognized his intellectual gifts and desired an education for their son, rather than involvement in the family business. So, in 1501, he enrolled at the University of Erfurt, where he was known as a diligent and talented student. A year later, Martin earned his bachelor's degree, followed by a master's degree four years later. Hans wanted his talented son to study law in order to pursue a lucrative career in that field, but a frightening experience in 1505 changed the course of Martin's life.

Traveling home on summer break, Luther was enveloped in a violent thunderstorm. Suddenly, a bolt of lightning struck near him, knocking him to the ground in abject fear. Luther uttered a spontaneous prayer of supplication and protection to the mother of the Blessed Virgin Mary: "Dear Saint Anne, I will become a monk."[24] Upon reaching home, Luther recounted the story to his astonished parents and friends, informing them of his new desire to become a monk. They tried to talk Martin out of such a seemingly rash decision, but two weeks after the storm, he entered the strict order of the Augustinian monks at Erfurt, a group that was focused solely on intellectual and spiritual pursuits to the exclusion of manual labor. In the monastery, Luther was known as an opinionated, impatient, and angry soul, always ready to debate

---

22. Indeed, as one historian has noted, "In most big libraries, books by and about Martin Luther occupy more shelf space than those concerned with any other human being except Jesus of Nazareth." John M. Todd, *Luther: A Life* (New York: Crossroad, 1982), xvi, quoted in James Kittelson, *Luther the Reformer: The Story of the Man and His Career* (Minneapolis: Augsburg Publishing House, 1986), 13.
23. Bainton, 17.
24. Robert Herndon Fife, *The Revolt of Martin Luther* (New York: Columbia University Press, 1957), 73. Saint Anne was also the patron saint of miners, the profession of Luther's father.

342 | CHAPTER SEVEN

passionately. He took his final vows in 1506, and nine months later was ordained a priest.

Recognizing his intellectual abilities, the order sent him to the University of Wittenberg in Electoral Saxony in 1508 to teach moral philosophy. Wittenberg was a small university town of two thousand inhabitants sixty miles southwest of Berlin. Elector Frederick III the Wise had established the new university only six years previously to rival the University of Leipzig, whose Dominican faculty taught according to the Scholastic method, which synthesized theology, Scripture, and Aristotelian philosophy, and focused on developing precise definitions by using reason through questioning.[25] The faculty at Wittenberg had embraced the new humanist education based on the philosophical teachings of William of Ockham (1285–1349), who advocated nominalism, a method that separated faith and reason and focused on the experiences of the individual. Luther continued his studies while teaching, eventually receiving his doctorate in 1512.

TRIP TO ROME

A dispute developed within the Augustinian order in 1510 wherein seven monasteries, observant of the rule of Saint Augustine, resisted a move to unite with other, less observant, groups. A meeting was called in Rome to resolve the issue. Luther, along with another monk, was chosen to represent the Erfurt monastery. After an arduous six-week journey to Rome, Luther was thoroughly disgusted by his experiences in the Eternal City. He did not speak the language and was shocked at the behavior of the Italian clergy. Many were not proficient in Latin and celebrated Mass too quickly, finishing it before Luther could read the Gospel of his own Mass.

---

25. Elector Frederick was an avid relic collector. In 1518, his collection contained seventeen thousand items, including relics of the Holy Innocents, a piece of the burning bush witnessed by Moses, part of Jesus' baby crib, fragments of hay and straw from the manger in Bethlehem, Jesus' swaddling clothes, fragments of the True Cross, two teeth of Saint Elizabeth, and a tooth of both Saint Matthew and John the Baptist. See Fife, 134. The university still exists and is now called the Martin Luther University of Halle-Wittenberg.

He was even shooed away from the altar by Italian priests because he was taking too long to celebrate Mass.[26] His monastic business concluded, Luther could not leave the city quickly enough. He had caught malaria while in Italy and suffered deeply from culture shock. Despite popular narratives to the contrary, the visit did not cause his rebellion from the Church or impact his faith.[27]

LUTHER AND SALVATION

Luther suffered from many physical health issues, including rapid heartbeat, severe anxiety, constipation, indigestion, hemorrhoids, severe kidney stones, ringing in his ears, and depression. In addition to his physical afflictions, Luther also suffered from extreme scrupulosity, which led him to frequent confession (sometimes daily and for hours at a time) and strict fasting, which could last for several days.[28] Obsessed with his own salvation, Luther was never convinced that he was justified in the eyes of God:

> I tried to live according to the rule and I used to be contrite, to confess and enumerate my sins; I often repeated my confession and zealously performed my required penance. And yet my conscience would never give me assurance, but I was always doubting and said, "You did not perform that correctly. You were not contrite enough. You left that out of your confession."[29]

Luther was a discontented monk who "would have been a troubled spirit in a tranquil age."[30] Luther's negative view of God,

26. Fife, 173.
27. Luther contributed to the myth that the visit to Rome was crucial in his move away from the Church, but he manufactured that excuse long after his trip and when already condemned for his heresy. See Fife, 176.
28. See Bainton, 34.
29. James M. Kittelson, *Luther the Reformer: The Story of the Man and His Career* (Minneapolis: Augsburg Publishing House, 1986), 84.
30. Bainton, 110.

perhaps caused in part by his tumultuous relationship with his earthly father, clouded his thinking. His spiritual director tried to help, telling him, "God is not angry with you, but you are angry with God."[31] Despite these words and his strict adherence to monastic rules, Luther could not be assured that God loved him:

> I lived without reproach as a monk, but my conscience was disturbed to its very depths and all I knew about myself was that I was a sinner. I could not believe that anything that I thought or did or prayed satisfied God. I could not love, nay, I hated the righteous God who punishes sinners. Certainly, and with intense grumbling (perhaps even blasphemy), I was angry with God and said, "As if it were indeed not enough that miserable sinners who are eternally lost through original sin and are crushed again by every kind of calamity through the Ten Commandments, God himself adds pain to pain in the gospel by threatening us with his righteousness and wrath!"[32]

Luther's internal struggles drove him to despair until, in 1513, he came to believe through his study and a creative interpretation of the Pauline epistles, especially the Letter to the Romans, that man is saved only through faith in Christ. Luther's theological revolution concerning justification is known as *sola fide* ("faith alone") and was revealed by the professor to his students in a series of lectures on the Letter to the Hebrews in 1517.[33] Luther advocated that man is justified in the sight of God through the actions of Christ, which man must accept by faith. Despite justification, man remains a sinful creature, since human nature was thoroughly corrupted as a result of original sin. Fundamentally, baptism and faith do not change man himself, but only God's dis-

31. Kittelson, 57.
32. Ibid., 134.
33. Daniel-Rops, *The Protestant Reformation*, vol. 2, 25.

position toward man. Man's evil is covered over with the mantle of Christ's righteousness so that God will not condemn him.[34] This erroneous teaching was partially a result of Luther's understanding of God, whom he saw as a tyrant and vengeful judge, not a loving father. For Luther, humans are not coheirs with Christ in the kingdom of God and adopted sons and daughters of the Father, but evil creatures whom God desires to purge with damning fire: "Is it not against all natural reason that God out of his mere whim deserts men, hardens them, damns them, as if he delighted in sins and in such torments of the wretched for eternity. ... I was myself more than once driven to the very abyss of despair so that I wished I had never been created. Love God? I hated him!"[35] Luther's heightened ego and stupendous willpower are reflected in his writings and preaching. He was thoroughly convinced his theological interpretation was correct, and he even believed his opponents knew in their consciences that he was right, even if they did not publicly acknowledge it.[36]

Luther excelled at preaching, a highly prized activity during the time period. He was a charismatic speaker, able to dominate an audience with his oratory. As a result, preaching would become a central focus of Protestant worship.[37] At times during his preaching, and also in his writings, Luther manifested violent anger. Aware of his temperament and inclination to anger, Luther explained: "I was born to go to war and give battle to sects and devils. That is why my books are stormy and warlike. I must root out the stumps and bushes and hack away the thorns and brambles. I am the great lumberjack who must clear the land and level it."[38] Although verbal and written abuse of one's opponents were the

---

34. Catholic teaching advocates that baptism and faith fundamentally restore the bond between man and God broken as a result of original sin. Man's nature is not corrupted but wounded. Christ's meritorious actions allow man to be in a state of sanctifying grace, which can be broken through man's sinful actions but restored again through the sacrament of confession.
35. Bainton, 44.
36. Fife, 448.
37. In 1528, Luther preached 195 sermons in 145 days. Bainton, 272–273.
38. Kittelson, 270.

order of the day, Luther elevated insults to a new level, frequently utilizing crude obscenities and expressions of bodily functions in his attacks and in explanations of his teachings. Luther's violent anger, intellectual gifts, and erroneous interpretation helped this previously little-known university professor became a household name in Christendom in the fall of 1517.

INDULGENCES AND THE 95 THESES

The doctrine of indulgences was the theological flash point for Martin Luther's dramatic entrance into the public consciousness of Christendom.[39] Indulgences are "the remission before God of the temporal punishment due to sins whose guilt has already been forgiven."[40] The Church is able to grant indulgences because she is "the minister of redemption"; with the authority given her by Christ, and the Church "dispenses and applies ... the treasury of the satisfactions of Christ and the saints" to the faithful.[41]

The granting of indulgences was not new at the time of Luther, but long-established Church teaching did not prevent sinful persons from abusing the practice. Some preachers erroneously asserted the authority to forgive sins for money, a claim condemned by Church officials. Although the practice of granting an indulgence for the penitential act of almsgiving (especially for a contribution to fund the building of a public utility — for example, a bridge or church) predates the sixteenth century, it was the rebuilding of Saint Peter's Basilica in Rome during the pontifi-

---

39. The following section is adapted from my booklet *20 Answers: The Reformation*, 44–47.
40. *Catechism of the Catholic Church*, 1471. The *Catechism* goes on to say that sin is a freely willed offense against God and neighbor, and it has the "double consequence" of eternal and temporal punishment. Mortal sin severs the relationship between God and man, which is the eternal punishment of sin — that is, the loss of eternal communion with God in heaven. But even venial sin "entails an unhealthy attachment to creatures [the temporal punishment of sin], which must be purified either here on earth or after death in the state called Purgatory" (1472). God forgives the guilt of sin through the sacrament of confession when true contrition of the penitent is present. This forgiveness satisfies the eternal punishment of sin, but the temporal punishment remains, which, through certain penitential actions — for example, prayers, works of mercy, and charity — prescribed by the Church, can be lessened (partial indulgence) or completely erased (plenary indulgence).
41. Ibid., 1471.

cate of Pope Leo X that raised Martin Luther's ire.

In 1515, Archbishop Albert of Mainz (and of Magdeburg and Halberstadt) approved the preaching of the Saint Peter's Basilica almsgiving indulgence in Luther's home diocese. The twenty-six-year-old had acquired a large debt through simony and approved the indulgence, in part because he would receive half of whatever was raised from the campaign, while the other half went to Rome. Johann Tetzel, a Dominican, one of the best-known and most successful indulgence preachers, came to the area for the campaign. Tetzel often preyed on the ignorance of the people in order to raise more money. He gave the impression that receiving an indulgence for almsgiving would free a soul from purgatory, saying such outlandish things as: "Can you not hear the voices of your dead father and mother pleading with you? A tiny alms, they are saying, and we shall be free from this torment. And you begrudge this to us?"[42] Although he probably never uttered the famous phrase, "As soon as the coin in the box clinks, the soul out of purgatory's fire springs," it is indicative of the general theme of his preaching.[43]

Irritated by the preaching of the indulgence and the abuse of some preachers, and convinced in his own interpretation of Scripture, Luther wrote what came to be known as the 95 Theses, published on October 31, 1517. The document was originally written in Latin, as Luther wanted other academics to read it and debate him on the propositions. Many of the theses concern the doctrine of indulgences, but Luther attacked other topics as well. The most problematic aspect of the 95 Theses was Luther's contention that the pope did not even have the authority to grant an indulgence. This questioning of papal authority (and Christ's gift of the keys to Saint Peter and his successors) caught Rome's attention. Luther sent a copy of his theses to Archbishop Albert with a cover letter. The archbishop forwarded the document to

---

42. Philip Hughes, *A Popular History of the Reformation* (New York: Image Books, 1960), 114.
43. The phrase has a rhythmic quality in the original German: "*Sobald das Geld in Kasten klingt, Die Seele aus dem Fegefeuer springt.*" See Fife, 255.

Rome and to theologians at the University of Mainz. The document soon spread to other universities, was printed in German in December, and soon circulated throughout German territory. Initially, Pope Leo X saw the matter as a dispute among religious orders — since Luther was an Augustinian, and most indulgence preachers were Dominicans — but theologians in Rome made him aware of the seriousness of Luther's teachings.

Throughout the early part of 1518, theologians in Rome investigated carefully Luther's writings. By the summer, he was formally charged with the "suspicion of disseminating heresy." The Master of the Sacred Palace, the Dominican Silvestro Mazzolini da Prierio (known as Prierias), summoned Luther to appear in Rome for trial within sixty days. Prierias wrote two works highlighting Luther's heretical beliefs, titled *Against the Presumptuous Theses of Martin Luther Concerning the Power of the Pope* and *Errors and Arguments of Martin Luther, Enumerated, Exposed, Repelled and Fully Ground to Pieces*. Luther answered by writing *Response to the Dialogue of Sylvester Prierias on the Power of the Pope*, in which he reaffirmed his teachings, rejected the authority of the Catholic hierarchy, and advocated the heresy of conciliarism. Despite the papal summons, Luther never appeared in Rome. He claimed he was too weak to travel and was afraid for his safety.[44] His secular ruler, Elector Frederick, proposed that Luther meet with Cardinal Cajetan, who was at Augsburg for the German Diet to discuss the Turkish threat.[45] Pope Leo agreed and ordered Cajetan to invite Luther to Augsburg, and to request that the friar recant his erroneous teachings. Failure to do so would lead to excommunication, and all temporal authorities would be requested to assist in apprehending him on pain of their own excommunication and interdict. Cajetan met with Elector Frederick and urged him not to support a heretic, to which Frederick argued that as Luther had not yet been declared a

---

44. Ibid., 286.
45. The Diet consisted of the House of Electors, the House of Princes, and the House of the Imperial towns; it was a political body called to address issues of importance to all German territories and overseen by the Holy Roman Emperor.

heretic he refused to arrest him or send him to Rome.

Eventually, Cajetan and Luther met in October 1518. Cajetan asked Luther in a friendly, fatherly, yet firm tone to recant his propositions (that the Church does not hold a treasury of graces from Christ and the saints, from which the pope can dispense indulgences, and that the sacraments are efficacious only by faith and not by their own operation). Cajetan instructed Luther using arguments from the writings of Thomas Aquinas. But Luther scorned the scholastics and Aquinas, and told the astonished Cajetan that only Scripture, the writings of the Church Fathers, or papal definitions would convince him. Cajetan then produced Clement VI's 1343 bull *Unigenitus Dei Filius*, in which the pontiff defined the doctrine of indulgences.[46] Cajetan may also have highlighted Pope Sixtus IV's 1476 bull which allowed indulgences to be applied to the souls in purgatory.[47] Luther infuriated the cardinal with a rejection of papal definitions, which he had previously indicated he would accept.

A few days later, Luther presented Cajetan with a written defense of his teachings based on his interpretation of Scripture and stated that he would submit if Pope Leo X pronounced him in error. Luther's verbal games tried Cajetan's patience. The cardinal dismissed the wayward monk, shouting, "Go and do not return unless you are ready to recant!" Luther yelled in response, "I will not become a heretic by contradicting the opinion with which I became a Christian: I will rather die, be burned, exiled, accursed."[48] Luther later apologized for his behavior — on the orders of his superior — but then requested the calling of an ecumenical council to address his concerns. Luther disliked Cajetan and the cardinal's adherence to Scholasticism, questioning "whether he is a Catholic Christian,"[49] and thought he was "a

46. See J. Neuner, S.J., and J. Dupuis, S.J., *The Christian Faith in the Doctrinal Documents of the Catholic Church* (New York: Alba House, 1996), 648.
47. Daniel-Rops, *The Protestant Reformation*, vol. 2, 10.
48. Letter from Luther to Carlstadt, October 14, 1518, quoted in Fife, 295.
49. Fife, 322.

vague, obscure, and unintelligible theologian … and therefore as unsuited to understand and judge in this matter as an ass to play the harp."[50] Any hope the cardinal may have had concerning a swift end to the Luther affair vanished during his interactions with the recalcitrant monk. A month after the unsuccessful meeting, Pope Leo X issued a bull reiterating the Church's teaching on indulgences so that "no one may pretend ignorance of the doctrine of the Roman Church."[51] Luther had been put on notice. Although his apology to Cajetan delayed the hammer of the Church and secular authorities, his heretical teachings were soon exposed to the rest of Christendom.

THE DISPUTATION AT LEIPZIG

Johann Eck was among the first to publish a response to Luther. Eck had begun his academic career at the young age of twelve when he entered the University of Heidelberg. He received his master's degree three years later from the University of Tübingen and a doctorate in theology at the age of twenty-four. Eck's academic interest extended to fields outside of theology, including languages (he learned Greek and Hebrew). With his incisive and analytical mind, Eck noticed the similarities between Luther's opinions and those of Jan Hus, the Bohemian heretic burned at the stake at the Council of Constance in the early fifteenth century. His work criticized Luther's teachings but did not mention the Augustinian monk by name (in keeping with the Catholic admonition to hate the sin and love the sinner). Luther responded to Eck's work by attacking the historical claims of the papacy, and in a private letter to his friend Georg Spalatin, he revealed his true thoughts, wondering "whether the pope is the Antichrist himself or his apostle."[52]

While he was a professor at Ingolstadt University, Eck's re-

50. Letter from Luther to Carlstadt, October 14, 1518, quoted in Fife, 294.
51. Fife, 306.
52. Ibid., 344.

sponse to Luther drew sharp attacks from Luther's colleague, friend, and fellow Augustinian Andreas Rudolph Bodenstein (known as Carlstadt). The disagreement led to a public debate at the University of Leipzig between Eck and Carlstadt on the topics of indulgences, penance, and free will. Luther, not content to let Carlstadt debate Eck alone, petitioned Duke George, the patron of the university, to allow him to join the debate, which was granted. Luther was also not pleased with the location of the debate, as the universities of Leipzig and Wittenberg competed with one another.[53]

The debate began on June 27, 1519, and lasted eighteen days. Eck, with his commanding voice and superior knowledge, clearly held the advantage. Carlstadt took too long to answer questions and had to flip through stacks of books before he answered. After four days of debate, Eck had carried the day. The main event between Luther and Eck followed, beginning on July 4. Eck knew that Luther shared opinions previously advocated by the proto-Protestants John Wyclif and Jan Hus; his strategy was to highlight Luther's links with them. This approach was particularly effective, as Leipzig was home to a large number of Bohemian Catholics who had fled their homeland during the wars that had followed the death of Hus. Luther initially tried to distance himself from Hus, claiming, "Never in all eternity will I agree to any schism."[54] Eck pressed the comparison, and, eventually, Luther admitted that some of Hus's teachings condemned at the Council of Constance "are plainly very Christian and evangelical, which it is not possible for the Church to condemn."[55] Eck was quick to emphasize Luther's disagreement with the actions of the Council of Constance, a council revered in Christendom because it had ended the Great Western

---

53. Leipzig was in Ducal Saxony, whereas Wittenberg was in Electoral Saxony. Luther accused Leipzig of envy and hatred of Wittenberg, writing that Leipzig was a "place of arrogance, greed, and usury." Ibid., 349.
54. Ibid., 360–361.
55. Ibid., 361.

352 | CHAPTER SEVEN

Schism. The debate turned to a discussion of papal primacy and authority, the crux of Luther's rebellion. During the discussion, Luther made the patently false statement that the council had not condemned Hus's denial of Roman primacy. He was quick to say that he was not advocating Hus's position, but was merely suggesting that papal primacy cannot be proved by Matthew 16:18–19. Eck pointed out to the assembly that the council had specifically condemned anyone who denied the Catholic interpretation of Matthew 16 as the proof-text for papal primacy. Luther was trapped and exposed as a heretic. Johann Eck had singlehandedly defeated and exposed Carlstadt and Luther at the Disputation at Leipzig.

Luther never again publicly debated a trained Catholic theologian. He wrote letters to friends after the debate that clearly showed his appreciation for the proto-Protestant Hus. He would later write in one of his famous 1520 treatises that Hus's "books and doctrines were unjustly condemned" by the council.[56] He also called Hus's heretical book *On the Church* the best book in four hundred years and referred to Hus as Saint John.[57] Finally, Luther believed that Hus was the true Christian, because even Saints Paul and Augustine unknowingly agreed with the Bohemian heretic.[58] The meeting with Luther fundamentally changed the course of Johann Eck's life. He made it his life's mission to refute the heresies espoused by Luther. Before and during the debate, Eck approached Luther and his writings with respect, but after confronting the arrogant Augustinian at Leipzig, Eck described Luther as "weak in scholarship but strong in biting and abusing. He is a liar and a Hussite."[59]

EXSURGE DOMINE — LUTHER CONDEMNED

Almost a year after the Disputation at Leipzig, Pope Leo X con-

---

56. He wrote this in his work *An Appeal to the Christian Nobility of the German Nation*.
57. Fife, 471,640.
58. Ibid., 471.
59. Ibid., 407.

demned Luther in the bull *Exsurge Domine* ("Arise, O Lord!"). The document listed forty-one heretical teachings contained in the works of Luther, judging them "either heretical, scandalous, false, offensive to pious ears or seductive of simple minds, and against Catholic truth."[60] Leo bemoaned the fact that Luther had not responded to repeated attempts at reconciliation, including the request to come to Rome in person to discuss his teachings. The pope expressed regret at the situation, but recognized his duty to safeguard the faithful from heresy. Luther was instructed to cease preaching and to submit a written recantation before the Church. If he failed to do so within sixty days of receipt of the bull, he would be declared an obstinate heretic and incur the penalty of excommunication.

Luther was not moved to repent by the pleadings of Leo, but became even more intransigent. Convinced he was correct in his interpretation of Scripture, and that the pope and his theologians were in error, Luther printed a reply to Leo's bull titled *Against the Execrable Bull of Antichrist*. He argued that the purpose of the papal document was to "compel men to deny God and worship the devil and all good Christians should trample it underfoot."[61] Luther raged throughout the work:

> But whoever wrote this bull, he is Antichrist. I protest before God, our Lord Jesus, his sacred angels, and the whole world that with my whole heart I dissent from the damnation of this bull, that I curse and execrate it as sacrilege and blasphemy of Christ, God's Son and our Lord. This bull condemns me from its own word without any proof from Scripture, whereas I back up all my assertions from the Bible. I ask thee, ignorant Antichrist, dost thou think that with thy naked words thou canst prevail against the armor of Scripture?[62]

60. Ibid., 497.
61. Ludwig von Pastor, *History of the Popes*, VII, 414, quoted in Carroll, *The Cleaving of Christendom*, 43.
62. Quoted in Bainton, 125.

Luther concluded his screed by "excommunicating" the pope, indicating that Christ at the Last Judgment would determine whose excommunication was authoritative. Luther's reply to the bull was in keeping with his general demeanor; he steadfastly refused to acknowledge any authority but his own. He centered his theological revolution on the destruction of papal and Church authority.

Besides publishing the vicious attack, in December 1520 Luther gathered a large assembly of faculty and students from the university to burn a copy of the bull at the town waste depository. Luther solemnly lit on fire a copy of *Exsurge Domine*, a copy of canon law, and several works of Scholastic theology, stating, "because you have condemned the truth of God, he also condemns you today to the fire. Amen."[63] The assembly sang the *Te Deum*, the traditional prayer of praise to God, while the burning commenced. Luther exhorted his followers that "he who does not resist the papacy with all his heart cannot obtain eternal salvation."[64] Many were displeased with Luther's rebellious actions, so he wrote a pamphlet defending the burning of the bull. *Why the Books of the Pope and His Disciples Were Burned* argued that, as a teacher of Scripture, Luther was duty-bound to "destroy false, seductive and unchristian doctrine."[65] In a reply to a critic, Luther's vehemence for the papacy reached new heights, as he advocated violence:

> If we punish thieves with the yoke, highwaymen with the sword, and heretics with fire, why do we not rather assault these monsters of perdition, these cardinals, these popes, and the whole swarm of the Roman Sodom, who corrupt youth and the Church of God? Why do we not rather assault them with arms and wash our hands in their blood?[66]

---

63. Fife, 580.
64. Duffy, *Saints and Sinners*, 202.
65. Fife, 582.
66. Bainton, 116.

With his words at the Disputation at Leipzig and his actions against Leo's bull, Luther clearly embraced the path of revolution, not reform. The disgruntled monk and university professor was convinced of his own righteousness. He desired to see his interpretation of Scripture, including his heretical notion of *sola fide*, dominant in theology.

THE THREE TREATISES

Luther wrote a friend, conscious that his actions placed him in revolution against the Church:

> I have cast the die: I now despise the rage of the Romans ... I will not reconcile myself to them for all eternity, nor have anything to do with them. Let them condemn and burn all that belongs to me. In return, I also will do as much for them; otherwise I could not kindle the fire that is to condemn and burn, before the eyes of the world, the whole papal system.[67]

If there was any doubt that Luther was a rebel and not a reformer, he erased all of it with the publication in the summer and fall of 1520 of three treatises, which formed the foundation of his heretical teaching and became bedrock Protestant principles. The first treatise, published in German in August, was titled *An Appeal to the Christian Nobility of the German Nation*. Luther exhorted the Holy Roman Emperor Charles V and the German nobility to rid the Church in German lands of its allegiance and unity with the 'Roman Church" and the pope. He giddily wrote about his proposed separation of the Church:

> And now farewell, unhappy, hopeless, blasphemous Rome! The wrath of God has come upon you in the

---

67. Von Pastor, *History of the Popes*, VII, 390, quoted in Carroll, *The Cleaving of Christendom*, 41.

end, as you deserved, and not for the many prayers which are made on your behalf, but because you have chosen to grow more evil from day to day. Let us then leave her that she may be the habitation of dragons, specters, ghosts, and witches, and true to her name of Babel, an everlasting confusion, an idol of avarice, perfidy, apostasy, or cynics, lechers, robbers, sorcerers, and endless other impudent monsters, a new pantheon of wickedness.[68]

In the first section of his *Appeal*, Luther identified three "walls" that Rome built around itself in order to maintain its power and to keep the people in bondage and separated from the true faith: the beliefs that spiritual power is greater than temporal power, that the pope alone can interpret Scripture, and that the pope alone can call an ecumenical council. Luther exhorted the nobles to remember "in this matter we are not dealing with men, but with the princes of hell."[69] In his second section, Luther attacked the papacy as an office, arguing that the pope should do "nothing else but weep and pray for Christendom and set an example of utter humility."[70] He castigated the pope for the avarice of the clergy and the extent to which money ruled the papal curia, writing, "Rome has become so expensive today that it allows no one to practice knavery unless he has first bought the right to do so."[71] In the last section of his book, Luther provided twenty-seven proposals to "reform" the Church, which ranged from the practical to the ridiculous. He advocated for an end of pilgrimages to Rome, for the German nobility to take complete control of the Church, for the suppression of the mendicant religious orders, for the abolition of feast days, and for the cessation of the canon-

---

68. Martin Luther, *An Appeal to the Christian Nobility of the German Nation, Three Treatises* (Minneapolis: Fortress Press, 1970), 4.
69. Ibid., 10.
70. Ibid., 26.
71. Ibid., 41.

ization of saints. Among his most absurd proposals was a call for married priests, because mandatory clerical celibacy caused the Great Schism with the Eastern Church, and "not every priest can do without a woman, not only on account of human frailty, but much more on account of keeping house."[72] Luther believed the pope had no real power to enforce celibacy, just as he could not "forbid eating, drinking, the natural movement of the bowels, or growing fat."[73] The wayward monk also desired the permanent ban of Aristotle's works, primarily because Scholastic theologians used them. Luther's ire for Aristotle produced outbursts in which he called the Greek philosopher "the damned, arrogant, sarcastic heathen"[74] and a belief that "God has sent him as a plague upon us on account of our sins."[75] *An Appeal to the Christian Nobility of the German Nation* became one of Luther's most popular works. The four thousand copies of the first printing sold out in two weeks. His call for the nobility to take control of the Church was a descent into schism, which, unfortunately, was embraced by many secular princes within the decade.

Luther's second treatise of 1520 was published in October and written in Latin, as the intended audience was theologians. *On the Babylonian Captivity of the Church* represented Luther's total break with the Church. Luther chose the title to recall the Babylonian conquest and subsequent exile of Israel, as described in the Old Testament. Luther believed the sacramental system of the Church had enslaved Christians in the tyranny of the papacy by requiring them to participate in the sacraments to receive grace. He opined that the Church's emphasis on sacraments removed people from the only authoritative source of God's Divine Revelation: the Scriptures. Luther denied that the sacraments are efficacious signs of grace by themselves; rather, he proposed that the recipient's faith was required for the sacraments to be effective. He defined

---

72. Ibid., 67.
73. Ibid., 68.
74. Fife, 60.
75. Luther, *An Appeal to the Christian Nobility of the German Nation*, 93.

sacraments as "a word of divine promise by which faith may be exercised."[76] At the beginning of the treatise, Luther accepted three sacraments: baptism, Eucharist, and penance; but, by the end of his book, he had rejected Penance as a sacrament, instead believing it a useful practice only. When discussing the Eucharist, Luther advocated the Hussite position of Communion under both species (bread and wine) for the laity, and argued extensively that the Mass is not a sacrifice but merely a celebration of Christ's promise of the forgiveness of sins. Luther rejected the Catholic doctrine of transubstantiation, arguing for consubstantiation: that the bread and wine are not transformed into the Body and Blood, Soul, and Divinity of Christ but remain present, along with Christ's Real Presence, after the words of consecration. Concerning marriage, Luther wrote: "Nowhere do we read that the man who marries a wife receives any grace from God. There is not even a divinely instituted sign in marriage, nor do we read anywhere that marriage was instituted by God to be a sign of anything."[77] Luther personally detested divorce, even recommending bigamy rather than the separation of the spouses.[78] Finally, Luther rejected the Sacrament of Holy Orders and instead promoted the "priesthood of all believers," arguing that there is no difference between priests and laity apart from the administration of the sacraments and preaching.

Luther's last 1520 treatise was titled *The Freedom of a Christian*, to which he attached an open letter to Pope Leo X. In this treatise, Luther argued that no commandments can be kept properly because of man's sinfulness, but humanity is not condemned for that failure since Christ died for all sins, writing: "A Christian is a perfectly free lord of all, subject to none. A Christian is a perfectly dutiful servant of all, subject to all."[79] Luther reiterated his belief in justification by faith alone (*sola fide*) and argued that a person

---

76. Martin Luther, *On the Babylonian Captivity of the Church*, *Three Treatises* (Minneapolis: Fortress Press, 1970), 219.
77. Ibid., 220.
78. Ibid., 235–236.
79. Martin Luther, *The Freedom of a Christian*, *Three Treatises* (Minneapolis: Fortress Press, 1970), 277.

is condemned only for unbelief: "No good work helps justify or save an unbeliever. On the other hand, no evil work makes him wicked or damns him; but the unbelief, which makes the person do evil and damnable works. Hence when a man is good or evil, this is effected not by the works, but by faith or unbelief."[80]

By the end of 1520, Luther's three treatises had proved that the monk was not interested in authentic reform, but was rather advocating for a destruction of the Church and for her replacement with an organization made in his image. Luther's subsequent writings affirmed the extent of his rejection of Catholic doctrine and hatred of the Church. He advocated for the total depravity of human nature as a result of original sin, and he denied the gift of free will, believing instead that human will, even after Christ's sacrifice, was completely captive to sin. He referred to the Church as the "whore of Babylon" and desired her eradication. In a 1521 pamphlet titled *On the Abuse of the Mass*, Luther continued his assault on the pope: "The abominable and horrid priesthood of Papists came into the world from the Devil. ... The Pope is a true apostle of his master the hellish fiend, according to his will he lives and reigns."[81] Luther worked closely with the artist Lucas Cranach to portray the pope as the Antichrist in numerous books and pamphlets. The heretical monk also desired an end to the Sacrifice of the Mass, writing: "If I succeed in doing away with the Mass, then I shall believe I have completely conquered the Pope. If the sacrilegious and cursed custom of the Mass is overthrown, then the whole must fall."[82] Luther's rebellion concentrated on four main areas: the understanding of sin and man's justification; a distortion of the role of faith; a rejection of the sacramental system and faulty understanding of the sacraments themselves; and a rejection of the authority of the Church, specifically as exercised by the pope.[83]

---

80. Ibid., 298.
81. Grisar, *Luther*, II, 84–85, quoted in Carroll, *The Cleaving of Christendom*, 56.
82. Grisar, *Luther*, II, 320, quoted in Carroll, *The Cleaving of Christendom*, 59.
83. See Daniel-Rops, *The Protestant Reformation*, vol. 2, 72.

CATHOLICS RESPOND TO LUTHER

Many faithful scholars rose to the defense of the Church against Luther's false teachings. A group of Dominicans at Frankfurt, along with the faculty at the universities of Leipzig, Cologne, and Louvain, joined the effort first begun by Johann Eck. Hieronymus Emser, who knew Luther personally, penned the work *Against the Un-Christian Book of Martin Luther, the Augustinian, to the German Nobility*. The Dominican Jakob Hochstraten from Cologne urged the pope to defend the Faith against Luther's insidious attacks, exhorting him to "arise, arise with the spirit of a lion and drive out the disturber of the Christian faith!"[84] Augustin von Alfeld, a Franciscan at Leipzig, wrote a defense of the papacy. Thomas Murner, a Franciscan from Strasbourg, took issue with Luther's attack on the Mass. Perhaps the most famous defense against Luther was published by the monarch of England. King Henry VIII, who enjoyed studying theology, wrote a work titled *Defense of the Seven Sacraments* after reading Luther's *On the Babylonian Captivity of the Church*. As a result, the pope granted Henry and all English monarchs the title "Defender of the Faith." Luther responded to the king's book by writing a letter addressed to Henry, in which his opening salutation was: "From Martin Luther, minister at Wittenberg by the grace of God. To Henry, King of England by the disgrace of God." In the work, Luther called the king "a nit which is not yet turned into a louse, a brat whose father was a bug, a donkey who wants to read the psalter, a sacrilegious murderer, a chosen tool of the Devil, a papistical sea-serpent, a blockhead and as bad as the worst rogues whom indeed he out rivals, an abortion of a fool, a limb of Satan."[85] Saint Thomas More, recognizing Luther's true nature, called him "an ape, ass, drunkard, a lousy little friar, a piece of scurf,

---

84. Ibid., 410.
85. Hartmann Grisar, *Luther*, II (St. Louis: Kegan Paul, Trench, Trubner, 1914), 153, quoted in Carroll, *The Cleaving of Christendom*, 58–59.

a pestilential buffoon, a dishonest liar."[86] Luther did not take kindly to any form of criticism, even friendly advice. He firmly believed that his rude and vulgar responses to his detractors were the result of their behavior, not his own.[87]

THE EMPEROR DEFENDS THE FAITH — THE DIET OF WORMS

Charles V had been born and raised in the Netherlands, and was "an awkward, unprepossessing boy, with a small thin body, a narrow face, an under slung jaw, and hesitant speech."[88] He also suffered from a facial deformity that made it difficult to chew food properly (which led to digestive problems) and a speech impediment (he spoke with a stammer). In 1516, at the age of sixteen, the boy became king of Spain and one of the most powerful rulers in Christendom when his grandfather, Ferdinand II, died. Charles had been tutored by Adrian of Utrecht, the future Pope Adrian VI (r. 1522–1523), and did not speak a word of Spanish.[89] Three years later, Charles was elected Holy Roman Emperor, although his election was filled with political intrigue. Pope Leo X did not favor his candidacy because Charles had claim to the throne of Sicily, and Leo did not want to be surrounded by territory ruled by the same individual.[90]

Luther's actions in 1520 (the burning of the papal bull and the publication of his three treatises) showed Pope Leo X that the monk was obstinate in his heresy. So, on January 5, 1521, Leo issued the bull *Decet Romanum pontificem*, officially excommunicating Luther. Hieronymus Aleander, the papal legate to German

---

86. Peter Ackroyd, *The Life of Thomas More* (New York: 1998), 230, quoted in John Vidmar, O.P., *The Catholic Church Through the Ages* (New York/Mahwah, NJ: Paulist Press, 2005), 184.

87. See Fife, 528.

88. Warren H. Carroll, *The Glory of Christendom: A History of Christendom*, vol. 3 (Front Royal, VA: Christendom Press, 1993), 711.

89. Adrian VI was the last non-Italian pope until Pope Saint John Paul II was elected in 1978.

90. According to the Golden Bull of 1356, seven electors, three of whom were archbishops, elected the Holy Roman Emperor. So, although a man might have had a hereditary claim to the throne, his accession was not guaranteed.

territory, encouraged Emperor Charles to enforce the excommunication by also declaring Luther a heretic. Originally from Venice, Aleander was an excellent scholar and close friend of the humanist Erasmus. Aleander believed that Luther was a "heretic worse than a thousand Ariuses."[91] He knew the German situation was volatile, due to deep resentment against Rome, so he understood that enforcing Luther's excommunication would be a tricky endeavor for the emperor. Charles agreed that Luther must be dealt with and invited Luther to the Diet at Worms to answer the charges. He provided Luther with safe conduct, which was delivered by Charles' own herald. The safe conduct guaranteed Luther's immunity from arrest while he traveled to and from the Diet, and during his attendance at the meeting. Luther was given twenty-one days to arrive; he weighed the decision to go while writing anti-papal letters to friends and supporters. He indicated that the only recantation he would give at Worms was that "previously I said the pope is the Vicar of Christ, I recant. Now I say the pope is the adversary of Christ and the apostle of the Devil."[92] In another letter, he expressed joy at being condemned by the pope: "I call the pope the greatest murderer that the earth has ever borne, for he murders body and soul. God be praised that I am a heretic in his eyes and those of his papists."[93] While Charles awaited the arrival of Luther at Worms, he issued an imperial ban prohibiting the copying, printing, buying, and selling of Luther's works.

Luther finally decided to attend the Diet, and arrived in Worms on April 16, 1521, to the sound of trumpet blasts, the imperial herald announcing his arrival, and two thousand people assembling to greet him. Aleander was horrified at the reaction, writing, "In such a manner does the Saxon dragon raise his head; in such a manner do the Lutheran serpents multiply and hiss far and wide."[94] The next day, Luther appeared before the assembled

91. Fife, 573.
92. Bainton, 139.
93. Fife, 640.
94. Ibid., 654.

dignitaries in a small meeting room that was packed to the point of suffocation. Luther appeared frightened, constantly changing expressions and turning his head repeatedly. He sat behind a table full of his books. Johann von Ecke, the lawyer for the archbishop of Trier (no relation to Johann Eck who had debated Luther at Leipzig), spoke: "Martin Luther, His imperial Majesty has summoned you for two reasons: to know whether you acknowledge as by you the books before you, which have been attributed to you; and then, if you do acknowledge them, whether you stand by them or wish to revoke any of them."[95]

Luther responded first in German and then in Latin, declaring he could not and would not deny that he had written the books, but asked for time to consider whether he would recant them. He was given one day to answer the charge verbally. The emperor was unimpressed with Luther's appearance and remarked, "This man will never make me a heretic!"[96] When the day came, Luther entered into a tirade against the papacy before the assembly, saying, "No one can deny that through the laws of the pope and doctrines of man the conscience of the Christian world is held prisoner and the substance of the German people destroyed with incredible tyranny."[97] Luther admitted that in some of his books he may have been too frank, but he would not recant:

> Unless I am shown by the testimony of Scripture and by evident reasoning (for I do not put faith in pope or councils alone, because it is established that they have often erred and contradicted themselves), unless I am overcome by means of the scriptural passages that I have cited, and unless my conscience is taken captive by the Word of God, I am neither able nor willing to revoke anything, since to act against one's conscience

---

95. Ibid., 659.
96. Fife, 659.
97. Ibid., 664.

is neither sage nor honest. God help me, amen.[98]

Luther's refusal to recant after the multiple opportunities afforded by ecclesiastical and secular authorities proved his obstinate heresy, compelling the emperor to act. Charles issued a statement that allowed Luther to leave the Diet under the safe conduct, but also declared him a heretic wanted by the secular authorities:

> I am descended from a long line of Christian emperors of this noble German nation. ... They were all faithful to the death to the Church of Rome, and they defended the Catholic faith and the honor of God. I have resolved to follow in their steps. For it is certain that a single monk must err if he stands against the opinion of all Christendom. Otherwise Christendom itself would have erred for more than a thousand years. After having heard yesterday the obstinate defense of Luther, I regret that I have so long delayed in proceeding against him and his false teaching. I will have no more to do with him. I will proceed against him as a notorious heretic.[99]

The Diet passed an edict that delineated Luther's heretical statements and required all lands to regard him as a "convicted heretic." After twenty-one days — the time frame of the safe conduct — no secular ruler was permitted to harbor him, and his books were "to be eradicated from the memory of man."[100] Luther was now a hunted man. However, his secular ruler, Elector Frederick, intervened and hatched a plan to "kidnap" Luther on his way home from the Diet. Luther was surrounded by a group of armed men who whisked him away to the Wartburg castle, where he

---

98. Ibid. The popular narrative indicates Luther ended his statement with the famous quote, "Here I stand, I can do no other." In German, "*Ich kann nicht anders. Hier stehe ich.*" However, Luther never uttered the phrase; it was added later to an account of the Diet of Worms by the Lutheran theologian Georg Rörer.
99. Bainton, 145.
100. Ibid., 147.

lived incognito for ten months, assuming a fake name, growing a beard, and wearing layman's clothes.

While ensconced in Wartburg, Luther began work on a German translation of the New Testament.[101] Scornful of the standard Latin Vulgate translation, he based his edition on Hebrew and Greek texts. Luther's translation was colored by his false teachings and the desire to alter passages or to remove books in order to fit his theology. While translating Luke's Gospel, Luther struggled with the archangel Gabriel's acclamation to Mary that she was "full of grace." Luther wrote: "What German would understand that if translated literally? He knows the meaning of a purse full of gold or a keg full of beer, but what is he to make of a girl full of grace? I would prefer to say simply, '*Liebe Maria*' (Mary, full of love). What word is more rich than that word, *liebe*?"[102] In translating the Old Testament, Luther was motivated by a desire to "make Moses so German that no one would suspect he was a Jew."[103] Luther's flawed translation of the Bible was published in 1534. It was so popular that it was printed in three hundred editions in his lifetime and contributed to the use of High German as a standardized language among the German peoples.[104]

VIOLENCE BEGINS

Luther's writings circulated widely throughout German lands. Those who desired to rebel against secular authorities utilized his writings as justification. By 1525, violent insurrection exploded. The Peasants' Revolt threw German territory into a spasm of

101. Luther's Bible was not the first vernacular edition of the Scripture. The oldest known German translation of the Scripture was produced in the eighth century at the monastery of Monse. There were 36,000 German manuscript Bibles by the fifteenth century, and a complete vernacular German printed Bible (known as the Zürich Bible) appeared in 1529, three years before Luther's. See Johann Michael Reu, *Luther's German Bible: A Historical Presentation Together with a Collection of Sources* (Columbus, OH: Lutheran Book Concern, 1934), 20,27.
102. Bainton, 256.
103. Ibid., 255.
104. Daniel-Rops, *The Protestant Reformation*, vol. 2, 48.

bloodshed and destruction as armed groups rampaged across the land, killing, destroying churches and sacred art, and profaning the Eucharist. Erasmus wrote to Luther that "you would not recognize the rioters but they recognized you."[105] Although Luther had not specifically called for a peasant uprising, he knew it was the result of his writing and preaching.[106] The German nobility was alarmed at the violence and the speed of its progress. Those who harbored Luther from the secular and ecclesial authorities demanded he do something to stop the peasants, so Luther wrote yet another treatise. Published on May 4, 1525, this work, titled *Against the Murderous, Thieving Hordes of Peasants*, was a clarion call to the nobility to forcibly suppress the rebellion by any means. Luther wrote: "Let everyone who can smite, slay and stab, remembering that nothing can be more devilish than a rebel. It is just as when one must kill a mad dog."[107] He exhorted the princes to fight the peasants, since one "can win heaven more easily by bloodshed than by prayer" and one "cannot meet a rebel with reason: your best answer is to punch him in the face until he has a bloody nose."[108] The princes, embracing Luther's advice, began a murderous rampage that left over one hundred thousand peasants dead. When reviewing the carnage, Luther had a twinge of guilt and admitted responsibility (somewhat) for the devastating loss of life: "It was I who slew all the peasants in the insurrection, for it was I who commanded them to be slaughtered; their blood is on my head, but I throw the responsibility on our Lord God who instructed me to give this order."[109]

REJECTING THE PRIESTHOOD

Shortly after the publication of his major theological works in

105. Ibid.

106. See Daniel-Rops, *The Protestant Reformation*, vol. 2, 56.

107. E. G. Rupp and Benjamin Drewery, *Martin Luther, Documents of Modern History* (London: Edward Arnold, 1970), accessed September 19, 2018, http://zimmer.csufresno.edu/~mariterel/against_the_robbing_and_murderin.htm.

108. Ibid.

109. Hughes, *A Popular History of the Reformation*, 157.

1520, Luther wrote another book, dedicated to his father and titled *On Monastic Vows*. The work was a repudiation of the monastic life, as Luther believed that religious vows were not found in Scripture and conflicted with liberty and charity. In a letter to a friend, Luther provided his rationale: "I have decided to attack monastic vows and to free the young people from that hell of celibacy, totally unclean and condemned as it is through its burning and pollutions."[110] Luther's view of monasticism and celibacy were shaped by his own experience in Erfurt, where he indicated he had "lost both the salvation of my soul and health of my body."[111] Luther believed the religious vow was based on the false assumption that there is a special vocation of the ordained and religious. *On Monastic Vows* spread quickly, and resulted in a mass exodus from German monasteries and convents. Although it was a capital offense in the Empire to abduct a nun, Luther helped twelve nuns escape their convent in 1523. A year later, Luther publicly discarded his Augustinian habit. On June 13, 1525, he rejected the promises made at his ordination by entering into marriage with Katherine von Bora, one of the nuns he had helped to escape. Luther was forty-two at the time of his wedding, and Katherine was twenty-six. They had six children together and raised four related orphans. Luther gave three reasons for rejecting the priesthood and entering into marriage: to please his father, to spite the pope, and to seal his witness as a martyr.[112] His view of marriage as a martyrdom was confirmed by his statement that "I have humbled and debased myself so far by this marriage that the angels must be smiling — at least I hope so — and all the demons weeping."[113] Luther's book influenced his supporters and colleagues. Carlstadt renounced his priesthood in 1522 and married a fifteen-year-old girl. By the next year, Carlstadt was advocating the practice of polygamy. *On Monastic Vows*, and Luther's personal example, set the Protestant movement on the

---

110. Kittelson, 171.
111. Fife, 92.
112. Bainton, 225.
113. Grisar, *Luther*, I, 471, quoted in Daniel-Rops, *The Protestant Reformation*, vol. 2, 63.

path of a married clergy, with all that practice's attendant challenges, and contributed difficulties to any potential reunion with Rome.

Although Luther's writings had excited many secular rulers, very few openly declared their support of his rejection of papal and Church authority until 1525. In that year, secular princes began to convert to Luther's revolutionary movement. The first to do so was Duke Albrecht of Brandenburg-Ansbach, the Grand Master of the Teutonic Order and the cousin of Luther's ordinary, Archbishop Albert of Mainz. Other nobles, including Duke Johann of Electoral Saxony and Landgrave Philipp of Hesse, soon followed Duke Albrecht's turn to Protestantism. Luther was gaining supporters and fault lines were developing in the Church family, which would lead to war once the Holy Roman Emperor could focus his attention on the effects of Luther's heresy in his central territory.

THE SACK OF ROME

While Luther's revolt was in full swing in German territory, Pope Clement VII (r. 1523–1534) was involved in a fight for his very life. France and the Holy Roman Empire were at war over territory in northern Italy, and the pope entered into a defensive alliance with the French King Francis I. Emperor Charles V sent a 50,000-man imperial army, which included 22,000 Lutheran troops, who shouted "Long live our pope Martin Luther," on a march to Rome.[114] The imperial army defeated the French and advanced on the Eternal City. On May 6, 1527, they broke through the defenses and rampaged through the city. A cadre of Swiss Guards protected Pope Clement VII as he ran down the covered passageway from the Vatican to Castel Sant'Angelo. The remaining Swiss Guards stood their ground in Saint Peter's Square. The battle made its way even to the altar of the basilica. The captain of the Swiss Guards was wounded in the attack; his comrades carried him home to be

---

114. Daniel-Rops, *The Protestant Reformation*, vol. 2, 87.

with his wife, but imperial troops entered the house and killed him in front of her. The pope was safe, but Rome was ravaged. The Swiss Guards paid the price for their admirable service; of the 189 Guards on duty that day, only forty-two lived to see another.[115] The imperial army sacked the city for more than a week. A contemporary recorded the devastation and its impact:

> In Rome, the chief city of Christendom, no bells ring, no churches are open, no Masses are said, Sundays and feast days have ceased. The rich shops of the merchants are turned into stables; the most splendid palaces are stripped bare; many houses are burnt to the ground; in others the doors and windows are broken and carried away; the streets are turned into dunghills. The stench of the dead bodies is terrible; men and beasts have a common grave, and in the churches I have seen corpses that dogs have gnawed. In the public places tables are set close together at which piles of ducats are gambled for. The air rings with blasphemies fit to make good men, if such there be, wish that they were deaf. I know nothing wherewith I can compare it except it be the destruction of Jerusalem.[116]

Priests were murdered and nuns dragged through the streets. A church-run orphanage was destroyed and all the children in it killed, along with the patients in a Catholic hospital. The Blessed Sacrament was profaned and an elderly priest killed because he refused to give the Host to a donkey.[117] Nearly 12,000 people died as a result of the sack.

---

115. Robert Royal, *The Pope's Army* (New York: Crossroad, 2006), 75. May 6 became an important date in the history of the Swiss Guards and remains so, as new recruits are sworn in on that day annually.
116. Von Pastor, *History of the Popes*, 427, quoted in Royal, *The Pope's Army*, 85.
117. Ibid., 84.

When the news reached the emperor, he was deeply saddened and apologized for his army's excess. He had not ordered the destruction and was not happy with the commanders who had allowed the travesty to take place. The pope remained in Castel Sant'Angelo until the imperial army finally left. The physical damage took months to repair, and the political ramifications continued for years. Unfortunately, the event prevented the emperor from focusing on the destructive force of Luther's heresy.

THE ADVANCE OF THE PROTESTANT MOVEMENT

The Protestant movement continued to gain ground in German territory during the remaining years of the 1520s and into the 1530s. Many German towns allowed Protestant theologians to preach publicly, which resulted in conflict with Catholics. Town authorities determined that, for the sake of peace, only one religion was allowed. In many cases, the new Protestant religion was chosen, and laws were passed to ban the celebration of Mass. A destructive wave of iconoclasm broke out. Statues were torn down, sacred art destroyed, altars smashed, and churches emptied of beautiful works of art intended to glorify God. Carlstadt described the necessity of the activity: "Organs belong only in theatrical exhibitions and palaces of princes. Painted images hanging on church walls are despicable. The idols painted on the altar panels are even more harmful and devilish."[118] Luther did not approve of the iconoclasm, and this issue was one of many to divide the early Protestant revolutionaries. Frequently, Church land and property were confiscated by secular rulers in order to enrich themselves, which contributed to the permanent break in Christian unity. Those newly enriched feared reunion with Rome, as it meant possible financial loss.

The imperial Diet met in 1529 to discuss the ongoing Ottoman Turkish threat on the southern borders. Many believed

---

118. Ozment, *The Serpent and the Lamb*, 123.

the Turkish advance was due to God's anger over the presence of heretics in the Empire.[119] The emperor could not focus completely on eradicating heresy because of the Ottoman military threat, but he needed peace in the Empire to effectively deal with the Turks. He was alarmed by the many cities and territories that had banned the celebration of the Mass and the resulting conflict with those loyal to the Church. So, in April 1529, the Emperor issued a decree that upheld the Edict of Worms (which had condemned Luther as a heretic eight years previously) and stipulated that no further religious changes should be made. Additionally, the decree commanded that the celebration of the Mass should be allowed throughout the Empire. Several nobles and the representatives from fourteen cities (including Nuremburg, Ulm, Constance, and Strasbourg) issued a formal written protest against Charles' decree, especially the stipulation concerning the Mass. This protest over the celebration of the Mass gave the name to the heretical movement sweeping central Europe: Protestantism.

Charles was now convinced that the divide between Catholics and Protestants was fixed. The religious situation required at least a temporary resolution, then, once the political and military situation was resolved, he could return to the eradication of heresy and spiritual disunity. At the next imperial Diet, which met in Augsburg in 1530, Charles invited the Protestants to develop a statement of their beliefs, in the hopes the that statement would provide a construct for fruitful dialogue with Catholic theologians, and perhaps lead to a settlement of religious differences. At the Diet, Luther was represented by his friend Philip Schwarzerd, known as Melanchthon (1497–1560). Melanchthon, an illustrious professor of Greek at Wittenberg, wrote a draft statement of Protestant beliefs and sent it to Luther, who approved. Protestant nobles signed the document and presented it to the emperor on June 25, 1530. Known as the Augsburg Confession, the document

---

119. Kittelson, 220.

was not a comprehensive statement of Protestant teachings but was divided into two parts: doctrines held in common with Catholics, and doctrines held in disagreement. In the section on teachings at issue, Melanchthon condemned the celebration of Mass, transubstantiation, the sacrament of confession, monastic vows, and priestly celibacy. The emperor gave the document to a group of Catholic theologians led by Johann Eck, the longtime nemesis of Luther. They reviewed the document and provided a report to the emperor that outlined the incompatibility of Protestant teachings with the Catholic faith. Charles issued a proclamation ordering Protestants not to publish any new theological writings, to refrain from proselytizing, and to stop persecuting Catholics. Luther responded to the emperor's decree:

> The Augsburg Confession must endure, as the true and unadulterated Word of God. Not even an angel from Heaven could alter a syllable of it, and any angel who dared to do so must be accursed and damned. The stipulations that monks and nuns still dwelling in their cloisters should not be expelled, and that the Mass should not be abolished, could not be accepted. Of all the horrors and abominations that could be mentioned, the Mass was the greatest.[120]

The Protestant rejection of Charles' decree ensured that the religious differences with Catholics could not be peacefully resolved.

THE BIGAMY OF PHILIP OF HESSE

Landgrave Philip of Hesse was young, handsome, and promiscuous. Married to Christine of Saxony, Philip grew tired of the relationship and, after embracing Luther's heretical teachings,

---

120. Johannes Janssen, *History of the German People at the Close of the Middle Ages* (London, 1910), V, 297, quoted in Carroll, *The Cleaving of Christendom*, 106.

wrote the professor a letter in 1526, asking if a Christian might have more than one wife. Luther responded that although polygamy was common in the Old Testament, it was not allowed for a Christian. Additionally, bigamy was against imperial law. Although initially rejected by Luther, Philip continued to pursue the idea and even received permission in 1539 from Martin Bucer, another Protestant revolutionary, to marry Margaret von der Sale, even though he was still married to Christine. However, Margaret (and her mother) would only agree to the dual marriage if both Luther and Melanchthon agreed it was permissible. This time, Luther changed his mind, telling Philip that bigamy should not be allowed for everyone, but it was acceptable in this case, as long as Philip kept the arrangement secret. So, Philip contravened secular and spiritual law and "married" Margaret. However, the secret arrangement soon became known, and people were rightfully outraged. Initially, Luther and Bucer told Philip to lie about the bigamy. Luther wrote, "What harm is there in telling a good bold lie for the sake of making things better and for the good of the Christian Church?"[121] He later retracted his support by writing, "If anyone thereafter should practice bigamy, let the Devil give him a bath in the abyss of hell."[122] Luther's fluctuating support of bigamy clearly illustrated the major issue with his revolution. In seeking to rid the German people from the "tyranny" of the papacy, he merely replaced papal authority with his own. Luther contradicted himself, and many of his initial supporters developed their own interpretations of Scripture and Christian doctrine, which led to fractures within the early Protestant movement. Destruction and division, as with all previous heresies, became the hallmark of the rebellion.

LUTHER'S LAST WRITINGS

Toward the end of his life, Luther finished his prodigious writing

---

121. Carroll, *The Cleaving of Christendom*, 178.
122. Bainton, 293.

career with several vehement works attacking the two groups of people he hated most: the Jews and the popes. In 1543, Luther published the treatise *On the Jews and their Lies*, wherein he advocated an eight-point plan to rid German lands of Jews, either by religious conversion or by forcible expulsion. Luther disliked the Jews and believed they were damned because of their refusal to accept Jesus as the Messiah. Luther called for Jewish homes, schools, and synagogues to be burned. He wanted their sacred writings confiscated and their rabbis forbidden to teach. He who had benefited from safe conduct exhorted the authorities to refuse the same treatment to Jews. Jewish money should be confiscated, and they should not be allowed the practice of usury. Luther also demanded forced labor for the Jews:

> I recommend putting a flail, an ax, a hoe, a spade, a staff, or a spindle into the hands of young, strong Jews and Jewesses and letting them earn their bread in the sweat of their brow. ... For it is not fitting that they should let us accursed Goyim toil in the sweat of our faces while they, the holy people, idle away their time behind the stove, feasting and farting, and on top of all, boasting blasphemously of their lordship over the Christians by means of our sweat. No, one should toss out these lazy rogues by the seat of their pants.[123]

Luther wanted the nobility to take his words to heart and exercise their duty to rid their territory of the Jews "like a good physician who, when gangrene has set proceeds without mercy to cut, saw, and burn flesh, veins, bone, and marrow."[124] The secular rulers should show no mercy to the Jews; rather, they should "drive them out like mad dogs, so that we do not become partakers of their abominable

123. Luther, *On the Jews and the Lies*, part 11 in *Luther's Works* Martin H. Bertram, translator (Philadelphia: Fortress Press, 1971), accessed September 19, 2018, http://www.ccjr.us/dialogika-resources/primary-texts-from-the-history-of-the-relationship/luther-1543.
124. Ibid.

blasphemy and all their other vices and thus merit God's wrath and be damned with them. I have done my duty. Now let everyone see to his."[125] Luther's anti-Semitic screed and general attitude toward Jews influenced German Protestantism. Although the Jewish people had suffered in many ways throughout Europe for centuries, Luther's polemic was taken to heart due to his popularity and standing among many Germans, who looked upon him as a national hero.[126]

Luther published his last work in March 1545, turning his ire once more to what he believed was the source of all evil in the world: the papacy. *Against the Pontificate at Rome, Founded by the Devil* called the pope "the vicar of the devil; an enemy of God; an opponent of Christ; and a destroyer of the Church; a teacher of all lies, blasphemy, and idolatries; an antichrist; a man of sin and a child of perdition; a genuine werewolf."[127] After many years of contemplating what should be done to the pope and cardinals, he outlined his vision for the end of the papacy: "He should be seized, he and his cardinals and their tongues should be torn from their throats and nailed in a row on the gallows tree. I would like to curse the Pope and his supporters so that thunder and lightning would strike them, hell-fire burn them, the plague, syphilis, epilepsy, scurvy, leprosy, carbuncles, and all manner of diseases attack them."[128]

THE END OF MARTIN LUTHER

As his death drew near, Luther reflected on his life's work. When

---

125. Ibid.
126. In the twentieth century, Luther's vision for the eradication of the Jewish people from Germany would manifest in the policies and actions of the National Socialist government. Many historians overlook (or are ignorant of) the role Luther played in fostering German Protestant anti-Semitic attitudes over the centuries. William L. Shirer, an American journalist living in 1930s Germany when the Nazis came to power, saw the link: "It is difficult to understand the behavior of most German Protestants in the first Nazi years unless one is aware of two things: their history and the influence of Martin Luther. The great founder of Protestantism was both a passionate anti-Semite and a ferocious believer in absolute obedience to political authority. He wanted Germany rid of the Jews. Luther's advice was literally followed four centuries later by Hitler, Goering and Himmler." William L. Shirer, *The Rise and Fall of the Third Reich: A History of Nazi Germany* (New York: Touchstone, 1990), 236.
127. Kittelson, 290.
128. Janssen, *History of the German People*, VI, 271–272, quoted in Carroll, *The Cleaving of Christendom*, 189.

reviewing the events in German territory over the previous twenty-five years, Luther was taken aback at what had transpired from his preaching and writing. He lamented the "misery, corruption, scandal, blasphemy, ingratitude, and wickedness" that had infected his native land.[129] He bemoaned the fact that since his revolution had begun the main result was not an increase in religious fervor but a greater indifference to faith. Pained, he wrote that he was "the sole author of this movement."[130]

In January 1546, while passing through a town (with a large population of Jews, as he noted), Luther contracted an illness. The next month, weak from the sickness and other health issues, Luther suffered a stroke and died. After Luther's death, a doctor discovered an inscription on the wall near his deathbed. The unrepentant heretic had scrawled into the wall one last insult for the pope: *Pestis eram vivus moriens ero mors tua, papa* ("I was your plague while I lived; when I die, I shall be your death, O pope!").[131]

There is no doubt that Martin Luther's life and work greatly impacted the family of God. It is unfortunate that his brilliant intellect, stupendous power of will, and steadfastness were not given in faithful service to the Church. Instead, these personal qualities assisted Luther in dividing the family of God — a division it continues to suffer, in violation of Christ's command that all Christians remain united in the Church.

JOHN CALVIN — A CALCULATING SOUL

The Chauvin family came from the northern area of France, from "the people that have no vineyards."[132] John was the second of six children, born to Gerard Chauvin and Jeanne Lefranc in the town

---

129. Janssen, *History of the German People*, VI, 276–277, quoted in Carroll, *The Cleaving of Christendom*, 188.
130. Ibid.
131. Daniel-Rops, *The Protestant Reformation*, vol. 2, 106–107.
132. Hilaire Belloc, *How the Reformation Happened* (Rockford, IL: TAN Books and Publishers, 1992 [1928]), 79.

of Noyon, about sixty miles north of Paris.[133] Gerard provided for his family with income drawn from ecclesial employment as a notary apostolic, episcopal secretary, and procurator fiscal of the cathedral chapter. Later in his life, Gerard was accused and convicted of financial irregularities, which led to his excommunication. John was a bright, diligent, high-strung young man who was "cold and resolute, reserved, but capable of terrible violence and as severe to others as he was to himself."[134] A scholarly individual, John suffered from chronic insomnia, migraines, and stomachaches, which were exacerbated by his extreme fasting. Although Calvin's life and work would be intertwined with Martin Luther's, no two different men have ever been connected. While Luther was highly volatile, rude, gregarious, and emotional, Calvin was ruled by logic, reason, and overwhelming seriousness.

John was sent to the University of Paris to study by his father in 1520, and likely came into contact with the writings of Luther during his studies. He studied philosophy, especially the nominalism of William of Ockham, whose thought had influenced Luther. Initially, Calvin's father envisioned an ecclesial career for his son, so the focus of John's studies was theological and philosophical. But, in 1525, Gerard changed his mind. He now believed a legal career was best for John, so the young man was sent to the University of Orléans to study civil law. Four years later, Calvin was at the University of Bourges, engaging in legal studies as well as learning Greek.

Calvin's acceptance of Protestant teachings during his time at Bourges was a different experience from Luther's formulation of heresy and fomenting of rebellion.[135] Calvin had been eight years old when the Augustinian published the 95 Theses. He was a layman, not a dissatisfied priest and religious like Luther. Calvin ex-

---

133. Chauvin was the family name. When young John went to Paris to study he Latinized his name, as was the academic custom of the time, to Ioannis Calvinus, or Jean Calvin in French and John Calvin in English.
134. Daniel-Rops, *The Protestant Reformation*, vol. 2, 138.
135. There is debate over the precise year that Calvin became Protestant, but it is generally believed he converted sometime in the 1530s.

plained his rejection of the Catholic faith as a God-directed conversion, but provided few details into the exact workings of his mind on the radical decision to reject the faith of his ancestors.[136]

Nicholas Cop, the rector of the University of Paris and a friend of Calvin, asserted the Protestant teachings of *sola fide* and *sola scriptura* in his November 1, 1533, inaugural address as rector. This public address led to Cop's arrest, along with that of fifty friends and associates, by the secular authorities. Calvin, due to his association with Cop, was implicated and fled Paris. During 1534 he wandered throughout France as a fugitive under the alias Charles d'Espeville and briefly met another fugitive heretic: Michael Servetus. The two would meet again twenty years later in Geneva.

In October 1534, numerous signs appeared in Paris and other French cities attacking the Holy Sacrifice of the Mass. Known as the "Placard Affair," the posters were the work of Antoine Marcourt, a follower of the Swiss Protestant revolutionary Ulrich Zwingli. King Francis I, enraged, ordered a manhunt for suspected Protestants, which led to the arrest of two hundred persons (and execution of twenty over the following three months), including several of Calvin's friends. In January 1535, Francis promulgated heresy laws that made it a capital offense to harbor heretics. Those who gave information about wayward Christians were promised a portion of the property of those arrested. Calvin saw the writing on the wall and knew he was no longer safe in his native land, so he fled France and went to the Swiss town of Basel.

In 1536, when Calvin was twenty-six years old, he published a book that made him famous throughout Europe. The full title of the book was *The Basic Teaching of the Christian Religion Comprising Almost The Whole Sum of Godliness and Whatever Is Necessary to Know on the Doctrine of Salvation*, but it became known as *The Institutes of Christian Religion*. Over the next twenty years, Calvin continued

---

136. See T. H. L. Parker, *John Calvin: A Biography* (Louisville, KY: Westminster John Knox Press, 2006 [1975]), 200.

to revise the *Institutes* in multiple and expanded editions, so that what "began as an oratory ... ended as a cathedral."[137] The second edition, published in 1539, was three times longer than the first. He revised the work a third time while in Strasbourg in 1543. Another edition came in 1550. The last and definitive edition was published in 1559, comprising eighty chapters that were divided into four books. Originally written in Latin, the French translation of the *Institutes* first appeared in 1541 based on the second edition. The work was eventually translated into English (in 1561), German, Dutch, Italian, Spanish, Hungarian, and Greek. It became the most widely read book of the sixteenth century and made Calvin one of the most popular French authors.[138]

The *Institutes* was an attempt by Calvin to systematize Protestant theology, which heretofore had been found in the various writings of multiple Protestant authors, especially Luther. Calvin's work was the first to organize Protestant belief into a single volume. The first edition was Calvin's personal statement of belief, as well as a framework of instruction in the basics of the Christian religion as interpreted by the author. He structured this edition like a catechism, including sections on the Ten Commandments and commentary on the Apostles' Creed and the Lord's Prayer. Later editions changed the work from a catechism to an introduction and guide to the study of the Bible, guided by Calvin's scriptural commentary.

The *Institutes* espoused the main Protestant teachings of *sola fide*, *sola scriptura*, the depravity of man, the sacraments, the Church, and Calvin's unique interpretation on predestination and the elect. Calvin explicated the Protestant belief that "man is justified by faith alone." He answered the challenge that if that is the case then charity was optional by writing that "true holiness of life is also essential."[139] However, he pointed out that good works

---

137. Ibid., 163.

138. See Daniel-Rops, *The Protestant Reformation*, vol. 2, 161.

139. John Calvin, *The Institutes of Christian Religion*, 3:3:1, Tony Lane and Hilary Osborne, eds. (Grand Rapids: Baker Academic, 1987), 151.

have no value in determining salvation, since "no believer ever performed a single deed which, if tested by God's strict justice, could escape condemnation ... because the deed is tainted by his sins it is stripped of all merit."[140] Calvin affirmed the Protestant belief that "the Scriptures are the only place in which God has chosen to record his truth for a perpetual reminder."[141] Like Luther, Calvin viewed human nature as completely corrupted (as a result of original sin) and deprived of God's sanctifying grace, writing in the first pages of the *Institutes* that "man... is rotten to the core and so wretched."[142]

Calvin rejected Catholic teaching that the sacraments are efficacious works of themselves, believing instead that they are "useless if not received in faith."[143] He agreed with Luther that there are only two sacraments, baptism and Eucharist, although he differed in his understanding of Christ's presence in the Eucharist. Calvin walked a middle ground between Luther, who believed in a consubstantial presence of Christ with the bread and wine in the Eucharist, and Zwingli, who believed there was no Real Presence of Christ in the sacrament. Calvin advocated that Christ gave himself to the Christian in a real manner at the moment of reception, but in a purely spiritual union. As with Luther, Calvin rejected the celebration of the Mass, referring to it as a sacrilege. Calvin knew that one effective attack against the Protestant movement was the historical continuity of the Catholic Church, so he created the narrative that the Church had become corrupt and, therefore, represented a radical departure from the early Church.[144] He believed that his interpretation of Divine Revelation represented a return to the true Church. Calvin rejected the understanding of the Church as a divinely instituted and organized body of believers united in faith with the Vicar of

---

140. Calvin, *Institutes*, 3:14:11, in Lane and Osborne, 192.
141. Calvin, *Institutes*, 1:7:1, in Lane and Osborne, 41.
142. Calvin, *Institutes*, 1:1:3, in Lane and Osborne, 23.
143. Calvin, *Institutes*, 4:14:17, in Lane and Osborne, 256.
144. Calvin, *Institutes*, 4:1:11, in Lane and Osborne, 235.

Christ, the pope. Instead, for Calvin, the Church was the general body of Christian believers throughout the world.[145]

Calvin also asserted in the *Institutes* that humanity was divided into two groups, the elect and the damned: "Scripture clearly proves that God, by his eternal and unchanging will, determined once and for all those whom he would one day admit to salvation [the elect] and those whom he would consign to destruction [the damned]."[146] Calvin's interpretation of predestination led to charges that, since God has already determined a man's fate, there is no reason for him to act virtuously. Calvin countered by arguing that man must still act morally; not in order to be saved, but because he is saved, or at least has the potential for salvation, by his faith in the salvific actions of Christ. Those who act virtuously may very well be members of the elect. Additionally, Calvin opined, "God rewards those who live good lives with many material blessings."[147] So, if one is blessed materially, it could be a sign that person is a member of the elect, whereas those who are poor or downtrodden manifest God's disfavor and rejection from the elect. This emphasis on material conditions as a sign of eternal favor or disfavor contributed to the Protestant view of labor and developed a unique way of life, especially in the city of Geneva.

ESTABLISHING THEOCRACY — GENEVA

Calvin decided to leave Basel and planned to travel to Strasbourg, a Protestant stronghold, but his friend Guillaume Farel (1489–1565) convinced him to move to Geneva instead. Geneva, formerly attached to the Italian duchy of Savoy, had recently become a fully independent, self-governing city-state republic. A well-fortified wall enclosed the city of ten thousand souls. The government was comprised of an executive group of four men,

145. Calvin, *Institutes*, 4:1:7, in Lane and Osborne, 233.
146. Calvin, *Institutes*, 3:21:7, in Lane and Osborne, 216.
147. Calvin, *Institutes*, 3:14:2, in Lane and Osborne, 190.

elected each January by a general assembly of male citizens who were assisted by the City Council. The City Council, a group of twenty-five men elected by the Council of 200, served as the central administrative body and enforced the legislation passed by the Council of 200. In the early 1530s, Protestant elements took control of the city government. Religious riots, including a wave of iconoclasm, the suspension of the celebration of Mass, and the expulsion of all religious orders, rocked the city in 1535. The following year, the government voted to embrace the Protestant movement. When Calvin came to the city, he assumed the role of pastor with the primary duties of preaching, enforcing Christian discipline, and organizing the Protestant church. Calvin also established an international printing house in the city with a specific aim of flooding France with heretical books.[148]

Calvin and Farel collaborated on a first attempt to organize the church and city according to their Protestant principles. In 1537, they published the work *Articles on the Organization of the Church and Its Worship at Geneva*. In the *Articles*, Calvin and Farel mandated citywide attendance at weekly church services and divided the city into quarters. An "overseer" presided over each quarter of the city, with the charge of reporting on the moral faults of citizens to the ministers of the church. Those who were reported to the authorities but failed to repent were excommunicated. Calvin convinced the city government to enact legislation prohibiting commerce on Sunday during the sermons: "Neither butchers, nor tripe sellers, nor others, nor second-hand dealers shall stay open beyond the last stroke of the great bell; there is to be no singing of idle songs and no playing of games of chance, nor are the pastry cooks to cry their wares during the time of the sermon."[149]

Genevans were not pleased with Calvin and Farel's attempt to enforce their Protestant teachings. Violence, directed at Calvin, erupted in the city. Many accused the refugee of being a secret

---

148. See Diarmaid MacCulloch, *The Reformation: A History* (New York: Penguin Books, 2003), 197.
149. *Opera Calvini* (*Corpus Reformatorum*) 21, 207, quoted in Parker, 88.

French agent sent to destabilize the city. Calvin was not fazed by the violence; he pressed on with implementing the *Articles* because he "belonged to that family of terrifying and sublime men who, like Savonarola and Robespierre before and after him, dream of creating man's salvation or happiness without them, despite them, and even against them."[150] The city government did not share Calvin's zeal or fortitude so, in order to restore peace in the city, they exiled the preacher. He left Geneva and went to Strasbourg, his initial destination eighteen months previously, where he became the pastor of a French Protestant congregation in the city.

Calvin's time in Strasbourg was primarily spent preaching and revising the *Institutes*. He also met and married a widow named Idelette de Bure. Idelette died in 1549. Calvin never remarried, but focused all his energy and life on advancing the Protestant cause.

THE WAR AGAINST JOY

After Calvin's departure from Geneva, the city descended into political instability. The hope of restoring peace by exiling Calvin proved fruitless. Eventually, the sentiment arose in the City Council that only a strong and impassioned spiritual leader could restore peace and unity to the city; so they asked Calvin to return. No doubt, Calvin was shocked and had every reason to reject the invitation, yet he returned in 1541. Upon his return to the city, Calvin mounted the pulpit and continued the commentary on the Bible at the exact passage where he had been forced to stop years before.[151] Calvin revised his plan for the ecclesial organization of Geneva in a new work titled *Ecclesiastical Ordinances*. He organized the church hierarchically with offices of pastors, doctors, elders, and deacons. Learning from his previous failed attempt to

---

150. Daniel-Rops, *The Protestant Reformation*, vol. 2, 178.
151. Ibid., 176.

establish a theocracy in Geneva, Calvin made sure that refugee French Protestants loyal to him — rather than native Genevans — staffed all church offices.[152] The church in Geneva was tasked by Calvin to preach the Gospel, administer the sacraments, teach the faith, train the faithful in obedience, and care for the sick. Pastors were elected by other pastors and confirmed by the City Council. They took an oath to faithfully serve God and defend Calvin's *Ordinances*. They met weekly to study Scripture and quarterly for a session of fraternal correction. The primary function of pastors was preaching; they were expected to do so four days a week. Although Calvin did not identify as a pastor, but a doctor, he excelled at preaching and gave two hundred sermons a year.[153] Pastors also baptized, celebrated the Eucharist four times a year, and ministered to the sick. Doctors were catechists who focused on language studies and Scripture commentaries. Elders were responsible for the administration of church discipline. Deacons were divided into two classes: administrators oversaw the distribution of charity, and executives dispensed charity and cared for the sick. The City Council adopted the *Ordinances* on November 20, 1541, and allowed Calvin to mesh ecclesial regulations with secular laws.

During his second stay in Geneva, Calvin established a theocracy in which the personal lives of the people in the city were under his direct jurisdiction, a situation best described as the "war against joy."[154] Calvin required Genevans to confess their sins to a civil magistrate in a court of law and established biannual visitations, where a commission of ministers and elders visited every house in the city to check on the spiritual lives of all citizens. The commission asked questions about the inhabitants' religious participation, and searched for any sign of allegiance to the Catholic Church. Ledgers were kept, wherein people were marked as pious, lukewarm, or corrupt. The city government passed legis-

---

152. MacCulloch, 239.
153. John Calvin, *The Institutes of Christian Religion*, Tony Lane and Hilary Osborne, eds., 12.
154. Belloc, *How the Reformation Happened*, 79.

lation that made adultery, pregnancy out of wedlock, blasphemy, idolatry, heresy, and striking a parent capital offenses. Additional legislation prohibited dancing, singing outside of church, staging or attending theatrical plays, wearing jewelry, playing cards or dice, wearing makeup, and falling asleep during a sermon. Restrictions were placed on children's names (which could only be taken from the Bible) and the length of a woman's hair. Calvin exceeded the tolerance of the people when he closed all the taverns in the city. Recognizing his error, Calvin worked with city officials to establish five government-controlled taverns. These bars were nonprofit enterprises which required patrons to say prayers before and after eating and drinking, and prohibited swearing, slandering, and dancing.

The inhabitants did not accept Calvin's rules and regulations unconditionally, and several high-profile cases serve to illustrate life in Calvin's Geneva. At a dinner party in his own house in January 1546, Pierre Ameaux criticized Calvin, calling him an "evil and ambitious man from Picardy, the preacher of false doctrine."[155] Someone informed the authorities, and Ameaux was arrested and tried before the City Council. He was ordered to pay a fine and publicly recant his attack on Calvin. The Council of 200 reduced his punishment to merely issuing an apology to Calvin. Calvin, incensed at the reduction of the punishment, refused to preach. People clamored for the return of their preacher, so the Council of 200 changed the sentence to suit Calvin's wishes. Ameaux was required to walk around the city carrying a lighted torch, bareheaded and dressed only in a shirt. He was made to fall to his knees three times and beg for mercy. Additionally, a gallows was constructed in front of his office as a reminder to conform to the teachings of Calvin. In another case, Jacques Gruet nailed a piece of paper with threats against the clergy to one of the pulpits in the city. His house was searched. One of Calvin's books was found with the words "all

---

155. Daniel-Rops, *The Protestant Reformation*, vol. 2, 182.

rubbish" written in it. Gruet was arrested, tortured, and behead-ed.[156] A woman was exiled from the city for saying that "what Jesus Christ said is quite enough for us."[157] Calvin's war against joy claimed many victims who were exiled, excommunicated, and executed for their opposition to his rule and interpretation of the Christian faith.

THE CURIOUS CASE OF MICHAEL SERVETUS

Michael Servetus (1511–1553) was a Spanish intellectual with varied interests in medicine, anatomy, astronomy, meteorology, geography, law, mathematics, cartography, and theology. In his 1531 book *Seven Books on Errors about the Trinity* Servetus denied the existence of the Trinity. He sent a copy of the work to Calvin for his opinion. Calvin retorted that the book confirmed its au-thor was "certainly a son of Satan!"[158] Servetus's book caught the attention of the Spanish Inquisition, which ordered his arrest for heresy. The Spanish renegade fled his native land and settled in France under an assumed name, and he somehow managed to become the personal physician to the archbishop of Vienne. Several years after the publication of his heretical work, Servetus sent a letter to Calvin, asking his opinion on three theological questions.[159] Calvin replied, but Servetus disputed his answers in another letter. Calvin responded with a longer letter of more detailed answers and sent a copy of his *Institutes* to the inquisi-tive Spaniard. Servetus then sent the copy of the *Institutes* back to Calvin with criticisms in the margins. Servetus told Calvin that his belief in the Trinity, which is a "triad of impossible mon-strosities ... is not proved by any Scriptures properly under-

---

156. Ibid., 183.
157. Ibid., 195.
158. Ibid., 186.
159. The questions focused on whether the crucified man Jesus was the Son of God and what was the manner or type of this sonship; whether the kingdom of God is in men, when it begins, and when is a man regenerated; and whether baptism demands faith like the Lord's Supper, and why baptism was instituted in the new covenant.

stood."[160] He then ridiculed the Genevan preacher by writing that Calvin's belief in the Trinity "shows that your knowledge is ridiculous, nay, a magical enchantment and a lying justification."[161] Calvin was incensed at Servetus's insults. In a letter to Farel, Calvin wrote about the Spaniard's request to come to Geneva: "He would like to come here if it is agreeable to me. But I do not wish to pledge my word for his safety. For, if he comes, I will never let him depart alive, if I have any authority."[162] Sadly, Calvin's threat would become a gruesome reality for Servetus.

Servetus's self-imposed exile in France came to a close when his disguise was discovered and he was arrested on charges of heresy in 1553. The French authorities declared that Servetus was "to be burned alive in a slow fire until his body becomes ashes. For the present, the sentence is to be carried out in effigy and his books are to be burnt."[163] Servetus escaped prison and while on the run made plans to settle in Italy, but, on the way, he detoured to Geneva. On August 13, 1553, he attended a sermon preached by Calvin and was recognized and arrested. While Servetus sat in a Geneva jail, Calvin wrote a list of theological accusations against Servetus, which were used against him in his trial. The City Council found Servetus guilty of Calvin's charges and condemned him to die by burning at the stake. Calvin requested the more humane death of beheading, which was rejected. Michael Servetus, whose main crime was embracing heresy in opposition to Calvin's heresy, was burned at the stake on October 27, 1553.

THE IMPORTANCE OF CALVIN

John Calvin's tireless work produced several important effects for the Protestant movement. He organized the theocratic city-state in Geneva, providing an example for Protestants through-

---

160. *Opera Calvini (Corpus Reformatorum)* 8, 653, quoted in Parker, 147.
161. Ibid.
162. *Opera Calvini (Corpus Reformatorum)* 12, 283, quoted in Parker, 148.
163. *Opera Calvini (Corpus Reformatorum)* 8, 786, quoted in Parker, 150.

out Europe of how church and state could be intertwined to govern the people of God. Through his *Institutes*, he systematized Protestant theology and provided a manual for the study of Protestant teachings. His teachings on predestination, and his belief that material blessings were the sign of God's favor, created a way of life and a work ethic that dominated Protestant thought for centuries.

Calvin's teachings spread throughout Europe through his books and extensive letter-writing. The creation of the Geneva Academy in the summer of 1559 educated a cadre of Protestant missionaries who could take his teachings throughout the world. At the time of Calvin's death, the Academy had 1,500 students; nearly 90 percent came from outside the Swiss cantons, including Russia.[164] Perhaps the most famous Protestant missionary who spent time in Geneva with Calvin was the Scotsman John Knox, who spread Calvin's teachings in his native land and helped overthrow the Catholic Mary Stuart, Queen of Scots. Knox enjoyed his time in Geneva and counted Calvin a personal friend. He referred to Geneva as "the most perfect school of Christ that ever was in earth since the days of the apostles."[165]

Toward the end of his life, Calvin reflected on his work and gave his followers unintentionally ironic advice:

> I have taught faithfully, and God has given me grace to write what I have written as faithfully as it was in my power. I have not falsified a single passage of the Scriptures, nor given it a wrong interpretation to the best of my knowledge; and though I might have introduced subtle senses ... I cast that temptation under my feet and always aimed at simplicity. I pray you make no change, no innovation ... because all changes are dangerous and sometimes hurtful.[166]

---

164. Hughes, *A Popular History of the Reformation*, 260.
165. Quoted in John Calvin, *The Institutes of Christian Religion*, Lane and Osborne, eds., 12.
166. Parker, 189–190.

Calvin had suffered from ill health, exacerbated by his workaholic tendencies, throughout his life. In 1558–1559, he was stricken with a serious fever that affected his lungs. He had barely recovered when he strained his voice preaching, which caused a violent coughing episode, resulting in a burst blood vessel in his lung.[167] His ailments, poor diet, and lack of proper sleep eventually caused his death in 1564. Calvin's body was laid in state, but due to concern over creating a cult of Calvin, he was buried in a common cemetery without a headstone.[168]

RADICAL REFORMERS

The core of Protestant teaching centers on the rejection of the teaching authority of the Catholic Church and the investment of this authority in the individual. As such, it was not surprising that various Protestant groups interpreted the Scriptures and Christian doctrine differently. Although Luther and Calvin were the main protagonists in the story of the Protestant Revolution, other actors were involved in the drama unfolding across Christendom in the sixteenth century.[169] Groups who did not agree with the Lutherans (who referred to themselves as "evangelical") or the Calvinists (who became known as the "Reformed"), were labeled as "radicals." Of the many Protestant groups in the "radical" camp, the two main sects stemmed from Ulrich Zwingli and the Anabaptists.

Ulrich Zwingli (1484–1531) was one of ten children. His father, the mayor of their village, desired that his children receive a good education. Zwingli was sent to Basel, Bern, and Vienna for school, but felt called to the priesthood. Ordained in 1506, Zwingli was sent to a parish church in the village of Galrus. Unlike the monastic university professor Martin Luther, Zwingli

---

167. Ibid., 185.
168. Eventually, a stone was added in the nineteenth century in the spot traditionally believed to be his grave.
169. The following section is adapted from my booklet *20 Answers: The Reformation*, 24–27, 64.

spent his priesthood as a pastor of souls, dealing with the spiritual and material needs of everyday people; he even spent some time as a military chaplain. He was greatly impacted by meeting the humanist and reformer Erasmus in Basel, and by Erasmus's writings, especially his 1516 translation of the New Testament.

A few years later, in 1518, Zwingli moved to Zürich, where he embraced the revolution against the Church and spent the rest of his life. He preached against indulgences in 1521 and advocated *sola scriptura*. A year later, he told his congregation they did not have to obey the Lenten fast, which led to the scandal of the Zürich printer Christoph Froschauer and his twelve companions publicly eating sausages during the penitential season. Zwingli publicly cast aside his promise of celibacy in 1522 (privately, he had been flouting that promise for years) when he married a widow with three children.

Zwingli was a popular preacher and motivator. Zürich embraced his radical teachings in 1523 and, two years later, officially banned the celebration of Mass. There was no university in Zürich, unlike Wittenberg, so the civil authorities, not professors, led the process of revolt from the Church. Zwingli embraced many of Luther's teachings but also disagreed with him, especially concerning the Eucharist. The disagreement became a source of distraction for both men and threatened to split the Protestant movement into different factions. The secular ruler Philip of Hesse wanted to repair the breach between Luther and Zwingli, so he invited them, Martin Bucer, and Johannes Oecolampadius to Marburg in 1529 to discuss their differences. Philip believed the Colloquy of Marburg would result in unanimity, but his hope was forlorn. Luther and Zwingli attacked each other for their respective teachings on the Eucharist. Zwingli denied Luther's idea of consubstantiation and advocated that the Eucharist was merely a symbol and remained simply bread and wine. Calvin encouraged his fellow revolutionaries to keep their disagreements private: "It is of the greatest importance that no suspicion of the divisions between us be passed on to future generations; for it is ridiculous beyond measure that, having broken with everyone, we should from the very beginning of our own reform agree so little among ourselves."[170]

Zwingli encouraged those Swiss cantons that had embraced the Protestant movement to join forces in an alliance known as the Christian Civic Union. This alliance engaged in aggressive warfare against the Catholic cantons. Peace was eventually achieved by a settlement which allowed for male citizens to determine the religion of an area by majority vote. In 1531, Zwingli and his supporters, emboldened by the peace agreement, initiated an economic blockade on the Catholic areas of Switzerland. This aggressive action prompted Catholic rulers to form an army, which marched on Zürich and routed the Protestant army in a battle on the mountain above the old Cistercian monastery at Kappel. Zwingli, attired in battle armor, was cut down and killed. When news reached Luther that Zwingli had died in battle, he remarked, "It is well that Zwingli ... lie dead on the battlefield. ... Oh, what a triumph this is, that [he has] perished. How well God knows his business" and lamented that "I have little hope for him [to be in heaven]."[171]

Luther was not the only person who disagreed with Zwingli's teachings. In Zürich, a group known as the Anabaptists, who believed that baptism could not be administered to infants or children, formed in opposition to Zwingli and his followers. The Anabaptists advocated adult baptism and performed "rebaptisms" on adults who embraced the sect's heretical teachings. Anabaptists also rejected military service, oath taking, and the use of the death penalty by civil authorities. They were a community-focused group where Scripture was the rule of law, although each member was allowed to interpret Scripture as he believed. Luther agreed with Zwingli that the Anabaptists represented a radical departure from Christian doctrine and wrote

170. Daniel-Rops, *The Protestant Reformation*, vol. 2, 86.
171. First quote from Hughes, *A Popular History of the Reformation*, 153; second quote from Kittelson, 242.

a pamphlet against them titled *On Infiltrating and Clandestine Preachers*. Luther believed the Anabaptists corrupted his idea of the priesthood of all believers by allowing anyone, regardless of authority, training, or education, to preach, which was an abomination and the work of Satan.[172]

Melchior Hoffman, an early Anabaptist leader, embraced apocalyptic ideas and preached that the Second Coming would occur in 1533 in the city of the New Jerusalem, which he identified as Strasbourg. City officials arrested him, and many of his followers were rounded up by imperial authorities and executed for heresy. The persecution prompted Hoffman to order his remaining followers to cease adult baptisms until the Second Coming. Hoffman's incarceration left a leadership vacuum, into which stepped the Dutchman Jan Matthijszoon (also known as Matthys). Matthijszoon, who called himself "the prophet," believed that the Anabaptists should use violence to spread their movement, so he ordered his followers to seize the German city of Münster in 1534. He also ordered the destruction of all the city's churches, and declared all material possessions to be held in common.

Matthijszoon was killed in a sortie from the city and was succeeded by Jan Beukels, also known as John of Leiden. John instituted even more radical teachings, declaring compulsory polygamy in imitation of Old Testament figures. John took sixteen wives, and, when one wife asked permission to leave Münster, he publicly cut off her head.[173] John proclaimed himself "King of the World" in September 1534 and even minted symbolic gold and silver coins, which were distributed throughout northern Europe.[174] John's reign was short-lived, as an allied Catholic and Protestant army recaptured Münster in 1535. John and two assistants were condemned to death and torn to pieces by red-hot

---

172. See Kittelson, 242.
173. Janssen, *History of the German People*, V, 460–463, quoted in Carroll, *The Cleaving of Christendom*, 169.
174. MaCulloch, 206.

tongs. Their bodies were placed in iron cages atop the cathedral and remained there as a sign to all heretics for more than three hundred years.[175]

Secular authorities arrested and executed Anabaptists throughout Christendom, especially during the years 1527–1533, as their radical ideas were deemed a critical threat to society.[176] Eventually, the Anabaptists developed into separate groups, including direct descendants, known as the Amish, Mennonites, and Hutterites, and later branches, such as the Bruderhof.

THE ENGLISH ACCIDENT

The rebellion against the Church was a continental European affair, until England joined the fray.[177] In England, there were no firebrand university professors or philandering disgruntled priests whose heretical teachings gained popular support, creating a groundswell against the Catholic Church. Rather, the "English Accident" occurred due to a king who wanted a divorce.[178] The story of England in the sixteenth century is crucial to an understanding of the Reformation as a whole, for if England had not fallen, the Protestant movement may not have become permanent.[179]

The Tudor family's claim to the English throne was tenuous. When the Welsh usurper Henry Tudor, Duke of Richmond, defeated King Richard III (r. 1483–1485) at the Battle of Bosworth Field in 1485, the Plantagenet line came to an end, and the Tudor dynasty began. Henry VII died in 1509, and his

---

175. Daniel-Rops, *The Protestant Reformation*, vol. 2, 100.
176. Eight hundred of the one thousand Anabaptists executed by the secular authorities were killed during that time. See C.P. Calsen, "Executions of Anabaptists 1527–1618: a research report," MQR 47 (1973), 115–152, quoted in MacCulloch, 167.
177. The following section is adapted from my booklet *20 Answers: The Reformation*, 27–32.
178. The phrase is Hilaire Belloc's from his work *How the Reformation Happened*.
179. See Hilaire Belloc, *Characters of the Reformation* (Rockford, IL: TAN Books and Publishers, Inc., 1992 [1936]), 16.

second-born son, also named Henry, became king. Henry VIII (r. 1509–1547) was a passionate man who exhibited little self-restraint. He had an exaggerated fear of death, so he never risked his life in combat and was terrified of epidemics. Intelligent and well-educated, he enjoyed reading and writing on theological topics. The king was also strongly attached to the Catholic faith and had a special devotion to the Blessed Sacrament.

Henry married his brother Arthur's widow, Catherine of Aragon, in 1509, after receiving a dispensation from Pope Julius II. The marriage produced five children, though only one, a daughter named Mary, survived. Although Catherine was Spanish (the daughter of Queen Isabel and King Fernando), she was beloved by the English people and was known for her pious, unselfish, and joyful personality. Henry was faithful to Catherine for nearly the first decade of their marriage, but then began to pursue other women. Most of his mistresses were content with royal attention and affection, but Anne Boleyn wanted to be queen. Anne completely controlled Henry, as Cardinal Lorenzo Campeggio observed: "This passion of the King's is a most extraordinary thing. He sees nothing, he thinks of nothing but his Anne, he cannot be without her for an hour, and it moves one to pity to see how the King's life, the stability and downfall of the whole country, hang upon this one question."[180]

Blinded by passion, in 1527 the king met with Cardinal Thomas Wolsey (1473–1530), the archbishop of York and lord chancellor of England. Henry wanted Wolsey to acquire a declaration of nullity for his union with Catherine, so he could marry Anne. Wolsey, confident the pope would grant the request, sent representatives to Rome. However, Pope Clement VII was in no position to acquiesce to the whims of the English king. Rome had been recently occupied and sacked by the imperial troops of Charles V. The pope, having barely escaped with his life, and

---

180. Geoffrey de C. Parmiter, *The King's Great Matter; a Study in Anglo-Papal Relations 1527–1534* (London, 1967), 84, quoted in Carroll, *The Cleaving of Christendom*, 122.

still surrounded by Charles V's army, was not in the mood to entertain Henry's request, especially since Catherine of Aragon was Charles V's aunt.

The pope allowed Cardinal Wolsey to initiate a marriage tribunal in England which would gather evidence and provide a report to the pope, who would make the final decision. The marriage tribunal opened in May 1529. Never before in European history had a reigning king and queen stood before an ecclesiastical court on the state of their marriage. All the bishops of England were present. Two — John Fisher of Rochester and King Henry Standish of St. Asaph — served as the queen's counselors. Henry's case rested on his concern with marrying his brother's widow, even though Pope Julius II had granted a dispensation to allow it. Catherine maintained that her marriage to Arthur Tudor was never consummated and, therefore, not a valid marriage in the eyes of the Church.[181] At one session, Catherine approached Henry; renewed her undying love and loyalty to him; announced she was a virgin when they married, despite her marriage to his brother; and requested he end the trial. The king was not moved by the impassioned plea of the queen and said his conscience was troubled because he had married his brother's wife. After Henry's rebuff, Catherine read a document protesting the trial in England, and she requested its transfer to Rome.

After the royal testimony and evidence were presented, the bishops voted. All but one (John Fisher) sided with the king and recommended that the pope grant a declaration of nullity. Catherine sent a formal protest to the pope, who suspended the tribunal and remanded the case to Rome for further study. The king was incensed at the papal action and took his anger out on Cardinal Wolsey, who was charged in October 1529 with putting papal bulls into effect without royal authorization and or-

---

181. Catherine maintained this position throughout her life. It is entirely plausible, as she was married to Arthur for only four months before his sudden death.

dered to resign as lord chancellor. His royal position was given to the lawyer and friend of the king, Thomas More. Wolsey died in 1530, admitting: "If I had served God as diligently as I served the king, he would not have deserted me in my old age."[182]

Henry became impatient at the pope's delay (ultimately, the decision took seven years). So, when Thomas Cromwell (1485–1540), one of the king's advisers, approached him with a plan to expedite the process, Henry listened.[183] Cromwell reasoned that the king was sovereign in his lands, so why should a foreign ruler — the pope — hold such authority and power in England? Cromwell recommended that the king threaten the pope with schism unless his marriage to Catherine was annulled. At the urging of Cromwell, Henry began the process of separating the Church in England from Rome. In 1531, the king ordered the English clergy assembled at an ecclesiastical meeting to agree to laws granting the king authority over the Church. At first, the clergy resisted, but eventually, they caved under royal pressure. The following day, after the submission of the clergy, Thomas More resigned his position as lord chancellor.

That same year, Thomas Cranmer (1489–1556), a priest and former professor at Cambridge University, was appointed chaplain and religious adviser to Anne Boleyn. Cranmer was secretly a Lutheran who ingratiated himself to the king. In January 1532, Cranmer was appointed English ambassador to the imperial court of Charles V, where he made contact with other Lutherans. While in Nuremberg, Cranmer met a Protestant woman and secretly married her, despite his priestly promise of celibacy. Later in the year, news reached Cranmer that he had been appointed archbishop of Canterbury. During his episcopal ordination, Cranmer was required to take an oath of loyalty and obedience to the pope, but before the ceremony, he took a secret oath against the pope, stating that the public oath was for

---

182. Daniel-Rops, *The Protestant Reformation*, vol. 2, 238.
183. Thomas Cromwell was the great-great uncle of Oliver Cromwell.

show. In 1533, on his own authority and in violation of papal orders, Cranmer opened another marriage tribunal to determine the validity of the king's marriage. He pronounced Henry's marriage to Catherine invalid and witnessed the king's "marriage" to Anne Boleyn. Anne was crowned as queen of England, but the English were not pleased at this show of disrespect to Catherine. Anne, already pregnant at her wedding, gave birth to a daughter, Elizabeth, in 1533. Cranmer baptized the girl and served as her godfather.

Clement VII issued his decision on the king's marriage in March 1534, ruling Henry's marriage to Catherine was valid. Henry, angered at the pope's decision, sought to settle the matter by calling Parliament to issue several pieces of legislation.[184] In April 1534, Parliament passed the Act of Succession, which stipulated that the king's "marriage" to Anne was valid and that his daughter Elizabeth was legitimate and the heir to the throne (passing over Henry and Catherine's daughter Mary). The act also stipulated that anyone who called into question the validity of the king's marriage to Anne was guilty of high treason. Anyone slandering the marriage was liable to imprisonment at the king's desire and forfeiture of all property. Citizens were subject to take the Oath of Succession, agreeing with the contents of the act, which included a denial of papal authority. In November, Parliament passed the Act of Supremacy, which declared the king the supreme head of the Church in England. This act also required English subjects to take an oath, and refusal to swear it was treason, punishable by death. The English hierarchy acquiesced to the king's demands and issued a joint declaration, stating, "the Bishop of Rome has not, in Scripture, any greater jurisdiction in this kingdom of England, than any other foreign bishop."[185]

In April 1535, royal commissioners were sent throughout

---

184. These included the Heresy Act, the Ecclesiastical Appointments Act, the Ecclesiastical Laws Act, and the famous Acts of Succession and Supremacy.
185. Hughes, *A Popular History of the Reformation*, 197.

England to require the Oath of Supremacy of all religious houses. In London, a group of Carthusian monks made a three-day spiritual preparation for the arrival of the commissioners. They went to confession, asked pardon of each other for offenses committed, and celebrated a Mass of the Holy Spirit. When the commissioners arrived and demanded they take the oath, the entire charterhouse refused. Three monks were arrested and put on trial for treason. They denied any malice toward the king, which was required for conviction. The jury wanted to acquit the men, but Cromwell threatened the jury with death, so the monks were convicted. In May, the three Carthusians were hanged, drawn, and quartered.[186]

Although most of the bishops in England sided with the king, one bishop, John Fisher (1449–1535), refused to cater to Henry's personal whims. The king ordered his imprisonment in the Tower. While Fisher was incarcerated, Pope Paul III created him a cardinal in the hopes that the king would not dare execute a prince of the Church. Henry reacted by saying: "Well, let the pope send him a hat, when he will. But I will so provide that whensoever it cometh he shall wear it on his shoulders, for head he shall have none to set it on."[187] Fisher was tried and convicted of treason and beheaded on June 22, 1535. His head was mounted on a spike on London Bridge for two weeks, as a sign for others, and then thrown into the Thames.

Thomas More knew where events in England were headed when the clergy submitted to the king's outrageous demands in 1531. After he resigned as lord chancellor, he spent time with his family. When the commissioners demanded he take the Oath of Succession, he steadfastly refused. More was arrested and imprisoned in the Tower of London for fifteen months, during which time he wrote letters and was allowed visits with his family. Like Fisher, he was tried and convicted of treason. During

---

186. See footnote 229 for a description of this horrible way to die.
187. E.E. Reynolds, *St. John Fisher*, 264, quoted in Carroll, *The Cleaving of Christendom*, 159.

the trial, More stated it was as impossible for England to "refuse obedience to the See of Rome than might a child refuse obedience to his own natural father."[188] More was sentenced to death by hanging, drawing, and quartering, but the king changed the method of execution to beheading. When the time came, More tied his own blindfold and told the crowd that he would die "the king's good servant, but God's first."[189] Thomas More's head was also placed on London Bridge, but his daughter Margaret prevented it from being thrown into the Thames.

The woman who wanted to be queen and not just a royal mistress did not have long to live herself. Henry grew tired of Anne Boleyn and turned his affections toward Jane Seymour, one of her ladies-in-waiting. In 1536, Cromwell brought charges of adultery and incest against Anne. The king's lackey, Thomas Cranmer, declared the marriage of Henry and Anne invalid. On May 19, 1536, Anne Boleyn was beheaded.

Henry continued his attack on the Church by dissolving England's monasteries. The suppression of the monasteries, Thomas Cromwell's brainchild, was primarily motivated by greed and resulted in the complete stamping out of monasticism throughout England.[190] The king took the Church's land and redistributed the assets to his loyal supporters, after which nobles were hesitant to support a future reunion with Rome for fear of losing their land and wealth.

Before the dissolution of the monasteries, the common belief among the English was that the king and pope were involved in a political dispute. After, however, a Yorkshire lawyer named Robert Aske decided enough was enough and launched a rebellion. Nearly thirty thousand men joined the revolt, known as the Pilgrimage of Grace, and succeeded in seizing the city of York. In December 1536, the leaders of the rebellion formulated their

---

188. E.E. Reynolds, *The Field is Won: The Life and Death of St. Thomas More* (Milwaukee: Bruce Publishing Company, 1968), 367–368, quoted in Carroll, *The Cleaving of Christendom*, 160.
189. Carroll, *The Cleaving of Christendom*, 160.
190. In 1535, there were 825 religious houses in England; by 1540, none was left. See Vidmar, 210.

demands to the king. They called for the restoration of papal authority and the monasteries, the reform of Parliament, and the re-legitimatization of Princess Mary. The Duke of Norfolk met with the rebels and promised them a royal pardon if they put down their arms. He also told them he would ask the king to hold a special parliament to restore the monasteries. A week later, the king invited Robert Aske to dinner at the royal court. He wined and dined Aske, and told him the monasteries would never be restored. The rebellion petered out. In July 1537, Robert Aske was arrested and executed.

At this point in time, the Church in England was only in schism and had not yet embraced heresy. Henry VIII, except for rejecting papal supremacy over the Church in England, remained faithful to the Church's doctrine. He had Parliament pass the Act of Six Articles Abolishing Diversity of Opinion in 1539 that, among other things, affirmed transubstantiation. The majority of Englishmen were still Catholic in belief and practice, though they were also loyal to their king.

OUR LADY APPEARS

While Luther led the rebellion against the Church in Europe, halfway around the world, Hernán Cortés and five hundred Spaniards in eleven ships landed at Veracruz (in modern-day Mexico) on Good Friday 1519. This was a Christian army in the service of King Charles, whose goal was to spread the true Light of Christ in the New World. Cortés was a skillful military leader, tactician and motivator — skills necessary to safely guide his army through the dangers of dealing with the Aztecs.

The Aztec Empire comprised fifteen million people; 250,000 lived in Tenochtitlán, the capital city, the future Mexico City. The warlike Aztecs conquered neighboring tribes both to expand their empire and to provide human sacrifices to their gods. Every Aztec city and large town had a central square in which a temple pyramid rose to the sky. The victim was laid on the pyramid's altar, and a priest would cut out his beating heart and hold it aloft for the worshipers to see. Aztec law mandated 1,000 human sacrifices a year in every temple, an annual total of nearly 20,000 victims.[191] The Aztecs believed their false gods — including the Hummingbird Wizard, who was the Lover of Hearts, Drinker of Blood, and the Lord of the Dark — demanded human sacrifices. The Aztecs also worshiped the serpent god; they announced the beginning of each sacrifice by beating a large drum made with snakeskins. In the year 987, Ce Acatl Topiltzin, a priest who served the god Quetzalcoatl, vehemently opposed human sacrifice and was expelled from the empire. A prophecy foretold that the priest would return from the sea in the year 1519 to abolish the practice of human sacrifice. When the Spaniards made contact with the Aztecs, Cortés invited the royal ambassadors from Montezuma II to Easter Mass and dinner. The Aztecs were astonished when Cortés reacted angrily to their attempts to season their dinner with human blood. They believed Cortés' visit was the culmination of the prophecy of the anti-human-sacrifice priest.

Ultimately, nasty and bloody violence broke out between the Aztecs and Spaniards over the next two years. Eventually, the Aztecs were defeated by the much smaller contingent of Spanish troops, allied with other tribes who hated the Aztecs.[192] Within a few years, and after some setbacks, Cortés had eradicated the practice of human sacrifices, but the Spanish conquistador sincerely wanted the Aztecs to embrace the Gospel of Jesus Christ. Missionaries worked tirelessly among the indigenous people of Mexico for a decade, but their efforts produced negligible results. However, that situation changed in 1531.

Saint Juan Diego (d. 1548) was one of the few native peoples

---

191. Victor Davis Hanson, *Carnage and Culture: Landmark Battles in the Rise of Western Power* (New York: Anchor Books, 2001), 195.

192. The Aztec way of war focused on capturing prisoners to be used for sacrifice, rather than killing the enemy, and was heavily dependent on leaders. Aztec troops could not function effectively if their leaders were killed. The Spanish had armor, firearms, and cannons, and focused on decisive engagements. See Hanson, *Carnage and Culture*, Chapter 6.

who had converted to the Faith after the Spanish conquest. On December 9, he was on his way to attend Mass when, crossing over Tepeyac hill, he heard singing and saw a brilliant white cloud. Before the cloud was a beautiful young woman, who spoke to him identifying herself as a merciful mother and asking for the building of a church. The woman asked Juan to take her request to Bishop Juan de Zumárraga, a Franciscan and former hermit who was known as a protector of native peoples in New Spain. Juan Diego obeyed the lady's request and went to Bishop Zumárraga to relay her message. The bishop doubted Juan's story and told him he needed proof. On the way home, the lady appeared to Juan again and told him she would give the requested sign the next day. Unfortunately, Juan had to care for his sick uncle and did not travel to Tepeyac. The following day, December 12, on his way to fetch a priest to anoint his uncle, he walked to Tepeyac, where the Blessed Mother appeared to him again, telling him to go to the top of the hill and bring her flowers. Juan thought the request odd, as the hill was a desert with only cactus, thistles, and thorn bushes, but he obeyed. To his amazement, he found beautiful roses. He picked the roses and brought them to Our Lady, who arranged them in his *tilma* (cloak). Juan took his special delivery to the bishop. When he opened his *tilma*, the roses dropped to the ground revealing a miraculous image of Mary, in native Aztec dress, on the fabric. Bishop Zumárraga fell to his knees. The miraculous image of Our Lady of Guadalupe helped to further evangelization efforts in Mexico, as people understood the various iconography in the *tilma* (the Virgin appeared like a native in traditional clothing, was pregnant, and was crushing the head of a serpent). By the time of the deaths of Juan Diego and Bishop Zumárraga in 1548, there were nine million baptized native people in Mexico.[193] While souls were leaving the family of God in Europe due to the Protestant Revolution, the Blessed Mother was at work in

---

193. Carroll, *The Cleaving of Christendom*, 623.

the New World, ensuring new souls were brought to the light of her son and into his Church.

ENGLAND EMBRACES HERESY

King Henry VIII died in 1547 and was succeeded by Edward VI (r. 1547–1553), his son by his third of six wives, Jane Seymour. Edward was only nine years old when his father died. It was during Edward's reign that England moved from schism to heresy. The architect of Protestantism in England was Archbishop Thomas Cranmer, who told Edward at his coronation that the young monarch should see "idolatry destroyed, the tyranny of the Bishop of Rome banished from your subjects, and images removed."[194] Seven months after Henry's death, Cranmer published the *Book of Homilies*, in which he advocated central Protestant teachings, such as *sola fide* and *sola scriptura*. Cranmer's plan to move England into full-blown Protestantism included inviting leading Protestant revolutionaries, such as Martin Bucer, to live and work in England. A wave of iconoclasm swept over England in 1548. In the same year, the House of Lords authorized clerical marriage and divorce for adultery. Parliament also repealed Henry's *Six Articles Abolishing Diversity of Opinions*.

Cranmer's next step in turning England Protestant involved the liturgy, which he revised in his *Book of Common Prayer* in 1548. The liturgy in the *Book of Common Prayer* was intended to replace the Mass. He removed all references to the Mass as a sacrifice and outlawed Eucharistic processions and adoration. Parliament approved Cranmer's liturgy and mandated its use, beginning at Pentecost 1549. The populace rioted in response. But Cranmer's Protestant colleagues were not satisfied; Bucer and Calvin both told Cranmer the new liturgy was still too much like the old Catholic Mass and urged him to revise it. Cranmer's second edition renamed the liturgy

---

194. Ibid., 223.

the "Lord's Supper" and eliminated all references to the sacra-ments. Once again, Parliament passed legislation authorizing the revised liturgy and mandated that all English subjects at-tend it on Sunday. Laws were also passed to prohibit people from attending Catholic Mass; the punishment was six months to life in prison.

Cranmer displayed his heretical teachings even further in 1550 when he wrote about the Eucharist: "Christ called bread his Body and wine his Blood, and these sentences be figurative speeches ... the substance of the bread and wine do remain still. ... In plain speech, it is not true that we eat Christ's Body and drink his Blood."[195] In March of the same year, Cranmer published a new rite for the ordination of priests which be-came known as the Edwardian Ordinal. This new rite made no mention of the priest acting *in persona Christi* and reenacting Christ's sacrifice on the cross at Mass. Indeed, the Ordinal as-sumed there was nothing sacred or unique about priestly ser-vice, as priests were only "messengers, watchmen, pastors, and stewards of the Lord" whose function is "to teach, to admon-ish, to feed, and to provide for the Lord's family."[196] Cranmer's ordination rite was contrary to the Catholic understanding of the priesthood and broke the chain of apostolic succession in England.[197]

King Edward died from tuberculosis in 1553 at the age of sixteen. Cranmer and his Protestant friends were afraid that Mary Tudor, the legitimate heir, would stop their heretical movement if she ascended to the throne. Before he died, Ed-ward declared (without the consent of Parliament) the Prot-

---

195. Ernest C. Messenger, *The Reformation, the Mass, and the Priesthood* (London, 1937), I, 429, quoted in Carroll, *The Cleaving of Christendom*, 229.

196. Carroll, *The Cleaving of Christendom*, 228.

197. Pope Leo XIII confirmed this break in the nineteenth century in *Apostolicae Curiae*, wherein the pope declared Anglican orders null and void. Leo wrote, "In the whole English Ordinal, not only is there no clear mention of sacrifice, of consecration ... of power of consecrating and offering sacrifice, but every trace of these things which had existed in those prayers of the Catholic rite not wholly rejected was deliberately removed and struck out." See Carroll, *The Cleaving of Christendom*, 266.

estant great-granddaughter of Henry VII, Lady Jane Grey, his successor. Grey's unpopular reign lasted only nine days.[198] Parliament sensed the popular support for Mary Tudor and declared her queen.

THE CATHOLIC QUEEN OF ENGLAND

Mary Tudor, thirty-seven years old at her accession as queen of England, was faced with a serious problem: she was unmarried and childless. English Catholics were afraid that, without an heir, the crown would pass to Mary's Protestant half-sister Elizabeth. The search for a suitable spouse consumed the first year of Mary's reign. The Holy Roman Emperor Charles V suggested his son, Philip, who was twenty-six years old, and Mary agreed. Many of her subjects were not in favor of the union, however, because they feared foreign intervention in English affairs. The planned wedding moved forward despite internal and external opposition. Prince Philip arrived in England, but he only spoke Spanish, which Mary could understand but not speak well. Mary spoke in French to Philip, who could understand the language but not speak it. The couple married on July 25, 1554. In order to allay English fears about a foreign takeover should Mary die, Philip was not crowned king and would not inherit the kingdom if an heir was not produced. Additionally, Philip was not given the customary landed estates of an English royal consort. Mary loved Philip and wanted the politically arranged marriage to work, but Philip did not love Mary in return, and disliked living in England. Unfortunately, the marriage did not produce children, despite belief early in the union that Mary was pregnant. Catholics continued to fear the possibility of the crown passing to the Protestant Elizabeth.

Mary had been raised in the Faith by her devout mother,

---

198. Grey and her husband were executed in 1554 for treason.

Catherine of Aragon. The new queen loved the Church and practiced her faith purposefully, commenting that she "would far rather lose ten crowns than put my soul in peril."[199] She respected her half-brother Edward's Protestant faith and allowed his funeral rites to be celebrated according to Cranmer's liturgy, but did not attend the service. Instead, she had a Requiem Mass offered for the repose of his soul. Mary firmly believed the reason she had become queen was to restore the Catholic faith to England. She knew it would be a difficult task, as five years of Edward's policies and initiatives, overseen by the zealous Protestant Cranmer, had greatly harmed the Church. The altars had been stripped, sacred art destroyed or removed, liturgical music changed, and the vestments, sacred vessels, and missals needed for the celebration of Mass were destroyed.[200] Although the majority of the English populace had remained attached to the Catholic faith during Edward's reign, a large-scale catechetical effort was needed to undo the effects of a half-decade of Protestant propaganda, illustrated by the common Edwardian prayer, "From the tyranny of the Bishop of Rome and all his detestable enormities, good Lord deliver us."[201]

The first step in the restoration of the Faith in England began in 1553 with Parliament's repeal of the annulment granted to Henry VIII for his marriage to Catherine. All the religious legislation passed under Edward was also repealed by Parliament, and the Mass was celebrated once more in England. Protestant leaders and intellectuals fled the country in droves, although some remained.

The man most responsible for the Catholic restoration was Cardinal Reginald Pole (1500–1588), cousin of the queen and papal legate to England. As a young scholar, Pole had studied in Italy and France and stayed overseas during Henry's mar-

---

199. Daniel-Rops, *The Protestant Reformation*, vol. 2, 302.
200. See Eamon Duffy, *Fires of Faith: Catholic England under Mary Tudor* (New Haven and London: Yale University Press, 2009), 3–4.
201. Ibid., 117.

riage debate, primarily because he did not support the king. Pole urged Parliament to vote for the restoration of the Faith in England, saying: "I come to reconcile, not to condemn. I come not to compel but to call again. I am not come to call anything in question already done, but my commission is of grace and clemency to such as will receive it."[202] Parliament convened in the fall of 1554 to discuss the matter of returning the country to the Catholic fold. Mary's husband, Philip of Spain, urged Parliament to vote in the affirmative on the question of rejoining the Church, saying: "The mercy of God now calls you to return, through obedience to the Roman pontiff, to the flock of Jesus Christ, incorporating yourselves in His Catholic Church. Vote for this measure, and may God enlighten your understanding and move your hearts."[203] Parliament overwhelmingly voted to return to the Church on November 30, 1554, and asked Cardinal Pole for absolution for the schism and adoption of heresy, which he granted in the name of the pope.

At the end of January 1554, Parliament restored the heresy laws, which made it illegal to embrace Protestant teaching. The bishops discussed how to implement the restoration. They ruled that every adult parishioner was required to go to confession to their parish priest and be absolved from the schism. Additionally, they initiated a concerted preaching campaign to catechize the populace.[204] Cardinal Pole initiated a restoration program that included the establishment of four diocesan seminaries (in York, Lincoln, Wells, and Durham) to train men for the priesthood.[205] Pole knew that the key to successfully implementing the restoration, as well as an authentic reform of

---

202. D. A. Bellenger and S. Fletcher, *Princes of the Church: A History of the English Cardinals* (Stroud, 2001), 81, quoted in MacCulloch, 282.
203. William T. Walsh, *Philip II* (New York, 1937), 145–146, quoted in Carroll, *The Cleaving of Christendom*, 240.
204. Duffy, *Fires of Faith*, 15,19.
205. These schools provided inspiration for the Church-wide movement to institute seminaries in every diocese as part of the reform initiatives from the Council of Trent. Ibid., 8.

the Church, required properly trained and formed clergy. The cardinal believed bishops should be pastoral, theologically well formed, and loyal to the pope. The queen allowed sixteen of the bishops who had served her father and half-brother to keep their dioceses, and made twenty new episcopal appointments. The new bishops were all university-educated theologians; many had suffered for the Faith under the previous royal regimes.[206]

Part of the Catholic restoration focused on the bishops who had led the heretical movement in England under Edward — specifically, Archbishop Thomas Cranmer. There was no man in the realm who had more contributed to Mary Tudor's difficult life than Cranmer. On his own authority, he had declared the king's marriage to Mary's mother invalid, making her illegitimate. She watched and silently suffered while Parliament, instigated by Cranmer, stripped the queenship from her mother and gave it to the king's mistress, and then was humiliated when Parliament recognized her half-sister Elizabeth as the legitimate heir. When Mary came to the throne, the archbishop was arrested and put on trial for perjury of his consecration oath, defiance of the pope, and heresy. Over the next three years, Cranmer struggled to prolong his life while simultaneously staying true to his beliefs. He agreed at one point to accept papal supremacy of the Church, only because the queen ordered it; this recantation was rejected. After the Royal Council condemned him to death by burning at the stake, Cranmer continued to prolong the inevitable. As the date of his execution drew near, Cranmer wrote two prepared speeches to present at the place of execution. One speech was a statement of belief in Catholic teaching. The other was one last recantation, in which he repudiated all previous recantations and denied papal authority and the Real Presence of Christ in the Eucharist. Uncertain as to which speech he would deliver

206. Ibid., 23.

in the morning, he brought both with him to the place of execution. At the moment of truth, Cranmer read the Protestant speech and ended by condemning the pope: "As for the pope, I refuse him as Christ's enemy and the antichrist, with all his false doctrine."[207] Cranmer was burnt at the stake as a heretic and enemy of the crown; as he died, he extended his writing hand into the flames. The day after Cranmer's death, Cardinal Pole was installed as the archbishop of Canterbury.

Mary also desired to root out Protestant revolutionaries who were a threat to her reign. Although the underlying threat was political, Mary's government pursued these individuals as part of the Catholic religious restoration. In so doing, she ensured that she would be known by the nickname given to her by Protestant propagandists: "Bloody Mary." Mary viewed Protestantism as sedition and adherence to Catholic teaching as allegiance.[208] Her view was influenced, in part, by Wyatt's Rebellion in 1554, which had been inspired by a Protestant agenda to rid England of Mary and her Catholic restoration. The persecution of Protestants was a government operation, not a movement of the Church, although the bishops investigated those arrested by royal commissioners for heresy.[209] Initially, the government's focus was on leading clerics of the Protestant movement in England, but then it switched to outspoken laypeople. Ultimately, 228 men and 56 women were executed for their Protestant beliefs between February 1555 and November 1558.[210] London witnessed the largest number of executions (113, nearly 40 percent), and most executions involved one or sometimes a handful of heretics.[211] Most of the condemned had been previously arrested, dealt with leniently

---

207. Carroll, *The Cleaving of Christendom*, 249.
208. Duffy, *Fires of Faith*, 89.
209. Ibid., 114.
210. Ibid., 79. The numbers of those executed over that period of time break down as follows: 75 in 1555, 85 in 1556, 81 in 1557, and 43 in 1558 (Duffy, *Fires of Faith*, 128).
211. Ibid., 128,130. The largest number executed at one time was thirteen men and women in June 1556.

by the Church, and released. Once free, if they continued their anti-Catholic stance, they were arrested again and executed by the government. Many spent a year in jail before their execution and were given multiple opportunities to repent. As a group, those arrested denied the Real Presence of Christ in the Eucharist and papal authority.[212] Although the burnings are difficult for modern sensibilities to understand, they were in keeping with the contemporary worldview and not considered cruel or unusual. In fact, Mary remained popular in England, despite the executions.[213]

Queen Mary became seriously ill in September 1558 and, by November, was near death. The overarching Catholic fear — that Mary's Protestant half-sister Elizabeth would assume the throne — was near fulfillment. On November 17, 1558, while morning Mass was being celebrated in her room, the Catholic queen of England died. The news was given to a sickly Cardinal Pole, who succumbed later that evening to his illness. The two great Catholic restorers of the Faith in England had died on the same day.

ELIZABETH I — PERSECUTOR OF CATHOLICS

Although Elizabeth, the daughter of Henry VIII and Anne Boleyn, ascended the throne at the death of Mary Tudor, in Catholic eyes, the legitimate heir to the throne was Mary Stuart, Queen of Scots. Mary Stuart was the granddaughter of Margaret Tudor, Henry VIII's sister, and had been queen of France briefly (1559–1560) during her marriage to King Francis II (r.

---

212. Ibid., 99,142.

213. Hilaire Belloc addressed this point: "There are two legends which it is important to discard ... first the legend that the burning of people alive struck contemporaries with a peculiar horror, as it strikes us; secondly, the legend that the English people, largely indifferent to religion, were sickened by the active persecution of the unpopular minority and thereby turned against the faith of their fathers. Both of these legends are historically false" (*How the Reformation Happened*, 96). It is unjust and scandalous that Queen Mary, a brave, intelligent, and faith-filled woman, has been given the moniker "Bloody" and is known as such by the general populace.

1559–1560). Mary Stuart was queen of Scotland (1542–1567) and devoted to the Church. Unfortunately, Mary's reign in Scotland was filled with political and religious intrigue. John Knox (trained in Geneva by John Calvin) fomented religious revolution in his native land. Knox was a tough man who had spent two-and-a-half years as a French galley slave. He was also an ardent anti-Catholic, who said he "feared one Mass more than ten thousand enemies" and whose rallying cry was, "No more Mass, death to the priesthood!"[214] He wrote a treatise in 1558, titled *The First Blast of the Trumpet Against the Monstrous Regiment of Women*, wherein he attacked Mary Stuart's mother (Mary of Guise) and argued that political rule by women was forbidden by natural and divine law. The attack on the Catholic Church in Scotland intensified in 1560 and was aided by a malformed and immoral clergy, which made it easy for Protestants to criticize the Church. By 1563, Knox openly preached that Mary Stuart should embrace Protestantism or be overthrown and executed. Eventually, Mary was forced to flee Scotland in 1567 and abdicate the throne, leaving her son James as king (James VI of Scotland and later James I in England). Mary Stuart sought exile in England, where Elizabeth I imprisoned her for twenty years. Advisers to Queen Elizabeth urged her to kill Mary because of her claim to the English throne. Elizabeth initially demurred but eventually caved to the pressure, ordering Mary's execution in 1587.

Elizabeth I became queen of England at the death of her half-sister Mary Tudor and reigned for forty-five years (1558–1603). Raised Protestant from birth, Elizabeth refused Communion at her coronation and declined to attend Mass on her first Christmas as queen. Modernity has created a false narrative of "Bloody Mary" and "Good Queen Bess." Elizabeth is seen as a strong, independent, intelligent "Virgin Queen" who led her people into an era of unprecedented prosperity. This

---

214. Hughes, *A Popular History of the Reformation*, 330.

picture of Elizabeth is not historically accurate and "a more monstrous scaffolding of poisonous nonsense has never been foisted on posterity."[215] In reality, Elizabeth was a figurehead monarch controlled behind the scenes by powerful men, the latter of whom had been enriched by the dissolution of the monasteries and had an economic incentive to prevent the permanent restoration of the Catholic faith in England.

One of these men was William Cecil (1520–1598), who had been secretary of state under Edward VI and was given that position again under the new queen. Cecil spent the next forty years keeping England Protestant. He "did the essential work of changing England from a Catholic to a Protestant county. It was he who eradicated the Faith from the English mind ... it was he who instituted and maintained a reign of terror, the long endurance of which at last crushed out the Mass from English soil."[216] Cecil viewed Catholics as a national security threat and created the myth that one could not be a Catholic and a loyal Englishman. He established an intelligence service that would be the envy of any modern totalitarian regime, using it effectively to hunt and persecute English Catholics. In the history of the Church, there is perhaps "no more dedicated, brilliant, indefatigable, and deadly enemy of the Catholic Church ... than William Cecil."[217]

Parliament passed the Acts of Supremacy and Uniformity in 1559, the first salvos in a long legislative campaign to eradicate the Catholic faith in England. The Act of Supremacy declared Elizabeth the Chief Governor of all Spiritual and Ecclesiastical Affairs in England, and it required all clergy and university professors to take an oath of loyalty to her as head of the Church. The first refusal to do so would be punished by confiscation of property and, possibly, life imprisonment;

---

215. Belloc, *Characters of the Reformation*, 102.
216. Ibid., 118.
217. Carroll, *The Cleaving of Christendom*, 258.

any subsequent refusal brought the death penalty.[218] The Act of Uniformity restored Cranmer's second edition of the *Book of Common Prayer* as the official liturgical rite in England and required every citizen to attend Church of England services; refusal to do so was punished by heavy fines. The Act of Uniformity also declared it a crime to say that the pope was the head of the Church in England.[219]

Other anti-Catholic legislation was passed throughout Elizabeth's reign, including a 1581 act that made it treason (punishable by death) to convert an Englishman to the Catholic faith and a capital offense to convert oneself.[220] In 1585, harboring or assisting a Jesuit priest became a crime of aiding and abetting rebellion.[221] Parliament also made it illegal to leave England without government approval, a law enacted to prevent Englishmen from studying for the priesthood on the Continent.[222] This law ensured that any man returning to England as a Catholic priest after 1559 was considered a traitor to the crown, and he was liable to suffer capital punishment if caught. In an attempt to force Protestantism on the English people, Parliament passed the Thirty-Nine Articles in 1563, which included such Protestant beliefs as *sola scriptura*, married clergy, rejection of papal authority, and denial of transubstantiation.

The attack on the Church in Elizabethan England required a response, especially if the Faith was to survive, even in an underground status. Cardinal William Allen soon grasped the need for Englishmen to be trained abroad for the priesthood and sent back to England to minister to the underground Church. In 1568, he established a seminary, known as the English College, across the Channel in Douai.[223] Students concentrated on learning Greek,

---

218. See Alice Hogge, *God's Secret Agents: Queen Elizabeth's Forbidden Priests and the Hatching of the Gunpowder Plot* (New York: HarperCollins, 2005), 51.
219. Hughes, *A Popular History of the Reformation*, 315.
220. See Carroll, *The Cleaving of Christendom*, 386, and Hogge, 86.
221. Carroll, *The Cleaving of Christendom*, 385.
222. See Hogge, 14.
223. The college was initially established at the city of Douai in French Flanders (now part of France) but moved to Reims in 1578. A campus in Rome was also founded in 1575 and remains to the present day.

Hebrew, and Latin, which helped in studying Scripture. Apologetics was also a focus, as Allen believed the struggle in England "was to be a war of words and will in which the sharpest weapons would be the combatant's ability to argue his cause clearly and persuasively, and his unwavering belief in the rightness of that cause."[224] Concerned that English authorities would see his priests as spies or agents of a foreign power, Allen established strict rules in the hopes that they would instead be seen as agents of God. For example, seminarians were forbidden to discuss English politics, or to debate the extent of the pope's authority over secular rulers or whether he could depose them. Even the name of Elizabeth was not to be mentioned at the school.[225] Elizabeth's government was not mollified and ordered all Englishmen studying abroad to return within four months.[226]

Once ordained, the seminary's graduates returned home clandestinely, at risk of their lives, to care for the persecuted faithful. One such priest, Cuthbert Mayne (1544–1577), arrived secretly in England on April 24, 1576. He ministered to the underground Church for just over a year, until he was arrested on June 8, 1577, for possession of a papal bull and an *Agnus Dei* sacramental (a small wax disc made from the Paschal candle, impressed with an image of the Lamb of God and blessed by the pope, which had been outlawed in England and considered a treasonous possession in 1571).[227] Father Mayne was charged with crimes against the state and sentenced to death. He was given the opportunity to save his life by recanting his Catholic faith, which involved swearing on a Bible that Elizabeth was the head of the Church. Mayne took the Bible, made the sign of the cross, and said, "The queen never was, nor is, nor ever shall be the head of the Church!"[228] As a result, Mayne was condemned to death by being hanged,

---

224. Hogge, 54–55.
225. Ibid., 59.
226. See Carroll, *The Cleaving of Christendom*, 385.
227. Hogge, 61.
228. Martin Haile, *An Elizabethan Cardinal: William Allen* (London, 1914), 140–141, quoted in Carroll, *The Cleaving of Christendom*, 382.

drawn, and quartered.[229] Saint Cuthbert Mayne was the first of many martyred priests in Elizabethan England.

Two years after Cuthbert's martyrdom, the superior general of the Society of Jesus began to send English-born Jesuit priests back home to assist the persecuted Catholics. Edmund Campion (1540–1581) was one of the first two English Jesuits to return home as a priest.[230] Campion had been a brilliant student at Oxford, once even debating in the presence of Queen Elizabeth. He was ordained a priest in the Church of England in 1568, but soon thereafter, he experienced a profound crisis of conscience. In 1569, he left Oxford for Ireland and, in 1572, fled to Cardinal Allen's English College to study for the Catholic priesthood. While there, he heard God's call to enter the Jesuits and walked from Douai to Rome to request admission.[231] He was accepted, and in 1580 was ordered to England, where he arrived in disguise after a daring crossing. There, he was persuaded to write a defense of the Faith, to be read only if he was captured. But it was given unsealed to a fellow Catholic who shared it with others, and it quickly circulated throughout England, becoming known as "Campion's Brag." Campion was ultimately betrayed and captured. While in prison, he was visited by Queen Elizabeth, who offered him freedom and a public office if he became Protestant. Campion replied that he accepted Elizabeth as his queen but not as head of the Church.[232] He suffered cruel tortures, including the rack and the ripping out of all his fingernails. At his trial in November 1581, he was charged

---

229. A gruesome and horrible way to die, hanging, drawing, and quartering was first used in 1241 and became the standard punishment for treason. It continued to be used until 1870 in England and 1950 in Scotland. "Drawing" meant being dragged by a horse to the execution site, where the convict was hanged just to the point of death; then, while he was still alive, his stomach, entrails, and heart were cut out of his body and thrown into a cauldron of boiling water. His head was then chopped off and shown to the assembled crowd with the cry, "Behold the head of a traitor! So die all traitors!" The head was then parboiled in a mixture of salt water and cumin, and stuck on a pole at London Bridge as a deterrent. Quartering involved dismembering the body and sending parts to the four corners of the kingdom. See Hogge, 142.
230. The other was Robert Persons (1546–1610).
231. See Hogge, 67.
232. See Carroll, *The Cleaving of Christendom*, 386.

with attempted murder of the queen. The jury disbelieved the charge but were bribed by the government to ensure a conviction. Campion defended his actions by recalling the past history of England and its attachment to the Catholic faith:

> In condemning us, you condemn all your own ancestors — all the ancient priests, bishops, and kings — all that was once the glory of England, the island of saints, and the most devoted child of the See of Peter. For what have we taught, however, you may qualify it with the odious name of treason that they did not uniformly teach? To be condemned with these old lights — not of England only, but of the world, by their degenerate descendants, is both gladness and glory to us.[233]

Campion was hanged, drawn, and quartered on December 1, 1581, becoming the first Jesuit to die for the Faith in England. In a literal manifestation of Tertullian's axiom that the blood of the martyrs is the seed of the Church, Henry Walpole, who was present at Campion's execution, was splattered by Campion's blood, which inspired him to become Catholic. Walpole fled England to study for the priesthood, returned home after ordination, and in 1595 suffered martyrdom.

The Elizabethan authorities persecuted not only priests but also the laity. Margaret Clitherow (1556–1586) was a joy-filled wife and mother who had been raised Protestant but who converted to the Faith. In 1576, her name appeared on a list of "recusants" — citizens who refused to attend Church of England services as mandated by the government. She was arrested four different times for her Catholic activities, the last of which occurred because she dared to hide priests, an act of treason.

---

233. E. E. Reynolds, *Campion and Parsons: The Jesuit Mission of 1580–1* (London, 1980), 194, quoted in Carroll, *The Cleaving of Christendom*, 387.

Brought before the court, she refused to enter a plea, saying, "I know of no offense whereof I should confess myself guilty."[234] Saint Margaret was executed while pregnant with her fourth child by being pressed to death on the feast of the Annunciation, March 25, 1586.[235] Despite the cruel persecution of Catholics under Queen Elizabeth, the Church in England survived, and conversions continued.

Pope Saint Pius V (r. 1566–1572) attempted to end the persecution of Catholics under Elizabeth by issuing a bull of excommunication in 1570: "Elizabeth, the pretended queen of England and the servant of crime ... having seized the crown and monstrously usurped the place of supreme head of the Church in all England ... has once again reduced this same kingdom, which had already been restored to the Catholic faith ... to a miserable ruin."[236] The bull absolved the English people from loyalty to Elizabeth, in hopes that a rebellion would force her from the throne. Unfortunately, Elizabeth and her advisers exploited the bull as proof that one could not be both Catholic and a loyal Englishman.[237]

THE SPANISH ARMADA

The cry of persecuted Catholics was heard in the Catholic kingdom of Spain. Thirty years into Elizabeth's reign, His Catholic Majesty Philip II launched an armada with the express aim

---

234. Hogge, 210.
235. The standard practice of pressing to death was to strip the prisoner, lay him or her on the ground, and place heavy weights on the body over a period of three days. On the third day, the prisoner's hands and feet were tied to posts and a sharp stone was placed under the back; weights were then put on a plank on top of the prisoner. In Margaret's case, the executioner took pity and went right to the third-day practice. Ultimately, 896 pounds of weight were placed on top of her, which forced the sharp stone next to her back into her body, breaking her ribs to the point that they protruded through her skin. She died fifteen minutes later. See Hogge, 211.
236. Pius V, *Regnans in Excelsis*.
237. Pope Gregory XIII (r. 1572–1585), the successor of Pius V, modified the implementation of this bull by instructing Catholics, in view of the pastoral situation in England, to obey the English government in civil matters, and declaring it unlawful to attempt to depose Elizabeth until the political and military conditions were more favorable. See Hogge, 73.

of providing relief to English Catholics, as indicated in a letter written by one of the Armada's chaplains before sailing from Lisbon:

> There also will await us the groans of countless imprisoned Catholics, the tears of widows who lost their husbands for the faith, the sobs of maidens who were forced to sacrifice their lives rather than destroy their souls, the tender children who, suckled on the poison of heresy, are doomed to perdition unless deliverance reaches them in time; and finally myriads of workers, citizens, knights, nobles and clergymen, and all ranks of Catholics, who are oppressed and downtrodden by the heretics and are anxiously looking to us for their liberation.[238]

The invasion preparation began in 1584 as Philip ordered the assembly of ships needed to conquer England. The audacious plan required the Armada of 130 ships, mostly converted grain transport vessels, to sail from Spain through the English Channel, avoid confrontation with the English Navy, and arrive unscathed in the Spanish Netherlands, where the invasion troops were waiting. The soldiers would then row to the transport ships in boats and barrages. Curiously, Philip entrusted command of this ambitious undertaking to the thirty-seven-year-old Don Alonso Pérez de Guzmán el Bueno, the Duke of Medina Sidonia, who had no significant naval experience. Alexander Farnese, the Duke of Parma, an experienced soldier, commanded the land forces. Farnese did not like the invasion plan, primarily because he lacked adequate seafaring vessels to get his men from land to the awaiting Armada. Unfortunately, for the Armada to succeed,

---

238. David Howarth, *The Voyage of the Armada: The Spanish Story* (Guilford, CT: The Lyons Press, 2001 [1981]), 47. The Armada was also a response to years of English raiding on Spanish ships, an effort to stop English support of Protestant rebels in the Spanish Netherlands, and a fulfillment of Philip's promise of protection to Mary Stuart.

everything had to happen exactly according to plan — an event that has rarely occurred in any military endeavor throughout history.

The Armada left Lisbon in May 1588. Every sailor was required to go to confession before departure. The men were emboldened by Pope Sixtus V's (r. 1585–1590) granting a plenary indulgence to all participants, in keeping with the conditions of the crusading movement. The English spotted the Armada in transit and a sea skirmish followed in which the Armada lost several ships, but the vast majority reached the rally point in the Low Countries. Unfortunately, communication issues hampered the readiness of the infantry, so the Armada had to wait six days before the embarkation process began. The English took advantage of the situation by sending eight fire ships on the night of July 28 to wreak havoc on the anchored transport ships. The fire ships forced the Spanish fleet to sea, and in the chaos the English attacked on the morning of July 29. This Battle of Gravelines resulted in the loss of hundreds of Spanish lives and three ships. Medina Sidonia now acknowledged the futility of the hoped-for invasion and ordered the Armada's retreat home to Spain by sailing around the western coast of Scotland and Ireland. This long voyage resulted in further loss of ships and men. Ultimately, the Spanish lost half the Armada and tens of thousands of men. King Philip's great plan to conquer England, end the persecution of Catholics, and restore the Faith ended as an unmitigated disaster.

Elizabeth died in 1603. She never married and had no heirs, so the throne passed to James, the son of Mary Stuart, Queen of Scots, and the great-grandson of Margaret Tudor, Henry VIII's sister. He ruled as King James I of England (r. 1603–1623) and James VI of Scotland, and is best known for commissioning a new English translation of the Bible in 1611, known as the "King James Version." The government's anti-Catholic persecution continued under James, especially after the 1605 Gunpowder Plot failed to blow up Parliament. In 1606, Parliament passed a series of anti-Catholic laws that barred Catholics from the medical and legal professions, forbade them from carrying weapons, and required Catholics to swear an oath that James was the rightful sovereign and head of the church in England.

Sixty years later, the grandson of James I ruled England as James II (r. 1685-1688). While in exile in France during the English Civil War and subsequent interregnum, James II converted to the Catholic faith along with his wife, Anne. His conversion was kept secret for years. The monarchy was restored in 1660 under Charles II, James' brother. When Charles died, James II ascended the throne, but his rule was short-lived as he was overthrown in 1688 and replaced by the Protestants William of Orange (a Dutchman who ruled as William III) and Mary II (James' daughter) in what is known as the "Glorious Revolution." The 1701 Settlement Act mandated that no Catholic could ever be the monarch of England, nor could a monarch marry a Catholic. The latter stipulation was repealed in 2015, but the former remains in force. Protestantism had permanently won the day in the land of Saint Augustine of Canterbury.

THE POLITICAL EFFECTS OF THE PROTESTANT REVOLUTION

The Protestant movement radically altered the political landscape of Europe while shattering the sense of unity that had been exhibited in Christendom for centuries. In mid-sixteenth-century France, the monarchy was politically weak but popular, and backed strongly by the Catholic Church. France was concerned with its Hapsburg neighbors, who controlled the Holy Roman Empire to the east and Spain to the west. The Catholic monarchy found itself supporting Protestants outside its borders, because the religious revolution weakened France's political enemies while vigorously opposing the movement within its borders.

The people of France were overwhelmingly Catholic and, in some areas of the country (notably Paris), fiercely so. However,

Protestant teachings infiltrated France, and a series of religious wars were fought from 1562 to 1598, which included the infamous St. Bartholomew's Day Massacre in 1572, during which Protestants, known in France as Huguenots, were killed, first in Paris and later throughout the country.

When King Charles IX died in 1574, the new king, Henry III (r. 1574–1589), tried to reach a peace settlement with the Protestants. Some groups in French society were displeased with the king's peace overtures and concessions to the Huguenots. Consequently, Jacques Clément, a deranged monk, assassinated the king in 1589. Before he succumbed to his wounds, the childless Henry III named Henry of Navarre (of the house of Bourbon) his successor. This was a controversial decision because Henry of Navarre, although baptized Catholic, had embraced Protestantism. The Catholic citizens of Paris steadfastly refused to acknowledge Henry as king, so he besieged the city for six months, bringing terrible suffering and death to the Parisians. King Philip II of Spain sent an army from the Spanish Netherlands to break the siege, which prompted Henry of Navarre to negotiate an end to the conflict.

Ultimately, Henry renounced his Protestantism and returned to the Catholic faith in order to be recognized as king, as Henry IV (r.1589–1610). Legend holds that Henry defended his decision by noting that "Paris is worth a Mass." A few years later, Henry ended the religious wars in France by signing the Edict of Nantes, which granted unlimited freedom of conscience and restricted religious liberty to the Huguenots in certain areas. King Louis XIV (r. 1643–1715) later revoked, in 1685, the privileges granted to the Protestant minority. The Faith was maintained, barely, in the land known as the "Eldest Daughter of the Church."

Spain was shielded from the Protestant movement because Cardinal Ximenes de Cisneros (1435–1517), confessor to Queen Isabel and archbishop of Toledo, had begun a reform movement in the late fifteenth century. This movement, along with the establishment of the Inquisition, helped strengthen the ties of the people to the Church and kept Spain free from the influence of heresy. However, change did come to Spain. Emperor Charles V began the process of divesting his power in 1555, when he gave his son Philip rule of the Spanish Netherlands. The emperor exhorted Philip to defend the Church and respect his subjects. The following year, Charles abdicated the thrones of Castile, Aragon, Sicily, and the Indies in favor of Philip. The imperial title was given to Charles' brother Fernando in 1558. The great Holy Roman Emperor, who had faced the arch-heretic Martin Luther thirty years earlier, returned to Spain to live in the Monastery of Yuste, spending his remaining years in quiet prayer, study, and penance. Charles died on September 21, 1558. His body was buried under the high altar of the monastery, arranged so that when a priest celebrated Mass, he stood over the emperor's chest and head as a perpetual sign of humility.[239]

Protestant revolutionaries attacked the Church in the Spanish Netherlands in 1566. Over a four-day period, more than four hundred churches were sacked: tabernacles were broken open, the Eucharist profaned, and relics of saints scattered. In one blasphemous episode, a Dutch nobleman destroyed the altar in his chapel with an axe and proceeded to feed consecrated Hosts to his pet parrot.[240] The bloody conflict in the Low Countries continued for the next eighty years, until 1648. The end result of the violence was the breakup of the region into seven northern Protestant provinces, known as Holland (the Netherlands), and ten southern Catholic provinces, known as Belgium.

Germans suffered as a result of the movement begun by Martin Luther. After the Diet of Worms in 1521, Charles V was embroiled in conflicts with the Ottoman Turks and the French for the next twenty years and unable to effectively combat the spread of Protestantism in imperial territory. The emperor was able to give the Protestant troubles his full attention in 1546, at which

---

239. Daniel-Rops, *The Protestant Reformation*, vol. 2, 293. His body was later moved by Philip II to a tomb in the Basilica of San Lorenzo de El Escorial.
240. See Carroll, *The Cleaving of Christendom*, 323.

time he went to war against the Schmalkaldic League, a Protestant defensive alliance. Catholic forces won a victory at the Battle of Mühlburg in 1547, after which Charles V appropriated Julius Caesar's famous quote: "I came, I saw, God conquered." Peace reigned for the next few years, until Protestant forces allied with France to restart the war in 1551. After four years of indecisive fighting, a peace was again reached in 1555 at Augsburg, where it was decreed that the religion of a region would be determined by the faith of the secular ruler. Known by the Latin phrase *cuius regio, eius religio* ("whose region, his religion"), the settlement was no real peace. Rather, it sowed the seeds for further conflict in the next century.

In 1629, Holy Roman Emperor Ferdinand II (r. 1619–1637) ordered the restoration of all Church lands taken during the Protestant troubles in the sixteenth century. France, which still opposed Protestants at home while supporting them abroad, intervened. Religious war, known as the Thirty Years' War (1618–1648), once more erupted in German territory.[241] Cardinal Richelieu (1585–1642), initially the secretary of state and later chief minister for King Louis XIII, was concerned with strengthening the power of the king throughout France and projecting French hegemony throughout the Continent by entering into alliances with Protestants in order to check Hapsburg power. He convinced the Protestant king of Sweden, Gustav II Adolph (sometimes known as Gustavus Adolphus, one of the best generals in Christendom), to join the fight. Gustav turned the tide in favor of the Protestant army until he was killed at the Battle of Lützen in 1632. The bloody fighting continued for another sixteen years, until a treaty was signed at Westphalia, with Catholic and Protestant representatives meeting in separate cities thirty miles apart.[242] The two sides agreed that the territorial position, as it

---

241. French policy was explained by Cardinal Richelieu, who said, "The interests of a state and the interests of religion are two entirely different things." P. Sonnino, "From D'Avaux to Dévot: Politics and religion in the Thirty Years War," *History* 87 (2002), 192, quoted in MacCulloch, 499.
242. MacCulloch, 485.

had existed in 1624, was to be maintained, which left Protestant forces entrenched in northern German territory and Catholics in the south. The Thirty Years' War was one of the most devastating wars in German history, as a quarter of the population was killed (around 4.5 million people).[243]

The Catholic Church suffered significant change as a result of the Protestant movement. Her political influence was severely curtailed, and she was no longer recognized as a force in the public life of Europe. The Church was viewed no longer as *the Church*, but as *a church*. This new outlook ultimately rejected the authority of the Church as the guardian and interpreter of God-given objective truth, and produced indifferentism (all religions are the same), religious skepticism, and secular humanism.

Although the most visible effects of the Protestant movement were corporate, there were also individual effects. The Protestant rebellion, with its focus on the individual, isolated the soul, and destroyed the communal quality of the Christian faith as lived in the society of Christendom.[244] A Christian looked no longer to the corporate authority of the Church for the truth, but to himself and his personal religious experience.[245]

The Protestant movement unleashed violence on a grand scale throughout Christendom, which forced secular rulers to contemplate how to prevent such sectarian violence from repeating. The solution was the complete separation of religion from politics and the privatization of religious belief. Faith was no longer something common to society but was now the province of the private individual. This societal shift produced the concept of a subjective *rights-based* worldview, rather than a worldview established on God-given objective truth. Citizens were provided the *right* to worship as they pleased by the state, or, in some rare cases

---

243. Steven Ozment, *A Mighty Fortress: A New History of the German People* (New York: HarperCollins Publishers, 2004), 121.
244. The thoughts on the effect of the Reformation in this paragraph are taken from Hilaire Belloc, *How the Reformation Happened*, 175–178.
245. Ibid.

(like the American experiment), civil government recognized the inherent religious right of citizens and guaranteed religion's free expression.[246]

There was a reason why the Church and secular rulers were concerned about heresy — it breeds violence and disunity. There is no more evident proof of that axiom than the violence and discord unleashed on Christendom in the century of the great divorce of the family of God.

---

246. See Brad S. Gregory, *The Unintended Reformation: A Religious Revolution Secularized Society* (Cambridge, MA: Harvard University Press, 2012).

EIGHT

The Great Reform

> *"Whom shall we accuse my fellow bishops? Whom shall we declare to be the authors of such great misfortune? Ourselves; we must admit that much, with shame and with repentance for our past lives. Storm and tempest have arisen on our account, my brethren, and because of this let us cast ourselves into the sea. Let judgment begin with the House of God; let those who bear the sacred instruments of the Lord be purged and reformed!"*[1]
>
> CARDINAL CHARLES OF LORRAINE AT THE COUNCIL OF TRENT

The young Basque boy, one of thirteen children, was surrounded by siblings. Four of his brothers became soldiers and were killed in combat. The little boy admired his brothers and knew from an early age he wanted to be a soldier, too. He dreamed of earthly glory and heroic feats

---

1. Henri Daniel-Rops, trans. John Warrington, *The Catholic Reformation: Volume 1*, 119.

on the battlefield. When war began in 1521 between France and Spain, he answered the call to defend Pamplona from the French. During the siege, the young man came face to face with the ugly realities of war, and its death and destruction. He was severely wounded when a French cannon ball hit his leg and broke a bone in several places. Captured by the French, the wounded soldier was treated by French doctors, but he nearly died from their incompetent care. He received viaticum and, on the vigil of the feast of Saint Peter, fervently prayed to the first pope to intercede for his life. His prayers were answered, and the leg healed. While convalescing, the soldier read a book on the life of Christ, as well as a collection of books on the lives of the saints. His hospital experience and these books stirred the young man to deeper faith, but it was a vision of the Blessed Mother and the Christ Child that moved him to dedicate the rest of his life to God. The recovered soldier left the hospital and put away his weapons, resolved to fight only for Christ and the Church. At first, he pursued his spiritual goals alone, living in a cave, practicing extreme fasting, and spending hours kneeling in prayer. Eventually, the hermit realized that in order to be useful to others he needed to further his studies. He left the cave and, in 1528, went to Paris. While in France, Ignatius of Loyola met other young men with similar dreams and goals of doing something great for the glory of God. They founded the Society of Jesus, which formed the backbone of the Catholic Reformation.

THE REFORM BEGINS

Before the Protestant Revolution, the Church was already engaged in reform. In the fifteenth century, small associations of lay faithful gathered to read and study Scripture and discuss theology. In several areas of Christendom, reform efforts began in dioceses and religious orders. The Catholic reform was undertaken for love of God and the Church, and was centered on active prayer. The axiom of this Catholic movement was to "reform oneself" first, after which the reform of the larger Church would follow. As in past initiatives, the lead agents of reform were popes.

Pope Clement VII died in 1534 and was succeeded by Alessandro Farnese, who took the name Paul III (r. 1534–1549). Alessandro had been created a cardinal forty years earlier by the infamous Pope Alexander VI. Alexander's mistress had been Alessandro's sister, Giulia, so he was derogatorily known as "Cardinal Petticoat." In his youth, Alessandro lived an immoral life, fathering four illegitimate children. It seems the cardinals believed his papacy would be short; he was the oldest living cardinal (at sixty-seven) and appeared weak and sickly. But the new pope "possessed a character of enormous strength together with the shrewdest intelligence" and had one of the longest pontificates in a century.[2] Paul had a bit of the Renaissance popes in him: He engaged in nepotism, appointing nephews to the College of Cardinals and making one of his illegitimate sons the commander of papal armies. He was an immensely popular pope who enjoyed a good party and staged bullfights and horse races for the people of Rome. Paul was also a patron of the arts, commissioning Michelangelo to paint the Last Judgment scene in the Sistine Chapel. However, unlike the Renaissance popes, Paul embraced the need for reform in the Church. He laid the foundation for the Catholic Reformation, which he planned in three stages: reform of Rome and the papal curia, calling an ecumenical council, and papal implementation of reforms. While engaging in all three stages, Paul focused his energies on calling an ecumenical council; it would consume most of his pontificate.

Paul III first called for a council to discuss the reform of the Church in 1536. He set the location as Mantua and the date of commencement as May 1537. Recognizing the need for the Church to prepare adequately before the council, Paul established a Reform Commission headed by the Venetian Gasparo Contarini (the Englishman Cardinal Pole was also a member). The commission issued its report in March 1537 and recognized that the sale of spiritual offices and privileges, pluralism, ill-formed and ignorant clergy, and heretical teachings in universities had con-

---

2. Daniel-Rops, *The Catholic Reformation*, vol. 1, 108.

431 | CHAPTER EIGHT

tributed to the cleaving of Christendom. The Reform Commission focused blame on those within, rather than those outside, the Church for the destruction of Christian unity.

THE COUNCIL OF TRENT (1545–1563)

The pope's plan for the council was thrown into chaos in the summer of 1536 when war broke out between France and the Holy Roman Empire over control of Milan. Francis I informed the pope that French bishops would be unable to participate in the scheduled council, due to the war. The Duke of Mantua, in whose city the council was supposed to convene, informed Paul III that due to the security situation, he could not guarantee the safety of the council fathers without thousands of troops paid at papal expense. Paul, concerned that the presence of armed soldiers in the city would lead to charges that the council fathers were coerced, made the difficult decision to postpone and relocate the council. Vicenza agreed to host the council in May 1538, and Paul III called bishops to the city, but few arrived. Once more, the council was postponed. Three years later, Paul III and Charles V met in Italy to discuss the council. Charles suggested the imperial city of Trent as the new location. The city was geographically well-situated on the main road from Italy to German territory. Paul III agreed and issued a bull calling for the council to meet at Trent in November 1542. Three papal legates arrived in Trent, but no bishops came until January 1543. By the spring, only twelve bishops had arrived, primarily because of the war. The council was once again suspended. Eventually, after peace was achieved, the great reform council commenced the Catholic Reformation in March 1545.[3]

The first meeting of the Council of Trent occurred from

3. This effort is sometimes referred to as the "Counter-Reformation," but that is a misnomer and a Protestant term. The Church did not counter the Protestant "Reformation"; she engaged in an authentic Catholic reform. Additionally, the Protestant movement was not a reformation, but a revolution; therefore, there was no original reformation to counter.

1545–1547, with poor attendance from Christendom's bishops. Bishop Cornelio Musso, a gifted orator, preached at the opening Mass and reminded his fellow bishops that the purpose of the gathering was "to defend the faith and the sacraments, to restore charity among Christians, [and] to eliminate from the body of the Church the poison of covetousness and ambition."[4] Procedures were established so that only bishops and the heads of religious orders could vote on documents prepared by various committees. Three types of meetings were established to conduct conciliar business: Particular Congregations, General Congregations, and Sessions. Particular Congregations were meetings of theologians, who gathered to debate a proposed decree previously written in committee. The debates occurred in the presence of the assembled bishops. The bishops then gathered alone under the presidency of the papal legates in a General Congregation to discuss the decree. Finally, a Session was called, open to the public, wherein the final version of the decree was read and voted on for acceptance or rejection. The council conducted twenty-five sessions in total. The first meeting focused on decrees concerning Sacred Scripture and Sacred Tradition. It reaffirmed the canon of Scripture as the seventy-three books contained in the Vulgate, which was declared a fully authentic translation of the Bible. Council fathers also developed decrees on original sin and justification, indicating that man's nature is not depraved as a result of original sin but is deprived of sanctifying grace (which is restored at baptism) and suffers from concupiscence. Faith alone, the council declared, is not sufficient for justification; it must be both accompanied by hope and illustrated by good works. The council also began a doctrinal review of the sacraments, defined baptism and confirmation, and passed reform decrees outlawing absenteeism and pluralism. Unfortunately, several bishops contracted (and one died from) typhus brought by a papal army marching through

---

4. Hubert Jedin, *A History of the Council of Trent*, vol. I (St. Louis, 1957), 577, quoted in Warren H. Carroll, *The Cleaving of Christendom: A History of Christendom*, vol. 4 (Front Royal, VA: Christendom Press, 2000), 191.

Trent. The council fathers voted to reconvene in Bologna in forty days, but the proposed change in location angered Charles V. Paul III suspended the council once more.

Four years later, Paul III had been succeeded by the sixty-two-year-old Cardinal Giovanni Maria Ciocchi del Monte, who took the name Pope Julius III (r. 1550–1555). Del Monte had been the senior papal legate at the first meeting of Trent and was eager to restart the council's work. Julius issued a bull summoning bishops to meet again at Trent in 1551. At this second meeting, the council fathers passed documents on the Sacrament of the Eucharist, affirming the doctrine of transubstantiation. Documents on the Sacraments of Penance and Extreme Unction (Anointing of the Sick) were also passed. In 1552 when a Protestant army conquered Innsbruck, which was only 110 miles from Trent, the council's work was once more suspended.

In the intervening decade between the second and third meetings of the council, Pope Julius III died and was succeeded by Giovanni Angelo Medici, who took the name Pius IV (r. 1559–1565). Pius IV was a sixty-year-old canon lawyer who engaged in nepotism by creating his twenty-two-year-old nephew, Charles Borromeo, cardinal and appointing him secretary of state. This third meeting was the most productive and well-attended, with more than 250 attendees. Decrees concerning the hierarchical structure of the Church, the religious life, purgatory, the veneration of relics, the intercession of the saints, and indulgences were passed. The council also focused on the clergy in this meeting, calling for the creation of a seminary in each diocese to properly form and train men for the priesthood. A minimum age of twelve was established for entrance into the seminary as well as for ordination (twenty-four). Bishops were reminded that spiritual weapons, such as excommunication and interdict, which had been used for temporal issues, were to be used appropriately and sparingly. Discipline canons directed at the episcopacy were also instituted, including some that required bishops to live in their diocese and not be absent for more than three months at a time (and never during the seasons of Advent and Lent). Bishops were exhorted to be attentive to the needs of their clergy and laity, to visit all parishes in the diocese at least once a year, and to preach every Sunday. The council fathers also highlighted the importance of the Petrine ministry in the Church, in response to the incessant Protestant attacks against the papacy as the Antichrist. Additionally, the council fathers desired the revision and publication of the Roman Missal, and the breviary, and called for the creation of a universal catechism. Pius IV closed the council on December 4, 1563, and promulgated its decrees. The Council of Trent ushered in a new era in the life of the Church, as "the work of unification was at the same time a work of purification and rejuvenation. There was indeed, in 1563, a revitalized Catholic Church, more sure of her dogma, more worthy to govern souls, more conscious of her function and her duties."[5]

Throughout Church history, the work of councils must be implemented for its decrees to take root and affect the life of the Church. Usually (though not exclusively), that implementation requires a strong pope who makes that initiative the top priority of his pontificate. The decrees of the Council of Trent were implemented primarily through the work of Pope Saint Pius V (r. 1566–1572).

THE FATHER OF THE CATHOLIC REFORMATION

Cardinal Michele Ghislieri, a Dominican, was elected pope in 1566, taking the name Pius V. Five days after his election, he addressed the cardinals, exhorting them to personal reform by avoiding scandal. He firmly believed the clergy should lead by example, recognizing that the ordained "must enlighten men's minds, [and] enliven their hearts by the example of our holiness and our virtues."[6] Pius enforced his vision of a reformed clergy by removing bishops guilty of heresy and imprisoning those who

5. Daniel-Rops, *The Catholic Reformation*, vol. 1, 189.
6. Ibid., 153.

refused to live in their diocese. He chose only virtuous men to become cardinals.

Pius V began the implementation of Trent in 1566 by promulgating the first universal catechism. A revised breviary for the praying of the Divine Office followed two years later. Pius knew that the liturgy was crucial in a reformed Church, so he issued a new Roman Missal in 1570. He required that it be used uniformly throughout the Church, unless a diocese had a special liturgy in use for more than 200 years (such as in Milan). These initiatives ensured that the conciliar decrees became operative in the life of the Church. The work of Pius V in the Catholic Reformation produced a reinvigorated Church, no longer timid or cowering as a result of the damage from the Protestant movement, but focused on the tasks of reform, recovery, and missionary activity.[7]

The "dirty work" of bringing conciliar documents into the lives of everyday people was done by holy men and women in contact with everyday society. Mystics, missionaries, and martyrs comprised the reforming saints who restored the family of God after the great divorce that ruptured the unity of Christendom.

THE SOCIETY OF JESUS

Ignatius Loyola (1491–1556) had been a soldier, but during a time of convalescence had a profound conversion to live the Faith more fully. Long hours of silent meditation as a hermit led Ignatius to write a series of *Spiritual Exercises* for his own use. The *Exercises* were translated into Latin in 1534 and published as a book to help the faithful. The *Exercises* are a method of self-conquest and self-government structured on a series of meditations, prayers, and examination of conscience. "The *Spiritual Exercises* were not written to be read, however carefully, but to be translated into

---

7. This vibrancy was expressed in the religious art of the time, the main patron of which was the Church, in the works of Bernini, Rubens, and Caravaggio. See Kenneth Clark, *Civilisation: A Personal View* (New York: Harper & Row, 1969), 175.

reality and lived."[8] Ignatius's book encapsulated the fundamental theme of the Catholic Reformation: reform oneself!

Ignatius traveled to the Holy Land in 1523 to live as a religious, but the Franciscan provincial refused to allow him to stay, so he returned to Spain. Contemplating his future and how he could be of service to others, Ignatius realized he needed to study, so he enrolled at the University of Paris in 1528. There he met a group of like-minded young men who desired to do something great for God. On the solemnity of the Assumption, August 15, 1534, Ignatius and his six companions formed a holy association known as the Society of Jesus. The group vowed to live the evangelical counsels of poverty, chastity, and obedience, and added an additional vow to go to Jerusalem to evangelize Muslims. They knew how difficult it would be to fulfill that last vow, so they agreed that if their efforts to reach the Holy Land were unsuccessful after a year, they would go instead to Rome and place themselves at the service of the pope. Their evangelization mission to Muslims did not come to fruition, so they traveled to Rome, where Paul III approved their religious order.

Ignatius's military background permeated the Society. The Jesuits saw themselves as soldiers participating in the combat of spiritual warfare. Membership was highly selective, with a long and rigorous novitiate and training period. Education, crucial to the life of the Jesuit, comprised fourteen years of classical studies, philosophy, and theology. Jesuits ordained to the priesthood were required to be at least thirty years old. The Society focused their efforts on encouraging the faithful to frequent the sacraments, especially the Eucharist. The Jesuits encouraged daily reception of the Eucharist, which was a radical departure from Catholic practice at the time.[9] The Jesuits also focused on education, especially catechesis and classical languages, and instituted and staffed universities throughout Christendom. By the seventeenth centu-

8. Daniel-Rops, *The Catholic Reformation*, vol. 1, 57.
9. Reception of the Eucharist was not a frequent occurrence among the faithful, as the "Easter Duty" instituted by the Fourth Lateran Council in 1215 mandated Communion once a year.

ry, the Society contained more than fifteen thousand members.

REFORMING SAINTS — MYSTICS

Teresa was born into a large Catholic family of thirteen children (nine boys and four girls). Sadly, her mother died when she was only twelve years old. At age twenty, Teresa entered a Carmelite monastery, but did not at first take her religious vocation seriously. She enjoyed the conversations and frivolities allowed in the convent at the time. But her life changed drastically when she contracted a serious illness and fell into a coma for four days. Her fellow Carmelites believed she had died, but Teresa recovered and decided to reform her life and help the Carmelites return to a more strict and ascetical life. Her reformed order became known as the discalced (shoeless) Carmelites, receiving papal approval in 1580. Teresa's influence spread throughout Spain, despite a brief encounter with the Spanish Inquisition, as she founded a total of seventeen reformed convents. She desired her religious daughters to be "solitary, silent, disdainful of the body and its demands, but gay as children; humble, but never forgetting the dignity of their souls; submissive, but to the Holy Spirit; in love, but in love with Christ; stripped of everything, but queens of the world."[10] Teresa experienced spiritual ecstasies, at times emerging physically drained and speechless, and was even known to levitate. She recorded her thoughts on the spiritual life and her relationship with Christ in several books, including her *Autobiography*, *Way of Perfection*, and *Interior Castle*. Teresa died on October 5, 1582, and was canonized by Pope Gregory XV (r. 1621–1623) in 1622.[11]

Teresa's compatriot in reforming the Carmelite order was John of the Cross (1542–1591), who had also joined the Carmelites at the age of twenty. John met Teresa in 1567 and, motivated by the encounter, started his first reformed community for men

---

10. Daniel-Rops, *The Catholic Reformation*, vol. 1, 175.
11. Pope Paul VI also gave her the high papal recognition of Doctor of the Church in 1970.

in 1568. Unfortunately, John's zeal caused friction with members of the order. In 1577, he was imprisoned by his fellow brothers in Toledo and subjected to physical and moral deprivations. Eventually, he was able to escape and continue the reform.[12] John lived an all-consuming spiritual and ascetical life; he once scourged himself until he bled for having taken a small piece of food before dinner because he had felt faint.[13] Like Teresa, John wrote books on the spiritual life, including *The Dark Night of the Soul*, *The Ascent of Mount Carmel*, *The Spiritual Canticle*, and *The Living Flame of Love*. His spiritual axiom was that the soul must empty itself of self in order to be filled with God. Saint John of the Cross died on December 14, 1591, and was canonized by Pope Benedict XIII (r. 1724–1730) in 1726.

REFORMING SAINTS — ACTIVISTS

Charles Borromeo (1538–1584), despite gaining his ecclesiastical position through nepotism, became one of the most important saints of the Catholic Reformation. Charles was appointed the archbishop of Milan at the young age of twenty-one and became the first resident archbishop in nearly a century. His archdiocese contained over 2,000 parishes and 3,000 priests. Unfortunately, Charles soon learned that many priests were devoid of spiritual zeal and concern for their entrusted flock, and they were deficient in Latin. Many of the parishes had been neglected to the point of abandonment or were being used as barns. Monasteries became secular entertainment venues for balls, banquets, and wedding receptions. Charles plunged himself tirelessly into the difficult task of reforming the archdiocese. He established seminaries, as called for by Trent, to properly form and train his new clergy. He introduced the confessional as a regular piece of church furniture in order to facilitate greater participation in the sacrament

---

12. Benedict XVI, Wednesday General Audience on Saint John of the Cross, February 16, 2011, in *Holy Men and Women of the Middle Ages and Beyond* (San Francisco: Ignatius Press, 2012), 201.
13. Daniel-Rops, *The Catholic Reformation*, vol. 1, 178.

of confession.[14] Charles also realized that young people needed proper education in the Faith, so he instituted a vibrant catechetical program, staffed with trained catechists who were required to make a public profession of faith and use approved materials. Charles established schools and recruited teachers: at his death, the Archdiocese of Milan boasted 740 schools, 3,000 teachers, and 40,000 students.[15] Saint Charles Borromeo went to his eternal reward on November 3, 1584. Pope Paul V (r. 1605–1621) canonized Charles in 1610.

The diocese of Rome also needed reform. Philip Neri (1515–1595) took it upon himself to be a reformer of souls through his personal example. Philip lived a simple, holy life, walking through the streets of Rome preaching and exhorting those he met to serve and love God. As a priest, Philip spent long hours in the confessional. He believed priests needed one another's support to live holy lives, so he founded the Congregation of the Oratory (Oratorians), a gathering of diocesan priests living in community without vows. The members would gather daily to read a passage from a spiritual work and discuss its applicability. The Oratorians frequently met for prayer in the catacombs, in order to be strengthened by the heroic witness of the early Christians. After a lifetime of service to the clergy and people of Rome, Saint Philip Neri died on May 26, 1595, and was canonized by Pope Gregory XV (r. 1621–1623) in 1622.

REFORMING SAINTS — MISSIONARIES TO PROTESTANT TERRITORY

Placed on a renewed and restored foundation, the Church engaged in her integral duty of evangelization:[16] "Mother Church would not allow herself to become exclusively preoccupied with

14. Diarmaid MacCulloch, *The Reformation: A History* (New York: Penguin Books, 2003), 412.
15. Ibid.
16. The following section is adapted from my book *The Real Story of Catholic History: Answering Twenty Centuries of Anti-Catholic Myths* (El Cajon, CA: Catholic Answers Press, 2017), 229–232.

the tasks of reconstruction and defense. What she had now lost in Europe she would recover elsewhere, all over the world."[17] Missionary activity during the Catholic Reformation was focused on two fronts: predominantly Protestant nations, and the new colonies established overseas during the Age of Discovery.

The Jesuit Dutchman Peter Canisius (1521–1597) has been called the "Second Apostle to the Germans." Peter entered the Society when he was twenty-two years old and earned a doctorate in theology in 1549. Peter wrote a brief catechism titled *Summary of Christian Doctrine*, which was published in 1555, for the purpose of teaching Protestants about the Catholic faith. His book was eventually published in three versions for different audiences. It went through two hundred editions and was translated into fifteen languages, including Japanese and Amharic. Instead of engaging in polemics, Peter sought common ground with Protestants, whom he called "separated brethren." Peter also understood the importance of education; he founded numerous schools and colleges throughout Christendom. His example and teaching helped many become Catholic. He died on December 21, 1597, and was canonized by Pope Pius XI (r. 1922–1939) in 1925.

Another missionary to Protestants was Francis de Sales (1567–1622), who, in 1594, only a year after being ordained a priest, volunteered to work in the Calvinist stronghold of Geneva and its environs. A few years later, in 1602, he was ordained bishop of Geneva, but he was forced to reside in Annecy, France, as the Calvinist city would not allow the residence of a Catholic bishop. Francis wrote many tracts and pamphlets explaining the Catholic faith. He provided catechetical instruction and was a renowned spiritual director. He propagated devotion to the Sacred Heart of Jesus and to guardian angels. He also encouraged frequent reception of the Eucharist. His spiritual treatise, *Introduction to the Devout Life*, is still avidly read. Francis' love for the poor

---

17. Henri Daniel-Rops, trans. John Warrington, *The Catholic Reformation*, vol. 2, (Garden City, NY: Image Books, 1964 [1955]), 14.

and his humble asceticism drew many thousands of Protestants to the Church. He died on December 28, 1622, and was canonized by Pope Alexander VII (r. 1655–1667) in 1665.

THE AGE OF DISCOVERY
AND CHRISTOPHER COLUMBUS

Missionary activity to new lands was made possible by the Age of Discovery, which was ushered in by Prince Henry the Navigator (1394–1460) of Portugal.[18] Prince Henry studied ocean currents and wind movement in order to improve navigation for sailing ships. He sent Portuguese ships and sailors down the West African coast, seeking a trade route to India. He also invented the caravel, a light ship that was perfect for long-distance, uncharted exploration. Prince Henry and his sailors inaugurated the age of explorers, finding new lands and creating shipping lanes for the import and export of goods, including consumables never before seen in Europe. These efforts also created fierce competition among the sailing nations of Europe, each striving to outdo the other in finding new and more efficient trade routes. It was into this world of innovation, exploration, and economic competition that Christopher Columbus was born.

A native of the Italian city-state of Genoa, Columbus became a sailor at the age of fourteen. He learned the nautical trade while sailing on Genoese merchant vessels and became an accomplished navigator. On a long-distance voyage past Iceland in February 1477, Columbus learned about the strong east-flowing Atlantic currents. He believed a journey across the ocean could be made because those currents would be able to bring a ship home.[19] Columbus formulated a plan to seek the East by going west, in order to increase trading opportunities and finance a crusade to retake Jerusalem. Such an ambitious undertaking required

---

18. The following section is adapted from my book *The Real Story of Catholic History*, 247–251.

19. The sailors of Columbus's day did not believe the earth was flat, as is commonly believed in the modern world, but were concerned about their ability to get home after sailing across the ocean.

royal backing, which he sought first from King João of Portugal, as the Portuguese were leaders in nautical exploration. Rebuffed by the Portuguese king, Columbus dispatched his brother to King Henry VII of England, while he managed to acquire a royal audience with King Fernando and Queen Isabel of Spain in May 1486. Impressed by Columbus and his daunting plan, the queen convened a commission to study his proposal. But the commission was concerned that Columbus had miscalculated the ocean's width, and that the journey would take longer and pose greater risk than Columbus estimated. They recommended rejecting Columbus's proposal.[20] At first, Queen Isabel concurred, but she later changed her mind and granted everything Columbus needed for the voyage. On August 3, 1492, he embarked from Spain with ninety men on three ships: the *Niña*, *Pinta*, and *Santa María*. After thirty-three days at sea and having traveled three thousand miles, Columbus's flotilla spotted land (the Bahamas), which he claimed in the name of the Spanish monarchs.[21] On this first voyage, Columbus also reached the islands of Cuba and Hispaniola. He stayed four months in the New World; then he arrived home to fanfare on March 15, 1493, after an absence of seven months and eleven days.

Columbus made four voyages to the New World, each bringing its own discoveries and adventures. His second voyage included many crewmen from his first, but also some new faces, such as Ponce de León, who later won fame as an explorer himself. On this second voyage, Columbus and his men encountered the fierce tribe of the Caribs, cannibals who practiced sodomy and castrated boys captured from neighboring tribes. Columbus rec-

---

20. The commission believed it would take Columbus three years to go from Spain to Asia. See Samuel Eliot Morison, *Admiral of the Ocean Sea: A Life of Christopher Columbus*, vol. 1 (Boston: Little, Brown, 1942), 131–132, cited in Carol Delaney, *Columbus and the Quest for Jerusalem* (New York: Free Press, 2011), 63. Columbus's calculation was in fact incorrect; he made the ocean 25 percent smaller than it is. See Morison, *Admiral*, vol. 1, 87, cited in Delaney, *Columbus and the Quest for Jerusalem*, 60.
21. Columbus's modern-day detractors view that as a sign of imperial conquest. It was not: it was simply a sign to other European nations that they could not establish trading posts on the Spanish possession. See Delaney, *Columbus and the Quest for Jerusalem*, 92.

ognized the Caribs' captives as members of a peaceful tribe he had met on his first voyage, so he rescued and returned them to their homes.[22] This voyage included stops in Puerto Rico and the Virgin Islands.

The third voyage was the most difficult personally for Columbus. He was arrested by Francisco de Bobadilla, who replaced him as Governor of the Indies, on charges of mismanaging the Spanish trading enterprise in the New World. Columbus was sent back to Spain in chains, but he was exonerated by the monarchs when they heard his full report of the situation in the Indies. Columbus's fourth and final voyage took place from 1502 to 1504, with his son Fernando among the crew. This crossing of the Atlantic was the fastest ever: sixteen days. The expedition visited Honduras, Nicaragua, and Costa Rica, and was marooned for a time on Jamaica.

Columbus greatly desired the evangelization and catechesis of the native populations he met on his voyages. His first words to the natives of Hispaniola were, "The monarchs of Castile have sent us not to subjugate you, but to teach you the true religion."[23] He realized that the Indians needed more than just baptism: they needed instruction in the Faith. Hence, he was deeply disappointed in the missionary priest who accompanied him on his second journey. The priest refused to learn the natives' language in order to catechize, rather than just baptize, them.[24] In a 1502 letter to Pope Alexander VI, Columbus asked the pontiff to send missionaries to the indigenous peoples of the New World so they could learn of and accept Christ. In his will, Columbus established a fund to finance missionary efforts to the lands he had discovered.[25] The efforts of Columbus and other explorers during the Age of Discovery allowed the Church to bring the Gospel to corners of the world where it had never been heard.

---

22. Ibid., 130.
23. Daniel-Rops, *The Catholic Reformation*, vol. 2, 27.
24. Delaney, 153.
25. Ibid., 159.

REFORMING SAINTS — MISSIONARIES TO ASIA

A founding member of the Society of Jesus, Francis Xavier (1506–1552) traveled tens of thousands of miles — to India, New Guinea, the Philippines, Japan, and an island off the coast of China — over a ten-year period. He arrived in India on May 6, 1542, and "within a period of thirty days Francis converted more Hindus than all his Portuguese predecessors had done in 30 years."[26] Francis continued his missionary journey with stops in New Guinea in 1545 and the Philippines in 1546. Three years later, Francis was in Japan, where he studied the culture, became fluent in Japanese, and worked hard to develop a native clergy. His work in Japan produced fruit, as several thousand people accepted the Faith. Unfortunately, Francis Xavier died off the coast of China in 1552 at the young age of forty-six. He knew that he was laying a foundation for future missionaries: "I pray God to give me the grace to open the way for others, even though I myself accomplish nothing."[27] Pope Gregory XV canonized Francis in 1622.

Within a decade of Francis Xavier's departure for China, six Jesuit missionaries operated in Japan, and the entire village of Nagasaki had converted. By the late sixteenth century, hundreds of thousands of Japanese became Christians. But the 1630s witnessed the worst period of persecution in Japan, and thousands were martyred for the Faith. A favorite torture tactic by the Japanese authorities was "the pit": victims were hung upside down from a gallows over a pit filled with excrement in an effort to influence them to apostatize.[28] Many Christians were forced to repudiate the Faith by stepping on a picture of Christ or a crucifix.

Despite horrific tortures, terrible governmental persecution, and the absence of priests, the Faith was maintained in Japan. Lay catechists led secret Christian communities, to whom they taught

---

26. Daniel-Rops, *The Catholic Reformation*, vol. 2, 60.
27. Ibid., 65.
28. This form of torture was portrayed in the 2016 Martin Scorsese film *Silence*, which was based on the 1966 book of the same name by the Catholic Japanese author Shusaku Endo.

Catholic prayers and doctrines. When Japan was "reopened" to foreigners in the nineteenth century, the Jesuits returned after a more than two-hundred-year absence and were astonished to find thousands of Catholics maintaining the Faith.

Unlike in Japan, the Faith in China, which had been brought by the Jesuits, was extinguished by a general persecution. It was later rekindled by the Jesuit missionary Matteo Ricci (d. 1611). Ricci had entered the Society at the age of nineteen and learned from the great Jesuit cardinal and theologian Saint Robert Bellarmine (1542–1621) and from the Jesuit mathematician and astronomer Christopher Clavius (1538–1612). Ricci left Europe in 1582 on his mission trip to China. He learned Chinese, translated the Ten Commandments, and published a catechism. Ricci also used his scientific knowledge to spread the Gospel in China, knowing the Chinese were interested in science. He made clocks, globes, and maps and showed them to the Chinese, which provided an opportunity for Ricci to talk about the Faith. Ricci was a master of the "accommodation method," whereby missionaries would adopt local clothing and customs (as long as they were not antithetical to the Gospel) in order to attract converts. Ricci's evangelization efforts produced fruit in China, but the culture and traditions of that land worked against the Faith. Conversions were never numerous relative to the population.

MISSIONARY ACTIVITY IN
THE NEW WORLD — SPAIN

Permanent Spanish colonization and evangelization efforts in the New World began with a settlement in St. Augustine, Florida, in 1565, forty-two years before the first English settlement at Jamestown.[29] Spanish activity extended to areas that are today known as Mexico, Chile, Peru, Colombia, Ecuador, Dominican Republic, the American Southwest, and California. Many of the

---

29. The following section is adapted from my book *The Real Story of Catholic History*, 233–236.

Spanish conquistadors were committed to the evangelization and fair treatment of the native peoples. Chaplains accompanied their expeditions to provide for the spiritual needs of the indigenous peoples as well as the Spanish. It is true, however, that some conquistadors were bent on finding gold and exploiting the natives. Some Spaniards were nothing less than barbaric. When a priest dared to rebuke a sadistic governor for throwing children to his hungry dogs, the governor ordered a child cut up in the priest's presence.[30] Another governor ordered the execution of five thousand natives just so he could watch them die.[31] Some native chiefs were tortured until their tribes paid ransoms, but, instead of releasing them, the Spanish authorities wrapped the chiefs in straw and threw them into raging fires.[32] Catholic missionaries protested this behavior, in most cases to no avail. Bishop Juan de Zumárraga, most famously known for his role in the appearance of Our Lady of Guadalupe in 1531, fought against the enslavement of the Indians, even excommunicating certain Spanish colonial authorities in Mexico.

Another bishop who fought for the native peoples was the Spanish lawyer and priest Bartolomé de las Casas (1474–1566). De las Casas came from a family of adventurers. His father had sailed on Columbus's first voyage to the New World, and Bartolomé knew the great Genoese explorer personally. At first, Bartolomé lived a normal colonial life in Hispaniola, which unfortunately included mistreatment of the natives, but later he had a change of heart. He set his slaves free, became religiously devout, and was ordained a Dominican priest. He focused his new life on preaching the Gospel and speaking out against colonial abuses of the native peoples. The colonial authorities labeled Bartolomé a madman and tried to convince royal officials in Spain to ignore his frequent reports about the abuse of

30. Henri Daniel-Rops, *Heroes of God: Eleven Courageous Men and Women Who Risked Everything to Spread the Catholic Faith* (Manchester, NH: Sophia Institute Press, 2002), 59.
31. Ibid.
32. Ibid.

the Indians. Recognizing that his written reports were ineffective, and concerned that they might not even be reaching the king, Bartolomé traveled to Spain and complained in person to King Fernando. In all, he made five trips across the Atlantic to report to the king on the plight of the native peoples. He also documented colonial abuse and condemned slavery in his book *A Short Account of the Destruction of the Indies*. In 1542, thanks to Bartolomé's efforts, King Charles I (who was also Emperor Charles V) laid down stricter laws that protected the native peoples. The king also appointed Bartolomé bishop of Chiapas in southern Mexico. As bishop, de las Casas ordered his priests to question all colonists in confession about their behavior toward the Indians. The bishop also instructed confessors to refuse absolution to penitents if they did not return stolen Indian property or if they refused to free their slaves.[33] The colonists responded by rioting and attacking priests. When word of the upheaval reached the king, he ordered de las Casas to come to Spain to discuss the situation; the bishop never returned to the New World. When news of his death at the age of ninety-two in 1566 reached the colonies, spontaneous funeral ceremonies broke out in hundreds of native villages. For centuries afterward, he was remembered as "Father to the Indians."[34]

Peter Claver (1580–1654) arrived in Cartagena (in today's Colombia) in 1610. The Jesuit priest made it his life's mission to serve the African slaves who were being imported by Portuguese slave traders to the New World, where the Spanish colonists needed many laborers to farm the land and mine for gold. Approximately one thousand African slaves from Guinea, Congo, and Angola arrived in Cartagena each month.[35] Pope Urban VIII (r. 1623–1644), in *Commissum Nobis* condemned the slave trade and forbade Catholics to displace Africans from their na-

33. Daniel-Rops, *Heroes of God*, 72.
34. Ibid., 66,75.
35. Pierre Suau, "St. Peter Claver," *Catholic Encyclopedia*, vol. 11 (New York: Robert Appleton Company, 1911), accessed September 20, 2018, http://www.newadvent.org/cathen/11763a.htm.

tive country.[36] Despite the pope's condemnation, African slaves continued to arrive in Cartagena, which became the main slave market in the New World. Claver ministered to these poor souls and declared himself "the slave of the negroes forever."[37] Because the slaves came from different African countries and spoke different languages and dialects, Peter developed a cadre of translators, whom he trained as catechists. It is estimated that his forty-four years of work among the slaves resulted in the baptism of more than three hundred thousand Africans, including some who were Muslim.[38] Peter died on September 8, 1654, and was canonized on January 15, 1888, by Pope Leo XIII (r. 1878–1903), who said, "No life, except the life of Christ, has so moved me as that of Saint Peter Claver."[39]

Junípero Serra (1713–1784) entered the Franciscan order in 1730 and later became a university professor. At age thirty-five, he volunteered for the New World missions. After an eighteen-month sea voyage, he arrived in Mexico. On the way from Veracruz to Mexico City, a scorpion stung him. The wound never properly healed, afflicting him with a limp for the rest of his life.[40] In the New World, Father Serra volunteered for service at the remote Sierra Gorda Indian missions, where he taught farming techniques and livestock while tending to the Pame Indians; he also translated the catechism into the Pame language. In 1767, Father Serra went to California, where he was tasked with founding missions along the six-hundred-mile Spanish colonial supply line. He eventually established the missions of San Carlos, San Antonio, San Gabriel, San Luis Obispo, San Francisco, San Juan Capistrano, Santa Clara, and San Buenaventura. He frequently clashed with the Spanish military and civil authorities over their treatment of Indians. Father Serra died on August 28, 1784, and

36. See Joel S. Panzer, *The Popes and Slavery* (New York: Alba House, 1996), 31.
37. Suau, "St. Peter Claver."
38. Ibid.
39. Angel Valtierra, S.J., *Peter Claver: Saint of the Slaves* (Westminster, MD: Burns and Oates, 1960), 266, quoted in Carroll, *The Cleaving of Christendom*, 644.
40. Daniel-Rops, *Heroes of God*, 123.

was canonized by Pope Francis (r. 2013–present) in 2015.

THE CHURCH AND SLAVERY

During the colonization of the New World, the Church dealt with an issue that had occupied her attention in earlier centuries but had been absent from European life for a long time.[41] The Church had been born into the imperial Roman world where slavery was the lynchpin of society and complete abolition of slavery was unthinkable and impractical.[42] Despite societal acceptance of slavery, the Church made no distinction between slaves and freedmen in her membership. The equality of believers in a highly class-stratified society was one of the attractions that the Church held for the people of Rome. Once Emperor Constantine legalized the Church in 313, her teachings influenced Roman laws and policies, and those teachings did have an effect on individual Roman converts.[43] One former slave even became pope![44] Still, slavery continued in Europe, even after the collapse of imperial rule in the late fifth century. But as the Church's influence increased, the institution of slavery decreased, until it was completely eradicated in Christendom.

Slavery returned to European society in the fifteenth century, upon the conquest of the Canary Islands and the discovery of the New World. But, from 1435 to 1890, a succession of popes condemned the slave trade and slavery in no uncertain terms. The first pope to do so was Eugenius IV (r. 1431–1447), who, in his 1435 bull *Sicut Dudum* (issued fifty-seven years before Columbus's first voyage), demanded that Christians free all enslaved natives of the Canary Islands within fifteen days; failure to do so would in-

41. The following section is adapted from my book *The Real Story of Catholic History*, 292–294.
42. See Warren H. Carroll, *The Founding of Christendom: A History of Christendom*, Volume 1 (Front Royal, VA: Christendom College Press, 1985), 540.
43. There is a record of a slave master who, in 355, became a Christian and as a result emancipated his Egyptian slave girl. See Henry Chadwick, *The Church in Ancient Society: From Galilee to Gregory the Great* (Oxford. UK: Oxford University Press, 2001), 81.
44. Callistus I, who reigned from 217 to 222.

cur automatic excommunication.[45] In 1537, Pope Paul III issued a bull, *Sublimus Dei*, teaching that native peoples "are not to be reduced to slavery and that whatever happens to the contrary is to be considered null and void."[46] In 1591, Gregory XIV (r. 1590–1591) promulgated *Cum Sicuti*, which was addressed to the bishop of Manila in the Philippines and reiterated his predecessors' prohibitions against enslaving native peoples. In the seventeenth century, Urban VIII (r. 1623–1644) promulgated *Commissum Nobis* (1639) in support of King Philip IV's edict prohibiting enslavement of the Indians in the New World.

The African slave trade in the New World was also condemned by Pope Innocent XI (r. 1676–1689), during whose pontificate the Holy Office ruled that the capture of Africans for the purposes of slavery was not permitted.[47] In 1741, Benedict XIV (r. 1740–1758) issued *Immensa Pastorum*, which reiterated that the penalty for enslaving Indians was excommunication.[48] Gregory XVI (r. 1831–1846) issued *In Supremo* in 1839 to condemn the enslavement of Africans. Pope Leo XIII promulgated two bulls on the subject of slavery. The first, *In Plurimis* (1888), encouraged the bishops of Brazil to support the recent abolition of slavery in that country. The second, *Catholicae Ecclesiae* (1890), urged the bishops of the world to support the end of the African slave trade and to encourage the evangelization of Africa by financially supporting the missions.

Despite the many papal condemnations, European colonists continued to enslave Africans and New World natives until the nineteenth century. Papal denunciations of slavery were so harsh and so frequent that the colonial Spanish forbade the publication of papal documents in the colonies without prior royal approval.[49]

---

45. See Panzer, *The Popes and Slavery*, 75–78.
46. Ibid., 81.
47. Ibid., 37.
48. Ibid., 42.
49. Kenneth Scott Latourette, *A History of Christianity*, vol. 2 Revised Edition (San Francisco: Harper San Francisco, 1975), 944, quoted in Rodney Stark, *Bearing False Witness: Debunking Centuries of Anti-Catholic History* (West Conshohocken, PA: Templeton Press, 2016), 173.

Sadly, the colonists of the New World, including the later English settlers in what became the United States, continued to subjugate their fellow human beings in bondage. Thankfully, holy men and women worked tirelessly to minister to slaves and continued to call for the eradication of the pernicious evil of slavery.

While Europeans were enslaving indigenous people in the New World and Africans for transport to the colonies, thousands of Christians living around the Mediterranean Sea suffered the same fate. Muslim marauders from the Barbary Coast (modern Morocco, Algeria, and Tunisia) harassed Christian towns, destroying churches, capturing Christians as slaves, and desecrating the dead.[50] Muslim pirates, operating from the sixteenth to the eighteenth centuries, were responsible for the enslavement of 1.25 million Christians in a concerted campaign to provide manpower for the Ottoman Turkish military and society.[51]

MISSIONARY ACTIVITY IN THE NEW WORLD — FRANCE

French missionary efforts in the New World began when Jacques Cartier explored the Saint Lawrence Seaway in the sixteenth century.[52] Samuel de Champlain established the city of Quebec in the early seventeenth century. By the mid-eighteenth century, the colony of New France was wealthy and populous. Among the nearby Native American tribes, the Algonquin and Huron were the most receptive to the Faith, so missionary activity focused on them.[53] Still, converts were few, and many of the Indians were hostile to the missionaries, whom they would blame for any ca-

---

50. See R. C. Davis, *Christian Slaves, Muslim Masters: White Slavery in the Mediterranean, the Barbary Coast, and Italy, 1500 – 1800* (London: Palgrave Macmillan, 2003).
51. Darío Fernández-Morera, *The Myth of the Andalusian Paradise: Muslims, Christians, and Jews under Islamic Rule in Medieval Spain* (Wilmington: ISI Books, 2016), 166.
52. The following section is adapted from my book *The Real Story of Catholic History*, 236–238.
53. The French word *hure* means "boar's head," which the French used to describe the Hurons because they styled their hair to make it look like the stiff bristles on a wild boar's head. See Daniel-Rops, *Heroes of God*, 99.

lamity that befell the tribe or one of its members.

Despite the challengers and hardships of missionary life, holy men and women continued to answer the call to spread the Gospel among the native peoples of modern-day New York state and Canada. Saint François de Laval (1623–1708), the first bishop of New France, worked tirelessly to establish the Church on a firm foundation in the New World. In 1663, he founded the first seminary in New France. Laval traveled extensively throughout Quebec, ministering to his people. He died on May 6, 1708, and was canonized by Pope Francis in 2014. Saint Marie Guyart's (1599–1672) husband died when she was eighteen years old; in 1631, she entered the Ursuline convent at Tours.[54] Marie decided to go to the missions in New France and arrived in Quebec in 1639, where she founded a school for girls.[55] Marie learned the Iroquois, Algonquin, and Huron languages, and published catechisms in these languages. She worked for thirty-three years in the New World until her death on April 30, 1672; she was canonized by Pope Francis in 2014.

Missionary work among the native peoples of New France was both arduous and dangerous. The journey from the main French colonial outposts to Huronia was eight hundred miles. Missionaries who traveled it faced many natural obstacles, as well as unfriendly Iroquois tribes. In the mid-seventeenth century, the Iroquois Confederacy began a campaign of annihilation against the Hurons, and the black-robed Jesuit missionaries were caught in the crossfire.[56] Eight Jesuit priests and lay workers, known collectively as the North American Martyrs, shed their blood for Christ in the New World in the years 1642–1649.[57]

René Goupil (1608–1642), a lay Jesuit trained as a surgeon, found use for his skills in the mission fields. He, along with Isaac

---

54. Saint Angela de Merici founded the Ursulines in 1535 to minister to women, especially orphaned girls and prostitutes.
55. She is also known as Saint Marie de l'Incarnation. Her school for girls is still operating in present-day Quebec City.
56. The Iroquois Confederacy comprised the Mohawks, Senecas, Oneidas, Onondagas, and Cayugas.
57. Pope Pius XI canonized the eight North American Martyrs on June 29, 1930.

Jogues, was captured and tortured on a trip to Huronia while carrying supplies from Quebec. On September 29, 1642, René was tomahawked to death for having made the Sign of the Cross before eating. When the old Mohawk who had ordered René's execution later saw Isaac Jogues also cross himself before a meal, he said: "There you have exactly what we hate! Now you know why they killed your companion and why they will kill you. Our neighbors the Dutch do not make this sign."[58] René was the first of the North American Martyrs to give his life for Christ in New France.

Isaac Jogues (1607–1647) was the fifth of nine children and, at age seventeen, entered the Society of Jesus. Ordained in 1636, Isaac later volunteered for the missions in New France. He traveled extensively in what was to become New York State. A group of friendly Native Americans brought him to a beautiful lake on the feast of Corpus Christi; Isaac named the body of water the Lake of the Blessed Sacrament.[59] Isaac was abducted with René Goupil and suffered in captivity for a year. Yet he continued to model the Christian life to the Mohawks, even caring for a sick tribesman who had earlier tortured him by ripping out his fingernails.[60] Eventually, Isaac escaped and made his way back to France, where accounts of his missionary travels in the publication *Jesuit Relations* made him something of a celebrity. Although he could have continued to live comfortably in France, Isaac's zeal for souls impelled him to request reassignment to New France, which was granted. Unfortunately, his second stint in the New World was short-lived. He was once again captured by the Mohawks and later tomahawked to death, along with the lay Jesuit worker Jean de la Lande (1615–1646).

Antoine Daniel (1601–1648) translated the Our Father into

58. Angus MacDougall, *Martyrs of New France* (Midland, Ontario: A Martyr's Shrine Publication, 1992), 5.
59. The English renamed the body of water Lake George, after their king, when they defeated the French in the Seven Years' War (1756–1763).
60. Daniel-Rops, *Heroes of God*, 111.

the Huron language. One day, he had just finished celebrating Mass when the Iroquois attacked the Huron village. During the chaos, Father Daniel ministered to and comforted the dying and wounded Hurons, until he was shot with arrows and musket balls. As he lay dying, he called out the name of Jesus. The Iroquois threw his body into a burning house.

The year 1649 was the bloodiest for the Jesuit missionaries, as four men joined the ranks of the martyrs. Jean de Brébeuf (1593–1649) had been one of the first missionaries to arrive in New France in 1625. Jean evangelized for several years, until British military campaigns forced him to return home to France. Returning to New France, Jean wrote a set of instructions for missionaries that reflected his deep love and concern for the Huron people. He told his fellow and future missionaries to love the Hurons unconditionally, to eat the food they offered, to carry something during portages, and to always appear cheerful.[61] Jean also published a catechism and a dictionary in the Huron language for use by other missionaries. Jean wrote of his time with the Hurons in letters sent back to France, which were compiled and published under the title *Huron Relation of 1635*. In these stories, Jean explained how the Hurons loved and cared for one another, practiced hospitality, and, despite the absence of Christian teaching, followed natural law concerning marriage by having only one spouse and following the laws of consanguinity. Jean even noted how the Hurons practiced temporary sexual abstinence during the time a mother nursed her child. When the Iroquois Confederacy declared war on the Hurons, Jean was captured by a Mohawk war party in March 1649, along with his brother priest Gabriel Lalemant (1610–1649), who had been in New France for six months. Jean was beaten, tied to a stake to be burned, and had scalding water poured over his head in a mockery of baptism. Additionally, a collar of red-hot tomahawk heads was placed around his neck and a red-hot iron thrust down his throat. Despite these

---

61. See MacDougall, 36.

horrific punishments, he did not utter a word of protest throughout the ordeal. Gabriel Lalemant suffered horrible tortures along with Jean. Gabriel's eyes were gouged out and burning coals were placed in the sockets. A hatchet blow to the head killed him. When both men died, the Mohawks cut out their hearts and ate them.[62]

Charles Garnier (1606–1649) was ordained a priest for the Society of Jesus in 1635. A year later, he arrived in New France, where he served among the Hurons and contracted smallpox. Charles was killed in December 1649 during an Iroquois raid. The last Jesuit to die in New France in 1649 was the youngest of them all, and had narrowly escaped martyrdom previously. Although Nöel Chabanel (1613–1649) had no facility for the Huron language, he vowed to remain among the tribe for the rest of his life. A Huron apostate from the Faith, Louis Honareenhax, killed Father Chabanel in the belief that doing so would be a service to his family and tribe, because they had suffered calamities after becoming Catholic.[63]

The blood of the North American Martyrs would prove to be the seed of a future saint. Ten years after the death of Saints Isaac Jogues and Jean de la Lande, a young Mohawk girl was born in the village of their martyrdom. Kateri Tekakwitha (1656–1680) was the daughter of an Algonquin mother and a Mohawk father. When she was four years old, her parents and brother died from smallpox, which she also contracted. The disease left her disfigured, with scars on her face and impaired eyesight. The villagers called her "Tekakwitha," or "she who bumps into things." French Jesuits evangelized the tribe, and Kateri embraced the Faith at the age of eighteen. As a result of her conversion, she was ostracized from the tribe, so she left and settled in a village near Montreal. Five years later, on the feast of the Annunciation in 1679, Kateri made a perpetual vow of virginity. On April 17 of the following year, at the young age of twenty-four, she died. Known as the

---

62. Ibid., 44–45.
63. Ibid., 69.

"Lily of the Mohawks," Kateri was canonized by Pope Benedict
XVI (r. 2005–2013) in 2012.

THE STRUGGLE AGAINST THE TURK

While Christendom was moving toward the Protestant Revolt,
the Ottoman Turks were invading Christian territory in an effort
to subjugate Europe. Brave warriors fought to preserve Western
civilization and Christendom against the Turkish scourge. The
crucial struggle occurred in the sixteenth century at the height of
the Protestant crisis, but several important engagements occurred
in the fifteenth century. After the Ottoman Turks captured and
ransacked Constantinople in 1453, they continued their march
through Christian territory with an eighty-thousand-man army,
reaching Belgrade (modern-day Serbia), an important town in the
Kingdom of Hungary, in 1456.[64] Pope Callistus III (r. 1455–1458)
asked all abbots, archbishops, and bishops to pray, fast, and do
penance on the feast of Saints Peter and Paul for the city's deliv-
erance, and called a crusade to defend the city. Christian warriors
answered the pope's call, and the Crusade army, with the saintly
priest John of Capistrano (1386–1456) in its midst, reached the
city in time to defend it against the Turkish horde. Throughout
the heavy fighting, which descended into hand-to-hand combat
at times, John of Capistrano held aloft a papal crucifix. Mehmet
II, the conqueror of Constantinople, was wounded in the fighting
and called off the attack. The city was spared, but the march of
the Turks into Europe would continue.

In the year 1480, the town of Otranto was in the crosshairs
of the mighty Ottoman Empire. Sitting on the heel of Italy
near the Adriatic Sea, Otranto provided a strategic base of operations for an invasion of Italy and for the ultimate destruction of Christendom. The Muslim invasion force was ruthless

---

64. The following section is adapted from my book *The Glory of the Crusades* (El Cajon, CA: Catholic
Answers Press, 2014), 207–208, 214–231.

and unmatched in its savagery. They massacred more than half of the town's residents; the archbishop was seized while celebrating Mass, taken outside the cathedral, and sawed in two.[65] As an example to the rest of the townspeople and all inhabitants of Italy, Pasha Ahmet, the Muslim commander, decided to execute 813 men. They were exhorted to convert to Islam, but a tailor named Antonio Primaldi bravely told the sultan he was willing to die a thousand deaths for Christ, which emboldened his fellow captives.[66] The next morning, on the vigil of the Assumption of the Blessed Mother, the men were led to the hill overlooking the city. Pasha Ahmet ordered the executioner to behead Antonio Primaldi first. One Muslim executioner was so moved by the faith of the martyrs that he converted to the Faith on the spot, and joined them in dying for Christ.[67] The Church honored the brave witness of these men, and they were officially declared martyrs by Pope Benedict XVI in July 2006 and canonized by Pope Francis in May 2013.

The Ottoman Empire entered its zenith during the reign of Suleiman the Magnificent (r. 1520–1566). Every sultan was required to add a new piece to the Ottoman Empire, but Suleiman was not content to add one or two territories; he wanted to rule the entire world. During his forty-six-year reign, Suleiman's forces conquered Baghdad, Belgrade, Budapest, and Rhodes. Suleiman primarily wanted to control the Mediterranean Sea, the strategic body of water at the center of the Western world. Suleiman's march across the Mediterranean began with the siege of the island of Rhodes in 1522, where a Turkish invasion force had been beaten back by Christians in 1480.

---

65. Twelve thousand of the 22,000 inhabitants were killed during the invasion. Roger Crowley, *1453: The Holy War for Constantinople and the Clash of Islam and the West* (New York: Hachette Books, 2005), 241.

66. Giovanni Laggetto, *Historia della guerra di Otranto del 1480.*, quoted in Matthew E. Bunson, "How the 800 Martyrs of Otranto Saved Rome," *This Rock* (Catholic Answers), Volume 19, Number 6, July 2008, http://www.catholic.com/magazine/articles/how-the-800-martyrs-of-otranto-saved-rome.

67. Saverio de Marco, *Compendiosa istoria degli ottocento martiri otrantini*, in Bunson, "How the 800 Martyrs of Otranto Saved Rome."

This time, although the outnumbered Knights Hospitallers, commanded by Master General Phillip Villiers de L'Isle Adam, fought bravely, they were eventually forced to surrender. Suleiman was so impressed by the courage of the knights that he allowed the survivors to leave the island with their weapons. The knights wandered Europe for a few years, looking for a permanent home. In 1530, Holy Roman Emperor Charles V gave them the island of Malta for the annual rent of one falcon.

Suleiman followed his success at Rhodes with a land campaign aimed at the Kingdom of Hungary. Battle was joined between Suleiman's army and the forces of King Louis II (1506–1526) on August 29, 1526. The Hungarians were outnumbered but fought bravely. Unfortunately, King Louis was killed during the retreat, along with two archbishops, five bishops, and thousands of soldiers. The Christian defeat allowed Suleiman to capture Hungary's capital city of Buda and ravage the countryside. The Turks were now only fifty miles from Vienna, the gateway to Europe, which they assaulted in 1529 but were unable to capture. They would return to the city on the Danube in the seventeenth century.

As Suleiman the Magnificent neared the end of his life, one regret from his younger days haunted him: letting the Knights Hospitallers leave Rhodes in 1522, instead of annihilating them when he had the chance. Suleiman told his advisers, "Those sons of dogs, whom I have already conquered and who were spared only by my clemency at Rhodes forty-three years ago, I say now that for their continual raids and insults they shall finally be cursed and destroyed."[68] Revenge was not the only reason to attack Malta: the Knights used the Mediterranean island as a base of operations to hamper Turkish shipping, including pilgrim traffic to Mecca. Suleiman knew that "Malta was simply too central, too strategic, and too troublesome to be ignored indefinitely."[69] He assembled an army of 40,000 warriors, 100 artillery pieces,

---

68. Tim Pickles, *Malta 1565: Last Battle of the Crusades* (New York: Osprey Publishing, 1998), 14.
69. Roger Crowley, *Empires of the Sea: The Siege of Malta, the Battle of Lepanto, and the Contest for the Center of the World* (New York: Random House, 2009), 90.

458 | CHAPTER EIGHT

and 100,000 cannonballs to attack the little island in the middle of the Mediterranean.[70] He was certain of victory.

The Knights Hospitallers had been established on Malta for almost forty years when the huge Ottoman invasion fleet arrived. The island's defense was manned by only 500 Knights and 8,000 Maltese militia and mercenaries from Spain and Italy.[71] As in previous engagements with the Ottomans, the Knights were woefully outnumbered. The master general of the order, Jean de La Valette, was seventy years old, a fifty-year member of the order and a veteran of the siege of Rhodes. Knowing the situation was desperate, he sent a summons to all the Knights in Christendom to come to the island's defense. La Valette knew the island must hold out against the Ottomans. Failure to do so would give the Muslims a strategic base from which to launch an invasion of Sicily and, ultimately, Italy, threatening Rome and the very heart of Christendom.

The Ottomans arrived on Malta in May 1565. From the beginning, their time on the island was marked by division and difficulty. Suleiman had divided the operation between two commanders, Mustapha Pasha and Piyale. Mustapha Pasha commanded the army; he was a veteran of the Persian and Hungarian campaigns and the siege of Rhodes. Piyale was the inexperienced admiral of the 180-ship fleet. Friction between the commanders and each man's desire for glory and the sultan's pleasure handicapped the campaign. The Ottoman landing was unopposed. They soon arrived at the main harbor, where La Valette had placed his troops in several forts. Fort Saint Elmo controlled the harbor passes and was the most strategic place on Malta. Mustapha Pasha and Piyale agreed on the need to capture Saint Elmo; no Ottoman ship was safe attempting to sail into the harbor as long as the Knights controlled the fort.

The fight for Fort Saint Elmo began on May 25, 1565. Ot-

---

70. Numbers of troops from Pickles, *Malta 1565*, 23; number of artillery pieces from Crowley, *Empires of the Sea*, 95–96.
71. Crowley, *Empires of the Sea*, 111.

toman engineers estimated the fort would fall within a week. But the Christians held their ground and made the Ottomans pay dearly for every inch of territory. As the fight for the fort slogged into June, both sides engaged in fierce hand-to-hand combat and heavy sniper activity. Turkish artillery pounded the fort, lobbing six thousand cannon balls per day. It was only a matter of time before the fort fell into Ottoman hands. The defenders knew the time was near when a cannonball decapitated the fort's commander on the twenty-sixth day of the siege. The remaining Knights and soldiers believed they could withstand only one more attack, which came on June 23. Only sixty defenders were left, and the two senior officers were unable to stand due to their wounds. They sat in chairs in the breach to fight; both were shot dead in the final assault.[72] As the Turks poured into the fort, they made quick work of the remaining defenders. Only five Maltese soldiers were known to have survived the final assault; they ran down to the shore and swam across the harbor.[73] Some soldiers tried to surrender to the Turks to save their lives, but these were lined up on a wall and shot. The bodies were then hung upside down, the heads and chest were split open, and the hearts ripped out.[74] The thirty-one-day siege resulted in 4,000 Turks and 1,500 Christians killed.[75] Although the Turks could absorb the losses better than the Christians, it was a heavy price to pay for such a small, yet strategic, fort. Mustapha Pasha, looking across the harbor to the main fortress of Saint Michael the Archangel, remarked, "Allah! If so small a son has cost us so dear, what price shall we have to pay for so large a father!"[76]

Mustapha Pasha hoped to demoralize the remaining Christian troops across the harbor. He ordered some of the bodies of

72. Desmond Seward, *The Monks of War: The Military Religious Orders* (New York: Penguin Books, 1995), 283.
73. Pickles, *Malta 1565*, 45.
74. Crowley, *Empires of the Sea*, 139.
75. Ibid., 142.
76. Bradford, *The Great Siege*, 123, quoted in Warren H. Carroll and Anne W. Carroll, *The Crisis of Christendom: A History of Christendom*, vol. 6 (Front Royal, VA: Christendom Press, 2013), 827.

the Knights to be stripped of their armor, their hearts ripped out, and heads cut off. Each headless corpse was then marked with a cross cut into their chest and finally nailed by the hands and feet to a wooden cross, placed in the water, and floated across the harbor to the Christian defenses.[77] La Valette responded to the Ottoman atrocity by beheading captured Muslim soldiers, loading the heads into his cannons, and firing them into the Muslim camp. This nasty exchange illustrates the fact that both sides knew this was a fight to the death, with huge stakes for either the advancement of the Muslim banner or for the safety of Christendom.

The battle for Malta continued for two more months. La Valette urged his Knights and soldiers to fight bravely against overwhelming odds while also participating in direct combat. Wounded by a Turkish grenade during one assault, La Valette refused to leave the front, saying, "How can it be possible for a man of my age to die more gloriously than among my brethren and my friends in the service of God, in defense of our holy religion?"[78]

As the calendar turned to September, the Christian defenders received the blessing of good news on the feast of the Nativity of the Blessed Virgin Mary; ten thousand Spanish troops, the long-awaited relief force from Sicily, arrived in eighty ships.[79] The Spanish reinforcements began their march toward the harbor to relieve La Valette's troops on September 11, 1565. Mustapha Pasha knew defeat loomed on the horizon; after losing a battle to the Spanish troops, he ordered a general retreat. Malta was saved.

The siege of Malta proved an epic and costly struggle for the center of the Mediterranean. The Turks lost 50 percent of the fighting strength of their invasion force, whereas La Valette lost 50 percent of his Knights and 2,500 Maltese troops.[80] An addi-

77. Seward, The Monks of War, 284; and Crowley, Empires of the Sea, 140.
78. Vertot, Histoire des Chevaliers Hospitaliers de S. Jean de Jerusalem, vol. IV, 51, quoted in Seward, The Monks of War, 286.
79. Crowley, Empires of the Sea, 176.
80. Number of Knights killed from Diane Moczar, Islam at the Gates: How Christendom Defeated the Ottoman Turks (Manchester, NH: Sophia Institute Press, 2008), 157. Number of Maltese killed from Crowley, Empires of the Sea, 185.

tional 7,000 Maltese men, women, and children died during the siege.[81] Pope Pius IV offered La Valette the cardinal's hat for his valiant defense of Malta, but the humble warrior refused the offer. He would live another five years, dying from a stroke suffered during the summer heat after he returned from a hunt. He was buried on the island he so gallantly defended.

Although the Ottomans faltered at Malta, they remained a strong force. Selim II (r. 1566–1574), the successor of Suleiman the Magnificent, conquered Cyprus in 1571, but his sights were on a much more impressive prize: Rome. He called the Eternal City the "red apple" because he believed it was ripe for the plucking. Pope Pius V, aware of the Turkish threat to Rome and Christendom, wrote letters to the major European secular rulers, pleading with them to unite in the face of the Ottoman threat. Most ignored the papal exhortation. Despite the lack of response, Pius kept pressing for an alliance to mitigate the Ottoman threat. Eventually, the persistent pontiff proved successful in his efforts. A Holy League alliance between Spain, Venice, and the Papal States was formed on March 7, 1571.

THE BATTLE OF LEPANTO

Selim and his military advisers knew that a successful invasion of Rome required a massive fleet, which they began to assemble. The fleet was ready by the fall of 1571; plans were made to conquer Rome and, eventually, Christian Europe. The Ottoman campaign required crafting large numbers of oared galleys.[82] These galleys were ships with limited range that operated in the littoral areas near the shore. They rarely ventured into open ocean and could only do so for short periods of time, because they required vast

---

81. Francisco Balbi di Correggio, *The Siege of Malta, 1565*, trans. Ernle Bradford (Rochester, NY: The Boydell Press, 2005), 189.
82. The best image of galley warfare comes from the 1959 movie *Ben Hur* starring Charlton Heston; although that movie was set in the time of the Roman Empire, the sixteenth-century Mediterranean oared galley was not much different from the Roman vessels portrayed in the movie.

amounts of potable water for the oarsmen. Originally, volunteers manned the oars, but, by the sixteenth century, chained slaves and conscripts — especially Christian slaves captured by Muslim pirates — provided the manpower. Life as a galley oarsman was akin to servitude in hell, as "the galley was an amoebic death trap, a swilling sewer whose stench was so foul you could smell it two miles off."[83] Galleys were periodically sunk to cleanse the filth. As the deployment season of 1571 came to a close, the Ottoman fleet anchored in their fortified port of Lepanto, situated at the mouth of the Gulf of Corinth. Lepanto was a strategic location; an attacker would waste valuable energy and time trying to row against the prevailing Mediterranean wind to get into the gulf, while the defender could sit and wait to attack until exhaustion took the enemy fleet out of action.

Ali Pasha commanded the Ottoman fleet in 1571, which consisted of 300 war galleys, 100,000 men, and 14,000 Christian galley slaves. The Holy League fleet, consisting of 208 ships, had assembled in Naples in August. It was commanded by Don Juan of Austria, the twenty-four-year-old illegitimate son of Holy Roman Emperor Charles V. Among the 26,000 Holy Leaguers was the future well-known Spanish author Miguel de Cervantes.[84]

The fleets engaged in combat on Sunday morning, October 7, 1571. Chaplains scattered throughout the fleet blessed the Christian troops and granted them general absolution. Don Juan left his flagship, the *Real*, with the words "Very well, let's fight!" to his staff, and sailed in a light frigate past the fleet's galleys.[85]

---

83. Crowley, *Empires of the Sea*, 77.
84. Cervantes fought well in the battle, was wounded, and suffered the loss of using his left hand for the rest of his life. Despite his wound, Cervantes later wrote that the battle was "the greatest day's work seen for centuries." Jack Beeching, *The Galleys at Lepanto* (New York: Charles Scribner's Sons, 1982), 216. Cervantes would recall the Battle of Lepanto in his most famous work, *Don Quixote*, when he wrote, "Those Christians who died there were even happier than those who remained alive and victorious," quoted in Victor Davis Hanson, *Carnage and Culture* (New York: Anchor Books, 2001), 253.
85. P. de Bourdeille de Brantome, *Oeuvres complétes*, ed. L. Lalanne, vol. 3 (Paris: Hachette BNF Book, 1864), 125, quoted in Crowley, *Empires of the Sea*, 256.

Carrying a crucifix, he urged his men on: "You have come to fight the battle of the Cross — to conquer or to die. But whether you die or conquer, do your duty this day, and you will secure a glorious immortality."[86] Don Juan moved his fleet into the shape of a cross — a formation that took three hours to complete, due to its intricacy and the number of galleys.[87] The Christian oarsmen were pressed hard as they sailed against the prevailing wind to the mouth of Lepanto.

Aware that the Christian fleet was outside the gulf and eager for battle, Ali Pasha chose to leave the sheltered anchorage and venture forth to win victory for the sultan. He formed his galleys into the shape of a crescent, a traditional Muslim land and sea military formation. It was symbolic, but it also effectively used the Islamic strategy of encirclement and annihilation. At the Battle of Lepanto, the cross and the crescent literally clashed for control of the center of the world.

Don Juan was confident of victory. He trusted in the Lord and had special weapons, which he believed gave his outnumbered fleet the advantage. The Venetians had outfitted six large transport ships, which they called galleasses, with side-mounted, as well as bow-mounted, cannons — fifty guns in total. Contemporary naval convention used only bow-mounted cannon on galleys, which limited the number of available pieces. The galleasses were towed into position by other ships and did not need oarsmen, so the extra room on the deck was filled with five hundred arquebusiers. These special ships wreaked havoc on the Ottoman fleet at the beginning of the battle, devastating the center formation of Ali Pasha's ships. Don Juan's use of these galleasses revolutionized naval warfare; soon, side-mounted cannons became the naval norm. In addition, Don Juan relied on special spiritual weapons. Each man in the fleet was given a rosary and was asked to pray to Our Lady for victory in the battle.

---

86. G. K. Chesterton, *Lepanto*, ed. Dale Ahlquist (San Francisco: Ignatius Press, 2003), 62.
87. For the amount of time it took to form up, see Crowley, *Empires of the Sea*, 257.

As the battle continued, the right wing of Admiral Doria's Christian fleet was in trouble. His flagship was under heavy assault, and his force was greatly outnumbered. Fierce fighting waged across the ships. The wind prevented Doria from using his sails and releasing his oarsmen to join the fight. The situation was desperate, but suddenly, the prevailing wind changed direction, allowing the Christians to gain the upper hand.[88] There was no natural explanation for why the wind moved when it did, but on Admiral Doria's flagship was a copy of the image of Our Lady of Guadalupe. The archbishop of Mexico, Don Fray Alonso de Montúfar, aware of the Ottoman threat to Christendom, had commissioned a small reproduction of the sacred image. The reproduced image had been touched to the real *tilma* of Juan Diego and sent to King Philip II with instructions to give it to the Holy League. It is no coincidence that, at the moment of direst need, Our Lady came to the rescue of Admiral Doria's flotilla and miraculously saved the day at Lepanto.

The Battle of Lepanto ended in an overwhelming victory for the Christian forces. The final tally was 237 Turkish galleys destroyed or captured and 25,000 dead Ottoman troops. The Holy League fleet lost only twelve ships.[89]

While Don Juan was assessing his grand victory, and before news reached Rome, Pope Pius V was meeting with his treasurer. He suddenly stood up, went to the window, and said, "This is not a moment for business; make haste to thank God, because our fleet this moment has won a victory over the Turks."[90] In commemoration of the salvation of Rome and Christendom, in 1572 Pius V established the annual celebration of the feast of Our Lady of Victory. A year later, his successor, Gregory XIII (r. 1572–1585), changed the name to the feast of Our Lady of the Rosary, to highlight the important role played by that special spiritual weapon in

---

88. Crowley, *Empires of the Sea*, 260.
89. Ibid., 276.
90. Moczar, *Islam at the Gates*, 192.

the victory over the Ottoman Turks.

VICTORY AT VIENNA

A little more than a hundred years after the victory at Lepanto, Christendom was once more threatened by the Ottoman horde. The Turks had solidified their hold on the Balkans, and they were gathering strength for an attack on the gateway of Europe, the highly cultured and strategic city of Vienna.

Holy Roman Emperor Leopold I (r. 1658–1705) engaged in a diplomatic policy of appeasement with the Ottomans because he was more concerned about his belligerent neighbor, King Louis XIV (r. 1643–1715) of France. Some of Leopold's advisers believed the once-mighty Ottoman military was weak and ineffective compared to the strong and large standing army of the Sun King. Concerned with French intentions and military might, Leopold entered into a peace treaty with the Ottoman Turks in 1665. Despite the treaty, Muslim and Christian warriors fought frequent, but neither large nor decisive, border clashes. Hedging his bets, Leopold entered into defense treaties with other European nations, including Poland, to come to his aid should the Turks invade. The treaty with the Turks was set to expire in 1684, but the emperor was confident it could be extended. Unbeknownst to him, the Ottomans had decided a year earlier to break the treaty and invade Austria.

Mehmet IV (r. 1648–1687), the son of Ibrahim the Debauched and a Russian concubine, became sultan of the Ottoman Empire at the young age of seven. Mehmet gave executive powers to his grand viziers, as his desire for outdoor sport precluded his attention to political, military, and diplomatic affairs. At a meeting on August 6, 1682, his advisers persuaded Mehmet that the time was right to break the treaty with Leopold, invade imperial territory, and conquer Vienna. The invasion commenced in 1683, with an army of one hundred thousand men under the command of the grand vizier Kara Mustapha (1634–1683). Kara

Mustapha was a veteran of numerous military campaigns and a ruthless commander willing to accept heavy casualties. He also hated Christians; overly confident of victory, he openly bragged that he would stable his horses in St. Peter's Basilica.[91] The Ottoman army crossed the frontier in late June 1683, rampaging and pillaging as they marched.

Vienna was not prepared for a siege. The outer defensive fortifications had been badly maintained over the years, and extensive suburbs near the main defenses limited effective fields of fire on an advancing army. Rüdiger von Starhemberg was appointed commander of Vienna's defenses, and quickly recognized that the best he could hope for was to hold out long enough for the allied relief force to reach the city. The Ottoman army arrived at the city on July 14 and, as was their tradition and custom, arranged their camp around the city in the shape of a crescent.[92] In short order, Kara Mustapha encircled the city and cut it off. Throughout the siege, the Ottoman army bombarded the Viennese with music as a form of psychological warfare. The residents of the city of music returned the favor so that, at times, one could hear a melodious tune wafting over the siege lines.[93]

As soon as news reached Leopold I that the Turks were on the move, he reached out to his allies and begged them to come to Vienna's aid. Jan Sobieski (r. 1676–1696), the King of Poland, responded to his treaty obligations, raising a relief army. He left Warsaw with an army of twenty thousand men, mostly cavalry, on the way to Cracow, where the rest of his troops were ordered to assemble. Along the march, Sobieski stopped to pray at the shrine of Our Lady of Czestochowa.[94] Entrusting the success of his military efforts to the intercession of the Blessed Mother, his army

91. Ibid.
92. Simon Millar, *Vienna 1683: Christian Europe Repels the Ottomans* (New York: Osprey Publishing, 2008), 44.
93. John Stoye, *The Siege of Vienna: The Last Great Trial Between the Cross and Crescent* (New York: Pegasus Books, 2006), 108.
94. Ibid., 131.

began the march to Vienna on the solemnity of the Assumption of the Blessed Virgin Mary, August 15, 1683. His forces were buoyed by the knowledge that Pope Blessed Innocent XI (r. 1676–1689) had granted the crusading plenary indulgence to all who fought for the defense and relief of Vienna.[95]

Starhemberg and his defenders fought valiantly for a month, but by the end of August and into early September food was scarce in the city. Flour supplies were running low, so bakers ceased making full loaves of bread. Instead, they made smaller pieces that they shaped in the form of a crescent to remind the inhabitants of the reason for their meager rations.[96] Disease was also rampant; out of an original complement of 13,000 troops, Starhemberg's effective defenders had dwindled to 5,000. It was only a matter of time before the Ottomans broke into the city.

The allied relief army arrived near Vienna on September 9. Sobieski prepared to attack the Ottomans using the high ground of the Kahlenberg Mountain on the outskirts of Vienna. The battle began on September 11, 1683, as Kara Mustapha ordered his troops to attack the Christian forces. The unseasonal heat of the day increased the suffering of the soldiers. Both sides were so exhausted by midday that they stopped to regroup and rest. The battle continued through the day until about 5:00 p.m., when Sobieski unleashed his elite armored cavalry, the Winged Hussars, in a cavalry charge that demolished the Ottoman line.[97] The rout was complete; the Ottoman army fell into disarray. Kara Mustapha was captured and later executed on December 25.[98] Polish troops were the first into the city. They were greeted with cheers

---

95. Ibid., 138.

96. Millar, *Vienna 1683*, 93. These small pastries acquired the name *croissant* for their crescent shape and are usually associated with France, but their origin stems from the siege of Vienna and are rightfully considered Austrian. Legend has it that the French adopted the tasty pastry when Marie Antoinette, who was born in Vienna, brought the item with her to France.

97. Known as "winged" hussars because the men wore a wooden frame on their back containing eagle, ostrich, swan, or goose feathers.

98. Ibid., 89.

and prayers of thanksgiving by the beleaguered defenders. Sobieski sent a victory message to Pope Innocent XI that echoed
Charles V's line at the Battle of Mühlberg: "We came, we saw,
God conquered."[99] The pope credited the Christian victory over
the Ottomans and the salvation of the city to the intercession of
the Blessed Mother. He established the feast of the Most Holy
Name of Mary as a result.[100]

The Ottoman campaign to capture the gateway to Europe
and destroy Christendom was a risky operation. Its success would
have ensured Ottoman hegemony over Eastern Europe and
opened up the approaches to Western Europe. Its failure began
the decline and ruin of the Islamic empire. After the victory at
Vienna, the Hapsburgs began the long process of liberating the
Balkans from Ottoman rule. Eventually, the Ottoman Empire became known as the "sick man of Europe" — an empire in name
only.[101]

The success of the Protestant Revolution was due, in part, to
the Ottoman Turkish military campaigns in Europe, which occupied the attention of Holy Roman Emperor Charles V. The
Catholic Reformation succeeded, in part, because the forces of
Christendom faced the Turkish threat and emerged victorious at
Malta, Lepanto, and Vienna, thereby emboldening the Church.
The Catholic Reformation had restored the Church's luminosity,
infused her with missionary zeal, and strengthened her for the
difficult centuries ahead. The Church "no longer doubted the future, as she had once seemed tempted to do. Difficult days might
come; the Word, of which she is the depository, would conquer."[102]

---

99. L. Pukianiec, *Sobieski a Stolica Apostolska na tle wojny z Turcja* (1683–1684) (Vilnius: Zorza Printing House, 1937), 1, quoted in Stoye, *The Siege of Vienna*, 174. Charles V's quote was adopted from Julius Caesar's famous phrase, "I came, I saw, I conquered."
100. Moczar, *Islam at the Gates*, 207.
101. The Turks allied with the German Kaiser in the First World War, declaring their participation a *jihad* in the name of Allah, but they chose the wrong side, and the victorious Allied powers disbanded the Ottoman Empire with the sweep of a pen in 1918. For the Turks declaring World War I a *jihad*, see Norman Housley, *Contesting the Crusades* (Malden, MA: Blackwell Publishing, 2006), 157.
102. Daniel-Rops, *The Catholic Reformation*, vol. 2, 218.

NINE

The Modern Attack

> *"Either the Catholic Church (now rapidly becoming the only place*
> *wherein the traditions of civilization are understood and defended)*
> *will be reduced by her modern enemies to political impotence, to*
> *numerical insignificance, and so far as public appreciation goes, to*
> *silence, or the Catholic Church will ... react more strongly against*
> *her enemies than her enemies have been able to react against her;*
> *she will recover and extend her authority, and rise once more to*
> *the leadership of civilization which she made, and will thus recover*
> *and restore the world."*[1]
>
> HILAIRE BELLOC

War loomed on the horizon. The man who had given his life in service to the Church had seen it coming for decades. Born into a family dedicated

---

1. Hilaire Belloc, *The Great Heresies* (Rockford, IL: TAN Books and Publishers, 1991 [1938]), 155.

to working for the Church (his grandfather, father, and older brother had been canon lawyers and papal advisers), he entered the seminary at the age of eighteen. He was a gifted linguist, learning Greek, Latin, English, French, German, Spanish, Portuguese, and Aramaic. He learned Hebrew from a Jewish friend, in whose house he was a frequent guest. Ordained on Easter Sunday 1899, the young man spent a brief time as a parish priest before his intellectual gifts were directed to the service of the Church. He went to the university and earned doctorates in theology and canon and civil law. Recognizing his unique talents, Pope Benedict XV assigned him to the Vatican Diplomatic Service. When war raged across Europe in 1914, he worked in the newly established Prisoners of War Bureau, which was charged with maintaining a registry of prisoners from all combatants and arranging their exchanges. The young priest saw firsthand the devastating effects of war. Sadly, it was not the only time he witnessed the ravages of war in his lifetime. As the First World War neared its end, he was appointed papal nuncio to Bavaria and then ambassador for all Germany after the armistice was signed. He witnessed firsthand the upheaval in postwar Germany and also saw the political rise of radical groups, like the National Socialist Workers' Party, and radical men, like Adolf Hitler. Extremely troubled by their racial ideology and policies, the priest warned the German people in frequent public speeches, to no avail. The Nazis and Hitler came to power. As Vatican secretary of state, the man continued his campaign against the evil ideology taking root in Germany, crafting the only encyclical originally written in German. When the pope died in 1939, the cardinals knew they had only one choice for a successor: Eugenio Pacelli, who took the name Pius XII.

THE GALILEO AFFAIR

The Church is not opposed to science. She teaches that faith and reason are not incompatible, but each must be comprehended within its respective area. Faith is concerned with the truths of divine revelation, which are metaphysical — that is, beyond physics — whereas science is concerned with observations of the material world.[2] Because faith and science are aspects of one truth, they cannot contradict each other. In fact, Church teaching that reason is a gift from God, and that nature is orderly and intelligible, is what made possible the explosion of scientific discovery and knowledge in Christian Europe. Most of the dramatic scientific advances in the sixteenth and seventeenth centuries were made by faithful Christian scholars, based in Christian universities, who stood on the shoulders of the Catholic scholars and scientists of preceding centuries.[3] Catholic clergy pioneered many fields of science during the time of rapid discoveries in the seventeenth, eighteenth, and nineteenth centuries. The fathers of geology (Nicolaus Steno, 1638–1686), Egyptology (Athanasius Kircher, 1602–1680), and modern atomic theory (Roger Boscovich, 1711–1787) were Catholic priests. The father of genetics, Gregor Mendel (1822–1884), was an Augustinian friar. Members of the Society of Jesus spearheaded many scientific advances; no fewer than thirty-five craters on the moon are named for Jesuits.[4] In all, the vast majority of scientists who made great advancements in their fields were men of Christian faith.[5]

The modern myth of an anti-science Catholic Church centers on the figure of Galileo Galilei (1564–1642). The "Galileo affair" is one of the most misunderstood and mischaracterized episodes in Church history, the truth of which centers on the arrogance and duplicity of Galileo himself, who, "though not plagued with a martyr complex, considered himself a martyr without seeing that he

---

2. The following section is adapted from my book *The Real Story of Catholic History: Answering Twenty Centuries of Anti-Catholic Myths* (El Cajon, CA: Catholic Answers Press, 2017), 145–151.

3. See Rodney Stark, *Bearing False Witness: Debunking Centuries of Anti-Catholic History* (West Conshohocken, PA: Templeton Press, 2016), 144. These scholars and scientists include Robert Grosseteste (1168–1253), an English bishop, who made contributions to optics, physics, and astronomy; Saint Albert the Great (1206–1280), a Dominican university professor and botanist who made advances in geography, astronomy, and chemistry; Roger Bacon (1214–1294), a Franciscan who contributed to the knowledge of mathematics, astronomy, the physiology of eyesight, and optics, and concocted a recipe for gunpowder; and Nicole D'Oresme (1325–1382), bishop of Lisieux, who proved that the earth turns on its axis.

4. Ibid., 4.

5. Sixty percent, in fact. See Stark, *Bearing False Witness*, 153–155.

was largely responsible for bringing martyrdom upon himself."[6]

The story of Galileo's struggle with the Church begins with the Polish scientist Nicolaus Copernicus (1473–1543). An uncle, who was a Catholic bishop, raised Copernicus and sent him to study at the universities of Cracow, Bologna, and Padua. In 1530, Copernicus put forth his theory that the earth revolves around the sun (heliocentrism), which was well received by Pope Clement VII. In 1533, the pope invited the German astronomer Johann Widmannstadt to give a public lecture on the theory in the Vatican gardens.[7] Several years later, Copernicus published his theory in his *Six Books on the Revolutions of the Celestial Orbits*, which he dedicated to Pope Paul III. His theory and book were well received in Catholic circles, though not in Protestant ones. Martin Luther wrote: "People give ear to an upstart astrologer who strove to show that the earth revolves, not the heavens or the firmament, the sun, and the moon. This fool wishes to reverse the entire science of astronomy; but Sacred Scripture tells us that Joshua commanded the sun to stand still, and not the earth."[8] John Calvin derided Copernicus's theory, calling those who believed it "frantic people who would like to change the order of nature."[9] Copernicus was careful to treat heliocentrism as a theory, not proven fact. Although it did find supporters, most scientists did not accept it, because the prevailing scientific thought accepted the Aristotelian-Ptolemaic geocentric view of the universe.

Galileo was born on February 15, 1564, in Pisa, but the family returned to their ancestral home of Florence when he was a ten-year-old boy. Galileo initially believed he had a religious vocation and spent time in a monastic community. His father wanted him to become a doctor, so he enrolled at the University

---

6. Stanley L. Jaki, *Galileo Lessons* (Pinckney, MI: Real View Books, 2001), 17.

7. Jerome L. Langford, *Galileo, Science, and the Church*, 3rd ed. (Ann Arbor, MI: University of Michigan Press, 1992), 35.

8. Ibid.

9. B. Cottret, *Calvin: A Biography* (Grand Rapids, MI: Eerdmans, 2000), 285–286, quoted in MacCulloch, 686.

of Pisa in 1581 but, due to financial difficulties, did not complete his studies. Galileo traveled to Rome in 1587 and met with
several scientists, including the Jesuit Christopher Clavius. His
Roman friends helped him secure an appointment as a professor
of mathematics at the University of Pisa in 1589. Galileo left
Pisa after a few years to accept the chair of mathematics at the
University of Padua. While in Pisa, Galileo met Maria Gamba,
who became his mistress and with whom he had a son and two
daughters. In 1610, Galileo returned to Florence where he held
the position as the personal mathematician and philosopher for
the Duke of Tuscany.

Galileo published the book *Sidereus Nuncius* (*The Starry Messenger*) in March 1610. The work contained findings from his
astronomical observations with the telescope.[10] After the publication of his book, Galileo was invited to Rome, where he was
well treated by cardinals, bishops, Jesuit scientists, and where he
participated in a long audience with Pope Paul V (r. 1605–1621).
The following year, Galileo observed the phases of Venus with his
telescope, which he argued could only be explained if Venus or-
bited around the sun and not the earth. Galileo was convinced by
his astronomical observations that Copernicus's heliocentric theory was true; he began to publicly support it. Although Galileo's
observations "certainly demolished geocentrism as part of Aristotelian cosmology and physics," they did not provide "physical
proof" of heliocentrism as he claimed they did.[11] (Indeed, incon-
trovertible proof of the Copernican theory was not achieved until
1838 by Friedrich Wilhelm Bessel, who made the first successful
measurement of stellar parallax.[12])

Although some high-ranking officials in the Church were
initially supportive of Galileo's work, others believed the Coper-

---

10. Although it is sometimes claimed that Galileo invented the telescope, the real inventor of the
telescope was the German-Dutch eyeglasses maker Hans Lippershey (1570–1619); however, Galileo
did make improvements to the telescope, including increasing its magnifying power.
11. Jaki, 9,18.
12. Stellar parallax is the "apparent displacement of a celestial body brought about by the change in
position of the observer." See Langford, 43.

nican theory contradicted Scripture, which, in various passages, seems to indicate that the sun revolves around the earth.[13] Other scientists besides Galileo, including the Carmelite friar Paolo Foscarini (1565–1616), argued for the truth of heliocentrism. Foscarini affirmed Copernicus's theory in his 1615 book *Opinion of the Pythagoreans and Copernicus Regarding the Motion of the Earth*. Foscarini tried to show that the heliocentric theory was not contrary to Scripture. He sent a copy of the book to Robert Cardinal Bellarmine (1542–1621) in Rome, who praised Foscarini for advocating heliocentrism as theory rather than provable scientific fact. Bellarmine noted that current exegesis and theological interpretation of Scripture supported geocentrism and could not change until physical proof of heliocentrism was provided.

The Church was very sensitive to Protestant charges about her interpretation of Scripture, and this fact undergirded her reaction to Galileo. Galileo was not content to teach Copernicus's thought as theory; he earnestly believed it was true, and he wanted the Church to support his belief. Friends, both clergy and lay, urged Galileo to bide his time and be patient, but he pressed the issue by traveling to Rome in 1615, where he met with his friend and patron Cardinal Alessandro Orsini (1592–1626). Galileo told Orsini that he had proof of the heliocentric theory. He believed that the tides of the sea proved the earth moved, arguing they could not occur if the earth was stationary. Orsini discussed the issue with Pope Paul V, who referred the matter to the Roman Inquisition. The Inquisition met to discuss the Copernican theory on February 26, 1616, and ruled that the motion of the earth was not "directly contrary to Scripture, but opposed to a doctrine which pertained to the faith according to the common consensus of learned theologians."[14] Cardinal Bellarmine informed Galileo that the Inquisition prohibited the public teaching and defense of

---

13. See Joshua 10:12–14 and Psalms 92:1.
14. Langford, 90. The ruling, with the eyes of hindsight, was imprudent and a scientific matter not within the competency of the Inquisition. It was not an infallible teaching of the Church, as it was "issued in a reformable manner by a fallible authority." See Langford, 101.

the Copernican theory, but allowed that it could be investigated privately. Afterward, Galileo met with Paul V, who assured the scientist he was not in trouble.

Galileo abided by the Inquisition's decision for the following eight years, but at the election of his friend and supporter, Maffeo Barberini, as pope — taking the name Urban VIII (r. 1623–1644) — Galileo once more traveled to Rome. In 1624, Galileo met with the pope, who believed the Copernican theory needed more discussion and scientific observation and should not be treated as proven fact or used to answer theological questions.

In 1629, Galileo began to write a book that he hoped would provide "a most ample confirmation of the Copernican system."[15] He titled the book *Dialogue Concerning the Two Chief World Systems* and structured it as a four-day conversation between three philosophers in Venice. The first philosopher argued in favor of the Copernican theory. The second philosopher served as a neutral referee and commentator, and the third character argued in favor of the standard Aristotelian view. The third philosopher was also the butt of the jokes of the first philosopher, who called him *Simplicio*, or "simpleton/idiot." Galileo utilized arguments favored by Pope Urban VIII for the Aristotelian view in the mouth of the third philosopher (which greatly angered the pontiff when the book was published). The first day of dialogue consisted of the first philosopher urging the reader to abandon the Aristotelian cosmology. The second focused on the possibility that the earth moved. The third day was a discussion concerning the evidence for and against the Aristotelian and Copernican theories, and the fourth day was a presentation of Galileo's "proof" for Copernicanism: the tides.

The book was published in 1632 and quickly sold out its first printing. Although confident in his argument supporting heliocentrism, Galileo "did not prove that the earth moves. He did succeed in showing that it is not impossible for the earth to

---

15. Ibid., 116.

move."[16] In the end, Galileo's book was a huge gamble. Galileo thought "he could compel the Church to see its mistake, revoke the prohibition, and adopt the new astronomy."[17] Pope Urban established a special commission to review Galileo's book. The commission ruled that Galileo had violated the injunction of the 1616 Inquisition, which forbade publicly treating the Copernican theory as truth. As a result of the commission's findings, Galileo received a summons from the Roman Inquisition to answer for his book. The scientist arrived in Rome on January 23, 1633. Contrary to standard practice, the seventy-year-old Galileo was not required to stay in an ecclesiastical jail; rather, he luxuriated in a five-room suite at the Tuscan embassy, where he was given a personal servant. The Inquisition questioned him during four meetings about his violation of its 1616 ruling. Galileo admitted he went too far in the *Dialogue*. He offered to publish an addition to it arguing against the Copernican theory.[18] He even denied the Copernican theory was true, although his book clearly articulated support for it. The Inquisition deliberated and eventually ruled in June 1633 that Galileo's writings were "vehemently suspect of heresy." The *Dialogue* was placed on the Roman Index of Prohibited Books, and Galileo was required to publicly recant his teaching, which he did.[19] As part of his penance, he was sentenced to three years' imprisonment, which was immediately commuted.

---

16. Ibid., 127.

17. Ibid., 133–134.

18. Ibid., 145.

19. Galileo's book was not banned throughout Christendom; as an example, it was never placed on the Index in Spain. Galileo never uttered the phrase "yet it moves" under his breath after his recantation, as is believed in modern retellings of the proceedings against him. Giuseppe Baretti concocted this false addition to the Galileo Affair in his book *Italian Library*, published in 1757. Galileo's recantation consisted of the following statement: "I, Galileo, swear that I have always believed, do believe, and with God's help will in the future believe all that is held, preached, and taught by the Holy Catholic and Apostolic Church. I must altogether abandon the false opinion that the sun is the center of the world and immobile, and that the earth is not the center of the world and moves, and that I must not hold, defend, or teach, in any way, verbally or in writing, the said false doctrine, and after it had been notified to me that the said doctrine was contrary to Holy Scripture. I have been judged to be vehemently suspected of heresy, that is, of having held and believed that the sun is the center of the world and immobile and that the earth is not the center and moves. I abjure, curse and detest the aforesaid errors and heresies and also every other error and sect contrary to the Holy Church." See Langford, 154.

He lived in limited house arrest with freedom of movement. He was also required to recite the seven penitential psalms once a week for three years, but his petition that his daughter, a Carmelite nun, be allowed to say them for him was granted. Galileo was neither tortured during the course of his trial, nor was he even shown the instruments of torture, which was standard inquisitorial practice. He continued to make scientific observations for the rest of his life and died in 1642, the year of Isaac Newton's birth.

In an effort to set the historical record straight, Pope Saint John Paul II (r. 1978–2005) established a commission to study the Galileo affair. In 1992, the commission issued a report stating that "it is in that historical and cultural framework [i.e. in the aftermath of the Reformation when the Church was under severe attack], far removed from our own times, that Galileo's judges, incapable of dissociating faith from an age-old cosmology, believed, quite wrongly, that the adoption of the Copernican revolution, in fact not yet definitively proven, was such as to undermine Catholic tradition, and that it was their duty to forbid its being taught. This subjective error of judgment, so clear to us today, led them to a disciplinary measure from which Galileo 'had much to suffer.'"[20]

Ultimately, the Galileo affair illustrates that the different yet complementary areas of faith and science must be respected: "The lesson [of Galileo and the Church] lies. ... in its dramatic verification of what disaster can come to science or faith when either of these is extended beyond its proper boundaries and enters the domain of the other."[21] Science should not seek to answer metaphysical questions that are the proper domain of revelation and theology — which, in turn, must respect the method and authentic observations of science. In other words, "Revelation is about the way of going to heaven and not about the way the heavens go."[22]

---

20. Robert P. Lockwood, "Galileo and the Catholic Church," accessed September 20, 2018, http://www.catholicleague.org/galileo-and-the-catholic-church/.
21. Langford, 180.
22. Jaki, 24.

THE "ENLIGHTENMENT"

As the family of God moved into the seventeenth and eighteenth centuries, the revolution in theology brought about by Protestantism influenced philosophical thinking; the world moved from the Age of Faith to the Age of Reason, which was dominated by intellectuals who disliked religion and desired to discredit the Church and her influence in society.[23] The intellectuals of the age believed a society without religion would be "enlightened," better off free from the shackles of the Church, which was seen as "worn out, immature, inherently hypocritical, hostile to progress, and above all, unreasonable."[24] French author Denis Diderot (1713–1784) captured the view of these writers when he said, "Man will never be free until the last king is strangled with the entrails of the last priest."[25]

The "Enlightenment" developed a new understanding of philosophy. The Catholic understanding of philosophy viewed it as the second highest science, after theology, and taught that the proper philosophical method involved reasoning based on observation of reality. Enlightened thinkers wanted to remake philosophy into a mathematically-expressible science, and believed theology and philosophy were incompatible. This method ultimately divorced philosophy from reality and focused on man and his mind. Enlightened philosophers were preoccupied with knowledge, and began with the question, "How do we know we know anything?" One of the major questions of knowledge at the time concerned the certainty of existence — and one philosopher sought a way to definitively answer that question.

René Descartes (1596–1650) was a devout, Jesuit-educated Catholic, and a one-time soldier who had fought in the nasty and brutal Thirty Years' War. Descartes, considered the "Father of

---

23. Thomas Paine, the American War of Independence propagandist and author of *Common Sense*, coined the term "Age of Reason" while in prison in Paris in 1793–1794. See Stark, *Bearing False Witness*, 91.

24. Brennan Pursell, *History in His Hands: A Christian Narrative of the West* (New York: Crossroad, 2011), 192.

25. Stark, *Bearing False Witness*, 194.

Philosophy," developed the method of rationalism. He wanted to bring certitude to the philosophical question of human existence; he reasoned that, if everything was in doubt and nothing was assumed to be certain, then the only certainty is that we doubt. He rationalized that the only certain, clear, and distinct idea that cannot be doubted is that man thinks — and if he thinks, he exists, which Descartes succinctly described with the Latin phrase *cogito ergo sum* ("I think; therefore I am"). Descartes also reasoned that the next certain idea is that God exists. He did not intend to develop a philosophical method that would lead to skepticism and the denial of God's existence, but philosophers who came after him utilized his methodology to do so. This fundamental shift in human reasoning invaded all forms of intellectual pursuits during the Enlightenment, and led to the creation of a man-centered society that, at best, rejected God and the Church — and, at worst, actively persecuted Christians and sought the eradication of the Church from the public square. Enlightenment thinkers realized that if their method of reason was to change society, they needed to control the centers of higher learning, the universities, which were controlled by the Jesuits.

The Society of Jesus numbered nearly 23,000 men at the end of the eighteenth century and managed hundreds of universities and seminaries in Europe. The Jesuits became the target of the Enlightenment not only because of their control of higher education, but also because their loyalty to the Roman pontiff represented a strong obstacle to central state authority. Additionally, their defense of indigenous people in the New World colonies angered many secular rulers. The attack against the Society began in Portugal. The Marquis de Pombal became the chief minister for King Joseph in August 1750 and began a propaganda campaign against the Jesuits. In 1755, he convinced the king to sign a decree denouncing them and ordering their expulsion from Portugal and Brazil.

France was the scene of the next assault on the Jesuits. The French thinker and author François-Marie Arouet (1694–1778), who took the name Voltaire, waged a fierce campaign of satire and ridicule against the Church. He was one of the authors of the *Encyclopedia*, a collection of articles on various subjects, many of which contained attacks on the Church. Voltaire was arrested because of his writings and spent prison time in the Bastille, as well as exile in England. Although educated by the Jesuits, he actively sought their suppression. In 1773, he wrote: "Once we have destroyed the Jesuits, we shall have our own way with the infamous thing [the Church]. [When the Jesuits are suppressed] in twenty years there will be nothing left of the Church."[26] The *Parlement* in 1761 issued a decree banning French subjects from entering the Society, banned the Jesuits from teaching theology, and prohibited attendance at Jesuit-run schools.[27] Three years later, the *Parlement* urged King Louis XV (r. 1715–1774) to completely suppress the order. On December 1, 1764, the king expelled the Jesuits from France and all its dominions. Despite the Society's expulsion from Portugal and France, the papacy still supported the Society. Pope Clement XIII (r. 1758–1769) issued a bull in support of the order in 1765.

Sadly, the next attack against the Jesuits occurred in the home country of their founder, Saint Ignatius Loyola. In Spain, King Charles III (r. 1759–1788) relied on two Italians as his chief ministers, both of whom hated the Jesuits. They convinced the king to order the suppression of the Society from Spain and its territories in April 1767. Although Clement XIII remained steadfast in support of the Jesuits despite increasing secular pressure, his successor did not. In the "papacy's most shameful hour," Pope Clement XIV (r. 1769–1774) issued an order of suppression against the Society of Jesus on July 21, 1773.[28] Clement wrote,

---

26. Martin P. Harney, *The Jesuits in History* (New York: The America Press, 1941), 292, quoted in Warren H. Carroll and Anne Carroll, *The Revolution against Christendom: A History of Christendom*, vol. 5 (Front Royal, VA: Christendom Press, 2005), 83.

27. The French *Parlement* comprised thirteen provincial sovereign courts of law staffed by the nobility and acted as the registrar and approval authority of royal decrees.

28. Eamon Duffy, *Saints and Sinners: A History of the Popes* (New Haven, CT: Yale University Press, 2006), 246.

"After a mature deliberation, we do, out of our certain knowledge, and the fullness of our Apostolic power, suppress and abolish the said Company; we deprive it of all activity whatever, of its houses, schools, colleges, hospitals, [and] lands."[29] Clement indicated in his order of suppression that he made this decision partly because the Jesuits had sowed seeds of dissension and discord among secular rulers, other religious orders, and in the universities. The Society effectively ceased to exist for a generation until it was reestablished by Pope Pius VII (r. 1800–1823) on August 7, 1814.

JANSENISM

In the sixteenth and seventeenth centuries, a heresy developed in France that still echoes in the modern world. Initially formulated by Michel de Bay (d. 1589), who was influenced by the Protestant teachings of Martin Luther, the heresy derived its name from the Dutch bishop Cornelius Jansen (d. 1638), who adopted and elaborated on de Bay's teachings.[30] Jansen had been a professor at the University of Louvain, where he had published a book on Saint Augustine's thoughts on the doctrine of grace. Jansen interpreted Augustine with a Lutheran and Calvinist bent. He believed that justification is a special grace that does not require personal cooperation, and that good works do not contribute to salvation. Jansenism also embraced other Protestant doctrines, including the depravity of man and the irresistibility of God's grace. Additionally, Jansenists believed that grace is not given to everyone, only a select few, a doctrine similar to Calvinist predestination. Adopting a Lutheran understanding, Jansenists saw God as a fearsome judge, not a loving Father. The sect maintained the sacraments but believed they could only be received after careful and prolonged deliberation — especially the Eucharist, which was infrequently received by the lay faithful. Jansenist priests were known

---

29. Clement XIV, *Dominus ac Redemptor*, quoted in G. B. Nicolini, *History of the Jesuits: Their Origin, Progress, Doctrines and Designs* (London: George Bell and Sons, 1876).
30. De Bay's teachings were condemned by Rome in 1560 and he retracted them.

482 | CHAPTER NINE

for giving severe penances in confession as well. The Jansenists clashed with the Jesuits, whom they accused of laxity. Jansenists disliked the Jesuit policy of encouraging frequent reception of the Eucharist. The severity practiced by the Jansenists was presented as a form of public piety and attracted adherents. In 1653, Pope Innocent X (r. 1644–1655) established a special commission of cardinals to examine the teachings of Cornelius Jansen, which recommended the condemnation of several.

The French writer and thinker Blaise Pascal (1623–1662), attracted to the extreme penances and ascetical life of the Jansenists, joined the group in 1646. Pascal promoted the Jansenist cause in his 1656 book *Provincial Letters*. Pascal is most known for his incomplete work *Pensées* (which was published eight years after his death). In this work, Pascal outlines the paradox of man — who is capable of the worst atrocities, but who can create the most beautiful pieces of art; who can love and hate, bring life and death to others. Most famous is Pascal's "Wager," in which he argues for the acceptance of the Christian faith because, if it is not true, then one loses nothing by accepting it; but, if it is true, then one gains everything by accepting it. Pascal's defense of Jansenism helped the heresy spread. Opposition from King Louis XIV (r. 1643–1715) and condemnation from Pope Alexander VII (r. 1655–1667), who required all clergy and religious to sign a statement against Jansenism, effectively reduced the heresy to a small sect around the abbey of Port-Royal.

GALLICANISM

Although King Louis XIV was not keen to see the spread of the Jansenist heresy throughout France, he was no champion of the Church. Louis XIV desired absolute control over France. He worked to consolidate his power over the French nobility, which he primarily did through the use of his palace at Versailles. The size of the palace "made it possible for the King to summon and house there all the important nobility of France" in order to influence them to support his policies.[31] Louis XIV thought the Church in France should be subject to the king, but not in the English way (with the monarch as the head of the Church). Louis respected the papacy (to an extent) and wanted the Church in France to be doctrinally loyal to Rome while also possessing unique local powers that kept her semi-independent from the pope and more controllable by the monarch. This view became known as Gallicanism. Louis attempted to isolate the Church in France from the pope, which culminated in the 1682 Gallican Articles. These stated that the pope had no secular power, the pope could not depose temporal rulers, secular rulers were not required to obey the pope in temporal matters, the pope was subject to ecumenical councils, the pope's decisions could be overturned by a council, and the pope must respect the ancient customs afforded the Church in France. Pope Innocent XI condemned the Gallican Articles, but they formed Louis's interaction with the Church throughout his reign. Both Jansenism and Gallicanism were attacks against the Church in France, but it would take something much more radical to destroy the Faith in the "Eldest Daughter of the Church."

THE FRENCH REVOLUTION AND THE PERSECUTION OF THE CHURCH

By 1789, the Catholic Church in France appeared to be on solid ground.[32] The Church was organized into 139 dioceses, including 40,000 parishes staffed by 128,000 priests and women religious. She owned 10 percent of the land in France.[33] The country was 98 percent Catholic but was divided into enlightened opponents (mostly intellectuals, artists, and businessmen); enlightened Catholics; Jansenists; practicing Catholics (those who fulfilled the minimum required of the Faith); and pious Catholics (the

31. Carroll, *The Revolution against Christendom*, 6.
32. The following section is adapted from my book *The Real Story of Catholic History*, 299–303.
33. All statistics are from Cardinal Walter Brandmüller, *Light and Shadows: Church History amid Faith, Fact and Legend*, trans. Michael J. Miller (San Francisco, CA: Ignatius Press, 2009), 190.

largest group).[34] France itself was one of the most powerful nations in the world. Its longtime rival, England, had a formidable navy but had just suffered a devastating loss in the American War of Independence (1775–1783) — thanks, in part, to French military assistance to the colonies.

But the long and costly war had run the nation into debt from which it could not recover. Indeed, by the late 1780s, half the royal budget was spent on paying the interest on loans.[35] Enemies of the Church believed the financial crisis could be solved by appropriating the wealth and property of the Church, as had been done in the Protestant nations of Europe. King Louis XVI (r. 1774–1792) did not view that suggestion favorably, but he knew something radical had to be done for the nation to recover. Louis XVI was a good king but was prone to indecision. He loved his people. He refused to increase taxes, ended government control of the grain trade (which reduced the price of bread), made the courts more just, abolished torture of accused prisoners, and ended the custom that required peasants to work on public roads two weeks a year without pay. Though a devout Catholic who loved the Church, he clashed with the increasingly powerful and wealthy nobility.

In the midst of the financial crisis, Louis turned for strength and support to his wife of almost twenty years, Marie Antoinette (1755–1793). The queen was a very independent woman who did not like the subordinate role usually reserved for the wives of French kings. Her mother, Maria Theresa, had reigned for forty years as the Holy Roman Empress. Marie, one of sixteen children, was raised a devout Catholic. At the age of sixteen, she married the future Louis XVI, which required her to move from Austria to France. The marriage produced three children: Marie-Thérèse Charlotte, Louis Joseph (the Dauphin), and Louis Charles. Despite her love for her adopted country, some groups in French society continued to regard her as a foreigner (she was

---

34. Ibid.
35. Pursell, 200.

pejoratively called "The Austrian"). Contemporary journalists depicted her as "a murderous, hedonistic, sexually insatiable lesbian plotting to betray the country to … her native Austria."[36] She was dubbed "Madame Deficit" for her allegedly extravagant lifestyle.[37] Although at first she had thrown elaborate parties and lived ostentatiously, her lifestyle changed as she matured, and her concern for the common people increased.[38]

Enemies of the Church and the monarchy told false stories about the queen to discredit both institutions. One of the most well-known false narratives about Queen Marie was her alleged indifference to the suffering of her subjects during the financial crisis of the 1780s. After the French Revolution, anti-Catholic historians invented the story of how, when told that the starving people of Paris had no bread to eat, she replied, "Let them eat cake." There is no basis for believing she ever said the phrase, and it was never attributed to her during the Revolution. It first appears in Jean-Jacques Rousseau's *Confessions*, which he finished writing in 1769, a year before Marie married Louis and moved to France.[39] The infamous quote was most likely attributed to Maria Theresa of Spain, the first wife of Louis XIV, who had died seventy-two years before Marie Antoinette was born.[40] In reality, Queen Marie cared very deeply for the sufferings of the French people, as illustrated by her establishment of soup kitchens in Paris to feed the hungry.

Faced with the financial crisis, Louis XVI was uncertain what policy to pursue, so he abolished the *Parlement* and convened the Estates-General, a representative advisory body that had not met in 175 years.[41] Discord among the members of the Third Estate,

---

36. David A. Bell, "Five Myths about the French Revolution," *Washington Post*, July 9, 2015, https://www.washingtonpost.com/opinions/5-myths-about-the-french-revolution/2015/07/09/6f27c6f0-25af-11e5-b72c-2b7d516e1e0e_story.html.

37. Hilaire Belloc, *Marie Antoinette* (New York: Tess Press, 1909), 190.

38. Ibid., 77.

39. Carroll, *The Revolution against Christendom*, 116.

40. Ibid., 117. The queen also hated wine and only drank water. See Belloc, *Marie Antoinette*, 77.

41. French society was divided into three estates as follows: First Estate (clergy), Second Estate (nobility), and Third Estate (commoners).

who had double the representation of the other estates but held the same number of votes, eventually led to the creation of a National Assembly, tasked with crafting a national constitution. In the summer of 1789 revolutionaries in Paris stormed the Bastille, a medieval fortress turned royal prison that had become a symbol of the supposed tyranny of the monarchy.[42] Thus began one of the most catastrophic political and religious revolutions in history, whose proponents saw two main obstacles: the monarchy and the Church. Over the next four years, they would abolish one and do grievous harm to the other.

After the revolutionaries seized control in 1789, they imprisoned the royal family in the Tuileries Palace. Less than two years later, Louis, Marie, and their children attempted to escape to the frontier, but were arrested and brought back to Paris. In the summer of 1792 an armed mob descended on the Tuileries and took Louis and Marie into custody, despite a heroic but futile stand by six hundred Swiss Guards.[43] A month later, the monarchy was officially abolished. While the king was incarcerated, the revolutionaries moved against the Church. Church lands were confiscated in November 1789, followed by the suppression of religious orders, the closing of churches, and an attack on marriage and the family by allowing divorce. On July 12, 1790, the revolutionary government passed the Civil Constitution of the Clergy, which officially separated the Church in France from Rome. The government assumed control of the Church, citizens elected their bishops, diocesan boundaries were redrawn to match civil jurisdictions, parishes were closed, and clergy were considered employees of the state. French clergy were required to take an oath of fidelity to the government, a scene reminiscent of Henry VIII's England. However, unlike in England, the overwhelming majority of French bishops refused, and only 24 percent of priests took

---

42. Contrary to popular belief, the Bastille was not important to the monarchy; it was being considered for demolition due to high maintenance costs.
43. The Guards initially fought bravely but were ordered to lay down their arms by the king. See Carroll, *The Revolution against Christendom*, 154.

the oath.[44] The following year, in September, the National Assembly was replaced by a Legislative Assembly where no Church participation or representation was allowed. In another year, this assembly was replaced by the Committee of Public Safety, which inaugurated and maintained the Reign of Terror.

A wave of killing began in September 1792, when radicals took control of Paris and went on a killing spree that saw hundreds of bishops, priests, and religious murdered in one day for refusing to take the oath required in the Civil Constitution of the Clergy. Eventually, over a thousand people, mostly clergy, were killed that month. The next year witnessed the height of the terror, which began with the execution of King Louis XVI in January. Nine months later, Queen Marie was tried on preposterously false charges of holding orgies at Versailles, sending money from the national treasury to Austria, and sexually abusing her son. Convicted on all accounts, she was sentenced to death, paraded through the streets of Paris in front of thirty thousand people, and beheaded by the guillotine.[45] The revolutionaries then embarked on a de-Christianization campaign to rid France of its Catholic culture and history. The Gregorian calendar was changed to a "calendar of reason" with new names for the months and a new ten-day week, in order to abolish Sunday as the day of worship. September 22 was established as New Year's Day to commemorate the date in 1792 on which the monarchy was officially overthrown. Churches were confiscated and turned into "temples of reason." A prostitute was crowned "Goddess of Reason" in the Cathedral of Notre Dame.

The Catholics of France were not idle as revolution overtook their country. In the Vendée region of southwest France, a Catholic uprising took place from March to December 1793. The troops from the Vendée marched into battle under the banner of the Sacred Heart of Jesus and, if not for a sniper's well-placed

---

44. Emmet Kennedy, *A Cultural History of the French Revolution* (New Haven, CT: Yale University Press,1989), 151, quoted in Stark, *Bearing False Witness*, 196
45. Carroll, *The Revolution against Christendom*, 234.

shot that killed the leader, the movement might have succeeded in stopping the revolution.[46] The failure of the uprising resulted in a government genocide of the Catholic people of the Vendée, which killed hundreds of thousands.[47]

The Reign of Terror came to an end in 1794, in part due to sixteen Carmelite nuns. When the Terror began, the nuns of Compiègne had offered their lives to God, if necessary, to stop the wave of murder sweeping their beloved France. In July 1794, they were arrested, convicted of being Catholic nuns, and sentenced to death by the guillotine. From the novice to the mother superior, they bravely went to their deaths confident of God's loving providence. Ten days later, the Reign of Terror ended when one of its chief architects, Maximilien Robespierre, was killed. All told, the French Revolution exacted a bloody toll of human lives, as tens of thousands were killed in Paris and more throughout France, including a thousand priests and several bishops.[48] The tragic period ripped apart the fabric of a once vibrant and beautiful Catholic society, leaving a deep and lasting wound in the family of God.

NAPOLEON BONAPARTE

After the Reign of Terror, the Directory was established in 1795 to craft some semblance of organized government once again in France. When riots broke out in Paris, the Directory called upon a young artillery officer named Napoleon Bonaparte to restore order. A year later, Napoleon was on his way to ultimate power in France. He led a successful military campaign in 1798 to Italy, which resulted in the French Army's conquest of Rome. Napoleon arrested Pope Pius VI (r. 1775–1799), declar-

---

46. As Warren Carroll aptly described, ".There are times when the course of history for a century or more is shaped by how straight one man shoots." See Carroll, *The Revolution against Christendom*, 221.
47. See Reynald Secher, *A French Genocide: The Vendée*, trans. George Holoch (Notre Dame, IN: University of Notre Dame Press, 2003 [1986]), 212.
48. Donald Greer, *The Incidence of the Terror during the French Revolution: A Statistical Interpretation* (Cambridge, MA: Harvard University Press, 1935), cited in Stark, *Bearing False Witness*, 97.

ing him to be "Pius the Last," and brought him to France, where he died in captivity. The French ruler believed he had succeeded where so many others had failed; he had ended the papacy. The cardinals assembled in Venice and elected a successor to Pius VI, Barnaba Chiaramonti, who took the papal name Pius VII (r. 1800–1823). In the year of Pius VII's election, Napoleon gave a surprise speech in Milan wherein he welcomed the return of the Church in France, saying: "I am sure that the Catholic religion is the only religion that can make a stable community happy. France has had her eyes opened through suffering, and has seen that the Catholic religion is the single anchor amid the storm. Tell the pope that I want to make him a present of thirty million Frenchmen."[49] The next year, the French government and the Church entered into a concordat that established the Catholic faith as the privileged religion of France. The concordat allowed Napoleon to nominate bishops with papal confirmation. Clergy were required to take an oath of allegiance to the state and were supported by governmental revenue. All Church land confiscated during the revolution remained the property of the state. Napoleon affixed an appendix to the concordat that stipulated papal documents could not be published and bishops could not leave their diocese without governmental approval. Pius VII refused to sign the appendix, so it was dropped from the final approved agreement.

Pius VII traveled to France in 1804 to witness the coronation of Napoleon and Josephine as emperor and empress of France. Five years later, Napoleon annexed the Papal States to the French Empire, for which he was excommunicated. Undeterred, Napoleon demanded the pope abdicate control of the Papal States, which Pius refused. Once more, Napoleon resorted to kidnapping the pope. He brought him to France, where he was kept in exile for six years. Pius returned to Rome on May 24, 1814, after an allied army defeated Napoleon and exiled him to the island of Elba. The pope

---

49. Duffy, *Saints and Sinners*, 262.

declared May 24 a feast in honor of Our Lady, Help of Christians.[50] Napoleon escaped his exile on Elba and returned to France for his famous one hundred days. After losing the battle of Waterloo on June 18, 1815, he was exiled once more, and died in 1821.

THE INDUSTRIAL REVOLUTION

One of the most profound societal transformations occurred in the nineteenth century with the advent of the Industrial Revolution. European society changed from a primarily agrarian to an urban culture, which impacted traditional family life. Men, women, and children worked long hours in factories and lived tightly concentrated in cities. A surging population aided the rise of the industrial age. In 1700, the population of Europe was 110 million, and by the end of the century, that number had nearly doubled to 190 million.[51] In the United Kingdom, as an example, the population in 1821 was twenty-one million. Only a decade later, it had increased to thirty-two million, even after accounting for the million people who emigrated to Canada, the United States, Australia, New Zealand, and South Africa.[52] England became the first urbanized society; in 1851, 38 percent of the population lived in cities of over 5,000 people.[53] The European landscape was permanently altered; the number of cities with a population of over 10,000 people grew from 150 in 1500 to 360 in 1800.[54] The Church adapted to meet the spiritual needs of the new urbanized civilization. Christendom witnessed not only a notable change in societal structure, but also in the political arena. By the mid-nineteenth century, political revolution was trending. In 1848, nearly every major European nation suffered from socialist

---

50. See Warren H. Carroll and Anne W. Carroll, *The Crisis of Christendom: A History of Christendom*, vol. 6 (Front Royal, VA: Christendom Press, 2013), 6.
51. Pursell, 191.
52. William L. Langer, *Political and Social Upheaval 1832–1852* (New York, 1969), 203, quoted in Carroll, *The Crisis of Christendom*, 212–213.
53. Carroll, *The Crisis of Christendom*, 217.
54. Pursell, 191.

upheaval that transformed the political map of Christendom.

MODERNISM

Concomitant with the political revolutions in the nineteenth century, a theological revolution waged a pernicious campaign of heresy within the Church. This attack was "a wholesale assault upon the fundamentals of the Faith — upon the very existence of the Faith."[55] Given the name "Modernism," this new heresy attacked the Faith from within, seeking to change not the teachings of the Faith but how those teachings were understood. The heresy took root in biblical scholarship, but it also infiltrated other disciplines. Modernist thinkers attacked the supernatural aspects of the Faith, seeking natural explanations for the miraculous. A Modernist Scripture scholar, for example, would not deny that Moses and the Israelites walked dry-shod across the Red Sea, but would argue that that event was due to a natural, non-miraculous explanation such as a mighty wind or low tides. Ultimately, by stripping away the supernatural, Modernism produced skepticism and moral relativism — where morality becomes a construct of humanity, rather than a plan from God for eternal happiness. As in past centuries, the Church recognized the evils of this new heresy, combatting it through the actions of holy popes and by calling an ecumenical council.

PIO NONO

When Pope Gregory XVI died in 1846, the cardinals chose Giovanni Mastai-Ferretti as his successor. Mastai-Ferretti took the papal name Pius IX (r. 1846–1878) who, at fifty-two-years old, was the youngest pope in centuries. His youth served him well, providing the Church with the second longest papal reign at

---

55. Hilaire Belloc, *How the Reformation Happened* (Rockford, IL: TAN Books and Publishers, 1992 [1928]), 143.

thirty-two years (only Saint Peter reigned longer). Pius IX was a genial, unpretentious, and jovial man who loved tobacco and playing jokes on people. At a papal audience, an Anglican clergyman approached the pontiff and asked for his blessing. Pius acquiesced but used the Latin prayer for the blessing of incense: "May you be blessed by him in whose honor you are to be burned."[56] When a nun approached Pius and asked for his autograph on a picture, he wrote, "Fear not, for it is I."[57]

Early in his pontificate, Pius IX expressed a desire to embrace the modern world. He supported new technological inventions by bringing gas street lighting to Rome and establishing a commission to install a railway system in the Papal States. However, in 1848, political revolutions swept throughout Europe, affecting the Papal States. Pius's openness to the world was challenged. Riots broke out in Rome, and a gruesome scene occurred on November 15, 1848. The prime minister of Rome, Count Pellegrino Rossi, was murdered in the presence of the pope and other dignitaries. A revolutionary infiltrated the gathering, sneaked up behind Rossi, and slashed his neck with a hunting knife. Rossi's blood spurted on members of the crowd, including the pope.[58] The events of that night forever remained in Pius's memory and shaped his interaction with political and nationalist groups for the remainder of his pontificate. Soon thereafter, mobs formed outside the Quirinal Palace (the papal residence), demanding the following democratic reforms in the Papal States: the calling of a constituent assembly for the purpose of creating a democratic government, papal support of Italian nationality, and papal recognition of the separation of temporal and spiritual powers.[59] The pope refused these demands, angering the mob. Shots were fired into the palace, killing the pope's secretary. Pius left Rome for

56. Duffy, *Saints and Sinners*, 293.
57. Ibid.
58. Christopher Hibbert, *Garibaldi and His Enemies* (Boston: Little Brown, 1965), 36–37, quoted in Carroll, *The Crisis of Christendom*, 119–120.
59. Carroll, *The Crisis of Christendom*, 120.

the safety of Naples, fleeing under the disguise of an ordinary priest.[60] Pius IX remained in Naples for two years and requested the intervention of Catholic secular rulers to maintain order in Rome. Eventually, the French answered his summons, occupying the city as a security force in the summer of 1849 (they would stay until 1870). The pope returned to Rome on April 12, 1850, and made the Vatican his residence instead of the Quirinal, as it was more secure. Pius's firsthand witness of the violence unleashed by revolutionary, nationalistic, and democratic forces moved him to reject liberalism and its democratic principles.

As a response to the Enlightenment teaching that faith and science are incompatible, Pius published the encyclical *Qui Pluribus* in 1846. The pope taught that faith and reason are not in opposition, but complement each other: reason can be used to help lead one to faith, and faith answers questions outside the purview of science. A few years later, in 1854, Pius IX solemnly proclaimed the dogma of the Immaculate Conception of Mary.[61] Four years later, Our Lady appeared to young Bernadette Soubirous at Lourdes and confirmed the pope's teaching by referring to herself as the Immaculate Conception. In addition to his devotion to the Mother of God, Pius was devoted to the Sacred Heart of Jesus. He placed the feast on the universal liturgical calendar in 1856.

THE FIRST VATICAN COUNCIL

Pius IX decided to combat the pernicious evil of the Modernist heresy with the publication of an encyclical and the calling of an ecumenical council. In 1864, Pius released the document *Quanta Cura*, to which was affixed a *Syllabus of Errors*, a condemnation of eighty heretical propositions in matters religious, philosophi-

---

60. Ibid., 121.
61. In the document *Ineffabilis Deus*, he wrote, "The Most Blessed Virgin Mary at the first moment of her conception was, by singular grace and privilege of the Omnipotent God, in virtue of the merits of Jesus Christ, Savior of the Human race, preserved from all stains of original sin."

cal, and political.[62] The *Syllabus* led many to believe the Church was against pluralistic and democratic forms of government. It is true that the Church was reluctant to embrace new political ideologies, thanks largely to her experience during the French Revolution.[63] This historical memory and the experience of Pius's pontificate, along with increasing attacks on religion in general and the Church in particular, fostered the view within the Church that her survival depended on strong governments and leaders and a rejection of modernity.[64] The result was an insular Church that was in danger of becoming irrelevant. Pius understood that danger. He told his cardinals on December 6, 1864, that he intended to call an ecumenical council.

A commission of five cardinals was established to explore the papal proposal for a council and to shape the agenda. The cardinals recommended the council discuss the issues of pantheism, naturalism, communism, Protestantism, socialism, and indifferentism. Additionally, the commission called for the creation of a new universal catechism, the reform of canon law, the reassertion of papal primacy, and a definition of papal infallibility.[65] In preparation for the council, Pius IX wrote to the patriarchs of the Eastern Orthodox churches and to Protestant groups, urging them to unite with the Catholic Church. He asked Protestants to "reconsider their position in the face of the innumerable sects into which Protestantism was broken up, and the consequent dilution of Protestant doctrines, and to return to the fullness of the Catholic faith and to Catholic unity from which their fathers had broken away."[66] Unfortunately, these groups did not heed the pope's plea. Pius wanted the council to accomplish three goals:

---

62. Such as pantheism, atheism, indifferentism (belief that all religions are the same), and communism.

63. Whose popular political slogan "Liberty, Equality, and Fraternity" in reality meant "atheism, murder and theft." Eamon Duffy, *Ten Popes Who Shook the World* (New Haven, CT: Yale University Press, 2011), Kindle ed., location 899.

64. Ibid.

65. Carroll, *The Crisis of Christendom*, 133.

66. Cuthbert Butler, *The Vatican Council, 1869–1870* (Westminster, MD: Newman Press, 1962), 76, quoted in Carroll, *The Crisis of Christendom*, 134–135.

to restate the faith in areas where it had been attacked by Modernism, specifically faith and reason; to discuss the relationship between Church and state in light of the new governmental systems; and to issue a doctrinal statement on the Church. Most of the goals were met at the council, some only partially.

The First Vatican Council opened on December 8, 1869, with more than six hundred bishops in attendance. It was the first council attended by bishops from the United States. The council met only for seven months because the outbreak of the Franco-Prussian War in July 1870 necessitated the withdrawal of French troops from Rome. Fearing the safety of the gathering, Pius suspended the council indefinitely.[67] As a result, the council produced only two documents: one on faith and reason, and one on papal primacy and infallibility. The conciliar document *Dei Filius* was a response to the Enlightenment, Modernism, and the belief in the triumph of reason over faith. *Dei Filius* argues that objective, God-given truth exists and can be known by human reason. It condemned the teaching that God did not make the universe *ex nihilo* (out of nothing). The existence of God can be known by human reason alone, but Divine Revelation instructs man about God. Last, *Dei Filius* teaches that faith and reason are complementary, since both have God as their author.

The document *Pastor Aeternus* dealt with the role of the papacy and the charism of papal infallibility. Peter received true primacy of jurisdiction in the Church from Christ, and his successors enjoy this privilege as well. The pope, therefore, has full and supreme power of jurisdiction over the universal Church. The charism of infallibility is a gift given by the Holy Spirit to the Church and, in a special way, to the pope. Infallibility does not mean the pope is perfect, but rather that when he teaches, under certain conditions, the Church knows the possibility of error is not present. *Pastor Aeternus* identified the conditions upon which the pope can teach infallibly: the pope must utilize his role as the

---

67. It was not officially closed until 1960, when the Church prepared for the Second Vatican Council.

universal teacher of the Church (and not simply as the bishop of Rome); he must exercise the full weight of his supreme apostolic authority; it must be a personal act, free from coercion, not the ratification of conciliar documents; he must intend to define the teaching infallibly and to be definitively held by the faithful; the teaching must be promulgated; and, finally, the teaching must concern a matter of faith or morals. There was great debate at the council over the doctrine of papal infallibility. Some saw the desire to promulgate the teaching as a way to centralize Church governance in the Roman Curia. Others believed it was inopportune to define the doctrine. Many bishops in countries with a majority Protestant population believed the pronouncement would hinder their catechetical efforts. Others believed Catholics would not fully understand the doctrine and elevate the pope to an inappropriate status. In the end, the document passed by a large majority vote. The council hoped to craft a document on the Church as a whole, not just the papacy, but the political events of the day shortened its work. A fuller treatment of the Church in a conciliar document would have to wait for another council.

When French troops left Rome in 1870, Italian nationalists occupied the city and Papal States. Pius IX was powerless to stop the invasion, which dissolved the Papal States after nearly a thousand years. The territory was absorbed into the new united nation of Italy. Pius remained in the Vatican and refused to leave its confines for the remaining eight years of his pontificate, considering himself a prisoner.

KULTURKAMPF

After the Prussian Army secured a victory in the Franco-Prussian War, which France had foolishly begun, a new united German Empire came into existence under Prussian leadership, through the actions of Otto von Bismarck (1815–1898). Bismarck desired the unification of the German people in a shared culture and religion. He saw the Catholic Church as an obstacle to that dream, especially in the populous Catholic regions of Bavaria and the Rhineland. The fifteen-year *Kulturkampf*, or "culture war," followed. Bismarck was concerned about the First Vatican Council's *Pastor Aeternus*. He viewed the pope as a foreign ruler who should have no authority in the new Germany, so he enacted a series of anti-Catholic laws and persecutory measures to isolate the Church in Germany from Rome. A pulpit law was passed in 1871 that severely penalized any clergy member who criticized the government. The following year, laws were enacted that forbade religious instruction in school and refused legal recognition to Catholic marriages celebrated in a parish. Jesuits were expelled from Germany, and bishops were accused of being foreign enemy agents. Church appointments had to receive approval by secular governors. Bishops and priests were arrested and imprisoned, monasteries were closed, Church land and schools were seized, and diplomatic relations with the Vatican were severed. The effect on Catholic Germans was incredible, as, Father Karl Jentsch wrote, "every day the Catholic had to read … that he was an enemy of the Fatherland, a little papist, a blockhead, and that his clergy were the scum of humanity."[68] German Catholics nonviolently resisted these measures and formed their own political party, the Center Party, which won seats in the Reichstag in the 1874 national elections. The following year, Pius IX issued the encyclical *Quod nunquam* about the situation in Germany and declared Bismarck's anti-Catholic laws invalid. Eventually, an agreement was reached: the Church allowed for state approval of clerical appointments, state control of public education, and state supremacy in law, and the state allowed Catholics the freedom to publicly practice the Faith without fear of harassment and persecution. Although the *Kulturkampf* was over, the Church would face persecution in Germany again in the not-too-distant future.

---

68. George J. Marlin, "The Original Culture War," *The Catholic Thing*, May 18, 2011, https://www.thecatholicthing.org/2011/05/18/the-original-culture-war/.

CONDEMNING MODERNISM

As the family of God entered the twentieth century, a holy priest with a strong devotion to the Blessed Sacrament, who had always seen himself as a catechist, was elected successor of Saint Peter. Giuseppe Melchiorre Sarto enjoyed his time as a parish pastor, but he accepted the cardinals' decision to make him the universal pastor. In appreciation for the pontificate of Blessed Pius IX, he took the papal name Pius X (r. 1903–1914) and initiated a mini-reform by reorganizing the Roman Curia, initiating the re-codification of canon law, and reforming the breviary and liturgy. Pius X recognized the importance of teaching the Faith and continued his practice of teaching religious education to children. He encouraged frequent reception of the Eucharist, lowering the age of first Communion to the age of reason so that young people could receive the necessary grace as they matured. Despite the work of Blessed Pius IX and the First Vatican Council to eradicate Modernism, it persisted. So, in July 1907, Pius X issued the encyclical *Lamentabili*, in which he condemned sixty-five Modernist errors. Later that same year, he issued *Pascendi Dominici Gregis*, calling Modernism "the synthesis of all heresies." In 1910, Pius X required all professors at pontifical institutions of higher learning to take an oath against Modernism and to teach faithfully the Church's doctrines. These measures helped stem the tide of the heresy, but it would rear its ugly head more forcefully in the latter twentieth century.

THE SUICIDE OF CIVILIZATION

It is difficult to find one month and year in the history of humanity that was more important to the lives of millions than August 1914. A few months earlier, a murder had placed Europe on the path to unprecedented death and destruction. The heir to the Austro-Hungarian Empire, Archduke Franz Ferdinand, and his wife, Sophie, were brutally gunned down in Sarajevo by Serbian revolutionary

Gavrilo Princip. Distraught at the death of his beloved nephew, the aged Emperor Franz Josef issued an ultimatum to Serbia, which amounted to an Austrian takeover of the country. The Serbians rejected the imperial demand, and Austria declared war on tiny Serbia. Politically, Europe was enmeshed in a collection of alliances that automatically triggered the mobilization of armies if certain conditions were met. The Russians were allied with Serbia. Once war was declared by Austria, Tsar Nicholas II had no choice but to order Russian mobilization, which triggered a reaction in Germany. The previously prepared German war plan (the Von Schlieffen Plan), in the event war broke out in Europe, called for the army to push into Belgium, avoid French defenses, and make a sweeping turn into the heart of France to capture Paris. The Germans knew that Great Britain would enter the war once they invaded Belgium, so speed was of the essence. In the span of five weeks, all Christian Europe had mobilized for the "war to end all wars."

The First World War (1914–1918) did not end war, but it did bring battlefield casualties in numbers never before seen in human history. After advancing into Belgium and France, the Germans were stopped, and all sides on the Western Front dug defensive trenches stretching for a thousand miles. Neither side was able to break the stalemate, even with the advent of new technological weapons, such as the tank and airplane. Years of death and inch-long territorial gains resulted. In the first three weeks of the war, more than a million men were killed, wounded, or missing; in 1915, more than four million; in 1916, more than two million on the Western Front alone.[69] Individual battles produced large-scale casualties over small land areas. The Battle of the Somme in 1916 was particularly ghastly, as more than 600,000 French and British men were killed or wounded for a total gain of eight miles — a macabre ratio of six-and-a-half men for every inch of territory.[70] On the first day of that battle, July 1, the British Army

---

69. Carroll, *The Crisis of Christendom*, 257.
70. Ibid.

suffered its worst casualty total in its history: 60,000 men (18,000 killed in action). Nearly one-third of all German males were killed, maimed, or incapacitated by illness or injury as a result of the war.[71] The most depressing thought about the Great War is that there was no good reason for it:

> The First World War is a mystery. Its origins are mysterious. So is its course. Why did a prosperous continent, at the height of its success as a source and agent of global wealth and power and at one of the peaks of its intellectual and cultural achievement, choose to risk all it had won for itself and all it offered to the world in the lottery of a vicious and local internecine conflict?[72]

One man consistently urged the belligerents to make peace. He was the Vicar of Christ and had been elected to the papacy at the very beginning of the war on September 2, 1914. Giacomo Paolo Giovanni Battista della Chiesa was a short man, so much so that the smallest pre-made pontifical robes at the conclave did not fit him. A trained diplomat from Genoa, he had served as undersecretary of state for Popes Leo XIII and Pius X and had been created a cardinal only three months before his papal election. He took the papal name Benedict XV (r. 1914–1922) and spent his pontificate dealing with the war and its impacts. Benedict abided by three principles during the war: maintaining perfect neutrality, extending charity to all victims of the war, and calling for peace at every opportunity.[73] Neutrality allowed the Church to remain above the political disputes, even though this position angered both sides of the conflict. It also enabled the Church to be a voice of reason throughout the conflict, calling on each party to conduct their wartime actions in accordance with the moral law.

---

71. Steven Ozment, *A Mighty Fortress*, 240.
72. John Keegan, *The First World War* (New York: Alfred A. Knopf, 1999), 426.
73. Pope Pius XII also adopted these principles when the next war began later in the century.

When that did not occur, the pope could lodge public and private protests concerning the conduct of the combatants. The pope was especially concerned with the impact of the war on families. He created the Prisoners of War Bureau, which facilitated communication between POWs of all sides and their families. The Vatican also crafted prisoner exchanges, especially for wounded soldiers and fathers of three or more children. Benedict made generous aid donations from the Vatican treasury. In fact, he gave away so much money that after the war the treasury did not have enough funds to pay for his funeral expenses. Throughout the conflict, the pope urged an end to hostilities, a reduction in armaments, respect for the freedom of the seas, and the settling of disputes by international arbitration.[74] Many of Benedict's peace ideas were incorporated into U.S. President Woodrow Wilson's famous Fourteen Points, although Wilson did not give credit to the pope.[75] After the war ended on the feast day of Saint Martin of Tours, November 11, 1918, the pope exhorted the victors to make peace without demanding reparations from Germany. Unfortunately, they refused to listen and created the Treaty of Versailles, which laid the foundation for the Second World War due to its severe penalties against Germany.

Benedict XV contracted pneumonia and died in January 1922, after a pontificate marked by a war in which Europe committed the suicide of civilization.

OUR LADY OF FÁTIMA

Mary, the Mother of the Church and Help of Christians, warned of the impending war and its effects by her frequent appearances in the Marian Century (1830–1930.)[76] In 1830, she appeared to

---

74. See Carroll, *The Crisis of Christendom*, 279.
75. Indeed, he was most dismissive of Benedict XV's 1917 plea for peace, saying, "What does he want to butt in for?" Walter H. Peters, *The Life of Benedict XV* (Milwaukee: The Bruce Publishing Company, 1959), 148–149, quoted in Carroll, *The Crisis of Christendom*, 280.
76. The following section is adapted from my book *The Real Story of Catholic History*, 305–309.

Saint Catherine Labouré (1806–1876) to give the world the Miraculous Medal. Further appearances occurred in France at La Salette in 1846, Lourdes in 1858, and Pontmain in 1871. Mary also appeared in Knock, Ireland, in 1879 and, in the midst of the First World War, in Portugal to three shepherd children.

In 1916, Lúcia dos Santos (age ten), Francisco Marto (nine), and his sister Jacinta Marto (seven) were visited by an angel, who referred to himself as the Angel of Peace and the Angel of Portugal. He taught the children prayers of reparation and asked them to make sacrifices for the conversion of sinners.[77] The angel's visit prepared the children for something greater: the appearance of the Blessed Mother.

Mary appeared to the children in the hills of central Portugal, at a place known as the Cova de Iria, on May 13, 1917. She was bathed in a white light, wore a white mantle, and held a rosary in her hand. She taught the children a prayer and told them she would appear to them on the thirteenth day of every month for the next five months. She instructed the children to "say the Rosary every day, to obtain peace for the world and an end to the war."[78] The next month, Mary appeared again, as promised, and told the shepherd children that God wanted to establish a devotion to her Immaculate Heart. The following month, July 1917, she made her only specifically political request: asking for "the consecration of Russia to my Immaculate Heart. If they listen to my requests, Russia will be converted and there will be peace. If not, she will scatter her errors through the world, provoking wars and persecutions of the Church."[79]

To the simple shepherd children, this request must have seemed odd. They had probably never even heard of Russia, nor could they have intuited on their own the awful danger that nation would pose to the world. Yet, later that same year, the

---

77. Diane Moczar, *Ten Dates Every Catholic Should Know: The Divine Surprises and Chastisements That Shaped the Church and Changed the World* (Manchester, NH: Sophia Institute Press, 2005), 159.
78. William Thomas Walsh, *Our Lady of Fátima* (1958, repr., New York: Image, 1990), 52.
79. Ibid., 81–82.

Bolsheviks came to power in Russia under the leadership of Vladimir Ilyich Ulyanov, also known as Lenin, who had been sent by the Germans to sow revolution in his home country. The Bolsheviks, atheists inspired by the writings of Friedrich Engels and Karl Marx, attacked religion with the goal of creating a proletarian state. Russia had suffered from serious political instability, as the First World War took a toll on the nation. Tsar Nicholas II and Tsarina Alexandra (who was under the influence of Rasputin) became disillusioned with the war and were unable to deal effectively with the military and economic crisis afflicting their country. Before the revolution, the Catholic Church had a sizable presence in Russia, but within twenty years of the rise of the Bolsheviks, that presence was substantially reduced — from 5,300 Catholic churches and chapels to only two.[80] By 1925, 200,000 Catholics and every Catholic bishop in Russia had been imprisoned or murdered.[81] In the 1940s, the Soviet government systematically persecuted Catholics in Ukraine, Lithuania, Latvia, and Estonia, and attempted to force them to join the state-recognized Orthodox Church. Clearly, when Our Lady spoke of Russia to the shepherd children, she knew exactly what sort of evil was brewing there and offered a spiritual remedy.

Mary also gave the children "three secrets," which included a terrifying vision of hell and a vision of a bishop dressed in white who was struck down.[82] Finally, Our Lady promised that, in October, she would tell the children her name and perform a miracle visible to all. October 13, 1917, was a dark, damp, rainy, and cold day in Fátima, Portugal. Tens of thousands of people gathered to witness the promised miracle.[83] The chil-

---

80. Robert Royal, *The Catholic Martyrs of the Twentieth Century: A Comprehensive World History* (New York: The Crossroad Publishing Company, 2000), 44.

81. Ibid., 51.

82. The vision of the bishop in white who is struck down is said to have come to pass on May 13, 1981, when Mehmet Ali Agca shot Pope Saint John Paul II in St. Peter's Square.

83. Estimates vary for the number of people who gathered that day. Most range from 50,000 to 70,000 people. All accounts agree it was a very large number.

dren saw a vision of Saint Joseph with the Child Jesus, and then Our Lady told them: "Have them build a chapel here in my honor. I am the Lady of the Rosary. Let them continue to say the Rosary every day. The war is going to end."[84] While the shepherd children were focused on the vision of the Holy Family, the spectators saw something quite extraordinary, supernatural, and terrifying. It has been described as the "dance of the sun." Multiple eyewitnesses described it as something like a "fireworks display," telling how their clothes and the ground, previously soaked from the rain, miraculously became completely dry.[85] People twenty-five miles away also witnessed the miracle of the sun, which lasted ten minutes. Even the managing editor of *O Seculo*, the largest newspaper in Lisbon, Avelino de Almeida — who was a Freemason, hostile to the Church, and who came to the event in order to prove it was a sham — witnessed the miraculous dance of the sun and reported on what he had experienced.[86]

The Miracle at Fátima was a sign to the world to turn to the Lord and refrain from sin. Unfortunately, the world did not listen, and Our Lady's prophecy of another horrific world war came true. Two of the three shepherd children lived for only a few years after that miraculous October day. Francisco and Jacinta Marto died from influenza in the pandemic that swept the world after the war. Lúcia dos Santos became a religious, first as a member of the Institute of the Sisters of St. Dorothy in 1925 and later as a Discalced Carmelite. She survived to hear of the shooting of Pope Saint John Paul II in 1981, and she was present for the beatification of Francisco and Jacinta on May 13, 2000.[87] She died on February 13, 2005, at the age of ninety-eight.

---

84. Walsh, *Our Lady of Fátima*, 144.
85. See Carroll, *The Crisis of Christendom*, 314.
86. See Walsh, *Our Lady of Fátima*, 147.
87. The two were canonized saints on May 13, 2017, the centennial of Our Lady's appearance at Fátima.

REVOLUTION AND PERSECUTION IN MEXICO

The twentieth century witnessed the rise of three political ideologies that brought destruction and death to the world and persecution to the Catholic Church.[88] Communism, National Socialism, and Fascism may appear to be at odds in their teachings, but each of these ideologies has the same fundamental worldview: the individual is subservient to the state. The utilitarian outlook of humanity embraced by these movements was sacrosanct, and anyone or anything opposed to that fundamental tenant was an enemy of the state. As the ideologies took root in numerous countries of the world, their leaders and supporters sought to discredit and limit the power of the Catholic Church, which, in some cases, also produced violent and bloody persecution. The same year Our Lady appeared at Fátima, a socialist, anti-Catholic constitution was established in a country visited by the Blessed Mother in centuries past: Mexico.

The 1917 Mexican Constitution was the fruit of the Mexican Revolution, which had begun in 1910. The constitution was designed to radically alter Mexican government and culture by severely restricting the Catholic Church. The constitution mandated a secular education and outlawed Catholic schools, unless they used a purely secular curriculum; outlawed monastic orders; forbade public worship outside the confines of churches; placed restrictions on owning property by religious groups; and attacked Catholic clergy. Priests were forbidden to wear clerical attire, stripped of their right to vote, and forbidden to comment on public affairs or criticize government officials. The constitution also outlawed the presence of foreign missionary clergy in Mexico. Although the new constitution severely restricted Mexico's religious practice, enforcement of the anti-Catholic articles was loose — until 1924, when the virulent anti-Catholic Plutarco

---

88. The following section is adapted from my article "Blessed Miguel Pro: Anti-Fascist Martyr," *Catholic Answers Magazine Online*, November 22, 2017.

Calles was elected president.

In the summer of 1926 Calles implemented the Law for the Reforming of the Penal Code, which added specific punishments for violations of the anti-Catholic articles of the constitution. Priests were fined five hundred pesos for wearing clerical garb and were subject to five years' imprisonment for criticizing the government. In response, the bishops in Mexico called for an economic boycott against the government. The bishops asked Catholics to stop attending movies and plays, and to refuse to ride in public buses and streetcars. Catholic schoolteachers reacted to the bishops' request by refusing to teach in the secular schools.

The persecution became so horrible that on November 18, 1926, Pope Pius XI (r. 1922–1939) issued the encyclical *Iniquis Afflictisque* concerning the events in Mexico. Pius noted that Calles's new law was "much worse than the original law itself" and added insult to the persecution, as "wicked men have tried to place the Church in a bad light before the people; some, for example, uttering the most brazen lies in public assemblies. But when a Catholic tries to answer them, he is prevented from speaking by catcalls and personal insults hurled at his head."[89] The pope sadly recalled that Calles's actions had resulted in violent persecution of the Church: "Priests and laymen have been cruelly put to death in the very streets or in the public squares which front the churches."[90] Pius XI also praised the Mexican hierarchy and people for their patience and "extraordinary virtue" in dealing with an intolerable situation. He acknowledged the work of Catholic organizations, especially the Knights of Columbus, for their efforts on behalf of the Mexican bishops, clergy, and faithful. Unfortunately, the Catholic response resulted in more repressive measures. Bishops were stripped of citizenship and expelled in 1927. Priests were arrested and killed;

---

89. Pius XI, *Iniquis Afflictisque*, 12.
90. Ibid., 16.

those who remained in Mexico were forced to minister to the Catholic faithful in secret, always aware they could be betrayed, tortured, and executed.

One priest who stayed was the Jesuit Miguel Pro (1891–1927). Pro was the oldest child of a large Catholic family. When his sister entered the convent, Pro felt a call to the priesthood, and received permission to enter the Jesuit novitiate. His seminary studies were interrupted by the troubles in Mexico, so he was sent to the United States for a time and then to Europe. Pro was ordained in 1925 and returned to Mexico shortly thereafter. He regularly donned a variety of disguises while ministering to the people in order to escape detection as a Catholic priest. Eventually, Pro and two of his brothers were arrested by the government on trumped-up charges of participating in a plot to assassinate former president Álvaro Obregón in 1927. The Calles government did not allow Miguel Pro a trial, condemning him to die by firing squad. On the morning of November 23, 1927, Pro was led to the place of execution. As he passed the assembled soldiers, he blessed and forgave them. His last request, which was granted, was to spend a moment on his knees in prayer. After his prayer, Pro refused a blindfold, raised his arms parallel to the ground in the form of cross, and uttered his last words, "*Viva Cristo Rey* (Long Live Christ the King)!" The execution was well attended by journalists. The government desired to utilize Pro's death as a deterrent to Catholic armed defense, and believed the sight of a priest at the moment of death would demoralize the populace, so pictures of his execution were widely distributed. When the pictures circulated among the people, they had the opposite effect — people treated the pictures with great devotion, and Pro's death became a rallying cry for the persecuted faithful. As a result, the government banned the publication and distribution of the pictures, declaring it a treasonous act to even possess a copy.[91]

---

91. Royal, *The Catholic Martyrs of the Twentieth Century*, 18.

"Viva Cristo Rey" became the battle cry of the Cristeros, Mexican Catholic freedom fighters who took up arms against the federal government in order to protect the Church and their right to worship. The Cristeros waged a two-year war in defense of Catholics against the government. The war ended in a negotiated settlement brokered by Dwight Morrow, the U.S. ambassador to Mexico. Calles stepped down and was replaced by a moderate president. The bloody persecution ended, but the evil ledger of Calles's activities was full. Nearly three hundred thousand people, mostly Catholics, had been killed.[92] Calles's attack affected the Church in Mexico for decades, but he did not accomplish his goal of eradicating the Church.

THE SPANISH CIVIL WAR

By the end of the nineteenth century, all vestiges of Spain as a world power had collapsed, primarily as a result of the Spanish-American War (1898), in which Spain lost most of its overseas possessions.[93] A deep political and social rift occurred in Spanish society as different factions vied to reform the country — including anti-Catholic groups, such as the Communist Party, which was a larger percentage of the population in Spain than in 1917 Russia.[94] The early twentieth century saw sporadic but increasing violence against the Church, including the assassination of the archbishop of Saragossa in 1923 and the destruction of churches in Madrid and Seville in 1931. Anti-Catholic forces believed a revolution akin to the one in France needed to occur in Spain, along with the confiscation of Church property. In the 1931 elections, the results were unfavorable to the conservative (especially monarchist) parties with which the Church had been compelled to ally itself. As a result, King Alfonso XIII (r. 1902–1931), a stabilizing force in a rapidly destabilizing en-

92. Ibid., 40.
93. The following section is adapted from my book *The Real Story of Catholic History*, 183–185.
94. Royal, 114–115.

vironment, fled to England. His departure created the Second Spanish Republic, which launched an initially nonviolent persecution of the Church.

In the summer of 1933 Pope Pius XI (r. 1922–1939) issued an encyclical, *Dilectissima Nobis*, specifically about the "oppression of the Church in Spain." Critics then and since have maintained that the Church brought persecution upon itself by embracing the conservative political parties in Spain — a charge Pius XI refuted: "Universally known is the fact that the Catholic Church is never bound to one form of government more than to another, provided the Divine rights of God and of Christian consciences are safe. She does not find any difficulty in adapting herself to various civil institutions, be they monarchic or republican, aristocratic or democratic."[95]

Three years later, new elections were held. Although the conservative Nationalists (composed mostly of Catholics and monarchists) received more votes than the Republicans (also known as the Popular Front, which was comprised of socialists, communists, and anarchists), they won fewer seats in the Spanish parliament. Violence erupted in July 1936 when the Nationalist leader Calvo Sotelo was assassinated — the last straw for conservative army officers, who had been alarmed at the state of Spanish society. On July 18, 1936, a group of officers initiated a military coup, which sparked the beginning of the Spanish Civil War.

General Francisco Franco, who was aware of the coup and supported it, left his posting in the Canary Islands and traveled to Spanish Morocco to mobilize Nationalist troops. Franco was politically conservative and an enemy of the Popular Front. Although he did accept military assistance from fascist Italy and Nazi Germany, he was not himself a fascist. This led to one of the enduring myths about the war: that the Nationalists were a group of elitist army officers and nobles supported by

95. Pius XI, *Dilectissima Nobis*, 3, accessed September 20, 2018, http://www.vatican.va/holy_father/pius_xi/encyclicals/documents/hf_p-xi_enc_03061933_dilectissima-nobis_en.html.

the Church that had much to lose with a Popular Front victory.[96] This false narrative impacted American opinion, which was divided along religious lines; Protestants and Jews supported the Republicans, and Catholics supported the Nationalists.[97] In Spain, Republican attacks on Catholics were widespread and ferocious. Ultimately, Republican forces killed 6,832 priests and religious, including 284 nuns. In all, 12 percent of the Spanish clergy were murdered (85 and 30 percent in the dioceses of Barbastro and Madrid, respectively), some publicly by being put in an arena with wild animals — a sight not seen in Europe since the Roman persecutions.[98] Nearly 50 percent of all churches in Spain were destroyed. Almost 1,000 members of the clergy who were killed have been canonized, and another 2,000 causes for canonization have been opened. The Spanish Civil War left a lasting mark on Spanish society and the Church. The Church is frequently portrayed as a willing ally of Franco and the Nationalists; in reality, she reluctantly supported them only because the Republicans were violent atheists who persecuted the Church. Ultimately, the horrific loss of life on both sides during the Spanish Civil War was the direct result of anti-religious political factions in Spain, eager to reenact the French Revolution, albeit on a much bloodier scale.

FASCIST ITALY AND NAZI GERMANY

The rise of fascism and National Socialism in post-World War I Europe sought to significantly limit the Church's influence. These groups even substituted their ideology and leaders for the

96. See Royal, *The Catholic Martyrs of the Twentieth Century*, 118; and Donald Prudlo, "American Catholics and the Spanish Civil War," accessed September 20, 2018, http://www.catholicculture.org/culture/library/view.cfm?recnum=8444.
97. The false narrative was also aided by the participation of famous volunteers who fought for the Republicans, including George Orwell (who later repudiated his youthful Marxist leanings) and Ernest Hemingway, who, as a journalist, supported the Republican cause against Franco.
98. Numbers of deaths and destruction of churches from Warren H. Carroll, *The Last Crusade: Spain: 1936* (Front Royal, VA: Christendom Press, 1996), 212,213. Account of priests killed by wild animals in Royal, 125.

Christian faith in the minds and hearts of the people. In order to protect the Church against persecution and safeguard her independence, a series of diplomatic agreements, or concordats, was negotiated and signed during the pontificate of Pope Pius XI. The pope was a shrewd diplomat and scholar who focused his papal policy on reaching concordats with the nations of Latvia (1922), Bavaria (1924), Poland (1925), Romania (1929), Austria (1933), and Germany (1933). These concordats provided the Church, at the very least, the ability to cite legal and internationally recognized documents when complaining about her treatment in various countries. Pius XI did not believe, especially in the case of Nazi Germany, that these agreements would prevent actual persecution.

In Italy, Pius XI and the fascist government of Benito Mussolini finally settled the "Roman Question" about the pope's international legal status. When Italian nationalists had conquered and absorbed the Papal States into a unified Italy toward the end of the nineteenth century, Pope Blessed Pius IX had refused to acknowledge the takeover. From that time, the pope and the nation of Italy coexisted in an awkward relationship. Mussolini was keen to regularize that relationship. As a student of history, he wrote: "[The] history of Western Civilization from the time of the Roman Empire to our days show that every time the state clashes with religion, it is always the state which ends defeated."[99] So, Mussolini's government and the papacy negotiated the Lateran Treaty in 1929 that created the sovereign Vatican City State, comprising 108 acres in the heart of Rome. The Catholic faith was designated the sole and official religion in Italy, Catholic education was made compulsory in all schools, holy days were considered state holidays, and the Church acknowledged the united nation of Italy and agreed to divorce herself from active political participation. The pope was finally provided a legal and interna-

---

99. Camille Cianfarra, *The Vatican and the War* (New York: E. P. Dutton & Company, 1944), 69, quoted in Ronald J. Rychlak, *Hitler, the War, and the Pope* (Huntington, IN: Our Sunday Visitor, 2000), 35.

tionally recognized sovereign territory of his own.

The Church watched carefully as the National Socialist Workers' Party (Nazis) rose to prominence in the Weimar Republic, the post-World War I government in Germany. The German bishops noted the racist ideology that spewed from the mouths of Nazi leadership and warned their flocks against this evil on five separate occasions from 1920 to 1927 — as did Eugenio Pacelli, the papal nuncio in Germany. When Hitler and the Nazis came to power in 1933, the Church finalized a concordat that had been in negotiation before the change in the German government. The Church desired the concordat in the hopes of avoiding Nazi persecution and establishing a legal basis for protest of Nazi abuses against the Church and Catholics. Pius XI wanted to ensure that the Nazis would allow independent Catholic organizations, freedom for Catholic schools, free communication with Rome, and government recognition that baptized Jews were Christians. In return, Nazis demanded the Church cease all political activity.

Of course, the Nazis had no intention of abiding by the dictates of the concordat. They arrested priests, searched Catholic youth club buildings, and closed Catholic publications during negotiations. Five days after the concordat was signed, the Nazis attacked the sanctity of marriage and family life by announcing a new sterilization law and a stipulation that allowed divorce for non-belief in Nazi teachings. Hitler and his henchmen knew that the best manner to inculcate their ideology in the minds of the people was to indoctrinate the youth, which is why they placed such emphasis on the Hitler Youth Program. The Catholic Youth League was an obstacle to their plan, so they moved to disband it. The government decreed in 1935 that only Hitler Youth groups could play organized sports, wear uniforms, and march in parades. They purposefully held Hitler Youth meetings on Sunday mornings, forcing Catholic parents to choose between Mass and youth meetings. The following year, all pretenses were wiped away, as the Nazis outlawed all youth groups except the Hitler Youth. The Nazis also attacked Catholic education and the Catholic press in order to stifle all resistance to the state.

Concerned with the state of affairs in Germany, Pius XI issued an encyclical in 1937 titled *Mit Brennender Sorge* (*With Burning Sorrow*). It is the only encyclical originally written in German, and was addressed to the German bishops. Pius addressed the signing of the concordat with the Nazis, indicating it was done with "many and grave misgivings" but was necessary to protect the Church and the faithful.[100] While the Church strove to diligently uphold the agreement, Pius acknowledged that the Nazis "emasculated the terms of the treaty, distorted their meaning, and eventually considered its more or less official violation as a normal policy."[101] In the encyclical, Pius attacked the core ideals of National Socialism, particularly its racist policies:

> Whoever exalts race, or the people, or the State, or a particular form of State, or the depositories of power, or any other fundamental value of the human community, however necessary and honorable be their function in worldly things, whoever raises these notions above their standard value and divinizes them to an idolatrous level, distorts and perverts an order of the world planned and created by God; he is far from the true faith in God and from the concept of life which that faith upholds.[102]

Although Pius did not mention Hitler by name in the encyclical, he clearly spoke out against the Nazi leader and his cult of personality: "Should any man dare, in sacrilegious disregard of the essential differences between God and his creature, between

---

100. Pius XI, *Mit Brennender Sorge*, 3.
101. Ibid., 5.
102. Ibid., 8.

the God-man and the children of man, to place a mortal, were he the greatest of all times, by the side of, or over, or against, Christ, he would deserve to be called prophet of nothingness."[103] The Nazis, incensed after reading Pius's encyclical, banned its publication and dissemination in Germany. In retaliation, they began a propaganda campaign against Pius XI, calling him a Jewish sympathizer because his mother was half-Jewish.

Pius XI was unintimidated by the Nazis and continued to illustrate his displeasure with Nazi ideology. When Hitler visited Mussolini in Rome in May 1938, Pius left the city, and the Vatican newspaper ran a front-page article condemning Nazi racial teachings. Later that year, when Jewish businesses were attacked throughout Germany in the *Kristallnacht*, Pius spoke out against the attacks. Vatican Secretary of State Eugenio Pacelli assisted German bishops in acquiring visas for Jews to emigrate from Germany to safer countries.[104] When Italy adopted anti-Jewish racial laws similar to the Nazi Nuremberg racial laws, Pius told a group of Belgian pilgrims visiting the Vatican in September 1938 that "it is impossible for a Christian to take part in anti-Semitism. It is inadmissible. Through Christ and in Christ, we are the spiritual progeny of Abraham. Spiritually we are all Semites."[105] The valiant defender of the weak and persecuted died on February 11, 1939, months before the world was once again plunged into a destructive and murderous war. On hearing the news that Pius XI had died, Mussolini remarked, "At last, that stubborn old man is dead."[106] Pius XI's actions against Nazi and fascist ideology laid the foundation for the continued actions of the Church under his successor. The Italian dictator did not know who would succeed Pius XI, but that man proved to

---

103. Ibid., 17.
104. Ultimately, two hundred thousand Jews were able to flee Germany with Vatican help. See Gordon Thomas, *The Pope's Jews: The Vatican's Secret Plan to Save Jews from the Nazis* (New York: St. Martin's Press, 2012), 8.
105. http://www.ccjr.us/dialogika-resources/primary-texts-from-the-history-of-the-relationship/pius-xi1938sept6, accessed September 20, 2018.
106. Duffy, *Saints and Sinners*, 344.

be just as stubborn and concerned for the weak, the powerless, and the persecuted.

POPE PIUS XII

Eugenio Pacelli came from a family dedicated to serving the Church, and so it was no surprise that he entered the seminary at age eighteen.[107] Ordained a priest on Easter Sunday in 1899, Pacelli served a brief tour as a parish priest before earning doctorates in theology and canon and civil law. He later entered the Vatican diplomat training program, with an initial assignment to the Prisoner of Wars Bureau in 1914. A few years later, in 1917, he was appointed papal nuncio to Bavaria, and in 1920 was made nuncio for all of Germany. During his time in Germany, he witnessed the rise of Adolf Hitler and the Nazi Party. He criticized Nazi policies in forty public speeches between 1918 and 1929.[108] Pacelli was created a cardinal in 1929 and appointed Vatican secretary of state by Pope Pius XI. Throughout his tenure as secretary of state, Pacelli continued to warn the world about the Nazis and their evil ideology.

Days after Hitler used the Enabling Act of 1933 to become dictator, Cardinal Pacelli ordered the nuncio to Germany "to intervene with the government of the Reich on behalf of the Jews and point out all the dangers involved in an anti-Semitic policy."[109] At Lourdes in 1935, Pacelli told a group of 125,000 people that the Nazis are "possessed by the superstition of race and blood."[110] In 1936, he traveled to the United States, where he praised Jewish contributions to the nation, denounced anti-Semitism, and expressed concern about the broadcasts of the anti-Semitic "radio priest" Father Charles Coughlin. In 1938, Pacelli issued a letter

---

107. The following section is adapted from my book *The Real Story of Catholic History*, 187–191.
108. David G. Dalin, *The Myth of Hitler's Pope: How Pope Pius XII Rescued Jews from the Nazis* (Washington, D.C.: Regnery Publishing, Inc., 2005), 63.
109. Margherita Marchione, *Did Pius Help the Jews?* (New York: Paulist Press, 2007), loc. 600, Kindle.
110. Ibid, loc. 692.

to the world's bishops, asking them to appeal to their national governments to generously grant visas to Jews trying to escape Nazi Germany.[111] Bishop Fulton Sheen once recalled a meeting with Cardinal Pacelli in Rome where "the cardinal pulled out a number of German newspapers from a file and began reading and translating them. For over an hour he spoke with considerable vehemence against Hitler and Nazism."[112]

Pacelli's efforts to warn the world about the dangers of Nazism and to assist the Jewish people continued when he was elected pope on March 2, 1939 (in one day — the briefest conclave in three hundred years), taking the name Pius XII (r. 1939–1958).[113] As one Berlin newspaper editorialized, "The election of Cardinal Pacelli is not accepted with favor in Germany because he was always opposed to Nazism."[114]

On October 20, 1939, Pius XII promulgated his fist encyclical, *Summi Pontificatus*, which attacked Nazi and fascist ideology. He described two errors affecting the modern world: the forgetfulness of the law of human solidarity and charity, and the rise of the totalitarian state. Pius illustrated that the central problem of a totalitarian form of government is its focus on the state over the individual, and its exaltation of the state and its leader to the level of idolatry.[115] Once again, the Nazis were not pleased with the outspoken criticism of the pope.

When Germany invaded Poland in September 1939, starting the Second World War, Pius XII embraced the earlier wartime policies of Pope Benedict XV: neutrality, charity to those affected by the war, and calls for peace at every opportunity. The pope knew the Nazis would continue their persecution of the Jewish

---

111. Benedict XVI, *Light of the World: The Pope, the Church, and the Signs of the Times: A Conversation with Peter Seewald*, trans. Michael J. Miller and Adrian J. Walker (San Francisco: Ignatius Press, 2010), loc. 1498, Kindle.
112. Fulton Sheen, *Treasure in Clay: The Autobiography of Fulton J. Sheen* (Garden City, NY: Doubleday, 1980), 46.
113. Pacelli was the first Roman-born pope in over two hundred years, and was elected on his birthday.
114. Rychlak, 110.
115. See Pius XII, *Summi Pontificatus*, 35, 51–53.

people, so he sent top-secret orders to the nuncio to Poland to assist Jews, and to the nuncio to Turkey (Angelo Roncalli, the future Pope Saint John XXIII), to "prepare thousands of baptismal certificates to give the Jews, which will allow them passage through Turkey to the Holy Land."[116] Additionally, in a letter, *Opere et Caritate*, to his nuncios dated December 23, 1940, Pius instructed them to work with local bishops to help the Jews escape persecution.[117] The letter was kept secret at the time "for the same reason the International Red Cross and the World Council of Churches had avoided making any public statement that would increase the suffering of the Jews."[118]

Although Pius's wartime actions have come under scrutiny and attack in the modern world, the historical record is clear. He did as much as he could, given the circumstances, to assist the Jewish people in their hour of utmost need.[119] Continuing a long tradition of papal defense of the Jews, Pius spoke out against Nazi treatment of the Chosen People. His Christmas addresses of 1941 and 1942 were praised by *The New York Times* editorial board, which called the pope "a lonely voice in the silence and darkness enveloping Europe."[120] But Pius understood that he had to tread carefully in his public pronouncements, knowing that strong papal condemnation of the Nazis' treatment of the Jews could make a bad situation worse. As he put it in an address to his cardinals on June 2, 1943, "Every word We address to the competent authority on this subject, and all Our

116. Thomas, 49.
117. Marchione, *Did Pius Help the Jews?*, loc.315–316, Kindle.
118. Thomas, 198.
119. For modern critics of Pius's wartime actions, see Rolf Hochhuth's *The Deputy* (1963), John Cornwell's *Hitler's Pope* (1999), James Carroll's *Constantine's Sword: The Church and the Jews—A History* (2001), and Daniel Jonah Goldhagen's *A Moral Reckoning: The Role of the Catholic Church in the Holocaust and its Unfulfilled Duty of Repair* (2002), among others.
120. Popes who protected the Jewish people from persecution include Saint Gregory the Great, Callistus II, Innocent III, Clement VI, Boniface IX, Martin V, Alexander VI, Julius II, and Leo X. The Papal States were usually the best place for Jews to live and work throughout European history. Secular rulers expelled Jews from their lands in France (Paris in 1182; the whole country in 1306), England (1290), Hungary (1390), Austria (1422), Spain (1492), and Portugal (1497). For Pius's Christmas addresses, see Marchione, *Did Pius Help the Jews?*, loc. 138–139, Kindle, and Rychlak, *Hitler, the War and the Pope*, 166,179,196.

518 | CHAPTER NINE

public utterances, have to be carefully weighed and measured by Us in the interests of the victims themselves, lest, contrary to our intentions, We make their situation worse and harder to bear."[121]

There was ample reason for Pius's caution: when the Dutch bishops publicly denounced Nazi mistreatment of Jews in 1942, the Nazis retaliated by increasing the number of Jewish deportations — including some Jews who had converted to the Catholic faith, like the Carmelite Saint Edith Stein (Teresa Benedicta of the Cross) and her sister. Holland witnessed the largest percentage of Jews deported during the war (79 percent of the total Jewish population).[122] As a result, bishops in Nazi-occupied territory, as well as Jewish leaders, cautioned Pius against speaking out too forcefully against the Nazis.

Despite the risk, Pius continued to promote efforts to assist Jews in Nazi-occupied territories as best as possible throughout the war. After Mussolini's downfall and the German conquest of Italy, the Nazis rounded up twelve thousand Jews in Rome for deportation to concentration camps. When news reached the Vatican, Pius XII ordered Secretary of State Cardinal Luigi Maglione to inform the German ambassador, Ernst von Weizsäcker, that the pope would publicly denounce the deportation unless it was stopped. The message was sent up the Nazi leadership chain to Heinrich Himmler, who ordered a cessation of the deportation operations.[123] When the Roman Jewish community was threatened with deportation unless they met a Nazi demand for gold, Pius offered to make up the difference if the Jews were short the amount.[124] He instructed Italian bishops to hide Jews in monasteries and convents, and he also hid many in his own summer residence, Castel Gandalfo.

---

121. Marchione, *Did Pius Help the Jews?*, loc. 712,717, Kindle.
122. Pinchas E. Lapide, *Three Popes and the Jews* (New York: Hawthorn Books, Inc., 1967), 202.
123. Of the 12,438 Roman Jews, 1,007 were arrested and sent to Auschwitz in the time it took for the stop order to be received. Of the 1,007, only 196 survived the war. See Thomas, 230.
124. See Thomas, 156–157.

After the war, individual Jews and many Jewish organizations thanked Pius XII and the Church for the heroic activity of the pope and other Catholics.[125] Isaac Zolli, the chief rabbi of Rome during the war, converted to the Faith and took the baptismal name Eugenio due to the witness of the pope toward the Jews. Zolli considered Pius XII a great friend to the Jews, saying of him, "No hero in all history was more heroic than Pope Pius and his readiness to defend the children of God."[126] Indeed, the actions of Pius XII and the Catholic Church during the Second World War resulted in the rescue of 860,000 Jews from the Nazis, 37 percent of Jews who survived the war.[127]

Pius was also gravely concerned about Nazi atrocities against Catholics throughout the war period. When the Germans invaded Poland, they arrested Catholic priests, imprisoned them, and executed thousands, including the Franciscan friar Saint Maximilian Kolbe (1894–1941), who gave his life at Auschwitz for another man.[128] The Nazis wanted to eradicate the Christian faith from Germany. They attempted to do so both nonviolently, through propaganda and the exaltation of Hitler as supreme leader, and violently, through the arrest, torture, and execution of Christians who criticized the government and its nefarious policies. Pius remained neutral throughout the war, but it was clear on both sides that he desired an Allied victory and was grateful when that occurred, although the Church would continue to suffer for decades in those areas conquered by Soviet Russia.

The Second World War dominated Pius XII's pontificate, but he continued to shepherd the Church for years after that calamitous event. He wrote forty encyclicals, including *Mystici Corporis Christi* (1943) on the Church as the Mystical Body of Christ, *Di-*

---

125. The list of grateful Jews includes the World Jewish Congress, the American Jewish Committee, the Jewish Theological Seminary of America, the Anglo-Jewish Association, the Union of Italian Jewish Communities, the United Jewish Appeal, Golda Meir, Albert Einstein, Sir Martin Gilbert, and Pinchas Lapide.
126. Thomas, 157.
127. Lapide, 215.
128. See Rychlak, 121–122.

vino Afflante Spiritu (1943) on biblical scholarship, and *Humani Generis* (1950), which discussed Darwinism and evolution. Perhaps his most enduring legacy to the Church was the proclamation in 1950 of the dogma of the Assumption of the Most Blessed Virgin Mary, who, Pius wrote, "having completed the course of her earthly life, was assumed body and soul into heavenly glory."[129]

In the history of the papacy, it is difficult to find a pope who experienced more challenging circumstances to his reign than Pius XII. He truly showed a deep love of Christ, the Church, and all men throughout dangerous and heart-wrenching times. He was a true hero of God.[130]

The family of God suffered mightily in the devil's century, when the Evil One did his utmost to destroy the Church and turn men's hearts away from the Father. More than one hundred million people died in the twentieth century due to the evils of political ideologies that served man rather than God. The world was adrift after the modern attack and in desperate need of the saving message and grace of Jesus. His Church responded to that need and laid a framework for the Faith as it approached the third millennium.

---

129. Pius XII, *Munificentissimus Deus*, 44.
130. There should be no doubt of Pius's personal sanctity, which has already been recognized in his proclamation as Venerable by Pope Benedict XVI in 2009. In God's time and with utmost justice, he will one day be recognized as Saint Pius XII.

TEN

Hope and Mercy

"We must summon fresh energy for tackling the problem of how to announce the Gospel anew in such a way that this world can receive it, and we must muster all our energies to do this."[1]

POPE BENEDICT XVI

After serving the Polish pope faithfully for twenty-three years, the German cardinal was looking forward to retiring in peace, but God had other plans. When he was elected the successor to his beloved friend, Cardinal Joseph Ratzinger accepted God's plan and put on the shoes of the fisherman, taking the name Benedict XVI.

Joseph Ratzinger was born during the early morning hours of Holy Saturday, April 16, 1927, in Marktl am Inn in Upper Bavaria. He was the

1. Benedict XVI, *Light of the World: The Pope, the Church, and the Signs of the Times: A Conversation with Peter Seewald*, trans. Michael J. Miller and Adrian J. Walker (San Francisco: Ignatius Press, 2010), loc. 1727, Kindle.

youngest of three children born to Mary and Joseph Ratzinger. As Joseph matured, he gradually came to believe God was calling him to the priesthood, and at the age of nineteen he entered the seminary in Munich. During the Second World War, he was conscripted into the German Army at the age of sixteen and spent a year as an anti-aircraft battery observer. After the war, he returned to his studies and was ordained a priest in 1954. He wrote his dissertation on Saint Augustine and received a doctorate in theology. He became a lecturer in dogmatic theology in the German universities of Münster, Tübingen, and Regensburg. During his years as a professor, Ratzinger published many essays and books, and was called to attend the Second Vatican Council as a theological expert to the German episcopate. He was ordained a bishop in 1977, installed in the Archdiocese of Munich, and was later created a cardinal by Pope Saint Paul VI. Five years later, Pope Saint John Paul II called the cardinal archbishop to Rome to serve as the prefect of the Congregation for the Doctrine of Faith, the curial office in charge of maintaining doctrinal orthodoxy. He served in this office for over twenty years, gaining a public reputation, through the media, as the "Panzer Cardinal" or "God's Rottweiler." Privately, he was known as an intelligent, charitable, and astute theologian who loved the Church and desired the Gospel truth to be proclaimed boldly and authentically.

Throughout the tumultuous twentieth century, the German pope had seen the suffering and evil brought by war, and the hope and joy brought by the reconstruction of Germany following the conflict. He had participated in a momentous ecumenical council and served God's people in times of change, crisis, and challenges. He faithfully fulfilled the role of Vicar of Christ (which he had never desired), but the old professor wanted peace and retirement and did not believe he was capable of vibrantly leading God's people anymore. So, he shocked the Church and the world by abdicating the chair of Saint Peter — an event the Church had not experienced in nearly six hundred years — to make way for a different pope as the family of God continued its march through history.

GOOD POPE JOHN

The world was in need of faith, hope, and love. The two world wars had devastated the spiritual as well as the material lives of twentieth-century people. The skepticism born in the Enlightenment had produced moral relativism, that led to the horrific atrocities of the wars. Darkness, despair, and fear remained. Pius XII thought calling an ecumenical council might be the answer, but he died before any serious plans were made. Some influential members of the Church did not see a need for a council. There was no major heresy threatening the doctrines of the Church, they reasoned, and it was best for the family of God to focus on itself and repair the damage inflicted by persecution.

The cardinals assembled in conclave upon the death of the heroic Pius XII and elected the seventy-seven-year-old Patriarch of Venice, Cardinal Angelo Roncalli, as pope. Roncalli took the name John XXIII (r. 1958–1963). Although he reigned for only five years, his pontificate was one of the most important in modern Church history. John XXIII was a jovial priest who exuded personal warmth and holiness. He was ordained in 1904, and he earned a doctorate in canon law. Roncalli served as secretary to a bishop, as well as a seminary professor, early in his priesthood. When the First World War broke out, Roncalli was drafted into the Italian Army, where he served as a chaplain and a member of the medical corps. After the war, he was appointed the president of the Italian Society of the Propagation of the Faith. Several years later, Roncalli entered the Vatican Diplomatic Corps as the papal representative to Bulgaria, a country that had been without such representation for six hundred years. Roncalli excelled as a diplomat and received postings to Turkey, Greece, and France. His time in Turkey and Greece helped him acquire familiarity with Islam and the Greek Orthodox Church. His experience during the war solidified in his mind the need for an extraordinary event in the life of the Church — one that would help modern man overcome his despair and skepticism.

Less than three months after his election, John XXIII spoke to the cardinals, telling them of his desire to hold an ecumenical council: "Standing before you I tremble somewhat with emotion but am humbly resolute in my purpose to proclaim… a general council for the universal Church."[2] It had been seventeen years since the end of the Second World War. He prayed the council would be a new Pentecost in the life of the Church and provide an opportunity for the Church to proclaim Christ to a broken world. He rejected the view held by many in the Curia that there was no need for a council. The Church must not become insular and reject the world, John XXIII reasoned; rather, she should actively engage modernity. The pope focused the tasks of the council on *aggiornamento* (renewal), *ressourcement* (return to the sources), and the defense and advancement of the truth. The Church must be renewed, John argued, in order to help modern man form a lasting relationship with Christ and his Church. The Church should return to the ancient sources of the Faith, with renewed emphasis on Scripture and the writings of the Church Fathers. Finally, John believed the "sacred deposit of Christian doctrine should be guarded and taught more efficaciously."[3] The pope did not want the council to debate the finer points of theology, but to center its attention on how the truth is presented. In his opening speech, John indicated that "the substance of the ancient doctrine is one thing, and the way in which it is presented is another."[4] The pope understood that modern man would not simply acquiesce to the Church's teaching because it was proclaimed; he would want to know why he must believe the Gospel. The pope hoped the council would focus on developing new ways to demonstrate the validity of the Church's teachings. As such, John XXIII did not believe the council needed to issue condemnations, as was cus-

---

2. Giuseppe Alberigo, *A Brief History of Vatican II*, trans. Matthew Sherry (New York: Orbis Books, 2006), 1.
3. John XXIII, *Gaudet Mater Ecclesia* (opening speech at the inauguration of the Second Vatican Council), 11.
4. Ibid., 15.

tomary with previous councils. The jovial pope hoped his council would bring fresh impetus to the Church.

THE SECOND VATICAN COUNCIL (1962–1965)

Preparatory work for the council began on February 6, 1959, when a small group of ten members, all Italians representing the Curial congregations, gathered to collect materials. Pope John also sent letters to the world's bishops, asking them to send in proposals for topics to be discussed at the council — over 2,000 responses were received.[5] The Central Preparatory Commission was created, including more than a hundred members and nearly thirty additional theological consultants, to develop schemas or documents for the council fathers to review, debate, and vote on. Initially, seventy schemas were developed, but only sixteen were eventually adopted, as most were modified or dropped during the course of the council.

Pope John XXIII joyfully opened the twenty-first ecumenical council in Church history, the first in nearly a hundred years, on October 11, 1962. Nearly three thousand bishops from around the world gathered at the Vatican to participate in the historic event.[6] One thousand accredited journalists were present to document the proceedings. Each day began with Mass, the procession of the book of Scripture to the main altar, and the recitation of the Creed. All documents were written in Latin, and all speeches were given in the ancient language of the Church. Joseph Ratzinger noted, "It was not uncommon that glowing panegyrics in favor of Latin were themselves delivered in labored pidgin Latin, while the most forceful advocates of the vernacular could express themselves in classical Latin."[7] The

5. Alberigo, 11.
6. The largest group was from Europe (1,041) and the largest national group was the Italians (379), but nearly 60 percent of the bishops were from areas of the world (Asia, Africa, North and South America) not represented at all in previous councils. See Alberigo, 21.
7. Joseph Ratzinger, *Theological Highlights of Vatican II* (New York: Paulist Press, 1966), loc. 289, Kindle.

council's business was conducted over four sessions from October 1962 to December 1965. However, the man behind the vision of the council died in the summer of 1963 after the conclusion of the first session, provoking serious discussion as to whether the council would continue.

Giovanni Battista Montini was a career diplomat for the Vatican and, after spending more than thirty years working in the Secretariat of State, was appointed archbishop of Milan in 1955. Chosen to succeed Pope Saint John XXIII,[8] Montini took the papal name Paul VI (r. 1963–1978) to signify his commitment to reform and missionary efforts. Pope Paul was "a complex man, affectionate, capable of deep and enduring friendship, yet reserved, prone to fits of depression, easily hurt."[9] Paul focused his efforts on Church reform. He established a mandatory retirement age for bishops (75), increased the number of cardinals, and decreed that cardinals over the age of eighty could not hold curial office or vote in a conclave. He was committed to Christian unity, working diligently throughout his pontificate to increase understanding and mutual respect with the Orthodox. Paul was also the first pope to travel the world extensively, which increased the prestige and influence of the papal office. He made a pilgrimage to the Holy Land in 1964. He traveled to India (in 1964), the United States (becoming the first reigning pope to visit that nation, in 1965), Portugal and Turkey (1967), Colombia (1968), Switzerland and Uganda (1969), and conducted a ten-day visit to eight Asian-Pacific countries (1970).

The biggest question facing Paul in the early stages of his pontificate was whether or not he would continue the ecumenical council. Paul decided to complete John's dream, but made some procedural changes allowing for greater dialogue and debate at the council. Paul wanted the council to produce a document about the inner nature of the Church, continue the renewal of the Church, promote Christian unity, and open a fruitful dialogue with the

8. Pope John XXIII was canonized along with Pope John Paul II by Pope Francis in April 2014.
9. Eamon Duffy, *Saints and Sinners: A History of the Popes* (New Haven, CT: Yale University Press, 2006), 368.

modern world.[10] The next three conciliar sessions accomplished these Pauline goals by producing sixteen documents, which included four major constitutions that form the foundational teachings of the council. The four constitutions deal with the Church in terms of her source of belief, her inner nature, her worship, and her mission in the modern world. The first was *Sacrosanctum Concilium* (Constitution on the Sacred Liturgy) which discussed the role and function of the liturgy. The council fathers desired the renewal of the liturgy, with an emphasis on the active participation of the faithful. Latin was to be preserved in the liturgy, though allowances were made for the vernacular language in order to increase lay participation. In 1969, Paul VI promulgated the *Novus Ordo Missae*, which reformed the Sacred Liturgy.

The next major document was *Lumen Gentium* (Dogmatic Constitution on the Church), which focused on the inner nature of the Church. The Church is the instrument of salvation and a communion, which is a "complex reality that coalesces from a divine and human element."[11] The totality of Christ's revelation, sacraments, and authority is contained in the Catholic Church. The document explores the nature and role of the Church with chapters on the people of God, the laity, religious life, the hierarchical structure of the Church, the universal call to holiness, and the role of the Blessed Mother in the economy of salvation. The source of the Church's belief is discussed in the document *Dei Verbum* (Dogmatic Constitution on Divine Revelation), which identifies the sacred deposit of the Word of God as both Sacred Scripture and Sacred Tradition and teaches "it is not from Scripture alone that the Church draws her certainty about everything which has been revealed."[12] Scripture is divinely inspired; it "firmly, faithfully, and without error teaches" what is needed for salvation.[13] The proper interpretation of Scripture is discussed in

---

10. Alberigo, 43.
11. *Lumen Gentium*, 8.
12. *Dei Verbum*, 9.
13. Ibid., 11.

Dei Verbum, along with the role of the magisterium, or teaching authority of the Church. The Church venerates Sacred Scripture as she does the Body of the Lord, and desires easy access for all to the Word of God. Additionally, the faithful are encouraged to study Scripture in order to deepen their faith.

The last major document of the council was *Gaudium et Spes* (Pastoral Constitution on the Church in the Modern World), which was promulgated to explain the presence of the Church and her activity in the modern world.[14] In the opening paragraphs of the document the conciliar fathers provide an overview of the situation of the world at the time of the council. The world had entered into a new stage of history, with dramatic cultural and societal transformations. The world contains immense amounts of wealth and resources, yet there is also hunger, poverty, and illiteracy. The modern world is more united than any past civilizations, yet there is still conflict. Modern society has undergone rapid change so that traditional values are being questioned, and people have abandoned the practice of religion on a scale unprecedented in human history. The council fathers noted that "the modern world shows itself at once powerful and weak; capable of the noblest deeds or the foulest; before it lies the path to freedom or to slavery."[15] It is the hope of the Church that modernity chooses the path to freedom by embracing the Gospel of Jesus Christ. The document is divided into two parts: the Church and man's calling, and a discussion of some problems of special urgency. The dignity of the human person is rooted in being created by God in his image and likeness; all men are called to fulfillment by giving of themselves to others.[16] Offenses against human dignity include abortion, euthanasia, torture, slavery, and prostitution. The Church has an active role to play in the modern world, and is concerned with the dignity of human life, so she fights against offenses to that

---

14. See *Gaudium et Spes*, 2.
15. *Gaudium et Spes*, 9.
16. See *Gaudium et Spes*, 24.

dignity. The faith should be practiced in public and is not simply a private matter. The Church should be allowed a voice in the public sphere, not relegated to passive observance of the actions of governments. In the second section, the council fathers discussed several areas of concern in the modern world, including marriage and family life and, more specifically, the purpose of marriage, human sexuality, and contraception. In the economic and social arena, the Church exhorts wealthy nations to exercise benevolent responsibility for poorer nations. Politically, the disagreements between nations should be settled peacefully and without recourse to war, if possible. *Gaudium et Spes* provided a platform for the Church to engage with the modern world, one of the goals of Pope Saint John XXIII when he called the council.

When Pope Paul VI closed the Second Vatican Council on December 8, 1965, there was much hope for the renewal of the Church. In many places, authentic renewal and reform did in fact bloom as a result of the council. However, in other areas of the Church, particularly in the Western world, the reform and renewal were hijacked by those with a different agenda. They used the council as cover for nefarious experiments, causing much confusion and loss of faith. Catechetical instruction suffered, and the liturgy was mocked. Paul VI worked diligently to authentically implement the conciliar decrees, but, as he met stiff resistance from primarily European and North American bishops and theologians, he questioned whether there was another force focused on disrupting the New Pentecost. In a homily given on June 29, 1972, the pope identified this opposing force as Satan. The crisis in implementing the council, at least in certain parts of the Church, is not attributable to the council itself, as some have argued; it is the result of the ideology of the Enlightenment, the heresy of Modernism, and the cultural revolution of the West in the 1960s. The council was a great gift of the Holy Spirit and is a sure compass by which the Church can take her bearings in the new millennium of the Faith.[17]

HUMANAE VITAE

Three years after the close of the Second Vatican Council, Pope Paul issued the encyclical *Humanae Vitae*, which focused on the subject of married love and the transmission of life. It is perhaps the most contentious and well-known (although not well-read) pontifical intervention in Church history. The document, issued at the height of the Western "sexual revolution," was the fruit of Paul's reflections and prayer from the reports of a commission established to study the morality of using the new birth control pill. Paul emphasized in his encyclical that married couples have a unique mission from God to bring forth new human life as co-creators. Marriage is a divine institution and, as such, the actions within marriage are governed by divine mandates. The marital act has a twofold purpose: uniting the spouses more intimately in love, and providing the means for the procreation of children. Married life should imitate divine love, which is free, total, faithful, and fruitful. As a result, Paul VI taught, in keeping with the constant teaching of the Church through the centuries, that the use of contraception in any form is inadmissible, and that "each and every marital act must remain open to the transmission of life."[18] Paul reminded married couples of their duty to exercise responsible parenthood by learning about the biological processes of the body, especially the fertility cycle of women, and to make a "well-thought out and generous decision to raise a large family, or by the decision, made for grave motives and with respect for the moral law, to avoid a new birth for the time being, or even for an indeterminate period."[19]

The reaction to *Humanae Vitae* was marked by great outcry, especially because news reports had speculated the pope would

17. See John Paul II, *Novo Millennio Inuente*, 57.
18. Paul VI, *Humanae Vitae*, 11.
19. Ibid., 10.

allow married couples to use the birth control pill. Catholic theologians staged protests, and an entire generation of Catholics was raised to ignore this important and beautiful teaching.[20] Pope Paul was shocked at the reaction and deeply saddened by the response of many clergy to his encyclical. It was his seventh encyclical in the sixth year of his pontificate, and, although he reigned for another ten years, it would be his last.

After guiding the Church through the completion of the Second Vatican Council, reforming the Curia, establishing the missionary outreach of the papacy through personal travel, and reaffirming the beauty and truth of marriage and human sexuality, Pope Paul VI was called home to his eternal rest on August 6, 1978, and was canonized by Pope Francis on October 14, 2018.

THE HEROIC HOLY FATHER

After the brief thirty-three-day reign of Pope John Paul I, the cardinals gathered once more in conclave in the year of the three popes (1978) to elect a universal shepherd for the Church. Somewhat surprisingly, they elected the fifty-eight-year-old Cardinal Archbishop of Cracow, Karol Wojtyła, who took the papal name John Paul II (r. 1978–2005). John Paul II was the youngest pope elected since Blessed Pius IX in the nineteenth century, and the first non-Italian pope since Adrian VI (r. 1522–1523) in the sixteenth century. The Polish pope had experienced profound suffering in his life, which led to a deep relationship with Christ. By the time he was twenty-one, his entire family had died, and he witnessed the horrible occupation of his beloved Poland by the Nazis, which had forced him to study clandestinely for the priesthood. His deep faith was exemplified in the first words he uttered as pope, "Be not afraid," the standard angelic greeting in Scrip-

---

20. The most famous protestor was Charles Curran, a priest of the diocese of Rochester, New York, and a professor at The Catholic University of America in 1968. Curran pursued a life of dissent from Church teaching and was eventually removed from the faculty at CUA. He moved to Texas and taught at Southern Methodist University.

ture. John Paul II embodied these words throughout his pontificate, especially by challenging the Soviet Empire (which fell, in
part, as a result of his efforts), by his commitment to evangelization, and by his frequent utterance of the phrase to the youth of
the world. Perhaps no greater display of his faith occurred when
he personally forgave his attempted assassin, Mehmet Ali Agca,
in 1981.

Pope John Paul II pursued four main goals during his twen-
ty-seven-year pontificate: spreading the Gospel and establishing the New Evangelization, implementing the Second Vatican
Council, explicating the Church's teachings on marriage and human sexuality, and preparing the Church to enter the third millennium of the Christian faith. Recognizing that the Church's
primary mission is evangelization, the pope focused on a "New
Evangelization" to areas that had already received the Gospel but
were no longer practicing the Faith authentically. He made more
than one hundred apostolic visits across the world. He established
World Youth Days in order to reach young people, and boldly
challenged them to live the Faith deeply and openly give witness
to their hope, love, and faith in Christ. His extensive writings
contained conciliar themes, and he frequently quoted from the
sixteen documents of the Second Vatican Council. During his
pontificate, the fruit of the council was born with the publication
of the revised Code of Canon Law in 1983 and the universal *Catechism of the Catholic Church* in 1992. John Paul's primary lasting
theological contribution came from the 129 Wednesday general audiences in which he explored the truth of marriage, love,
and human sexuality. Known popularly as the "Theology of the
Body," this catechesis provided a new and deeper way to understand the teachings contained in *Humanae Vitae*. Finally, the pope
saw in the approach of the new millennium a unique opportunity
for his pontificate. He prepared the Church to enter into this
new phase of history with a three-year theological focus on the
Trinity, leading to the Great Jubilee of 2000. He tasked the International Theological Commission with reviewing the Church's

history and purifying her memory, so that she could enter the new millennium acknowledging the past sins of her members and ask God for forgiveness.[21] John Paul knew it was not enough to prepare the Church to enter the third millennium, but that a blueprint for the way ahead in the new era was also required. His apostolic letter *Novo Millennio Ineunte* provided the foundation for the Church's activity in this new era.

The Polish pope left the Church an abundance of writings: fourteen encyclicals, eleven apostolic constitutions, fifteen apostolic exhortations, forty-five apostolic letters, and five books.[22] This rich philosophical and theological corpus is one part of an enduring legacy of one of the most important papacies in Church history. John Paul exhorted the faithful to live the universal call to holiness (outlined in the Second Vatican Council document *Lumen Gentium*) and provided the Church a multitude of witnesses to emulate in that pursuit by canonizing 482 saints (the most ever during one pontificate) and beatifying over one thousand holy individuals. John Paul II gave the Church a rich theology, a renewed emphasis on evangelization and holy living, and a new image of the pope and his role in the modern world. He helped end one of the most repressive and brutal political regimes in history. He died on April 2, 2005, and was canonized by Pope Francis on April 27, 2014.[23]

The two men who followed Saint John Paul II in the papacy, Benedict XVI (r. 2005–2013) and Francis (r. 2013–present),

21. See the document *Memory and Reconciliation: The Church and the Faults of the Past*. Contrary to popular understanding and inaccurate media portrayals, the pope did not apologize for events in the Church's history, but asked God for forgiveness: "[The Church's] … request for pardon must not be understood as an expression of false humility or as a denial of her two-thousand-year history, which is certainly rich in merit in the areas of charity, culture, and holiness. Instead she responds to a necessary requirement of the truth, which, in addition to the positive aspects, recognizes the human limitations and weaknesses of the various generations of Christ's disciples."

22. Examples of these writings include: *Redemptor Hominis* (1979), *Veritatis Splendor* (1993), *Evangelium Vitae* (1995), *Ex Corde Ecclesia* (1990), *Familiaris Consortio* (1981), *Ordinatio Sacerdotalis* (1994), *Crossing the Threshold of Hope* (1994), and *Memory and Identity* (2005).

23. His pontificate was truly one of the greatest in Church history, and he may be designated with the title "the Great" and join the ranks of only three men in the history of the papacy with such a title. Some historians have already bestowed the title on him; see Warren Carroll's *The Crisis of Christendom*.

have continued his vision for the papacy and the Church by embodying the theological virtues of faith, hope, and love and by exhorting the faithful to do likewise. The history of the Church clearly illustrates that the Holy Spirit sent by Christ at Pentecost two thousand years ago continues to guide, guard, and animate the family of God. The family has survived violence and persecution, and continues to faithfully conduct the mission given to it by Christ to, "Go therefore and make disciples of all nations."[24]

THE FUTURE OF THE FAMILY

The situation of the Church in the modern world is full of hope, but it also contains areas of deep concern. Studying Church history provides plentiful examples for the family of God to know how to respond to the challenges of modernity. The family exists today in a post-Christian civilization, which presents a host of unique challenges and opportunities. The modern Western post-Christian world suffers from an identity crisis and a deep historical amnesia. As such, society is not based on a sure foundation, making it susceptible to new forms of immorality and a frightening lack of appreciation for the dignity and worth of every human person. Unmoored from the sure foundation of Christ and his Church, modern society drifts in a sea of confusion that only a renewed evangelization and catechetical effort can correct.

In 1929, the Catholic author, historian, and politician Hilaire Belloc (1870–1953) wrote a fascinating analysis titled *Survivals and New Arrivals*. Belloc believed it was of utmost importance to survey the contemporary attacks on the Church and what she might expect in the way of opposition in the future. He categorized these attacks into survivals, the main opposition, and new arrivals. "Survivals" were the old, unsustainable forms of attack, weakened as effective opponents of the Church. Among these "survivals," Belloc counted the foundational Protestant tenant of

24. Matthew 28:19.

sola scriptura; the belief in the supremacy of material causes and rejection of the spiritual world; the economic theory which boasted
that Protestant nations were wealthy and industrious, and Catholic countries poor and lazy; the historical attack in which critics of
the Church sought to discredit her through false historical myths;
and the recourse to physical science for explanations of supernatural events. Belloc identified the "Main Opposition" as national-
ism, the worship of state or leader; anti-clericalism, in which the
state interferes in ecclesial affairs; and the modern mind. Belloc
argued that the modern mind was not so much an attack as a resistance. Modernity renders faith unintelligible by developing a
mentality entrenched in pride, ignorance, and intellectual sloth.
Fighting against the modern mind proves elusive (Belloc likened
it to "fighting smoke") because it is impossible to argue "with a
man who always argues in a circle."[25] The modern mind is fed by
universal compulsory education, in which the populace is indoc-
trinated with information rather than taught formation in virtues
and critical thinking, and by the popular press, which feeds the
modern mind's dislike of thinking and increases "that sloth by
providing sensational substitutes."[26] The "New Arrivals," which
Belloc foresaw attacking the Church, comprised neopaganism
and Islam. Neopaganism would focus its attack on the moral
teachings of the Church, especially marriage and family life, and
seek to overthrow the very foundations of civilization. Belloc believed that when neopaganism matured, the Church would face
"not the present isolated, self-conscious insults to beauty and
right living, but a positive coordination and organized affirma-
tion of the repulsive and vile."[27] Belloc predicted the resurfacing
of Islam, which at the time of his writing was a fanciful idea; the
once-great Ottoman Empire had disintegrated after its defeat in

---

25. Hilaire Belloc, *Survivals and New Arrivals: The Old and New Enemies of the Catholic Church* (Rockford, IL: TAN Books and Publishers, Inc., 1992 [1929]), 115.
26. Ibid., 127.
27. Ibid., 136. This has most assuredly come to pass in the present age with gender-identity, trans-
gender, and homosexual movements.

the First World War, and the disunited and weak Muslim world was occupied by European colonial powers.

Almost a decade after *Survivals and New Arrivals* was published, Belloc wrote *The Great Heresies* (1938), in which he stated, "It has always seemed to me possible, and even probable, that there would be a resurrection of Islam and that our sons and grandsons would see the renewal of that tremendous struggle between the Christian culture and what has been for more than a thousand years its greatest opponent."[28] Belloc's prophecy has come to pass, as the late twentieth century saw the rapid expansion of Muslim immigrants to the Western world, especially in Europe. Islamic terrorist groups came to the world's attention in the late twentieth and early twenty-first centuries when they unleashed a wave of violence, bloodshed, and Christian persecution, which has become so intense that "the single most dangerous thing in the world to be, right now, is a Christian in a Muslim country."[29] Christian populations have radically decreased in the ancient Christian lands that are now Islamic-occupied countries.

Although Belloc was concerned for the Church's future, he knew there was a great opportunity for the Church as she defends herself against the survivals, main opposition, and new arrivals. Christians are a hope-filled people, because Christ Jesus has already won the final battle. However, the Church is called not to passively await the Second Coming, but to engage in the skirmishes of modernity, primarily through evangelization and catechesis. Belloc rightly argued that the "success or failure of our effort against the New Paganism will depend much more on letting people know what the Catholic Church is, than upon anything else."[30] He understood, thirty-three years before the Church acknowledged the same at the Second Vatican Council, that the key to future successful evangelization and catecheti-

---

28. Hilaire Belloc, *The Great Heresies* (Rockford, IL: TAN Books and Publishers, Inc., 1991 [1938]), 73.
29. Joseph Bottum, "Who Will Defend Mideast Christians?", *USA Today*, February 7, 2011.
30. Belloc, *Survivals and New Arrivals*, 159.

cal efforts lies in "the right conduct of the presentation of the Faith."[31] The Church, Belloc knew, was the lynchpin of civilization. The Catholic Church built, shaped, maintained, and sustained Western civilization. If her influence declines, "civilization will decline with her and all the effects of tradition."[32] Faced with these challenges, the Church can assess if she is making headway against the forces of modernity by whether or not her faithful are suffering persecution. "When that shall once more be at work it will be morning."[33]

OUR ROLE IN THE STORY OF GOD'S FAMILY

The family of God faces a unique challenge in the modern world as secularization increases and Christian civilization recedes. Most of the once-Christian Western world has rejected the Faith, with those nominally identifying as Christian no longer practicing the Faith even once or twice a year.[34] This rejection of faith has led to declining populations and an increase in immorality, resulting in concerted and sustained attacks against marriage, human sexuality, and the dignity of the human person. The family of God is truly at a crossroads. We can be tempted to focus on self-preservation, to ignore the world's problems, but Christians are called to be missionary people of hope, engaged with the world — even if it leads to persecution. However, no program of reform or renewal will succeed "unless God stands in the center and becomes visible again in the world," and that must happen through the personal witness of individual Christians.[35] In his second encyclical *Spe Salvi* (*Saved in Hope*), Pope Benedict XVI challenged the members of God's family to bring the Gospel light to others:

---

31. Ibid., 166.
32. Ibid., 165.
33. Ibid., 167.
34. See the results of the 2006 World Values Survey (http://www.worldvaluessurvey.org/WVSOnline.jsp) that indicated 60 percent of Frenchmen, 46 percent of Britons, 53 percent of Dutch, and 25 percent of Americans never attend Church.
35. Benedict XVI, *Light of the World*, loc. 170, Kindle.

Life is like a voyage on the sea of history, often dark
and stormy, a voyage in which we watch for the stars
that indicate the route. The true stars of our life are
the people who have lived good lives. They are lights
of hope. Certainly, Jesus Christ is the true light, the
sun that has risen above all the shadows of history.
But to reach him we also need lights close by — people who shine with his light and so guide us along our
way.[36]

Catholics in the modern world have a unique role to play in the
divine drama of history. We have each been given a specific role
that only we can fulfill. The challenge is to discover that role and,
with God's grace, live it out each day in our homes, workplaces,
and society. An important part of that role is studying and knowing our Catholic history in order to defend the Church when she
is attacked by those opposed to the Gospel. Knowledge becomes
most effective when we share it with others, so we must also hand
on our family story so that future generations will know the truth
of the greatest organization in human history. Confident in our
membership in the family of God and learning from the men and
women, our brothers and sisters in faith, who have gone before
us, let us be people of light and transform the world for Christ.

36. Benedict XVI, *Spe Salvi*, 49.

Bibliography

Alberigo, Giuseppe. *A Brief History of Vatican II*. Translated by Matthew Sherry. New York: Orbis Books, 2006.

Aquilina, Mike. *The Fathers of the Church: An Introduction to the First Christian Teachers*. Expanded ed. Huntington, IN: Our Sunday Visitor, 2006.

Baker, G. P. *Constantine the Great and the Christian Revolution*. New York: Cooper Square Press, 2001.

Bainton, Roland H. *Here I Stand: A Life of Martin Luther*. New York: Mentor Books, 1950.

Barraclough, Geoffrey. *The Crucible of Europe: The Ninth and Tenth Centuries in European History*. Berkeley and Los Angeles: University of California Press, 1976.

Becher, Matthias. *Charlemagne*. New Haven, CT: Yale University Press, 2003.

Beeching, Jack. *The Galleys at Lepanto*. New York: Charles Scribner's Sons, 1982.

Belloc, Hilaire. *Characters of the Reformation: Historical Portraits of 23 Men and Women and Their Place in the Great Religious Revolution of the 16ᵗʰ Century*. Rockford, IL: TAN Books and Publishers, 1992 [1936].

———. *Europe and the Faith*. Rockford, IL: TAN Books and Publishers, 1992 [1920].

———. *The Great Heresies*. Rockford, IL: TAN Books and Publishers, 1991 [1938].

———. *How the Reformation Happened*. Rockford, IL: TAN Books and Publishers, 1992 [1928].

———. *Marie Antoinette*. New York: Tess Press, 1909.

———. *Survivals and New Arrivals: The Old and New Enemies of the Catholic Church*. Rockford, IL: TAN Books and Publishers, 1992 [1929].

Benedict XVI. *Church Fathers and Teachers: From Saint Leo the Great to Peter Lombard*. San Francisco: Ignatius Press, 2010.

———. *Church Fathers: From Clement of Rome to Augustine*. San Francisco: Ignatius Press, 2008.

———. *Holy Men and Women of the Middle Ages and Beyond.* San Francisco: Ignatius Press, 2012.

———. *Jesus, the Apostles, and the Early Church.* San Francisco: Ignatius Press, 2007.

———. *Light of the World: The Pope, the Church, and the Signs of the Times: A Conversation with Peter Seewald.* Translated by Michael J. Miller and Adrian J. Walker. San Francisco: Ignatius Press, 2010.

Bennett, Rod. *The Apostasy that Wasn't: The Extraordinary Story of the Unbreakable Early Church.* El Cajon, CA: Catholic Answers Press, 2015.

Blumenthal, Uta-Renate. *The Investiture Controversy: Church and Monarchy from the Ninth to the Twelfth Century.* Philadelphia: University of Pennsylvania Press, 1995 [1988].

Bostom, Andrew G., ed. *The Legacy of Jihad: Islamic Holy War and the Fate of Non-Muslims.* Amherst, NY: Prometheus Books, 2005.

Brandmüller, Cardinal Walter. *Light and Shadows: Church History amid Faith, Fact and Legend.* Translated by Michael J. Miller. San Francisco: Ignatius Press, 2009 [2007].

Bury, J.B. *Ireland's Saint: The Essential Biography of St. Patrick.* Edited by Jon M. Sweeney. Brewster, MA: Paraclete Press, 2010.

Calvin, John. *The Institutes of Christian Religion.* Edited by Tony Lane and Hilary Osborne. Grand Rapids, MI: Baker Academic, 1987.

Cantor, Norman F. *In the Wake of the Plague: The Black Death and the World It Made.* New York: Harper Perennial, 2002.

Carroll, Warren H. *The Building of Christendom.* Vol. 2 of *A History of Christendom.* Front Royal, VA: Christendom College Press, 1987.

———. *The Cleaving of Christendom.* Vol. 4 of *A History of Christendom.* Front Royal, VA: Christendom Press, 2000.

———. *The Founding of Christendom.* Vol. 1 of *A History of Christendom.* Front Royal, VA: Christendom College Press, 1985.

———. *The Glory of Christendom.* Vol. 3 of *A History of Christendom.* Front Royal: Christendom Press, 1993.

———. *The Last Crusade: Spain: 1936.* Front Royal, VA: Christendom Press, 1996.

Carroll, Warren H., and Anne Carroll. *The Crisis of Christendom.* Vol. 6 of *A History of Christendom.* Front Royal, VA: Christendom Press, 2013.

————. *The Revolution against Christendom*. Vol. 5 of *A History of Christendom*. Front Royal, VA: Christendom Press, 2013.

Catherine of Siena. *Letter to Gregory XI, Saint Catherine of Siena as Seen in Her Letters*. Edited by Vida D. Scudder. New York: E. P. Dutton, 1906.

Chadwick, Henry. *Augustine of Hippo: A Life*. New York: Oxford University Press, 2009.

————. *The Church in Ancient Society: From Galilee to Gregory the Great*. Oxford: Oxford University Press, 2001.

————. *The Early Church*. Revised ed. New York: Penguin Books, 1993.

Chesterton, G. K. *Lepanto*. Edited by Dale Ahlquist. San Francisco: Ignatius Press, 2003.

Clark, Kenneth. *Civilisation: A Personal View*. New York: Harper & Row, 1969.

Clement of Rome. *The Epistle to the Corinthians*. Translated by James A. Kleist, S.J. New York: Paulist Press, 1946.

Comby, Jean. *How to Read Church History: From the Beginnings to the Fifteenth Century*. Vol. 1. New York: Crossroads, 2001.

Crowley, Roger. *Empires of the Sea: The Siege of Malta, the Battle of Lepanto, and the Contest for the Center of the World*. New York: Random House, 2009.

————. *1453: The Holy War for Constantinople and the Clash of Islam and the West*. New York: Hachette Books, 2006.

Dalin, David G. *The Myth of Hitler's Pope: How Pope Pius XII Rescued Jews from the Nazis*. Washington, D.C.: Regnery Publishing, 2005.

Daniel-Rops, Henri. *The Catholic Reformation*. Translated by John Warrington. 2 vols. Garden City, NY: Image Books, 1964.

————. *Heroes of God: Eleven Courageous Men and Women Who Risked Everything to Spread the Catholic Faith*. Manchester, NH: Sophia Institute Press, 2002.

————. *The Protestant Reformation*. Translated by Audrey Butler. 2 vols. New York: Image, 1963.

Delaney, Carol. *Columbus and the Quest for Jerusalem*. New York: Free Press, 2011.

Di Correggio, Francisco Balbi. *The Siege of Malta, 1565*. Translated by Ernie Bradford. Rochester, NY: The Boydell Press, 2005.

Duffy, Eamon. *Fires of Faith: Catholic England under Mary Tudor*. New Haven,

CT: Yale University Press, 2009.

———. *Ten Popes Who Shook the World*. New Haven, CT: Yale University Press, 2011.

———.*Saints and Sinners: A History of the Popes*. New Haven, CT: Yale University Press, 2006.

Eusebius. *The History of the Church from Christ to Constantine*. Translated by G. A. Williamson. New York: Penguin, 1965.

Fernández-Morera, Darío. *The Myth of the Andalusian Paradise: Muslims, Christians, and Jews under Islamic Rule in Medieval Spain*. Wilmington, DE: ISI Books, 2016.

Ferrill, Arthur. *The Fall of the Roman Empire: The Military Explanation*. London: Thames and Hudson, 1986.

Fife, Robert Herndon. *The Revolt of Martin Luther*. New York: Columbia University Press, 1957.

France, John. *Victory in the East: A Military History of the First Crusade*. New York: Cambridge University Press, 1994.

———. *Western Warfare in the Age of the Crusades, 1000–1300*. Ithaca, NY: Cornell University Press, 1999.

Gies, Joseph, and Frances Gies. *Cathedral, Forge, and Waterwheel: Technology and Invention in the Middle Ages*. New York: HarperCollins, Kindle Edition, 2010.

Goldsworthy, Adrian. *The Complete Roman Army*. London: Thames & Hudson, 2003.

———. *How Rome Fell: Death of a Superpower*. New Haven, CT: Yale University Press, 2009.

Graham, Henry G. *Where We Got the Bible: Our Debt to the Catholic Church*. Rockford, IL: TAN Books and Publishers, 2004 [1992].

Grant, Michael. *Constantine the Great: The Man and His Times*. New York: Charles Scribner's Sons, 1993.

Gray, Tim, and Jeff Cavins. *Walking with God: A Journey through the Bible*. West Chester, PA: Ascension Press, 2010.

Gregory, Brad S. *The Unintended Reformation: A Religious Revolution Secularized Society*. Cambridge, MA: Harvard University Press, 2012.

Gregory of Tours. *History of the Franks*. Translated by Lewis Thorpe. New York: Penguin Books, 1974.

Guarducci, Margherita. *The Primacy of the Church of Rome: Documents, Reflections, Proofs.* Translated by Michael J. Miller. San Francisco: Ignatius Press, 2003.

Hallam, Elizabeth, ed. *Chronicles of the Crusades: Nine Crusades and Two Hundred Years of Bitter Conflict for the Holy Land Brought to Life Through the Words of Those Who Were Actually There.* New York: Weidenfeld and Nicolson, 1989.

Hanson, Victor Davis. *Carnage and Culture: Landmark Battles in the Rise of Western Power.* New York: Anchor Books, 2001.

Hoffman, Matthew Cullinan, trans. *The Book of Gomorrah and St. Peter Damian's Struggle Against Ecclesiastical Corruption.* New Braunfels, TX: Ite Ad Thomam Books and Media, 2015.

Hogge, Alice. *God's Secret Agents: Queen Elizabeth's Forbidden Priests and the Hatching of the Gunpowder Plot.* New York: HarperCollins, 2005.

Holland, Tom. *The Forge of Christendom: The End of Days and the Epic Rise of the West.* New York: Doubleday, 2008.

———. *In the Shadow of the Sword: The Birth of Islam and the Rise of the Global Arab Empire.* New York: Doubleday, 2012.

Housley, Norman. *Contesting the Crusades.* Malden, MA: Blackwell Publishing, 2006.

———. *Fighting for the Cross: Crusading to the Holy Land.* New Haven, CT: Yale University Press, 2008.

Howarth, David. *The Voyage of the Armada: The Spanish Story.* Guilford, CT: Lyons Press, 2001 [1981].

Hughes, Philip. *The Church and the World the Church Created.* Vol. 2 of *A History of the Catholic Church.* London: Sheed and Ward, 1993 [1979].

———. *A Popular History of the Catholic Church.* Garden City, NY: Image Books, 1947.

———. *A Popular History of the Reformation.* New York: Image Books, 1960.

———. *The World in which the Church was Founded.* Vol. 1 of *A History of the Catholic Church.* 2nd ed. London: Sheed and Ward, 1998.

Ignatius of Antioch, *Epistle to the Romans.* Translated by James A. Kleist, S.J. New York: Paulist Press, 1946.

Jaki, Stanley L. *Galileo Lessons.* Pinckney, MI: Real View Books, 2001.

John Paul II. *Memory and Identity: Conversations at the Dawn of a Millennium.*

New York: Rizzoli, 2005.

Josephus, *The Wars of the Jews*. Translated by William Whiston, A.M., Peabody, MA: Hendrickson Publishers, 2006.

Kamen, Henry. *The Spanish Inquisition: A Historical Revision*. New Haven, CT: Yale University Press, 1997.

Karsh, Efraim. *Islamic Imperialism: A History*. New Haven, CT: Yale University Press, 2006.

Keegan, John. *The First World War*. New York: Alfred A. Knopf, 1999.

Kittelson, James. *Luther the Reformer: The Story of the Man and His Career*. Minneapolis: Augsburg Publishing House, 1986.

Langford, Jerome L. *Galileo, Science, and the Church*. 3rd ed. Ann Arbor: University of Michigan Press, 1992.

Lapide, Pinchas E. *Three Popes and the Jews*. New York: Hawthorn Books, 1967.

Laux, John. *Church History: A Complete History of the Catholic Church to the Present Day*. Rockford, IL: TAN Books and Publishers, 1989.

Le Goff, Jacques. *Saint Louis*. Translated by Gareth Evan Gollrad. Notre Dame, IN: University of Notre Dame, 2009.

Lukacs, John. *The Future of History*. New Haven, CT: Yale University Press, 2011.

Luther, Martin. *Three Treatises*. Minneapolis: Fortress Press, 1970.

Maalouf, Amin. *The Crusades through Arab Eyes*. Translated by Jon Rothschild. New York: Schocken Books, 1984.

MacCulloch, Diarmaid. *The Reformation: A History*. New York: Penguin Books, 2003.

MacDougall, Angus. *Martyrs of New France*. Midland, Ontario: A Martyr's Shrine Publication, 1992.

Madden, Thomas F., ed. *The Crusades: The Essential Readings*. Malden, MA: Blackwell Publishing, 2006.

———. *The New Concise History of the Crusades Updated Edition*. New York: Rowman & Littlefield Publishers, 2005.

Marchione, Margherita. *Did Pius Help the Jews?* New York: Paulist Press, 2007.

Michuta, Gary. *Hostile Witnesses: How the Historic Enemies of the Church Prove Christianity*. El Cajon, CA: Catholic Answers Press, 2016.

Millar, Simon. *Vienna 1683: Christian Europe Repels the Ottomans*. New York:

Osprey Publishing, 2008.

Moczar, Diane. *Islam at the Gates: How Christendom Defeated the Ottoman Turks.* Manchester, NH: Sophia Institute Press, 2008.

————. *Ten Dates Every Catholic Should Know: The Divine Surprises and Chastisements that Shaped the Church and Changed the World.* Manchester, NH: Sophia Institute Press, 2005.

Möhring, Hannes. *Saladin: The Sultan and His Times, 1138–1193.* Translated by David S. Bachrach. With an intro and preface by Paul M. Cobb. Baltimore: Johns Hopkins University Press, 2005.

Murdoch, Adrian. *The Last Pagan: Julian the Apostate and the Death of the Ancient World.* Rochester, VT: Inner Traditions, 2008.

Neuner, J., and J. Dupuis. *The Christian Faith in the Doctrinal Documents of the Catholic Church.* 6th ed. New York: Alba House, 1996.

Nicolle, David. *Hattin 1187: Saladin's Greatest Victory.* Oxford, UK: Osprey Publishing, 1993.

————. *Poitiers AD 732: Charles Martel turns the Islamic Tide.* New York: Osprey Publishing, 2008.

Ozment, Steven. *A Mighty Fortress: A New History of the German People.* New York: HarperCollins, 2004.

————. *The Serpent and the Lamb: Cranach, Luther, and the Making of the Reformation.* New Haven, CT: Yale University Press, 2011.

Panzer, Joel S. *The Popes and Slavery.* New York: Alba House, 1996.

Parker, T.H.L. *John Calvin: A Biography.* Louisville: Westminster John Knox Press, 2006 [1975].

Pernoud, Régine. *The Crusaders.* Translated by Enid Grant. San Francisco: Ignatius Press, 2003.

————. *Martin of Tours: Soldier, Bishop, Saint.* Translated by Michael J. Miller. San Francisco: Ignatius Press, 2006.

————. *The Retrial of Joan of Arc: Evidence for her Vindication.* Translated by J.M. Cohen. San Francisco: Ignatius Press, 2007 [1955].

————. *Those Terrible Middle Ages: Debunking the Myths.* Translated by Anne Englund Nash. San Francisco: Ignatius Press, 2000 [1977].

Peters, Edward, ed. *The First Crusade: The Chronicle of Fulcher of Chartres and Other Source Material.* 2nd ed. Philadelphia: University of Pennsylvania Press, 1998.

————. *Inquisition*. Berkeley: University of California Press, 1988.

————. *Torture*. Expanded ed. Philadelphia: University of Pennsylvania Press, 1985.

Phillips, Jonathan. *The Second Crusade: Extending the Frontiers of Christendom*. New Haven, CT: Yale University Press, 2007.

Pickles, Tim. *Malta 1565: Last Battle of the Crusades*. New York: Osprey Publishing, 1998.

Pirenne, Henri. *Mohammed and Charlemagne*. Mineola, NY: Dover Publications, 2001 [1954].

Pursell, Brennan. *History in His Hands: A Christian Narrative of the West*. New York: Crossroad, 2011.

Queller, Donald E., and Thomas F. Madden. *The Fourth Crusade: The Conquest of Constantinople*. 2nd ed. Philadelphia: University of Pennsylvania Press, 1997.

Ratzinger, Joseph. *Theological Highlights of Vatican II*. New York: Paulist Press, 1966.

Ratzinger, Joseph, and Marcello Pera. *Without Roots: The West, Relativism, Christianity, Islam*. New York: Basic Books, 2007.

Rega, Frank M. *St. Francis of Assisi and the Conversion of the Muslims*. Rockford, IL: TAN Books and Publishers, 2007.

Rengers, O.F.M. Cap., Christopher. *The 33 Doctors of the Church*. Rockford, IL: TAN Books and Publishers, 2000.

Reu, Johann Michael. *Luther's German Bible: A Historical Presentation Together with a Collection of Sources*. Columbus, OH: Lutheran Book Concern, 1934.

Ricciotti, Giuseppe. *The Age of the Martyrs: Christianity from Diocletian (284) to Constantine (337)*. Translated by Rev. Anthony Bull, C.R.L. Rockford, IL: TAN Books and Publishers, 1999 [1959].

Riley-Smith, Jonathan. *The Crusades, Christianity, and Islam*. New York: Columbia University Press, 2008.

————. *The Crusades: A History*. 2nd ed. New Haven, CT: Yale University Press, 2005.

————. *The First Crusaders, 1095–1131*. Cambridge, UK: Cambridge University Press, 1997.

————. *The Oxford Illustrated History of the Crusades*. New York: Oxford University Press, 1995.

Robinson, J. H. *Readings in European History*. Boston: Ginn, 1905.

Royal, Robert. *The Catholic Martyrs of the Twentieth Century: A Comprehensive World History*. New York: Crossroad Publishing, 2000.

―――. *The Pope's Army: 500 Years of the Papal Swiss Guard*. New York: Crossroads, 2006.

Rychlak, Ronald J. *Hitler, the War, and the Pope*. Huntington, IN: Our Sunday Visitor, 2000.

Secher, Reynald. *A French Genocide: The Vendée*. Translated by George Holoch. Notre Dame, IN: University of Notre Dame Press, 2003 [1986].

Seward, Desmond. *Eleanor of Aquitaine: The Mother Queen of the Middle Ages*. New York: Pegasus Books, 2014 [1978].

―――. *Jerusalem's Traitor: Josephus, Masada and the Fall of Judea*. Cambridge, MA: Da Capo Press, 2009.

―――. *The Monks of War: The Military Religious Orders*. New York: Penguin Books, 1995 [1972].

Shannon, Christopher, and Christopher O. Blum. *The Past as Pilgrimage: Narrative, Tradition, and the Renewal of Catholic History*. Front Royal, VA: Christendom Press, 2014.

Sheen, Fulton. *Treasure in Clay: The Autobiography of Fulton J. Sheen*. Garden City, NY: Doubleday, 1980.

Shirer, William L. *The Rise and Fall of the Third Reich: A History of Nazi Germany*. New York: Touchstone, 1990.

Spencer, Robert. *The Truth about Muhammad: Founder of the World's Most Intolerant Religion*. Washington, D.C.: Regnery Publishing, 2006.

Stark, Rodney. *Bearing False Witness: Debunking Centuries of Anti-Catholic History*. West Conshohocken, PA: Templeton Press, 2016.

―――. *God's Battalions: The Case for the Crusades*. New York: HarperOne, 2009.

Stoye, John. *The Siege of Vienna: The Last Great Trial Between the Cross and Crescent*. New York: Pegasus Books, 2006.

Strayer, Joseph R. *The Albigensian Crusades*. Ann Arbor: University of Michigan Press, 1992 [1971].

Sumption, Jonathan. *Age of Pilgrimage: The Medieval Journey to God*. Mahwah, NJ: HiddenSpring Books, 2003.

Thomas, Gordon. *The Pope's Jews: The Vatican's Secret Plan to Save Jews from the Nazis*. New York: St. Martin's Press, 2012.

Tyerman, Christopher. *God's War: A New History of the Crusades*. Cambridge, MA: Belknap Press of Harvard University Press, 2006.

Undset, Sigrid. *Catherine of Siena*. Translated by Kate Austin-Lund. San Francisco: Ignatius Press, 2009 [1954].

Vidmar, O.P,, John. *The Catholic Church Through the Ages*. New York and Mahwah, NJ: Paulist Press, 2005.

Wallace-Hadrill, J.M. *The Barbarian West 400–1000*. Cambridge, UK: Basil Blackwell, 1985.

Walsh, William Thomas. *Our Lady of Fátima*. New York: Image, 1990 [1958].

Weidenkopf, Steve. *The Glory of the Crusades*. El Cajon, CA: Catholic Answers Press, 2014.

———. *The Real Story of Catholic History: Answering Twenty Centuries of Anti-Catholic Myths*. El Cajon, CA: Catholic Answers Press, 2017.

———. *20 Answers: The Reformation*. El Cajon, CA: Catholic Answers Press, 2017.

Wells, Peter S. *Barbarians to Angels: The Dark Ages Reconsidered*. New York: W. W. Norton, 2008.

Wilken, Robert Louis. *The Christians as the Romans Saw Them*. 2nd ed. New Haven, CT: Yale University Press, 1984.

———. *The First Thousand Years: A Global History of Christianity*. New Haven, CT: Yale University Press, 2012.

Woods Jr., Thomas E. *How the Catholic Church Built Western Civilization*. Washington, D.C.: Regnery Publishing, 2005.

Index

| A |

| C |

| E |

| F |

| G |

| H |

| I |

| M |

| P |

| Q |

I R I

I S I

| T |

Acknowledgments

This book is the fruit of over a decade of teaching at the Christendom College Graduate School. I am grateful for the opportunity to teach at that great institution. Thanks also to the faculty and staff of the school for their support and encouragement. Additionally, I thank all my students for making me a better teacher by their questions, academic work, and dedication to the Church.

Sincere thanks are in order to my family, especially my beloved wife, Kasey, whose love and support enabled me to complete this task. I am thankful for my children, Maddie, Maximilian, Thérèse, Luke, Jeb, and Martin, and their patience during the writing of this book. I owe extreme gratitude to Jaymie Stuart Wolfe, who approached me to undertake this project, shepherded it through the initial process at Our Sunday Visitor, and developed the title. I extend my appreciation to Rebecca Willen for her expert editing of the manuscript. Thanks are also in order to Todd Aglialoro at Catholic Answers Press for his support of my work during the last few years and for his permission to utilize some of that work in this book.

Last, I give thanks to Saint Anthony of Padua, whose intercession throughout this project enabled its completion.

About the Author

Steve Weidenkopf teaches Church History at the Christendom College Graduate School of Theology in Alexandria, VA. He is the author of *The Glory of the Crusades* (2014), *The Real Story of Catholic History: Answering Twenty Centuries of Anti-Catholic Myths* (2017), and *20 Answers: The Reformation* (2017). He is the creator, co-author, and presenter of the adult faith formation program *Epic: A Journey through Church History* and is a popular author and speaker on the Crusades and other historical topics.